D0515707

DISCARDED

The Student's Encyclopedia of Judaism

THE
STUDENT'S ENCYCLOPEDIA
OF
JUDAISM

EDITOR-IN-CHIEF *Geoffrey Wigoder*
COEDITORS *Fred Skolnik and Shmuel Himelstein*
EDUCATIONAL EDITOR *Barbara Sutnick*

NEW YORK UNIVERSITY PRESS
New York and London

NEW YORK UNIVERSITY PRESS
Washington Square
New York, NY 10003
www.nyupress.org

Planned and produced by G.G. The Jerusalem Publishing House, Jerusalem, Israel.
Copyright © 2004 by G.G. The Jerusalem Publishing House, Ltd.
39, Tchernichovski Street, P.O.B. 7147, Jerusalem 91071, Israel.

Typesetting by Raphaël Freeman, Jerusalem Typesetting.

A Cataloging-in-Publication Data record for this book is available from the Library of Congress.
LC Control # 2003065125, ISBN 0-8147-4275-0 *cloth*

New York University Press books are printed on acid-free paper,
and their binding materials are chosen for strength and durability.

Manufactured in China

10 9 8 7 6 5 4 3 2 1

CONTENTS

ACKNOWLEDGMENTS

The Publishers wish to express their appreciation to the following individuals and institutions for their help:

For the color illustrations:
p.57: Coll. IMJ Photo P.A. Ferrazini; *p.58:* British Museum; *p.59:* Coll. IMJ Photo D. Harris; *p.60:* Wolfson Museum Hechal Shlomo Synagogue, Jerusalem Photo D. Harris; *p.125:* Coll. IMJ Photo D. Harris; *pp.126–127:* Coll. Schocken Library, Jerusalem Photo D. Harris; *p.128:* Coll. Eric Estorick, London Photo IMJ N. Slapak; *p.193:* IMJ Stieglitz Coll. Photo A. Ganor; *pp.194–195:* Coll. IMJ Shrine of the Book. Photo A. Ferrazini; *p.196:* Coll. IMJ; *p.261:* Coll. IMJ Photo D. Harris; *pp.262–263:* Coll. IMJ Photo D. Harris; *p.264:* Coll. IMJ; *p.313:* The British Library; *p.314:* Photo D. Harris; *p.315:* JPH Photo D. Harris; *p.316:* JNUL Photo D. Harris; *p.349:* Coll. IMJ; *p.350:* Tel Aviv Museum; *p.351:* Coll. Jewish Museum, NY Photo Art Resources, NY;

For the black and white illustrations:
Aaron: The British Library; *Ablution:* IMJ Photo D. Harris; *Abraham:* JNUL/Laor Coll. Photo D. Harris; *Abravanel:* Coll. Royal Library, Copenhagen; *Acrostics:* The British Library; *Agricultural Laws:* Archeology Museum Istanbul, (copy) IMJ Photo H. Burger; *Akedah:* IMJ; *Aliyah:* GPO Photo A. Ohayon; *Angels:* Coll. IMJ Photo R. Milon; *Apostasy:* Coll. IMJ Photo D. Harris; *Astrology:* A. van der Heyden; *Ark:* Yad Vashem Archives, Jerusalem; *Ark of the Covenant:* GPO; *Ashkenazim:* Coll. IMJ Photo D. Harris; *Assimilation:* Courtesy of Beth Hatefutsoth, Tel Aviv; *Asylum:* IAA. Photo D. Harris; *Ba'al Shem Tov:* JNUL Photo Beth Hatefutsoth, Tel Aviv; *Ba'al Teki'ah:* GPO Photo D. Harris; *Bar Mitzvah:* GPO Photo M. Milner; *Belz:* Yad Vashem Archives, Jerusalem; *Ben-Gurion, David:* General Zionist Archives; *Bet Midrash:* IAA Photo IMJ/K. Meyerowitz; *Bible:* (p.48) Coll. Ben Zvi Institute, Jerusalem, (p.49) IAA Photo IMJ/D. Harris; *Bible Commentaries:* Coll. Ben Zvi Institute, Jerusalem; *Bimah:* Courtesy Mrs. Sarah Shammah in memory of her parents Tera and Ezra Shammah, IMJ Archives; *Birth:* IMJ Photo D. Harris; *Bread:* IAA; *Buber:* Photo R. Kneller; *Burial:* JPH Photo D. Harris; *Burning Bush:* Photo Zev Radovan; *Chabad:* GPO Photo G. ben Amos; *Cherub:* IAA Photo IMJ/N. Slapak; *Christianity:* Öffentliche Kunst Sammlung Basel; *Circumcision:* IMJ Photo D. Harris; *Community:* State Jewish Museum, Prague; *Creation:* Coll. Sarajevo National Museum; *Daniel:* Photo Alinari Firenze; *David:* Photo Museum for Music and Ethnology, Haifa; *Day of Atonement:* Coll. IMJ; *Dead Sea Scrolls:* IMJ; *Dew, Prayer for:* JNUL; *Dietary Laws:* Vatican Library, Rome; *Dowry:* Photo IMJ/H. Burger; *Ecclesiastes:* British Library; *Ehad mi Yode'a:* Coll. Bill Gross, Tel Aviv; *Elijah ben Solomon Zalman:* JNUL/Schwadron Coll. Photo D. Harris; *Emancipation:* JNUL; *Ethiopian Jews:* GPO Photo A. Ohayon; *Eulogy:* State Jewish Museum, Prague; *Evil:* IMJ Photo R. Milon; *Exodus:* Museum of Jewish Art, Jerusalem. Photo D. Harris; *Eybeschütz, Jonathan:* Sir Isaac & Lady Edith Wolfson Museum, Hechal Shlomo, Jerusalem; *Ezrat Nashim:* IMJ Photo D. Harris; *First Fruits:* IMJ. Photo H. Burger; *Four Species:* Photo D. Harris; *Funeral:* State Jewish Museum Prague; *Genesis:* IMJ. Photo D. Harris; *Genizah:* Beth Hatefutsoth, Tel Aviv; *God, Names of:* IMJ Photo D. Harris; *Golden Calf:* Rijksmuseum, Amsterdam; *Grace After Meals:* IMJ Photo R. Milon; *Gur:* Yad Vashem Archives, Jerusalem; *Hanukkah:* GPO Photo Y. Sa'ar; *Hasidism:* D. Mandrea; *Hasmoneans:* Reifenberg Coll. on loan from Bank Leumi Photo IMJ; *Herzl, Theodor:* GPO; *Hillel:* IMJ Photo D. Harris; *Holocaust:* Yad Vashem Archives, Jerusalem; *Idolatry:* Bibliothèque Nationale, Paris; *Incense:* IAA; *Ingathering of the Exiles:* IMJ Photo Y. Lehman; *Israel Land of:* GPO; *Jacob:* Wolfson Museum, Hechal Shlomo, Jerusalem Photo D. Harris. *Jacob ben Asher:* Vatican Library, Rome; *Jerusalem:* GPO Photo M. Milner; *Job:* IMJ Photo D. Harris; *Joshua:* Oesterreichische National Bibliothek; *Judah Halevi:* Library of the Jewish Theological Seminary, New York; *Kapparot:* Royal Library, Copenhagen; *Kiddush Cups:* IMJ Stieglitz Coll. Photo A. Ganor; *Kook, Abraham Isaac:* General Zionist Archives; *Lag ba-Omer:* GPO Photo M. Milner; *Lamentations:* IMJ Photo D. Harris; *Leaven, Search for:* IMJ Photo D. Harris; *Levirate Marriage:* IMJ Photo N. Slapak; *Leviticus, Book of:* IMJ/Shrine of the Book; *Luria, Isaac:* Royal Library Copenhagen; *Magen David:* Photo JPH/A. Van der Heyden; *Magic:* Royal Library Copenhagen; *Mahzor:* Royal Library, Copenhagen; *Maimonides, Moses* (right) JNUL Schwadron Coll., *Maror:* Royal Library, Copenhagen; *Marranos:* IMJ Photo D. Harris; *Matzah:* GPO Photo Y. Roth; *Memorial Light:* GPO Photo M. Milner; *Mendelssohn, Moses:* Zentralbibliothek, Zurich; *Menorah:* IAA, Courtesy Prof. Avigad; *Mezuzah:* IMJ Photo D. Harris; *Mishnah:* JNUL; *Moon:* Coll. Erica and Ludwig Jesselson, New York Photo IMJ/R. Milon; *Moses:* IMJ Photo H. Burger; *Mother:* IAA; *Mysticism:* JNUL; *Nahmanides:* IMJ Photo D. Harris; *New Year for Trees:* GPO; *Noah:* Photo N. Garo; *Orthodoxy:* Photo G. Geffen; *Passover:* GPO Photo C. Herman; *Peace:* IAA; *Petihah:* Library of the Jewish Theological Seminary, New York; *Piyyut:* Vatican Library, Rome; *Prayer:* GPO; *Prayer before a Journey:* JNUL; *Priestly Blessing:* Photo R. Milon; *Priestly Garments:* IMJ; *Purim:* (top and bottom) Photo D. Harris; *Reading of the Law:* IMJ Photo D. Harris; *Red Heifer:* Schocken Library, Jerusalem; *Reform Judaism:* Photo Y. Lehman; *Sabbath:* Photo Z. Radovan; *Samaritans:* JPH Photo A. van der Heyden; *Saul:* IMJ; *Schneersohn, Menahem Mendel:* GPO; *Scroll of the Law:* Bildarchiv Photo, Marburg; *Seder:* GPO Photo D. Eldan; *Shavu'ot:* Photo D. Harris; *Shofar:* GPO Photo A. Ohayon; *Sigd:* GPO; *Simhat Torah:* GPO Photo G. ben Amos; *Solomon:* IMJ Photo D. Harris; *Soloveichik:* GPO; *Song of Songs:* IMJ Photo IMJ; *Spinoza, Baruch:* Yad Vashem Archives, Jerusalem; *Sukkot:* Photo D.Harris; *Szold Henrietta:* Schwadzon Coll.; *Tallit:* Coll. Mrs. Morpugo, Sde Eliahu. Photo IMJ/D. Harris; *Tashlikh:* GPO Photo Y.Sa'ar; *Tefillin:* Courtesy Genya Markon, Photo M. Haziza; *Temple Mount:* Photo Werner Braun; *Torah Ornaments:* (p.347) IMJ Stieglitz Coll. Photo A. Ganor, (p.348) Yad Vashem Archives, Jerusalem; *Tribes, Twelve:* JPH; *Western Wall:* Photo D. Mandrea; *Wine:* IMJ Photo D. Harris; *Yad:* IMJ Stieglitz Coll. Photo A. Ganor; *Yeshivah:* Photo Guill, Baltimore. Courtesy Ner Israel Rabbinical College; *Zion:* IMJ Ethnography Coll. Photo R. Lobell; *Zunz, Leopold:* Jewish National and University Library, Jerusalem.

Charles Scribner's Sons, for the use of the essay on "Peace" by Prof. Aviezer Ravitzky from *Contemporary Jewish Religious Thought* by Arthur A. Cohen and Paul Mendes Flohr (1987).

Weidenfeld and Nicolson Ltd., for the translation of Aleinu le-Shabbe'ah from *A Jewish Book of Common Prayer* by C. Raphael (1986).

IMJ = Israel Museum, Jerusalem; GPO = Government Press Office, Jerusalem; JNUL = Jewish National and University Library, Jerusalem; IAA = Israel Antiquities Authority; JPH = Jerusalem Publishing House Ltd.

The Publishers have attempted to observe the legal requirements with respect to copyright. However, in view of the large number of illustrations included in this volume, the Publishers wish to apologize in advance for any involuntary omission or error and invite persons or bodies concerned to write to the Publishers.

CONTRIBUTORS

Yaacov Adler
Lecturer in Ancient Hebrew Literature, Bar Ilan University, Ramat Gan.

Marc D. Angel, Ph.D.
Rabbi, Spanish and Portuguese Synagogue, Shearith Israel of the City of New York; First Vice-President of the Rabbinical Council of America.

David Applebaum, M.D.
Rabbi; physician, Jerusalem.

David Assaf, Ph.D.
Professor of Jewish History, Tel Aviv University, Tel Aviv.

Yehuda Bauer, Ph.D.
Professor Emeritus, The Avraham Harman Institute of Contemporary Jewry, Hebrew University, Jerusalem.

Adina Ben-Chorin
Researcher and editor, Jerusalem.

Scbalom Ben-Chorin
Professor D. Theology h.c., Jerusalem.

Tovia Ben-Chorin
Rabbi, Har-El Synagogue, Jerusalem.

Alexander Carlebach, Ph.D.
Former Chief Rabbi of Northern Ireland. Jerusalem.

Bernard Casper, Ph.D.
Former Chief Rabbi of South Africa. Jerusalem.

Jonathan Chipman, Ph.D.
Rabbi; editor and translator, Jerusalem.

Yosef Dan, Ph.D.
Professor of Jewish Studies, Hebrew University, Jerusalem.

Uri Dasberg
Rabbi; researcher, Zomet-Torah and Science Institute, Gush-Etsion.

David Jay Derovan
Rabbi; educator, Jerusalem.

Jackie Feldman, M.A.
Shalom Hartman Institute for Advanced Jewish Studies, Jerusalem.

Sir Monty Finniston, F.Eng. FRS
Industrialist, London.

Seymour Freedman, Ph.D.
Writer, Jerusalem.

Albert H. Friedlander, Ph.D.
Rabbi, Westminster Synagogue, London.

Theodore Friedman, Ph.D.
Rabbi; former President of Rabbinical Assembly of America, Jerusalem.

David Geffen, Ph.D.
Rabbi; researcher, Jerusalem.

Ilana Goldberg, M.A.
Researcher, Hebrew University, Jerusalem.

Hanna Goodman
Writer, educator, Jerusalem.

Itshak Gottlieb, Ph.D.
Senior Lecturer, Department of Bible, Bar Ilan University, Ramat Gan.

Reuven Hammer, Ph.D.
Professor of Rabbinic Literature, Schechter Institute of Judaic Studies, Jerusalem.

Shmuel Himelstein, Ph.D.
Rabbi; editor and translator, Jerusalem.

Ida Huberman, M.A.
Lecturer, Beth Berl College, Kefar Saba.

Boaz Huss, Ph.D.
Senior Lecturer, Department of Jewish Thought, Ben Gurion University of the Negev, Beersheba.

Moshe Idel, Ph.D.
Max Cooper Professor of Jewish Thought, Department of Jewish Thought, Hebrew University, Jerusalem.

Julian G. Jacobs, Ph.D.
Rabbi; Senior Minister, Liverpool Old Hebrew Congregation.
Louis Jacobs, Ph.D.
Author and Rabbi of the New London Synagogue.
Lord Jakobovits
The Chief Rabbi of the United Hebrew Congregation of the British Commonwealth, London.
Rahel Sharon Jaskow
Coordinator, International Directory of Women's Tefilla Groups
Michael Klein, Ph.D.
Professor of Bible and Targumic Literature;
Dean of the Hebrew Union College-Institute of Religion, Jerusalem.
Michael L. Klein-Katz
Rabbi; educator and lecturer, Jerusalem.
Daniel Lasker
Associate Professor, Department of History, Ben Gurion University of the Negev, Beersheba.
Sidney B. Leperer, Ph.D.
Rabbi; Lecturer in Jewish History, Jews' College, London.
Mendell Lewittes, D.D.
Rabbi; Editor of Shanah be-Shanah. Jerusalem.
Sheldon Lilker, D.H.L.
Rabbi; author, Kibbutz Kefar ha-Maccabi.
Norman Linzer, Ph.D.
Professor, Wurzweiler School of Social Work, Yeshiva University. New York.
Chaim Mayerson
Educator and translator, Jerusalem.
Tirzah Meacham, Ph.D.
Department of Near Eastern Studies, University of Toronto, Ontario, Canada.
Moshe Miller
Rabbi; editor and translator.
Barry Mindel
Translator, Jerusalem.
Aryeh Newman, M.A.
Senior Lecturer, E.F.L. Department, Hebrew University, Jerusalem.
Isaac Newman
Coordinator Hebrew Studies, Middlesex Polytechnic; Rabbi; Barnet, Herts., England.
Avi Ofer, B.A.
Translator and editor, Jerusalem.
Shalom Paul, Ph.D.
Professor, Chairman of the Department of Bible, Hebrew University, Jerusalem.
Chaim Pearl, Ph.D.
Rabbi Emeritus, Conservative Synagogue Adath Israel of Riverdale, N.Y., Jerusalem.
Chaim Rabin, Ph.D.
Professor Emeritus of Hebrew Language, Hebrew University, Jerusalem.
Aaron Rakefet, D.H.L.
Rabbi; Professor of Responsa Literature, Gruss Institute of Yeshiva University, Jerusalem.
Aviezer Ravitzky, Ph.D.
Professor of Jewish Philosophy, Hebrew University, Jerusalem.
Uri Regev, LL.B.
Rabbi; Director of Israel Program, Hebrew Union College-Institute of Religion, Jerusalem.
Nissim Rejwan
Journalist, writer specializing in Middle East and Israeli politics and culture, Jerusalem.
Meir Rikin
Researcher, Hebrew University, Jerusalem.
Henry Romberg, M.D.
Physician, Jerusalem.
David Rosen
Dean of Sapir Center. A.D.L. Liaison to the Vatican. Former Chief Rabbi of Ireland. Jerusalem.
Yaakov G. Rosenberg
Rabbi; Vice Chancellor Emeritus of Jewish Theological Seminary. Jerusalem.
Yael Rossing, M.A.
Researcher, Shalom Hartman Institute for Advanced Jewish Studies, Jerusalem.

James Rudin
Rabbi; American Jewish Committee, New York.
Moshe Sachs, Ph.D.
Researcher, Jerusalem..
Eliahu Schleifer, Ph.D.
Associate Professor of Jewish Music, Hebrew Union College-Institute of Religion, Jerusalem.
Fern Seckbach, M.A.
Researcher, Jerusalem
Abraham Shafir, Ph.D.
Lecturer, Department of Bible, Beth Berl College, Kefar Saba.
Mark Elliott Shapiro, M.A.
Editor and translator, Jerusalem.
Marc I. Sherman, M.L.S.
Director of Academic Research Information Systems, Research Authority of Tel Aviv University, Tel Aviv.
Suzan Laikin Shifron
Reconstructionist Rabbi, Kefar Saba.
Vivian Charles Silverman, M. Phil.
Rabbi, Central Synagogue, London.
Gabriel A. Sivan, Ph.D.
Writer and lecturer, Jerusalem
Fred Skolnik
Senior Editor, Encyclopedia of Jewish Life, Jerusalem.
Yoram Skolnik
Researcher, Jerusalem.
David Solomon, Ph.D.
Lecturer, Central Teachers College for Extension Studies, Tel Aviv.
Dora Sowden
Dance critic, Jerusalem.
Iris Spero, M.S.L.S.
Librarian, Jerusalem.
Shubert Spero, D. Phil.
Rabbi Emeritus, Young Israel Congregation, Cleveland, Ohio. Irving Stone Professor in Jewish Thought, Bar Ilan University, Ramat Gan.
Benjamin Stein
Cantor, Jerusalem.
Shafer B. Stollman
Editor, Jewish Agency Publications, Jerusalem.
Sefton D. Temkin, Ph.D.
Rabbi; Professor Emeritus, State University of N.Y., Albany.
Yoel Tobin, Ph.D.
Fellow of the Shalom Hartman Institute for Advanced Jewish Studies, Jerusalem.
Moshe Tutnauer
Rabbi, educator, Jerusalem.
Shalva Weil, Ph.D.
Institute of Research on Education, Hebrew University, Jerusalem.
Mendel Weinberger
Rabbi, columnist, Jerusalem.
Geoffrey Wigoder, D. Phil.
Editor-in-Chief, Encyclopedia Judaica; Director, Oral History Department,
Institute of Contemporary Jewry, Hebrew University, Jerusalem.
Walter Zanger
Rabbi, author, columnist, and guide, Jerusalem.
Benjamin Zvieli
Rabbi; former director of religious broadcasting, Israel Radio and Television, Jerusalem.

EDITORS
Adina Ben-Chorin; Sam Freedman; David Geffen; Evelyn Katrak; Michael L. Klein-Katz; Chaim Mayerson; Linda C. Newman;
Susanna Shabetai; Stacy Weiner.

BIBLIOGRAPHY
Marc I. Sherman

INTRODUCTION

The *Student's Encyclopedia of Judaism* is a basic reference work that explores all areas of the Jewish religion. Using material from the award-winning *New Encyclopedia of Judaism*, the *Student's Encyclopedia* has been completely rewritten for a new audience, presenting a wide range of subjects in clear, concise language.

The development of the Jewish religion covers a period of nearly 4,000 years. In this time, while the great works that are at the core of Judaism were being produced – the Bible, the Mishnah, the Talmud, and the codes and commentaries of the later rabbis – the Jews were fully engaged in an often tragic history. That they survived and also produced great cultural monuments is due largely to their faith. In their daily lives the Jews studied and prayed, observed Jewish law and affirmed the existence of their God. In time new ideas and trends challenged the observant Jew: the Haskalah, Zionism, the reforming religious movements. All this is part of the story of Judaism and all this is given ample space in the *Student's Encyclopedia of Judaism*.

Thus, in around 1,000 entries, the reader will find broad surveys of the ideas and views that are part of the Jewish heritage on subjects touching every aspect of human life, the everyday and the holy, the private and the public. All facets of daily, Sabbath and holiday prayer and ritual are covered, including customs and folk traditions, and all the leading biblical and rabbinical figures receive biographical entries. Both traditional and modern issues are discussed from the standpoint of the Reform, Conservative, and Orthodox movements and special attention is paid to the subject of women, including an entry on the feminist movement. To broaden the framework still further, entries of historical interest have been added, like those on the Kingdoms of Israel and Judah, the Hasmoneans, Herod, the Zealots, and Bar Kokhba, as well as surveys of the Haskalah and Zionism and such phenomena as Anti-Semitism and the Holocaust.

Additional features enhancing the *Encyclopedia* are its numerous illustrations and sidebars. The latter include the sayings of the sages, texts of prayers and other documents, and summaries of all the biblical books. Finally, a list of books for further reading will guide the student in expanding his or her knowledge.

The *Student's Encyclopedia of Judaism* is the work of many scholars representing the entire spectrum of Jewish thought and practice. Its aim is to present as complete a picture as possible of the Jewish faith in all its variety and richness. It is a book that we hope will accompany the reader for many years to come.

HOW TO USE THE ENCYCLOPEDIA

Entries are arranged in alphabetical order. As many are found under their familiar Hebrew names (*tefillin, tallit, menorah,* etc.), they are also cross referenced against the corresponding English terms. Thus, under Phylacteries, Prayer Shawl, Candlestick, etc., the reader will be referred to the proper place to find the relevant entry. The same holds true in the opposite case, where the entry is given under its English name. Thus, under *bris* or *brith* the reader will find "see CIRCUMCISION" and under *siddur* "see PRAYER BOOK."

In the Index the reader will find all main entries accompanied by their corresponding page numbers and references to other main entries where the same subject is mentioned. Thus the listing for Aaron in the Index will be *AARON 1 → Blessing and Cursing, Consecration, etc. Subjects without a main entry will likewise be indexed against the entries where they are discussed. Thus, ACRONYMS → Acrostics, etc.

The key to exploiting the *Encyclopedia* fully is its extensive system of cross references within the entries themselves. These are indicated by small capital letters directing the reader to other main entries where supplementary information may be found or a term defined. In this way a user reading the *Encyclopedia* selectively will find in each entry all the possible links to other entries in the *Encyclopedia*. It is hoped that in this way the reader will be led to explore a given subject thoroughly with all the information made available throughout the *Encyclopedia*.

Bible quotations are usually based on the new translation of the Jewish Publication Society of America but other standard translations have also been used and on occasion the contributor has chosen to supply his own version, as with translations from the Talmud. References to the Bible cite chapter and verse (e.g., Ex. 6:16–20 for verses 16–20 in chapter 6 of the Book of Exodus). For the Mishnah and Jerusalem Talmud, the chapter and paragraph (*mishnah*) are cited (*RH* 1:1), while for the Babylonian Talmud the page is given (*Ket.* 3a or *Sanh.* 72b). (Each new page in the Babylonian Talmud starts on the left-hand side and is called "a" while its reverse side is called "b.") The key to all source abbreviations is given in the List of Abbreviations. Where place names and personal names have a familiar English form, these have been used; otherwise they have been transliterated. Frequently used words and terms are explained in the Glossary and the Rules of Transliteration give the English equivalents of Hebrew letters and signs.

RULES OF TRANSLITERATION

Hebrew	English	Hebrew	English	Hebrew	English
א not transliterated (e.g., at end of word)					
א or אַ or אָ	a	ו	v	ס	s
א or אֶ or אֵ	e	ז	z	ע	not transliterated
אוֹ or אֹ	o	ח	h (as in (C)haim)	פּ	p
אוּ or אֻ	u	ט	t	פ	f
אִי or אִ	i	י	y	צ	ts
בּ	b	כּ	k	ק	k
ב	v	כ	kh	ר	r
ג	g	ל	l	שׁ	sh
ד	d	מ	m	שׂ	s
ה	h (also at end of word)	נ	n	תּ or ת	t

VOWELS

Hebrew	English	Hebrew	English
◌ָ	a	◌ֵ	e
short ◌ָ	o	◌ִ	i
◌ַ	a	◌ֶ	e
◌ֹ	o	◌ְ	e
◌ֻ	u	◌ֻ	o
אֵ◌ ◌ֵי	ei	◌ַ	a

vocal sheva – e
silent sheva – not transliterated

ABBREVIATIONS

Akkad.	Akkadian	*Hor.*	Horayot	*Orl.*	Orlah
Ar.	Arakhin	Hos.	Hosea	*Pes.*	Pesahim
Arab.	Arabic	*Hul.*	Hullin	Phoen.	Phoenician
Aram.	Aramaic	Isa.	Isaiah	pl.	plural
ARN	Avot de-Rabbi Natan	Jer.	Jeremiah	Prov.	Proverbs
AZ	Avodah Zarah	Josh.	Joshua	Ps.	Psalms
BB	Bava Batra	Judg.	Judges	R.	Rabbi (title)
BCE	Before Common Era (BC)	*Kel.*	Kelim	*RH*	Rosh ha-Shanah
		Ker.	Keritot	Ruth R.	Ruth Rabbah
Bekh.	Bekhorot	*Ket.*	Ketubbot	Sam.	Samuel
Ber.	Berakhot	*Kid.*	Kiddushin	*Sanh.*	Sanhedrin
Bets.	Betsah	*Kil.*	Kilayim	*Shab.*	Shabbat
Bik.	Bikkurim	*Kin.*	Kinnim	*Sh. Ar.*	Shulhan Arukh
BK	Bava Kamma	Lam.	Lamentations	*Shek.*	Shekalim
BM	Bava Metsia	Lam. R.	Lamentations Rabbah	*Shev.*	Shevi'it
c.	circa	Lat.	Latin	*Shevu.*	Shevu'ot
Can.	Canaanite	Lev.	Leviticus	*Sif.*	Sifrei
CE	Common Era (AD)	Lev. R.	Leviticus Rabbah	*Sof.*	Soferim
cent.	century	lit.	literally	Song	Song of Songs (Canticles)
Chr.	Chronicles	LXX	Septuagint		
Dan.	Daniel	*Ma'as.*	Ma'aserot	Song R.	Song of Songs Rabbah
Dem.	Demai	*Ma'as. Sh.*	Ma'aser Sheni	*Sot.*	Sotah
Deut.	Deuteronomy	Macc.	Maccabees	Sp.	Spanish
Deut. R.	Deuteronomy Rabbah	Maim.	Maimonides	*Suk.*	Sukkah
Eccl.	Ecclesiastes	*Mak.*	Makkot	*Ta'an.*	Ta'anit
Eccl. R.	Ecclesiastes Rabbah	*Makh.*	Makhshirim	*Tam.*	Tamid
Ed.	Eduyyot	Mal.	Malachi	*Tanh.*	Tanhuma
EH	Even ha-Ezer	*Meg.*	Megillah	Targ.	Targum
Er.	Eruvin	*Mekh.*	*Mekhilta*	TB	Babylonian Talmud
Est.	Esther	*Men.*	Menahot	*Tem.*	Temurah
Est. R.	Esther Rabbah	Mic.	Micah	*Ter.*	Terumot
Ex.	Exodus	*Mid.*	Middot	TJ	Jerusalem Talmud
Ex. R.	Exodus Rabbah	Midr.	Midrash	*Toh.*	Tohorot
Ezek.	Ezekiel	*Mik.*	Mikva'ot	*Tos.*	Tosafot
ff.	following	Mish.	Mishnah	*Tosef.*	Tosefta
fl.	flourished	*MK*	Mo'ed Katan	*Uk.*	Uktsin
Fr.	French	Nah.	Nahum	*Yad.*	Yadayim (Maim., Y = Mishneh Torah) ad
Gen.	Genesis	*Ned.*	Nedarim		
Gen. R.	Genesis Rabbah	*Neg.*	Nega'im	*Yal.*	Yalkut
Germ.	German	Neh.	Nehemiah	*YD*	Yoreh De'ah
Git.	Gittin	*Nid.*	Niddah	*Yev.*	Yevamot
Gk.	Greek	Num.	Numbers	Yid.	Yiddish
Hag.	Hagigah	Num. R.	Numbers Rabbah	*Zav.*	Zavim
Hal.	Hallah	Ob.	Obadiah	Zech.	Zechariah
Heb.	Hebrew	*OH*	Orah Hayyim	Zeph.	Zephaniah
HM	Hoshen Mishpat	*Ohol.*	Oholot	*Zev.*	Zevahim

GLOSSARY

(plural and adjectival forms in parentheses)

ACROSTIC: letters at beginning of lines in religious poetry that together spell out words or names.

AGGADAH (AGGADOT; AGGADIC): non-legal portions of the Talmud and Midrash.

AHARONIM: later rabbinical authorities.

ALEINU: prayer recited at the end of each daily service.

AMIDAH: prayer of "Eighteen Benedictions" recited in every service.

AMORA (AMORAIM; AMORAIC): sage of the talmudic era.

ARK: niche or cupboard in synagogue for Scrolls of the Law.

ASHKENAZI(M): Jew of medieval German tradition and descent.

ASSIMILATION: becoming part of a foreign culture.

AV BET DIN: head of Jewish law court.

AVOT: ethical tractate of the Mishnah.

BARAITA: statement of *tanna* not found in Mishnah.

BAR MITZVAH: attainment by a boy of his religious majority (for a girl, bat mitzvah).

BET DIN (BATTEI DIN): rabbinical law court.

BET MIDRASH: study center, often part of synagogue.

BIMAH: reader's desk or platform in the synagogue.

CANAAN: another name for the Land of Israel.

CHABAD: Hasidic movement

CHALLAH (CHALLOT): white loaf of bread baked for Sabbaths and festivals.

CONSERVATIVE: movement in Judaism which permits modifications in *halakhah.*

CUBIT: about 18 inches (45 cm).

DAYYAN: religious judge.

DIASPORA: Jewish communities outside the Land of Israel.

EMANCIPATION: the granting of civil rights to Jews in their countries of residence.

ENLIGHTENMENT (Heb. *Haskalah*): a movement to spread modern ideas among the Jews.

ERETS ISRAEL: the Land of Israel.

ESSENES: ascetic movement in Second Temple times.

EXILARCH: lay head of the Jewish community in Babylon.

FIRST TEMPLE PERIOD: from building of the First Temple c. 950 BCE to its destruction by the Babylonians in 586 BCE.

GABBAI (GABBA'IM): Jewish community official; synagogue warden.

GALUT (GOLAH): Exile, Diaspora.

GAON (GE'ONIM; GEONIC): title given to leading Babylonian sages of the 6th–12th centuries.

GEMARA: commentary on Mishnah incorporated in Talmud.

GET: bill of divorcement.

HAFTARAH: reading from the Prophets chanted after the Reading of the Law.

HAGGADAH (HAGGADOT): book from which the traditional "narrative" is recited at the Passover *Seder.*

HAKKAFOT: circuits, especially around the synagogue.

HALAKHAH (HALAKHOT; HALAKHIC): Jewish religious law.

HALITSAH: ceremony effecting release from obligation of levirate marriage.

HALLEL: "Psalms of Praise" (113–118) recited on festive occasions.

HAMETS: leavened bread.

HANUKKAH: festival, commemorating victory of the Maccabees.

HASIDIM (HASIDIC): adherents of various pietist movements, especially one founded in Eastern Europe in 18th century.

HASKALAH: Jewish Enlightenment movement.

HAZZAN: synagogue cantor or "reader."

HEDER: primary religious school.

HELLENISM: the embracing of Greek culture among Jews and other peoples after Alexander's conquests in the fourth century BCE.

HERESY: beliefs opposed to official religious doctrine.

HIGH HOLIDAYS: Rosh ha-Shanah (the Jewish New Year) and the Day of Atonement (Yom Kippur).

HOL HA-MO'ED: intermediate (semi-festive) days of Passover and Sukkot.

HOLY OF HOLIES: the most sacred place in the Sanctuary (Tabernacle) and Temple, where the Ark of the Covenant was kept.

HOSHANA RABBAH: seventh day of the festival of Tabernacles.

KABBALAH (KABBALISTIC): Jewish mystical tradition.

KADDISH: hymn of praise chanted by the reader or mourners in public worship.

KARAITES: sect founded in eighth century CE rejecting the Oral Law.

KETUBBAH: marriage contract.

KIDDUSH: "sanctification" blessing on Sabbaths and festivals.

KOHEN (KOHANIM): Jew of priestly descent.

KOL NIDREI: formula recited on the eve of Day of Atonement.

KOSHER: conforming to the Jewish dietary laws (*kashrut*).

LAG BA-OMER: semi-holiday during the Omer period.

LEVIRATE MARRIAGE: marriage of childless widow with husband's brother

MA'ARIV: evening prayer service.

MAFTIR: last portion of the Law read on Sabbaths, festivals, etc.

MAGEN DAVID: hexagram which became major Jewish symbol.

MAHZOR: festival prayer book

MARRANOS: descendants of Jews of Spain and Portugal who had been forcibly baptized but secretly observed Jewish rituals (also known as Anusim, Conversos, and Crypto-Jews).

MASKILIM: adherents of the Jewish Enlightenment (Haskalah).

MASORAH (MASORETIC): body of traditions concerning Bible text.

MATZAH: unleavened bread.

MENORAH: temple candelabrum which became major Jewish symbol.

MESSIAH: savior and redeemer expected to come at the End of Days.

MEZUZAH: container carrying parchment scroll with Torah verses, affixed to doorposts.

MIDRASH (MIDRASHIM; MIDRASHIC): exposition of Scripture, both aggadic and halakhic.

MIKVEH: ritual bath.

MINHAG: local customs; prayer rite.

MINHAH: afternoon prayer service.

MINYAN: prayer quorum of at least ten adult males.

MISHNAH (MISHNAIC): first rabbinic codification of the Oral Law.

MITNAGGEDIM: "opponents" of Hasidism.

MITZVAH (MITZVOT): religious commandment; honor allocated to a worshiper in synagogue.

MUSAF: additional prayer service.

NASI: President of Sanhedrin.

NE'ILAH: Concluding Service on the Day of Atonement.

NEOLOGY: Reform Jewish trend in Hungary.

NOVELLAE (Heb. hiddushim): rabbinic commentary deriving original conclusions.

OMER: period of semi-mourning between Passover and Shavu'ot.

ORAL LAW: body of legal rules traditionally given by God to Moses and passed on from generation to generation.

ORIENTAL JEWS: Jews in Islamic and Asian lands, not of European origin.

ORTHODOX: subscribing to the beliefs and practices of traditional Judaism.

PAGANISM: the worship of many gods.

PARASHAH: weekly Torah reading

PHARISEES: rabbinical movement in Mishnaic times.

PILGRIM FESTIVALS: Passover, Shavu'ot, and Sukkot.

PIYYUT (PIYYUTIM): liturgical poetry.

PROGRESSIVE: term for Reform Judaism.

PURIM: feast celebrating the deliverance of Persian Jewry.

RABBI: qualified teacher of Judaism (variants include Rav, Rabban, Reb, Rebbe).

RECONSTRUCTIONISM: movement in U.S. Judaism regarding Judaism as a civilization.

REFORM: movement in Judaism advocating major departures from halakhah and traditional belief (also called Liberal).

RESPONSA: authoritative replies to halakhic questions.

RISHONIM: earlier rabbinic authorities.

ROSH HA-SHANAH: New Year festival.

ROSH HODESH: new moon semi-festival.

SADDUCEES: movement of aristocrats and priests in Second Temple times.

SAGES: the early (tannaitic and amoraic) rabbis.

SANHEDRIN: ancient Israel's supreme court.

SAVORAIM: Babylonian scholars in 6th century CE.

SECOND TEMPLE PERIOD: period from rebuilding of Temple (c. 520) to its destruction in 70 CE.

SEDER: home service on Passover eve.

SEFER TORAH: Scroll of the Law.

SEPHARDI(M): Jew of Spanish-Portuguese tradition and descent.

SEPTUAGINT: first Greek translation of the Bible.

SHABBATEAN: adherent of the pseudo-messianic and heretical movement founded by Shabbetai Tsevi.

SHAHARIT: morning prayer service.

SHAVU'OT: Festival of Weeks or Pentecost.

SHEHITAH: ritual slaughter.

SHEKHINAH: the Divine Presence.

SHEMA: "Hear, O Israel" profession of Jewish faith.

SHEMINI ATSERET: festival that concludes Sukkot.

SHOFAR: ceremonial ram's horn blown on the New Year and other solemn occasions.

SHULHAN ARUKH: major codification of Jewish law.

SIDDUR: prayer book.

SIMHAT TORAH: festival of the Rejoicing of the Law.

SUKKOT: festival of Tabernacles, the "Feast of Booths."

TABERNACLE (Heb. mishkan): the shrine accompanying the Israelites in the desert after the Exodus and housing the Holy of Holies.

TALLIT (TALLITOT): prayer shawl worn by Jewish males.

TALMUD (TALMUDIC): basic codification of Jewish law, comprising the Mishnah and the Gemara.

TALMUD TORAH: religious school.

TANNA (TANNAIM; TANNAITIC): sage of the Mishnaic era.

TARGUM: Aramaic translation of Bible.

TEFILLIN: "phylacteries" worn at weekday morning prayers.

TISHAH BE-AV: Ninth of Av fast day commemorating the Temple's destruction.

TORAH: the Pentateuch or Five Books of Moses; Jewish religious teaching in the widest sense.

TOSAFOT: comments on Talmud by successors of Rashi, 12th–14th century (tosafists).

TOSEFTA: collections of tannaitic statements (baraitot) not found in Mishnah.

TRACTATE (Heb. massekhet): book of the Mishnah or Talmud.

TSADDIK: Hasidic leader.

TSITSIT: fringes attached to prayer shawl or undergarment.

TU BI-SHEVAT: semi-festival of New Year for Trees.

YESHIVAH (YESHIVOT): Babylonian or Palestinian Academy; modern talmudic college.

YOM KIPPUR: Day of Atonement.

ZOHAR: principal work of Jewish mysticism.

AARON Elder brother of MOSES, younger brother of MIRIAM, and a member of the tribe of Levi. Aaron was appointed by God to be Moses' spokesman to Pharaoh and the Israelites around the time they were leaving Egypt. With his miracle rod, he brought the first three plagues upon the Egyptians. Later on, he supported Moses during the battle with the AMALEKITES at Rephidim (Ex. 6–8). Once the Tabernacle was built, Aaron became the HIGH PRIEST and his sons and descendants inherited the right to serve as the Israelites' priests (Ex. 28–29; Lev. 8).

There were three major crises in Aaron's life. The first one happened when Moses went away for 40 days. The people demanded a God they could see, and Aaron made the GOLDEN CALF (Ex. 32). The second was the death of Nadab and Abihu, two of Aaron's four sons, after they brought a "strange fire before the Lord" (Lev. 10). The third was when Aaron's cousin KORAH started a rebellion because he wanted to replace Aaron as the High Priest (Num. 16). Because they disobeyed God

Aaron the High Priest. From an anthology of texts on the Bible, religion, grammar, astrology, etc. Northern France, c. 1280.

at the Waters of Meribah, Aaron and Moses were punished. They were not allowed to enter the Promised Land. Aaron was stripped of his special clothes, which his son Eleazar then put on. Aaron died on Mount Hor (Num. 10).

The rabbis saw Aaron as a model spiritual figure and the ideal priest. He was close to the people, settled their arguments and worked for peace among the Israelites. He inspired Hillel's saying: "Be a disciple of Aaron, loving peace and pursuing peace, loving your fellow creatures and attracting them to the TORAH" (*Avot* 1:12). Aaron is one of the seven "invisible holy guests" (USHPIZIN) whom observant Jews invite to their *sukkah* on the festival of SUKKOT.

ABBAHU (fl. 300 CE). Prominent rabbi of Erets Israel, head of the Academy in Caesarea. He was the spokesman of the Jewish community in Erets Israel before the Roman authorities, because he was rich and spoke Greek. He was a student of R. JOHANAN BEN NAPPAHA. The first three sections of the book of *Nezikin* were written at his Academy and later became a part of the Jerusalem Talmud. Christianity was the official religion during his time. A great deal of Abbahu's teachings were directed against Christianity and Jews who were becoming Christians (see MINIM). He made a number of laws, which were written in the Jerusalem Talmud and accepted throughout Erets Israel. He is also quoted in the Babylonian Talmud. He has several famous sayings. For example: "Be among the persecuted rather than the persecutors" (*BK* 93a) and "When sinners repent, they can achieve more than the wholly righteous" (*Ber.* 34b).

ABBAYE (c. 280–338 CE). Together with RAVA, the most prominent Babylonian rabbis of their time. Abbaye lost both of his parents as an infant. He was raised by an uncle, RABBAH BAR NAHMANI, who hired a nurse to take care of Abbaye. He often quoted her folk wisdom and home remedies. Abbaye had two teachers: Rabbah, who was the head of the Academy in Pumbedita, Babylonia, and R. Joseph ben Hiyya, who taught Abbaye about the traditions of the *tannaim* and the *amoraim*. Abbaye became the head of the Academy in Pumbedita after Rabbah. Abbaye's argument with Rava on the subject of Jewish law can be found throughout the Talmud. He was known for his strong moral character and good temper. When the *halakkah* was in doubt he used to say: "Go out and see how people act in such situations" (*Ber.* 45a, etc.). He used to quote proverbs that were popular in his time, which shows that he was not removed from society.

ABLUTIONS   Ritual washing that ranges from immersing the whole body (*tevilah*) to pouring water over the hands (*netilat yadayim*). According to the TORAH (Lev. 11:30), if people or objects become unclean through contact with unclean sources they must immerse their entire body in a natural spring, river, or MIKVEH (ritual bath). Some examples of unclean sources are contact with a dead body, menstruation, contagious diseases, and leprosy. People attending the services at the TEMPLE also had to perform ablutions because they had to be in a state of ritual purity. The PRIESTS had to perform ablutions before they did their duties or ate the special food they had received as offerings or tithes. The HIGH PRIEST underwent five immersions on the DAY OF ATONEMENT, the holiest day of the year.

Copper receptacle with a wide mouth and two handles for the ritual washing of the hands (netilat yadayim) *involving pouring water over the right hand and then over the left. Central Europe, 19th century.*

When the Temple stood, the ashes of the RED HEIFER were used in ritual purification. Since the Temple was destroyed, the ashes of the red heifer are no longer used and many kinds of purification are out of use. There are some forms of ablution that are still used: ritual immersion of women after their menstrual period or childbirth, purification of cooking utensils made by non-Jews, immersion of converts on their CONVERSION to Judaism, and washing the hands before eating bread (see GRACE BEFORE MEALS) and after sleeping and using the toilet.

Both hygiene and holiness are taken into account. The first step in any ablution is a thorough cleaning. All foreign objects must be removed, so that nothing comes between the person or object and the purifying waters.

In the Second Temple period, a few Jewish sects paid particular attention to ritual ablution. These sects included the Hemerobaptists ("morning bathers"), the ESSENES, and the Qumran community (see DEAD SEA SCROLLS). It is likely that John the Baptist was close to one of these groups, and from him the custom of baptism passed into CHRISTIANITY.

ABOMINATION   The word "abomination" usually stands for one of three different Hebrew words in Bible translations: *to'evah, shekets,* and *piggul.*

To'evah is the strongest term, and was originally used for an action that offends the religious beliefs of a people. For example, the Egyptians considered raising cattle to be a *to'evah* (Gen. 46:34). Therefore the Hebrews, who were shepherds, had to live apart from the Egyptians in a separate district of Egypt. The same word is later used for animals that may not be eaten (Deut. 14:3; see DIETARY LAWS). An even greater abomination is IDOLATRY, and the idols themselves are called *to'evah* (Deut. 7:26). Forbidden sexual relations are perhaps the most serious *to'evah* (Lev. 18:22–28, 20:13; Deut. 22:5).

Shekets refers to unclean fish, seafood, birds, and insects (Lev. 11:10–13). It also used to describe idol worship in the prophets (Jer. 4:1).

The meat of most sacrifices had to be eaten within a certain amount of time. If meat was left over beyond that time, it became *piggul* and could no longer be eaten.

ABORTION   The issue of abortion involves several Jewish laws. If the fetus were considered a living being, then abortion would be murder. This is the most serious consideration, and the rabbis of the TALMUD did not agree about this point. There are also laws against causing any kind of injury to one's body and destroying human seed. All rabbinic authorities agree that abortion for social or economic reasons is against Jewish law.

In Jewish law, a mother may have an abortion in order to save her life. It is more important to save the mother than to save the fetus because the mother is already alive. Some rabbis allow an abortion if the fetus has a serious disease, such as Tay-Sachs. Others allow an abortion if the pregnancy puts the mother's mental health in danger. The Talmud says that a fetus is formed only after 41 days, and some rabbis therefore allow an abortion if the fetus is less than 41 days old.

ABRAHAM   Father of the Jewish people, first of the three PATRIARCHS, son of Terah. There were ten generations from ADAM to NOAH and ten from Noah to Abraham. Abraham was born in the year 1948 after the CREATION of the world (1812 BCE). At first his name was Abram, which means "the father is exalted," but he was then renamed Abraham by God, which means "the father of many nations" (Gen. 17:5). After Terah's death, God told the 75-year-old Abraham to move with his wife SARAH "to the land which I will show you." This was the land of CANAAN. God also promised to make him into a great nation (Gen. 12).

Abraham spent much of his life wandering. He is portrayed as a peaceful man with many flocks. God promised to give him the land of Canaan in a COVENANT ceremony (Gen. 15) and also told Abraham to circumcise himself and all his male descendants as a sign of this promise.

When Abraham was in his eighties, he and Sarah still had no children. Sarah offered her handmaiden, Hagar, to Abraham as

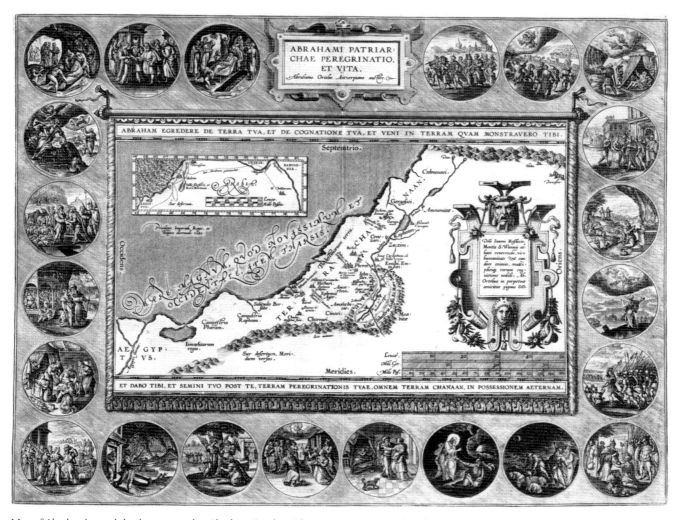

Map of Abraham's travels by the cartographer Abraham Ortelius. The 22 vignettes surrounding the map show the major events of the Patriarch's life, from the time he left Haran to his death. Beginning at the top right, clockwise: Abraham leaves Mesopotamia with his family; God promises Abraham to make him into a great nation; the Patriarch builds an altar to the Lord; God appears and promises Abraham the Land of Canaan; he sets out to Lot's rescue; upon his return, he is greeted by Melchizedek, the king of Salem; God renews his promise to Abraham; the three angels predict that Sarah will bear him a son; the birth of Isaac; Hagar and Ishmael are banished; the covenant with Abimelech; the supreme test: God orders the sacrifice of Isaac; Sarah's death and burial; the marriage of Isaac and Rebekah; Abraham's burial in the Cave of Machpelah at Hebron, next to Sarah. From Additamentum IV Thiatri *orbus terrarum, Antwerp 1590.*

a concubine (unofficial wife). Hagar then gave birth to Ishmael. God promised Abraham that he would still have a child with Sarah, and when Sarah was ninety and Abraham one hundred years old, Isaac was born. Isaac became Abraham's heir. When Isaac was born God tested Abraham and told him to kill Isaac as a sacrifice. Abraham was about to do so when an angel prevented the sacrifice (see AKEDAH). Abraham died at the age of 175 and was buried in the cave of Machpelah in Hebron.

There are many rabbinic legends about Abraham. He was the father of MONOTHEISM, the first person who believed there was only one God. This belief led him to smash all the idols in his father's store. Nimrod, the ruler, had him thrown in a fiery furnace, but Abraham came out of the furnace unharmed.

Abraham is also seen as the model of HOSPITALITY and of *hesed*, kindness to others. He began the tradition of praying the MORNING SERVICE.

ABRAHAM BEN DAVID OF POSQUIÈRES (known as *Ravad*; c. 1125–c. 1198). He was born in Provence and he was a student of Moses ben Joseph of Norbonne and Meshullam ben Jacob of Lunel. Ravad was one of the most important French TALMUD scholars of his time. He established a *yeshivah* at Posquières. He was very wealthy, so he supported many of the needy students at his *yeshivah*. He was known as *ba'al hassagot,* which means the great critic, because he wrote critical notes on several famous books, including the *Mishnah Torah* of MAIMONIDES. Ravad was opposed to the Talmud becoming just a code of law. For this reason he criticized Maimonides, who had not given any sources or explanations in the *Mishnah Torah*. He also disagreed with Maimonides' philosophy.

Few of Ravad's books can still be found. He wrote a commentary on the MISHNAH, but only two of the six parts have survived. A few of his RESPONSA are in a book called *Temim De'im* (Perfect in Knowledge). His commentary on the SIFRA, a MISRASH on the book of Leviticus, also still exists. His students were Isaac Hacohen of Narbonne and Abraham ben Nathan of Lunel.

ABRAVANEL (ABRABANEL), ISAAC BEN JUDAH   (1437–1508).
Statesman, Bible commentator, and philosopher. Abravanel worked for Alfonso V, the king of Portugal. When the king died, Abravanel was accused of spying so he ran away to Toledo, Spain, where he served King Ferdinand and Queen Isabella. In 1492 the Jews were forced to leave Spain. Abravanel tried to convince the king and queen to let the Jews stay, but he did not succeed. When the Jews were expelled from Spain, he went with them to Naples. There too he worked for the king.

Abravanel was a student of Joseph Hayyun, the rabbi of

Page from an illustrated Haggadah *with a commentary (appearing in smaller letters on the right) by Isaac Abravanel. Central Europe, 1741.*

Lisbon. He studied both TALMUD and secular subjects and wrote a long commentary on the TORAH and the PROPHETS. In his commentaries he used ideas he had learned from the secular world. He wrote several books of Jewish philosophy and also three works that argue with people who thought Jesus was the MESSIAH. Abravanel believed that there would soon be a living Messiah in the world, who would be arriving in around the year 1503.

Abravanel's oldest son, Judah (c. 1469–c. 1535), was known in Italy as Leone Ebreo. He wrote a book called *Dialoghi di Amore*.

ABULAFIA, ABRAHAM BEN SAMUEL   (1240–after 1291).
Spanish Kabbalist. When Abulafia was 20, he decided to leave Spain to search for the SAMBATYON River. According to legend, the TEN [Lost] TRIBES still live on the river's other side. While in Italy, he began to study philosophy, and soon went on to study KABBALAH. He was most interested in the mystical meaning of Hebrew letters and the GEMATRIA (number codes) of Hebrew words. He believed that the secrets of the creation of the world were found in different combinations of Hebrew letters and words.

Abulafia lived a simple life and avoided pleasures. He believed that God had appeared to him. He later predicted that the age of the Messiah would begin in the year 1290, and therefore tried to convert Pope Nicholas III to Judaism. However the pope had Abulafia put in prison and brought to Rome. Fortunately the pope died before he could carry out the harsh punishment that he had in store for Abulafia. Little is known of Abulafia's later years, in which he constantly wandered from place to place; nor do we know how and where he died.

Abulafia's form of Kabbalah combined very complicated ideas with clear and logical ones. He viewed it as a natural continuation of the work of the great scholar MAIMONIDES, whom he considered to be in some ways a mystic. Abulafia's form of Kabbalah later became one of the bases of the 16th century Kabbalah that grew out of Safed in Erets Israel.

ACADEMIES   The original schools of higher Jewish learning established in Erets Israel and Babylonia. Both the WRITTEN LAW and the ORAL LAW were taught by the rabbis at these academies. Our earliest written account of houses of learning is found in the APOCRYPHA (Ecclus. 51:16, 23, 29). There the word "sitting" (*yeshivah* in Heb.) is used to describe a house of study (see also *Avot* 2:7). Because seating arrangements were important in the study hall, it came to be called a YESHIVAH. In Babylonia, the Aramaic word for seating, *metivta*, was used (*Yev.* 105b).

The TALMUD academies had a wide range of functions: center of rabbinic learning and discussions, high court of law (see BET DIN), ORDINATION of worthy students as rabbis, and determining the New MOON every month and thus fixing the CALENDAR.

Both teachers and students had to work to earn a living, since they were not paid by the academy. Classes were therefore held in the early morning and at night, which also allowed students time to prepare for the next session (*Shab.* 136b). Students could join the academy at any age, but only the most accomplished became teachers. The president of an academy was voted into office by its scholars, and he was called the *rosh yeshivah* ("head of the session"; *Ber.* 57a). His election had to be approved by the Babylonian EXILARCH.

Erets Israel (also called "Palestinian") Academies   Academies probably did not exist in Erets Israel outside of JERUSALEM before the Temple was destroyed in the year 70. There may have been a small academy in Yavneh, 25 miles west of Jerusalem. According to Jewish tradition, when the Romans mounted a siege against Jerusalem, Rabbi JOHANAN BEN ZAKKAI arranged to have himself smuggled out of the city in a coffin and brought before the Roman commander, Vespasian. In exchange for the rabbi's promise not to rebel against the Romans, Vespasian was willing to grant his request: "Give me [an academy at] Yavneh and its sages!" (*Git.* 56b).

Johanan made Yavneh the central point in a network of academies that spread from Erets Israel to Babylonia and even to Rome. It is said that Rabbi AKIVA attracted thousands to his academy in Bene Berak, Israel. When the BAR KOKHBA rebellion against Rome failed in 135 CE, much of central and southern Israel was destroyed. The Jewish communities, along with their academies, moved to the northern part of the country. The Yavneh academy moved first to Usha and then to Sepphoris, where Rabbi JUDAH HA-NASI edited the final version of the MISHNAH.

Tiberias became the location of the major academies during the time that the Jerusalem Talmud was edited. Although closed from about 400–520, the Tiberias academy remained active until the seventh century, one century after the Arabs conquered the region. The other academies in Erets Israel vanished by the fourth century.

Babylonian Academies   It is likely that there were already academies in Babylonia by the first century BCE. Under Rav Shila and Abba bar Abba, the academy at Nehardea became Babylonia's Jewish spiritual center in about the year 200 CE. When RAV (Abba Arikha) became its leader, its ties to Erets Israel became stronger, because Rav had been ordained there. Rav then founded a new academy in Sura, which remained active for nearly 800 years and drew over 1,000 full-time students. Twice a year, during the Hebrew months of Elul and Adar, thousands of people gathered at the academies to study Talmud (see KALLAH MONTHS). Most of the Babylonian Talmud was edited in Sura. SAMUEL (Mar) became the head of the academy at Nehardea. He and Rav became the first leading pair of scholars in Babylonia (see ZUGOT). The Nehardea Academy was destroyed in 259 by allies of the Romans and rebuilt by Judah bar Ezekiel in Pumbedita. It remained there until the ninth century.

The age of the Talmud was followed by the age of the *ge'onim* (see GAON), the leading rabbis at Sura or Pumpedita, which began in 589. During this period, the Babylonian academies con-

tinued to grow in importance. Jewish communities throughout the world sent their religious questions to the *ge'onim,*. These questions and their answers formed the RESPONSA literature. Jewish law codes were also written by the *ge'onim* at the academies (see CODIFICATION).

For information on the later academies, see YESHIVAH.

ACROSTICS   A poem in which sets of letters spell out words or appear in a special order. In many Hebrew prayers, each line begins with the next letter of the Hebrew alphabet in alphabetical order. There are examples of acrostics in the Bible, mostly in the book of Psalms (Psalms 37, 111–112, 119, 145). Using acrostics made it easier to remember the psalms or prayers by heart in the time before printed prayer books were available. In some cases, the first letter of each line spells out the author's name (e.g., MAOZ TZUR, LEKHAH DODI).

Acrostics were also used in the poetry of the Middle Ages and especially in the KABBALAH, an important set of mystical books. ANIM ZEMIROT is an example of a PIYYUT – a poem used in prayer – that is an acrostic sung at the end of Sabbath services. There are also a number of songs and hymns sung at the end of the Passover SEDER that use acrostics.

Acronyms are a similar form, also used frequently in the

Acrostics from an initial word-panel for a liturgical poem for Shavu'ot, from a prayer book with commentary. Southern Germany, c. 1320.

Middle Ages. In an acronym, the first letters of a group of words are used to form a new word. This new word is then used as an abbreviation of the original phrase. For example, RASHI (Rabbi Shelomo Yitshaki), RAMBAM (Rabbi Moses ben Maimon) and RAMBAN (Rabbi Moses ben Nahman).

ADAM AND EVE   First human couple in the world, according to Genesis 1:26–30. The Bible actually presents two descriptions of the creation of Adam and Eve. In Genesis 1, God creates both male and female in His likeness, and gives them the ability to reproduce and the power to dominate all other living creatures. In Genesis 2 and 3, in a more detailed description, Adam is created from the dust of the earth and placed in the Garden of EDEN. He is responsible for tending the garden. But when God sees that "it is not good for man to be alone," He puts the man into a deep sleep and makes him a mate out of one of his ribs.

In the biblical story, Adam and Eve are allowed to eat anything that grows in the Garden of Eden except the fruit of the Tree of Knowledge (of good and evil). However, a serpent living in the garden tempts the woman and she samples the fruit of this tree. God confronts the three and punishes each one. God tells Adam that he will from then on earn his bread "by the sweat of his brow." Eve will be dominated by her husband and is condemned to suffer pain in childbirth. The snake must crawl the earth on its belly and eat dust.

The story of Adam and Eve explains the origin of evil in the world. The world was "very good" when created, but a single act of disobedience introduces problems. Instead of being a caretaker in an ideal Garden of Eden, man will now have to work hard to survive. The ethical message in the Torah's version of the creation of humans makes it unique among the creation traditions of the ancient Near East.

ADAR   Twelfth month of the Jewish religious CALENDAR. When the year is a leap year, a second month of Adar is added to the year. Normally, Adar consists of 29 days and coincides with February/March. The Bible mentions the month several times by name, particularly in the Book of ESTHER.

A number of important events in Jewish history took place in Adar. On the third day of the month, the rebuilt TEMPLE in JERUSALEM was dedicated (Ezra 6:14–16). The traditional date for the birth and death of MOSES is Adar 7. The 7th of the month is also the traditional date of the minor fast observed by members of the Jewish BURIAL SOCIETY to atone for any disrespect they may have accidentally shown toward the dead. The major holiday of the month is Purim, which falls on the 14th (or 15th in Jerusalem and certain other cities).

In a leap year, there is a first Adar (*Adar Rishon*) consisting of 30 days and a second Adar (*Adar Sheni*) consisting of 29 days. All the events of Adar are celebrated in the second Adar.

The special joy associated with the holiday of Purim extends to the entire month of Adar. The Talmud states: "When Adar comes in, rejoicing is increased" (*Ta'an.* 29a).

ADDIR BI-MELUKHA   ("Mighty in Kingship"). Alphabetical ACROSTIC hymn included in the Passover SEDER by ASHKENAZIM. Each of the eight stanzas mentions two aspects of God and a different class of angels singing praises to God. This is followed by the chorus, *Ki Lo Na'eh* ("For to Him praise is becoming"). The composer was probably a French or German Jew.

ADDIR HU   ("Mighty is He"). Alphabetical ACROSTIC hymn included in the Passover SEDER by ASHKENAZIM. Each stanza of *Adir Hu* builds up an alphabetical list of God's qualities and attributes. The chorus calls upon God to restore His SANCTUARY without delay. The hymn was probably composed in 14th century Germany.

ADDITIONAL SERVICE   (Heb. *Musaf*). Prayer service added after the MORNING SERVICE on the SABBATH, the New MOON, PILGRIM FESTIVALS, and the HIGH HOLIDAYS. The Additional Service replaces the additional (*musaf*) sacrifice that, according to the Bible, was brought on these days to supplement the daily morning sacrifice (see SACRIFICES AND OFFERINGS). Even so, the Talmud records that the *Musaf* prayer was already known in the Second TEMPLE era (*Suk.* 53a), even though the *musaf* sacrifice was still being offered at that time.

RABBIC VIEWS OF ADAM AND EVE

Adam's dust was gathered from all parts of the world.

A single man was brought forth at creation, indicating that to destroy one human life is to destroy a whole world and to preserve one life is to preserve a whole world, so that no man should ever say to another: "My father was superior to yours!" God's greatness was thereby established, for when a human being uses one die to stamp coins, all of them emerge alike; yet when God stamps men with the die of Adam, each of them is in some way different. Thus all have the right to say: "The world was created for my sake!"

Adam was created from the dust, and Eve from Adam; but henceforth it will be in God's image only – not man without woman, nor woman without man, and neither without the Divine Presence.

A heretic said to Rabban Gamaliel: "Your God is a thief, for is it not written that He caused Adam to fall asleep and then stole one of his ribs?" Gamaliel's daughter promptly told this heretic that she was sending for the police, as thieves had stolen a silver jug from the house, leaving a golden one in its place. "I wouldn't mind such thieves breaking into my house!" said the heretic, to which Gamaliel's daughter replied: "Then why criticize our God? If He took a rib from Adam, it was only to enrich him with a helpmate!"

The Additional Service is generally recited immediately after the Morning Service, although according to Jewish law it can be recited at any time during the day. The order is: Half KADDISH, followed by the Additional Service, which consists of a special AMIDAH prayer, with the standard three opening and three concluding benedictions of the *Amidah*. Except for the Additional Service of ROSH HA-SHANAH (New Year), all the *Amidah* prayers contain a single middle blessing. This central blessing mentions the importance of the day, asks God to restore the Jews to their land and Temple, and quotes the Bible verses about the *musaf* sacrifice that was offered in the Temple on that day. The Rosh ha-Shanah *Amidah* is special because its middle section contains three blessings. After each blessing, the SHOFAR is sounded (except on the Sabbath).

The *Amidah* of each additional service is first read silently by the congregation and then repeated aloud by the leader. On the New Moon and the intermediate days of the pilgrim festivals, the standard KEDUSHAH is recited in the third benediction; on Sabbaths, the High Holidays and the pilgrim festivals (including HOSHANA RABBAH), a special extended *Kedushah* is recited. On the first day of Passover, the seasonal Prayer for DEW is added to the *Musaf*. On SHEMINI ATSERET a special Prayer for RAIN is added to the reader's repetition of the *Musaf*.

ADMOR (Heb. acronym of *Adonenu Morenu ve-Rabbenu* – "Our lord, teacher, and master"; also called "Rebbe"). Title of honor given to highest leaders in Hasidic communities (see also TSADDIK).

ADONAI See GOD, NAMES OF

ADON OLAM ("Lord of the Universe"). Opening words of a popular SYNAGOGUE hymn. Some suggest that *Adon Olam* was written by the 11th century poet Solomon IBN GABIROL, though not everybody accepts this. The prayer is one of the most popular of all hymns. It is a "mono-rhyme," with the same rhyming sound at the end of each verse. It expresses trust in God, man's one and only Creator, Guardian, and Redeemer.

Adon Olam appears in several places in the PRAYER BOOK. We find it at the beginning of the MORNING SERVICE, at the end of the ADDITIONAL SERVICE for the Sabbath and festivals, and at the end of the NIGHT PRAYERS before going to sleep.

ADOPTION Jewish law does not consider adoption as an actual replacement for the natural parents. It does, however, recognize adoptive relationships in certain ways. For example, an individual is permitted to take on responsibility for the physical, emotional, and social well-being of a child. In such cases, the death of the adoptive parent does not end the relationship with the adopted child. According to Jewish law, the parents' heirs must continue to provide for the child. A rabbinical court (BET DIN) can remove children from the custody of their natural parents, and place them in a more suitable home, if the children are being endangered.

ADON OLAM

Reigned the Universe's Master,
Ere were earthly things begun;
When His mandate all created,
Ruler was the name He won.
And alone He'll rule tremendous
When all things are past and gone,
He no equal has, nor consort,
He, the singular and lone,
Has no end and no beginning;
His the scepter, might and throne.
He's my God and living Savior,
Rock to Whom I in need run;
He's my banner and my refuge,
Fount of weal when call'd upon.
In His hand I place my spirit,
At nightfall and at rise of sun,
And therewith my body also;
God's my God – I fear no one.

On the other hand, in Jewish law the natural parents are still required to provide for the child's needs if the adoptive parents are unable to do so. The adopted child does not automatically inherit from the adoptive parent – a special provision must be made in the will. Because adoption does not change the personal status of the child, no prohibitions regarding marriage or divorce exist between the child and members of the adoptive family.

The list of adoptive relationships in the Bible is short. For example, SARAH wishes to have a child through her handmaiden (Gen. 16:2), who she would presumably raise as her own; MOSES is adopted by Pharaoh's daughter (Ex. 2:10); Esther is adopted by her uncle Mordecai (Est. 2:7).

ADRET, SOLOMON BEN ABRAHAM (known as *Rashba*; c. 1235–1310). Rabbinical authority in Spain. He was born in Barcelona, where he served as rabbi for half a century. He was a student of Jonah ben Abraham Gerondi and NAHMANIDES. Adret's writings include all branches of rabbinic literature. He produced commentaries on 17 books of the Talmud; his law code, *Torat ha-Bayit* ("The Law of the House"), deals with the Jewish home, including DIETARY LAWS and FAMILY PURITY. He is also the author of thousands of RESPONSA on all aspects of Jewish law, in answer to questions addressed to him by Jewish communities from northern Europe to Erets Israel. These Responsa are thought to have been part of the groundwork for the great law code, the SHULHAN ARUKH.

He was an important defender of Jewish rights (see DISPUTATIONS). He composed a work challenging the charges of Raymond Martini, a Dominican monk, who portrayed Judaism in an unfavorable light in his *Pugio Fidei* ("Dagger of Faith").

ADULT   In Jewish society, reaching puberty changes one's status from child to adult – for most matters. However, because individuals are different, it is hard to tell when this change takes place. For this reason the rabbis created a basic timeframe for establishing adulthood that applies to everybody. However, the rules are different for men and women. For women, a girl passes to the new status of adult in two stages. When she turns 12, she is given the status of "young woman" (na'arah). Then at the age of 12 years and six months, she receives the new status of "adult" (bogeret). For men, a boy passes immediately to the new status of "adult" (gadol) when he reaches the age of 13 years and one day. He can then be counted for a prayer quorum (MINYAN) along with other adults of similar status.

What exactly does adulthood mean? For one, it means that the new adult is now morally responsible for his/her actions. Before adulthood the father is responsible for the actions of his minor child (see BARUKH SHE-PETARANI). In addition, the new adult must now observe the commandments and may act on behalf of other adults in the synagogue. Outside the synagogue, the new status brings with it the right to represent other adults in matters of Jewish law. It also brings full responsibility in Jewish civil and criminal courts.

While this timeframe is generally correct, the rabbis also created a number of exceptions to the rule. For example, the Talmud states that individuals were not subject to heavenly punishment for sins committed before the age of 20 (Shab. 89b). On the other hand, certain vows taken even during the year before BAR MITZVAH were considered binding. Regarding marriage, in talmudic times girls could become engaged from the age of three. Boys could be engaged only from the age of nine (Nid. 5:4–5).

In Israel today, both men and women may marry only from the age of 17; before that they need special permission from the court.

ADULTERY   (Heb. ni'uf). The prohibition against adultery is one of the TEN COMMANDMENTS. Adultery means specifically voluntary sexual relations between a married or engaged woman and someone other than her husband.

As part of the Ten Commandments, adultery is one of the most serious of all sins. In the Bible, both the man and the woman can receive the death penalty (defined by the rabbis as strangulation). According to the Talmud, the adulterer and the adulteress receive eternal punishment, even in the hereafter (BM 58b). In addition, the basic law of adultery was strengthened by another biblical commandment, the law of SOTAH (Num. 5:12–31). This law allowed a husband who suspected his wife of adultery to impose on her the ordeal of the "waters of bitterness" to test if she was guilty or innocent. In post-biblical times, a husband who has good reason to suspect that his wife has been unfaithful may divorce her; if the case is proven in court, he must divorce her (see DIVORCE).

The Talmud treats adultery with even greater seriousness. The prohibition is counted among the seven basic NOACHIDE LAWS that apply to all human beings. Adultery is also one of three offenses – along with murder and idol worship – for which a Jew must allow himself to be killed rather than sin (Sanh. 74a). The seriousness extends even to the next generation: the offspring of adultery is a mamzer, an illegitimate child who carries a stigma within the community (see ILLEGITIMACY).

As a theme, adultery receives special treatment in all three sections of the Hebrew Bible. The stories of SARAH and Abimelech (Gen. 20) and JOSEPH and Potiphar's wife (Gen. 39) treat adultery as a sin against God. King DAVID is later punished for this offense (II Sam. 12:9ff). The first nine chapters of the Book of Proverbs contain advice to young men about how to avoid having an unfaithful wife. In addition, the relationship between God and Israel is portrayed as a marriage and the worship of false gods is described as adultery or prostitution (Ezek. 16:15ff; Hos. 2:4; Ex. 34:15–16; Num. 15:39).

While Jewish law condemns relations between a married man and an unmarried woman, such relations do not count as adultery and the child of such a union is not considered a mamzer.

AFIKOMAN   See SEDER

AFTERLIFE   Anyone who has read the Jewish prayer book knows that it is difficult to imagine Judaism without a belief in the afterlife. The second of the 18 blessings that make up the daily AMIDAH is devoted entirely to the theme of RESURRECTION (rebirth) of the dead. Even so, modern scholars see the development of a full-fledged belief in the afterlife as a gradual addition to Jewish belief.

The TORAH does not specifically state that there is life after death. It assumes that when people die they go to sheol – the grave – which may mean nothing more than a burial plot (Gen. 37:35). In the PROPHETS (second section of the Hebrew Bible), this begins to change. For example, SAUL communicates with the dead prophet SAMUEL, which clearly shows that he continued to exist after death (I Sam. 28). Later Bible stories hint at resurrection, but they refer to resurrection of the entire people (Ezek. 37). By the time of the later books of the Writings (third section of the Hebrew Bible), we begin to see resurrection applying to individuals (Dan. 12:2). Still, we do not yet see a fully developed belief in the afterlife.

By the time of the Maccabees (2nd cent. BCE) the idea of the afterlife had taken a more definite shape. By this time REWARD AND PUNISHMENT began to apply to life after death. God promised the righteous that they would see Israel restored (II Maccabees 12:44). Apocalyptic literature (writings about "the end of days") contrasts the "world to come" with "this world" (Apocalypse of Enoch 71:15). Finally in the period of the MISHNAH (2nd cent. CE), the concept of individual, physical resurrection after death is clearly defined and widely accepted. Mishnah Sanhedrin 10:1 states: "All Israel has a portion in the world to come, except one who says, 'There is no resurrection of the dead.'" Scholars widely agree that, from this point on, the belief in the afterlife as the reunion of body and soul before the time of God's judgment became part of mainstream Judaism.

The TALMUD and MIDRASH discuss a number of other subjects related to the afterlife. These include: the fate of those who are neither completely righteous nor completely wicked, descriptions of heaven and hell, the location of hell, etc. In general, the rabbis taught that the righteous would receive their reward in the world to come, while the wicked would be punished.

The Middle Ages represented the golden age of Jewish intellectual life. It is not surprising to find a wide range of beliefs about the afterlife in the major writings of the period, including the idea of an afterlife without physical resurrection. SAADIAH GAON (Babylonia, 882–942 CE) suggested that there were two resurrections for the righteous: the first, a physical one, when the age of the Messiah begins; the second, when they enter the world to come, was a purely spiritual state. The wicked were condemned to eternal suffering (*The Book of Beliefs and Opinions* 6:1, 6:7, 7:113). MAIMONIDES took this idea even further. He wrote: "In the world to come, the body and the flesh do not exist, but only the souls of the righteous alone" (*Yad, Teshuvah* 3:6). Maimonides was severely criticized for his denial of physical resurrection. In his later writings he seems to have changed his views on this subject.

The Middle Ages also represent the golden age of Jewish MYSTICISM. Unlike the philosophers who struggled with the idea of the afterlife, the mystics wrote much on the subject. In particular, they describe the details of the soul after death. In his mystical writings, NAHMANIDES (c. 1194–1270) described three worlds that follow this one: the world into which the soul enters to be judged, the future messianic world in which the soul is judged and resurrected, and the world to come in which the "the body will become like the soul and the soul will cleave (attach) to knowledge of the Most High" (*Gate of the Reward*). According to the ZOHAR, the soul is divided into three parts – *nefesh*, *ruah*, and *neshamah* – each of which experiences a different fate after death. Elsewhere in the KABBALAH, we find a belief in *gilgul* or the TRANSMIGRATION OF SOULS after death. Originally, this meant that the soul was reborn into another body as punishment for extraordinary sin. However, in time, *gilgul* was understood as an example of God's mercy, since the reborn soul would have an opportunity to correct the sins of its previous life.

With the coming of the time of the EMANCIPATION, the afterlife became a less central issue in Jewish belief. As a rule Orthodox Jews still believe in resurrection, and therefore refer to it in their prayer book. In contrast, early American REFORM JUDAISM rejected the idea of an afterlife. It saw belief in "bodily resurrection and in Gehenna (hell) and Eden (heaven) as places for eternal punishment and reward" as "ideas not rooted in Judaism" (Pittsburgh Platform, 1885).

The belief in an afterlife has taken the full course of Jewish intellectual history to develop. In different eras, more or less attention was given to thought and writings about the afterlife, depending on how relevant the idea seemed to people at the time.

AFTERNOON SERVICE Daily afternoon prayer service known as *Minhah*, which translates as "meal offering." This is because the afternoon service replaced the afternoon meal (grain) offering that took place daily in the Temple (see Kings 16:15). According to the rabbis, the patriarch ISAAC started the tradition of the Afternoon Service.

The order of the Afternoon Service is as follows: Psalm 145 (ASHREI), the AMIDAH, the reader's repetition of the *Amidah*, TAHANUN supplications, and ALEINU. The service also includes various additions – both in the *Amidah* and in the service itself – for specific days, such as fast days, New Moon, HANUKKAH, etc. Half-KADDISH is recited before the silent *Amidah*, and the full *Kaddish* before *Aleinu*. The mourner's *Kaddish* follows *Aleinu*. In the Sephardi service, *Minhah* includes reciting a description of the sacrifices before *Ashrei*.

The Afternoon Service can be recited at any point during the afternoon. Afternoon begins half an hour after midday (halfway between sunrise and sunset). As one of the three daily services, *Minhah* is ideally recited with a prayer quorum (MINYAN).

AGE AND THE AGED Jewish attitudes towards age and the aged are discussed in all the classic books. These attitudes fall into three basic categories: respect for parents, honoring the aged, and responsibility to care for the elderly.

The Bible regards long life as a blessing (Isa. 65:20; Ps. 92:15). It teaches that one must honor one's parents (Ex. 20:12; see Lev. 19:3). In addition, one must "rise before the aged and honor the face of the old man" (Lev. 19:32). Finally, in Psalms we read: "Do not cast me off in old age when my strength fails; do not forsake me" (Ps. 71:19).

In the Bible people lived longer in earlier time periods than they did at later stages in history. From the CREATION until the time of NOAH, ages of 900 and more were common. By the time of the patriarchs this had changed: ABRAHAM lived 175 years, ISAAC 180 years, JACOB 147 years, SARAH 127 years, and MOSES lived to be only 120. Finally, a verse in Psalms establishes the number of years a person can expect to live: "The span of life is seventy years or, given strength, eighty years" (Ps. 90:10). Life expectancy has basically not changed since the days of the Psalmist.

The Bible offers long life as the reward for honoring one's parents (Ex. 20:12), as well as for the performance of certain other commandments (Deut. 22:7; Deut. 25:15; Deut. 6:2).

Even so, the definition of long life has decreased with time.

The TALMUD adds much to our understanding of the aging process. According to *Avot* 5:22: "At sixty a man attains old age, at seventy one attains gray-haired old age, at eighty the gift of special strength, at ninety he bends beneath the weight of years, at a hundred he is as if he were dead and had passed away from the world." Jewish law requires us to show respect and rise

SAYINGS ABOUT THE AGED

If the old say "tear down" and the children "build"—tear down. For the construction of the old is construction; the "construction" of the young is destruction.

If a person studies when he is old, to what may he be compared? To ink written on paper that is blotted out. For the ignorant, old age is like winter; for the studious, it is harvest time.

An old man in the house is a burden; but an old woman is a treasure.

Do not dishonor the old; we shall one day be among them.

Two octogenarians employed at bookbinding in one of ten workshops of "Life Line for the Old" in Jerusalem.

before every person of 70 years or more. Mature wisdom – the type that comes with the experience of age – can be attained at any age. But it is most commonly found in people who have lived a long time – for this reason they must be respected. Other opinions in the Talmud hold that the biblical commandment "to rise before the aged" refers to a person who is both old and wise in TORAH learning.

Beyond the issue of respect, Jewish law is concerned with the care of the elderly. In ancient times, this was closely linked with honoring one's parents, since the family looked after the elderly. Where there was no family, the aged were taken care of by the community. In recent centuries, a home for the aged has become an important community institution.

AGGADAH (lit. "narration"). Refers to non-legal sections of classical rabbinic texts. HALAKHAH (Jewish law) is made up of legal arguments and decisions; *aggadah* is made up of moral stories, history, ethical statements, folklore – and everything else that cannot be classified as *halakhah*.

The *aggadah* makes up about one-third of the Talmud. It includes legends connected to Bible stories and the biographies of rabbis and Jewish heroes. In many places the *aggadah* adds to the Bible story, supplying details that are not present in the Bible itself. In addition, it includes a wealth of Jewish folklore that is not connected in any way to the Bible. The *aggadah* is a rich source on ANGELS and DEMONS, and for many of the customs of ancient Jewish communities.

Aggadah stories are often difficult to understand and tend to deal with deep moral and spiritual matters, such as the nature of God. Unlike technical writing on Jewish law, the *aggadah* freely moves from subject to subject. It reflects the opinion of

The Hebrew letter bet *as the first letter of the Bible is a subject for a rabbinic aggadah.*

the writer, since it does not have to end in an important legal decision.

Originally, the *aggadah* was not collected in any particular book and did not have the logic and organization that is part of legal writings. However this has changed somewhat. Over the centuries many efforts have been made to bring *aggadah* stories together in a single collection. In the 15th century the Spanish scholar Jacob Ibn Habib created *En Ya'akov*, a special edition of the Talmud that was only *aggadah*. In the modern period, Hayyim Nahman Bialik and Y.H. Rawnitzki compiled *Sefer ha-Aggadah*, which is organized according to theme. Louis GINZBERG authored *The Legends of the Jews* in English, which roughly follows the order of history described in the Bible.

AGNOSTICISM AND ATHEISM   Two different beliefs about the existence or non-existence of God. The atheist flatly denies that there is a God. The agnostic claims that man has no way of knowing if there is such a thing as God, since this is beyond human thought processes; but he does not rule out the possibility that a God could existence.

Although there are some Jews today who say they are agnostics, the idea of agnosticism does not appear in traditional Jewish religious literature.

The word "atheism" has no translation into the Hebrew language, because in ancient Israel everyone believed in supernatural forces. For the prophets of the Bible, who continually wrote about God, the question was not "does God exist," but rather "should a person believe in one God or many?"

The rabbis of the Talmud also took for granted the existence of God. In fact, those they attacked as *kofer ba-ikkar* ("one who denies the main belief" – *Sanh.* 39a–b) were those who said "there is neither judgment nor Judge" (Gen. R. 26:14; Lev. R. 28:1). These people challenged God's sense of justice, not His existence. Even the famous heretic ELISHA BEN AVUYA was not accused of atheism, but of denying that there is a personal God who "cares" about individuals and who rewards or punishes according to a person's actions.

We first hear of atheism in Jewish sources in the Middle Ages, when MAIMONIDES and other Jewish philosophers developed "proofs" of God's existence. (Christian and Muslim scholars were also producing such "proofs" at this time.) Even so, these philosophers never doubted God's existence; they were more concerned with the MIN or "heretic" who denies God's unity or creative power.

Only since the Age of Enlightenment (18th century; see HASKALAH) have Jewish thinkers really begun to grapple with atheistic ideas. Many new ideas arose during that time to challenge the idea of one God who maintains harmony in the universe and controls the fate of humanity. Since World War II, Jewish scholars have had to face the issue of loss of faith in God after the Nazi HOLOCAUST.

Even though many modern Jews claim that they are atheist or agnostic (and may also practice few Jewish customs or commandments) they still consider themselves to be Jews. This is because Jewish identity is made up of many elements besides religious belief, such as the Jewish people, cultural traditions, and the Jewish homeland. See also SECULARISM, HUMANISTIC JUDAISM, ZIONISM.

AGRICULTURAL LAWS   Jewish society in Bible times revolved around farming, and many of its laws related to agriculture. One entire section of the MISHNAH – ZERAIM (lit. "seeds") – focuses on agriculture, and many parts of the Talmud do as well. Biblical agricultural laws apply only to land within the borders of biblical Israel (Later, the rabbis imposed a few laws on Jews living outside the Land of Israel as well.)

The Jewish calendar and festivals are largely connected to agriculture. PASSOVER is the "festival of spring" (Ex. 13:4). On its second night a measure of barley was harvested and brought to the Temple (see OMER). SHAVU'OT is the Harvest Festival (Ex. 23:16); it marks the end of the barley harvest and the beginning of the wheat harvest. It is also the festival when the First Fruits are brought to Jerusalem (Num. 28:26). SUKKOT is the Festival of Ingathering (Ex. 23:16), when the grain is brought from the fields into the barns.

ROSH HA-SHANAH also has an agricultural side. One tenth of all the calves born from one New Year to the next were set aside for the priests.

Farmers in Israel were required to set aside a portion of their crops for the priests (see SACRIFICES AND OFFERINGS). In addition, 1/10 of the crops went to the levites (priests' assistants). In the first, second, fourth, and fifth years of the seven-year agricultural cycle (see SABBATICAL YEAR) farmers had to bring another 1/10 of the crops to Jerusalem (Lev. 27:30–31). In the third and sixth years of the seven-year cycle, farmers were expected to give 1/10 of their crops to the poor (Deut. 14:28–29).

Farmers also had to take care of the poor during the harvest. All grain that was dropped while harvesting, forgotten in the fields, or found growing in the corners of the fields was left for the poor (Lev. 19:9; Deut. 24:19).

In the case of trees, no fruits may be eaten during the first three years of a tree's life. The fruit of the fourth year was to be taken to Jerusalem and eaten there, or else the money from its sale was spent in Jerusalem. From the fifth year onwards, the fruit could be used as desired (Lev. 19:23–25).

Biblical law does not allow different types of seeds to be planted in the same area (see MIXED SPECIES; Lev. 19:19). Rabbinic law added that one may not graft one type of tree onto another.

Every seventh year of the seven-year agricultural cycle, farmers are not permitted to tend their fields. People and animals are given free access to whatever grows in any field in Israel during that year. The Bible promises that farmers who keep this law will be blessed with such a bountiful crop in the sixth year of the cycle that it will be enough for three years, until the next new crop can be harvested (Lev. 29:1–5).

Since the destruction of the Second Temple in 70 CE, most rabbis consider the agricultural laws to be rabbinical, rather

The so-called Gezer Calendar incised on soft limestone with a listing of the year by agricultural tasks: the (two) months of harvest; the (two) months of sowing; the (two) months of late planting; the month of reaping flax; the month of reaping barley; the month of reaping and measuring; the (two) months of (vine) tending; the month of summer (fruit). Eight agricultural activities are listed; since four of them are in association with the plural "months," the latter must indicate a two-month period. In the margin of the calendar are the first three letters of the Hebrew alphabet. This agricultural calendar is dated to the 10th century BCE, and is one of the earliest Hebrew inscriptions known.

than biblical, laws. This has allowed for the relaxation of most of these rules. For example, during the past century, the practice of leaving the land untended was extremely difficult for the newly founded Jewish settlements in pre-State Israel. Chief Rabbi KOOK therefore created a system in which the land was temporarily sold to a non-Jew during the Sabbatical year. Jews could then work the fields on behalf of their non-Jewish owners and avoid starvation. Rabbi Kook's ruling was rejected at first by many rabbis throughout the world. Over time, however, it has come to be accepted practice in Israel.

AGUNAH   (lit. a wife "forsaken" or "anchored"; Ruth 1:13). In Jewish law, a woman remains married to her husband for life unless he gives her a bill of DIVORCE (Heb. *get*) or until his

death can be proven. Therefore, in cases where the husband refuses to give a *get*, or where the husband cannot provide a *get* (for example, if he is in captivity or mentally ill), or when the husband's death cannot be proven (for example, death at sea), the wife remains married in the eyes of the law. She may not remarry, and the child of any union with her is considered a *mamzer* (see ILLEGITIMACY).

Freeing an *agunah* to remarry is one of the most difficult problems in all of Jewish law. On the one hand, the rabbis pitied the woman who was chained to an absent husband. They looked for solutions to free her. In talmudic and medieval times, they allowed a woman to remarry on the basis of hearsay testimony that the husband had died, or on the basis of only one rather than the two witnesses that are usually required in a Jewish court (*Git.* 3a; *Yev.* 122b). They encouraged husbands to write a conditional divorce (*Git.* 73a) before leaving on a dangerous journey or for war (*Ket.* 9b).

On the other hand, the rabbis could not allow remarriage until the woman's existing marriage was properly dissolved. To do so would be the same as encouraging ADULTERY. Therefore, only when a strong legal basis existed for relaxing the law did the rabbis tend to allow remarriage.

In recent times, the Chief Rabbinate and Chief Chaplaincy of the State of Israel have dealt with *agunot* created by the Holocaust. Most often victims of the death camps disappeared without a trace. If a woman survived and her husband died, there were usually no witnesses to testify that they saw the body. In such cases the Rabbinate took a liberal approach. Wherever there was no record of marital discord or reason to suspect that the husband might have deserted his wife, they assumed that the husband would have returned if he could have. On this basis they allowed the wife to remarry. Elsewhere in Israel's history, the widows of all the sailors who disappeared when the destroyer *Eilat* and the submarine *Dakar* were lost at sea (1967–8) were allowed to remarry – even though the bodies had not been recovered. In more common cases, Israel's rabbinical courts often award high alimony to wives or even imprison husbands who refuse to give a *get*.

In the Diaspora, the CONSERVATIVE movement inserts a clause in the marriage contract that helps the civil courts to use their powers to enforce a *get*. For REFORM Jews, who do not accept the *halakhah*, the problem of the *agunah* does not exist.

AHAI (OR AHA) OF SHABHA   (680–752). Talmudic scholar of the geonic era. Ahai was born and educated in Babylonia. He moved to the Land of Israel (c. 750) when he was passed over for election as GAON of Pumbedita. He is best known for his collection, *She'iltot,* which stands as the first major halakhic (see HALAKHAH) work to be completed after the close of the Talmud. One of R. Ahai's primary goals was to spread knowledge of the Babylonian Talmud to readers in the Land of Israel.

The *She'iltot* consists of 182 halakhic and aggadic (see AGGADAH) discussions in Aramaic. It follows the order of the weekly readings from the TORAH. Each *she'ilta* is divided into five sections. It begins with an introduction containing laws related to the theme of the *she'ilta*. It continues with the legal questions to be discussed. Next, the *she'ilta* quotes related passages from the Talmud. The third section answers the legal questions set out in section two. Finally, in the last section, R. Ahai offers his sermon on the theme.

AHARONIM   ("later ones"). Jewish legal experts who were active in the late Middle Ages after the period of the RISHONIM ("early ones"). While scholars disagree as to when exactly the period of the AHARONIM begins, the appearance of R. Joseph CARO'S SHULHAN ARUKH in 1565 is a reliable starting point. The SHULHAN ARUKH influenced the content and the direction of the legal discussions of the AHARONIM. It is common to see the AHARONIM quote from the SHULHAN ARUKH, even if it is to disagree.

AHAVAH RABBAH   ("[With] great love"). The first words of the blessing that comes before SHEMA in the MORNING SERVICE. There are actually two versions of this blessing – *Ahavah Rabbah* and AHAVAT OLAM – with *Ahavat Olam* appearing in the EVENING SERVICE immediately before *Shema*.

Ahavah Rabbah thanks God for the gift of TORAH. It requests special understanding to appreciate and obey the commandments. The blessing contains thanks for having been selected as God's chosen people. It concludes with a prayer for the INGATHERING OF THE EXILES, which calls for the return of all Jews to Israel.

AHAVAT OLAM   ("[With] everlasting love"). The first words of the blessing that comes before SHEMA in the EVENING SERVICE. There are actually two versions of this blessing – *Ahavat Olam* and AHAVAH RABBAH – with *Ahavah Rabbah* appearing in the MORNING SERVICE immediately before *Shema*.

Ahavat Olam thanks God for the gift of TORAH and its commandments. It sees the Torah as an eternal heritage in which the Jew can find happiness on earth and in the world to come (see AFTERLIFE).

AKEDAH   (Heb. *Akedat Yitshak*, the "binding of Isaac"). Refers to the story of the binding of Isaac in Genesis 22:1–19. In the biblical story, Abraham is commanded by God to sacrifice his son as a BURNT-OFFERING. After a journey of three days, Abraham is about to carry out the commandment. At the last possible moment, a voice from heaven tells him not to harm the boy. Abraham notices that a ram is caught in a thicket by its horns. He offers the ram in place of his Isaac.

One of the most powerful biblical tales, the *Akedah* has generated much rabbinic commentary. The MIDRASH describes a confrontation between God and Satan. Satan points out that at the celebration made by Abraham in honor of Isaac's birth, Abraham failed to offer even a single thanksgiving sacrifice. God responds by saying that Abraham would offer the boy himself if commanded. In other *midrashim* there are actually two versions

The Akedah. "Abraham's Sacrifice" by Rembrandt, 1655 etching.

of the story. In one group of legends, Abraham is the hero (cf. Lev. R. 29:8) for having passed God's fearsome test. Elsewhere (Gen. R. 56:11), Isaac – who is 37 years old at the time – is the hero for not having protested.

The *Akedah* was of great interest to the medieval Jewish philosophers. Contemporaries of SAADIAH GAON saw in the *Akedah* proof that God was not perfect – after all, God cancels His own command. Saadiah replied that all God required of Abraham was a willingness to obey. Once Abraham had shown his readiness to carry out the command, there was no reason for him actually to do it. MAIMONIDES asks: since God knows everything, he already knew that Abraham would pass the test. Therefore, what purpose is served by actually putting him through the ordeal? Maimonides answers that the real purpose of the story is to demonstrate the height to which man's love for God should aspire (*Guide* III, 24).

The *Akedah* is so powerful a theme that it is included in several places in the High Holiday prayer service. For example, it is referred to in the *Selihot* recited daily during the TEN DAYS OF REPENTANCE. It is mentioned in the ZIKHRONOT section of the ADDITIONAL SERVICE *Amidah* for the New Year (ROSH HA-SHANNAH). Finally, on the second day of the New Year, the *Akedah* is read from the TORAH.

Akedat Yitshak is the title given to R. Isaac Arama's well-known commentary on the Torah (15th cent. Spain).

AKIVA BEN JOSEPH   (c. 45–135 CE). Rabbi of the MISHNAH; spiritual hero; one of the TEN MARTYRS. R. Akiva was an unedu-

Rabbi Akiva in a Passover Haggadah. *Spain, 14th century.*

cated shepherd who began studying at the age of 40. His loyal wife, Rachel, encouraged him to leave home to study TORAH. He was a student of both ELIEZER BEN HYRCANUS and JOSHUA BEN HANANIAH. When he returned, he founded his own Academy in Bene Berak. SIMEON BAR YOHAI, R. NEHEMIAH, JUDAH BAR ILAI, Johanan ha-Sandelar, R. MEIR, and YOSE BEN HALAFTA are among his thousands of students.

R. Akiva was the leading rabbinic scholar of his generation. He is unique among the rabbis of the Talmud because he is respected as both a legal master and as a master of the AGGADAH., R. Akiva created one of the two major systems of rules for deriving laws from the Torah used in the Talmud (see HERMENEUTICS). He is also credited with giving order to the mass of legal traditions that existed until his day (see HALAKHAH). Regarding the *aggadah*, R. Akiva is quoted widely on ethical subjects. For example, his version of the GOLDEN RULE reads: "The Torah's greatest principle is: 'What is hateful unto you, do not do unto your neighbor'" (*Sifra* to Lev. 19:18). He also offered a solution to the philosophical puzzle of how

---

SAYINGS OF RABBI AKIVA

He who sheds blood impairs the Divine image.

If a husband and wife are worthy, the *Shekhinah* (Divine Presence) abides with them; if they are not, fire consumes them.

Who is wealthy? The man who has a virtuous wife.

Whoever neglects to visit a sick person is like one who sheds blood.

More than the calf wants to suck, the cow wants to suckle [i.e., the teacher wants to teach even more than the pupil wants to learn].

As a house implies a builder, a dress a weaver, a door a carpenter, so the world proclaims God, its Creator.

---

free will can exist when God already knows every outcome: "Everything is foreseen, yet freedom of choice is granted. The world is judged favorably, yet all depends on the prevalence of good deeds."

When the Jews rebelled against Rome under the leadership of Simeon BAR KOKHBA (132 CE), R. Akiva became an enthusiastic supporter. His students fought in the rebellion, and thousands lost their lives. R. Akiva defied the Emperor Hadrian's edict outlawing the teaching of Torah, and was arrested at the advanced age of 90. He was tortured and executed by the Romans at Caesarea. According to the account in the Talmud, his executioners tore his flesh with iron "combs." In his final moments, R. Akiva recited SHEMA, pronouncing the last word (*Ehad*, "One") with his dying breath.

ALBO JOSEPH (c. 1360–1444). Spanish Jewish philosopher; student of Hasdai CRESCAS. Joseph Albo is best known for his *Sefer ha-Ikkarim* ("Book of Principles"). His basic presentation of the teachings of Judaism has been extremely popular over the centuries. In this work he claims that Judaism can be explained by three basic principles that all Jews must believe: that God exists, that God revealed Himself to human beings, that there is Divine reward and punishment. He also puts forth six other important philosophical ideas and eight further explanations of the three basic principles.

Albo was an expert in Bible, Talmud, and Jewish philosophy, as well as Islamic philosophy and Christianity. Because of his genius and scholarship, he was selected to represent the Jewish community in the Tortosa DISPUTATION of 1413–14.

ALEINU LE-SHABBE'AH ("It is our duty to praise [the Lord of all things]"). Opening words of one of the most ancient Jewish prayers – often called simply *Aleinu*. Scholars disagree about the origin of the *Aleinu*. One tradition is that the author was JOSHUA; another says it was RAV (3rd cent., Babylonia). Others claim the men of the Great Assembly wrote the prayer in Second Temple times.

The prayer consists of two paragraphs. The first refers to Israel as the Chosen People. The second paragraph mentions God's kingship on earth in our day, but also looks forward to a perfect world in the times of the Messiah. In this future world, all people will unite under the kingship of God. The prayer fits perfectly into the MALKHUYYOT (Heb. "verses of kingship") section of the ADDITIONAL SERVICE for the New Year because of this theme of kingship.

Beginning in the 12th century, *Aleinu* was included in other prayer services. Jews living in Western Europe recited it as part of the MORNING SERVICE. Later, it was appended to the *Musaf* service for the DAY OF ATONEMENT. Finally, it was added as the concluding prayer for the afternoon and evening weekday services. Only later did it enter the Sephardi rite.

The *Aleinu* prayer became a hymn of faith, almost as popular as the SHEMA. In a tragic example: On May 26, 1171, in Blois, France, more than 30 Jews were burned to death in a BLOOD

LIBEL. As the flames erupted around them, the martyrs sang not *Shema* –but *Aleinu*.

ALFASI, ISAAC BEN JACOB (1013–1103). Talmud scholar and writer of laws. Also known as the *Rif* (= Rabbi Isaac Fasi), R. Isaac Alfasi was born in Algeria and then moved to Fez, Morocco, where he stayed until 1088. At the age of 74, he was forced into exile in Spain, where he lived out the remainder of his life. It was in Lucena that he founded a major center of Talmud study.

Alfasi's main work is his *Sefer ha-Halakhot* ("Book of Legal Decisions," also known as "Alfas"). Called the "little Talmud" (*Talmud Katan*), the *Alfas* is a shortened version of the massive Babylonian Talmud. Alfasi eliminates all AGGADAH, shortens the legal arguments, and deals only with laws that were applicable in his day. (He does not include, for example, laws concerning the Temple, which had been destroyed.) Important laws – like TEFILLIN, MEZUZAH, and SEFER TORAH – are collected from throughout the Talmud and grouped in separate categories under the title *Halakhot Ketanot* ("Minor Legal Decisions"). Alfasi always concludes each legal grouping with the decision according to the Babylonian Talmud.

Before Alfasi's time, Sephardi scholars applied themselves to both Jewish and secular studies. He concentrated purely on the study of Talmud. His expertise made him the greatest legal authority of his age. Hundreds of his RESPONSA (responses to legal questions) have survived in which he applied his vast knowledge to the legal questions he received from many Jewish communities.

AL HA-NISSIM ("For the Miracles"). Prayer of thanksgiving added to the AMIDAH and GRACE AFTER MEALS on the festivals of HANUKKAH and PURIM. *Al ha-Nissim* includes a brief description of the historic events associated with the holiday. It thanks God for the miracles performed on behalf of the forefathers. The origin of the prayer text can be traced to the time of the Talmud. But in the modern period some communities have added a new version of *Al ha-Nissim* to be recited on Israel's INDEPENDENCE DAY.

AL HET ("For the Sin"). Opening words of the "Great Confession of Sins" recited on the DAY OF ATONEMENT. The entire *Al Het* sequence is the long confessional that is recited nine times during the Day of Atonement. It covers the range of sins between God and man that must be confessed publicly in order for the penitential ritual to be fully effective.

The entire phrase that opens each line is *al het she-hatanu lefanekha* ("for the sin we have committed before you"). The declaration is in the first person plural. This ties in to the themes of shared responsibility and shared forgiveness associated with the holiday. The list of sins contained in *Al Het* is a complete list for everyone to recite – whether or not the individual has actually committed the sin. For example, in the Ashkenazi version of the prayer there are 44 lines, which comes out to two sins for each letter of the Hebrew alphabet. The Sephardi version contains one sin for each letter. By reciting the entire list of sins – in the first person plural – the individual binds his fate to that of the larger Jewish community.

ALIYAH ("going up"). Term with four different meanings in Jewish tradition. (1) Immigrating to the Land of Israel (whereas, emigration from Israel is called *yeridah*, "going down"). This popular usage actually derives from the Bible (see Gen. 13:1, 46:4, and Ezra 1:3). (2) *Aliyah le-Regel* ("going up for the festival") refers to the PILGRIMAGE TO JERUSALEM that was performed at

Reception ceremony for new immigrants from the U.S.A. at Ben Gurion Airport.

each of the three festivals annually. (3) *Aliyah la-Torah* ("going up to [the reading of] the TORAH") refers to the honor given to those called to participate in the Reading of the Torah in the synagogue. (4) *Aliyah [la-shamayim]* also is used in the Bible to refer to those few individuals who ascended directly to heaven. These include ENOCH (based on Genesis 5:23–24) and ELIJAH (II Kings 2:11). The rabbis also ascribed direct ascent to heaven to MOSES and BARUCH.

ALKALAI, JUDAH BEN SOLOMON HAI (1798–1872). Sephardi rabbi and forerunner of ZIONISM. Alkalai was born in Sarajevo and studied in Jerusalem. At an early age, he began to see the Return to Zion as a national act that would bring about redemption through human effort. He argued for the creation of Jewish colonies in the Land of Israel. He preached that the

talmudic idea of *teshuvah* ("repentance") actually implied *shivah* ("return") – that is, authentic penitence involved returning to the Land of Israel. He was vehemently opposed by the rabbis of his day.

Following the Damascus BLOOD LIBEL of 1840, Alkalai worked tirelessly to encourage settlement in Israel. He traveled throughout Europe in search of financial and political support; he published a steady stream of books and pamphlets arguing for settlement of the land. He founded societies wherever he went for the purpose of purchasing land from the Ottoman (Turkish) rulers. In the final analysis, he was a man who lived before his time. None of his efforts succeeded.

ALLEGORY   Allegory is a literary device that conveys one idea beneath the surface of another. Allegories can be found in classic Jewish literature in all periods of history. Typically they rely on narrative, extended metaphors, figurative speech, etc. to deliver a religious message.

In the Bible, various allegories are found. Good and evil are personified, as are wisdom and folly. Ezekiel's riddle of the eagle and the vine (Ezek. 17:1ff.) is an allegory of the first Exile; his vision of the dry bones (37:1–14) is a symbol for the national rebirth in Zion. He portrays Samaria and Jerusalem as adulterous sisters (2:2–45), which is a theme adopted by later prophets (Hos. 1:2–2:15).

The rabbis in the MIDRASH accepted figurative interpretations of the Bible. As a rule, whenever the Bible created the impression that God had a physical form, they regarded the allegorical meaning as the only legitimate one. For example, in Genesis 11:5 in the story of Babel, the Midrash comments: "'The Lord went down to look at the city' – Everything is revealed to God, yet He had to go down to see for Himself! The text wishes to point out a moral – that one should never pass judgment on the basis of hearsay, but go first and see for oneself" (*Tanhuma, ad loc.*). Elsewhere, the rabbis used long allegories that could even restate the plain meaning of the text. For example, the Song of Songs was interpreted as an extended metaphor for the love between God and Israel, even though the plain meaning of the text portrays the love between a man and a woman. Elsewhere, one sage boldly declares regarding JOB, "it was an allegory – he never existed and it never happened at all" (*BB* 15a).

Because an allegorical interpretation of a biblical text essentially conflicts with the plain meaning, rules developed to limit the use of allegory. SAADIAH GAON ruled that allegorizing was permitted only when the literal meaning conflicted with good sense, reason, or other accepted texts. Add to this when a specific rabbinic tradition existed for interpreting the text as an allegory.

In the medieval period, many of the major figures – MAIMONIDES and NAHMANIDES, for example – used allegorical interpretations in their writings. The medieval *Seder* song HAD GADYA is an allegory, and forms part of the Passover *Haggadah*.

ALTAR   Place of SACRIFICES AND OFFERINGS to God. In biblical times an altar served several functions. Animal sacrifices were placed on the altar to be burnt; blood from the sacrifice was sprinkled on the horns of the altar (the corner extensions). In the early period – that is, before the Torah formalized the rules of the SANCTUARY – altars stood in open fields and non-priests brought the sacrifices. These altars were erected near an ancient tree (*asherah*) or near a pillar (*matsevah*) and served the additional purpose of marking an important historical event. For example, MOSES built an altar at Rephidim, where he had defeated the AMALEKITES (Ex. 17:15). These altars were usually built on the crest of a hill and were known as *bamot* (high places).

The Book of Deuteronomy repeatedly calls for centralization of sacrifice in the "place that the Lord shall choose" (Deut. 12:11–14, 14:23, 16:16, etc.). This meant destroying the *bamot* that had been a regular part of the popular religious practice. The prophets often denounced the *bamot* even after their use had been forbidden, which indicates that it took a long time for people to fully let go of the practice.

The TORAH lists three rules that govern the construction of an altar. An altar could be of either earth or stone. The stones had to be "unhewn" – that is, they could not be shaped by an iron tool (Ex. 20:21,22). The Talmud explains that the altar was created to lengthen man's life, whereas iron (the sword) was created to shorten it (*Mid.* 2:4). Finally, the altar could have no steps leading up to it for fear of exposing the nakedness of the priest performing the service. An earthen ramp was used instead (Ex. 20:23).

The altar served an additional purpose that was not related to sacrifices. In ancient times one who had committed murder could not be harmed if he held on to the horns of the altar. The altar served as a place of ASYLUM; the murderer could not be touched. Asylum did not apply to everyone: he who "schemes against another and kills him treacherously" – unprovoked premeditation – was not protected by the altar (Ex. 21:14).

In the aftermath of the destruction of the Temple, the rabbis stressed the altar as a symbol of atonement. They taught that it was replaced by acts of charity. Elsewhere, the table in the Jewish home was seen as a substitute for the altar, and many familiar customs derive from this comparison (*Tos.* to *Sot.* 15:11–13).

AL TIRA MI-PAHAD PITOM   ("Be not afraid of sudden terror"). Opening words of a sequence of three biblical verses recited after ALEINU LE-SHABBE'AH in the Ashkenazi prayer book (Prov. 23:25, Isa. 8:10, 46:4). The message of the three verses is that the people of Israel can rely on God's protection, no matter how dire the moment may seem.

ALTRUISM   Devotion to the interests of others. In rabbinic terms, an altruist is one who performs a good deed simply for its own sake or *le-shem shamayim* – "for the sake of heaven." Likewise with respect to studying TORAH, an altruist is one who learns "for its own sake" (*li-shemah*). The rabbis had a dual attitude towards the performance of good deeds. They saw the highest good in a deed performed for altruistic motives. At the same time, they recognized that most people fall short of the ideal. Therefore, in the words of the Talmud, "a man should always occupy himself with Torah study and the observance of the precepts. For even if does not do so altruistically at first, he will do so by persevering in the end."

AMALEK, AMALEKITES   Son of Eliphaz (Gen. 36:12). The Amalekites were a warlike desert tribe that fought with Israel throughout the biblical period. They first attacked the Israelites near Rephidim in the Sinai desert, but were defeated by JOSHUA. At this time it was decreed that the hatred of Amalek would be "from generation to generation" (Ex. 17:8–16); the Jewish people must try to completely destroy Amalek.

In rabbinic tradition Amalek represents the typical, long-standing enemy of the Jews. In fact Haman (of the PURIM story) is counted as a direct descendant of Agag, the Amalekite king. In popular usage the term Amalek stands for an enemy of the Jews.

AMEN   A word meaning "truly" or "so be it," used to answer a prayer that one has heard. There are 14 examples of the use of this word in the Bible. The *amen* response has been widely used in Jewish prayer since the time of the Second Temple. CHRISTIANITY has adopted the use of *"amen"* as well. In general the rule is that people should answer all BENEDICTIONS (blessings) that they hear – except for those they have made themselves – with *"amen."* According to a rabbinic AGGADAH, the term is an acronym for EL MELEKH NE'EMAN ("God, faithful King"; *Shab.* 119b; see ACROSTICS).

AM HA-ARETS   (lit. "people of the land"). In the Bible, *am ha-arets* usually refers to the people who live in a place, either Israelites or foreigners. By Mishnah times, however, the term had taken on a very negative meaning and was used for uneducated people whose religious observance could not be trusted. HILLEL declared: "An *am ha-arets* cannot be truly religious" (*Avot* 2:5). The rabbis warned that one should be careful about eating the crops of an *am ha-arets,* because the proper TITHES might not have been taken. They also expected that the *am ha-arets* would neglect his children's education (*Sot.* 22a) and take the laws of PURITY too lightly. They even doubted if the *am ha-arets* had a place in the AFTERLIFE (*Ket.* 111b). Today an *am ha-arets* (in Yiddish, *amoretz*) is simply a person who is ignorant of Jewish religious matters.

AMIDAH   (lit. the "standing [prayer]"). The central prayer of every prayer service. In the Talmud it is called *Ha-Tefillah –* "The Prayer." It is also called the *Shemonah-Esrei* ("Eighteen"), because its weekday version originally was made up of 18 blessings (see BENEDICTIONS). The number increased to 19 during Second Temple times, when an additional blessing was added. The *Amidah* is recited standing with feet together. Ideally it is

---

SOME RULES FOR SAYING THE AMIDAH

1. The prayer must be said while standing and facing the Ark (i.e. generally in the direction of Jerusalem).

2. It is recited silently by each worshiper, with every word said clearly to oneself.

3. The feet are placed together; one begins the *Amidah* by taking three steps forward, as if approaching God, and ends by taking three steps backwards.

4. At the beginning and end of the opening blessing, the worshiper bows the head at the word *Barukh*, bends the knees at the work *Attah*, and straightens up at the word *Adonai*. This is later repeated at *Modim* and after *Ve-khol ha-Hayyim*.

5. The Amidah is recited aloud after each person has said it silently, and the congregation responds with *"Amen"* after every blessing.

6. Worshipers may be seated during the repetition, but all rise for the responsive reading of the *Kedushah*.

7. No conversations or interruptions are allowed during the *Amidah*. One must also not make disturbances that will distract others.

8. When the Priestly Blessing is said, worshipers respond with *ken yehi ratson* ("May it be [God's] will") after each verse.

---

said in synagogue with a MINYAN (prayer quorum) but may also be said on one's own if no *minyan* is available. The rabbis point out that the *Amidah* prayers have come to replace the daily SACRIFICES AND OFFERINGS that were once brought to the TEMPLE (*Ber.* 26b).

The *Amidah* has three sections. The opening section is known as *Shevah* ("Praise [of God]") and is made up of three blessings. The closing section is called *Hoda'ah* ("Thanks [to God]") and is also made up of three blessings. The central section varies in length and subject according to the day on which the prayer is said. During weekdays it is a series of 13 requests to God for such things as knowledge, the ability to repent, forgiveness, healing, and the ingathering of the Jewish people to the Land of Israel. On FESTIVALS and the SABBATH, the central section concerns itself mostly with the day at hand and does not include requests. The PRIESTLY BLESSING is part of the *Amidah* on some festivals in the Diaspora and on Sabbaths and festivals in Israel.

Just before beginning to recite the prayer, the worshiper takes three steps back and then three steps forward. At the end, these three steps are taken again and one also bows three times (left, right, and front). This symbolizes that one is approaching God's throne when saying the prayer and then backing away when finished. The prayer is said silently, with the lips moving to help increase concentration on its meaning. The worshiper also bends the knees and bows during the first and second to

```
╔══════════════════════════════════════════════════╗
```

BLESSINGS OF THE AMIDAH

Weekdays
Avot ("Patriarchs" – praises the God of history)
Gevurot ("God's Might")
Kedushat Ha-Shem ("God's Holiness")
Da'at or *Binah* ("Knowledge and Insight")
Teshuvah (Repentance")
Selihah ("Forgiveness")
Ge'ulah ("Redemption")
Refu'ah ("Healing")
Birkat ha-Shanim ("For a Prosperous Year")
Kibbuts Galuyyot ("Ingathering of the Exiles [to Israel]")
Hashavat ha-Mishpat ("Restoration of Justice")
Birkat ha-Minim ("Against Heretics")
Al ha-Tsaddikim ("For the Righteous")
Binyan Yerushalayim ("Rebuilding Jerusalem")
Mashiah ben David ("Messiah from the line of King David")
Kabbalat Tefillah ("Acceptance of Prayer")
Avodah ("Temple Service")
Hoda'ah ("Thanksgiving")
Birkat Shalom ("For Peace")
Elohai Netsor – Concluding Prayers

Sabbaths, New Moon
(Rosh Hodesh) and
Pilgrim Festivals
Avot
Gevurot
Kedushat Ha-Shem
Kedushat ha-Yom
Avodah
Hoda'ah
Birkat Shalom
Elohai Netsor

Rosh ha-Shanah
Avot
Gevurot
Kedushat Ha-Shem

(Morning, Afternoon
and Evening services):
Kedushat Ha-Shem
Avodah
Hoda'ah
Birkat Shalom
Elohai Netsor

(Additional Service):
Malkhuyyot ("Sovereignty")
Zikhronot ("Remembrance")
Shofarot ("Shofar Verses")
Avodah
Hoda'ah
Birkat Shalom
Elohai Netsor

Day of Atonement
Avot
Gevurot
Kedushat Ha-Shem
Kedushat ha-Yom
Avodah
Hoda'ah
Birkat Shalom
Seder Viddu'i ("Confession")
Elohai Netsor

last blessings while saying the prayer silently. If it is said in a *minyan*, the prayer leader will recite the entire series out loud, with all congregants answering "AMEN" after each blessing. This is to ensure that those who have difficulty saying the prayer on their own will be able to fulfill their requirement to do so.

During the repetition the third blessing, KEDUSHAH, is chanted responsively.

AMORA (pl. *amoraim*; lit, "speaker" or "commentator"). Sage of the TALMUD. They lived in both Erets Israel and Babylonia from the time that the MISHNAH was completed (c. 200 CE) until the completion of the Talmud (c. 500 CE). There were eight generations of *amoraim* in Babylonia and five in Israel, totaling about 2,000 rabbis who have been clearly identified. Their discussions fill both the Jerusalem and Babylonian Talmuds as well as the MIDRASH AGGADAH. The *amoraim* often disagreed with one another, and all opinions were faithfully recorded. An *amora* was not, however, allowed to contradict a statement of the *tannaim* (see TANNA) who came before him in the time of the Mishnah. The basic focus of the debates of the *amoraim* was to interpret the Mishnah and to explain how the view expressed there is connected to the Bible.

By carefully analyzing the Mishnah, the *amoraim* were able to point out what seemed to be contradictions between two laws stated there. They then proceeded to interpret either the parts of the Mishnah or its sources in order to make them consistent with one another. These discussions also generated a great body of talmudic law that supplemented the more obvious laws of the Mishnah.

Some *amoraim* focused mainly on matters of HALAKHAH (law), while others were particularly known as "rabbis of the AGGADAH" (legend). *Amoraim* from Erets Israel were called RABBI, and those from Babylonia had the title of *Rav*. The *amoraim* of Babylonia recognized that their colleagues in Erets Israel were more direct successors of the rabbis of the Mishnah. Therefore, when differences of opinion could not be solved between the *amoraim* of Babylonia, questions were often sent to the ACADEMIES of Erets Israel for a final decision.

Although they spent a great deal of their time engaged in scholarship, *amoraim* had to support themselves and their families just like all other citizens. They were, however, exempt from taxes and other duties to the community.

AMOS (mid-8th cent. BCE). Earliest of the "writing" PROPHETS. The Book of Amos appears as the third of the Minor Prophets in the Bible. Amos was a shepherd and farmer from Tekoa, in Judea. God called upon him to preach to the sinful inhabitants of the Northern Kingdom of Israel and to bring them to repent (see REPENTANCE). Amos repeatedly criticized the priests and rulers of Israel for their corrupt ways, weakening of religious practice, and taking advantage of other citizens. At the shrine in Bethel, he warned both priests and worshipers that they would soon be destroyed if society did not mend its evil ways. He was the first to speak about the idea of EXILE, a generation before this fate would befall the people. King Jeroboam II forced this disturber of the peace to leave his kingdom (7:10–13), and Amos returned to Tekoa to record his prophecies.

Amos insisted that taking responsibility and not seeking privilege should be the way of the Chosen People: "You alone

<table>
<tr><th colspan="2">BOOK OF AMOS</th></tr>
</table>

1:1–2:16	Prophecies against foreign nations and against Israel
3:1–5:17	Reprimands against Samaria
5:18–6:14	Prophecies of woe
7:1–9:6	Visions (locusts, judgment by fire, basket of fruit) forecasting doom
9:7–15	Hope and promise of a return to God's favor

have I singled out from all the families on earth, which is why I will make you accountable for all your sins" (Amos 3:2). He warned that true religion could not be separated from a just and moral society. Amos was a great social reformer who had demanding standards for relating to both God and human beings. He proclaims that God will not excuse the sins of Israel any more than He will those of other nations. The aim of people should be to "hate evil and love good, and establish justice in the gate" (ch. 3–6). He stresses that the people must urgently repent to avoid the disaster that God has planned for them as a punishment for their many sins (ch 7–8). Finally, he describes a future Golden Age in which social justice and a just kingship will be restored and when God and His surviving people will be reunited (ch. 9).

AMRAM (BEN SHESHNA) GAON (c. 810–874). Head of the Babylonian Academy of Sura from 858. He wrote over 200 RESPONSA in answer to questions about Jewish law, and these shed light on the religious life of Jews in his time. He is best known for his *Seder Tefillot* ("Order of Prayers"), the oldest surviving Jewish prayer book. It was the first work to provide a logical arrangement of the prayers for every occasion, together with their complete texts, laws and customs of prayer, and rules of SABBATH and FESTIVAL observance.

AMULETS Objects worn or kept close by as a protection against evil, both natural and supernatural. Some people believe that these objects ward off evil and misfortune (see EVIL EYE) because of what is written on them, where they come from, or to whom they have belonged. The Talmud mentions the practice of hanging or wearing parchments on which were written quotes from the Bible. Maimonides disapproved of amulets, but most other rabbis did not object to them. Their use was widespread throughout both Eastern Europe and the Orient.

Special amulets could be prepared for various needs, for example to cure BARRENNESS, heal the sick, or protect the pregnant or laboring mother and her baby. The words written on amulets could include the Priestly Blessing (Num 6:24–26), the Names of God written in different ways, or other mystical writings. They were written either on paper or on small metal objects and sometimes worn as jewelry. Traditional Judaism does not consider the MEZUZAH to be an amulet, but many still wear small ones as a "good luck" charm.

ANGEL OF DEATH The angel who takes a person's soul from the body at the time of death. While death generally is believed to be in God's hands, the Bible sometimes refers to a host of "destroying angels" (Ex. 12:23, II Sam. 24:16; Isa. 37:36) and other messengers of death. SATAN, the evil inclination, and the Angel of Death are one and the same in the eyes of the Talmud.

These beliefs gave rise to many folk tales and superstitions connected with death, burial, mourning, and even childbirth (see LILITH). The Angel of Death was often thought of as a death-dealing doctor, which led the 12th century Spanish poet Joseph Ibn Zabara to joke: "Both the doctor and the Angel of Death kill, but only the doctor charges a fee!" Rabbi NAHMAN OF BRATSLAV added, along these lines: "It was difficult for the Angel of Death to slay everyone in the world, so he found doctors to assist him!"

Jews sing about the Angel of Death at the end of the Passover SEDER. In the song, HAD GADYA, he stands for the Christians who persecuted Jews (see ANTI-SEMITISM) and whom God would finally punish. In the Bible it says that "righteousness (*tsedakah*) delivers from death" (Prov. 10:2, 11:14). Therefore, righteous practices such as giving CHARITY, Torah study, and careful observance of *mitzvot* were believed to overcome the Angel of Death.

ANGELS Heavenly beings. The word "angel" is the translation of the Hebrew word *malakh*, which literally means messenger – a messenger of God. Angels appear in many books of the Bible, and their existence is taken for granted in almost all traditional Jewish literature. Even so, angels never became a central Jewish concern or even a well-developed area of Jewish thought

In the Bible, angels seem to be needed as messengers between God and His world. They do not take away from God's oneness, since they are lesser creatures. Except in the Book of DANIEL, angels have no names and no will of their own. Human beings never pray to them in any way. They appear most often in the form of human beings and are appointed for a certain mission. They might deliver a message from God, explain a prophecy, carry out God's orders, etc. A second type of angel is made up of members of the heavenly court, who surround God and praise Him (e.g. Isa. 6:1–7). These are divided into several subgroups: *seraphim* (Isa. 6:2), *cherubim* (Ezek. 10:3, see CHERUB), *hayyot* – living creatures (Ezek. 1:5), and *ofannim* – wheels of God's chariot (Ezek. 1:16). The book of ZECHARIAH contains many references to angels.

Most other ancient religions had angels, and in religions with many gods and other divine beings, angels were no doubt worshiped. However, the religion of Israel viewed angels as no more than messengers, which set the Jewish idea apart from those of surrounding peoples. The MISHNAH itself contains no mention of angels, but other Jewish works of the time do

Silver amulet with a loop at the top, and an inscription in six lines with dividing strips including the names of the angels Michael, Gabriel, Raphael, and Uriel. Kurdistan, 19th century.

(see BARAITA). The Talmud discusses the creation of angels, their groupings, and includes them as characters in many stories. While angels seem to be superior to most human beings, righteous people are better than angels (e.g. TJ, *Shab.* 6:10). The Talmud mentions that the names of angels came from the Babylonian Exile (TJ, *RH* 1:2).

Angels receive a great deal of attention in Jewish MYSTICISM. The types of angels in this literature include angels of severe judgment, angels of mercy, evil angels, and ministering angels. Some have masculine qualities and others are feminine. They are arranged into groups in heaven, and may sometimes come to earth in human form. According to the ZOHAR, every human being has a good angel and an evil one – the good one is strengthened when the person does good deeds and the evil one grows in power when the person sins. A whole host of angels serve evil forces, and these tempt people to act sinfully and then report to God about their sinful acts. Because of the great power many believed that angels had, AMULETS and other devices were created to ward off the evil ones. Even though many rabbis disapproved of people's focus on angels, they were not concerned that Jews would actually worship them.

In the KEDUSHAH prayer, perhaps the climax of the daily and festival synagogue services, there is a description of the angels praising God. Worshipers, in fact, "imitate" the angels during this prayer by standing with feet tightly together (in keeping with the tradition that these angels had only one leg) and rising up on the toes to reach closer to heaven. The popular *Shalom Aleikhem* prayer, chanted at the Sabbath table, speaks to the two angels that traditionally accompany each person home from the synagogue on Friday night.

Angels tend to be understood as symbols in modern interpretations of Judaism. REFORM JUDAISM has removed all mention of them from the prayer book. (See also ANGEL OF DEATH.)

ANI MA'AMIN ("I believe"). A section in the Ashkenazi PRAYER BOOK that lists the 13 PRINCIPLES OF FAITH of MAIMONIDES. The final verse, which reads "I believe in perfect faith in the coming of the MESSIAH" was set to music. It was sung by many Jews on their way to their deaths in the Nazi gas chambers as a way of expressing their belief that they will be redeemed by God in the future.

ANIMALS, ATTITUDE TO In the first chapter of the Bible we read that God gives humans "the right to rule over the fish of the sea, the birds of the air, the cattle, the whole earth, and every creeping thing" (Gen. 1:26). In the ancient world, most religions involved animal sacrifices. The Bible also laid down a detailed procedure for SACRIFICES AND OFFERINGS, which was observed by the Israelites until the destruction of the Temple in 70 CE. At the same time, Bible law demanded the humane treatment of animals, including feeding them on time, sparing them needless pain, and not overworking them. As it says in Proverbs: "A righteous man knows the needs of his beast" (12:10). For example, an animal that is threshing wheat may not be muzzled (Deut. 25:4); animals, like humans, must have a day of rest (Ex. 20:10, 23:12; Deut. 5:14); and a lost animal must be returned to its owner (Ex. 2:4). One of the major rules given to NOAH (see NOACHIDE LAWS) forbade eating the limb of a living animal (Gen 9:4), which had been a widespread practice at the time.

The rabbis added to the biblical laws that prevent suffering to animals (*tsa'ar ba'alei hayyim*). They taught that many SABBATH laws could be broken to save an animal's life or to relieve its pain (*Shab.* 128b). They prohibited castration (*Shab.* 111a) and ruled that people must feed their animals before sitting down themselves to eat. Although it is permitted to eat meat, many authorities believe that the method required by the DIETARY LAWS for slaughtering animals for food (see SHEHITAH) is as humane as possible. Because animals must be slaughtered in a special way in order to be eaten, the sport of hunting never caught on in the Jewish world.

AN'IM ZEMIROT ("I shall chant hymns"). The opening words of the "Hymn of Glory" (*Shir ha-Kavod*), believed to be written by the German mystic JUDAH HE-HASID (d. 1217). The poem

AN'IM ZEMIROT

AN'IM ZEMIROT

(partial poetic translation by Israel Zangwill)

Sweet hymns shall be my chant and woven songs,
For Thou art for which my spirit longs –
To be within the shadow of Thy hand
And all Thy mystery to understand…
In Thee old age and youth at once were drawn,
The gray of old, the flowing locks of dawn,
The ancient Judge, the youthful Warrior,
The Man of Battles, terrible in war,
The helmet of salvation on His head,
And by His hand and arm the triumph led…
Deem precious unto Thee the poor man's song,
As those that to Thine altar did belong.

---

is an alphabetical acrostic (see ACROSTICS) that uses half-line rhymes in each line.

The writer drew on biblical, rabbinic, and mystical ideas and phrases in this song of praise to the Creator. The symbolic language describes God almost in human terms, although the poet clearly did not mean for it to be taken literally. Solomon LURIA and others felt that the poem was too holy to be sung in the synagogue. Jacob EMDEN and ELIJAH Gaon of Vilna thought it should be said on SABBATHS and FESTIVALS only. Until recently, however, many congregations recited it daily. Today the common practice is to sing it on Sabbaths and festivals, either at the end of the service or before the READING OF THE LAW. It has become a widespread custom for a child to lead the singing of An'im Zemirot, perhaps to balance the deeply spiritual language with a child's innocence.

ANINUT   Hebrew term used to describe the status of a person whose close relative (father, mother, sister, brother, son, daughter, or spouse) has just died but has not yet been buried (see BURIAL). During that time, making the proper funeral arrangements should be the only concern of the mourner. Therefore the *onen* (person in *aninut*) is forbidden from performing any positive commandments (e.g., saying prayers, putting on a TALLIT). The *onen* is also not permitted to eat meat or drink wine.

If the death occurs late on Friday and the FUNERAL will not be until Sunday, the special laws of *aninut* are suspended during the Sabbath, because funeral arrangements cannot be made on the Sabbath.

ANOINTING   In Bible times, people and objects that were dedicated for holy purposes were anointed with oil. Prophets and kings were also anointed at an initiation ceremony. For individuals, oil was poured from a pitcher over their head. As for objects, JACOB poured oil over the pillar that he built at the place where he had a vision of God (Gen 28:18) and the entire SANCTUARY was anointed when it was completed (Ex. 40:10).

According to the rabbis, the oil for anointing was produced according to a special formula. The instructions were hidden away when the First Temple was destroyed. Since that time anointing has not played a role in Jewish ritual.

ANTHROPOMORPHISM   (from the Greek word meaning "human form"). Describing God in human terms. The Bible contains many anthropomorphisms, such as "the image of God," "the hand of the Lord," "His outstretched arm," "the eyes of the Lord," or "His footstool." These phrases were never taken literally in Judaism, because of the strong belief that God has no body. However, the rabbis explained, "the Torah speaks in human language" (*Ber.* 31b); in other words, the Bible uses human language to describe God, because this is the only language people can understand. Therefore, when we read about God's "outstretched arm," this is to help us think about His power. Similarly, the expression "the eyes of the Lord" helps us understand that God can see everything. Maimonides explained that the common biblical phrase "and the Lord spoke" is not at all to be taken literally, because God does not actually speak. The expression symbolizes the mystical communication that took place between God and Moses, which is beyond human understanding.

In a similar way, phrases that describe God's "feelings" – God willed, God regretted his oath, God showed anger or love – are also not to be taken literally. These expressions are called anthropathisms and are to be understood in much the same way that we understand anthropomorphisms.

ANTI-SEMITISM   Hatred of the Jews. The term was first used in 1879 by Wilhelm Marr, who wrote anti-Jewish propaganda in Germany. Quotations by Latin and Greek writers show that anti-Semitism dates back at least to classical times. The Jews were accused, among other things, of laziness because they rested on the seventh day. Throughout history, anti-Semites have based their false accusations on hearsay and distorted information. Judaism's absolute refusal to accept the gods of other nations (see MONOTHEISM) increased the anger of peoples who saw no reason not to worship many gods. In addition, observing the commandments, especially the DIETARY LAWS, kept Jews from socializing fully with their Gentile neighbors.

The birth of CHRISTIANITY brought with it a new, more extreme form of anti-Semitism. Christians believed that they were the "new Israel," and that they had replaced the Jews as God's CHOSEN PEOPLE. They further taught that the Jews were responsible for the death of Jesus.

In the Muslim world, Jews were officially viewed as second-class citizens, and their rights were restricted (see ISLAM; DHIMMI LAWS). In better times, they suffered from laws that forced them to wear special badges or clothing, forbade them from riding on animals, or restricted the building of new synagogues. In worse times, they were subject to violent attacks and forced conversions.

The Middle Ages was a deadly one for European Jews.

Anti-Semitic cartoon showing Russian Jewish immigrants taking over New York and forcing Americans to head west. From the Judge, *1892.*

Beginning in 1096, large armies of Christian Crusaders began traveling from Europe towards the Holy Land to claim it for Christianity. They destroyed scores of Jewish communities on their way, maiming and murdering their residents. In those years, many Jews fell victim to BLOOD LIBEL charges, based on the bizarre notion that Jews used the blood of Christian children to bake their special PASSOVER bread (see MATZAH). If a Christian child disappeared during the weeks before Passover, rumors spread by anti-Jewish troublemakers could lead to the massacre of an entire Jewish community.

Many restrictions were placed on Jews in the Christian world. They were not permitted to own land or belong to trade unions. One of the few businesses open to them was money lending (see USURY), a practice forbidden to Christians. Jews were at times forced to pay unreasonably high taxes and in the later Middle Ages they were forced to live in ghettoes. Many attempts were made to cause Jews to convert to Christianity, including forcing them to listen to Christian sermons, participate in debates about religion that were heavily weighted on the Christian side (see DISPUTATIONS), and even undergo baptism (see MARRANOS).

Certain false accusations repeated themselves in anti-Semitic propaganda: the blood libel (see above); that Jews purposely destroyed Christian ritual objects; that Jews had wild desires to rape Christian women; that Jews would commit any crime for the sake of gaining more money. These ideas led regularly to pogroms – murderous attacks on Jewish communities by Christian mobs. In many cases, they were largely motivated by the desire to steal the possessions of the murdered Jews. In the late 19th and early 20th century, a wave of pogroms in Russia led to the mass emigration of Russian Jews to the United States and other Western countries.

Toward the end of the 19th century, anti-Semitism underwent a change, and Jews began to be considered a race more than a religion. German leaders began to spread the idea that the only way to deal with the Jews was to destroy the "Jewish race" entirely. This led to the vicious Nazi HOLOCAUST. Millions of Jews were systematically hunted down throughout Europe during World War II and murdered in gas chambers and in other brutal ways. Even Jews who had completely abandoned their religion were not spared.

Although there was a decline in anti-Semitism after World War II, pogroms were still carried out in Poland in 1946. When the State of Israel was created in 1948, violent anti-Semitism swept the Arab world, and tens of thousands of Jews living in Arab lands were forced to leave. In recent years, anti-Semitism has often been disguised as "anti-ZIONISM." Some modern anti-Semites also try to persuade others that the Holocaust never took place.

Since World War II, many Western Christian churches have condemned anti-Semitism and taken steps to change their traditional anti-Semitic teachings and prayers.

ANUSIM   See MARRANOS

APIKOROS   See EPIKOROS

APOCALYPSE   A form of literature that puts forth the idea that God is suddenly about to redeem the world and bring about sweeping changes in the social order. It describes such mysteries as the nature of God, heavenly beings (see ANGELS; DEMONS), journeys to heaven to commune with God, and the end of days (see AFTERLIFE). Jewish apocalypse literature was written during a time of terrible persecutions at the hands of the Syrian Greeks and the Romans during Second Temple times and after the destruction of Jerusalem. It reflects the strong belief on the part of the writers that God is about to step into the world and save the Jewish people by changing the course of history. Apocalypse writers believed that they were in "the last generation" between this world (or, "the rule of wickedness") and the next world, where righteousness would rule.

Jewish apocalypses are all written in the names of ancient biblical personalities – such as ABRAHAM, MOSES, or ENOCH (Gen. 5:24) – but their real authors are unknown. Except for the Book of DANIEL, which was included in the Bible, apocalypse literature belongs to the category of APOCRYPHA AND PSEUDEPIGRAPHA. Although many ideas found in apocalypse literature can also be found in the writings of the biblical PROPHETS, there are some important differences between the two. The most important is that the prophets called upon the people to repent and thus slowly bring about a better situation for the Israelites (or persuade God to prevent a future disaster). The apocalyptics (writers of apocalypse) expected a sudden, dramatic intervention by God, which would not even allow time for the process of REPENTANCE to take place.

The rabbis of the MISHNAH were suspicious of the early Christian and other influences that played a part in the development of Jewish apocalypse writings. They even warned the people: "These writings and the books of the heretics (those who deny God) are not to be saved from fire but are to be burnt wherever found, they and the Divine Names occurring in them" (*Shab.* 116a). Even so, echoes of apocalyptic beliefs found their way into later Jewish messianic movements (see SHABBETAI TSEVI) as well as Jewish MYSTICISM and HASIDISM.

APOCRYPHA AND PSEUDEPIGRAPHA   Collections of Jewish writings from the time of the Second Temple and shortly after that were not included in the Jewish Bible. They were originally written in a number of different languages – Hebrew, Aramaic, and Greek – and in different places, such as Erets Israel and Egypt. Some were included in the Christian Bible (see

CHRISTIANITY). They include works that have great historical accuracy, works that claim to be historical, fictional works that preach a religious message, works of philosophy and prophecy, and works that expand upon the Bible. The Apocrypha and the Pseudepigrapha were both rejected by the Jewish sages of the Talmud, who called them *Sefarim Hitsonim* ("external books").

Books known as Aprocrypha ("hidden books") were included in the Greek translation of the Bible, the SEPTUAGINT, and in Jerome's Latin Bible translation, the Vulgate. They became holy in the Greek Orthodox and Catholic Churches. These books include: Tobit, Judith, Baruch, the Epistle of Jeremiah, the Wisdom of Ben Sira (Sirach or Ecclesiasticus), the Wisdom of Solomon, I and II Maccabees, Esdras, and additions to ESTHER and DANIEL.

Pseudepigrahpa are books written in the name of a person other than their actual author. In most cases, the supposed writer was a religious leader or prophet. Most were written by early Christians. The pseudepigraphal books were preserved by different churches, but not included in the Christian Bible.

An example of apocryphal works that are extremely reliable as historical books are I and II Maccabees. They tell the history of the HASMONEANS, including the victory of JUDAH MACABEE over the Syrian Greeks. Many apocryphal or pseudepigraphal books retell Bible stories. The Book of Jubilees, for example, presents its own version of the biblical stories from the CREATION until the beginning of the Book of EXODUS. It is particularly interested in the REVELATION, when God appeared to MOSES and to the people at SINAI. The Wisdom of Ben Sira is the only apocryphal book that is directly quoted in the Talmud.

Although Judaism officially rejected the body of Apocrypha and Pseudepigrahpa, Jewish scholars throughout the Middle Ages remained interested in them and translated some into Hebrew. Since the time of the EMANCIPATION, when Jews began to engage in secular scholarship, many have been published in Hebrew translations.

APOLOGETICS AND POLEMICS   Defense of a belief and defending it against attacks. The beginnings of Jewish apologetics are in the Greek period, when Jewish writers tried to defend Judaism against the criticisms of Hellenism (belief that Greek culture and religion is superior) and paganism (the belief in many gods). Both the philosopher PHILO and the historian Josephus wrote books that defended Jewish beliefs and counterattacked pagan ones. The TALMUD and MIDRASH also contain apologetics, often in the form of imagined arguments between a clever rabbi and the Gentile philosopher or ruler, who loses the argument.

The rise of CHRISTIANITY, ISLAM, and even splinter groups that eventually broke away from Judaism (see KARAITES), increased the need for apologetic literature. Judah HALEVI's famous *Kuzari* is actually a 12th century Jewish apologetic. It is based on a fictional debate about religion (see DISPUTATION) between a Christian, a Muslim, and a Jew, who persuaded the king of the Khazars to become Jewish. Much polemic literature also grew up among ex-MARRANOS (who had once been forced to convert to Christianity) to persuade others that Judaism is superior to Christianity. Moses MENDELSSOHN's *Jerusalem* (1783) became highly influential in paving the way for the granting of civil rights to Jews in Western Europe.

The relative acceptance of Judaism in the modern world since World War II, with the exception of anti-ZIONISM, has led to a decrease in polemical writings and an increase in interfaith dialogue.

APOSTASY Abandoning one's religious belief to accept another; those who do so are called "apostates." The Bible's opposition to this practice is clearly seen in this warning: "If your brother … or your closest friend … tries to tempt you secretly saying, 'Come let us worship other gods' … do not agree or pay attention to him … but take his life" (Deut. 13:7, 9–10). All of the PROPHETS preach against IDOLATRY, which was still practiced among ancient Israelites. However, this was not actually apostasy, since the Israelites did not break their ties with their religion or people.

During the period of the HASMONEANS, when the Syrian Greeks ruled Erets Israel (2nd cent. BCE) many Jews became Hellenized. They turned their backs on Jewish traditions and adopted the gods and culture of their rulers. Under the leadership of JUDAH MACABEE, the foreign rulers were driven out and the entire nation returned to Jewish practice.

Under Roman rule, individual Jews turned to apostasy, which often meant that they became traitors to their Jewish brothers. At first, the followers of early CHRISTIANITY were considered to be part of the Jewish people. Once they began teaching, however, that Jesus was the son of God and that he had risen from the dead, the rabbis accused them of idolatry and apostasy. A final break between the two religions took place. The rabbis added an extra BENEDICTION to the AMIDAH prayer

Jews in a church in Rome, forced by priests and soldiers to remain seated and listen to a conversion sermon. Watercolor by Hieronymus Hess, 1829.

condemning groups that turned their backs on mainstream Jewish beliefs (see BIRKAT HA-MINIM).

During the Middle Ages, especially in Christian lands, Jews were often forced to convert or die. In a few cases, these converts became enthusiastic Christians who then helped Christian authorities in persecuting Jews (see DISPUTATIONS). With the period of EMANCIPATION in Western Europe, when Jews were welcomed into the general society, large numbers of educated Jews converted to Christianity. The Jewish German poet Heinrich Heine (1797–1856) called his conversion certificate his "entrance ticket into European civilization." Conversion to Christianity was also a way of avoiding the extra high taxes that Jews often had to pay.

According to Jewish law, apostates are considered dead, and close relatives even observe the rituals of MOURNING for them. On the other hand, conversion out of Judaism is not really recognized by Jewish law, and once a person is a Jew, that person is always a Jew.

Since the HOLOCAUST, the Roman Catholic and other major churches have stopped their efforts to convert Jews. However, certain fringe groups (see CULTS) such as "Messianic Jews" and "Jews for Jesus" still try to attract Jewish members. Although they may consider themselves to be part of the Jewish people, most Jews view them as apostates.

ARAKHIN ("Evaluations"). Fifth tractate (book) of the Order of KODASHIM in the Mishnah. Its nine chapters deal with laws of dedicating property – be it animals, produce, or money – to the TEMPLE (see Lev. 27:1–8, 16–24, 25: 25–34). Once dedicated, the property becomes "holy" and may not be used for everyday purposes without being redeemed.

ARAMAIC North Semitic language that is similar to Hebrew and written with the same letters (see ALPHABET). The first Arameans probably lived in the area of Ur in southeastern Mesopotamia, as did ABRAHAM's family (Gen. 11:31). Since Aramaic was written with a pen and ink, it spread more quickly than the picture languages of other ancient peoples, which were carved into clay tablets. It became an international language and was taken over by the Persians, who ruled the Near East from 529 BCE.

In the Bible, parts of the books of DANIEL and EZRA are in Aramaic. The TARGUM was an Aramaic translation that was read aloud along with the Hebrew text at public Bible readings. Aramaic was widely spoken in the Middle East through the sixth century CE, and is the language of most of the Babylonian TALMUD. A number of well-known prayers (see LITURGY) are recited in Aramaic, such as KADDISH, KOL NIDREI, and HA LAHMA ANYA. Many Jewish mystical works were written in Aramaic (see MYSTICISM, JEWISH), beginning with the ZOHAR (latter 13th century CE).

ARBA KOSOT ("four cups"). The four cups of wine that one must drink at the Passover SEDER. The original reason for four cups at the *Seder* comes from God's four-part promise in the Bible to free the Hebrew slaves from Egypt: "I will (1) bring you out of forced labor in Egypt, and (2) deliver you from their slavery. I will (3) redeem you with an outstretched arm … and I will (4) take you to be My people" (Ex. 6:6–7). The number four became central to the Passover HAGGADAH, which also includes the Four Sons and the Four Questions as well as the Four Cups.

Some sages in the Talmud also spoke of a fifth cup, based on "I will bring you into the land I swore" (Ex. 6:8). Many hold this to be the cup of ELIJAH, which is poured and set in the center of the table and not drunk, as a symbol of future redemption (see MESSIAH).

The requirement to drink four full cups of wine during the *Seder* applies to both men and women. Children should also be given small cups of wine so they can begin to take part in this ritual. Two are blessed and consumed before the Passover meal and two come after the meal. Ideally the wine should be red, but white wine or grape juice are also acceptable.

ARK, SYNAGOGUE   (or Ark of the Law). An enclosed cabinet at the front of a SYNAGOGUE that houses the SCROLLS OF THE LAW. In Hebrew, it is called *aron ha-kodesh* ("Holy Ark"); in the days of the MISHNAH it was called simply *tevah* ("chest"). Jewish

Ark of the Law in the rebuilt Bonn Synagogue, Germany.

law requires that great honor be paid to the scrolls because of their special holiness. The Ark that holds them must therefore be both beautiful and respected (*YD* 282). Throughout the ages Arks were built and beautifully decorated by fine artists in many artistic styles. The Ark itself is indeed holy – the next holiest object in the synagogue after the scrolls themselves. While one may sell synagogue furniture to buy an Ark, one may not sell an Ark even to build a synagogue (*Meg.* 26a).

In Bible times the Tablets of the Covenant, which contained the TEN COMMANDMENTS, were kept in a portable ARK OF THE COVENANT (Ex. 25:10–16). In many synagogues, an artistic version of the Ten Commandments often appears above the Ark in keeping with the historical tradition. The synagogue Ark is usually covered with a beautiful, embroidered curtain (PAROKHET), and an ETERNAL LIGHT burns continuously above it. Both of these are symbols of similar objects that existed in the Jerusalem TEMPLE. Larger Sephardi synagogues may contain two or three Arks.

The Ark is placed in the wall of the synagogue that faces Jerusalem, so that worshipers will face both the TORAH and the TEMPLE during prayer. In Jerusalem synagogues, the Ark faces the Temple Mount (see MIZRAH).

Whenever a Torah scroll is taken out for the Reading of the Law, the Ark becomes the focus of a dramatic ceremony. All worshipers rise and sing hymns of praise. The scroll, which is covered with silver ornaments, is paraded around the synagogue. When especially holy prayers are read, the doors of the Ark are opened (see PETIHAH) and congregants rise to show their respect.

ARK OF THE COVENANT   (Heb. *aron ha-berit*). The specially designed wooden chest that contained the TABLETS OF THE COVENANT. The Ark was built according to God's command by the craftsman Bezalel (Ex. 25:10ff., 37:1ff.). It was the most holy possession of ancient Israel.

The Ark was originally kept in the portable SANCTUARY that the Israelites brought with them as they wandered through the desert. It was carried in front of the people by the LEVITES, whenever the Israelites left one place and set out for another. It was also carried in front of the soldiers when the Israelites went to war. After the Jews conquered the Land of Israel in the time of Joshua, the Ark was kept in the Shiloh Sanctuary. King David later installed it in a special tent in Jerusalem. King Solomon, David's son, placed it in the HOLY OF HOLIES in the TEMPLE that he built.

According to the description of the Ark in EXODUS, it was an open rectangular chest 2.5 cubits (3¾ ft. / 1.10 meters) long and 1.5 cubits (2¼ ft. / 70 cm) in height and width. It was made of acacia wood and overlaid with pure gold. The whole upper surface of the Ark also had a covering plate (*kapporet*) of gold, which included two golden figures that faced each other with outstretched wings (see CHERUB). The Tablets of the Covenant were placed in the Ark, which was then placed in the Sanctuary's Holy of Holies.

The Holy Ark on wheels, carved on a stone found in the synagogue of Capernaum, on the shore of the Sea of Galilee, dating from the late 3ʳᵈ or 4ᵗʰ century CE.

The Ark served several purposes. First, it held the original stone tablets of the TEN COMMANDMENTS and also the second set of tablets. Secondly, when carried out to war it was a sign to the Israelites that God went ahead of them in battle (Deut. 1:30–33). "When the Ark was to set out, Moses would say: 'Advance, O Lord! May Your enemies be scattered, and may Your foes flee before You!' And when he halted, he would say: 'Return, O Lord, You who are Israel's myriads of thousands!'" (Num. 10:35–36). Finally, the Ark somehow symbolized God's presence among the people. For example, Moses was told that the Lord would meet with him between the two cherubs that sat on top of the Ark.

Following the destruction of the First Temple, the Ark of the Covenant was either hidden or lost. The Talmud suggests that JEREMIAH hid it or that it could have been taken to Babylon (*Yoma* 53b–54a; TJ, *Shek.* 6:1–2, 49c). It was not present in the Second Temple (*Yoma* 5:2). Today, a replica of the Ark is part of SYNAGOGUES throughout the world. (See ARK, SYNAGOGUE.)

ART   In general, the Jewish attitude towards art for its own sake has been somewhat negative throughout the ages. This was not true, however, of art that was created to beautify the SYNAGOGUE, Jewish ritual, or the LITURGY. While the modern period has shown a real change in the traditional attitude, the origins of Jewish art belong to the world of Jewish ritual.

The Bible has varied views towards art. On the one hand, it contains verses that forbid the making of pictures, statues, and sculptured images (Ex. 20:4; Deut. 5:8). This applies to the likeness of any person, animal, bird, fish, or other living creature and was largely a safeguard against IDOLATRY. On the other hand, when God commands the building of the SANCTUARY in the wilderness (Ex. 31:2–10), the many details given show

that the Sanctuary was designed for beauty and form as much as for function. In fact, God commands that only Bezalel, the master craftsman, was to build the Sanctuary and its vessels. Because of his artistic skills, he was entrusted with making the Sanctuary, the MENORAH, the curtains (PAROKHET), the ARK, and the various ritual objects.

The sages set guidelines for what was permitted or forbidden artistically. For example, three-dimensional sculptures and raised reliefs were forbidden, because they were considered close to idolatry. Therefore, Jews developed other art techniques that were both beautiful and permitted. These include: mosaics, illuminated manuscripts, metal engravings, embroidery, appliqué work, paper cuts, and decorated books, as well as flat reliefs on synagogues and gravestones. The unstable social conditions of Jewish life contributed to the character of Jewish art. Throughout the Middle Ages, Jews were expelled periodically from the countries where they lived. They therefore tended to concentrate on decorating portable objects, rather than sculptures or paintings that they would have to leave behind. Among the common artistic objects that have survived are SCROLLS OF THE LAW, TORAH ORNAMENTS, HANUKKAH lamps, KIDDUSH cups, candlesticks, SPICE BOXES, MARRIAGE documents (KETUBBOT), and ritual objects for the SABBATH and FESTIVAL celebrations. Certain symbols, such as objects from the TEMPLE and the MAGEN DAVID (Star of David), appear frequently in all forms of Jewish art.

Until modern times, individual Jewish artists were hardly known, although some of those who designed mosaics, illuminated manuscripts, painted synagogues, or created ritual objects have been identified. However, beginning in the period of EMANCIPATION (late 18ᵗʰ century), Jews became active in the art world. Some became famous painters; Jewish themes were the subject of art. For example, Morris Oppenheim (1799–1882) was a well-known portrait artist in Germany. He also painted biblical scenes and families observing Jewish festivals in the synagogue and home.

ARTICLES OF FAITH   See PRINCIPLES OF FAITH

ARTIFICIAL INSEMINATION   (creating a pregnancy by inserting sperm into a woman by artificial means). The Talmud is aware of the possibility of artificial insemination (e.g., *Hag.* 15a). However, it is only in the modern period that we have the medical technology for artificially producing a pregnancy. Rabbis today are dealing with this important halakhic (Jewish legal) issue in an effort to help couples who cannot have children another way.

Modern halakhic authorities limit the use of artificial insemination in several ways. First, the donor must be the woman's husband. He is recognized as the father of the child in all respects, including fulfilling the MITZVAH of bringing children into the world (see BIRTH). Even so, if artificial insemination is performed with a donor other than the husband, the child is not considered a *mamzer* (see ILLEGITIMACY). This is because no forbidden physical act occurred between the donor and the woman.

ARVIT   See EVENING SERVICE

ASARAH BE-TEVET   See TEVET, TENTH OF

ASCETICISM   Practice of self-denial as a spiritual discipline. Asceticism has been a religious value in Judaism from Bible times. Beginning with the Talmud, however, rabbis have tended to oppose extreme asceticism.

The main example of asceticism in the Bible is the *nazir,* who takes NAZIRITE VOWS. These were individual vows that included not drinking wine or cutting one's hair for a given period of time. According to the sages, vows of this type were taken into the period of the Second Temple. By this time, there were whole communities that practiced an ascetic lifestyle. The ESSENES are an example of one such community, and the religious climate of the times encouraged such practice.

After the destruction of the Second Temple, certain ascetic practices spread among the people. For example, the PERUSHIM (i.e., ascetics) were a popular movement that refrained from eating meat or drinking wine (*Tosef. Sot.* 15:11). They were expressing their extreme sense of mourning for the loss of the sacrifices (see SACRIFICES AND OFFERINGS). Rabbi Joshua challenged the *Perushim* publicly on the issue of not eating meat. He said: "Should we then not eat figs and grapes, from which the FIRST FRUITS were brought on SHAVU'OT? Should we not eat bread [like the showbreads that were offered]? Should we not drink water which was poured out as a SUKKOT ritual?" (*Tosef. Sot.* 15:12). The more moderate type of asceticism taught by the rabbis included a set number of fasts (see FASTING AND FASTS). In addition, various mourning practices were adopted during certain periods of the year, including not eating meat, cutting one's hair, drinking wine, or attending celebrations.

In the Middle Ages, the HASIDEI ASHKENAZ of Germany again began to adopt ascetic practices. JUDAH HE-HASID and ELEAZAR OF WORMS suggest in their writings that various forms of self-denial can lead to REPENTANCE. Those practicing MYSTICISM in Safed (16th century), under the influence of the *Hasidei Ashkenaz,* also adopted ascetic practices.

ASHAMNU   ("We are guilty"). Opening word of the "Shorter Confession" that is recited ten times on the DAY OF ATONEMENT. Like AL HET, the longer CONFESSION OF SINS, *Ashamnu* is an alphabetical acrostic (see ACROSTICS), with the last letter of the Hebrew alphabet (*tav*) repeated three times. *Ashamnu* is written in the first person plural to emphasize collective responsibility. When reciting it, the individual beats his breast each time a sin is mentioned.

While best known as part of the Day of Atonement, *Ashamnu* is also included in the SELIHOT for the TEN DAYS OF REPENTANCE. Some also recite it in the weekday TAHANUN prayer.

ASHAMNU

We are guilty, we have been faithless, we have robbed, and we have spoken basely;

We have committed iniquity, and caused unrighteousness;

We have been presumptuous, done violence, and have been false;

We have counseled evil, we have failed in promise, we have scoffed, revolted and blasphemed;

We have rebelled, we have acted perversely, we have transgressed, oppressed, and been stiff-necked;

We have done wickedly, we have corrupted ourselves and committed abomination;

We have gone astray, and we have led astray.

ASHER   See TRIBES, TWELVE

ASHER BEN JEHIEL   (known as the *Rosh* and also as *Asheri;* c. 1250–1327). Born in Germany, he was the leading student of Rabbi MEIR OF ROTHERNBURG. After his teacher's death, Asher became the leader of German Jewry. In 1303 he left Germany for Spain and became rabbi of Toledo. From there he was to become the spiritual leader of Spanish Jewry. The government gave his law court (BET DIN) there the power to impose severe punishments.

Asher brought to Spain the strict and narrow approach of the Franco-German tradition and made strict decisions of law. He did not approve of secular learning, because he did not believe it could be harmonized with religious tradition. Because of his influence, Spanish Jewry turned from scientific study to the study of TALMUD.

Asher wrote commentaries on the Talmud called *Tosafot ha-Rosh* ("Additions of R. Asher") and on the MISHNAH. He also wrote over 1,000 RESPONSA (legal decisions), which are a major source of information about Spanish Jewry. He is most famous for his law code, *Piskei ha-Rosh* ("Decisions of R. Asher"), which lists all the main opinions on each law and then shows how a legal decision may be gleaned directly from the Talmud. It forms the basis for the *Tur* law code of his son, JACOB BEN ASHER.

ASHI   (c. 335–c. 427 CE). Sixth generation Babylonian rabbi of the Talmud; also known as Rabbana. Rav Ashi was taught by leading scholars, including Rav Papa, Rav Kahana, and RAVA. For about 50 years (from c. 375) Ashi headed the Sura Academy in Babylonia (see ACADEMIES). The Academy blossomed under his leadership. In addition to being extremely learned, Rav Ashi maintained good relations with the Persian government. Together with Ravina, he made an important contribution to the final editing of the Babylonian Talmud.

ASHKENAZI, TSEVI HIRSCH BEN JACOB (c. 1660–1718). Rabbi and halakhic (Jewish legal) scholar known as "Hakham Tsevi," which was also the name of his major halakhic work. He was taught by his father and grandfather, both of whom escaped from Vilna to Hungary during the Cossack rebellion. He wrote his first legal decision (see RESPONSA) at age 16. He then studied in Salonika, Greece, and Belgrade, Yugoslavia, where he learned Sephardi traditions. When he returned to Hungary his life turned to tragedy. His wife and child were killed during the Austrian siege of Buda in 1686, and his parents went missing. Not until three years later, when he was living in Sarajevo, Yugoslavia, did he discover that his parents had been ransomed by the Jews of Berlin (see CAPTIVES, RANSOMING OF).

In 1710 he was elected chief rabbi of the Ashkenazi community of Amsterdam, Holland. His legal decisions were praised by all local rabbis. In 1713, Nehemiah Hayon, a follower of the false MESSIAH, SHABBETAI TSEVI, arrived in Amsterdam to preach among the people and spread his writings. Hakham Tsevi took the lead by placing Hayon and his writings under the ban of EXCOMMUNICATION. The chief rabbi of the Sephardi community in Amsterdam became very angry that he was not consulted in the matter and ruled against Hakham Tsevi's decisions about Hayon. Hakham Tsevi then resigned his post and became rabbi of Lemberg, Poland, where he died four months later.

ASHKENAZIM Jews tracing their roots to northwestern Europe in the early Middle Ages. In folkways, culture, and religious tradition they have important differences from Sephardim and "Oriental" Jewish communities. In the Bible, Ashkenaz was a grandson of Japheth and great-grandson of NOAH (Gen. 10:1–3). In the Talmud (*Yoma* 10a) and the prayer book of AMRAM GAON (9th cent.), Ashkenaz is identified with Germany. By the 11th century, it came to be a region spanning northeastern France, Lorraine, Flanders, and the Rhineland. Jews there spoke Old French or Middle High German. Within the next 200 years, the Jewish culture that had developed in the region also spread to all of France, England, parts of Germany, Switzerland, and northern Italy. In the late 13th and 14th centuries, Ashkenazim expelled from England and France fled to Germany, Austria, and Poland. Additional persecutions (see ANTI-SEMITISM) drove them even further east.

The traditions of Ashkenazi Jews come mainly from the Jerusalem Talmud, in contrast to those of the SEPHARDIM, which were largely Babylonian in origin. This applied specifically to the texts of standard prayers (see LITURGY; NUSAH), the forms of hymns (PIYYUT), verses of mourning (KINNOT), and prayers for forgiveness (SELIHOT). Perhaps because of the many Christian persecutions they suffered, the religious life of the Ashkenazim was narrower and less tolerant than that of the Sephardim. A very strict approach to interpreting and following Jewish law was demanded of Ashkenazim, and great Talmud scholarship was their badge of pride. Ashkenazim developed a complex civilization, with a tight COMMUNITY structure – including schools, synagogues, charity funds, courts, etc. – that

A Jewish couple from Warsaw. After L. Hollanderski, Les Israélites de Pologne. *Paris, 1846.*

marked their public life. Another special Ashkenazi possession, which followed them wherever they went for 1,000 years, was the YIDDISH language.

By the 18th century, Ashkenazim outnumbered Sephardim in the world. The 19th century saw many of them move to countries in the West after escaping the persecutions of czarist Russia. Just before World War II, they were 90% of the world Jewish population. The horrors of the Holocaust, which destroyed their European communities, reduced their numbers by six million. Even so, today they still form the world's Jewish majority, except in Israel, where Sephardim outnumber them somewhat.

The Ashkenazim can be credited with founding a range of key Jewish movements, such as HASIDISM, HASKALAH, Political ZIONISM, REFORM JUDAISM, NEO-ORTHODOXY and CONSERVATIVE JUDAISM.

ASHREI ("Happy are they"). First word of a well-known hymn of praise to God that is said several times a day in Jewish worship. It is made up of different parts of the Book of PSALMS (Ps. 84:5, 144:15, all of Ps. 145, and Ps. 115:18). Psalm 145 is an alphabetical acrostic (see ACROSTICS) that leaves out only the Hebrew letter *nun*. Verses 1–6 describe God's greatness; 7–10 focus on His lovingkindness; 11–13 praise His majesty; and 14–21 describe his never-ending kindness to all who worship Him.

According to the rabbis, one who recites *Ashrei* three times a day "is assured of life in the world to come" (*Ber.* 4b). In many Western (Orthodox and Conservative) synagogues, the entire congregation chants *Ashrei* responsively, or it is sung by a choir. In Reform congregations, it is often recited in English.

ASSEMBLY, GREAT   See GREAT ASSEMBLY

ASSEMBLY OF NOTABLES   See CONSISTORY

ASSIMILATION   Assimilation can be either active or passive. In Jewish history, there have been many examples of active assimilation, which has strengthened Jewish culture. In these cases, Judaism absorbed such things as language, music, diet, and dress from the outside world. Passive assimilation is less desirable, however, because it involves allowing forces in the outside world to change or destroy Jewish identity.

Passive assimilation occurred in Europe following the French Revolution, when Jews were permitted to leave their closed communities and join the educational institutions, business-es, and social frameworks of the world around them. Moses MENDELSSOHN (1729–1783) stressed the importance of secular education and speaking the local language. EMANCIPATION brought with it the opportunity for Jews to open themselves to the modern world, but it also broke down the well-developed communities that had kept Jewish traditions alive for centuries. Although it was not formally expected of Jews to embrace the Christian religion (see CHRISTIANITY), many chose to do so.

Nationalism grew in Germany and other parts of Central Europe, but it ironically did not keep the Jews from their desire to assimilate. On the contrary, many modern Jews wanted to be more and more German, to demonstrate that they were worthy members of the nation. The development of REFORM JUDAISM grew out of this trend as did NEO-ORTHODOXY, a more modern form of ORTHODOX JUDAISM.

The United States provided the ideal open society, only dreamed of by Jews of the European Enlightenment. Remaining part of a Jewish community was completely voluntary, which caused various types of SYNAGOGUES and Jewish organizations to make efforts to attract Jews to their membership. Although Reform Judaism tried to halt the tide of assimilation in America by offering Jewish religious experiences for those with the least Jewish background, they did so by including many imitations of Christianity in their practice.

A trend that began in the 1960s, which saw many Americans seeking to identify more strongly with their ethnic group, was also felt among Jews. Many Jews have since rediscovered their roots and become more Jewishly observant and less assimilated. Even so, a high percentage of INTERMARRIAGE shows that as-similation is still a major factor in the Western world.

ASTROLOGY   Study of the stars in the belief that they have an influence on human life and society. There is a variety of opinions among rabbis about astrology. Up until the Middle Ages, and even later, it seems that most of the great rabbis believed it was legitimate.

In a discussion in the Talmud (*Shab.* 156a), Rabbi Joshua ben Levi says that a person born on Sunday will be either totally good or totally evil, because light and darkness were created on Sunday, the first day of CREATION. Rabbi Hanina felt that the time of day one was born was more important, since the sun and each planet ruled a different time of the day. Rabbi JOHANAN, on the other hand, rejects the entire idea of astrol-ogy: "The Jews have no *mazzal*" – meaning that they are not dependent on the signs of the ZODIAC. Jews had the ability to overturn the fate that the stars may have set for them with their deeds.

A number of medieval scholars from very different Jewish communities, such as SAADIAH GAON and R. JUDAH LÖW of Prague, openly supported astrology and included it in their writings. Others, such as IBN EZRA, NAHMANIDES, and LEVI BEN GERSHOM believed that it had potential but doubted that astrologers were able to obtain correct readings of the stars. The mystical ZOHAR takes the importance of astrology for granted.

MAIMONIDES, perhaps the greatest halakhic (Jewish legal) ex-pert of all times, was strongly opposed to astrology and believed it to be sinful. He wrote in his *Mishneh Torah*, "Laws of Idolatry" (11:9): "One is forbidden to predict (favorable or unfavorable) times, even if one does nothing more than state these lies, for the simple people believe that these are true words coming

The metamorphosis of a Hanukkah candlestick into a Christmas tree, symbolizing the process of assimilation of Jews as they became wealthier. From the first issue of Schlemiel, a Jewish satiric newspaper, Germany, 1906

Signs of the zodiac from the mosaic floor of the Beit Alfa synagogue in the Land of Israel.

from the wise. Whoever is involved in astrology and plans his work or a trip based on the time set by those who examine the heavens deserves to be whipped, for it is written 'You shall not observe times' (Lev. 19:26)." He goes on to say "…it was with [astrology] that the ancient constellation-worshipers deceived the nations so that they might follow them. It is not proper for Israelites, who are wise, to follow these lies and to think for an instant that there is any value in them."

ASYLUM   Place of refuge. The idea that fugitives (people running from the law) should be given asylum was accepted in ancient societies, and this continued through the Middle Ages. The SANCTUARY, particularly the ALTAR, served as a place of refuge for the ancient Israelites. However, the Bible strictly limits the right of asylum by declaring: "When a man plots against another and kills him intentionally, you shall take him from My very altar to be put to death" (Ex. 21:14). For the Israelites,

Stone horned altar found at Meggido, dated to the 10th–9th century BCE. A person grasping the horns of the altar was granted temporary asylum.

only the person guilty of causing an accidental death could be given asylum (Ex. 21:13).

The altar was actually a place of only temporary asylum; from there the person guilty of involuntary manslaughter was escorted to a city of refuge. The Bible commands (Num. 35:9–34) that three cities of refuge be established in Transjordan (Deut. 4:41–43) and three in CANAAN (Josh. 20:7). The rabbis of the Talmud held that the 48 towns assigned to the LEVITES could also serve as cities of refuge. From the Talmud we learn something about how the asylum procedure worked: A person who has killed another person must be brought before the court, which will decide if the death was accidental or intentional. If judged accidental, the killer must remain in a city of refuge for the remainder of his life or until the death of the HIGH PRIEST.

Cities of refuge were important for protecting people from an even more ancient tradition: that of the BLOOD AVENGER. When a person was killed, either accidentally or intentionally, it was the duty of the family members of the victim to avenge the blood by killing the slayer. Only by remaining in a city of refuge could the killer avoid being killed by the family.

ATHEISM   See AGNOSTICISM AND ATHEISM

ATONEMENT   (Heb. *kapparah*). Making amends by a sinner to the offended party just before receiving FORGIVENESS for the SIN. Judaism sees the sinner as a person who is spiritually apart from God, from human beings, or from his true self. Atonement returns the sinner to a state of spiritual "at-one-ment" with God, other people, and the self. In Jewish teaching, atonement can only be achieved after a process of REPENTANCE. Repentance

involves recognizing and admitting the sin, feeling remorse, apologizing to the offended party, and resolving never to repeat the offense. If the offended party is a person, the sinner must ask forgiveness of that person before turning to God (*Yoma* 8:9). In Judaism the sinner must be the one to initiate the atonement process; God never takes the first step.

During Bible and Temple times, a person who committed an accidental crime against God would bring a sacrifice called a sin-offering (see SACRIFICES AND OFFERINGS). This was not seen as a "payment" to God, but rather a way of restoring one's relationship with God. Verbal CONFESSIONS of the sin always accompanied the sin-offering. The PROPHETS harshly criticized those who brought a sin-offering without repenting sincerely in their hearts.

With the destruction of the Temple and the end of the system of sacrifices, PRAYER became the way to restore a broken relationship with God. Fasting, acts of lovingkindness (GEMILUT HASADIM), and giving CHARITY were recommended by the sages as the path to atonement (*RH* 18a; *Ta'an.* 16a; *BB* 9a). In Judaism, the practice of restoring spiritual health is so important that the TEN DAYS OF REPENTANCE are set aside at the beginning of each year for focusing on repentance and atonement. The climax of this period is the DAY OF ATONEMENT, which is spent entirely in fasting and prayer.

ATSERET   see SHAVU'OT, SHEMINI ATSERET

ATTAH EHAD   ("You are One"). Prayer composed in the time of the *ge'onim* (c. 800, Babylonia; see GAON). The opening sentence comes from 1 Chronicles 17:21. It appears as an introduction to the blessing for SABBATH rest during the AMIDAH of the Sabbath AFTERNOON SERVICE. The prayer speaks of a three-way link between the One God, His Chosen People, and the MITZVAH of resting on the holy Sabbath.

ATTAH HORETA LA-DA'AT   ("It has been clearly shown to you"). Opening for a group of biblical verses that are said in both the EVENING and MORNING SERVICE of SIMHAT TORAH (Festival of the Rejoicing of the Law). *Attah Horeta* is said before all the Torah scrolls are removed from the ARK for the HAKKAFOT, processions around the SYNAGOGUE. Those who follow the Sephardi and Hasidic prayer traditions also read *Attah Horeta* on SABBATH and FESTIVAL mornings, when the scrolls are taken from the ark.

The verses give thanks and praise to God, ask Him to accept Israel's prayers, and express hope for God's REDEMPTION of Israel in the future.

ATTRIBUTES, DIVINE   See GOD

AUFRUFEN   See READING OF THE LAW

AUTHORITY, RABBINIC   Power of the rabbis to govern the religious life of the Jewish people. According to rabbinic tradition, the TORAH consists of the WRITTEN LAW and the ORAL LAW. The activities of the rabbis included interpreting the Written Law and passing on the traditions of the Oral Law. However, the right to interpret the law and the responsibility to safeguard the traditions was given only to those who were qualified and who had earned special status in their generation. The MISHNAH gives us the line of rabbinic authority: "MOSES received the Torah at SINAI, and handed it down to JOSHUA; Joshua [passed it to] the ELDERS; the Elders to the men of the GREAT ASSEMBLY" (Avot 1:1). In other words, rabbinic authority has two parts: the validity of the rabbinic tradition and the worthiness of the rabbis who maintained it.

After the destruction of Jerusalem in 70 CE, the Jewish world was thrown into turmoil. JOHANAN BEN ZAKKAI created a new center of rabbinic authority in Yavneh. However, with the defeat of the BAR KOKHBA uprising in 135 CE, the Jews were further dispersed, and maintaining a central rabbinic authority became impossible. Large Jewish populations, like the community in Babylonia, developed their own ACADEMIES. Centers also continued to exist in the Land of Israel. As a result, rabbinic authority became more localized and regional. Rabbinic leaders arose who had great influence in their immediate communities but had much less influence in other areas. Over the centuries, this process continued wherever Jews settled.

The authority of the rabbis to decide the law (see HALAKHAH) is central to the Talmud. We read there about a famous dispute (*BM* 59b) that illustrates the point. In the Talmud, R. ELIEZER's opinion was overruled by his colleagues. R. Eliezer caused various miracles to occur in order to prove his point. A heavenly voice (BAT KOL) even proclaimed that the law was according to R. Eliezer. R. JOSHUA BEN HANANIAH rejected the *bat kol,* saying: "The Torah is not in heaven; we do not listen to a heavenly voice [in matters of law]." In other words, once the Torah had been given to the people of Israel, only the rabbis had the power to decide the law. Neither miracles nor heavenly voices are important in a halakhic discussion; not even heaven can overrule the authority of a majority of rabbis.

The actual authority held by any particular rabbi depends on both his level of accomplishment as a rabbi and when he lived. The earlier sages (RISHONIM) have greater authority than the later sages (AHARONIM). The closer one lived to the REVELATION at SINAI, the greater one's authority. Rabbinic tradition holds that the earlier a sage lived, the more wisdom and even Divine inspiration he had. In contrast, actual halakhic practice is based on the decisions of the authorities that lived most recently. This is because later sages have available to them all the traditions of those who came before. They are therefore in a better position to apply these teachings to their times.

Down to the present day, authority rests with those who have been taught the traditions of the Written and Oral Law. Rabbinic ORDINATION is more than an academic degree: it brings with it the weight of authority. If the individual who has earned rabbinic ordination serves on a court of law (BET DIN) his authority is even greater (see DAYYAN).

Historically, there have been challenges to the entire system of rabbinic authority. During the Second Temple period, the SADDUCEES rejected many of the teachings of the early rabbis (PHARISEES). They disputed the right of the rabbis to decide the *halakhah* and Jewish belief. After the destruction of the Temple, the Sadducees disappeared. Another movement, the KARAITES, rejected the Oral Law. Karaites actually exist to the present day, although they now see themselves as a separate religion. Other movements that rejected the ways of mainstream Judaism include SHABBETAI TSEVI and his followers, and the FRANKISTS.

To some degree, HASIDISM – at least in its original form – was a challenge to rabbinic authority. It never, however, rejected the belief system of rabbinic Judaism. The Hasidim had their own group of spiritual leaders, "rebbes," who often challenged the authority and style of other rabbinic leaders. As a result, a fierce conflict took place between Hasidic Jews and *Mitnaggedim,* their mainstream opponents. It appeared at the time that this conflict could have resulted in a split in Judaism. However, as the years passed Hasidism became more moderate. Today, Hasidim are among the most traditional of all religious Jews.

In the United States today, widespread movements exist that challenge traditional rabbinic authority. The REFORM movement ordains its own rabbis. It rejects both the *halakhah* and the traditional "orthodox" rabbinate. CONSERVATIVE JUDAISM, another American movement, likewise ordains its own rabbis, but has adopted a more traditional attitude. Conservatism seeks to update the Oral Law in accordance with the decisions of its own rabbis. ORTHODOXY, the third major American movement, maintains a commitment to rabbinic authority in its traditional sense.

AUTOPSIES AND DISSECTION   See MEDICAL ETHICS, JEWISH

AV   Fifth month of the Jewish religious CALENDAR; 11th month of the Hebrew civil year counting from TISHRI. Av has 30 days and normally falls in July/August. There is no specifi-c reference to Av in the Bible, though the "fifth" month is mentioned. The Talmud already refers to Av by its name. In Second Temple times, the 15th of Av (see AV, FIFTEENTH OF) was a minor festival that gave Av a joyous character. But with the destruction of the Temple on the Ninth of Av (see TISHAH BE-AV), the month was forever associated with mourning. Tradition has it that both the First and the Second Temple were destroyed on the Ninth of Av. AARON is believed to have died on the first day of the month. Numerous other disasters have been associated with the month as well. According to the rabbis, "when Av comes in, we rejoice less" (*Ta'an.* 4:6, 29a).

Rituals of mourning mark the month of Av. The first nine days are the climax of THREE WEEKS of mourning that begin with the 17th of TAMMUZ, the previous Hebrew month. In some communities, people do not eat meat or drink wine during the nine days. Beginning with the Sabbath just after Tishah be-Av, the first of seven HAFTARAH readings of comfort and hope is read in the synagogue.

AV, FIFTEENTH OF (*Tu be-Av*). Folk festival in Second Temple times when young bachelors would select wives from among the unmarried girls. According to the Mishnah, on this day as well as the Day of Atonement, the young women of Jerusalem dressed in white dresses that were borrowed (so as not to embarrass the poorer women) and danced in the vineyards. The young men would go there to choose their brides (*Ta'an.* 4:8).

The Talmud gives a number of historical reasons for having a festival on this date. The most likely is that it was once connected to the sacrificial service of the TEMPLE. The 15th of Av is the last day in the season for chopping down trees for the fire that burned on the altar. It was feared that afterwards the heat of the sun would no longer be strong enough to dry out the trees properly.

In modern times, eulogies and fasting are banned on this day, and the TAHANUN prayer is not recited. In religious communities, the 15th of Av is one of the most popular days of the year to hold a wedding.

AV, NINTH OF See TISHAH BE-AV

AVELEI ZION ("Mourners of Zion"). Term originally from the Bible (Isa. 61:3). It applied to groups of extremely religious Jews who actively lived out their grief over the destruction of the Second Temple.

"Mourners of Zion" first appeared in 70 CE. They are mentioned in the Talmud, where the rabbis criticized their practices (*BB* 60b). From the Arab conquest of the Holy Land in 638 until the 12th century, the influence of the *Avelei Zion* grew. They abstained from daily work, and did not eat meat or drink wine. Diaspora communities supported them while they waited and prayed for the REDEMPTION. Their influence was felt in the lands of Israel, Yemen, Italy and Germany, where other groups adopted their customs. The most well known of the German "Mourners of Zion" was Meir ben Isaac Nehorai, the poet who composed the prayer *Akdamut Millin*.

The traditional prayer book refers to *Avelei Zion* in several places. In the Afternoon Service AMIDAH for TISHAH BE-AV, a special passage is added asking God to "console the mourners of Zion and the mourners of Jerusalem." A similar phrase is added to the GRACE AFTER MEALS said in a house of MOURNING. In addition, both at the cemetery and when entering the synagogue on Friday night, mourners are greeted with the formula: "May the Almighty console you among all other mourners for Zion and Jerusalem."

AV HA-RAHAMIM ("Merciful Father"). A special prayer recited in the synagogue in memory of Jewish martyrs and Jewish communities destroyed during the time of the First Crusade (1096–1099). It refers to the wholesale massacres that took place at the time in the Rhineland and southern Germany. Thousands of Jews were murdered, preferring death to baptism (see ANTI-SEMITISM). The author of the prayer is unknown.

Av ha-Rahamim is recited in Ashkenazi congregations. Some recite it on the Sabbaths before SHAVU'OT and TISHAH BE-AV, as well as at the end of each *Yizkor* memorial service. Most say it weekly, with the exception of the New MOON, the Sabbath preceding the New Moon, and on several other occasions during the year. It is said before ASHREI, after the Torah reading but before the SCROLLS OF THE LAW are returned to the ARK.

The prayer glorifies those who "laid down their lives for the sanctification of the Divine Name" – KIDDUSH HA-SHEM.

AVINU MALKENU ("Our Father, our King"). Opening words and refrain of the most ancient Jewish plea to God. It is recited on fast days (see FASTING AND FAST DAYS) and days of REPENTANCE. The origin of the *Avinu Malkenu* prayer can be traced to Rabbi AKIVA. Once, during a severe drought, only the prayer of Rabbi Akiva was answered. His words were: "Our Father our King, we have no king beside You. Our Father, our King, for Your own sake have mercy on us!" (*Ta'an.* 25b). As new disasters fell upon the Jewish people, the basic formula set out by Akiva expanded to include additional petitions (requests), all in the style he had set out. By the ninth century, the prayer included 25 lines (see AMRAM GAON). Today the Sephardi version has 32 lines, and the Ashkenazi version has 44 lines.

The content of *Avinu Malkenu* includes prayers for God's help in a range of ways, both for individuals and the community. They express the humility of the petitioner and ask that God overlook the worshiper's lack of merit. Instead, let the prayer be answered for the sake of the righteousness of Israel's martyrs and saints.

Avinu Malkenu is recited immediately after the AMIDAH of the MORNING and AFTERNOON SERVICE during the TEN DAYS OF REPENTANCE. It is also recited on all public fast days – except for TISHAH BE-AV. We do not say it when these days fall on a Friday afternoon or the Sabbath. When the DAY OF ATONEMENT falls on the Sabbath, it is recited only at the Concluding (NE'ILAH) Service. It is customary to open the ARK when reciting *Avinu Malkenu*.

AVINU SHE-BA-SHAMAYIM ("Our Father who is in Heaven"). *"Avinu she-ba-shamayim"* is a common name for God in Jewish LITURGY (prayers). It is based on the Bible's idea that God is the Divine Father (see Isa. 63:16; Jer. 31:9; Ps. 103:13; 1 Chr. 29:10). This notion also appears in the Talmud, where following the TORAH was described as "doing the will of Our Father in Heaven," on whom Jews could safely depend (*Sot.* 9:15).

Jewish liturgy uses different phrases to express different aspects of a person's relationship with God. At times God is portrayed as the King, and we are His servants (see AVINU MALKENU). This described a more formal, distant relationship, and we find it used when the worshiper is in trouble. *Avinu she-ba-shamayim* is used when the relationship is close, loving, and filled with a sense of obligation. Not only is God our Father, but just as a human father can be expected to have mercy on his child, so too can we hope and perhaps even expect that God will treat us with mercy.

When the Chief Rabbinate of Israel wrote the prayer for the Welfare of the State of Israel, it used the *Avinu she-ba-shamayim* form.

AVODAH ("service," "worship"). Term used for the HIGH PRIEST's Order of Service in the TEMPLE on the DAY OF ATONEMENT. The Bible provides the details of the ritual, which then become law in *Yoma* in the Mishnah. After a week of spiritual preparation, the High Priest entered the HOLY OF HOLIES to conduct the annual ceremony of ATONEMENT. This involved sacrificing a bull as his own sin-offering; a three-fold CONFESSION OF SINS, and saying God's holiest Name (Tetragrammaton; see GOD, NAMES OF) on behalf of himself and his family, the priesthood, and the entire people of Israel; drawing lots to decide which of two goats would be chosen as a scapegoat "for AZAZEL" and which for a sacrifice; and a concluding prayer for the welfare of the nation.

When the Temple was destroyed, a version of the *Avodah* was placed in the ADDITIONAL (*Musaf*) SERVICE of the Day of Atonement. By medieval times, various hymns were added to make the *Avodah* more beautiful and dramatic. Today, synagogue ritual surrounding the *Avodah* service still has some measure of the drama that was part of the original. For example, when the reader recites the *Ve-ha-kohanim ve-ha-am* ("When the priests and the people"), worshipers observe the ancient ritual of bowing their heads to the ground in keeping with what was done in the Temple.

AVODAH ZARAH ("Idolatry"). Eighth book of the Order NEZIKIN in the Mishnah. *Avodah Zarah* contains laws about the treatment of IDOLATRY and idolators. It includes laws that forbid business transactions with idolators, associating with them, and using their images; the commandment to destroy idols; and the prohibition against using or benefiting from wine made by idolators. The fourth chapter also records a discussion between the Romans and the Jewish elders concerning idolatry. "The Romans asked the elders, 'If God has no use for idol worship, why does He not destroy it?' The elders replied, 'If they worshiped a thing for which the world has no use, He would destroy it; but behold, they worship the sun, the moon, the stars, and the planets. Shall he make an end of His world because of fools?'" (*AZ* 4:7).

AVOT ("Fathers"). Ninth book of the Order NEZIKIN in the Mishnah; also known as *Pirkei Avot* ("Chapters of the Fathers").

Avot is a collection of rabbinic sayings that stress the importance of wisdom, Torah study, and religious observance in Jewish life. It has no halakhic (Jewish legal) content and no stories. There is also no *Gemara* – which exists for all other books of the Mishnah – to expand its meaning in the Talmud.

The first two chapters of *Avot* build a "chain of tradition" from MOSES to the men of the GREAT ASSEMBLY, from them to the schools of HILLEL and SHAMMAI, and finally down to Rabban GAMALIEL, who compiled the MISHNAH (see AUTHORITY, RABBINIC). About 40 scholars from the period of the Mishnah are quoted in chapters 3–4; most of the statements in chapter 5 are quoted without the name of the author.

Avot is read in the synagogue between PASSOVER and SHAVU'OT. This is actually an ancient custom that originated with the Babylonian Jews. Since there are six weeks between the two festivals, a sixth (post-Mishnaic) chapter was added for reading on the last Sabbath before Shavu'ot. This final chapter is known as *Baraita de-Rabbi Meir,* after the author of the first saying in the chapter. It was originally called *Kinyan Torah* ("Acquiring Torah") because the subject matter is Torah study.

AVOT DE-RABBI NATAN ("*Avot*" according to Rabbi Nathan). An early commentary on Mishnah AVOT that includes moral sayings by rabbis that did not appear in *Avot*. *Avot de-Rabbi Natan* is made up entirely of AGGADAH. It often illustrates the sayings of *Avot* with parables and stories drawn from the lives of the sages who appear in *Avot*. It is not exactly clear who Rabbi Nathan was, although some suggest he is R. Nathan ha-Bavli, who lived in the second-third century CE.

AVTALYON   See SHEMAYAH

AYIN HA-RA   See EVIL EYE

AZAZEL   Place in the wilderness to which one of two goats was sent as part of the DAY OF ATONEMENT service in the TEMPLE in JERUSALEM. This was the goat that carried the sins of Israel away with it (Lev. 16:22). As part of the ritual, the High Priest drew lots over two goats. He assigned one goat to be sacrificed and the other to be sent away "to *Azazel*" in the wilderness to be killed (see v. 8). The Talmud says that *Azazel* was a craggy cliff, over which the goat was thrown in the wilderness (*Yoma* 67b). According to the Talmud, the law of *Azazel* falls into the category of laws that man's intellect cannot understand (see HALAKHAH).

B

BAAL The most important Canaanite fertility god. The word Baal means "lord" in Phoenician and Canaanite. He was the god of wind and rain and responsible for animal and human fertility. His female partner was Ashtoreth.

Baal was considered the biggest threat to the Jewish religion in biblical times. The Israelites sinned, worshiping him many times. Many Israelites even sacrificed their children to him. JEREMIAH and HOSEA are two of the prophets who spoke against worshiping Baal (Hos. 2:10, 13:1, Jer. 19).

The best-known story about Baal took place on Mount Carmel. ELIJAH and the 450 prophets of Baal climbed the mountain to pray for rain and the God of Israel consumed the sacrifice of Elijah with fire. This proved to the Israelites that Elijah was the real prophet, and they must do as God commanded.

The Israelites were still attracted to Baal worship through the First Temple period.

BA'AL KERI'AH (master of reading). The person who chants the Torah reading in the synagogue. From the Second Temple period until the early Middle Ages each person who was called to the Torah would read his own portion. By about the ninth century CE, most Jews did not know the traditional melody (CANTILLATION); therefore they began to choose a person in each synagogue to chant the Torah. He was called a *ba'al keri'ah*. He would be responsible for every Torah reading throughout the year. (An exception is the Yemenite community, where each person still chants his own portion.)

Nowadays, most synagogues have a professional *ba'al keri'ah*. He is expected to chant the Torah portion very accurately. He uses a special pointer called a YAD as a guide. Young boys often read the Torah for the first time at their BAR MITZVAH and young girls in non-Orthodox synagogues do so at their BAT MITZVAH. There are special training programs for Jews of all ages to learn to be Torah readers. Recorded cassettes are also available.

BA'AL SHEM (pl. *Ba'alei Shem*; "Master of the Holy Name of God"). Title given to someone believed to possess the secret of the *Shem ha-Meforash* (Tetragrammaton; see GOD, NAMES OF). A *Ba'al Shem* was thought to be able to use the holiest name of God to perform miracles. There were *Ba'alei Shem* throughout the ages, from the HAI GAON in Babylonia to the Hasidei Ashkenaz in medieval Germany. The most important mystics in Spain were also *Ba'alei Shem*. In each time period the term *Ba'al Shem* meant something a little different.

The original *Ba'alei Shem* were rabbis and scholars. They used their "magical" powers to write AMULETS with holy names. Later on, men who practiced PRACTICAL KABBALAH and sold amulets were called *Ba'alei Shem*.

There were many legends and folk stories about *Ba'alei Shem*. People thought they could remove evil spirits (see DEMONS AND DEMONOLOGY, DIBBUK). Some people pretended they were *Ba'alei Shem*, but they did not have their powers. For example: SHABBETAI TSEVI and his followers.

BA'AL SHEM TOV (Israel ben Eliezer, known as the *Besht*, an acronym of *Ba'al Shem Tov*; 1698–1760). Founder of HASIDISM. It is very difficult to describe the life of the *Besht*, because there are no historical documents written about him. One book written about his life, *Shivhei ha-Besht* (1814–5), *In Praise of the Ba'al Shem Tov*, is mostly legend and hardly has any facts. However, historians have been able to find out the basic facts about his life by comparing different sources.

Israel ben Eliezer, the *Besht*, was born in Okup, a village

The bet midrash (study and prayer room) of Israel Ba'al Shem Tov, the founder of Hasidism, in Medzibezh, Podolia.

SAYINGS OF THE BA'AL SHEM TOV

*It matters not how many commandments you
fulfill, but the spirit in which you fulfill them.*

*Serve God with joy, because a joyful person has
much love for man and all of God's creatures.*

*If you want to pull your friend out of the mud,
do not be afraid of getting a little dirty.*

When God wants to punish man, He takes away his faith.

*The world is full of wonderful sights and great mysteries,
but one small hand in front of our eyes blocks the view.*

There is no room for God in one who is full of himself.

If your son has taken to evil ways, love him more than ever.

*When I die, I shall go out through one
door and then in through another.*

If you wish to live long, do not be famous.

When the Ba'al Shem Tov heard that some Hasidim in
Brody were being mistreated by *Mitnaggedim*, he said: "Our
opponents do this out of religious zeal. Since they get pleasure
out of persecuting us, because they believe it is a *mitzvah*,
why should we take their pleasure away from them?"

in the Carpathian Mountains. He started out as a healer and miracle worker. He used the Divine Name (the name of God) to work miracles, which is why he was called the Ba'al Shem Tov (Master of the Good Name). He later became a school teacher and *shohet* (slaughterer of kosher meat). Several other miracle workers also operated in the same area, and each had a circle of followers. Israel ben Eliezer's group was the largest one, and the other groups eventually joined him. They were called a *havurah kaddisha* or "holy company." Ben Eliezer, their spiritual leader, was known as a TSADDIK (righteous person), and his followers were called Hasidim. The position of *Tsaddik* was later passed down to the *Tsaddik*'s greatest student.

The Ba'al Shem Tov was not a great scholar, but he did know the Bible, the rabbinic AGGADAH (legend), and especially the KABBALAH very well. He did not write any books, but his students collected and wrote down his sayings. Each student recorded what the Ba'al Shem Tov had said from his own point of view, which makes it very hard to know what he really said.

One of the ideas that was most important to the *Besht* was DEVEKUT (attachment to God). Hasidim try to keep God in their mind all the time. Even when they are doing something ordinary, like eating or working, they are serving God. According to the Hasidim, when people study Torah, they should concentrate on loving God. The MITNAGGEDIM (those who were opposed to the Hasidim) believed that when people study Torah they should concentrate on what they are learning.

The Ba'al Shem Tov believed a simple Jew who was not a scholar could be more spiritual than a scholar. Even the most unlearned person can concentrate on being close to God. On the other hand, many scholars learn Torah to increase their knowledge. He gives an example of a scholar and a Hasid who are both learning the same part of the TALMUD, but each one of them sees the text from a different point of view. The *Besht* explains that the scholar is actually interested in the Talmud's complicated laws while the Hasid may not even be able to understand the text. The Hasid is studying only to become closer to God, therefore he is worshiping God when he reads the text.

The Hasidim say that the Ba'al Shem Tov had special powers because he was devoted to God. He used to smoke a pipe before he prayed in order to prepare himself to concentrate on becoming close to God.

The Ba'al Shem Tov had two children, Tsevi Hirsch and Adel. The Hasidim tell many stories about his daughter. Her children were Moses Hayyim Ephraim of Sudyklow (1740–1800) and Baruch, the *Tsaddik* of Medzibezh (1757–1810), who was the Ba'al Shem Tov's spiritual heir. Adel's daughter, Faige, was the mother of RABBI NAHMAN OF BRATSLAV. The Ba'al Shem Tov's students spread Hasidism throughout Europe. By the beginning of the 19th century, half the Jews in Europe were Hasidim.

BA'AL TEFILLAH ("master of prayer," also called *sheli'ah tsibbur*). The person who leads the prayers in a synagogue. Until the time of the *ge'onim* (starting 6th cent. CE), any Jew could be asked to lead the prayers as a volunteer. From then on a professional CANTOR usually served in place of the *ba'al tefillah*.

BA'AL TEKI'AH ("master of blowing the SHOFAR"). The person who blows the *shofar*, the ram's horn, on ROSH HA-SHANAH and

*A ba'al teki'ah ("master of the blowing"), wearing a prayer shawl, blows
the* shofar *(ram's horn) in a synagogue, Jerusalem.*

at the end of the DAY OF ATONEMENT. According to Jewish law, the *ba'al teki'ah* should be a learned person, who has learned how to blow the *shofar* properly. He must concentrate on blowing the *shofar* on behalf of the people listening.

The *ba'al teki'ah* recites the blessings and blows the different notes on the *shofar* in the correct order, which is not an easy task. Another person stands next to him and calls out each note before he blows it. There is always an extra *shofar* and another *ba'al teki'ah* ready in case of a problem.

BA'AL TESHUVAH (or *hozer bi-teshuvah*: "a person who has returned or repented"). Hebrew term for someone who returned to the laws of Judaism.

The rabbis praised the *ba'alei teshuvah*, and made rules to protect them. It is forbidden to remind a *ba'al teshuvah* of past sins. It says in the Talmud that "*ba'alei teshuvah* are often more righteous than people who were always righteous" (*Ber.* 34b; see also REPENTANCE).

The modern "*Ba'al Teshuvah* Movement" has grown very quickly. Most of the members of the movement are young people who are attracted to the ultra-Orthodox way of life. In the 1960s many American secular Jews became Orthodox. In Israel many people became *ba'alei teshuvah* after the Six-Day War (1967).

In the past, the *ba'al teshuvah* was a person who had left Judaism and had come back. The modern *ba'al teshuvah* is usually becoming religious for the first time, and usually studies Judaism in a special educational institute.

BABEL, TOWER OF   Tower built on the plain of Shinar in Babylonia (Genesis 11). It was built when "the whole earth spoke one language," after the great FLOOD. The Tower of Babel was supposed to reach the heavens and make the people who built it famous. People believed that if they built a tower they could reach heaven and would all stay in one place, instead of being scattered all over the world.

From the Bible's viewpoint, the builders committed more than one sin. They defied God's commandment to scatter themselves throughout the earth and fill it up and perhaps even tried to overthrow God by reaching the heavens. As a punishment, God introduced many new languages into the world, so they could no longer understand one another, and scattered them all over the world. In Hebrew the word Babel comes from the root *b-l-l*, which means "confuse." That is why it was called the Tower of Babel.

BABYLONIAN EXILE   See EXILE, BABYLONIAN

BABYLONIAN TALMUD   See TALMUD

BAECK, LEO (1873–1956). Rabbi, religious philosopher, leader of the German Jewish community and of the World Movement for Progressive Judaism. He was born in Lissa, which was then a part of Prussia, and studied at Liberal and Conservative rabbinical schools. He was a rabbi in several communities and then became a head rabbi in Berlin, where he taught at a rabbinical seminary.

When Hitler became chancellor of Germany in 1933, Baeck began to fight for the rights of the Jews. He was arrested many times. Each time he was arrested it became more dangerous for him to be in Germany. Jewish communities outside of Germany invited him to stay with them, but he felt that he should stay with the Jews in Germany. In 1943 he was taken to the Theresienstadt concentration camp. He set an example of strength and good spirit for the Jews there. He gave classes on Judaism and encouraged the Jews to keep their hope and faith. After the war, he moved to London, and became head of the World Union for Progressive Judaism.

Baeck wrote on Jewish history and Jewish thought. His most famous book was *The Essence of Judaism*. He believed that Jews are the CHOSEN PEOPLE, so they must be more moral than the rest of the world. Jewish law teaches how to treat other people fairly and with love, and in this way the Jews can save the world from evil. He also wrote a book that compares Judaism and CHRISTIANITY.

BAHIR, SEFER ("Book of Light"). Hebrew mystical book written at the end of the 12th century. It is the first book of the KABBALAH, and was written in the style of a MIDRASH. Each section explains a verse or story from the Bible. Rabbi Nehunya ben ha-Kanah is the speaker in the first section, and is probably the author of the book. The original book is not divided into sections or paragraphs; more modern editions are divided into 130 or 200 sections.

The Bahir is the first book that deals with the SEFIROT, ten different mystical levels of God's power in the universe. God's world is described as a tree whose roots reach deep to God and whose branches turn toward the world. These symbols became very important in the Kabbalah later on.

The author of the *Bahir* used older mystical sources such as the *Sefer Yetsirah,* but he gave new meaning to these texts.

BAHUR ("young man," literally "chosen one"). A Hebrew term that had various uses in the Bible, but later came to mean an unmarried Talmud student. Sometimes *bahur* meant "chosen warriors" (Jer. 48:15), but more often it meant a young man in the prime of his life or a youth ready to get married. From the Middle Ages onward, *bahur* specifically meant a young Talmud student in the early stages of learning at a YESHIVAH (rabbinical academy). Older, married students were called *avrekhim*. The biblical expression *tiferet bahurim* ("the glory of young men"; Prov. 20:29) was used for young men who were the pride of their community.

BAHYA BEN ASHER IBN HALAWA (known as Rabbenu Bahya; c. 1260–1340). Spanish Bible commentator and mystic. Very little is known about his life. He was a rabbi and preacher in Saragossa, and his Talmud teacher was Solomon ben Abraham ADRET. Bahya wrote several works. His most famous was a commentary on the PENTATEUCH, which used mystical ideas to explain the text. He made use of several different languages to translate and explain difficult words, as RASHI did. It was the earliest work of KABBALAH to be printed (1492). Bahya explained the Torah on four different levels. The most basic was *peshat,* the plain or literal meaning. The next level was DERASH, which was the way of MIDRASH or legend; the third was "the way of *sekhel*" or reasoning; the fourth "the way of *sod*" or mysticism (meaning Kabbalah). His commentary was very popular because of its clear explanation of complicated mystical ideas. Ten commentaries were written on Bahya's commentary.

BAHYA BEN JOSEPH IBN PAKUDA (11th cent.). Jewish philosopher in Spain. Almost nothing is known of his life, except that he was a rabbinical judge (DAYYAN). His most famous book is *Hovot ha-Levavot* ("Duties of the Heart"), which appeared in 1080. He believed that there are two important aspects of being a religious Jew. Observing Jewish laws and customs, such as keeping the SABBATH and FESTIVALS is only one part of being a Jew. "The duties of the heart," which means working on one's spirituality, is just as important as keeping the laws, but had been ignored by many rabbis. Bahya tried to balance the two. He taught that the "duties of the heart" are essential to being a complete person.

The book is divided into ten "gates" and each one deals with a different duty of the heart. For example: accepting God as one, worshiping God as the one and only Creator, humility, and repentance.

BAL TASHHIT (lit. "Do not destroy!"). This expression is taken from the biblical law that forbids destroying fruit trees (Deut. 20:19–20). The rabbi's expanded this law to mean that it is forbidden to destroy anything that man can use. This includes vandalism, wastefulness, and any other damage to property. A person may not even destroy his own belongings. A person who smashes china or furniture in anger or wastes hard-earned money on drink or gambling is compared to an idol-worshiper (*Shab.* 105b). Today, the same law would apply to a person who damages buses or park benches, burns down forests, or kills animals without reason.

BA-MEH MADLIKIN ("With what may one light the Sabbath lamp?"). First words of the second chapter of the Mishnah *Shabbat,* recited in the Friday night service. It discusses the different kinds of oil and wicks that may be used for the Sabbath candles, when one can put them out in an emergency, and the preparations that one makes before the Sabbath begins. The rabbis added a short passage about the TORAH's role in bringing world peace. Some authorities place *ba-meh madlikin* before the service to give people who are running late a chance to finish their Sabbath preparations before the actual service starts. RASHI and other rabbis placed it at the end of the prayers so that people who arrived late to the synagogue have a chance to finish their prayers and leave with everyone else.

Ashkenazim still do as Rashi taught, while SEPHARDIM and Oriental Jews recite this passage between KABBALAT SHABBAT and the EVENING SERVICE. Hasidim replace it with a passage from the ZOHAR.

BAN   See EXCOMMUNICATION

BARAITA (Aramaic for "external teaching"; plural *baraitot*). Any statement made by the rabbis in the times of the *tannaim* (see TANNA) that was not included in the MISHNAH. A *baraita* has less legal authority than a Mishnah statement, so if there is a contradiction between the Mishnah and the *baraita,* the law is according to the Mishnah. There are some exceptions to this rule.

The *baraitot* from Mishnah times are divided into several categories. Most *baraitot* either add to the Mishnah or quote a law not found in the Mishnah. Some quote a different version of the Mishnah. These *baraitot* start with the words *tanya* ("we have learned this") or *tanu rabbanan* ("our sages have taught").

There were also many later *baraitot* from the times of the *amoraim* (see AMORA). They usually explain the Mishnah, or add something to it. They do not contain different opinions.

Some collections of *baraitot* from the times of the *tannaim* were published as a unit. The *Baraita de-Rabbi Meir,* "on acquiring the Torah," was added on to the Mishnah as an extra chapter in the book of AVOT. The *Baraita de-Rabbi Yishma'el* ("of thirteen rules") is now a part of the daily prayers. The *Baraita de-Rabbi Eliezer* is often printed after the book of BERAKHOT in the Babylonian Talmud. (See HERMENEUTICS.)

BAREKHI NAFSHI ("Bless [the Lord], O my soul"). These are the first words of Psalm 104, which is a song of praise to God and his wonderful creation. ASHKENAZIM recite it after the Sabbath AFTERNOON SERVICE, between SUKKOT and PASSOVER. It is also read after the ADDITIONAL SERVICE on the morning of the New Moon (*Rosh Hodesh*). SEPHARDIM and Oriental Jews read it before the EVENING SERVICE, the night before the New Moon.

BAREKHU ("Bless!"). This is the opening word of the formal call to prayer. It is used in the MORNING and EVENING SERVICE, when praying in a MINYAN – a group of at least ten. The full text is *Barekhu et-Adonai ha-Mevorakh* ("Praise the Lord who is to be praised"). In answer, the congregation then says: *Barukh Adonai ha-Mevorakh le-olam va-ed* ("Praised be the Lord who is to be praised forever and ever"). When this prayer is recited the congregation stands. The same prayer is said by a person called to the READING OF THE LAW (reading of the Torah in synagogue).

There are several opinions about the purpose of *Barekhu,* and any other form of praising God. NAHMANIDES said that prayer and worship is for the good of man, since God does not need it. The mystics thought that prayer has a positive influence in heaven, which causes good things to happen on earth. Samson

Raphael HIRSCH said that by praising God, man can play a part in achieving God's plan.

When saying the word *barekhu*, the reader bows his head. He straightens up when saying God's name. In many communities, *Barekhu* is recited again at the end of the morning and evening service.

BAR KOKHBA, SIMON   Leader of the Second Jewish Revolt against Rome in Judea (132–135 CE). The First Jewish Revolt (66–73 CE) was not successful, because the Jews did not succeed in overthrowing the Romans. Even so, it was followed by about two generations of quiet, until Trajan tried to turn JERUSALEM into a Roman colony. He put a temple to Jupiter in Jerusalem and changed the name of the city to Aelia Capitolina. Rabbi AKIVA and the SANHEDRIN convinced the Jews that they would be better off without the Romans. The Jews began to plan the revolt very carefully, since they did not want to make the same mistakes they had made in the first revolt. When the Jews made weapons for the Romans, they gave them to the Romans with small defects. When the Romans gave them back, the Jews fixed the weapons and kept them. When Hadrian left the country, the Jews took the opportunity to start the rebellion.

Simon bar Kokhba, "the Son of a Star," was chosen to lead the revolt. Rabbi Akiva declared him to be the MESSIAH. Bar Kokhba was a charismatic leader, who ruled the nation during the revolt. He minted coins and passed laws. The revolt began in Modein, the home of the Maccabees. They captured Jerusalem and most of Judea and Samaria. An army was brought in from Britain to fight the Jewish rebels and it recaptured Jerusalem and the remainder of the places under Jewish control. The last town to fall was Bethar, in the Judean Hills. Bar Kokhba died in this town. After the revolt, the Jews were thrown out of Jerusalem and Jewish customs were outlawed. The Jews were not allowed to keep the Sabbath, study Torah, or circumcise their children. Many Jewish leaders were killed. From that time on, Jews no longer ruled in the Land of Israel.

Many people think of the Bar Kokhba Revolt as heroic. Others consider it a lost cause from the beginning, since the Jews could never have stood up to a powerful nation like the Romans. Their fight for religious freedom was a tragedy, but it was also what saved them. Other nations have disappeared from the earth, but the Jews have survived.

BAR MITZVAH   The time that a boy becomes an adult in religious matters, at the age of 13. After the age of 13, a boy is counted in a MINYAN, and is responsible for keeping the commandments (*mitzvot*). In the Talmud, a 13-year-old boy is called a *bar onshin* – one who can be punished for his actions.

A group of 13-year-old boys celebrating their bar mitzvah at the Masada fortress 1ˢᵗ century synagogue.

In Jewish law, a father is responsible for his son's actions until he turns 13. From then on he is responsible for himself.

According to the Talmud, a boy is able to participate in religious ceremonies as soon as he can understand them. This means that a boy could be called to the Torah, wear TEFILLIN, and fast on the DAY OF ATONEMENT before he was 13. In fact, no bar mitzvah ceremony is mentioned before the year 1400.

By the late Middle Ages, a Jewish boy could not wear *tefillin* or be called to the Torah until he was 13 years old. For this reason a bar mitzvah ceremony was developed. The main parts of the bar mitzvah ritual were praying with *tefillin* for the first time, and being called to the READING OF THE LAW.

Today, the most popular custom is for a boy to be called to the Torah at the Sabbath MORNING SERVICE after his 13th birthday. He recites the Torah blessings, perhaps chants some of the Torah portion, and chants a "portion of the law" (MAFTIR) and the HAFTARAH reading from the Prophets. The father recites a special blessing, BARUKH SHE-PETARANI, which means that the boy is now responsible for his own actions.

Some other religious and social customs have been adopted over the years. In almost all communities, the bar mitzvah boy gives a speech (*derashah*) on a Jewish subject. If the boy has learned the CANTILLATION (the special tune used when reading the Torah), he chants some or all of the Torah portion of that week. Some boys lead the prayers on Friday night or Sabbath morning. In many communities, the rabbi speaks to the boy in front of the congregation after the Torah reading, and a MI SHE-BERAKH is said for him. In many congregations, the women and girls throw candies at the bar mitzvah boy as soon as he has finished chanting his portion of the Torah.

At first, the family and friends of the bar mitzvah boy would have a bar mitzvah meal after the services or at the "third meal" (SE'UDAH SHELISHIT). Later on, families made a KIDDUSH for the whole congregation after the services. Nowadays, the bar mitzvah reception or dinner is a huge social event. The bar mitzvah boy receives gifts from his parents, relatives, and other guests.

REFORM JUDAISM, in the 19th century, replaced the bar mitzvah with a CONFIRMATION ceremony. This ceremony is held in the late teens and it is the same for boys and girls. Today many Reform Jews have a bar mitzvah as well. In all Jewish communities, a bar mitzvah is a good opportunity for a family to join a synagogue or start sending their children to Hebrew school or Jewish day school. Nowadays, there are programs for adults who want to have a bar mitzvah and did not have one as a child.

In Israel, many boys throughout the world have their bar mitzvahs at the WESTERN WALL in Jerusalem, on a Monday or Thursday morning. Another popular place for a bar mitzvah ceremony is Masada. (See also BAT MITZVAH.)

BARRENNESS   The condition of a woman who cannot have children. In the Bible, barrenness in people and in animals is a curse. One of the blessings in the Bible is: "There shall be no sterile male or female among you or among your livestock" (Deut. 7:14).

Of the four MATRIARCHS (mothers), three – SARAH, REBEKAH, and RACHEL – had difficulty getting pregnant. Sarah was 90 years old when she gave birth to ISAAC; Rebekah was barren for the first 20 years of her marriage; and Rachel too did not give birth for many years. Hannah, the mother of SAMUEL the prophet, could also not get pregnant for many years, so she prayed and begged God for a child. When she finally conceived, she promised that her child would serve God in the Tabernacle (1 Sam. 1). According to the AGGADAH (legend), God did not allow the matriarchs to get pregnant easily so they would pour their hearts out to Him.

The sages said that a childless person was "as good as dead" (*AZ* 5a). A scholar without children could not be part of the SANHEDRIN. In Jewish law, barrenness is a reason to get divorced. If a wife does not get pregnant after ten years of marriage, her husband can end the marriage (*Yev.* 64a) and marry another woman who can have children (see DIVORCE). Barren women developed many folk remedies and SUPERSTITIONS while trying to solve their problem.

BARUKH DAYAN HA-EMET   ("Blessed be the true Judge"). The short form of the blessing people say when they hear bad news (especially about death). A mourner also says it when performing the RENDING OF THE GARMENTS (*keri'ah*; tearing the clothes when a relative has died). This phrase is recited twice during a FUNERAL SERVICE. It is also recited when visiting ruins of Jewish holy places.

BARUKH HA-SHEM   ("Blessed be the Name [of the Lord]"). Phrase of thanksgiving, equivalent to "Thank God" or "Thank heaven." Sometimes people add to it, and say: *Barukh Ha-Shem yom yom*, "Blessed be the Lord every day."

BARUKH SHE-AMAR   ("Blessed be the one who spoke [and the world came into being]…"). Opening words of the first hymn in *Pesukei de-Zimrah* ("Passages of Song") in every MORNING SERVICE. According to tradition, this hymn was written by the men of the GREAT ASSEMBLY. It was first used in the prayer book of AMRAM GAON in the ninth century.

Barukh she-Amar is made up of two parts. The first is about God creating the universe and saving the people of Israel. The word *barukh* appears 11 times in this section. The second part is a benediction (*berakhah*), which begins and ends with the words "Blessed are You, O Lord."

When reciting this hymn, worshipers should stand and try not to interrupt their prayers from this part of the morning service until after the repetition of the AMIDAH (silent prayer).

BARUKH SHEM KEVOD MALKHUTO   ("Blessed be the Name of His glorious kingdom"). Words, from the Bible (Neh. 9:5) said right after the first sentence of SHEMA. The complete phrase, *Barukh shem kevod malkhuto le-olam va-ed*, has more than one translation. Some examples are "Blessed be His Name, whose glorious kingdom is forever and ever," and "Praised be His glorious sovereignty throughout all time." Traditionally, JACOB was the first to use this phrase, after his sons accepted the God of Israel (Deut. 2:25). Later on, MOSES heard the angels in heaven reciting these words. It was used instead of AMEN in the TEMPLE, especially on the DAY OF ATONEMENT. Every time the HIGH PRIEST said God's holiest Name, on the Day of Atonement, the Israelites answered with this verse.

Throughout the year, Jews recite *Barukh shem kevod malkhuto* twice a day, in the MORNING and EVENING SEVICE after the *Shema*. It is recited in a whisper because it is connected with the angels and as a sign of grief for the destroyed Temple. On the Day of Atonement it is read out loud, because the Jews, who are fasting, are like angels.

Orthodox ASHKENAZIM recite it when they put on their TEFILLIN. It is also recited three times, out loud, after the *Shema* at the end of the NE'ILAH service on the Day of Atonement.

BARUKH SHE-PETARANI ("Blessed be the One who has relieved me"). Blessing recited by the father of a BAR MITZVAH boy. The source of the blessing is in the MIDRASH: "A man should be responsible for his son until the boy is 13; he should then say 'Blessed be He who has relieved me of the punishment due on his account'" (Gen. R. 63:14). Parents are punished for their children's religious misbehavior until the child reaches the age of bar mitzvah. When a father recites this blessing, he relieves himself of the responsibility for his child. From that point on, the child is responsible for himself in Jewish matters. In Conservative synagogues, the blessing is not said, and in Reform congregations, SHE-HEHEYANU is recited instead. In some modern Orthodox congregations the blessing is recited for girls at their BAT MITZVAH, as well.

Nowadays, in spoken Hebrew and Yiddish, *Barukh she-petarani* is an expression that means "good riddance!"

BAT KOL (literally "daughter of a voice," meaning "an echo"). Term generally used in the Talmud for a voice of an angel, usually Gabriel, from heaven. The *bat kol*'s message is usually taken from the Bible. According to tradition, one *bat kol* announced MOSES' death, and another announced that God Himself would bury him.

There is a famous story about Rabbi Eliezer and a *bat kol*. Rabbi Eliezer disagreed with the other rabbis on a point in Jewish law, and he caused several miracles to prove that he was correct. The rabbis were not convinced, so he called upon heaven to intercede on his behalf. A *bat kol* announced that the law was according to Rabbi Eliezer's opinion. Still, the rabbis did not accept the *bat kol*'s ruling because the Torah "is not in heaven," meaning that disputes about the law should be solved by human beings in democratic ways.

BATLANIM (Hebrew for "men of leisure" or "idlers"; Yiddish *batlonim*). Originally a name for those with enough time to devote all or part of their day to Torah study and communal work. From early rabbinic times, there were always at least ten men in each community (*asarah batlanim*) who devoted their time to Torah study and prayers (*Meg.* 1:3, 3b, 5a; *Sanh.* 17b, *Ber.* 6b). RASHI defines *batlanim* as "ten persons who do not do any other work in order to be present in synagogue for morning and evening prayers," and devote themselves to the community. Until recently, these ten "men of leisure" were an important part of the community, and were often asked to decide legal questions. Then the institution became a system of paid "MINYAN men," who would recite KADDISH for families who could not do it themselves. This explains why the modern meaning of the word *batlan* is an idler or a ne'er-do-well. In Yiddish folklore, the *batlon* was a misfit, who was not too bright, and did not work very hard.

BAT MITZVAH (literally "daughter of the commandment"). A girl who has reached the age of 12 years and one day and is an adult according to Jewish law. A girl is not required by Jewish law to have any kind of ceremony, but she still becomes independent and responsible for her own Jewish decisions. In the mid-19th century, Rabbi Jacob Etlinger developed a ceremony equivalent to a BAR MITZVAH; however, it is not part of the synagogue service. The custom spread, and in the late 19th century, it was accepted by Rabbi Joseph Hayyim ben Elijah al-Haham, an important rabbi in Baghdad. He suggested holding a banquet in honor of the bat mitzvah girl, who would wear a new dress and say the SHE-HEHIYANU blessing.

Mordecai KAPLAN introduced the bat mitzvah ceremony as part of the synagogue service in the United Stated during the 1920s. It has become very popular, and each community has a different type of bat mitzvah ceremony. In American non-Orthodox communities, a 12-year-old girl celebrates her "coming of age" on a Friday night or Sabbath morning. She leads the services, might read the week's portion of the Torah, chants the appropriate portion from the Prophets (HAFTARAH), and sometimes gives a speech about a Torah-related subject. In Orthodox synagogues, the bat mitzvah girl participates less in the services. Some Orthodox communities invite the girl to be called to the Torah and chant her portion in a women's prayer group.

In most British and South African communities, a girl must take a course and pass a test in order to participate in the group bat mitzvah ceremony. In Israel, non-observant families arrange a special 12th birthday party with no religious aspect.

Lately, it has become popular for adults who did not have a bat mitzvah as a child, to have one as an adult. The congregation's rabbi or cantor gives them a special course to prepare them for the ceremony.

BAVA BATRA ("Last Gate"). Third tractate (book) of the Order of NEZIKIN in the Mishnah. It has ten chapters, which talk about owning, selling, and trading real estate. It also deals with the laws of inheritance, legal documents, and weights and measures.

BAVA KAMMA ("First Gate"). First tractate (book) of the Order of NEZIKIN in the Mishnah. It has ten chapters, which deal with the laws of damages and compensation. The last three chapters deal with damage by theft and violence.

BAVA METSI'AH ("Middle Gate"). Second tractate (book) of the Order of NEZIKIN in the Mishnah. It has ten chapters, which deal with property, lost and found, interest, and hiring workers. The first *mishnah* of the first chapter is one of the first things taught to a beginning Talmud student.

Opening page of the talmudic tractate Bava Metsi'ah.

BEDIKAT HAMETZ   See LEAVEN, SEARCH FOR

BE-EZRAT HA-SHEM ("With the help of the Name of God"). Phrase that is used to express trust in God. It was not used in ancient times, but in the Middle Ages, it became a standard expression used by many rabbis. Nowadays many Jews use the expression daily. Observant Jews write a abbreviation of *be-ezrat ha-Shem* in the corner of all their letters. *Be-siyyatta di-Shemayya*, "with the help of heaven," is the Aramaic equivalent, which is often used instead.

BEHEMOTH   See LEVIATHAN.

BEKHOROT ("Firstborn"). Fourth tractate (book) of the Order of KODSHIM in the Mishnah. It has nine chapters, which deal

with redeeming the firstborn child or animal. The Mishnah also discusses what happens when the firstborn animal has a blemish, giving ten percent of one's animals to charity, and the firstborn's special rights. See also FIRSTBORN, REDEMPTION OF.

BELZ Hasidic sect originally from the town of Belz, in Eastern Galicia. Rabbi Shalom Roke'ah (1783–1855), a student of Rabbi Jacob Isaac, founded the dynasty. He attracted followers from Poland, Galicia, and Hungary. His youngest son, Joshua Roke'ah (1825–1894), became the second Belzer Rebbe. He made the Belz court the most important Hasidic sect in Galicia. He was greatly opposed to the modern world and fought to protect the interests of the Orthodox community. He challenged the secular Shomer Israel organization in Lwow.

His son, Isaachar Dov, was an extreme anti-Zionist. During World War I, he fled to Hungary with many of his followers. They were able to return to Belz, which was then part of Poland, only in 1925. Aaron Roke'ah (1880–1957) took over the position of Rebbe after his father's death. He and his brother were the only members of the family who managed to flee the Nazis in World War II. They came to Erets Israel. After his death, his nine-year-old nephew, Issachar Dov, became the Rebbe. He was known for his independence. He broke away from the other HAREDIM (ultra-Orthodox Jews) in 1980, and formed a separate community.

Today, Belz is one of the largest Hasidic sects, with a center in Jerusalem and a large community in the Boro Park section of Brooklyn.

The Belz Rebbe attending a funeral, 1851.

BENEDICTIONS Blessings that are recited on various occasions. *Berakhah*, the Hebrew word for benediction, comes from the Hebrew word *berekh* (knee), since "bowing the knee" was a part of worshiping or praising God (Isa. 45:23; Ps. 95:6; Dan. 6:11; II Chr. 6:13). From the times of the PATRIARCHS until MISHNAH times, there were several types of benedictions, which each began with different words. The rabbis of the Mishnah (c. 90 CE) began to develop rules for the wording of the different types of benedictions. This process was completed in the times of the TALMUD (after 220 CE).

According to the Talmud (*Ber.* 12a, 40b), all benedictions must mention God's name and His Kingship. Therefore all formal benedictions must begin with the words *Barukh attah Adonai Elohenu Melekh ha-Olam*, "Blessed are You, O Lord our God, King of the Universe." This idea was in reaction to the Romans, who worshiped the emperor instead of God. The response to most benedictions is AMEN.

The ideal, according to Rabbi MEIR (*Men.* 43b), is to recite 100 blessings a day. Many of the benedictions are included in the daily prayers, such as the "18 Benedictions" in the AMIDAH. MAIMONIDES divided the rest of the blessings into three main categories. The first category is called *Birkhot ha-Nehenin* ("Benedictions for Enjoyment"), and includes all blessings for food, drink, and inhaling spices or perfumes. The source of these blessing can be traced to the Bible. The Talmud adds that "it is forbidden to taste anything before making a benediction. Since everything in the world belongs to God, neglecting to offer thanks for enjoyment is the same as stealing from Him (*Ber.* 35a).

A second category of blessings is called *Birkhot ha-Mitzvot* ("Benedictions for Performing Commandments"), which are recited when performing a MITZVAH. The blessings include the words *asher kiddeshanu be-mitzvotav ve-tsivvanu* ("Who has sanctified us with His commandments and commanded us…"), followed by the specific commandment (e.g. "to kindle the Sabbath light").

The third category is *Birkhot Hoda'ah* ("Blessings of Gratitude and Thanksgiving"). These blessings are recited on witnessing special events, including natural phenomena (earthquakes, lightning), and seasonal and family events (holidays, circumcision). This is to show that everything in life comes from God.

Reciting the benedictions, from morning until evening, reminds Jews constantly that they are dependant upon God. By reciting a blessing, a Jew can transform a daily activity into a religious experience.

BENEI ISRAEL ("Children of Israel"). Indian Jews from the Konkan coast of Maharashtra. The Benei Israel claim that they are members of the "lost tribes" that reached India as long ago as 175 BCE (see TRIBES, TEN LOST). According to their tradition, they were shipwrecked off the Konkan coast and lost all their holy books, remembering only the SHEMA prayer. They lived among the Hindus and adopted many of their customs. When David Rahabi discovered them, in the 18th century, they observed the SABBATH, the DIETARY LAWS, CIRCUMCISION, and many of the Jewish FESTIVALS, but had no synagogue. The New Year was only one day, several Jewish fasts had been forgotten, and HANUKKAH was unknown because it belonged to the time after the Benei Israel had left Erets Israel.

From 1750 onwards, the Benei Israel began to adjust to mainstream Judaism. Their first synagogue, named "Gates of Mercy," was built in Bombay in 1796. Cochin Jews helped them with different aspects of religious life. In the 19th century, Jews from Baghdad joined the Benei Israel of Bombay.

After the State of Israel was established in 1948, the Benei Israel began immigrating to Israel. By, 1960 there were several rabbis who would not marry Benei Israel to other Israelis, because they had doubts about their Jewishness. In 1962, The Chief Rabbinate instructed marriage registrars to examine the history of Benei Israel who wished to marry other Jews. Between 1962 and 1964, the Benei Israel organized strikes, and demanded to be recognized as "full Jews." In 1964, the Chief Rabbinate declared Benei Israel to be "full Jews in every respect." Some rabbis still refused to marry the Benei Israel, but this problem was solved in the 1970s when the chief rabbis declared again that the Benei Israel were "Jews in every respect."

BEN-GURION, DAVID (David Green; 1886–1973). Zionist leader and first prime minister of Israel. Ben-Gurion was born in Poland and became a Zionist under his father's influence. In 1906 he left for Erets Israel and became a farmer. He was active in the socialist Po'alei Zion Party, which called for Jewish labor, Jewish self-defense, and Hebrew culture. When World War I broke out, the Turks expelled him from Erets Israel. In the United States, he helped form a Jewish battalion called the Jewish Legion, which fought alongside the British Army in 1918. He was one of the founders of the Histadrut and its secretary-general for a number of years. He was also one of the founders

David Ben-Gurion.

of Mapai, the country's leading political party, and chairman of the Jewish Agency. He was dedicated to moving the Jewish people to an independent state.

During World War II, Ben-Gurion continued to fight for a Jewish state. The British issued a document called the "White Paper," which restricted the number of Jews allowed to enter Palestine. This caused a problem for the Jews in Palestine. On the one hand they had to support the British in their war against Nazi Germany, but on the other hand the British were not allowing the Jews to emigrate from Europe to Palestine. Ben-Gurion vowed to fight the British White Paper "as though there were no war" and to fight the Nazis "as thought there were no White Paper."

He proclaimed the State of Israel in 1948, and became the country's first prime minister and minister of defense. He was prime minister through the War of Independence and the Sinai campaign and resigned in 1963.

Ben-Gurion was one of the most important Jewish leaders of modern times. Golda MEIR called him "the greatest Jew of our generation." He saw the fulfillment of the Zionist dream, the State of Israel, as the only solution to the Jewish problem of homelessness. He had a major influence on the character of the State of Israel. He created the Israel Defense Force, the public school and the social security system. He thought the State of Israel should be a Jewish State and tried to preserve Jewish observance in public life in a modern, secular state.

BENJAMIN   See TRIBES, TWELVE

BENTSHEN   (Yiddish "bless"). Term used by many ASHKENAZIM to mean the act of reciting a BENEDICTION whenever required by Jewish law, especially GRACE AFTER MEALS. *Bencao* is a similar term used by Spanish and Portuguese Jews. The opening Hebrew phrase in Grace After Meals, *Rabbotai nevarekh*, "Gentlemen, let us pronounce the blessing," is often replaced by the Yiddish equivalent, *"Rabbosay, mir vilin bentshen."* The special book for Grace and Sabbath hymns is called a *bentsher.*

BERAH DODI   ("Hasten, my Beloved"). Opening words of three different hymns, written by three different authors, read in some ASHKENAZI congregations on PASSOVER. The phrase is taken from the SONG OF SONGS (8:14). The poems call out to God to redeem His people, a theme that appears in the Song of Songs.

BERAKHOT   See BENEDICTIONS

BERAKHOT   ("Benedictions"). First tractate (book) of the Order of ZERA'IM in the Mishnah. It has nine chapters that deal with the laws of reading the SHEMA, the time for reciting the AMIDAH prayed and the level of concentration it requires, the blessings recited over different foods, and the laws of GRACE AFTER MEALS. One of the chapters explains the differences between the schools of HILLEL and SHAMMAI on the subject of KIDDUSH and HAVDALLAH. The last chapter describes the blessings made when seeing lightning, hearing thunder, or hearing good or bad news.

BERIKH SHEMEH   ("Blessed be the Lord's Name"). Prayer in Aramaic recited by traditional congregations when the ARK is opened before the READING OF THE LAW on the SABBATH and FESTIVALS. This mystical prayer was said to be written by SIMEON BAR YOHAI, and is part of the ZOHAR. The prayer talks about man's role as an agent of God on earth and his duty to increase the good in the world. It also contains blessings and declares God to be King of the Universe. Both ASHKENAZIM and SEPHARDIM recite *Berikh Shemeh* right after the Ark is opened, while Yemenite Jews recite it right before the Torah reading. Some modern prayer books include a Hebrew translation.

BERIT MILAH   See CIRCUMCISION

BERLIN, NAPHTALI TSEVI JUDAH   (1817–1893). Lithuanian rabbinical leader and head of the Volozhin *yeshivah*. He was known (from the acronym of his Hebrew name) as the *Netsiv*, or "pillar," of Volozhin. Born in Mir, White Russia, he began learning in the *yeshivah* at the age of 13. He later married the daughter of the head of the *yeshivah*, Rabbi Isaac of Volozhin. When Rabbi Isaac died, his son-in-law, Rabbi Isaac Fried, became the head of the *yeshivah*, with Berlin as his assistant. When Fried died in 1853, some people wanted to appoint Berlin and Rabbi Joseph Baer SOLOVEICHIK as joint heads of the *yeshivah*, and some people wanted Soloveichik alone to run the *yeshivah*. Leading rabbis of the time were asked to choose, and they decided in favor of Berlin.

He had a far-reaching influence on the *yeshivah* and the number of students grew to 400 while he was the head. Berlin gave daily lectures on the Torah portion of that week and wrote several books. His most important works were his commentary on the PENTATEUCH, *Ha'amek Davar*, and his RESPONSA, *Meshiv Davar.*

Berlin was an active leader of the community, and openly declared his opinion on every major question of his time. He supported the Hibbat Zion ("Lovers of Zion") movement, and urged observant Jews to settle in Erets Israel. He disagreed with Samson Raphael HIRSCH (see NEO-ORTHODOXY), who wanted to establish separate Orthodox communities. In his later years, the Russian government wanted to limit the hours of Torah study in the *yeshivah* and add secular studies instead. The *Netsiv* would not agree to this, so the *yeshivah* was closed and the *Netsiv* was expelled from Volozhin.

The *Netsiv*'s younger son, **Meir Berlin (Bar-Ilan**; 1880–1949), became a leader of Mizrachi, a religious Zionist movement. He organized the American Mizrachi and the Teachers' Institute, which later became part of Yeshiva University. From 1926, Meir Berlin was active in Jerusalem. He founded and edited the Mizrachi newspaper *Ha-Tsofeh* (1937–), worked on the

Talmudic Encyclopedia (1947–), and wrote a Yiddish memoir and a biography of his father (*Rabban shel Yisrael*, 1943). Israel's modern Orthodox University, Bar-Ilan, is named for him.

BERNAYS, ISAAC (1792–1849). Rabbi and pioneer of NEO-ORTHODOXY. He was born in Mainz, Germany, studied at the rabbinical academy of Abraham Bing in Wurzberg, and was the first traditional German rabbi with a university education. He became the chief rabbi of Hamburg in 1821. He fought against the REFORM Jews and worked hard to attract intellectuals to traditional Judaism. He objected to the fact that unqualified reformers called themselves rabbis, so he took on the Sephardi title of HAKHAM instead of rabbi. He was especially opposed to the new Reform prayer book because it left out the hope of rebuilding Erets Israel. He revived the TALMUD TORAH school, delivered impressive German sermons, and put much effort into SYNAGOGUE worship. His teachings inspired Samson Raphael HIRSCH.

BERTINORO, OBADIAH BEN ABRAHAM YAREI DI (c. 1450–c. 1515). Rabbinic scholar and commentator on the MISHNAH, known also by the acronym *Ra'av* (= *Rabbenu Ovadiah mi-Bartenura*), His last name shows that his family's roots were in the northern Italian town of Bertinoro.

In 1485 he left for Erets Israel, passing through Naples, Salerno, Messina, Rhodes, and Egypt. During his journey he wrote three letters, which contained geographical, historical, and cultural information and are among the best-known Hebrew travel literature. After three years he arrived in Jerusalem, where he became the head of the community, with the help of Nathan ha-Kohen Sholal. The Jewish community in Jerusalem was small and poor, and Bertinoro succeeded in rebuilding it. When cultured Sephardi Jews arrived in 1492, after their expulsion from Spain, the community improved even more.

Bertinoro's commentary is as important to Mishnah study as RASHI's commentary is to Talmud study. He uses the commentaries of Rashi and MAIMONIDES to explain the Mishnah in a clear and direct way. NO standard edition of the Mishnah is printed without Bertinoro's commentary.

BERURYAH (2nd cent. CE). Wife of Rabbi MEIR and a scholar herself, daughter of Rabbi Hananiah ben Teradyon. She and her husband lived in Tiberias. The Talmud refers many times to her intellectual gifts and ability to argue with the rabbis. Berurya's opinions were given the same importance as those of the rabbis of her time, and her opinion was accepted at least once, by Rabbi JUDAH BAR ILAI.

Berurya's life was full of tragedy. Her father was tortured to death by the Romans, her sister was forced into prostitution, and her brother was killed by bandits. The Mishnah tells us that her two sons died suddenly one Sabbath afternoon. She told her husband only after he came home from the ACADEMY after the Sabbath had ended. She broke the news to him gently by asking him if a precious object left with her for safekeeping

should be returned. He replied: "Why of course it should!" She then showed him their sons' bodies and said: "The Lord has given, and the Lord has taken away; blessed be the name of the Lord" (Job 1:21).

BESAMIM   See SPICES

BET DIN (pl. *battei* din). A court of Jewish law. From the earliest times, the Israelites had a court system. At first MOSES judged the people "from the morning to the evening" (Ex. 18:13) until his father-in law, Jethro, advised him to appoint more judges. He then appointed judges "over thousands, hundreds, fifties, and tens." Any case too difficult for the judges would be passed upwards and eventually heard by Moses, who acted as the Supreme Court.

Later, after the Israelites entered the Land of Israel, judges also served as leaders of the people. Many of the kings, such as SOLOMON, were judges.

According to the Talmud, in Second Temple times, there were *battei din* of three, 23, and 71 judges. Each town had a *bet din* of three judges, which could rule on civil matters. A town of 120 or more men had a *bet din* of 23 judges, which could rule in cases involving physical or CAPITAL PUNISHMENT. Finally there was the SANHEDRIN, a court of 71 judges. If a smaller court could not reach a decision, the case would be passed to a larger *bet din*, and finally to the Sanhedrin. However, a case could not be appealed to a larger court if a person was not satisfied with the verdict. The Sanhedrin also dealt with announcing the New Moon and setting the Jewish calendar.

The Sanhedrin's decisions were final and no one was allowed to contest them. In fact if a TORAH scholar spoke against the Sanhedrin's decision, he was called a *zaken mamreh* – rebellious elder – and could receive the death penalty.

When JERUSALEM fell, JOHANAN BEN ZAKKAI arranged to move the Sanhedrin to Yavneh. The Sanhedrin lost some of its power and was unable to use capital punishment. Other Jewish centers were developed when the Jews were exiled to Babylonia, and they challenged the authority of the Sanhedrin in Yavneh. By 425 CE the Sanhedrin had broken up.

Before EMANCIPATION (when Jews were given equal rights), the Jews lived in their own independent communities. The *bet din* ruled on all legal questions: religious, personal status, or civil cases. The strongest punishment they had was HEREM, or excommunication. In Spain the *battei din* could use capital punishment. Later, the Council of the Four Lands (mid-16th cent.–1764), which controlled Jewish life in Lithuania and Poland, was given a great amount of power by the government. It was responsible for taxing the Jews, and was able to impose the *herem* and fines, which made sure that everyone cooperated with them.

In modern times, the Jews can go to regular courts to solve their disputes. The *battei din*, however, still exist. If two parties involved in a dispute agree in writing to accept the *bet din*'s ruling, it will rule on civil cases as well as personal cases. *Battei din* often deal with matters of Jewish divorce (See GITTIN) and in Israel they deal with the issue of CONVERSION. The *battei din* in Israel often disagree with the secular courts on different questions, such as non-Orthodox conversions.

BET HA-MIKDASH   See TEMPLE

BETH JACOB   See EDUCATION

BET MIDRASH   (lit. "house of study"). Center for religious learning, often part of a synagogue. The *bet midrash* has generally been the primary place of TALMUD study. According to legend, the first *bet midrash* was that of NOAH's son Shem and his son Eber. One of the earliest recorded examples, was the *bet midrash* of SHEMAYA AND AVTALYON (1st cent. BCE), which charged an entrance fee. When HILLEL, who later became one of the greatest scholars in Jewish history, was unable to pay it, he would climb to the roof and listen through the chimney.

From the Middle Ages, there was a *bet midrash* in every Jewish town. Young men would study there during the day, and those who worked would study for a few hours in the evenings. Today there are almost no communal *battei midrash*, but many synagogues have one that operates at specific hours of the day. Each YESHIVAH has a *bet midrash* which is the main place of study.

According to Jewish law, TORAH study is so important that a *bet midrash* is considered holier than a synagogue. It is permitted to sell a synagogue in order to build a *bet midrash*.

BETROTHAL   See MARRIAGE

BETSAH   ("Egg"). Seventh tractate (book) of the Order of MO'ED in the Mishnah. Its five chapters discuss the difference between what is considered work on the SABBATH and work on a FESTIVAL day (such as PASSOVER or the New Year). The tractate also explains the laws of MUKTSEH (things forbidden to be touched on the Sabbath and festivals), the preparation of food on holy days, and the idea of *shevut* – not working on the Sabbath and festivals. The tractate is named for its first word, but is also called *Yom Tov* (Festival Day) because of its subject.

BET SHAMMAI AND BET HILLEL   ("House of Shammai and House of Hillel"). Two rival schools of thought, which greatly influenced the development of the ORAL LAW. These two schools were run by HILLEL and SHAMMAI, the most important rabbis of the time in the last decades of the Second Temple and after it was destroyed. They have 316 recorded controversies, which deal with every subject in HALAKHAH (Jewish law). Shammai's school usually had the stricter opinion, but the law was most often according to Hillel's school.

An example of a disagreement between the two is the law of DIVORCE. According to the school of Shammai, a man could divorce his wife only if she committed adultery. According to Bet Hillel, a man could divorce his wife if he had any serious reason to do so. There is also a general difference in the way the two schools interpreted the Bible. Bet Shammai tended to interpret the text literally, while Bet Hillel would look for the meaning behind the words.

Since the 19th century, scholars have tried to explain the differences between Bet Shammai and Bet Hillel based on their lifestyles. The Shammaites were rich aristocrats, living in the country, who were known for being very conservative. The Hillelites were small merchants and workers who lived in the towns, and were considered more liberal.

When the Jews lived under Roman rule, the Shammaites wanted to make 18 new *gezerot* (rules) that would prevent the Jews from getting too close to the Romans. They outnumbered the Hillelites, so the laws were enforced. This caused much controversy between the two schools. Some 40 years later, the rabbis decided that the *halakhah* should always follow Bet Hillel. The Talmud (*Er.* 13b) tells the story of how the decision was made: "For three years, the schools of Shammai and Hillel argued, each insisting that its opinion was the *halakhah*. Then, a heavenly voice (BAT KOL) announced: 'both of them are the living words of God, but the *halakhah* is according to Bet Hillel.' Why is this? Because the Hillelites were pleasant and humble, teaching the opinion of both sides, and always taught Bet Shammai's view before their own."

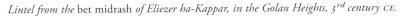

Lintel from the bet midrash *of Eliezer ha-Kappar, in the Golan Heights, 3rd century CE.*

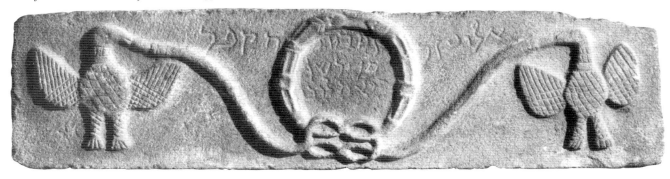

BIBLE   The common English name for the Hebrew Scriptures. "The Bible" comes from the Greek word *biblia,* which means "the books."

The popular Hebrew word for Bible is *Tanakh,* which is an acronym (TaNaKh) for the three sections of the Hebrew Bible, *Torah* (PENTATEUCH), *Nevi'im* (PROPHETS), and *Ketuvim* (HAGIOGRAPHA). The Christian term "Old Testament" is used to separate the Hebrew Scriptures from the New Testament.

The Bible is written mostly in the HEBREW language. Two words in Genesis (31:47), one verse in Jeremiah (10:11) and sections of the books of Daniel (2:46–7:25) and Ezra (4:8–6:18, 7:12–26) are written in ARAMAIC. The text is written in many different styles because it represents many periods of time and types of language.

Contents   The Hebrew Bible is divided into three sections.

1. Pentateuch (*Torah*). This includes the first five books of the Bible: GENESIS, EXODUS, LEVITICUS, NUMBERS, and DEUTERONOMY. The meaning of the word *Torah* is instruction. According to Jewish tradition, these books were written by MOSES, who was instructed by God.

The Five Books begin with the CREATION of the world and the history of the PATRIARCHS. They continue uninterrupted through the Law-giving at SINAI, until Moses' death before Israel entered the Land of Canaan. In the times of Ezra and Nehemiah, the Torah was divided into five parts and became known as the "five-volumed book" (Heb. *Hamishah Humshei Torah*), or *Humash,* which means Pentateuch.

2. Prophets (*Nevi'im*). This section is divided into two parts. The "Early Prophets" include JOSHUA, JUDGES, SAMUEL (I and II), and KINGS (I and II). These books are a continuation of the story line of the Pentateuch. The books of Joshua, Judges, and Samuel trace the history of Israel from the conquering of Canaan and the period of the Judges through the establishment of the rule of the kings in the times of SAUL and DAVID. The Book of Kings is about the two Jewish kingdoms of JUDAH and ISRAEL, until JERUSALEM's downfall in 586 BCE.

The "Latter Prophets" consist of the books of ISAIAH, JEREMIAH, EZEKIEL, and the twelve "Minor Prophets" (in Aramaic, *Terei Asar* – "the Twelve"): HOSEA, JOEL, AMOS, OBADIAH, JONAH, MICAH, NAHUM, HABAKKUK, ZEPHANIAH, HAGGAI, ZECHARIAH, and MALACHI. The name "Minor Prophets" does not mean that these books are less important, only that they are short and originally written on one scroll. The "Latter Prophets" are a collection of works dating from the end of the kingdoms of Judah and Israel until the early Second Temple period (8th to 5th cent. BCE).

The books of the Prophets mostly contained a record, in poetic form, of their various prophecies. They also included details about the lives of the prophets and the times in which they lived.

3. Hagiographa (*Ketuvim*). The third section of the Bible is a collection of different types of books. There are books of religious poetry (PSALMS and LAMENTATIONS); love poetry (SONG OF SONGS); WISDOM LITERATURE (PROVERBS, JOB, and ECCLESIASTES); historical books (RUTH, CHRONICLES (I and II), ESTHER, EZRA, and NEHEMIAH); and the book of DANIEL, which is a mixture. The name *Ketuvim* includes all of these styles of literature.

The Bible's division into three sections was not done according to style or subject matter, but according to the three stages in which they were added to the Canon (see below).

Canon   The term "canon" means a collection of holy writings to which nothing can be added or taken away. The canon has a certain amount of religious authority in its writings because the Bible is believed to be the word of God. For this reason, not every book was included in the canon. A process took place in which books were either made part of the canon or rejected. Many of the rejected writings were lost. The Bible became the focus of Jewish life, and the Jews became known as the "People of the Book."

There were several stages in canonizing the Bible. During King Josiah's time, an old copy of the "book of the Torah" was found (II Kings 22:23). The book was authentic, and it was immediately read aloud to the people of Israel. Right after that, the religious life of the Israelites began to be in keeping with this book, which is believed to be the Book of Deuteronomy. The next public reading is recorded in the time of EZRA (about 444 BCE), as described in Nehemiah 8–10. This was a further stage in the canonization of the Pentateuch. The Prophets became a set part of the Bible before the end of the Persian Empire and the Hagiographa was finally closed well into the Greco-Roman period.

In the times of the Talmud, there were still disagreements about whether certain books were part of the Bible or not. A debate occurred in the Talmud about Proverbs, Ecclesiastes, the Song of Songs, and Esther (*Meg.* 7a). The Wisdom of Ben Sira (Ecclesiasticus) was considered a holy book until the rabbis declared that it would not be part of the Bible. Many other works written at this time were accepted into the holy books of the Greeks and from there into the Christian literature, so they could not become part of the Bible. The Qumran sect had a much wider range of works in their canon. Some of these books were only discovered when the DEAD SEA SCROLLS were studied.

Text   The text of the Bible is made up of three graphic elements: (1) the consonants, (2) the vowel signs, (3) the accent marks. The accent marks are like musical notes used to chant the special melody of the Bible. Originally, only the letters themselves where written, and the pronunciation and melody were passed down orally. In the Middle Ages, the Masoretes added the vowel signs and accent marks to prevent those traditions from being lost. They developed what was called the Masoretic text, which was eventually accepted as the official text of the Bible.

There are some differences in the texts of the earliest manuscripts of the Bible, generally in the spelling or grammar. In some cases we find different wordings or ordering of entire sections of the Bible. Even in passages that appear more than once, differences can occur. For example, the TEN COMMANDMENTS appear once in the Book of Exodus (20:2–14) and again in the Book of Deuteronomy (5:6–9), with some changes.

The Samaritan Pentateuch (see SAMARITANS) is a Hebrew text of the first five books of the Bible. It was preserved within the Samaritan community as their Bible. It was clearly one of the versions of the Bible that was in circulation in the Second Temple period and later disappeared from Jewish communities. Other important sources of information about the original text of the Bible are ancient translations. The earliest and most famous translation is the SEPTUAGINT, which was done by secular Jews in Alexandria, around the third century BCE.

In the 1940s and '50s, ancient biblical scrolls were discovered in caves at Qumran in the Judean Desert. The DEAD SEA SCROLLS were the earliest manuscripts of the Bible and quickly became an extremely important source of information. Among the scrolls were versions of the Masoretic text, the Samaritan Pentateuch, and the Septuagint, dating from the third century BCE until 70 CE.

The last type of evidence are books that were not included in the Bible. These books often contained quotes from the Bible, but with some differences.

In the Talmud we find descriptions of the process of preserving a biblical text. An official Temple scroll was used for correcting all the other scrolls leading to the text that was accepted as

A page with verses from the Book of Psalms, from the Aleppo Codex, *the oldest complete manuscript of the Bible, dating from the 10ᵗʰ century.*

the only correct version of the Bible. *Soferim* (counters) counted the number of words in the scroll and established the middle word and letter of each book.

Critical Study of the Bible   The Bible text had so many contradictions and difficulties that a talmudic rabbi said: "The Torah was given scroll by scroll" (*Git.* 60a). Such discussions caused Jewish scholars to develop the system of HERMENEUTICS, which helped solve some of the problems. Hellenistic and Muslim scholars used these difficulties to try to prove that the Bible was not authentic. The medieval Jewish scholar Abraham IBN EZRA (1092–1167) hinted that some sentences in the Pentateuch could not have been written by Moses. He also pointed out the work of a second prophet in the second half of the book of Isaiah.

The first scientific Bible critic of modern times is Baruch SPINOZA (1632–1677). He thought that the Bible should be studied just like any other text, ignoring the religious tradition. He openly declared that the Pentateuch was not written by Moses, and in the years that followed, this was a main question for Bible critics. They divided the Pentateuch into four separate works, each with its own author, based on differences in the text, such as various names for God. A similar study was done on the rest of the Bible. Recently, scholars have taken more of an interest in the Bible as literature. They emphasize the entire text as a unit instead of breaking it up into ideas and laws.

In the 19ᵗʰ and 20ᵗʰ centuries, many important artifacts were found in archeological excavations of biblical sites, such as Hazor, Megiddo, Samaria, Jerusalem, and Lachish. These objects help paint a picture of what life was like in biblical times and therefore give new meaning to the text. In the areas surrounding Erets Israel, ancient texts have been preserved on monuments and in libraries. By studying the language of these sources, scholars have learned more about the language of the Bible. When historians studied ancient Canaanite literature, for example, they found that the Bible had inherited much of its language, subjects, and ideas from the Canaanites. Psalms in the Bible were found to be similar to Egyptian and Mesopotamian hymns.

The most obvious similarities between the Bible and Mesopotamian literature are the stories of the CREATION and the FLOOD. Although the plot and language are very similar, the moral of the story is different in each culture. The Bible does not have any magic or astrology in it, while almost all other holy books of the time did. By comparing the Bible to other holy books of the time, one can see that the Jewish religion specifically taught belief in one God. At the time, it was popular to worship many gods; therefore all literature except the Bible presents pagan traditions.

In Judaism   From the period of the Exodus (when the Israelites left the Land of Egypt) until Second Temple times, the Bible served as a vehicle that brought the commandments in the Pentateuch to the Jews. Later, Jewish life was mostly controlled by the ORAL LAW, which was based on the WRITTEN LAW in the Bible. Two types of rabbinic literature developed based on the Scriptures. The first was a "way of life," the HALAKHAH

Part of the Epic of Gilgamesh *on which the Babylonian version of the Flood is recorded. It is dated to c. 2000–1800 BCE. Parallels have been found in Mesopotamian literature with the story of Creation in the Bible.*

(Jewish law), based on the 613 commandments written in the Pentateuch (see COMMANDMENTS, 613). The rabbis traced every detail of Jewish life, from the cradle to the grave, to its source in the Pentateuch. The second was the MIDRASH and AGGADAH, which were collections of imaginative stories based on the weekly portion of the Torah and other parts of the Bible. These stories looked beyond the plain meaning of the text and created legend and folklore. The Midrash is also the source of Jewish mysticism, KABBALAH.

When the Temple was destroyed, the SYNAGOGUE became much more important to the Jewish community. Each house of prayer was considered a small Temple (*mikdash me'at*), and many of the details of the synagogue came from the Bible. Each daily service replaced one of the daily sacrifices. The Ark, which contained the Scrolls of the Law (manuscripts of the Pentateuch), replaced the ancient ARK OF THE COVENANT, which was in the holiest part of the Temple, and the ETERNAL LIGHT replaced the MENORAH (candelabra in the Temple).

The written words of verses from the Bible are often used for decoration in synagogues and manuscripts, especially in medieval Spain. Many of the prayers, such as the SHEMA and the PRIESTLY BLESSING, are taken directly from the Bible. Each week, a section of the Pentateuch is read in the synagogue on Monday, Thursday, and the Sabbath (see READING OF THE LAW). Special sections are read on the New Moon and all festivals and

fast days (see FASTING AND FAST DAYS). The HALLEL is a prayer of thanksgiving taken from chapters of Psalms, and it is recited on PILGRIM FESTIVALS and the New Moon. The rabbi's sermon is usually based on that week's portion of the Pentateuch. The MEZUZAH on the doorpost reminds a Jew of the Bible every time he walks through a door.

Education   Traditionally Jewish EDUCATION began with the Bible. A Jewish child started by learning Hebrew, the language of the Bible, and continued to study the weekly Torah portion (PARASHAH), then MISHNAH, TALMUD, and Jewish law.

From the Middle Ages until the 19th century, Ashkenazi Jews studied mostly the Talmud and Jewish law and neglected Bible studies. Sephardi Jews, on the other hand, studied the Bible extensively and could quote long passages from memory. Until today, North African Jews love the Hebrew Bible and are very familiar with it.

Nowadays, Jewish education revolves around the Bible. Many translations and commentaries have appeared that allow everyone to study Bible. In modern Israel, Hebrew is the spoken language, so the Bible can be read like a story book. Bible study is part of the school system, though religious and non-religious schools teach it differently. Children and new villages are given names from the Bible, talks on the weekly portion are broadcast on the radio each morning, and there is a worldwide Bible contest every year.

BIBLE COMMENTARY, JEWISH   One of the most important parts of Jewish life is understanding the BIBLE (see BIBLE, Canon). Once the Scriptures were finalized, Jews began to interpret their holy book. From the period of EZRA (5th cent. BCE) another thousand years were devoted to developing Jewish law (HALAKHAH), which was rooted in the Bible, and the MIDRASH (interpretations and folktales, also rooted in the Bible). Philosophical interpretations of the Bible were written in the Middle Ages, mostly in reaction to Christian and Muslim interpretations (see APOLOGETICS AND POLEMICS). Many commentaries as well as mystical works were written at that time.

According to Jewish tradition, both the WRITTEN LAW (the PENTATEUCH) and the ORAL LAW were given to MOSES by GOD at Mount Sinai. The Oral Law was necessary in order to understand the Written Law. Jews tried to find the true meaning of the text, and eventually developed the TALMUD, a collection of discussions about the laws. A "chain of tradition" was recorded in the MISHNAH (*Avot* 1:1): "Moses received the Torah from Sinai and passed it on to Joshua, and Joshua to the elders (the Judges), and the elders to the Prophets, and the Prophets passed it on to the Men of the Great Assembly."

The GREAT ASSEMBLY was established by Ezra at the beginning of the Second Temple period. He moved from Babylonia to Erets Israel to help set up a religious base in the Land of Judah. He called an assembly of all of the Jews and read the Pentateuch to them, declaring it as the constitution of the Jewish community. Ezra also committed himself to studying the meaning of the text. He was the head of a line of teachers called

SCRIBES (*Soferim*). Many of the Jews had forgotten their Hebrew while they were in EXILE in Babylonia, therefore the Scribes had to explain the meaning of the Bible text. They translated parts of it into ARAMAIC, and from these translations came the Aramaic version of the Bible, the TARGUM ("translation"). The Targum is one of the earliest Bible commentaries, because the translation was based on traditional interpretations of the Bible.

The *tannaim* (see TANNA) continued the work of the Scribes. They preserved legal (halakhic) traditions, and wrote commentaries on each verse of the Bible text. They developed four ways of explaining the text, which are known by the acronym PARDES ("Orchard"): PESHAT (the simple, literal explanation); *Remez* ("hint", the symbolic explanation); *Derash* (reasoning); and *Sod* (the "secret" or mystical meaning). Other rabbis made rules for interpreting the text. HILLEL first wrote seven rules, which grew to 13, then finally to 23 in the days of Rabbi Eliezer ben Yose the Gallilean (see HERMENEUTICS). Later on there were two schools of interpretation: the school of AKIVA,

which explained every word and letter in the Bible text, and the school of Rabbi ISHMAEL, which looked into the more general message of the text. A book of Midrash was written on each book of the Pentateuch.

From the seventh century onwards, Arab armies conquered North Africa and western Asia and spread Islam and Arabic throughout these areas. Arabic became the new written language of the region. SAADIAH GAON (882–942) translated the Bible into Arabic. His translation was studied along with the original Hebrew text. He wrote this translation mainly to counter the KARAITES, who believed only in the literal meaning of the Torah and rejected the Oral Law. His translation was philosophical and beautifully written and brought a new approach to Bible commentary.

From the times of the Talmud, rabbis have paid attention to the language of the Bible. The Talmud says that "wherever the word *Va-yehi* ["Now it came to pass…"] appears in the Bible, trouble begins" (*Meg.* 10b). Beginning in the tenth century

A page from Numbers with commentaries, in Hebrew. On either side are explanatory notes and biographies of the commentators, in English. From an educational brochure of the Jewish National Fund, printed in London in the 1930s.

1. THE TORAH. The passage shown is the commencement of the book of Exodus.

2. TARGUM. The **Targum** is a translation into Aramaic. (The word "Targum" means "translation"). It was made at approximately the end of the 1st Century. The **Targum** of the **Torah** is traditionally attributed to Onkelos, a proselyte to Judaism. It is a fairly literal translation but occasionally contains interpretations.

3. RASHI. Commentary of **Rabbi Shlomo Yitzchaki** (1040-1105). He lived and taught in Troyes, (France). His commentary contains explanations derived from the Talmud and Midrash and often he translates difficult Hebrew words into Mediaeval French.

4. RAMBAN. Commentary of **Rabbi Moshe ben Nachmon Gerondi** (1194-1270) also known as Nachmonides. He was a Spanish Talmudical scholar and physician. A great Talmudist, he was sympathetic towards **Cabalah** (Jewish mysticism).

In 1263, he participated in a public disputation before the King of Aragon. It lasted four days and, although the king sided with him, he was banished. He eventually settled in Palestine.

5. IBN EZRA. Avraham ben Meir (1093-1167) was a poet as well as commentator. Born in Spain, where he lived for a great deal of his life, he travelled in North Africa, Palestine, Persia, Italy and France. In 1158, he visited London. His commentary frequently stresses the grammatical structure of the Hebrew in the Chumash text. All his works, poet-

ical, philosophical and scientific, were written in Hebrew.

6. COMMENTARY ON IBN EZRA. The Commentary of **Ibn Ezra** itself presents various difficulties. This "Commentary" on Ibn Ezra's work was written by **Rabbi Shlomo Zalman Netter** in an attempt to render Ibn Ezra more understandable.

7. SFORNO. Obadia Sforno (1475-1550) lived in Italy. He too was a physician by calling. His commentary is largely devoted to a literal explanation of the text.

8. RASHBAM. Rabbi Shmuel ben Meir (1085-1174) was a grandson of the famous Rashi, and also lived in France. In his commentary, he is concerned with the simple meaning of the text. In addition to his commentary on the **Torah**, he also wrote a commentary on most of the "Prophets", ("Neviim").

9. MASSORAH. These are notes and rules concerning the actual text of the Torah. They are concerned with the writing, spacing and paragraphing of the text of a **Sefer Torah**. Observations are also made on the correct vowels of the text. The purpose is to ensure the accuracy and uniformity of text.

The Scholars responsible for the "Massorah" are referred to as "Massoretes". They lived from about the 6th to the 10th Centuries and their work was done mainly in Tiberias.

10. TOLDOT AHARON This gives the Talmudic reference when ever a Biblical phrase or sentence is quoted in the **Talmud**. *(See next page).*

in Spain, rabbis began to use grammar to interpret the Bible. Abraham IBN EZRA, the philosopher, poet, and grammarian, wrote a brilliant commentary on many of the books of the Bible. He attacked the Karaites and those who paid no attention to grammar. He carefully studied the language of the Bible, and suggested that Joshua had written the final verses of the Pentateuch and that there was a second Isaiah, who wrote the last 26 chapters of the Book of Isaiah.

David KIMHI, known by the acronym *Radak*, was a grammarian and commentator who wrote an extremely popular commentary on Psalms. He concentrated on the "plain" meaning of the text but did not ignore other aspects.

The philosophical and halakhic works of MAIMONIDES were a high point in Judeo-Spanish learning. Maimonides did not write a verse-by-verse commentary on the Bible, but rather explained difficult sections in his works. His most famous book was the *Guide for the Perplexed*, where Maimonides explained the Bible in a logical, symbolic way. Many scholars disagreed with his approach and challenged his followers for many centuries.

JUDAH HALEVI and NAHMANIDES both thought that the Bible should not be seen as logical. There are concepts in the Bible that the human mind cannot grasp, and therefore it is a mistake to explain these ideas symbolically. Nahmanides was also one of the first scholars to write a mystical commentary on the Bible.

The most important mystical work is the ZOHAR (c.1300), which was said to be written by SIMEON BAR YOHAI. It is a mystical Midrash on certain parts of the Bible that greatly influenced Jewish thought.

A similar mystical movement called HASIDEI ASHKENAZ began in Germany at that time, led by ELIEZER BEN JUDAH. The greatest Bible scholar and commentator came from the Hasidei Ashkenaz movement. Rabbi Solomon ben Isaac of Troyes, better known as RASHI (1040–1105), lived in the Christian world during the First Crusade. The Jews of that time were uneducated and persecuted by the Christians. Rashi wrote a running commentary on the Bible and Talmud. He insisted that "a passage should be explained according to its content," and his simple, clear explanations made the Bible an open book for children and uneducated workers. He used French words to explain difficult terms and paid attention to grammar and some midrashic explanations. Rashi's grandson, SAMUEL BEN MEIR (Rashbam), put even greater stress on the plain meaning of a text in his commentary on the Bible.

Isaac ABRAVANEL was the last Spanish commentator. He was opposed to the mysticism that was popular in Spain at that time, so he devoted himself to studying the Bible. His commentary is very long and repetitive, but has many important ideas. A generation later, in Italy, Obadiah SFORNO wrote a commentary on the Pentateuch that also rejected mysticism.

When the Jews of Eastern Europe where forced to move to ghettos (mid-16th century), Bible commentary was postponed for about 200 years. Attention was turned to Talmud instead. At the end of this period, a new type of Bible commentary was written by David Altschuler and his son. It was written as a running commentary in two portions. One, the *Metsudat Tsion* ("Tower of Zion"), explains words in the text, and the other, *Metsudat David* ("Tower of David"), explains the text itself. These commentaries along with Rashi, Ibn Ezra, Kimhi, Rashbam, Ralbag, and Nahmanides are printed in the standard edition of the Pentateuch.

In the 18th century, when European Jews were working for EMANCIPATION (equal rights), Moses Mendelssohn called upon the Jews to speak German instead of Yiddish. He thought they should study the Bible more, because it was universal, and study the Talmud less. Mendelssohn wrote a German translation of the Bible and later added his own commentary called the *Bi'ur*. Many Orthodox rabbis of the time banned the commentary because it departed too much from traditional views.

In other parts of Europe, Jews were beginning to study the Bible again. Samuel David Luzzatto (*Shadal*, 1800–1865), a traditional Italian rabbi, encouraged Bible study by writing a commentary of the Pentateuch and other books of the Bible. He also translated the Bible into Italian. Meir Leib Malbim wrote a commentary that proved that the Written and Oral Law are one.

From the 19th century, non-Orthodox Jewish scholars were largely influenced by Christian studies of the Bible. In the 20th century, however, "scientific" Bible study became less extreme, going back to a more traditional approach, based on the language, history, and religion of the people in the Bible. This was developed mainly by scholars at Jerusalem's Hebrew University.

BIGAMY   See MONOGAMY AND POLYGAMY

BIKKUR HOLIM   See SICK, VISITING THE

BIKKURIM   See FIRST FRUITS

BIKKURIM ("First Fruits"). Last tractate (book) in the Order of ZERA'IM of the Mishnah. It has three chapters that deal with the laws of the FIRST FRUITS of Erets Israel. In Temple times a farmer had to bring the first fruits of the SEVEN SPECIES to JERUSALEM (cf. Ex. 23:19, 34:26; Deut. 26:1–1). The Mishnah discusses who has to bring the first fruits, what one says when offering them, the differences between first fruits and other TITHES, and the colorful procession of people on their way to Jerusalem. *Androginos*, a fourth chapter, was added to the tractate. It discusses the legal problems of a hermaphrodite (person who has both male and female characteristics).

BIMAH ("platform"). A raised platform with a reader's table from which the Torah is read (see READING OF THE LAW) and some prayers are led in the synagogue. According to MAIMONIDES, "the *bimah* is built in the center of the synagogue so that congregants may ascend to read the Torah, and so those delivering the sermon may be heard by all."

Decorated wood bimah *in the center of the synagogue (now destroyed) of Zelwa, Poland.*

The Torah was first read publicly from a raised platform in the times of EZRA (5th cent. BCE). The Mishnah talks about such a platform in the Second Temple, and the Talmud mentions a platform that was built in the center of the Great Synagogue in Alexandria.

From the Middle Ages, the *bimah* was the focus of the synagogue's activity. It was usually placed at the center of the building, but this was not essential. In Spain and Italy the *bimah* was often found at the far end of the synagogue, against the western wall. When designing a synagogue, the relationship between the ARK and the *bimah* was always a major issue. In East European synagogues, the *bimah* was between the four large pillars that supported the roof of the synagogue, which were in the center of the building. In medieval Spain, it was raised on columns high above the worshipers (like the pulpit of a church or mosque), and there was a flight of stairs leading up to it. In some communities, the congregation sat between the *bimah* and the Ark, in others the space was left open. In Muslim lands the *bimah* was usually at the center, with the congregation sitting around it.

In the 19th century, REFORM JUDAISM moved the *bimah* forward, placing it in the area in front of the Ark. Although the exact placement of the *bimah* is a matter of CUSTOM and not law, Orthodox rabbis were opposed to changing the arrange-

ment of the synagogue. They saw any change of tradition as a step towards ASSIMILATION, and 100 Orthodox rabbis signed a declaration against attending synagogues where the *bimah* was not in the center. Eventually most synagogues moved the *bimah* to the front in order to save space.

BINDING OF ISAAC   See AKEDAH

BIRKAT HA-GOMEL   See GOMEL BLESSING

BIRKAT HA-MAZON   See GRACE AFTER MEALS

BIRKAT HA-MINIM   ("Benediction against Heretics"). Prayer dated from Hellenistic times, the 12th BENEDICTION of the weekly AMIDAH. The Talmud refers to is as a "benediction against Sadducees" (rival sect in Judaism), which caused many to believe it was written by Rabban Gamaliel II (*Ber.* 28b) some time after 70 CE and added later to the *Amidah*. It is more likely that it was written in the second century BCE, during the Maccabees' struggle against Jewish traitors (see HANUKKAH). After the Second Temple was destroyed, the survival of the Jewish people was on the line. There were many Jewish informers, who worked with the Romans, and groups of Jews were breaking away and becoming Christians. Rabbi Samuel ha-Katan adapted the already existing prayer and added it to the *Amidah* as the 19th benediction. The prayer was directed mostly at Judeo-Christians.

Birkat ha-Minim was a blessing that Judeo-Christians could not recite, nor could they answer "AMEN" when it was recited in the synagogue. This barred them from the synagogues and cut them off from the Jewish people. The text reads as follows: "For apostates [non-believers, see APOSTASY] who have rejected Your Torah, let there be no hope, and may Nazarenes [Christians] and heretics perish in an instant. Let all the enemies of Your people, the House of Israel, be speedily cut down … Blessed are You, O Lord, who shatters His enemies and humbles the arrogant."

The blessing was kept, with a few changes until the 13th century. In the 14th century, in Spain, it was seen as an attack against the Church, and the Jews were forced to take it out of the prayer book. In the Ashkenazi world some of the words were changed so it would not be directed specifically at Christians. REFORM JUDAISM tends to leave this prayer out altogether.

BIRKAT KOHANIM   See PRIESTLY BLESSING

BIRKHOT HA-SHAHAR   See MORNING BENEDICTIONS

BIRTH   "Be fruitful and multiply" (Gen. 1:28) is the first commandment in the Bible. However, man's first sin, eating from the Tree of Knowledge, led to a curse upon Eve: she and all her female descendants would suffer pain in childbirth (Gen. 1:16).

In biblical times, a woman gave birth in a kneeling position or sitting on a special stool. Midwives were highly respected.

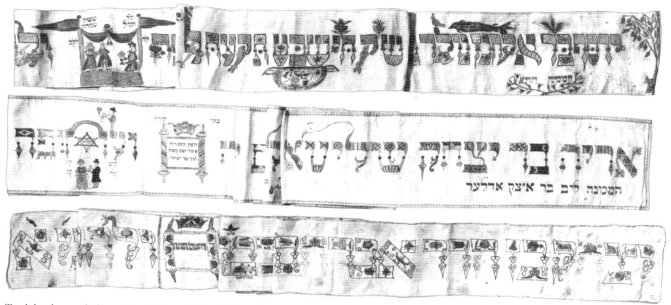

Torah binders made from strips of the swaddling cloth used at the circumcision of a child, embroidered later with good wishes for the future of the infant. Germany, 19ᵗʰ century.

A woman with many children was considered blessed, but BARRENNESS was a curse.

In Temple times, a mother was considered ritually impure for seven days after giving birth to a boy (14 for a girl). After that, for the next 33 days (66 for a girl), she could not enter the Temple or handle holy objects. When the "days of purification" ended, she had to bring two sacrifices. Nowadays, a woman who has given birth keeps the regular laws of NIDDAH.

According to Jewish law, if a woman is in danger during childbirth her life is saved before the baby's, because she is already alive. Once most of the baby's body come out, this is no longer true. According to the Jewish legal concept of PIKKU'AH NEFESH ("saving life"), it is permitted and even required to violate the Sabbath in order to save an unborn child. Therefore, anything that needs to be done in connection with childbirth must be done on the Sabbath. For three days after the baby is born, the mother is considered in mortal danger, so the Sabbath may be violated for her. This status continues for as long as the doctors find it necessary. The Mishnah says that a firstborn child delivered by Caesarean birth does not have the rights or the duties of a firstborn.

Many superstitions accompanied Jewish childbirth customs. AMULETS were placed above a pregnant woman's bed. After the birth, friends and family would say prayers to ward off LILITH, the DEMON who tries to kill newborn babies.

From the Middle Ages onwards, mothers would come to the synagogue after giving birth to recite the GOMEL blessing.

BIRTH CONTROL   The duty to have children is the first commandment in the Bible. ADAM was commanded to "be fruitful and multiply." Therefore using any kind of birth control is problematic, because it involves deliberately avoiding one of the commandments. Some methods of birth control are also specifically prohibited by the Torah.

If the woman or potential fetus would be in danger, it is permitted to use birth control. The Talmud discusses three categories of women who may (or must, according to some) use birth control: a minor below the age of 12 (who was allowed to marry at the time); a pregnant woman; and a nursing mother (*Ket.* 39a).

Modern rabbis have many disagreements on the subject of contraception. When it is permitted, rabbis prefer methods of contraception used by women because according to the sages, women are not technically included in the commandment to be fruitful and multiply. Oral contraceptives are the most accepted solution.

BITTER HERBS   See MAROR

BITTUL HA-TAMID   ("cancelation of the daily offering"). Ashkenazi practice which began in the Middle Ages. It allowed people to halt the prayers or Torah reading in the synagogue and focus public attention on an issue they felt needed to be discussed. It usually involved a moral wrong committed by an individual or protest against the Jewish authorities. Women were allowed to use this as well as men. During the 19ᵗʰ century, this right was used quite often in Czarist Russia. The government hired *khappers* whose job it was to kidnap young boys for a 25-year period of service in the army. Desperate mothers would resort to *bittul ha-tamid* to shame the *khappers* into returning their children. This custom is still occasionally used by pious Jews, but is mostly out of use.

BI'UR HAMETS   See LEAVEN, SEARCH FOR

BLASPHEMY   (Heb. *gidduf, heruf*). Anything a person says that shows contempt for God, or profanes God's Name. The third commandment (Ex. 20:7; Deut. 5:11) forbids "taking the Lord's Name in vain," and the penalty is death by stoning (Lev. 24:10–16, 23). Together with the prohibition of blasphemy is the prohibition to curse a leader of Israel. By Mishnah times, only a person who misused God's holiest four-letter name would be stoned. As the Jewish legal system lost its authority, the official punishment for blasphemy was changed to *herem* (EXCOMMUNICATION). See also BLESSING AND CURSING; HILLUL HA-SHEM.

BLESSING AND CURSING   The original meanings of the Hebrew word "blessing" (*berakhah*) were "gift," or "worship." The Bible often mentions blessing God. People give God their thanks or praise, and in return, receive God's blessing – spiritual or physical well-being. In Bible times, people believed that the spoken word had much power and would fulfill itself for good (as a blessing) or for evil (as a curse), according to God's will. Blessing and cursing therefore are always in the name of God, whether or not His name is mentioned.

The first blessing mentioned in the Bible is the blessing God gave the creatures of the sea and air: "Be fruitful and multiply" (Gen. 1:22). The serpent, who tempted Eve to eat of the fruit of the Tree of Knowledge (Gen. 3:14), was the first creature to be cursed by God (see ADAM AND EVE).

One of the most important of God's blessings is fertility. Throughout the ages, the Israelites are blessed with rain and cursed with drought, "Will I not then open the windows of heaven and pour you out a blessing that there shall be more than enough?" (Mal. 3:10). God's blessing can also be spiritual, such as His blessing to Abraham: "All the families of the earth shall bless themselves by you" (Gen. 12:2).

There are many examples in the Bible of a father blessing his sons and grandsons before his death. For example: ISAAC's blessing of JACOB and Esau (Gen. 27:27–29, 39–40) and Jacob's blessing of his grandsons (Gen. 48:8, 49:25–26). There are also many examples of friends who bless each other when meeting or parting, and the traditional response to a friend's greeting is "The Lord bless you!" (Ruth 2:4).

The people are often blessed by priests, kings, prophets, and leaders. Aaron blessed the people on the last day of the SANCTUARY's opening ceremony (Lev. 9:22) and there is a special PRIESTLY BLESSING in Numbers 6:22–26. This blessing is said in traditional synagogues daily by the *kohanim* (worshipers who are descendants of the priests), and also by parents to their children at the Sabbath table. At the dedication of the First TEMPLE, King SOLOMON (1 Kings 8:14, 54–55) blessed "the whole congregation of Israel."

Like blessings, curses are also in the Name of God, whether or not His Name is mentioned specifically. Sometimes people are cursed (Heb. *kelalah*) for something they have already done, as with CAIN after he killed Abel (Gen. 4:11–12), and sometimes people are cursed as a threat, as when JOSHUA cursed anyone who would try to rebuild the city of Jericho after it was destroyed (Josh. 6:26). In Deuteronomy 27:11–26, there is a dramatic ceremony where a series of curses is put upon anyone who does any of a list of forbidden things. Half of the Israelites were standing on Mount GERIZIM, and the other half on Mount Ebal to hear and respond "AMEN" to the curses read by the LEVITES.

Curses were taken very seriously, as can be seen in the story of Shimei son of Gera, a member of King SAUL's family. He cursed King DAVID randomly, and accused him of shedding innocent blood. Although the accusation was false, David commanded his son SOLOMON to bring Shimei's "gray head down to the grave in blood" (1 Kings 2:9). This helps explain why, in biblical law, cursing God or the king or one's parents is punishable by death (Ex. 22:27; 21:17; Lev. 20:9; 24:23; see BLASPHEMY).

In the times of the Talmud, standard blessings giving thanks to God were developed (see BENEDICTIONS). A special blessing is said before performing each commandment (MITZVAH), and a benediction is said when receiving good or bad news (*Ber.* 7a; *Pes.* 50a). The power of a blessing or curse is also mentioned in the Talmud: "Never underestimate the blessings [or curses] of an ordinary person" (*Ber.* 7a; *Meg.* 15a); and "A curse pronounced by a sage, even if groundless, is bound to be fulfilled" (*Ber.* 56a; *Mak.* 11a).

Cursing was forbidden, according to the rabbis of the Talmud: "Let yourself be cursed, rather than curse [someone else]" (*Sanh.* 49a). However, the curse *Yimmah shemo* (*vezikhro*) – "May his name and memory be wiped out" – is still applied today to enemies of the Jews, such as Hitler.

BLESSING OF CHILDREN   See PARENTAL BLESSING

BLINDNESS   In the Bible, blindness is mentioned in several places, for example the blindness of ISAAC (Gen. 27:1) and JACOB (Gen. 48:10) in their old age. In the Talmud, out of respect for the blind, different expressions rather than direct language are used for blindness such as *sagi nahor* – "a person with a great deal of light."

Jewish law shows much consideration to the blind. While a regular person must recite the AMIDAH prayer standing and facing the direction of JERUSALEM, a blind person must direct his thoughts to Heaven, without having to find someone to point him in the right direction. While he is required to say the blessings over the new MOON (*kiddush levanah*) and the HANUKKAH lights, a blind person does not recite the blessing over the HAVDALLAH candle, because he cannot see it, nor may he be called up to the READING OF THE LAW because one must be able to read the words, not only hear them.

In general, unlike deaf-mutes, the blind are treated by Jewish law as fully normal and restricted only by their physical limitations.

BLOOD (Heb. *dam*). The vital fluid which, according to the Bible, is the substance of life itself, "for the life of the flesh is in the blood" (Lev. 17:11). This explains the repeated prohibition against drinking the blood of animals and birds (e.g., Lev. 3:17, 7:26, 17:13; Deut. 12:23), which was a law unique to the Israelites in the ancient world. The Bible included this same prohibition in the NOACHIDE LAWS, which apply to all humanity. The punishment was KARET (being cut off from the community, or punishment from God, Lev. 7:27, 17:10–14). The blood of any sacrifice had to be poured over the horns of the altar or at its base and sometimes sprinkled on the SANCTUARY's curtain (Ex. 24:6, 29:21; Lev. 1:5, 4:7). At the inauguration of AARON and his sons, MOSES took some of the blood of a sacrifice and dabbed it on the lobe of Aaron's left ear, on the thumb of his right hand, and on the big toe of his right foot (Lev. 8:23). The blood of a bird was used to purify lepers (Lev. 14:4–7). The blood of any slaughtered animal or fowl had to be poured out and covered in dust (Lev. 17:12–13).

Among the pagan Canaanites, blood was considered the food of the gods. The prophets of the BAAL would gash themselves with knives until they were covered in blood (1 Kings 18), an act that is specifically prohibited by the Torah (Deut. 14:1).

In biblical sources, "blood" is often used for MURDER. Murderers are "men of blood" (Ps. 5:7), and murdering an innocent person is called "shedding innocent blood" (Lev. 20:9). Blood is also the bond of solidarity uniting a man with his family, allowing him to avenge a slain family member (see BLOOD AVENGER). In Jewish law, one cannot compensate for murder with money (Num 35:31–34). The shedding of innocent blood "defiles the land" and can only be compensated through the death of the murderer – "whoever sheds the blood of a man, by man shall his blood be shed" (Gen. 9:6).

Although many of these detailed rules disappeared with the destruction of the Temple, others remain a part of traditional Jewish life. One example is the rite of CIRCUMCISION, which involves a slight loss of blood; the child is called *hatan damim*, a "bridegroom of blood" (Ex. 4:25–26). The laws of FAMILY PURITY (based on Lev. 15:19ff) declare a woman ritually unclean and prohibit normal marital relations during her menstrual period and for a week after (see also NIDDAH).

The laws of *kashrut* (the Jewish DIETARY LAWS) can be seen as a direct outcome of the biblical prohibitions concerning blood. An animal meant to be eaten by Jews can only be killed by *shehitah* – a method of slaughter in which the blood is drawn out very quickly, causing minimum pain to the animal. Any leftover blood is then removed by a process of soaking and salting, after which the meat is kosher, and can be eaten by Jews. The animal's lifeblood must be covered with earth, unless it is collected and used as fertilizer. The dietary laws even prohibit the eating of an egg with a spot of blood attached to the yolk.

Because the Jews kept these laws so strictly, even the thought of drinking blood disgusted them. In the Middle Ages, by a grim irony, they were often accused of slaughtering a Christian child and using his blood for baking unleavened bread for the Passover SEDER. This was used as an excuse to massacre the Jews and confiscate their property (see BLOOD LIBEL).

BLOOD AVENGER (or "blood redeemer"; Heb. *go'el ha-dam*). Member of family required by ancient Jewish law to avenge bloodshed. The origin of this practice is in societies organized according to tribes and clans. If a person was killed, it was up to the closest member of his family to avenge his death by killing the killer; if not a member of the family than a member of the same clan or tribe. If they could not kill the killer they had to kill a member of the killer's clan. According to the Bible, any human bloodshed must be avenged (Gen. 9:6). If the murder is not resolved, it falls upon God to avenge it (Gen. 9:5; Deut. 32:43; II Kings 9:7). GIDEON killed Zebah and Zalmunah for killing his brothers (Judg. 8:18), Joab killed Abner for murdering his brother Asahel (II Sam. 3:27), and Absalom killed Amnon for having raped his sister Tamar (II Sam). To this day, among Bedouin Arabs, the rape and dishonor of a woman must be avenged by her family, who often take it upon themselves to kill the offender.

Biblical law provides special cities of ASYLUM for involuntary killers. The Talmud (in tractate MAKKOT) attempts to apply normal court procedures instead of having a family member avenge the blood.

BLOOD LIBEL (also "ritual murder"). False accusation that Jews used the blood of slain Christian children to prepare their MATZAH for PASSOVER. Originally, both Jews and early Christians were accused by pagans, who misunderstood Jewish and Christian customs. Ultimately the libel was turned against the Jews by Christians. The local clergy often started the rumor, and the result was usually attacks by mobs, executions, massacres, and expulsions in countless places throughout Europe, over a period of nearly a thousand years. The libels also led to the financial ruin of many Jewish communities. The Jews were also falsely accused of DESECRATION of Christian symbols and well poisoning.

The first recorded blood libel occurred in Norwich, England, in 1144, when a boy named William was allegedly tortured by Jews. Similar libels occurred in France, Germany, Italy, and Spain, spreading to Eastern Europe by the 17th century. There were blood libels which resulted in entire Jewish communities being burned alive. In modern times, there were two particularly horrible blood libels, the Damascus Affair in 1840 and the Beilis Trial in Kiev in 1911–13, both of which aroused worldwide protest. In the 1930s the Nazi's revived ancient accusations and began "investigations." In later years blood libels occurred in Soviet Russia. See also ANTI-SEMITISM.

BOBOV Hasidic sect founded by Solomon ben Meyer Nathan (1847–1906), a grandson of Hayyim Halberstam of Zanz. Solomon established his court in the town of Bobowa, Poland, in 1893. He also established a *yeshivah* of about 300 students. Bobov Hasidim are famous for their beautiful melodies, which were composed by Solomon's son Ben Zion, who perished in the Holocaust. Ben Zion's son Solomon established a Bobov center in the Boro Park section of New York and a small settlement near Bat Yam in Israel in 1959. There are tens of thousand of Bobov Hasidim in Brooklyn.

BODY Judaism generally differentiates between the body and the SOUL. According to the MIDRASH, man is the link between the earthly – his body – and the Godly – his soul. A person is considered the caretaker of his body, not its master; therefore one is not permitted to mutilate the body in any way. An operation is permissible only if it is for the general benefit of the entire body. For this reason, many rabbis do not permit plastic surgery, unless it is necessary for psychological reasons. SUICIDE is also forbidden. A body remains holy even after death, therefore AUTOPSY and CREMATION are prohibited. These prohibitions also have to do with the belief in RESURRECTION of the dead which would not be possible if the body were destroyed.

Unlike other systems, Judaism considers the body holy. There is even a blessing which is said after using the toilet, which thanks God for having created the amazing human body.

BOOK OF LIFE (Heb. *Sefer ha-Hayyim*). Heavenly "ledger" containing a record of man's actions and behavior throughout the year. This idea is only mentioned once in the Bible (Ps. 69:29), where hope is expressed that evil men "may be erased from the Book of Life and not be written down with the righteous."

The idea of the "book of life" was developed mostly by the rabbis of the Talmud. JUDAH HA-NASI warned: "Know what is above you – an Eye that sees, an Ear that hears, and a Book in which all your deeds are recorded" (*Avot* 2:1). Akiva declared that "the ledger is open, the hand records…" (*Avot* 3:16). According to the Talmud (*RH* 16b), three separate books are opened on the New Year (ROSH HA-SHANAH): one for the completely wicked, who are immediately condemned to death; one for the righteous, who are written down and sealed for life; and a third for ordinary people, who are held in suspense until the DAY OF ATONEMENT, when their fate is sealed. Between the New Year and the Day of Atonement are the annual TEN DAYS OF REPENTANCE, during which a person can repent and change his fate. The phrase "Inscribe us in the Book of Life" is repeated many times throughout the HIGH HOLIDAY prayers, and becomes "Seal us in the Book of Life" in the concluding service (*ne'ilah*) on the Day of Atonement. A traditional greeting for that time of year is "may you be inscribed and sealed for a good year." According to mystical sources, the final judgment is sealed on HOSHANA RABBAH.

BREAD (Heb. *pat* or *lehem*). In ancient Erets Israel, bread was the basic staple food, symbolizing an entire meal or one's livelihood. The MANNA that fell when the Israelites wandered in the desert was called "bread from heaven" (Ex. 16:4). It was used as an accompaniment to various types of SACRIFICES AND

Clay figurine of a woman kneading dough. From the Phoenician cemetery in Achziv, Israel, dating to the 6ᵗʰ–4ᵗʰ century BCE.

OFFERINGS. In the Sanctuary as well as the Temple, 12 loaves of SHOWBREAD were displayed on a table that stood before the ARK OF THE COVENANT.

Different methods were used to make bread in biblical times. The most common was to place the dough on the sides of an earthenware stove. If the dough baked before it rose, the result would be flat, unleavened bread, like the MATZAH which is eaten on PASSOVER. In the process of baking, a piece of the dough is taken and thrown into the fire; originally a gift of bread was made to the priest (Num. 15:20; see CHALLAH). This commandment is called *hafrashat hallah* – "taking of the bread," and a special blessing is recited when performing the commandment.

In the times of the Talmud, the practice began of reciting the *Ha-Motsi* blessing before eating bread (*Ber.* 38a; see GRACE BEFORE MEALS). Before the blessing there is a ritual washing of the hands (*Netilat Yadayim*; see ABLUTIONS). Any meal that begins with the blessing over bread must end with GRACE AFTER MEALS. The rabbis taught that bread should be handled with respect, not thrown around and not mixed with other garbage when it becomes stale.

On the Sabbath two loaves of bread are used for the BENEDICTION, in memory of the double portion of manna (*lehem mishneh*) which the Israelites received in the wilderness on Fridays (Ex. 16:22). A special embroidered challah cover is placed over the loaves before the blessing is recited on the SABBATH and FESTIVALS.

BRIBERY The Bible forbids the taking of bribes, "for bribes blind the clear-sighted and upset the pleas of those who are in the right" (Ex. 23:8). A curse is put upon one who takes bribes in a capital case (Deut. 27:25; Ezek. 22:12).

The Mishnah and Talmud also found bribery hateful. Judges were warned against taking bribes even for the purpose of acquitting the innocent or convicting the guilty (*Sif.* to Deut.

Opposite page: Two Torah Scrolls of the 19ᵗʰ century: on the right, in painted wood, from India; on the left, in wood with silver plaques, from Iran. Overleaf left: Aaron pouring oil into the seven-branched candelabrum as described in Exodus 37:17–24. From an illuminated manuscript of Benjamin the Scribe, c. 1280; possibly written in Troyes, France (British Museum). Overleaf right: Abraham and the Three Angels. Rothschild Miscellany, Northern Italy, c. 1450–1480

זה המעורה ואהרן הטוב שמן בנירות

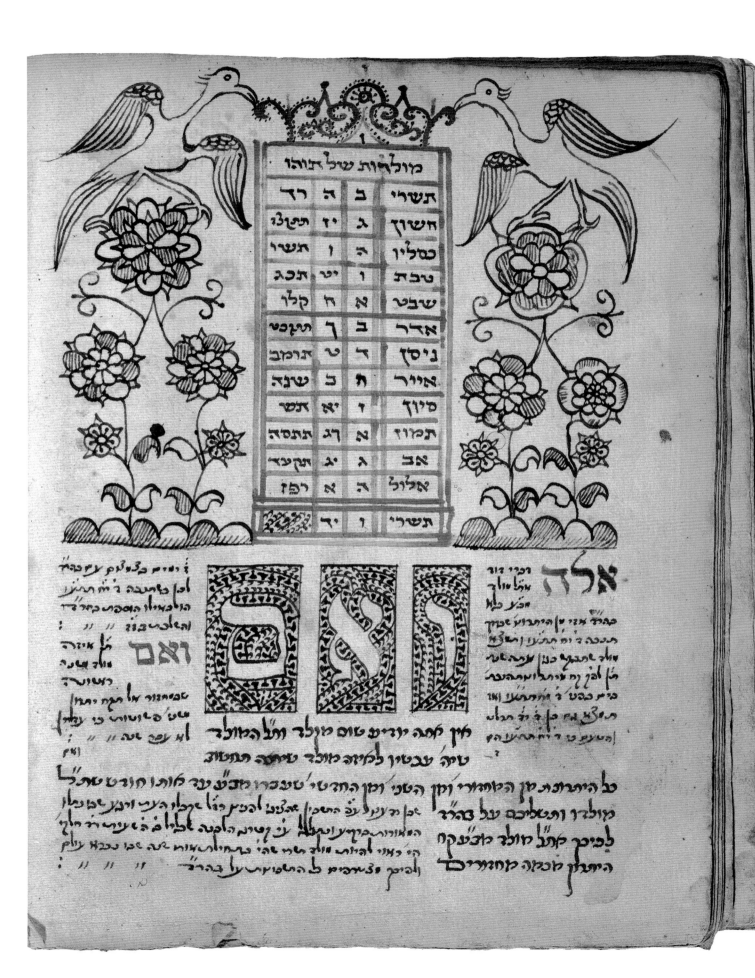

מולדות של דורהו			
תשרי	ב	ה	רד
חשון	ג	יז	תתקנ"ג
כסליו	ה	ו	תשרי
טבת	ו	יט	תכג
שבט	א	ח	קלו
אדר	ב	ז	תתקפט
ניסן	ד	ט	תרמב
אייר	ח	כ	שנה
סיון	ז	יא	אמש
תמוז	א	רג	תתרסה
אב	ג	יג	תתקעד
אלול	ה	א	רפז
תשרי	ו	יד	

אלה

מן האחה יודעא טוס מולד ותל המולד
טיה עבטון לחיה מולד טיאטא חתטוט

כל היתרתא מן הוחמרי וקן הטעי טעברו חב"ע עד אותו חודט שה"ל
מולדן ותטאליכה על בהרד
לביכך כתל מולד הבטעקה
היתרן מהמה מהומרים

פאר

16:19; *Ket.* 105a). Because bribes "blinded the clear-sighted," the Talmud said that a bribe-taking judge was in danger of physically lose his sight (*Pe'ah* 8:9; *Ket.* 105a). Judges were not allowed to accept even subtle non-monetary forms of bribery. Thus the Rabbi SAMUEL disqualified himself from judging the case of a man who had once helped him cross the river.

Jewish law also considers giving bribes a sin, based on Leviticus 19:14: "You shall not place a stumbling block before the blind," meaning one may not lead another to sin (Maim. *Yad; Sanh.* 23:2 *Sh. Ar., HM* 9).

BRIDEGROOMS OF THE LAW   Title given to the people who receive two special honors on the SIMHAT TORAH festival, when the annual cycle of reading the Pentateuch is concluded and begins again. During the Middle Ages, it was customary for one person to chant the final section of DEUTERONOMY and the first section of GENESIS from the same scroll. By the 12th century, the readings were divided between two people, and the original "Bridegroom of the Law" (*hatan Torah*) was joined by a "Bridegroom of Genesis" (*hatan Bereshit*). At one time, the first honor was given to the rabbi of the congregation and the second to the GABBAI. Nowadays, both honors are usually given to devoted, learned members of the community. In Sephardi Western congregations, a vote takes place each year to choose the recipients of the honor.

It is customary for the two "bridegrooms" to make a generous donation to charity and to throw candy to the children in their synagogue. In Oriental Jewish communities sweets are thrown at the "bridegrooms" as they approach and leave the reading platform. In Sephardi synagogues, the two "bridegrooms" often sit in special chairs of honor under a canopy. Nowadays, the "bridegrooms" usually provide a festive KIDDUSH or meal (SE'UDAH) for the entire congregation after the services.

Deputies were sometimes appointed to receive other minor honors, such as spreading a woolen prayer shawl (*tallit*) over the heads of all of the children present ("*kol ha-ne'arim*"), who then repeat the Torah blessings.

In Reform and egalitarian communities, women, known as *Kallot Torah*, may be honored with special readings on Simhat Torah. In many Conservative congregations wives accompany their husbands as they are called to the Torah reading.

BRIS, BRITH   See CIRCUMCISION

BRIT BAT   See SIMHAT BAT

BUBER, MARTIN   (1878–1965). Theologian, philosopher, educator, and Zionist thinker. Born in Austria, he grew up in the house of his grandfather, Solomon Buber, a well-known Midrash scholar. He received his Bible and Talmud education from his grandfather, as well as a love for Judaism.

At one point, Buber was involved with the ZIONISM of HERZL, but later moved away from Herzl's political Zionism. He believed that the Zionist movement should be based on reviving Jewish culture. He thought that Zionism should be a special kind of humanistic socialism which he called "the special way," and that Zionism should consider the needs of the Arabs as well and "develop the common homeland into a republic in which both peoples will have the possibility of free development." He and his colleagues established the *Der Jude* newspaper, in which they expressed their views.

Buber began his career as a writer by translating Hasidic tales and writing several books on the religious message of HASIDISM. Some of his books have been translated to English, including *For the Sake of Heaven* (1945), *The Legend of the Ba'al Shem* (1955), *Tales of Rabbi Nachman* (1956), *Hasidism and Modern Man* (1958), and *The Origin and Meaning of Hasidism* (1960).

Martin Buber.

In 1925, Buber began to publish a new German translation of the Bible, together with Franz ROSENZWEIG. After Rosenzweig's death, he continued the work alone, completing it in 1961.

Buber was appointed professor of religion at the University of Frankfurt, and held this position until the Nazis rose to power in 1933. For the next few years, he taught Judaism and brought spiritual strength to the Jews of Germany. In 1938, Buber could no longer continue teaching in Germany, and left for Palestine. He was appointed professor of social philosophy at the Hebrew University. He continued to work for a bi-national state in which Jews and Arabs would live and cooperate.

Buber describes the relationship between man and his fellow man and God as a dialogue. This dialogue is called the "I-Thou" relationship, and it is based on openness, mutuality, directness, and human sympathy. The "I-Thou" relationship is on its highest level when it brings man in contact with God.

For Buber, the Bible is a record of Israel's dialogue with God, and the laws of Judaism are part of Israel's response to God's

Opposite page: List of the months of the Jewish calendar. Poland, 1640.

revelation. This means that every generation must make its own response in its own dialogue with God. The laws accepted by one generation are not necessarily valid for the next generation, since each man has to follow what he believes to be God's law for him. This view was very different from traditional schools of Jewish thought.

Buber's writings have had a wide influence on modern Christian thinkers. Together with Rosenzweig, he was one of the pioneers of Jewish-Christian dialogue, referring to Jesus as "my brother."

BURIAL (Heb. *kevurah*). According to Jewish tradition, a deceased person must be buried in the ground or under stones. The Bible says: "Dust you are, and to dust you shall return" (Gen. 3:19). In ancient Israel, leaving a CORPSE unburied was a terrible dishonor. The greatest curse imaginable was that someone's remains should become food for "the birds of the air and the beasts of the earth, with none to fight them off" (Deut. 28:26). The Talmud teaches that the religious obligation to bury the dead comes from the respect shown to a criminal who had been hanged: "His corpse shall not remain all night on the tree, but you must bury him the same day" (Deut. 21:23).

In the Bible, burial is often referred to when DEATH is discussed. ABRAHAM purchased the cave of Machpelah (see HOLY PLACES) as a burial place for his wife SARAH (Gen. 23). This cave later became a sepulcher, in which all the patriarchs and matriarchs were buried, except for RACHEL. The Bible also tells us that MOSES was buried in Moab, where (according to rabbinic tradition) God Himself did the burial. The exact site of Moses' grave is unknown (Deut. 34:6).

Respectful burial of the dead has always been important to the Jewish people. In ancient times, Jews used caves and tunnels called catacombs for burial, although cemeteries are now set aside for Jewish burial (see CEMETERIES). Until the Middle Ages, it was standard practice to bury the dead in a stone or marble coffin, and then, after about a year, to remove the bones and bury them permanently in a crypt. This custom was called "gathering the bones" (*likkut atsamot*). The embalming of JACOB and JOSEPH (Gen. 50:2; 26) was an Egyptian custom which, like CREMATION, is now forbidden by Jewish law.

The mourners (close family members) are initially responsible for burying the dead, according to the Bible (Gen. 25:9). If there are no close family members, or they are unable to make the necessary arrangements, the community takes responsibility. The Talmud teaches that burying someone who dies without a family (*met mitzvah*) should be considered a supreme religious obligation, and comes before many other priorities. The same applies to an unidentified corpse found along the road: it must be buried as near as possible to where it was discovered (*Meg.* 28b; *BK* 81a). Even a High Priest, who normally is not allowed to come into contact with the dead, must bury a *met mitzvah* if there is no one else to do so (*Naz.* 7:1) Jews must also bury Gentiles if necessary, according to the SHULHAN ARUKH (*YD* 367:1).

Most Jewish communities have their own BURIAL SOCIETY, the *hevrah kaddisha*, a "holy brotherhood." Since burying the dead is a positive commandment, all those who take part in the funeral (pallbearers, gravediggers, etc.) should be Jewish whenever possible. "Escorting the dead" is considered one of the basic humanitarian deeds (GEMILUT HASADIM), for which there will be a reward in the afterlife (*Shab.* 127a). Burial society members who volunteer their services are considered to be performing "an act of true kindness" (*hesed shel emet*), for which no reward can be expected. A Jew is obligated to accompany a FUNERAL procession for at least a short distance (6 feet), failure to do so is considered mocking the dead (*Ber.* 18a; *Sh. Ar., YD* 361:3). The term *halvayat ha-met*, or *levayah* (from the Hebrew root meaning "to accompany"), means both the funeral procession and the service at the burial ground.

Burial should take place as soon as possible after death. Jewish law permits delay only when it is purely in honor of the dead: to prepare the shrouds or coffin or to allow close relative to reach the place of burial from far away. No burial may take place on the SABBATH or on the DAY OF ATONEMENT, and nowadays funerals are not held on the first and last days of PILGRIM FESTIVALS. In Israel, particularly in Jerusalem, a funeral may take place at night.

It has always been considered an honor to be buried in the Land of Israel, and some Jews living abroad buy burial plots and make arrangements in advance for that purpose. Otherwise, it is traditional to place some earth from the Land of Israel on the head or under the body of Jews buried out of Israel.

Within larger Jewish communities, a row is set aside in

Tombs and sarcophagi elaborately decorated in the necropolis of Bet She'arim, dating from the 2ⁿᵈ to 4ᵗʰ centuries CE. The underground tunnels are carved out of the soft chalk rock.

the cemetery for important rabbis and scholars. *Kohanim*, Jews who are descendants of the priests, may not come in contact with the graves because they are not permitted to become contaminated by the dead (see PRIESTS). For that reason an area near a broad pathway is usually set aside for the *kohanim*, so they can witness the funeral service and visit later without actually coming too near to the graves.

The members of the burial society prepare the body for burial by washing it thoroughly in a process called TOHORAH (or *taharah*, i.e., ritual purification) and then dress it in white linen shrouds (*takhrikhin*). All Jews are buried in a uniform white linen shroud so that all will be equal in death. In order to prevent the poor from being embarrassed, all Jews are buried in the same simple way with no decorations or expensive burial garments. For this reasons Jews do not generally lay flowers on the grave. The shrouded corpse is placed in a coffin or on a bier before the funeral service. In the Land of Israel, no coffin is used and the shrouded body is buried directly in the earth, except in the case of state or military funerals. MAIMONIDES ruled that Jews should be buried in a wooden coffin (*Yad, Evel* 4:4), which is the custom nowadays in the Diaspora. Observant Jews use only a plain wooden coffin, with no metal handles or decoration and no linings. Following the example of Rabbi JUDAH HA-NASI (TJ, *Kil.* 9:4), some drill holes in the bottom of the coffin so that the body may have more direct contact with the earth. Adult males are usually buried with their prayer shawls (TALLIT), and in some Oriental communities, the dead person's phylacteries (TEFILLIN) are also buried with him.

A marker is placed on the newly filled grave and a TOMBSTONE is put up at the end of the 30-day mourning period in Israel, or after 11 months in the Diaspora. It is forbidden by Jewish law to dig up a grave unless it is for the purpose of reburial in Israel (*Sh, Ar., YD* 363:1). A limb amputated from a person who is still alive must be buried. A stillborn child or one who died before the age of 30 days must also be buried, although the usual mourning laws do not apply.

Burial practice among REFORM JEWS is different from traditional Ashkenazi and Sephardi practice. Embalming and cremation are permitted; some Reform rabbis will even hold a funeral service in a crematorium. The deceased is buried in normal clothing, without a prayer shawl, and earth from the Land of Israel is not placed in the casket. See also FUNERAL SERVICE.

BURIAL SOCIETY (Heb./Aram. *Hevrah* or *Havurah Kaddisha*, i.e., "Holy Brotherhood"). Group of people who volunteer to look after the needs of the dying and the requirements of the dead. In Judaism, burial of the dead is a religious commandment (*mitzvah*), which comes even before the study of Torah. The burial of the dead was considered the obligation of the deceased person's close family. Burial societies are first mentioned in the times of the *amoraim* (*Ket.* 8b, etc.) and have been an important part of the Jewish community ever since. They usually consist of 18 people, since the Hebrew letters that add up to the number 18 spell *Hai*, "life."

It was considered a special honor to belong to a burial society, and the members were often the wealthiest and most learned men in the community, receiving special communal privileges. In England, in the 19th century, Sir Moses Montefiore was a member of the *Hevrah Kaddisha*. The services provided by the "holy company" began with reciting special prayers at the bedside of the gravely ill. They included ritual washing of the body (TOHOROH), BURIAL, and visits of consolation to the home of the mourners.

Women were also part of the society, seeing to the burial of other women. After a burial, the members would go to the ritual bath (MIKVEH) and then have a meal together. Once a year the members would fast and pray for forgiveness for any ritual disrespect they may have shown the deceased. After the fast day, the members would have a feast. Some of these customs are still observed in the Orthodox communities.

In 18th century Lithuania, the community set a limit on the fees the burial societies could charge for their services, in order to prevent extortion. In larger communities, an additional society called *Hevrah Hesed Shel Emet* ("Society of Lovingkindness") devoted itself to burying people who had no family. Today, the burial society is a major organization, and the fees that it collects are used to fund general community activity. There are often separate burial societies for Ashkenazim, Sephardim, Hasidim, and MITNAGGEDIM, because the burial customs vary slightly in each community.

BURNING BUSH The plant from which God revealed himself to MOSES in the wilderness of SINAI and told him to lead the Israelites out of Egypt, to freedom (Ex. 3:1–10). The amazing and miraculous feature of this bush was that it was "burning, yet it was not consumed" (3:2). This has been taken as a symbol of the idea that the people of Israel cannot be destroyed. The rabbis also wondered why it is that God should have chosen to reveal Himself in a lowly bush rather than a mighty tree.

A bush growing in St. Catherine's monastery on the traditional site of Mount Sinai is considered by the monks to be the original bush.

BURNT-OFFERING SEE SACRIFICES AND OFFERINGS

BUSINESS ETHICS The Jewish religion, based on the Torah, was supported by debates and sayings of accepted authorities in each time period. The Talmud and the legal works based on it therefore discuss basic rules of conduct in relationships of any kind, including business dealings between two people.

These rules were not taken directly from the Torah but were developed by the rabbis over time according to what seemed fair in light of the general ethics of Judaism. As a result, the laws are flexible and were changed in order to fit the changing society. *Tsedek* (fairness and justice) motivates Jewish business ethics, while *Hesed* (kindness) is an added consideration.

Jewish law appreciates hard work and industry. A part of the fourth commandment (the commandment to keep the

A trailing bush in St. Catherine's Monastery in the Sinai is said by the monks to have grown from the original burning bush.

SABBATH) is "six days shall you labor" (Ex. 20:9). The Mishnah teaches that "all study of the Torah without work must in the end be worthless and lead to sin" (*Avot* 2:2). This indicates that unemployment is immoral.

Jewish law was concerned that business should be fair to both the buyer and the seller. Charging reasonable interest on a business loan is allowed, but setting prices above the customarily accepted rate is called *hafka'at she'arim* ("profiteering"). It is forbidden even if the buyer agrees to the inflated price.

In the Mishnah period, a recognized authority would set fixed prices. In the times of the Talmud, market supervisors set only measurements, not prices. According to RASHI's commentary on the Talmud, "the townspeople were authorized to fix prices and measurements and workers' wages, which they may enforce by punishment" (i.e., fines). Various laws were made in order to prevent profiteering and inflation. For example, it was forbidden to hoard produce brought to the market, since this could cause prices to rise and affect the poor.

In Israel, nowadays, there are laws that fix prices of essential goods. There are also laws that protect tenants, such as maximum rents and laws preventing landlords from evicting tenants without specific cause. These secular laws are based on the rabbinic view.

The Bible discussed the fair treatment of workers (see LABOR LAWS). Workers were needed and valued and had to be treated fairly. One must not delay in paying a worker, which meant paying him daily (Lev. 19:13). Bondsmen (people who sold themselves into slavery in order to repay a debt) had to be treated humanely (see SLAVERY). Today there are trade unions that take responsibility for workers' rights, but from very early times such rights were protected by Jewish law (*BB* 8b). A Jewish person is considered a servant of God, therefore he could sell his labor, but not himself.

From ancient times, Jews have been associated with money lending, and in the modern age with high finance and banking. According to the Torah, loans were given as a type of charity and not as a business investment, therefore it is forbidden to collect interest when lending money to a Jew (Deut. 23:20). Similarly, no one must condemn a poor person who can not pay back a loan (Ex. 22:24). MAIMONIDES taught that "the highest level of charity is that of a person who helps a poor man by providing him with a gift or a loan, or by accepting him into a partnership, or by helping him find employment – in short, by placing him in a situation where he does not require other people's help" (*Mishnah Torah, Yad, Mattenot Aniyyim* 10:7–14). Recently, modern countries have taken this attitude towards Third World countries, helping them become financially independent.

When solving modern problems, Judaism looks for solutions that are based on biblical morality and rabbinic ethics. If the situation is entirely new, and such solutions are not available, the law is based on the principles of justice (*tsedek*) and kindness (*hesed*).

C

CABALA   See KABBALAH

CAIN AND ABEL   Two eldest sons of ADAM AND EVE (Gen. 4). They were born after their parents were driven out of EDEN for disobeying God. Cain was "a tiller of the soil" and Abel "a keeper of sheep." Both offered a sacrifice to God, but Abel's was received by God and Cain's was not. In a fit of jealous rage, Cain killed his brother and became the first murderer in history.

When God confronts him, Cain says, "Am I my brother's keeper?" To this God replies, "Your brother's blood cries out to Me from the ground!" (Gen 4:9–10). As a punishment, Cain is made to wander homeless for the rest of his life. This story is an example of the ancient rivalry between the farmer and the shepherd.

CALENDAR   According to the Jewish calendar, the CREATION is the starting point of all time, and therefore is the Year One.

The first known recorded Jewish calendar is the *Seder Olam*, and Rabbi YOSE BEN HALAFTA is credited with creating it in the second century. Its calculations are based on the six days of creation and the length of lives recorded in the Bible. Creation therefore corresponds to 3761 BCE in the secular calendar, and the year 2003–2004 is 5764 in the Jewish calendar.

The Jewish calendar is a lunar calendar, since it is based on the cycles of the MOON. Each cycle is a month, and there are 12 months in a year and 29 or 30 days in each month. The lunar year has approximately 354 days. Since the FESTIVALS must remain in their proper season according to the solar year, an adjustment must be made each year to the Jewish calendar to keep it in line with the secular calendar, which is 365 days long. Since the lunar year is 11 days shorter than the solar year, a 13th month is added to the Jewish calendar in certain years, making them leap years. In Temple times this was done periodically, after examining the agricultural situation at the end of the 12th

THE JEWISH CALENDAR

Name of month	Number of days	Special dates	Festival or commemoration
Nisan	30	15	Passover begins
Iyyar	29	5	Israel Independence Day
		18	Lag ba-Omer
Sivan	30	6	Shavu'ot begins
Tammuz	29	17	Fast of 17th of Tammuz
Av	30	9	Fast of 9th of Av
Elul	29	1	Rosh ha-Shanah (New Year) begins
Tishrei	30	10	Day of Atonement
		15	Sukkot begins
Heshvan	29 or 30	*called "Marheshvan" since it has no holidays*	
Kislev	29 or 30	25	Hanukkah begins
Tevet	29	10	Fast of 10th of Tevet
Shevat	30	15	New Year for Trees
Adar	29 (30 in leap year)	14	Purim
Adar II	29 (leap year only)	14	Purim celebrated in Adar II in leap years

month. Later, the calendar was fixed and written down, with a leap year seven times in every 19 years.

The Sanhedrin served as a central body that set the calendar for the entire Jewish world, so that all Jews would celebrate the festivals on the same days. We know the correct date of each festival from the Bible. The Bible tells us in which month each holiday occurs and how many days after the new moon. Since the new moon is tiny, and can be very hard to see in certain weather conditions, the Sanhedrin would receive witnesses from all over Israel to testify that they saw the new moon. The Sanhedrin would then announce the new moon throughout the Jewish world by means of a chain of bonfires that could be seen from one mountaintop to another. In later years, messengers were sent out to announce the new moon. Since Diaspora communities might not receive the news before the festival was to occur, the tradition of a SECOND DAY of festivals was introduced to avoid mistakes.

In 398, Hillel II introduced a permanent calendar based on mathematical and astronomical calculations. This made the system of witnesses and messengers unnecessary. In the 19th century, REFORM JUDAISM dropped the second day of festivals, claiming its observance is unnecessary now that we have a fixed calendar.

The names of the 12 Hebrew months are originally Babylonian. In the Bible, the months are usually identified by their number, with Nisan – the month of PASSOVER – being the first month of the year.

The Jewish day begins at sunset and ends at nightfall on the following evening). Therefore, the Sabbath and festivals all begin at sunset and end when three stars appear in the sky the next night.

CANAAN, LAND OF The name for the Land of ISRAEL from the time of ABRAHAM until the Second TEMPLE period. The Bible refers many times to the land and its inhabitants (*Kena'anim*). The Canaanite peoples included the Amorites, Canaanites, Jebusites, Hittites, and Philistines. They had a fairly advanced civilization and spoke a language similar to Hebrew.

God's promise to give to Abraham and his descendants "all the Land of Canaan" appears in several places in the Bible (Gen. 17:8; Num 34:2ff; Ps. 105:11, etc.). Its exact territory, however, is not clearly defined. In some places in the Bible we read that it covered about 6,000 square miles "from Dan to Beersheba" and west of the Jordan River; in others, parts of Lebanon, Syria, and Transjordan are included.

JOSHUA is commanded to fully conquer Canaan and destroy its inhabitants. However, it took centuries for the Israelites to gradually absorb these tribes. In the meantime, the Hebrews were constantly tempted by their IDOLATRY and are therefore harshly criticized by the PROPHETS.

CANDLES In ancient times, oil lamps were used for worship as well as to light homes. The candelabrum (MENORAH) that was lit daily in the Sanctuary, and later in the Temple, used a wick dipped in pure olive oil. The Mishnah (*Shab.* 2) discusses the substances that may and may not be used as oils and wicks for the SABBATH lights. Once candles became common, they generally replaced wicks and oil – as long as they were not made of tallow, a non-kosher fat (see BA-MEH MADLIKIN).

At least two candles are kindled just before the Sabbath in honor of the two-part commandment to "remember" and to "observe" the Sabbath day (Ex. 20:8; Deut. 5:12). This is traditionally a MITZVAH performed by the Jewish housewife (*Shab.* 2:6–7) and accompanied by a blessing (see BENEDICTIONS), but any adult may light the candles if she is absent. The Sabbath ends with the HAVDALAH ceremony, which includes the lighting of a candle made with at least two wicks. This is because the blessing "who creates the lights of fire" has "lights" in the plural.

In the case of the HANUKKAH lamp, lighting oil is preferable, because the miracle of Hanukkah involved a small bit of pure oil that was found in the Temple when it was liberated. A candle is also used in the search for LEAVEN on the eve of Passover and to light the synagogue when the Book of LAMENTATIONS is read on TISHAH BE-AV. Synagogues keep an ETERNAL LIGHT burning over the ARK, as a memory of the *Menorah* in the Temple, but this is often powered by electricity. It is the custom in some Orthodox communities for the parents of a bride and groom to carry candles as they walk their children to the MARRIAGE canopy.

In the Book of Proverbs we read: "The spirit of man is the lamp of the Lord" (20:27), so candles are traditionally lit when a person dies (see CORPSE; DEATH). A long-burning candle remains lit for seven days in a house of MOURNING, and then yearly on the anniversary of the death (YARTZEIT) and when MEMORIAL PRAYERS are said.

CANDLESTICK See MENORAH

CANTILLATION The art of chanting the Bible. Various portions of the PENTATEUCH are chanted throughout the year as part of the synagogue service (see READING OF THE LAW); on the SABBATH the HAFTARAH is also chanted from the PROPHETS; and on and FESTIVALS a reading is added from the HAGIOGRAPHA. In most cases a trained reader called a BA'AL KERI'AH chants the text, but it can also be read by a BAR MITZVAH boy, a BAT MITZVAH girl in most non-Orthodox settings, or another worshiper.

The art of chanting is ancient and may go back to Second Temple times. Various Jewish communities began to develop their own melodies from about the Middle Ages, and these have continued to grow and change ever since. Cantillation follows a system of notes called *te'amim*. There are 29 *te'amim*, some of which appear above the line and some below. They were developed together with the punctuation marks in the Bible in Babylonia and Erets Israel during the time of the Talmud. At first they were passed down orally but were later written. The sages assigned three functions to the *te'amim*: (a) to show which syllable in each word is to be accented, (b) to divide the verses of the Bible properly, which helps preserve their meaning, and (c) to show the pattern of melody that should be chanted for each verse. The signs for the *te'amim* must be memorized by the reader, because they only appear in printed texts; they are never copied into the Pentateuch scrolls that are read in the synagogue. The reader uses a book called a *tikkun* to practice. The *tikkun* has the printed text with *te'amim* and vowel points on one side of each page and a copy of the text as it appears in the scroll (i.e. with no *te'amim* or vowel points) on the other side.

CANTOR AND CANTORIAL MUSIC   The person who leads the SYNAGOGUE prayer service, called *hazzan* in Hebrew; his singing is called *hazzanut*. Unlike the *sheli'ah tsibbur* or BA'AL TEFILLAH, who also lead services, the cantor is a paid professional with training in music, voice, and prayer texts. In the Sephardi tradition, where the cantor relies more on traditional chants and melodies, voice training is not as important. The cantor is usually responsible for training BAR MITZVAH boys, as well as BAT MITZVAH girls in non-Orthodox settings.

The style and development of cantorial music in Europe was strongly affected by the society in which Jews lived. In Western Europe, as a result of the EMANCIPATION, Jews and their cantors were exposed to the culture and music of the times. Cantors underwent formal music training and began to write arrangements for traditional melodies as well as choir pieces (see CHOIRS AND CHORAL MUSIC). Talented cantor-composers began to write original melodies with echoes of more traditional forms.

Cantorial music in Eastern Europe developed entirely differently. Since Jews lived in small-town communities from the late Middle Ages onward, most cantorial traditions were passed along orally. Youngsters who showed promise studied with experienced cantors. The most popular cantors were those with the finest voices who sang new melodies or were able to entertain with their singing. Since not all small towns were able to support a full-time cantor, traveling cantors often went from village to village. They conducted especially festive Sabbath services when they were in town, and the best ones gave concerts with paid admission.

The last decade of the 19th century and the first two decades of the 20th became known as the "Golden Age of *Hazzanut*." There were a number of reasons for the tremendous popularity of cantorial music during these years. First, several *hazzanim* appeared with truly great voices, including: Gershon Sirota, Mordecai Herschman, Zavel Kwartin, and Yossele Rosenblatt. The growth in recorded music helped spread their popularity. In addition, the large number of immigrants from Eastern Europe tremendously enjoyed the connection that *hazzanut* held with the SHTETL, their former home.

In more recent years, even though there are now cantorial schools in the United States and Israel, cantorial music has become less popular. In the Orthodox community, aside from a few places where the tradition of a cantor is still strong, prayers are usually led by a rotation of synagogue members. Cantorial concerts are still well attended, but the average age of their audience is high.

CAPITAL PUNISHMENT   The Bible calls for capital punishment for a series of crimes, among them kidnapping, MURDER, IDOLATRY, DESECRATION of the SABBATH, BLASPHEMY, ADULTERY, INCEST, and various other sexual sins. It was an accepted form of punishment in the ancient world, and the Bible saw it as a way of preventing such crimes: "And all the men of his city shall stone him with stones, that he die; so shall you put away the evil from your midst; and all Israel shall hear and fear" (Deut. 21:21). Since executing the offender was seen as a way to rid society of evil, the court was forbidden to show mercy to those convicted of the worst crimes (murder, kidnapping, and idolatry). In addition, the Bible commands that the body of the executed be left on public display to serve as an example (Deut. 21:22). However, it was forbidden to leave the body on display overnight, "for he that is hanged is a reproach unto God; that you not pollute your land" (Deut. 21:23).

Two forms of capital punishment are mentioned directly in the Bible. The most common is stoning to death, in which all the people threw stones at the condemned person. In most cases the stoning was done by court order, but on several occasions the community rose up and stoned a person as an expression of their anger (Ex. 17:4; Num. 14:10; II Chr. 10:18). At times burning, most probably after the condemned was already dead by stoning, was called for in the case of sexual offenses (Lev. 20:14, 21:9).

Among other ancient peoples, an individual could be punished for the crimes of family members. However, the Bible ended this practice for the Israelites. The Bible limited responsibility for a crime to the criminal: "The fathers shall not be put to death for the children, neither shall the children be put to death for the fathers; every man shall be put to death for his own sin [only]" (Deut. 24:16).

Capital punishment can apply to animals as well. The ox that gores a human being to death (Ex. 25:28–29), as well as an animal involved in sexual relations with a human (Lev. 20:16), are to be put to death. This practice took place only among the Israelites.

The Talmud shows a shift in attitude away from executions. It made the conditions for carrying out capital punishment nearly impossible for a court to fulfill. We read that a SANHEDRIN that puts a person to death even only once in 70 years is considered to be bloodthirsty (*Mak.* 1:10). Capital crimes could only be tried before a court of 23 judges. The testimony of at least two acceptable witnesses was needed for conviction, and the accused had to be warned in advance in front of witnesses that the crime was punishable by death. (See also Maimonides, *Yad, Sanh.* 12.) The death penalty nearly disappeared from Jewish practice because of these limitations, but there were communities in Europe that continued to execute informers, even though this is not listed as a capital crime in the Bible (see Maimonides, *Yad, Hovel u-Mazzik* 8:10).

In addition to severely limited the cases in which the death penalty could apply, talmudic law added two additional forms of execution: slaying by sword and strangling. The rabbis believed that these two forms of death were more humane, in keeping with the law, "love your neighbor as yourself" (Lev. 19:17; *Ket.* 37b; *Sanh.* 45a). They also felt they did less damage to the body than in stoning and burning, and therefore the death was more like the taking of life by God (*Sanh.* 6:4; 45a).

Since the death penalty can be carried out only by a qualified Sanhedrin, there is no Jewish body considered suitable for administering capital punishment today.

The death penalty was officially removed as a possibility in most cases in the State of Israel in 1954. Until that time several death sentences were issued, but none was carried out. Capital punishment has remained, however, under the Crime of Genocide (racially motivated mass murder) Law and for treason committed in time of war. The only instance of capital punishment in the history of the State was the hanging of Adolf Eichmann (1962), convicted of genocide for his crimes during the HOLOCAUST.

CAPTIVES, RANSOMING OF   (Heb. *pidyon shevuyim*). A religious obligation which has had the highest priority in Jewish communities since Bible times. Because of the commandment "You shall not stand idly by the blood of your neighbor" (Lev. 19:16) and because captives were always in serious danger, the rabbis considered ransoming captives to be a major duty (*BB* 8a–b). Even a SCROLL OF THE LAW could be sold to raise money to ransom captives (*Tos.* on *BB* 8b). At the same time, Jewish law did not permit a community to bend to extortion, and therefore only "reasonable" amounts could be paid to ransom captives. The fear was that if inflated ransoms are paid, this will only encourage more kidnapping. MAIMONIDES and others held that even when lives may be at stake, the community must not make exaggerated efforts to release captives if doing so will endanger another person's security in the future. When MEIR OF ROTHENBERG (*Maharam*) was imprisoned in 1286 by the Holy Roman Emperor, he refused to allow fellow Jews to obtain his release in exchange for a huge sum. He chose to spend the remaining seven years of his life in prison rather than encourage others to kidnap Jewish scholars. Nevertheless, most communities had communal funds set aside for ransoming captives in keeping with the talmudic saying "All Jews are responsible for one another" (*Shevu.* 39a).

In modern times, Israeli authorities have been called upon to release large numbers of enemy prisoners in exchange for small numbers of prisoners of war or even the bodies of Israeli soldiers. If the prisoner release will not endanger Israeli security, every effort is made to redeem the captives and the bodies.

CARLEBACH, SHLOMO   (1925–1994). Rabbi, composer of many Jewish melodies that have already become classics. Carlebach grew up in Vienna, where his father was a rabbi. He came from a line of Polish Hasidic rabbis. When the Nazis rose to power, the family moved to the United States. Carlebach studied in the *yeshivah* in Lakewood, New Jersey. He then became close to the Lubavicher Rebbe (see SCHNEERSOHN, MENAHEM MENDEL), who sent him out to various Jewish communities to bring people closer to Judaism (1951–1955). However, the Rebbe came to disapprove of Carlebach's ways of reaching out to fellow Jews, and the two parted ways.

Over the next few years Carlebach moved from place to place reaching out to Jews in his own way, until he decided to study the guitar. One day he came to his guitar teacher with a melody he had written, and she wrote down the music for him. This was the first of hundreds of songs that Carlebach was to write, mostly based on words taken from prayers. Carlebach began to give popular concerts at which he performed his music with great energy, leaping into the air as he sang. His singing was mixed with stories and inspiring words about being Jewish. Most of what he earned playing music he donated to charity.

From 1959 he began to spend half his year in Israel and attracted many followers, both there and in North America. He opened the House of Love and Prayer in San Francisco, where there was no traditional separation between men and women. His unusual approach attracted still more followers.

With his death he became a larger-than-life figure. Today hundreds of synagogues use his melodies. Many also have "Carlebach SABBATHS" or "Carlebach MINYANS," where most of the service uses his music.

CARO, JOSEPH BEN EPHRAIM   (1488–1575). Greatest writer of Jewish law codes of the 16th century, author of the SHULHAN ARUKH ("*Set Table*"). Caro was born in Spain or Portugal and taken to Turkey as a child. He became a leading Talmud scholar. In 1536 he moved to Safed, in Erets Israel, where he became head of the rabbinical court (see BET DIN) and of an important Talmud academy. Caro believed that he was guided by a heavenly teacher (MAGGID) who was the "MISHNAH in human form," and who revealed to him secrets and mysteries of the Torah throughout his life. The mystical diary he wrote was called *Maggid Mesharim*.

Caro worked from 1522 to 1554 on his largest legal work, the *Bet Yosef* ("House of Joseph"). It traces each law in the Talmud through all the stages of its development, presents all the opinions of the various authorities on that law, and then states Caro's legal decision. The *Shulhan Arukh* (1564) was originally written for young students as a digest of the *Bet Yosef,* but became extremely popular among scholars at all levels. It focuses, however, only on Sephardi CUSTOM and practice, completely ignoring Ashkenazi traditions (see ASHKENAZIM, SEPHARDIM). Moses ISSERLES, an outstanding Polish expert in Jewish law,

ב"ה

אבן העזר

שלחן ערוך

באמשטרדם

Title page of the Shulhan Arukh, *Joseph Caro's most famous work. Published in Amsterdam, 1698.*

repaired this fault by writing a supplement, called *Mappah* ("Tablecloth"), which adds the practices of the Ashkenazi world. Orthodox Jews consider the decisions of the *Shulhan Arukh* to be binding until today.

CELIBACY Refraining from sexual relations. MARRIAGE is a commandment in Jewish tradition, and therefore celibacy is looked down upon. The first MITZVAH in the Bible, "be fruitful and multiply" (Gen. 1:28), made it clear that having children is a holy obligation. Many authorities view celibacy as a sin, and it was extremely rare for rabbis and other Jewish leaders to remain unmarried. As it says in the Talmud: "He who is without a wife is without joy, without blessing, without happiness, without learning, without protection, without peace; indeed he is no man" (*Yev.* 62b).

CEMETERY Area of land set aside for BURIAL of the dead. In Bible times, the general practice was to bury the dead in family tombs outside the city limits. Cemeteries developed during Talmud times.

A cemetery is known in Hebrew as *bet kevarot* ("place of graves"); *bet olam* ("house of eternity"); and even *bet hayyim* ("house of life") – the latter a traditional Jewish effort to avoid negative language. The land of the cemetery is considered to be holy, and it is reserved only for Jews. On the other hand, it is also a place of ritual IMPURITY, and *kohanim* (those descended from PRIESTS) therefore avoid entering a cemetery unless it is to bury an immediate family member. Respectful, serious behavior is required in a cemetery, and one is not permitted to eat, drink, read, or study there. Animals may not graze there, and it may not be used as a shortcut or a place to take a stroll. Visitors to the cemetery wash their hands upon leaving as a symbol of purification.

Each Jewish COMMUNITY is required to establish a cemetery. Private Jewish cemeteries have also come into existence. These sell graves to members of the Jewish public who do not have burial plots in community cemeteries.

Graves are arranged in rows and usually marked with TOMBSTONES. Jewish law calls for a distance of six handbreadths between graves. If necessary, one body may be buried above another, if there is a separating layer of earth the depth of six handbreadths. Customs for the arrangement of cemeteries can vary by community (see ASHKENAZIM and SEPHARDIM). Some have separate rows for men and women. Some bury in the order of the date of death; others have family plots. Traditionally, one area was reserved for rabbis and religious community leaders. Those who committed SUICIDE (unless not "of sound mind"), APOSTASY, or terrible crimess are usually buried near the cemetery wall. The SHULHAN ARUKH law code instructs that a wicked person should not be buried near a righteous person, and enemies should not be buried next to one another.

Cemeteries are surrounded by a wall or fence. Traditionally a building was built in the cemetery to serve as a chapel for FUNERAL services and sometimes also as a place to prepare the body for burial (see PURITY, RITUAL). In ancient times, cemeteries were not decorated with trees or plants. This practice is maintained in the old cemeteries of Jerusalem, Safed, Tiberias, and Hebron. Beautifying cemeteries with greenery has since become a widespread practice among Jews.

There are many customs for visiting graves. The most common times are at the end of the seven days of MOURNING; 30 days after burial; yearly on the anniversary of the death; and before the New Year (ROSH HA-SHANAH). At times of community trouble, people often prayed for God's mercy at the graves of holy people. However, the rabbis discouraged visiting cemeteries too frequently.

Among North African Jews it became the custom to honor the memory of a particularly holy person on the anniversary of death with a HILLULA. This involved a pilgrimage to the gravesite, where prayers were offered asking the saintly person to intervene with God to help those who were praying. The Hillula was usually a large festive community gathering, with bonfires lit, candles on the grave, and prayers through the night.

CENSORSHIP Destroying books (or sections of books) by those who find them problematic. Following a DISPUTATION (debate in which Jews were forced to face Christians) in Paris, France (1240), all copies of the TALMUD were collected and burned. After another disputation in Barcelona, Spain (1263), Jews were ordered to remove from their books all sections that Christians considered problematic. The Pope ordered all copies of the Talmud to be burned in Italy in 1554. This pattern of attacks on Jewish books was to continue for many centuries. Often the censor was a Jew who had turned to APOSTASY (i.e. taken on Christian belief), since few Christians knew the Jewish works well enough to find the sections that could be linked to CHRISTIANITY. In some cases, Jews made changes to their own texts and prayers to avoid offending the authorities.

In more recent years, the governments of Communist countries, such as Russia, practiced censorship. The worst censors of modern times were the Nazis, who undertook a campaign to burn all books by Jewish authors. In 1933 the Nazi list of targeted books included 12,400 titles.

In a different kind of censorship, some religious Jews have taken it upon themselves to read only Jewish books that have been approved by certain rabbis, who give the book a *Haskamah*. The *Haskamah* certifies that the book contains no inappropriate beliefs or morality.

CHABAD Hasidic movement founded by SHNEUR ZALMAN OF LYADY (1745–1813). Shneur Zalman's basic ideas stem from DOV BAER, the Maggid of Mezhirech, and from Dov Baer's son, Abraham "the Angel." Chabad theory is put forth in the *Tanya* and *Likkutei Torah* of Schneur Zalman; in the works of his son, Dov Baer (1773–1827); and of Dov Baer's disciple, Aaron ben Moses of Starosielce (1766–1828); and in the writings of later Chabad thinkers. The central branch of the Chabad dynasty passed through Dov Baer's family, which settled in Lubavich, Russia; today the terms "Chabad" and "Lubavich" mean the same.

"ChaBaD" is an acronym (see ACROSTICS) of (C)hokhmah, Binah, Da'at – "Wisdom," "Understanding" and "Knowledge." In the Kabbalah, these are the names of the higher SEFIROT (levels of God in the universe). This shows Chabad's focus on the processes of the Divine "mind," as opposed to other Hasidic systems that focus on Divine "emotions." For Chabad, thinking about God comes before true religious emotion – if one reverses the process, this distorts the worship.

Chabad understands the verse "The whole earth is full of His glory" (Isa. 6:5) to mean that there really is no world at all – only the Divine reality. This interpretation was problematic for some Jewish thinkers, since it seems to mean that God is in some way physically present. ELIJAH, the Gaon of Vilna, and the MITNAGGEDIM saw this as heresy, which explains the angry disputes that took place for some time between the Hasidim and *Mitnaggedim*.

Chabad thought includes the idea of trying to lose the individual self in God. Chabad believes that deep in the recesses of

The Chabad house in Ramat Shlomo, Jerusalem, an exact duplicate of the Lubavich house in New York.

the individual Jew is an authentic Divine spark. When a person succeeds in completely bypassing his ego, the Divine spark is awakened. To this day, some Chabad members can spend an hour or more reciting the SHEMA, singing softly to themselves, lost and totally absorbed in the Divine.

In 1940, the sixth Lubavicher Rebbe (leading rabbi of Chabad), Joseph Isaac Schneersohn, arrived in the United States and made Brooklyn, New York, the new center of Lubavich Hasidism. Menahem Mendel SCHNEERSOHN, the next Rebbe, turned Lubavich into a worldwide outreach movement. Many new approaches were created for approaching individual Jews and encouraging them to perform MITZVOT. Cable and satellite broadcasts, Chabad House centers on college campuses, and Chabad centers in hundreds of communities has made Lubavich active in over 50 countries. It now includes more than 200,000 followers around the world.

CHALLAH (also challeh, hallah) (1) Portion of dough set aside as a gift to the priests (Num. 15:18–21); (2) Sabbath loaf of bread. It is the Talmud's view that the law of "the first yield of your baking" applies only to the Jewish community in the Land of Israel, and is not binding in the Diaspora (*Ket.* 25a). Since ancient times, however, observant Jews throughout the world have practiced "separating the dough."

Challah laws apply only to dough prepared from one of the FIVE SPECIES of grain – wheat, emmer, barley, oats, or rye. Separation of the dough should take place immediately after it is kneaded; failing this, it should be taken from the newly baked bread. The rabbis determined that a baker must set aside a ¼₈ part of his dough, while the housewife (who prepares a smaller amount) must separate ¼₄. Dough weighing 1.25 kg. (about 2 lb 12 oz) and upwards requires challah to be taken.

The separation of challah is accompanied by the BENEDICTION: "Blessed are You, Lord our God, King of the universe who has sanctified us with His commandments and commanded us to separate challah from the dough."

CHANUKAH   See HANUKKAH

CHARITY   The Hebrew word for charity is *tsedakah*, from the root of the word meaning "justice." In Jewish sources, we learn that there is a difference between *tsedakah* and GEMILUT HASADIM ("acts of lovingkindness"). *Gemilut hasadim* includes all types of aid to others, such as lending one's possessions, visiting the sick, and escorting the dead at a funeral. *Tsedakah* is therefore one aspect of the overall system of *gemilut hasadim*.

The AGRICULTURAL LAWS of the PENTATEUCH made a point of providing for the poor. At harvest time, landowners were required to leave the corners of their fields for the poor. Grains that were dropped or left behind during harvest also belonged to the poor. At the end of each seven-year cycle of the SABBATICAL YEAR all debts were canceled, and in the third and sixth year of the cycle, a TITHE was given to the poor.

For the rabbis, the manner in which charity was given could add to the value of the deed. R. Eleazar said: "The reward that is paid for giving charity is directly related to the kindness with which it is given" (*Suk.* 49b). Charity, together with prayer and repentance during the TEN DAYS OF REPENTANCE, can cancel a harsh decree by God for the coming year. MAIMONIDES in his *Laws of Gifts to the Poor* (10:7ff.) notes eight levels of charity. The lowest level is giving reluctantly with the giver and receiver face to face, since this is a situation that can cause shame. A higher level is giving so that the receiver and giver do not know the identity of the other. The highest level is helping the poor person to become self-sufficient, for example, by helping him set up a business. In general people should give ¹⁄₁₀ of their yearly earnings to *tzedakah*, but no more than ⅕. The rabbis were concerned that people who give too much *tzedakah* might themselves need support one day.

The amount of *tzedakah* a person should receive is relative. HILLEL said that the person in need should receive enough to live according to the lifestyle he had before requiring support (*Ket.* 67b). At the same time, a person should do everything possible to avoid taking charity. When money is tight, advises

---

SAYINGS ABOUT CHARITY

A person must carefully fulfill the commandment to give charity, for this is a sign of a descendant of Abraham.

Israel will be redeemed through acts of charity.

As great as is the commandment to give charity, it is even greater to persuade another to give charity.

Charity is one of the things whose profits man enjoys in this would, but whose principal remains for the world to come.

Charity is equal to all the other commandments combined.

Everyone should give charity; even he who depends on charity should give to those who are less fortunate.

It is better not to give charity than to do so and shame the receiver publicly.

He who is generous to the poor makes a loan to the Lord.

Nobody ever becomes poor by giving charity.

Do not humiliate a beggar; God is beside him.

---

the Talmud, "Make your Sabbath into a weekday" (i.e. eat ordinary food rather than Sabbath delicacies).

Every town in which Jews live is required to have a charity fund (*kuppah*), with at least two individuals responsible for running it (Maimonides, *Laws of Gifts to the Poor,* 9:1). Some cities had an extra fund, called *tamhui*, which would collect food from various families and distribute enough for two meals each evening to those in need. All residents were required to contribute to the charity fund, including visitors who were in town for at least 30 days.

The Jewish COMMUNITY, from early days to the present, has contained various organizations that distribute charity to those in need. For example, in past centuries funds existed to provide hospitality to travelers, redeem those who had been taken captive, and bury the poor. Today's charitable organizations buy Passover supplies for the needy; support institutions of Torah learning; build and run hospitals; aid the sick, poor, and elderly; absorb needy immigrants from other Jewish communities; provide assistance to the needy in Israel; etc.

CHASTITY   Abstaining from forbidden sexual activity (in contrast to VIRGINITY, which is avoiding all sexual intercourse). Forbidden sexual activity, such as ADULTERY, INCEST, HOMOSEXUALITY, and relations with animals are considered absolutely repulsive to God, and the Bible issued numerous warnings against such practices. On the other hand, by refraining from such activities the Israelites could achieve a state of holiness. Forbidden sex is one of the three cardinal sins (along with MURDER and IDOLATRY); a person had to allow himself to be killed rather than commit such an act.

MARRIAGE is the ideal relationship between man and woman.

Within that framework, sex is permitted and is viewed as natural and good – a MITZVAH. In Judaism the sexual urge should not be repressed, as it is in other cultures, but rather channeled into marriage. In fact a husband and wife are not permitted to deny sexual relations to one another; to do so would be grounds for DIVORCE. Even within marriage, modesty and restraint are traditionally called for. During the NIDDAH period, when a woman is menstruating, and for several days after, chastity is required even in marriage. Husbands and wives refrain from touching one another until the wife immerses herself in a ritual bath (MIKVEH). The practice of chastity enables couples to achieve a holy state within marriage.

CHERUB   (Heb. *keruv*; pl. *keruvim*). Winged heavenly being that is mentioned frequently in the Bible. They were either messengers from God (see ANGELS) or one of a pair that was attached to the ARK OF THE COVENANT to guard it (Ex. 25:18–22, 37:7–9). After God expelled ADAM AND EVE from the Garden of EDEN, he posted cherubs to guard its entrance (Gen. 3:24). The throne of God Himself was supported by cherubs.

Carved decorations in the form of cherubs were placed on the walls, doors, and panels of the Temple. Cherubs could have the faces of humans or of animals (at times a lion, ox, or eagle). They sometimes appeared with several sets of wings and more than one face. Although they were not very important in Jewish ritual art, MAIMONIDES counted them among the angels (*Yad, Yesodei ha-Torah* 2:7).

A carved ivory cherub with two wings and one face. From Samaria, 9ᵗʰ century BCE.

CHIEF RABBINATE   A central form of Jewish religious authority that has existed since the Middle Ages. In medieval Europe, a "chief Jew" was sometimes little more than a tax collector and agent of the king; in other cases he might be the head of the rabbinical court (BET DIN); in some places he was both. Having a chief rabbinate allowed the Jewish community independence in running its own court system. Under the Holy Roman Empire, for example, MEIR OF ROTHENBURG was both a government-appointed administrator of the Jewish community and its spiritual leader.

In England, the "Chief Rabbi of the United Hebrew Congregations of the British Commonwealth" has been an elected position since 1844. No similar position exists in the United States. Other chief rabbinates exist today in the following countries: Argentina, Belgium, Denmark, France, Holland, Hungary, Israel, Italy, Rumania, South Africa, Sweden, Switzerland, Turkey, and Venezuela. All of these are Orthodox, except for the chief rabbinates of Sweden and Hungary, which are Conservative. All Diaspora chief rabbinates are funded by voluntary contributions.

The Chief Rabbinate of Israel is a state authority funded by the government. It has full control over matters of personal status, such as MARRIAGE, DIVORCE, and CONVERSION TO JUDAISM. The rabbinate runs a Jewish court system throughout Israel (see BET DIN). There are also chief rabbinates in Israel's major cities.

CHILDREN   Judaism has always placed a high value on having and raising children. The Jewish household traditionally revolved around the family and instilling children with Jewish knowledge and values. Jewish parents the world over hope to be blessed with children and grandchildren in whom they will be able to take pride. (See also FAMILY; MOTHER; PARENT AND CHILD.)

The verse "Be fruitful and multiply" (Gen. 1:28) is the first commandment in the Bible. It was understood that to fulfill the commandment a couple should have at least one boy and one girl. The Talmud says that one who is childless may be considered as dead (*Ned.* 64b); purposely avoiding having children is like murder (*Yev.* 63b). A couple that had been childless for ten years was once expected to divorce, but in modern times divorce for this reason is extremely rare.

The Bible says that children will suffer for their parents' evil actions "unto the third and the fourth generation" (Ex. 20:5). However, the rabbis believed that punishment would only be carried out on children who followed in their parents' evil ways (*Ber.* 7a). On the other hand, children will benefit from their parents' righteous behavior "to the thousandth generation" (Ex. 20:5–6).

The birth of a boy is celebrated by a SHALOM ZAKHAR party in his home on the first Friday night after his birth. NAMES are given to male infants at their CIRCUMCISION. Traditionally girls are named in the synagogue, when their father is called to the READING OF THE LAW. In recent decades, the custom of celebrating the birth of a daughter with a SIMHAT BAT ceremony has become popular.

The child's Jewish education traditionally begins at an early age at home, with the SHEMA prayer at bedtime and the Jewish FESTIVALS and DIETARY LAWS observed. The Mishnah states that boys are to study the Bible from the age of five, study Mishnah at ten, perform *mitzvot* (see MITZVAH) at 13, and study Talmud at 15 (*Avot* 5:21; see EDUCATION). Today the study of Mishnah and Talmud often begins at earlier ages. In previous eras, girls were not given formal schooling, but rather learned how to run a Jewish home from their mothers. Today girls in even the most traditional communities attend school.

Children are required to both honor (Ex. 20:12) and respect (Lev. 19:3) their parents. Honor requires that they provide food, drink, and personal needs. Respect means that the child does not sit in the parents' seat or contradict the parent in a conversation (*Kid.* 31b). The Bible (Deut. 21:18–21) even called for the death penalty in the extreme case of the REBELLIOUS SON, who carries out violent rebellion against his parents. However, children are supposed to disregard parents who tell them to violate the laws of Judaism.

A child born of a forbidden sexual relationship (INCEST or ADULTERY) is called a *mamzer* and may not marry another Jew, unless that Jew is also a *mamzer* (or a convert to Judaism). There is no stigma (disgraceful status) in Jewish law about a child born to an unwed mother.

CHILDREN'S PRAYERS AND SERVICES   Worship services specially created for, and often conducted by, Jewish youngsters. Teaching children how to recite daily prayers has always been a central part of religious education in the home and in the Jewish school. In observant homes, even very young children are taught to say brief prayers in the morning and at bedtime (see MODEH ANI, SHEMA). Other passages are added when they begin to go to school. Even small boys recite a blessing over their TSITSIT. Children are often also called up to lead the concluding hymn AN'IM ZEMIROT at the end of the Ashkenazi adult synagogue service. In Sephardi synagogues, children are invited to recite a verse from the prayers aloud and even read the HAFTARAH from the age of seven.

In the mid-19th century REFORM JUDAISM introduced shortened prayer services for boys and girls on Sabbath mornings or afternoons. They were usually conducted in the local language, with brief sections in Hebrew. This trend also appeared in CONSERVATIVE JUDAISM. Both movements have printed prayer books for "junior congregations" and youth camps. Short, illustrated prayer books have been published for children in the Orthodox world to encourage them to learn the prayers at an early age.

CHOIRS AND CHORAL MUSIC   Jews have been active since ancient times as singers and musicians. The LEVITES sang to beautify the services in the TEMPLE. Although they were accompanied by instruments, the choral music was central to the Temple service (*Suk.* 50b–51a; *Ar.* 11a). The opening of many psalms, "*La-menatse'ah*," probably refers to a choir conductor or musical director. The HALLEL service, originally also sung by the Levites in the Temple, was famous for its beauty.

The choir of the Second Temple was all male, could only be joined after serious training, and upheld the highest musical standards. After the destruction of the Temple, chanting of ordinary worshipers began to replace formal choirs in the SYNAGOGUE, and no musical instruments were allowed. Up until the 17th century, a prayer leader often conducted services with two assistants, an adult and a boy soprano (see CANTOR AND CANTORIAL MUSIC; MUSIC AND SONG).

In the late 16th century Jews were barred from Italian society, and many talented Jewish musicians began to channel their creativity into the synagogue. The outstanding pre-modern composer, Salomone de' Rossi, borrowed from Italian music in writing his ambitious *Songs of Solomon* (1622–23). He also wrote and conducted Hebrew choir pieces, which were mostly "echo poems," to be sung without instruments. De' Rossi inspired others in his day to write Hebrew cantatas and choral pieces in Provence and Amsterdam, as well as Italy. The practice of writing musical compositions to be sung as part of the worship service has continued to this day.

By the 19th century, the new approaches of REFORM JUDAISM introduced many changes to the synagogue service. Israel Jacobson trained a boys choir to sing Protestant-style hymns with ORGAN music in Germany (1809–18). In Reform congregations throughout Europe, synagogue MUSIC began to feature women and non-Jews in the choir, as well as instrumental music, and did away with the chanting style that was popular in more traditional congregations. From the early 1900s Orthodox synagogues in Europe began to introduce all-male choirs to increase worshipers' enjoyment of the service.

In the United States, the first synagogue to organize a choir in 1818 was the Orthodox Sephardi congregation Shearith Israel. Since then, choirs singing especially composed worship pieces have been enjoyed by all of the movements.

CHORIN, AARON   (1766–1844). Pioneer of REFORM JUDAISM in Hungary. When he was the chief rabbi of Arad (Transylvania), he sharply criticized Jewish customs that he believed to be superstitious (e.g. KAPPAROT). His attacks on traditional Jewish practice grew more and more severe until the other local rabbis wanted him removed from his position. Only intervention by the government kept him in his job.

Chorin felt that one should "not simply cling to the dry letter of the Law, but be guided by its spirit." He therefore called for many changes in Jewish practice, but he quoted the traditional ORAL LAW to justify his views. His reforms included: eliminating KOL NIDREI on the DAY OF ATONEMENT, permitting worship without a head covering (see COVERING THE HEAD), praying in Hungarian, playing the ORGAN in synagogue on the SABBATH and FESTIVALS, shortening the week of MOURNING, and permitting both writing and travel on the Sabbath.

CHOSEN PEOPLE   Judaism's belief that God chose the people of Israel from among the nations and made a special COVENANT (contract) with them. In the Bible, we read that God chose ABRAHAM to establish a special relationship with him and his descendants. God says about Abraham: "I will make of you a great nation … and all the families of the earth shall bless themselves by you" (Gen. 12:2–3) and "… I have singled him out, that he may instruct his children and his descendants to keep the way of the Lord, by doing what is just and right" (Gen. 18:18–19). At SINAI, the entire people of Israel is called upon to accept the covenant and enter into a special relationship with God: "Now, therefore if you will obey Me faithfully, and keep My covenant, you shall be My treasured possession among all peoples; for all the earth is Mine; but you shall be unto Me a kingdom of priests and a holy nation …" (Ex. 19:5–6). MOSES reminds the people before his death: "… the Lord your God chose you from among all other peoples on earth to be His treasured possession" (Deut. 14:2).

The Bible offers no clear reason for why God chose the people of Israel. Although rewards for the Israelites' proper behavior are certainly part of the covenant, the Bible does not hesitate to point out the dangers involved in being chosen: "I have known only you of all the peoples of the earth; therefore I will punish you for all your sins" (Amos 3:2). Chosenness also includes responsibilities toward the other nations: "I will make you a light unto the nations, so My salvation will reach the ends of the earth!" (Isa. 49:6).

The rabbis of the Talmud felt the relationship between God and the people of Israel to be intimate and loving. In fact, they viewed the beautiful, romantic love poetry of the SONG OF SONGS as a metaphor for the relationship between God and His nation (*Yad.* 3:5; *Tosef. Sanh.* 12:10). One MIDRASH shows the people choosing God at Sinai – when God tried to offer the Torah to a number of nations, only Israel agreed to keep its laws (*AZ* 2b–3a). The traditional PRAYER BOOK includes numerous blessings (see BENEDICTIONS) thanking God for choosing the people of Israel.

In the Middle Ages, two basic views developed about the idea of Israel's chosenness. MAIMONIDES believed that it was a matter of duty, not of rights. Holiness and a special place in the world were not to be taken for granted; Israel earns them by following all of God's laws. The second view, held largely by JUDAH HALEVI and followers of HASIDISM, is that Israel's uniqueness is unconditional, and Jewish souls have a special, holy quality no matter how the individual might behave. Persecutions of Jews by other peoples throughout history tended to strengthen the second belief, since the tormenters were clearly behaving in an inferior manner.

With the modern era and EMANCIPATION, the idea of the chosen people became difficult to explain in a world of "equal" nations. Abraham GEIGER, of early Reform Judaism, emphasized that Israel was chosen to bring God's message to the world. This meant that Jews were no better than other people and that Jews were meant to live scattered among the other nations. Other Reform thinkers insisted that it was Israel that chose God in keeping with the Midrash (see above). Mordecai KAPLAN, the founder of RECONSTRUCTIONISM, completely rejects the chosen people notion. He removed all mention of the idea from the many places in the worship service where it traditionally appears.

Most modern Jewish thinkers uphold the ideas of chosenness and covenant. Throughout the ages this belief has strengthened the Jewish people in times of crisis, given a sense of purpose to individual and national life, and motivated Jews to strive for moral and spiritual excellence.

CHRISTIANITY   Major world religion that arose out of JUDAISM. Christians believe that Jesus of Nazareth (1st cent. CE) was the MESSIAH, and that his coming fulfilled the prophecies from the Bible.

The Christian Bible is called the New Testament. It describes the life of Jesus, the son of Mary. Mary was believed to be a Jewish virgin who conceived and bore Jesus after a miraculous union with God, Jesus' father. Jesus was an observant Jew who attracted a number of Jewish followers. He preached about a "Kingdom of Heaven" that awaited those who sincerely repented their sins. He criticized the ethical behavior of the two major Jewish parties, the SADDUCEES and PHARISEES, but shared many ideas with both groups. As his following grew and people began to view him as the Messiah, Jesus was seen as a threat to both the Roman government in Erets Israel and to the Jewish leadership. This led to his arrest and crucifixion by the Romans. Jesus' heartbroken followers kept his spiritual message alive after his death, until it developed fully into the religion of Christianity.

Ecclesia *(Church) holding a cross, and* Synagoga *(Synagogue) holding a broken staff, a common motif in medieval Christian art.*

All of the early Christians were Jewish followers of Jesus who believed that he had risen from the dead and would soon return to earth as the Messiah. Under the influence of Paul of Tarsus (a Jews who at first was opposed to Christianity), the new religion expanded to include non-Jews. The Christians believed that the ethical teachings of the Bible were important, but that there was no longer any need to follow the commandments. Non-Jews were therefore welcomed into the new religion without the Jewish legal requirements for conversion (see CONVERSION TO JUDAISM). A break with Judaism occurred some time in the second century as the number of non-Jews among the Christians grew.

Early Christians were persecuted by the Romans, but in the fourth century, the Emperor Constantine made Christianity the official religion of Rome. From that time on, Jews who lived under Christian governments suffered persecution, discrimination, attempts at conversion, EXPULSIONS, and massacres. Christians accused the Jewish people of being responsible for the death of Jesus, the "son of God." They also saw the continued existence of the Jewish people, who did not accept Jesus as Messiah, as a threat to their belief system. Anti-Jewish stereotypes, even

identifying Jews with the devil, became part of Christian culture (see ANTI-SEMITISM).

Throughout the ages there have been various types of organized efforts on the part of the Christian world to publicly "prove" that Judaism should not continue to exist. Christian thinkers published attacks on Judaism called polemics, which were presented as logical arguments about the foolishness of Jewish belief (see APOLOGETICS AND POLEMICS). Jews often responded with apologetics in defense of Judaism. During the Middle Ages, Jewish leaders in several countries were forced to defend their religion in public debates with Christian leaders (see DISPUTATIONS). The anti-Jewish results were often known in advance. Forced conversions and other violent attacks against Jews were well known in the Christian world. Even in modern times, some Protestant groups continue to try to convert Jews to Christianity. The growth of groups such as "Jews for Jesus" are evidence of their efforts (see CULTS).

Despite the history of hostility between Judaism and Christianity, Christianity adopted many Jewish beliefs and practices, such as prayers and immersing in water (baptism for Christians; MIKVEH for Jews). Many believe that Jesus spent time with the Qumran community (see DEAD SEA SCROLLS), where he learned mystical ideas and practices.

Judaism has traditionally had a mixed attitude toward Christianity. The many years of persecution at the hands of Christians has understandably created much resentment. Many hold its belief in a son of God and the statues and images found in churches to be IDOLATRY. Others have pointed out the difference between Christian belief and forms of idolatry that involve many gods. Even so, in the modern period many Jews and Christians have met for respectful interfaith dialogues, in an effort to create better understanding between members of the two faiths (see INTERFAITH RELATIONS).

Since the HOLOCAUST, many Christians have begun to reexamine their own religion, because they are disturbed that their beliefs have led to Anti-Semitism. The Catholic Church issued a declaration condemning anti-Semitism and announcing that the Jews did not kill Jesus. Evangelical Christians have begun to speak out in praise of the Jews' rightful place in the Land of Israel. Many such Christians are active supporters of Israel and believe that the Jewish State is part of God's plan. Eastern Orthodox churches have not changed their teaching about Jews and Judaism, and traditional prejudices remain.

While there are many forms of both Judaism and Christianity, the differences between mainstream Judaism and mainstream Christianity are as follows:

1. Judaism accepts only one, unified GOD; Christianity believes in a Divine Trinity, including the Father, Son, and Holy Spirit, who are all viewed as God.

2. For Judaism, God has no body and can never be seen; Christianity believes that Jesus, the Son, was both a God and a human being

3. Judaism believes that people can do REPENTANCE for their sins and receive FORGIVENESS and acceptance by God through their own efforts; Christianity holds that humans are basically sinful, because of the original sin of ADAM AND EVE, and therefore need the sacrifice of Jesus to achieve forgiveness for their sins

4. Judaism describes a Messiah who will be a political and religious leader, a descendant of King David who will come in the future; Christianity holds that Jesus, their Messiah, was both human and God and that he will return to the world in the future. His task is to redeem humanity from the original sin of Adam

5. Judaism teaches that both the relationship between God and the People of Israel and the requirement to observe the commandments (see MITZVAH) are valid for all time; Christianity believes in a second covenant (agreement) between God and all humanity that was recorded in the New Testament. It is based on belief in Jesus, not on observance of the commandments. It holds that those who accept Jesus as Messiah have replaced the Jews as God's CHOSEN PEOPLE.

CHRONICLES, BOOK(S) OF (Heb. *Divrei ha-Yamim*).

I CHRONICLES	
1:1–1:54	Genealogical listing
2:1–9:1	Lists of the tribes of Israel
9:2–9:18	List of the inhabitants of Jerusalem
9:19–9:34	List of the Levites and their duties
9:35–9:44	List of the inhabitants of Gibeon
10:1–29:30	Monarchy during David's time

II CHRONICLES	
1:1–9:31	Solomon's reign
10:1–12:16	Rehoboam's reign
13:1–13:23	Abijah's reign
14:1–16:14	Asa's reign
17:1–20:37	Jehoshaphat's reign
21:1–21:20	Jehoram's reign
22:1–22:9	Ahaziah's reign
22:10–23:21	Athaliah's reign
24:1–24:27	Joash's reign
25:1–25:28	Amaziah's reign
26:1–26:23	Uzziah's reign
27:1–27:9	Jotham's reign
28:1–28:27	Ahaz's reign
29:1–32:33	Hezekiah's reign
33:1–33:20	Manasseh's reign
33:21–33:25	Amon's reign
34:1–35:27	Josiah's reign
36:1–36:4	Jehoahaz's reign
36:5–36:8	Jehoiakim's reign
36:9–36:10	Jehoiachin's reign
36:11–36:21	Zedekiah's reign
36:22–36:23	Proclamation of Cyrus

According to Jewish tradition, Chronicles is the last of the biblical books of Writings (see HAGIOGRAPHA) as well as the last book of the Bible. In many ways, it is a survey of Jewish history. It begins with a family history that starts with ADAM and ends just before the Jews' return to the Land of Israel from exile in Babylonia (538 BCE; see EXILE, BABYLONIAN). It focuses particularly on showing the house of King DAVID in a good light, from the beginning of his reign until the destruction of Jerusalem (586 BCE). The stories of SOLOMON, who built the

Temple, and the 19 kings of Judah all appear, but only those kings of the Northern Kingdom of ISRAEL who had dealings with the kings of Judah are mentioned.

Although many of these stories also appear in the books of II SAMUEL and KINGS, Chronicles includes details that are missing in the other books. Chronicles also leaves out stories from II Samuel and Kings about David and Solomon in which the monarchs behaved sinfully. It especially emphasizes the building of the Temple and the role of the PRIESTS and the LEVITES.

CHUMASH   See PENTATEUCH

CHUPPAH   See MARRIAGE

CIRCUMCISION   (Heb. *berit milah;* lit. "covenant of circumcision"). The removal of part or all of the foreskin that covers the glans of the penis. In Judaism, circumcision is performed on the eighth day of a male baby's life, providing he is in good health. The procedure is carried out by a properly qualified professional, called a *mohel,* who is an observant Jew highly trained in both the Jewish legal and medical aspects. Males who undergo CONVERSION TO JUDAISM are also circumcised as a sign of entering the COVENANT. If they have already been circumcised, a drop of blood is drawn ritually from the place of the circumcision.

Circumcision is a sign of the covenant between God and the descendants of ABRAHAM. We read in the Bible: "God said

Ritual circumcision implements and book of rules and prayers for circumcision. Germany, France, and Italy, 18ᵗʰ and 19ᵗʰ centuries.

to Abraham … such shall be the covenant between Me and you and your offspring to follow which you shall keep; every male among you shall be circumcised. You shall circumcise the flesh of your foreskin, and that shall be the sign of the covenant between Me and you. Throughout the generations, every male among you shall be circumcised at the age of eight days. Thus my covenant shall be marked in your flesh …" (Gen. 17:10–13). The Bible also reports that "Abraham was 99 years old when he circumcised the flesh of his foreskin, and his son Ishmael was 13 years old when he was circumcised" (Gen. 17:24–25).

Several other Bible stories focus on circumcision. When Shechem wants to marry Jacob's daughter, Dinah, her brothers object: "We cannot do this thing, to give our sister to a man who is uncircumcised, for that is a disgrace among us" (Gen. 34). In another story, Zipporah, the wife of Moses, "took a flint and cut off her son's foreskin" (Ex. 4). When Joshua brought the Israelites into the Land of Israel, he was commanded by God: "Make flint knives and proceed with a second circumcision of the Israelites" (Josh. 5). The term was also used symbolically in the Bible: "circumcision of the heart" (Deut. 10:16, 30:6; Jer. 4:4) was of a spiritual nature.

In the time of the Maccabees (see HASMONEANS) many Jews became ashamed of this practice, because it made them different from the Greek majority population in the bathhouses and sports arenas (see HELLENISM). Some Jews even tried to hide or reverse their circumcision, but the Greek king, Antiochus Epiphanes, forbade that practice. Centuries later, the Roman emperor outlawed circumcision, which set off the BAR KOKHBA revolt (132–135 CE).

This Jewish religious ceremony is performed even if the baby's eighth day falls on the SABBATH, a FESTIVAL, or the DAY OF ATONEMENT. As the ceremony is about to begin, the godmother (in Yiddish, *k'vatrin*) takes the baby from the mother and hands him to the godfather (SANDAK), who will have the honor of holding him during the ceremony on the special Chair of ELIJAH. The circumcision itself takes only a few seconds. When it is finished, a special blessing is said over a cup of wine, the baby is given some wine on a piece of cotton to calm him down, and the child receives his Jewish NAME. The ceremony, which can take place in a synagogue or at home, is followed by a festive meal.

Circumcision is observed by all Jews. In Reform Judaism, a doctor sometimes performs the procedure instead of a *mohel.* Female circumcision has never been a part of Judaism, and is in fact forbidden. A baby girl is traditionally welcomed into the covenant when her father is called to the READING OF THE LAW shortly after her birth. In recent years, many families have a SIMHAT BAT ceremony for their new daughters.

CITIES OF REFUGE   See ASYLUM

CIVIL MARRIAGE   According to Jewish law, MARRIAGE must be carried out "in accordance with the laws of Moses and Israel." Therefore, when a couple has a civil rather than a religious ceremony, the question of whether they are really married in the eyes of Jewish law must be addressed. If they are considered Jewishly married, then a Jewish bill of DIVORCE (*get*) is needed to end the marriage; if they are not considered married under Jewish law, then no *get* is needed to dissolve the union.

In general, Jewish law assumes that no man would want his acts of sexual intercourse to take place outside of marriage. In addition, sexual relations are one way to bring about a valid Jewish marriage. Therefore, any woman a man lives with could be considered to have become his wife with their first act of sexual intercourse.

Whether or not Jewish marriage actually occurs through the first act of intercourse has been a matter of debate among the greatest rabbis throughout the centuries. Some argue that those who choose a civil marriage do so because they have no interest in a Jewish marriage. Even so, a *get* is still traditionally required, just in case a valid Jewish marriage was created.

There are no civil marriages in Israel, where all marriages are conducted according to the religion of the bride and groom. There have been attempts to change this policy in favor of the option to allow civil marriage. Civil marriages that take place outside of Israel are recognized by the Jewish state.

CODIFICATION OF JEWISH LAW   Collections of halakhic (Jewish legal) rulings that are arranged in a clear and orderly manner (see HALAKHAH). They are an important part of halakhic literature. Codes are designed as guides to religious practice for laymen as well as for rabbis. They are generally made up of both civil and religious law and include moral as well as legal instruction. Law codes are based on TORAH law as interpreted by the rabbis of the MISHNAH and TALMUD.

The earliest rabbinic codes, called *halakhot*, were compiled in the first and second centuries CE under the leadership of Rabbi JUDAH HA-NASI. They were arranged either according to subject matter in the Mishnah and TOSEFTA, or according to the order of the laws as they appear in the Bible text in the MIDRASH HALAKHAH (see also MEKHILTA; SIFRA; SIFREI).

Law codes were not composed during Talmud times (third to sixth centuries), but a number appeared shortly afterwards, during the period of the *ge'onim* (see GAON). These codes organized the many legal decisions of the Talmud, which were usually not presented in an orderly fashion. The *She'iltot* of the eighth century Babylonian scholar AHAI OF SHABHA, the *Halakhot Pesukot* of YEHUDAI Gaon, and the HALAKHOT GEDOLOT of Simeon Kayyara are important examples. In his introduction, Kayyara lists the 613 commandments for the first time (see COMMANDMENTS, 613).

The later *ge'onim* (850–1000) published halakhic codes that each focused on a particular subject. Examples include the PRAYER BOOKS of AMRAM GAON and SAADIAH GAON, which also contained laws about prayer; Saadiah's many works on such subjects as legal contracts, INHERITANCE, VOWS, and DIETARY LAWS; and the *Sefer Mekah u-Memkar* ("Book of Buying and Selling") of HAI Gaon.

Isaac ALFASI, a Spanish authority, produced a code that followed the order of subjects in the Babylonian Talmud. He included only those parts of the Talmud that presented a practical legal decision and often added the comments of the *ge'onim*. His work, *Hilkhot ha-Rif,* soon became the standard law code for Sephardi Jewry. About two centuries later, ASHER BEN JEHIEL issued a code similar in style and importance for the Ashkenazi world called *Hilkhot* (or *Piskei,* "legal decisions of") *ha-Rosh* (see SEPHARDIM and ASHKENAZIM). Dozens of digests of Jewish law for Ashkenazim followed throughout the centuries, including those of ELEAZAR OF WORMS, Simhah Vitry, and Moses ben Jacob of Coucy.

The most authoritative law code for Sephardi Jews, the MISHNEH TORAH (completed 1185), was written by Moses MAIMONIDES ("*Rambam*" for short). It was, and remains to this day, the most complete and systematic collection of Jewish law ever written. A large number of commentaries by other experts have since been written on it.

Another classic code, the *Arba'ah Turim* (*Tur* for short) or "Four Rows" of JACOB BEN ASHER (the son of Asher ben Jehiel), appeared in the 16th century. It deals with all categories of law, except those concerning the TEMPLE, which had been destroyed. The *Tur* became the basis for the best-known code, the SHULHAN ARUKH ("Set Table") by Joseph CARO, written for the Sephardi world. Since many differences in custom and observance had arisen between Sephardi and Ashkenazi Jews, Moses ISSERLES of Cracow ("*Rema*" for short) wrote a commentary on the *Shulhan Arukh* for Ashkenazim, which he called *Mappah* ("Tablecloth"). He mostly followed the rulings of Maimonides' *Mishneh Torah.* Together the *Shulhan Arukh* and the *Mappah* became the accepted law codes for use by rabbis throughout the Jewish world.

Digests of Jewish law for particular communities, as well as those written on the level of the layman, continued to appear. Solomon Ganzfried of Hungary wrote a brief law handbook called *Kitsur* ("Shortened") *Shulhan Arukh,* which became extremely popular. The *Mishnah Berurah* ("Clear Code") by Israel Meir ha-Cohen Kagan (better known as the HAFETS HAYYIM) clarified the rulings of the *Shulhan Arukh* on the laws of PRAYER, the SABBATH, and FESTIVALS. Law codes with subjects arranged in alphabetical order first appeared in modern times; for example, the *Entsiklopedia Talmudit* ("Talmudic Encyclopedia"), published in Jerusalem.

COHEN, HERMANN   (1842–1918). German philosopher and interpreter of Judaism. At first he studied to be a rabbi, but then he turned to philosophy. In 1876, Cohen became professor of philosophy at the University of Marburg and remained there until he retired in 1912. He then continued teaching in Berlin.

Cohen established the "Marburg School" of philosophy, which taught about the dignity of man. He also engaged in defending Judaism (see APOLOGETICS AND POLEMICS) against those who accused the Talmud and Jewish law of being "racist," since they concern only Jews. Cohen defended the Chosen People idea by saying that Judaism's real goal is to unite all humanity by establishing God's kingdom on earth.

In his earlier years, Cohen felt that ethical behavior was the central idea in Judaism. Later in his life, he began to view faith in God as crucial for the individual Jew. He believed that people should strive to imitate God as much as possible, in an effort to live a holy life. The Jewish people could bring the MESSIAH more quickly by striving to be God-like, keeping the commandments, and living as a model community. Cohen therefore rejected ZIONISM, because he held that the Jews needed to do their spiritual work among the other peoples of the world.

COMMANDMENTS, TEN   See TEN COMMANDMENTS

COMMANDMENTS, THE 613   (Heb. *Taryag Mitzvot*). The laws recorded in the PENTATEUCH that God gave to MOSES, so that he could give them to the Children of Israel. The commandments (see MITZVAH) were to be observed by the Israelites as their part of the COVENANT between GOD and His people. Rabbi Simlai said in the third century that they totaled 613, which included 365 negative (forbidden) actions – like the days in the solar year. There were 248 positive duties, which correspond to the number of "limbs" in the human body (*Mak.* 23b). These numbers were accepted and used widely by later halakhic (Jewish legal) authorities.

The rabbis divided the commandments into categories in several different ways. *Hukkim* ("statutes"; see Lev. 18:4–5) are ritual laws "between man and God" for which we have no logical explanation. Included are the DIETARY LAWS, concerning which animals may and may not be eaten, and the prohibition against wearing a mixture of linen and wool in one garment (Deut. 22:11; see SHA'ATNEZ). Even though human reason questions *hukkim*, the Bible warns: "I am the Lord. I have decreed them and you have no right to question them (Lev. 18:5). *Mishpatim* ("judgments"; see Lev. 18:4–5), on the other hand, are laws that apply to relations among human beings. These laws are rational, such as laws against murder and theft, and would be adopted by society even if God had not commanded them.

The rabbis also distinguished between commandments "dependent upon the Land" – such as AGRICULTURAL LAWS – and those not dependent upon being in Israel – such as the commandment to place a MEZUZAH on one's doorpost.

The rabbis discussed the category of "positive commandments observed at specific times" – such as SUKKAH and PRAYER with a MINYAN – and those not dependent upon time – such as saying the GRACE AFTER MEALS. Women were traditionally exempt from many of the commandments that had to be fulfilled at certain times, in order to free them to care for the home and family. Women were also exempted from such obligations as studying Torah, commandments dealing with SACRIFICES AND OFFERINGS, and the duties of a father to his son – such as CIRCUMCISION and teaching him TORAH (*Kid.* 34a–36a).

However, women may voluntarily perform commandments from which they are exempt, and many do today.

Commandments can also fall into categories according to the periods of history that they are in effect. In the Middle Ages, the rabbis made a distinction between commandments that are in effect only when the TEMPLE is standing and those that apply at all times. Others, such as the JUBILEE and laws concerning Jewish slaves (Ex. 21:6ff), ceased to apply once the Ten Tribes were exiled from the kingdom of ISRAEL.

Maimonides ("*Rambam*" for short; 12ᵗʰ cent.), the great halakhic expert, wrote *Sefer ha-Mitzvot* ("Book of Commandments") where he lists each commandment and briefly points out its source in the Bible and Talmud. About a century later, Nahmanides ("*Ramban*" for short) criticized Maimonides work in several important areas. Maimonides claims, for example, that prayer is a positive commandment as early as the Pentateuch; Nahmanides insists that the command to pray comes later, from the rabbis and not the Bible. On the other hand, Nahmanides rules that it is a positive – and extremely important – commandment for Jews to settle in the Land of Israel; Maimonides does not include settling in Israel on his list.

Another important listing of commandments appears in *Sefer ha-Hinnukh* ("Book of Education") by Aaron ha-Levi of Barcelona, Spain (13ᵗʰ cent.). He describes each commandment in the order that is appears in the Bible, including how it should be performed, who is obligated to fulfill it (men, women, priests, etc.), and when and where it is in effect. Ha-Levi follows the rulings of Maimonides. In the Ashkenazi world as well (see ASHKENAZIM and SEPHARDIM), many codes appeared throughout the centuries to help the laymen understand the commandments and how to follow them.

For the differences between biblical commandments and those from rabbinic texts, see HALAKHAH; see also MITZVAH.

COMMUNITY, JEWISH   Jews have been organized into social units for thousands of years. The very first such group was the ancient Hebrew clan, the family of ABRAHAM the patriarch. The Bible tells us that this clan grew to a nation made up of twelve TRIBES during its years in Egypt. When the Israelite people returned to the land of Canaan after wandering in the desert for 40 years (see EXODUS), they changed from nomadic (wandering) shepherds to farmers. They began to settle in towns and cities, with leaders called ELDERS. In ancient ISRAEL, the area of each tribe (see TRIBES, TWELVE) could include several towns.

During the time of the Babylonian EXILE, Jewish communities developed a number of self-governing organizations, including the SYNAGOGUE. It was not only a house of prayer but also a focus of community activities. It held a school for children and a study hall (BET MIDRASH) for adults. In the Roman Empire, Jews had their own courts (see BET DIN), and this independent legal system remained part of Jewish life for all the centuries that followed.

At the end of the Second Temple period (70 CE), the two

major Jewish communities in the world – Erets Israel and Babylonia – were each headed by a central authority. In both cases, the religious leaders were also the general rulers, since the daily life of Jews was tied to Jewish law (HALAKHAH). In each community, the local leadership established such institutions as synagogues, law courts, schools, charitable organizations, and ritual baths.

In Central Europe during the Middle Ages, Jewish communities were led by the outstanding rabbi in the region. The Jews tended to live in a "Jewish quarter" of towns, where they followed the *halakhah*. As in Babylonia, each community had a good number of institutions that looked after all aspects of religious and communal life. The Jewish community collected its own taxes, both those needed for its own use and those that it handed over to the government. Special funds were set up for such purposes as the ransoming of CAPTIVES; caring for the SICK, the AGED, and WIDOWS; providing HOSPITALITY for visitors to town; providing the DOWRY for a poor bride; and supervising Jewish BURIAL. The synagogue was the community's center, but not only for prayer. It also housed the school, court, adult study hall, ritual bath, and even a "dance hall" for celebrations.

The court was staffed by religious judges (see DAYYAN). They could fine those who violated religious or communal laws or perhaps issue a ban of EXCOMMUNICATION for more serious crimes. The ability to carry out a death sentence was extremely rare (see CAPITAL PUNISHMENT). It was only considered in the case of Jews who informed against the community to outside enemies. In Poland-Lithuania, the Council of the Four Lands was a central body with elected representatives who governed all the Jewish communities in a wide region.

Seal of the Rousinov Community, Moravia, 19th–20th century. The inscription reads: "Gemeinde Neuraussnitz".

The Ottoman Empire recognized a chief rabbi (HAKHAM BASHI) as the Jewish community's representative in each province of the Empire.

This traditional pattern of close-knit, independent Jewish communities changed considerably when EMANCIPATION opened up the secular world to Jews in the 18th century. Once Jews were granted civil rights in Europe, their membership in the Jewish community became voluntary. They could choose, for example, whether to bring disputes to a Jewish religious court or to the general court of the country in which they lived. Napolean set up a central Jewish governing body called the "Grand Sanhedrin" in Paris (1807). It was not independent, however; it had to answer to the French government (see CONSISTORY).

Today many organizations supervise and coordinate work in all areas of Jewish communal life. Worldwide umbrella organizations, such as rabbinical councils and synagogue associations, unite similar bodies the world over. In Israel, caring for the social needs of citizens is the responsibility of the government, and programs are funded by taxes. In the Diaspora, all Jewish communal organizations are voluntary, in terms of who supports them and who uses their services. Yet they still serve similar needs among Jews in the modern world – caring for the sick, elderly, and poor; assisting Jews in danger; education; synagogues; burial services; etc. – as they have in Jewish communities for the past two thousand years.

CONCLUDING SERVICE (DAY OF ATONEMENT)   See NE'ILAH

CONFESSION   (Heb. *viddu'i*). Admitting that one has committed a SIN. This is the first step in seeking FORGIVENESS and ATONEMENT for improper behavior. True confession has several steps: admitting guilt (the act of confession itself), feeling regret and undergoing REPENTANCE for the wrong, apologizing to the injured party, and resolving never to repeat the sin. There are many examples of confession in the Bible. The stories of CAIN (Gen. 4:13), Judah (Gen. 38:36), SAUL (I Sam. 15:24), and DAVID (II Sam. 12:13) are some of the best-known. When bringing a SACRIFICE in the TEMPLE for an accidental sin, the person confessed the sin while placing his or her hands on the head of the animal to be sacrificed. While the Temple still stood, the HIGH PRIEST confessed the sins of all of the people during the DAY OF ATONEMENT.

Since the Temple's destruction (1st cent. CE) each person confesses directly to God; it is not the function of a priest or other leader to hear the confession. If the sin was against a human being, the sinner must confess to that person and pay for any damages before turning to God for forgiveness.

During prayers on the Day of Atonement, each worshiper recites two series of confessions. The short one is called ASHAMNU, and the long one is AL HET. Both are written as alphabetical ACROSTICS. The alphabetical form helped people remember the list of sins more easily before prayer books were widely available. Also, by including each letter of the Hebrew alphabet, it is as if the sinner is asking forgiveness for all possible sins "from A to Z." The confession is in the plural ("For the sins *we* committed…") to show that "all Jews are responsible for one another" (*Sanh.* 16b).

It is also a custom for a bridegroom to say the confession series during the AFTERNOON SERVICE just before the wedding. This is because the new couple is starting a new life together, and they want to begin it with a "clean slate." Confession is also said by or for a person who is near DEATH.

CONFIRMATION Public ceremony in which young people in their teens confirm their commitment to Judaism and the Jewish community. It is found mostly in non-Orthodox English-speaking congregations.

In Judaism the practice began in the first decade of the 19th century in Westphalia (now Germany). It was thought of as an addition to the BAR MITZVAH ceremony, which some felt takes place when a child is too young to really reaffirm commitment to Judaism. One of its purposes is to keep students in the religious school beyond the age of bar or BAT MITZVAH.

Today confirmation is usually a group ceremony for boys and girls about 15 years old who have completed a course of study in a congregational high school. The ceremony is usually held in the synagogue, and the content of the program varies considerably from congregation to congregation. In some synagogue schools, the confirmation class concludes with a trip to Israel.

CONGREGATION see KEHILLAH

CONSECRATION The act of making something or someone holy. It may be performed by God, or it may require human action. In the Bible, we read in the CREATION story that "God blessed the seventh day and made it holy" (Gen. 2:3). This shows that the consecration of the SABBATH day was a Divine act. On the other hand, since human beings set the CALENDAR according to the cycles of the MOON, the consecration of the FESTIVALS is a human act.

Various people or groups of people were also consecrated. The FIRSTBORN of Israel were consecrated to serve in the SANCTUARY (Ex. 13:2); later the Levites took their place. AARON was consecrated as HIGH PRIEST of Israel (Ex. 28:41), by means of ANOINTING his head with oil. Different items used in the Sanctuary were also anointed, by having oil poured over them (Ex. 40), in order to consecrate them.

Once the TEMPLE was destroyed, however, only three forms of consecration remained in Jewish life: that of a new SYNAGOGUE, a new CEMETERY, and a new home. None of these practices follow specific laws, but rather take place according to CUSTOM. In the case of a synagogue, the SCROLLS OF THE LAW are usually brought into the new prayer hall with music and dancing and are paraded around the room (see HAKKAFOT). Synagogue members hold a festive party and say

the SHE-HEHEYANU blessing, which thanks God for allowing them to reach this milestone.

When a new cemetery is consecrated, special prayers asking for FORGIVENESS are added to the morning service, and members of the BURIAL SOCIETY observe a fast. All present walk around the cemetery and say a prayer asking that no evil befall anyone and that there be no more death (i.e., because the MESSIAH arrives to bring a new world order).

The consecration of a new home is known in Hebrew as *hanukkat ha-bayit* ("Dedication of the Home"). A MEZUZAH is placed on the doorpost with a BENEDICTION and the *She-heheyanu* prayer is said. A festive meal is then usually served. If one moves into a new home in Israel, this meal is traditionally required – considered a MITZVAH – since settling the Land of Israel is a *mitzvah*.

CONSERVATIVE JUDAISM Religious movement that was born in the mid-19th century. It began when Zacharias FRANKEL, head of the Jewish Theological Seminary (a rabbinical school) in Breslau, Germany, found that he could no longer identify with either "old-fashioned" ORTHODOXY or modern REFORM JUDAISM. Frankel called for a more middle-of-the-road approach that would: keep traditions central to Judaism, adapt HALAKHAH (Jewish law) somewhat to the times, and relate to traditional Jewish texts with a modern approach. He wished to preserve tradition and encourage its growth. He also strongly favored the idea of establishing a Jewish homeland long before political ZIONISM even came into being.

The Jewish Theological Seminary of America was founded in 1886 by rabbis and scholars who supported Frankel's views. Solomon SCHECHTER became its president in 1902 and strengthened an institution that had nearly fallen apart. He brought outstanding scholars, such as Louis GINZBERG, to teach there. This made the Seminary one of the leading centers of Jewish scholarship in the Western world and the jewel of the Conservative movement. Seminary rabbis shaped Conservative belief with their scholarly, historical approach to understanding the development of Jewish life and law.

Schechter also founded several other organizations to meet the needs of the rapidly growing American Jewish community. In 1913 the United Synagogue became an umbrella organization of synagogues. It was Schechter's dream that his movement would serve all of the Jewish people and that it would promote Jewish unity. Although not all Jews – or even all American Jews – joined the movement, Conservative Judaism includes a wide range of beliefs and practices. It is more open to variety of expression and belief than are the other movements. Many of the large numbers of Jews who had immigrated from Eastern Europe found this quite suitable. Reform Judaism was foreign to them, and many were no longer able to uphold the strict ways of Orthodoxy. They appreciated the traditional feel of the synagogue in a congregation that did not expect a particular level of personal observance.

The Conservative movement grew rapidly after World War II.

With Louis FINKELSTEIN heading the Seminary, a West Coast Seminary – the University of Judaism in Los Angeles – opened in 1947. As Jews flocked to the suburbs, hundreds of new synagogues joined the United Synagogue. The Rabbinical Assembly had rabbis serving all over the world. The movement's own summer camp organization, Ramah, set the standard for creative Jewish camping in America. Other organizations that sprung up included United Synagogue Youth (USY), radio programs ("Eternal Light"), TV programs ("Frontiers of Faith"), the Solomon Schechter Day Schools, and New York's Jewish Museum. The Conservative movement has also published its own PRAYER BOOKS, HAGGADAH, and BIBLE COMMENTARY. The Rabbinical Assembly's Committee on Jewish Law and Standards ("Law Committee") makes innovations in Jewish law, but these are usually not accepted by the Orthodox world. Even within the Conservative movement, each rabbi is given great leeway in bringing Law Committee decisions into the congregation.

The Seminary became much more liberal under Gerson D. Cohen (1972–1985). The most important changes took place in the area of the status of WOMEN in public worship. By 1955, women could be called to the READING OF THE LAW in congregations that accepted this ruling. From 1973 women were counted in a prayer quorum (MINYAN). From 1983 women were admitted to the Seminary for rabbinical study, and the first woman rabbi was ordained in 1985. This issue threatened to split the movement, and indeed a small group of more traditional Conservative Jews formed the Union for Traditional Judaism by 1990. In recent years, most Conservative rabbis have accepted equality of women in all aspects of Jewish life. This has set the movement even further apart from Orthodoxy.

Summary of Conservative belief:
1. Judaism is a seamless mix of religion and nationhood, which has evolved from biblical times to the present day.
2. It is organized as a system of *mitzvot* that cover all aspects of human life and conduct as well as relationships among individuals and between humans and God.
3. Jewish law (*halakhah*) is flexible enough to meet the needs of modern people when interpreted creatively by knowledgeable, committed rabbinic authorities.
4. There is room within *halakhah* for change and for different opinions.
5. The modern scientific and historical approach to Jewish study is a positive development that helps us to make Judaism as creative today as it was in the past.

CONSISTORY   (Fr. *Consistoire*). A state-controlled Jewish communal organization that was first established by Napoleon in France (1808). Its purpose was to make French Jews "useful citizens" of France. The year before, Napoleon called together 71 leaders of the French Jewish community to form a "Great Sanhedrin," like the ancient SANHEDRIN that had once been the ruling body of the Jews in Erets Israel. The French "Great Sanhedrin" followed Napoleon's wishes and ruled that the religious teachings of Judaism were valid forever, but that the "political" laws – those that established the Jews as a nation – would no longer be in effect. Jews would no longer be allowed to have their own courts or to perform marriages and divorces within the Jewish community, as they had in the past. Marriages between Jews and non-Jews would be legal in France. Although Judaism was made an "official religion of France," Jews suffered from a series of laws that discriminated against them financially as well as nationally. The effect of these rulings was that many Jews lost their connection with traditional observance. Many were lost to Judaism through ASSIMILATION or APOSTASY.

Consistories were set up in many parts of France, and later in Belgium, Luxembourg, and Algeria. In each place, their purpose was to move control of Jewish community affairs into the hands of the government. Today, they still remain in Belgium and Luxembourg.

CONVERSION TO JUDAISM   (Heb. *giyyur*). The official adoption by a non-Jew of Jewish religion, observances and nationhood. This takes place when the non-Jew makes the decision to adopt the Jewish faith and religious practices and then undergoes the rituals of conversion in the presence of a BET DIN (Jewish religious court), which accepts the person into the Jewish nation. Judaism does not encourage conversion and respects the status of all non-Jews who follow the basic seven NOACHIDE LAWS. Thus, non-Jews who sincerely choose to take the large step of changing their religious and ethnic identity to a Jewish one are to be welcomed into the Jewish fold as *gerei tsedek* (righteous converts).

It is important that potential converts undergo an educational process to ensure that they are really interested in being Jewish. They are also given the basic tools necessary to live a Jewish life. Education programs vary from place to place and from community to community. Minimally, some of the major and some of the minor COMMANDMENTS must be taught. At the beginning of the process, converts must traditionally be discouraged with at least three warnings: (1) they will be joining a people with a history of persecution; (2) there will be many forbidden activities, such as performing work on the Sabbath and eating certain foods; (3) relationships with their own family may become very strained. Only once the candidate shows determination to become Jewish is conversion then encouraged. Once the conversion takes place, Jewish status becomes permanent, and the convert receives all of the responsibilities and privileges of a full-fledged Jew. Only children who were converted by their parents may opt out of their Judaism when they reach the age of BAR MITZVAH or BAT MITZVAH.

The basic rituals of conversion for a male are CIRCUMCISION and immersion in a MIKVEH (ritual bath). If the man is already circumcised, a small drop of blood is drawn from the penis to symbolize entering the "covenant of Abraham." Females are required only to immerse in the *mikveh*, which brings about an increase in holiness for converts of both sexes. At the time of the Temple, the convert was also required to bring a sacrifice.

Conversion has a long history in Judaism. According to the MIDRASH, ABRAHAM used to encourage men to join his new religion, and his wife, SARAH, approached the women. RUTH the Moabitess, who declared "your people are my people and your God is my God" is the model convert and the great-grandmother of King DAVID. One of the only forced conversions recorded in Jewish history was carried out in the second century BCE by John Hyrcanus. He forced the Edomites (Idumeans) to convert, and they eventually became loyal Jews. Another mass conversion took place many centuries later, when the Khazars converted.

In the Talmud we see some variety of opinion about the benefits of accepting converts to Judaism. In fact, the statement that "converts are as hard for the people of Israel to endure as is a sore" is interpreted in several ways (*Yev.* 47b). Some feared that converts could dilute the strength and purity of the Jewish people. Others argued that converts were often so careful and enthusiastic in their observance of Jewish law that they put other Jews to shame. In general, however, the rabbis recommended that Jews "not close the door" before potential converts. Indeed, large numbers of people at the time who were uncomfortable with the belief in many gods were attracted to Judaism, among them the grandparents of great rabbis.

Before the split between CHRISTIANITY and Judaism, early Christians (who still considered themselves Jews) accepted pagan converts to Judaism without requiring circumcision and immersion in a *mikveh*. This was, in fact, one of the main reasons that the rabbis determined that the Christians had become a separate people and religion. Once Christianity became the official religion of the Roman Empire, conversion to Judaism became illegal. Several centuries later, when Muslims conquered country after country, ISLAM also forbade conversion to Judaism.

ORTHODOXY will only accept converts to Judaism if their religious motivation is genuine. They must be prepared to lead a lifestyle that is fully observant of the commandments. Conversions performed by REFORM or CONSERVATIVE rabbis are not recognized in the Orthodox world, and the children of such female converts are not considered Jewish. While Conservative rabbis require the traditional rituals of conversion (circumcision and *mikveh*), they often perform conversions because of marriage to a Jewish spouse – an insufficient reason for conversion in Orthodoxy. Most Reform rabbis do not require the traditional rituals of conversion, but rather a course of study and a commitment ceremony. The differences in standards for conversion among the major religious movements is a serious issue.

CONVERSOS   See MARRANOS

CORDOVERO, MOSES   (1522–1570). Mystic (see MYSTICISM, JEWISH). He was born into a family of Spanish origin that lived in Safed, in the Land of Israel. He worked with R. Joseph CARO and may have taught Isaac LURIA, who arrived in Safed in the year Cordovero died. His most important work is *Pardes*

Rimmonim ("Pomegranate Orchard"), one of the deepest works of KABBALAH. Cordovero presents the Kabbalah as a system and organizes its symbols into a sequence that maps out the mystical world. He calls the uppermost hidden aspect of God the EN-SOF and then describes a series of levels of Godliness that reach down through the heavens. He believed that God's presence was in everything in the universe.

Cordovero was a scholar of the ZOHAR and wrote an important commentary on that major mystical work called *Or Yakar* ("Precious Light"). However, Cordovero brought his own original ideas to the *Zohar*'s teachings. He also wrote an ethical work that linked mystical beliefs to man's everyday moral behavior. Cordovero called for man to act as much as possible in IMITATION OF GOD in his ethical behavior.

CORPSE   Attending to the dead is considered the most selfless COMMANDMENT in the TORAH. Since humans were created in the image of God, the body must be honored and respected, even after DEATH. From the moment of death until BURIAL, the body must not be left alone. A *shomer* ("watcher") sits nearby reading PSALMS. The eyes and mouth of the deceased are closed, and the body is covered with a sheet. Burial traditionally takes place within a day of death. Just before burial, the body is washed and dressed in white garments by a *hevrah kaddisha* ("holy fellowship") of religious people, in a ceremony called TOHORAH ("ritual purification"). It is considered an especially important MITZVAH to attend to the body of a person with no relatives or to an unidentified corpse (*met mitzvah*).

Contact with the corpse of either a human or an animal brings with it a state of ritual impurity (see PURITY, RITUAL). In times when the TEMPLE stood in Jerusalem, all those who had tended to the dead – even though this is a great *mitzvah* – had to undergo purification before they could enter the Temple. Today, the descendants of the PRIESTS avoid entering cemeteries for this reason.

COSTA, URIEL DA   (1585–1640). Free-thinker and radical Jewish philosopher. He was born in Oporto, Portugal, as Gabriel da Costa (or Acosta). His family was descended from MARRANOS, who were forced to convert to CHRISTIANITY. After studying the Bible and working for the Catholic Church, he began to reject the Catholic religion. He decided to return to Judaism and fled to Amsterdam with his mother and four brothers. There the family was able to practice their Judaism openly.

Within a short while, Da Costa angered local rabbis by openly calling for the practice of "biblical" Judaism. He claimed that all the rabbinic development of HALAKHAH (Jewish law) that took place since Bible times was irrelevant. He refused to practice the ORAL LAW set down by the rabbis and also questioned accepted Jewish belief in the immortality of the soul (see AFTERLIFE). When his writings were published in 1624, the rabbis put him under a ban of EXCOMMUNICATION. He was accepted back into the community nine years later, but remained firm in his views.

He continued to reject rabbinic laws and began to challenge the Divine origin of the Bible itself. He wrote in his autobiography: "I began to ask myself whether the law of Moses should be considered the law of God, and I concluded that it was nothing more than human invention." He was again placed under a ban, which his own family upheld, and was punished by the rabbinic court (see BET DIN) with 39 lashes in an Amsterdam synagogue. This public humiliation eventually led him to commit suicide. His radical thinking later became the basis of the philosophy of SPINOZA.

COURT OF LAW   See BET DIN

COVENANT   (Heb. *berit*). An agreement or contract between two parties. There are many examples of covenants in the Bible. God tells NOAH of His plans to destroy all life on earth. However He makes a covenant with Noah that he and his family will be saved in the ark that Noah builds (Gen. 6:18). After the FLOOD, God makes a covenant with humanity, saying that He will never again destroy all life by a flood (Gen. 9:8). Covenants were also made between individuals (e.g., Gen. 21:28; Josh. 9:15).

Making a covenant usually involved a ceremonial act, such as eating a meal and making an oath (Gen. 26:26–33); passing between pieces of cut-up animals (Gen. 15:7–21; Jer. 34:18); or creation of a symbol, such as a rainbow, as when God promised never again to destroy the earth with a flood (Gen. 9:13).

Three covenants have been especially important in the Bible and in Jewish history: the "Covenant Between the Pieces," the covenant of CIRCUMCISION, and the covenant at SINAI.

The Covenant Between the Pieces   (Gen. 15:7–21). When Abraham asks God how he can be sure that he will inherit the land of CANAAN, God tells him to take several animals and to cut them in half. After Abraham arranges them in two rows on the ground, God promises Abraham that his descendants will inherit the land from "the river of Egypt to the great river Euphrates," but that the people will first undergo a long period of exile (i.e the slavery in Egypt; see EXODUS). A "flaming torch," which represents God, then passes between the animal parts to seal the covenant.

The Covenant of Circumcision   (Gen. 17). God appears to Abraham when he is 99 years old and promises to make His everlasting covenant with him. He then commands Abraham to circumcise himself and all male family members and slaves as a sign of the covenant. Abraham obeys, and from then on every newborn male child is to be circumcised at the age of eight days. This is a sign of his entering the Jewish people's covenant with God.

The Covenant at Sinai   (Ex. 19–24). The covenant at Sinai is a renewal and expansion of Abraham's covenant with God. It is the only example in the Ancient Near East of a covenant made between the Diety and an entire people. It serves as the basis for the everlasting relationship between God and the Jewish people.

About three months after the Exodus from Egypt, the children of Israel arrive at Mount Sinai. MOSES goes up the mountain and returns with a decree from God to establish a covenant with the people. It calls for the children of Israel to obey God's commandments. God will then consider them to be special among all other peoples, a holy nation, and a kingdom of priests. The people agree, and God reveals (see REVELATION) Himself to them as He gives them the TEN COMMANDMENTS. The people are absolutely terrified by the thunder, lightning, storm clouds and other expressions of God's presence. They demand that Moses receive the rest of the laws on their behalf, because they are too frightened to remain before God. Moses then returns to heaven to record the many additional laws, which are then submitted to the people for confirmation before the convent is sealed.

The idea of a covenant remained central in Jewish thought throughout history. God is seen as calling upon the Jewish people to be loyal to Him and to live according to the ritual and moral principles given at Sinai. In modern times, Orthodox thinker Rabbi Joseph Baer SOLOVEICHIK wrote that the covenant at Sinai had two basic parts. The first, the "Exodus from Egypt Covenant," binds all Jews to their shared history, suffering, and responsibility to the nation. The second, the "Sinai Covenant," makes following Jewish law central to Jewish life. REFORM thinker Eugene Borowitz believes that each generation can change the details of the covenant in keeping with modern conditions, as long as it remains true to the original spirit of the covenant.

COVERING THE HEAD   (Heb. *kissu'i rosh*). The Bible does not require any form of head covering for ordinary people, although the HIGH PRIEST wore a special cloth turban (Ex. 28:4, 29:6, etc.), and other PRIESTS wore a ceremonial cap (Ex. 28:40, 29:9; Lev. 8:13). In TEMPLE times, only those of high rank seemed to have covered their heads, as was the local custom.

In the Talmud, a variety of views are expressed about head coverings. In one, head covering for Jewish males was a matter of custom and therefore optional (*Ned.* 30b). Others were offended by bareheadedness, and some would not walk two paces bareheaded, since the presence of God is always above (*Kid.* 31a; *Shab.* 118b). The question of Jewish males praying bareheaded remained a hotly debated issue for many centuries. However, the sages all agreed that a married woman must not display the "crowning beauty" of her hair.

From the Middle Ages onward, most rabbis throughout the Jewish world considered covering the head a sign of love and respect for God, while bareheadedness was a sign of taking one's religion too lightly. In Christian Europe, where praying with the head uncovered was the norm, rabbis saw bareheadedness as an imitation of non-Jews and completely rejected it. It soon became Jewish CUSTOM for males to cover the head while praying, attending SYNAGOGUE, studying TORAH, and reciting BENEDICTIONS before and after eating. From the 18th century, the custom among Jewish men in Europe to wear a skullcap (Heb. *kippah*; Yid. *yarmulka*) at all times became so strong that it took on the force of law.

Modern Jewish movements, beginning in the 19th century, began to abandon or limit the use of a head covering. In REFORM JUDAISM, it was rejected altogether at first. However, some Reform Jews today (men as well as women) cover their heads for religious activities. In CONSERVATIVE JUDAISM, men and women usually cover their heads for religious activities but otherwise do not. In Orthodox circles, men cover their heads with a skullcap or hat at all times, and women do the same with a wig, hat, or scarf.

While the covering of a man's head is generally viewed as a pious (religious) act, the covering of a married woman's head has always been seen as a sign of her modesty. In Bible and Temple times, uncovering a woman's head in public was a humiliation (Isa. 3:17; Num. 5:18). Single girls were exempt from these rules, and the law was also less strict about uncovering a woman's hair at home. From the Middle Ages, fancy head coverings were worn by fashion-conscious women. The use of a wig first became fashionable among Ashkenazi women in the 18th century. Some rabbis objected, saying that the beauty of some of the wigs did not protect a woman's modesty. However, the practice of wearing wigs among Hasidic women – sometimes with a hat added – is very widespread (see HASIDISM).

COVETOUSNESS The inability to master one's cravings for the property of others. Envy and greed are moral SINS that are prohibited by the TEN COMMANDMENTS (Ex. 20:14; Deut. 5:18). The rabbis observed that envy and covetousness lead to other sins, therefore to violate the commandment against coveting is like violating the entire TORAH (*Pesikta Rabbati* 107a). Jewish ethical writers throughout Jewish history have therefore stressed the importance of building a just and civilized society in which people will be content with what they have and not covet others' lands, possessions, or spouses.

CREATION The origin of the universe is described at the beginning of the Bible, in the first two chapters of GENESIS. The belief that GOD created the heavens and the earth and all that is in them is one of the most important ideas in Judaism.

The Bible There are two descriptions of the creation of the

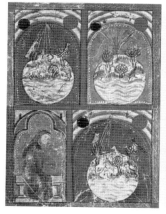

The creation of the world. Miniature from the Sarajevo Haggadah, *Spain, c. 1400.*

heaven and the earth in the Bible. In the first (Gen. 1:1–2:4), God creates the universe in six days and rests on the seventh. After each day of creating, we read that "God saw that it was good; and there was evening and there was morning…" – and then the number of the day is given. The high point of creation, humankind, is announced by the ANGELS on the sixth day: "Let us make man in our image, after our likeness" (Gen. 1:26). God creates human beings "in the image of God, male and female." God blesses the man and woman to "be fruitful and multiply, fill the earth and master it; and rule the fish of the sea, the birds of the sky, and all the living things …" (Gen. 1:28). Then, having finished the creation, God rested from His creative work on the seventh day, and He blessed this day and made it holy (see SABBATH).

In the second account of creation (Gen. 2:4–24), the ground is watered by an underground flow of water. A man is formed from the earth and brought to life by the breath of God. When none of the animals appear to be a suitable mate for the man, he is made to fall asleep, and a woman is created for him from his rib. The man and woman are then placed in the Garden of EDEN to tend it. (See also EVOLUTION.)

In Other Near Eastern Cultures Other peoples in the Ancient Near East have recorded creation stories that share elements with the Bible's account. In Ancient Egyptian stories, for example, the first man was created in the image of his creator god. In the Babylonian story, *Enuma Elish*, creation of heaven and earth is carried out by making a separation between waters, as in the Bible. The creation of heavens, land, sun, moon, stars, man, and then rest by the Divine creator follow the same order in both the Bible and Babylonian writings. Unlike the traditions of other peoples, however, the Bible's view is that One all-powerful God (and not a host of warring gods) created the entire universe and gave man the important role of ruling over it.

Rabbinic Literature In the time of the MISHNAH and TALMUD, creation came to be seen as a great mystery that one should not really try to explore. In the Mishnah we read: "Why does

---

THE CREATION OF THE WORLD ACCORDING TO GENESIS I

DAY ONE:	Light, Day, and Night
DAY TWO:	Sky
DAY THREE:	Land, Seas, and Vegetation
DAY FOUR:	Sun, Moon, and Stars
DAY FIVE:	Sea Creatures and Birds
DAY SIX:	Land Animals and Humans
DAY SEVEN:	Sabbath Rest

the story of creation begin with the [Hebrew] letter *bet*? Just as the letter *bet* is closed on three sides and only open in the front, you are not permitted to ask questions about what came before or what is behind it, but only from the actual time of creation" (TJ, *Hag.* 77c). Rabbi AKIVA insisted that the world was created by God out of nothing, a view which challenged the thinking of other groups at the time. In later Talmud times, the prohibitions against discussing and exploring the nature of creation were relaxed.

Kabbalah   The Kabbalah, or Jewish mystical tradition (see MYSTICISM, JEWISH), insists that there can be no knowledge of God without thinking deeply about the creation. Since God is hidden and unknowable, we can gather hints of God's ways only by viewing the "evidence" of His nature, which is revealed in the created world. Even so, God's decision to enter into the world through creation remains a constant mystery to man. Did God create by moving outside of Himself, as some believed? Did He, on the other hand, create by collapsing into Himself, and thereby leaving "room" for the universe? In Isaac LURIA's kabbalistic system, the creative process involved "the breaking of the vessels," which scattered sparks of holiness throughout the world. The job of the mystic is to gather up these sparks and return them to their proper places, which will bring perfection to the world (see TIKKUN).

Modern Times   Few modern Jewish thinkers take the Bible's account of creation literally. Franz ROSENZWEIG saw the root of God's love for man in that He created humankind as well as the universe. God therefore involves Himself in man's life (see REVELATION). Martin BUBER saw creation as "communication between Creator and creature." Humankind is God's partner; people can complete the act of creation and work toward bringing about a more perfect world.

CREED   See BELIEF; FAITH; SHEMA; PRINCIPLES OF FAITH

CREMATION   Burning a CORPSE to ashes. According to traditional Judaism, cremation of human bodies is completely revolting and absolutely forbidden by Jewish law. Since the BODY was created in the image of God, it must be treated with tremendous respect and honor; cremation is viewed as just the opposite. Burial in the earth is a positive commandment, taken from the Bible: "For dust you are, and to dust you shall return" (Gen. 3:19). Cremation is mentioned occasionally in the Bible, but it is usually associated with human sacrifices (Deut. 12:31) or reserved for serious criminals (Gen 38:24; Lev. 20:14).

The rabbis ruled that cremation is forbidden; even if that was the last request of the person who died. Jewish law does not permit a rabbi, or any other Jew, to be present at a FUNERAL when the body is to be cremated. The family of a person who was cremated at his own request does not observe the laws of MOURNING. The practice in CONSERVATIVE JUDAISM is very much like that of ORTHODOXY in the case of cremation. REFORM JUDAISM, however, does permit rabbis to perform cremation ceremonies.

CRESCAS, HASDAI   (c. 1340–c. 1410). Spanish Jewish philosopher and community leader (Crown Rabbi of Aragon). He was one of a group of Jewish leaders who won the renewal of Jewish rights from the king of Aragon. Despite his close ties with the king, his son was murdered in anti-Jewish massacres in Barcelona in 1391.

Hasdai's most important work, "A Refutation of the Principles of Christians," was written in Spanish. Its aim was to explain to Jews who might be attracted to CHRISTIANITY that Christian beliefs made no sense. His other well-known work, *Or Adonai* ("The Light of the Lord"), was written in Hebrew. It is a clear explanation of Jewish FAITH, according to Hasdai's view. In most cases, he disagrees with the philosophy of MAIMONIDES on such questions as the nature of GOD, PROPHECY, and the TORAH. Hasdai also sets out certain "true opinions" that every properly believing Jew must hold. These include CREATION, IMMORTALITY, RESURRECTION, REWARD AND PUNISHMENT, MESSIAH, and the effectiveness of PRAYER. He is the only medieval Jewish philosopher who claimed that human FREE WILL is not complete in order to explain how God can know everything in advance.

CRYPTO-JEWS   see MARRANOS

CULI (HULI), JACOB   (c. 1685–1732). Rabbinic scholar and Judeo-Spanish author. Culi was born and educated in Jerusalem, but he later moved to Constantinople, where he served as a rabbinic judge (DAYYAN). The disastrous movement of the false MESSIAH, SHABBETAI TSEVI, had attracted many, many Jews. Tsevi's followers were then devastated by religious disappointment when he turned to APOSTASY (denying his Jewish faith). Culi recognized that the Jews of the Ottoman Empire needed books that would bring them back to their traditional Jewish belief. He also felt that they needed written literature in their spoken Jewish language, Judeo-Spanish. Culi therefore wrote a massive guide to Judaism and the Sephardi way of life (see SEPHARDIM) called *Me-Am Lo'ez* ("From a People of Alien Speech"). It follows the order of the weekly TORAH portions and contains a wealth of commentary, MIDRASH, mystical thought from the *Zohar,* Jewish law and customs, ethical teachings, legends, and folktales. The first volume appeared in 1730 and was an immediate success. Less than half of the work was completed by the time Culi died. His students completed the multivolume set using Culi's notes.

Me-Am Lo'ez encourages trust in God, strong religious feeling, and gratitude for what one has. The work always enjoyed extremely wide popularity among Sephardi Jews. In recent years, appreciation of *Me-Am Lo'ez* has spread to the Ashkenazi world as well.

CULTS   The existence of destructive religious cults is a serious problem for Jewish communities in the United States, Europe, and Israel. These groups use trickery, family separation, psychological and physical abuse, and brainwashing techniques to exercise their power over members and new recruits. The percentage of membership of Jews in such cults is extremely high. Cults such as the Unification Church, Hare Krishna, and Scientology are among the best known. Cults that claim they can improve one's human potential, such as EST and Life Spring, also attract many Jewish members. Satan worship, one of the world's oldest cults, is also taking its toll.

"Hebrew Christian" missionaries are active in both the United States and Israel. The best known of these groups is "Jews for Jesus," who claim that one can be Jewish and Christian at the same time (see CHRISTIANITY). They have been sharply attacked by both Jewish and Christian leaders. They use Jewish symbols, such as the MATZAH (unleavened bread), HANUKKAH candelabrum, and MAGEN DAVID (Jewish star) to confuse Jews and make them believe they are dealing with an authentic Jewish group. Their use of Hebrew songs and prayers further manipulates both young Jews and the elderly into joining their cult.

Various agencies and organizations have been set up in the American Jewish community to battle cults. A massive education campaign has been mounted in Jewish schools, among youth groups, and on college campuses to help Jews understand that if they join a cult they risk various kinds of abuse and also separate themselves from the Jewish community. It also attempts to prepare young Jews to stand up to the cults' trickery and powerful manipulations.

CURSING   See BLESSING AND CURSING

CUSTOM   (Heb. *minhag*). A religious practice that grows out of a tradition established by the people rather than a specific law. Customs usually arise in a particular community or region. They are therefore often called *minhag ha-makom* ("local custom"). The Mishnah stressed that when traveling one must follow local custom to avoid strife (*Suk.* 3:11; *Ket.* 6:4; *BM* 7:1). Differences in custom often arose when there was a disagreement among rabbis about how to observe a law. One community might choose to follow the stricter opinion and the other the more lenient opinion. The rabbis believed that it was better for dif-ferent communities to vary their customs somewhat than for a complete split to arise in Judaism. Indeed the Talmud points out that great rabbinic leaders, of BET SHAMMAI AND BET HILLEL, differed over basic issues. Yet "they did not hesitate to [let their children] marry one another – which showed that there was affection and friendship among them" (*Yev.* 13b–14b).

In the course of time, differences arose in Jewish practice between Jews in Erets Israel and those in Babylonia. Later, differences grew between ASHKENAZIM and SEPHARDIM. Many of these took on the status of law when they were written down in the SHULHAN ARUKH and other law codes. For example, Rabbenu GERSHOM of Germany ruled in the tenth century that a man could no longer marry more than one woman. This ended the practice among Ashkenazi Jews, but not among Sephardim. Differences also arose between the two communities of Jews in matters of PRAYER (see also NUSAH) and foods eaten on PASSOVER. New customs were followed in the 16th century by the followers of the mystic Isaac LURIA, and from the mid-18th century by HASIDISM.

Jews sometimes adopted styles of dress and other customs from the non-Jewish world. For example, Hasidic Jews wear a Polish-style fur hat on Sabbaths and festivals known as a *shtraymel*. Old customs are sometimes preserved simply for the sake of tradition. The Aramaic language, widely spoken in talmudic times, is still used for some important prayers, even though most do not understand it today. However, many practices of the non-Jewish world were rejected and condemned by Jewish leaders (see HUKKAT HA-GOY).

Sometimes customs spread to neighboring Jewish communities, when Jews moved or married outside their hometown. However, local customs were meant to be carried from one generation to the next. Jewish tradition expects children to follow the custom of their father, even if it no longer applies in their situation. In fact, the idea that "what is customary in Israel [becomes] Torah" (*Tos.* to *Men.* 20b) is held by many Orthodox Jews. In some instances, popular custom was actually used to decide the law. When the sages of the Talmud were in doubt about a certain law they would say, "Go see what the people do," and that became the agreed-upon practice (*Ber.* 45a, 52a).

DAF YOMI ("daily page"). An organized approach to the daily study of the TALMUD. R. Meir Shapira of Lublin created this plan in 1923 to encourage Talmud students to study a *daf* (double-sided page) of Talmud each day. Students all over the world study the same *daf* on the same day. In this way, participants complete their study of the entire Babylonian Talmud once every seven years.

The number of people taking part in this program has increased steadily over the years. A large, worldwide celebration is held to mark the completion of each seven-year cycle. The ninth such celebration is scheduled for 2005.

DAN   See TRIBES, TWELVE

DANCE   Dancing has always been part of Jewish ritual and celebration. MIRIAM led the women in dance at the Red Sea (Ex. 15:20); the Israelites danced around the GOLDEN CALF (Ex. 32:19); and DAVID danced before the Lord (II Sam. 6:14). It seems that biblical men and women danced in separate groups, but mostly at the same celebrations. Some dances were in a circle and others in a line, with one person leading. In Second Temple times, young unmarried women danced in vineyards on the 15th day (full moon) of the summer month of Av while young men chose their brides (*Ta'an.* 4:8).

The Talmud records that rabbis danced at weddings (*Ket.* 17a), and dancing was part of the WATER-DRAWING FESTIVAL. In Jewish communities in Europe, dance was a very important part of life and there were special dances for occasions such as weddings and PURIM. Some rabbis were opposed to too much dancing, and most forbade men and women to dance together, for fear of sexual temptation.

A new form of Jewish dance came into being at the end of the 18th century: Hasidic dance (see HASIDISM). The BA'AL SHEM TOV saw dancing as a form of religious joy – but with men and women always dancing separately. Some Hasidim conclude their daily prayers with dancing.

Jews from the East developed their own styles of dance, mostly for weddings and religious festivals. When they arrived in modern Israel, Yemenite, Kurdish, Bokharan, Ethiopian, and Indian Jews brought this rich heritage with them. Modern Israeli dance, both religious and secular, has absorbed many Jewish cultural dance traditions. For Jewish communities all over the world, dancing in the synagogue with the TORAH scrolls is an important part of the SIMHAT TORAH festival.

DANIEL, BOOK OF   Biblical book that tells the story of Daniel, who had been exiled to Babylon after Jerusalem was destroyed by King Nebuchadnezzar. Daniel had been a young nobleman in Judea and was therefore trained to serve the king in Babylon. He is given the Babylonian name Belteshazzar, but refuses to eat the non-kosher food that he is served (see DIETARY LAWS). To avoid non-kosher meat, Daniel takes on a vegetarian diet, which makes him healthier than others of the king's servants, and this greatly impresses the king.

Nebuchadnezzar has a frightening dream, and the only one who can interpret it is Daniel. The king then appoints him to a high position in the government. Daniel later interprets another dream for the king, which predicts that the king will go mad. At a feast held by the new king, Belshazzar, strange writing appears on the wall. None of the Babylonian magicians or scholars can understand it, so Daniel explains that the

	BOOK OF DANIEL
1:1–1:21	Daniel and his three friends at the court of Nebuchadnezzar
2:1–2:49	Daniel interprets Nebuchadnezzar's dream
3:1–3:33	Daniel's three friends are saved from the fiery furnace
4:1–4:34	Another dream by Nebuchadnezzar is interpreted by Daniel
5:1–5:30	Belshazzar's feast and the writing on the wall
6:1–6:29	Daniel in the lions' den
7:1–7:28	The vision of the four beasts
8:1–8:27	The vision of the ram and the he-goat
9:1–9:27	The 70 years
10:1–12:13	The vision of the End of Days

Alexander the Great in combat with the Persians, based on the Vision of Daniel. From a mosaic at Pompei.

words predict that Belshazzar will be overthrown. This indeed happens that same night.

Daniel's jealous enemies have a law passed that forces everybody to pray to no one but the king for 30 days. Because of his religion, Daniel continues to pray to God three times a day. He is thrown into a lions' den as punishment, but comes out the next day unharmed.

The second part of the Book of Daniel contains four visions that are very strange and mysterious. Some people believe that they can be used to predict the End of Days and the coming of the MESSIAH, but most rabbis are very much opposed to such predictions. Most agree that the overall spiritual message of the book is that both the history and the future of the world are in God's hands.

Some parts of the book are written in Hebrew, but most is in Aramaic. According to Jewish tradition, the entire book was written by Daniel around 545 BCE. Modern scholars believe, however, that the first half of the book is several hundred years older than the second half.

In Jewish legend, Daniel was a descendent of King DAVID. The Talmud claims that Daniel was the wisest man of his time. Later sources credit Daniel for the fact that King Cyrus allowed the Jews to return to the Land of Israel and rebuild the TEMPLE.

DAVID   (c. 1040–c. 970 BCE). Israel's second and greatest king. He was born in Bethlehem of the tribe of Judah and was the son of Jesse and the great-grandson of Boaz and Ruth (see RUTH, BOOK OF). His early years were spent as a shepherd, but he later entered the court of King SAUL. When Saul fell out of God's

favor, the prophet SAMUEL rejected Saul and secretly anointed David as the new king (1 Sam. 16:13).

David used to play the harp for King Saul to comfort the king when he was unhappy. When David defeated Goliath in battle, he became a national hero. David married Saul's daughter Michal. He was so popular with his countrymen that Saul feared that David would steal the throne. Saul's early fondness for David turned to jealousy and hatred, and David was forced to flee from the palace to save his life. David lived in hiding to avoid Saul's many attempts to kill him. Saul's tragic end came when he and his son Jonathan were killed in battle by the Philistines on Mount Gilboa.

David was crowned king over Judah in Hebron (II Sam. 2:4) He then proceeded to conquer Israel's hostile neighbors, Philistine, Moab, Edom, Ammon, and Aram. He enlarged Israel's borders to create the largest empire in its history.

David conquered the city of Jerusalem and established a central capital there for Israel. He brought the ARK OF THE COVENANT there. Although he wanted to have the honor of building the TEMPLE in Jerusalem, the prophet NATHAN told him that a warrior such as himself would not be allowed to build a Temple of peace.

David's personal faults and problems are clearly recorded in the Bible. He commits ADULTERY with Bathsheba and then has her husband killed. Two of his sons, Absalom and Adonijah, try to stage revolts against him. David finally proclaimed his son SOLOMON as his heir.

In Jewish tradition, David is called "the sweet singer of Israel" and is given credit for writing the Book of PSALMS. He is mentioned in many prayers because of the belief that the MESSIAH will be descended from him. David has also been a favorite subject of Western literature, music, painting, and sculpture.

David playing the harp, depicted on the mosaic floor of a 6th-century synagogue in Gaza.

DAY OF ATONEMENT (*Yom Kippur*). Holiest and most serious day of the Jewish year. It is observed at the end of the TEN DAYS OF REPENTANCE, which begin on the New Year, ROSH HA-SHANAH. The day is observed as a 25-hour fast, from sunset until nightfall the next day. It is the only Jewish fast that is not postponed if it should fall on the Sabbath.

The Bible calls upon us "to make atonement before the Lord" and "afflict your soul" (Lev. 16:29–31, 23:27–32; Num. 29:7). The sages interpreted afflicting the soul as not eating and drinking, not wearing leather shoes, not washing, not using cosmetics and lotions, and not having sexual relations. They ruled that to make ATONEMENT, people must admit their SIN, undergo CONFESSION and REPENTANCE, and finally make atonement before God in order to receive FORGIVENESS. These practices, therefore, make up the special rituals of *Yom Kippur* observance, along with the work prohibitions of the SABBATH. It is the

hope of every worshiper to be written into the BOOK OF LIFE for the coming year.

The rabbis insisted that the Day of Atonement allows people to atone for sins against God, but not for those committed against another person. The injured party must first forgive the sinner before God will forgive the sin (*Yoma* 8:9). It is therefore the custom of pious Jews just before *Yom Kippur* to ask forgiveness of anybody they might have harmed during the previous year. Some Orthodox Jews immerse themselves in a MIKVEH (ritual bath) to purify themselves before the day.

In Jewish homes, a festive meal is eaten shortly before the fast begins. A MEMORIAL LIGHT is left burning to honor the memories of departed relatives. MEMORIAL PRAYERS are also recited in the synagogue. It is customary to wear white as a symbol of purity.

Five services are held on the day (three are held on all other days), beginning with the very solemn KOL NIDREI service just after sunset. Each service includes group confessions of both a long and a shorter list of sins. The confessions are made in the first person plural to show that all members of the community are responsible for one another. Important and well-known prayers include AVINU MALKENU, U-NETANNEH TOKEF, and the special AVODAH.

The Day of Atonement has always been the festival most widely observed by Jews, even those who observe few Jewish practices. In times of persecution, Jews fasted in secret (see MARRANOS). In modern Israel, Yom Kippur is the one day of the year when restaurants, places of entertainment and business, factories, and even the radio and television stations close down for 25 hours. In 1973 the Egyptian and Syrian armies launched a surprise attack on Israel, and that war became known as the Yom Kippur War.

Silver buckle on a brocade belt worn by rabbis and cantors on the Day of Atonement. Eastern Europe, 19th century.

DAY OF JUDGMENT The time when many believe that God will judge the world at the End of Days. The prophets also spoke often of this idea and the Day of the Lord, when all will accept God as ruler of the universe. The Day of Judgment is part of that time.

Prophets including Amos, Isaiah, Joel, Obadiah, Zephaniah, and Ezekiel all wrote about the Day of Judgment. They also used the phrases "on that day" and "the day of God's wrath." God's judgment will be felt through a series of disasters that will befall God's enemies, who are the enemies of Israel. The process will feature frightening changes in nature, such as the dimming of the sun and stars and great "trouble and distress, a day of devastation and desolation" (Zeph. 1:15). Idol worship will finally disappear from the world. Some prophets held that the wicked among the people of Israel will also meet with disaster. Ezekiel (13:5) saw the destruction of the TEMPLE as the Day of the Lord.

On the other hand, the Day of the Lord is also viewed as a day of great salvation. It is the day that Israel will be delivered from its enemies, and all those who mourn the destruction of Jerusalem will be comforted. For the wicked, however, it will be like a burning furnace. Before the coming of that "great and dreadful day," God will send the prophet ELIJAH to reconcile fathers and sons (Mal. 3:23–24).

In later literature, the Day of Judgment includes the revival of the dead (see AFTERLIFE; ESCHATOLOGY; RESURRECTION).

DAY OF THE LORD   See DAY OF JUDGMENT; ESCHATOLOGY

DAYS OF AWE   See HIGH HOLIDAYS

DAYYAN   ("judge"; pl. *dayyanim*). Judge in a rabbinical court of law (BET DIN). The Talmud describes courts of different sizes,

with three, 23, or 71 judges. Every community with over 120 adult Jewish males was expected to have a *bet din* with 23 judges.

Before EMANCIPATION, when Jews lived in their own communities, *dayyanim* would rule on questions of a religious, personal, or civil nature. Today, these courts deal mostly with questions of Jewish DIVORCE. In Israel, *dayyanim* are responsible for many other areas of personal law, including CONVERSION to Judaism.

DAYYENU   ("It would have been enough for us") Chorus and title of a traditional song of thanksgiving that is part of the Passover SEDER. It begins with the exclamation: "How many favors we have to thank God for!" It then goes on to say that being freed from Egypt would have been enough for us; all that God has done for us since then only adds to our gratitude. Fifteen such favors are listed, including the parting of the Red Sea, providing MANNA in the wilderness, the gift of the SABBATH, the giving of the TORAH, entering the Land of Israel, and the building of the TEMPLE. *Dayyenu* is sung in a joyful tune at the end of each verse.

DEAD, PRAYERS FOR THE   See MEMORIAL SERVICES

DEAD SEA SCROLLS   Collections of ancient scrolls and scroll fragments that were found near the Dead Sea. This outstanding archeological find has helped scholars better understand varieties of Jewish life in late Second TEMPLE times.

In 1947 Bedouin shepherds happened to find seven parchment scrolls in clay jars in a cave in the Judean Desert. Further

The caves of Qumran, discovery site of the Dead Sea Scrolls – the library of a Jewish sect, thought to be the Essenes – hidden in jars and found in 1947 by a young Beduin shepherd. Portion of Isaiah Scroll in Hebrew.

searches in the area led to thousands of other pieces of ancient scrolls, many of them quite damaged. Scholars from all over the world have been studying the scrolls since then. Most of the writings are in the Hebrew of the Second Temple era, with the remainder in Aramaic. Many of the scrolls proved to be ancient sections of the Bible, some were from other important religious works, and others describe the life of members of a sect that lived in Qumran in the last period of the Second Temple. Many scholars believe this sect was the same as the ESSENES.

The Qumran sect members believed that they had been chosen to have a "New Covenant" with God. Most spent their days engaged in prayer and worship, but some worked to support the community. They believed in PREDESTINATION, rather than the idea of free will that was taught by the mainstream PHARISEES. The sect had its own calendar, which means that it celebrated Jewish holidays at different times than did the rest of Israel. Ritual purity (see PURITY, RITUAL) was another extremely important element of their belief and practice.

It is most striking that they considered the Jerusalem Temple to be a place of pollution and disgrace. They therefore held their own holy communal meals at Qumran instead of participating in Temple rituals. They believed that a Great War would break out before the coming of the MESSIAH, in which the Sons of Light (sect members) would drive the Sons of Darkness (all others) out of the Temple.

Members of the sect participated in the Great Revolt against Rome (66–73 CE), which is when they met their end.

DEATH   The Bible is concerned with two main questions about death: 1) Why must people die, and what is the force that takes away life? 2) What happens to a person after death? In Genesis 3:19, God tells Adam that he will return to the earth from which he was taken. On the other hand, God expels ADAM AND EVE from EDEN because they sinned; if not for their sin, they might have eaten from the TREE OF LIFE and lived forever (Gen. 3:22–23).

BURIAL of the dead, particularly in the family tomb was very important in Bible times (Gen. 47:29–30, 49:29; 1 Kings 21:19). The TORAH forbids sacrificing to the dead or trying to communicate with them (Deut. 26:14), even though these were common practices in the Ancient Near East. The Bible describes death as going down to a place called *sheol* – a name that appears in no other ancient language. All are equal in *sheol* (Job 3:13–19), and there is no consciousness after death (Eccl. 9:4, 5; Job 14:21). On the other hand, in a few passages in the Bible, God saves a man from *sheol* and takes the person to Himself, e.g., ENOCH and ELIJAH. In later books, the Bible refers to the RESURRECTION of the dead (see AFTERLIFE). It is therefore very difficult to get a unified picture of the Bible's attitudes toward death and what follows.

According to traditional HALAKHAH (Jewish law), the exact moment of death occurs when breathing stops. With modern medicine, and the ability to use a respirator that "breathes" for an individual, definitions of death in *halakhah* have been

---

> **CONFESSION ON A DEATHBED**
>
> I admit before You, God, my God and God of my ancestors, that my cure and death are in Your hands. May it be Your will that You heal me with a complete healing. And if I die, may my death be an atonement for the sins, transgressions, and violations which I have sinned before You. Set my portion in the Garden of Eden, and let me merit the world to come, reserved for the righteous. Hear, O Israel, the Lord our God, the Lord is One.

changed. R. Moses SOFER wrote that death occurs when both breathing and the heart stops. R. Moses FEINSTEIN ruled that a person dies when the brain stem dies, since breathing cannot then take place on its own.

A critically ill, dying person is considered to be alive in all respects. Doctors must make every effort to save a dying patient (see MEDICAL ETHICS). One is not allowed to speed up the dying process. However, if an external obstacle is preventing death from occurring at its own pace, it may be removed. The example given is the case of a noise outside the window that is preventing a person from dying; this noise may be stopped to allow death to take its course (*YD* 339). One can pray for the death of a very ill person who is suffering terribly and wishes to die (*Hikkekei Lev* I, *YD* 50).

In rabbinic literature, death is viewed as something to fight; LIFE is to be cherished and preserved. Early death is seen as a misfortune and long life is a reward and a blessing. Even so, the prayer recited by mourners at the FUNERAL SERVICE praises God as the righteous Judge, and accepts His decree of death. Death is viewed as the most powerful form of ATONEMENT for a person's sins – even in cases when no other form of REPENTANCE will be effective.

In Jewish ritual, a CORPSE carries the highest level of impurity (see PURITY, RITUAL). Yet the sincerest respect must be shown toward the dying and to the body after the soul has departed. Neither a dying person nor a body is ever to be left alone. A dying person should be helped to make a final CONFESSION in a way that is not upsetting. Arrangements made for the care and burial of the body are called *hesed shel emet* (true kindness), since they can never be "paid back" by the dead person.

After death, the eyes and mouth are closed. The body is placed on the floor and covered with a sheet, and a lighted candle is placed near the head. In the home of the deceased, mirrors are covered. Before burial, the body is cleaned (see TOHORAH) and dressed in special white garments. Mourners pray for God's mercy on the soul of the deceased and recite the KADDISH prayer in the synagogue.

DEATH ANNIVERSARY   see YAHRZEIT

DEBORAH   (c. 12th cent. BCE). Judge and prophetess in ancient Israel. Deborah was a local judge who judged cases beneath a palm tree between Ramah and Beth El (Judg. 4:5). She is the only judge whom the Bible actually describes as judging the people.

Deborah had a Divine vision and ordered General Barak to take 10,000 men and march against the king of Hazor, who was ruling Israel harshly. Barak agreed, as long as Deborah would come with the troops into battle. With Deborah's encouragement, Barak drove the enemy general, Sisera, and his 900 chariots out of the land. Sisera fled and was killed by Yael, who drove a tent peg into his temple as he slept in her tent (Judg. 4:21). The Song of Deborah in Judges 5 is a victory poem that retells the story of the battle.

DECALOGUE   see TEN COMMANDMENTS

DEMAI   ("produce suspected of not having been tithed"). Third tractate (book) of the Order of ZERA'IM in the Mishnah. Its seven chapters discuss the requirements of tithing (see TITHE) produce bought from an *am ha-arets* (unlearned man) because it assumed that he had not tithed properly. The law against eating *demai* is lenient in some cases, permitting the suspect food to go to the poor or to Jewish soldiers.

DEMONS AND DEMONOLOGY   The term *shedim* ("demons") appears only twice in the Bible. In both cases, the people of Israel are accused of sacrificing to them. It was believed that demons lived among ruins and in the wilderness. Much more is written about demons in the MIDRASH, TALMUD, and other books of the time, probably because of Babylonian and Persian influence.

In one legend, fallen ANGELS married the daughters of men who gave birth to a race of giants. Their children were the demons, who harm human beings and lead them to sin. Demons are said to be like the angels in three ways and like people in three other ways. Like angels, they have wings to fly from one end of the earth to the other, they are invisible, and they know the future. Like people, they eat and drink, have children, and die. Demons are also able to appear in any way that they choose. They by far outnumber the human race.

Much advice has been written about how to avoid demons. For example, one should not go out at night, particularly on Wednesdays and Fridays when demons await their prey. Many prayers, charms, and AMULETS have appeared throughout the ages for a person to use in trying to drive them off. The Talmud tells of a number of rabbis who had encounters with various demons, but in each case the rabbi was able to best the demon. The famous rabbis HILLEL and JOHANAN BEN ZAKKAI understood the speech of demons.

In the Middle Ages, belief in demons and their ability to harm was widespread among both Jews and Christians. In the mystical book ZOHAR, God's influence in the world is said to have two opposite aspects: holiness and good and "the other side." "The other side" is the area of impurity and evil, represented largely by demons. When these two aspects are kept in balance, neither harm nor evil takes place. When humans sin, however, the balance is thrown off and demons and their harmful ways are able to dominate the world. The SHULHAN ARUKH contains a few laws that are based on a belief in demons. Some scholars, such as JUDAH HALEVI and NAHMANIDES, have argued that they exist. On the other hand, a number of leading rabbis have denied that demons exist. MAIMONIDES forbade the wearing of amulets and Abraham IBN EZRA said that those who believed in demons were sinners.

DERASH   (Heb. "text commentary"). A traditional method for interpreting the Bible. The rabbis developed rules and techniques for explaining the text in a way that brings out their moral or legal messages. This method was often used in writing a *derashah* ("sermon"). See also MIDRASH and HOMILETICS.

DEREKH ERETS   (lit. "the way of the world"). A system of proper behavior. According to the Mishnah, "He who pleases people also pleases God" (*Avot* 3:13) — because he knows how to behave, he creates a spirit of harmony around him. Rabban Gamaliel taught that "it is admirable to combine Torah study with *derekh erets*" (*Avot* 2:2), and by this he meant having a profession (and therefore not becoming a burden on society).

**SOME ADVICE FROM THE RABBIS
ON *DEREKH ERETS***

A person should not weep among those who are enjoying themselves and should not behave joyfully among those who are weeping.

One guest does not invite another to be a guest.

When visiting, do not ask to eat until it is offered to you.

Do not eat in company anything that causes an odor.

Do not drink with one gulp.

A sage with a stain on his clothes deserves to be punished.

Cleanliness brings holiness.

A servant who waits on a table should wear different clothes from those used for cooking.

Wear special clothes on the Sabbath.

Be eager to protect the honor of your friend.

Never utter an unworthy thought.

Avoid whatever is ugly.

There are seven ways of a wise person: not speaking before one who is wiser; not interrupting another's speech; not being quick to reply; asking according to the subject matter and answering to the point; speaking about first things first and last things last; admitting when one does not understand; acknowledging the truth.

Derekh erets includes courtesy, cleanliness and attention to one's appearance, avoiding rude language, and the respect due to parents and teachers. Samson Raphael HIRSCH added to the definition when he spoke of combining traditional Judaism with *derekh erets,* meaning secular culture.

DESECRATION   (Heb. *hillul*) Making unholy that which is considered holy; an improper action that removes holiness or purity from a person or object that had been holy or pure (see PURITY, RITUAL). For example, objects and foods that had been purified for use in the TEMPLE could be desecrated if they came into contact with impure objects, such as a CORPSE or somebody who had touched a corpse (without being purified). A priest who marries a divorced women, which he is not permitted to do, becomes a "*hallal,*" or desecrated priest (see PRIESTS).

Just as time can be made holy, for example in the case of the SABBATH, it can also be desecrated when Sabbath laws are not observed. It is also said that God's name is desecrated when a Jew acts publicly in a way that brings shame upon himself and, by extension, his people.

DESTINY AND DETERMINISM   See FREE WILL.

DEUTERONOMY, BOOK OF   Fifth and last book of the PENTATEUCH. It is known in Hebrew as *Devarim,* "Words," from its opening phrase. The rabbis called it *Mishneh Torah* (i.e., "the Repetition of the Torah") and the Greeks called it Deuteronomy (i.e. "Second Law"), because most of the book is a review of the three books that come before it: EXODUS, LEVITICUS, and NUMBERS. It has 34 chapters and 955 verses and includes the TEN COMMANDMENTS (5:6–18) and the first two paragraphs of the SHEMA prayer (6:4–9, 11:13–21).

In Jewish tradition, the book was dictated by God to MOSES. Moses delivered its contents verbally to the Israelites during the last 37 days of his life in order to prepare them to enter the Land of Israel after 40 years of wandering in the desert (see EXODUS). The last eight verses of the book take place after the death of Moses, which calls for an explanation. The Talmud offers two possibilities: (a) these last verses were written down by Moses' successor JOSHUA and not by Moses; (b) God dictated these last eight verses to Moses just before his death, "and Moses wrote them down in tears."

Modern scholars disagree about when the book was first written. Some say it was written by priests just before the time of King Josiah (i.e., before he found the book in the Temple in 622 BCE) to persuade the King that all worship should take place in the TEMPLE. Others say it is from after the time of the Babylonian exile (6th cent. BCE); others place it earlier still, during the time of King Hezekiah; and others say it is as early as the time of the Judges. Some say it is the work of LEVITES, whose job it was to preach the Law. Others have suggested that court scribes wrote it, because of its interest in political matters.

BOOK OF DEUTERONOMY	
1:1–1:5	Introduction
1:6–3:29	Moses' first speech: the lessons of the past
4:1–4:40	Moses' second speech: the uniqueness of God
4:41–4:43	Three cities of refuge in Transjordan
4:44–11:32	Moses' third speech: the Giving of the Law and reasons for obeying God
12:1–26:19	Laws and statutes which Israel must obey in the land they are to inherit
27:1–28:69	The blessing in reward for observing the Torah and the punishment for disobeying it
29:1–31:30	Moses' final speech: preparing for the entry into Canaan
32:1–32:52	The Farewell Poem of Moses
33:1–33:29	Parting benediction to the tribes
34:1–34:12	Death of Moses

Those who hold that the book was written down by Moses point out several reasons for this belief. First, they insist that the central message of the book is to forbid IDOLATRY, which was one of Moses' main concerns. Also, some of the laws that appear in Deuteronomy – such as appointment of judges, the behavior of kings, and contract law – are similar to those of other cultures in the Ancient Near East. In addition, the form of ancient Hebrew found in the book seems to come from the time of Moses.

DEUTERONOMY RABBAH   MIDRASH (part of MIDRASH RABBAH) on the book of DEUTERONOMY (see also MIDRASH AGGADAH). It is divided into 11 sections, like the 11 sections of the Torah reading cycle that Jews now follow. It is also made up of 27 homilies (i.e., stories that teach proper behavior), like the three-year Torah reading cycle that was once observed in the Land of Israel (see TRIENNIAL CYCLE). Each section is introduced by a simple question of law and an answer: "What is the law for a man of Israel? – Our sages taught…" Most of the homilies end with words of comfort.

DEVEKUT   ("cleaving" or "clinging"). Term describing a close attachment to God. The Bible sees *devekut* as the result of loving God and obeying His laws; its rewards are life in the Land of Israel, as God promised to the PATRIARCHS (Deut. 30:20).

In the Middle Ages the idea of *devekut* took on new meaning. The mystics saw it as complete concentration on the words and meaning of prayers, as a way of connecting to God (see KAVVANAH). As Abraham Abulafia described *devekut*, it could elevate the mind to a very high level of holiness. The mystics believed it could bring the soul into the presence of God and help a person achieve religious perfection (see MYSTICISM, JEWISH; LURIA, ISAAC). In the thought of HASIDISM, the idea received a broader interpretation. The BA'AL SHEM TOV taught that *devekut* is the supreme goal of religious life and is more important than studying TORAH. He believed that the practice of always striving for attachment to God is one that all Jews can undertake, even those who are not particularly learned.

DEVIL   See SATAN

DEVOTION   See KAVVANAH

DEW, PRAYER FOR   (Heb. *Tefillat Tal*). Name given to several prayers of request that form part of the AMIDAH during the dry season in the Land of Israel. The Bible recognizes that dew is extremely important to the Land of Israel (e.g., Gen. 27:28; Mic. 5:6; Ps. 133:3). The blessings of rain and dew are emphasized in the daily *Amidah*, which both praises God for causing them to appear, and requests them in the proper season. The prayers take on different forms in the services of Ashkenazi, Sephardi, and Oriental Jews.

According to an old tradition, the "heavenly stores of dew" are opened up at the beginning of PASSOVER in the spring. From

Part of the Prayer for Dew on a page from the Mahzor of Worms *illustrated with the signs of the Zodiac. Germany, 1272.*

the early Middle Ages it became the custom to recite special prayers for dew in the Land of Israel during the dry summer months and for rain during the winter months (see SHEMINI ATSERET; RAIN, PRAYERS FOR).

The prayer is made up of a long series of alphabetical acrostic poems (see ACROSTICS). It makes a connection between the rebirth of nature in the spring and the hope for the return of the people of Israel to its full glory in the Land of Israel. Few congregations recite the entire poem, but most recite a shorter version.

DHIMMI LAWS   Laws that applied to Jews and other religious minorities in Muslim lands. Jews and Christians were officially considered "protected" people (i.e., *dhimmi*), because they followed the Bible, which made them "People of the Book." They were therefore allowed to practice their religion, own property, and carry on business. They were not allowed to serve in the army. In return, they had to agree that the religion of Islam is superior, pay special taxes, follow certain dress codes, follow restrictions on riding animals, and often suffer various types of humiliations. The overall effect was to make *dhimmis* into second-class citizens.

The Dhimmi Laws were decreed by Omar II (717–720 CE). In different times and in different parts of the Muslim world they were applied more and less strictly. When the fanatical Almohads rose to power in North Africa and Spain (1146–1269), Jews were forced to convert to Islam and were no longer able to practice their religion openly. On the whole, however, Dhimmi Laws did not persecute Jews as severely as did anti-Jewish laws in the Christian world.

DIASPORA   See GALUT

DIBBUK   (or Dybbuk). An evil spirit, or the soul of a wicked person who has died, that has attached itself to the body of a living person. The dibbuk is believed to be a foreign being inside a person that speaks through his throat and causes the person spiritual and emotional distress.

The idea of evil spirits entering the body was common among Jews during the time of the Second Temple and the Talmud. In the Middle Ages many Jews and Christians believed that certain souls of the dead could not find rest and therefore entered the bodies of living people.

Among the early mystics, the idea was that the soul of a deceased righteous person would join with a living soul to strengthen the living person (see MYSTICISM, JEWISH; TRANSMIGRATION OF SOULS). Only later did followers of Isaac LURIA in Safed concern twhemselves with evil dibbuks. They wrote detailed instructions for chasing them away. From the 16th century on, ceremonies for getting rid of dibbuks became quite common. A famous play, called *The Dibbuk*, written by S. An-Ski in 1916, is one example of literary writings about dibbuks.

DIETARY LAWS   A set of laws concerning which foods are KOSHER, or permitted for observant Jews to eat. This set of laws is known in Hebrew as laws of *kashrut* ("fitness").

The first dietary laws in the Bible forbid the eating of blood and the limb of a living animal (Gen. 9:4). The Bible gives clear criteria for land animals that are permitted: "Every animal that has true hooves that are split in two and that chews its cud, you may eat" (Lev. 11:3). Animals that meet only one requirement such as the pig, which has split hooves but does not bring up its cud, or the camel, which brings up its cud but does not have a split hoof, are forbidden.

The Bible does not give criteria for birds, but rather lists the birds that are forbidden (Lev. 11:13–19; Deut. 14:12–18). From these two lists, the rabbis came up with a list of 24 forbidden birds. Water animals must have fins and scales. Therefore, shellfish and water mammals may not be eaten.

The Bible permits four types of locusts to be eaten (Lev. 11:21–22); however, the rabbis restricted them because they are difficult to identify. All other creatures that crawl on the earth are forbidden, as is the milk and eggs of forbidden fish and animals. One exception is honey, which is a permitted food, even though bees are not.

The dietary laws also deal with the health of the animal, the way in which the animal is slaughtered, and how the meat is prepared for eating. All kosher land animals and birds must be slaughtered by a professional *shohet* using a method known as SHEHITAH. The animal's throat is slit rapidly with a very sharp knife, and death comes almost immediately. The *shohet* then inspects the dead animal to be sure that it was healthy. If the animal was ill or seriously injured, the meat is labeled "*tref*" (see TEREFAH) and is sold to a non-kosher butcher. People who demand of themselves a particularly high level of Jewish observance may choose an extra-strict standard of *kashrut* known is Hebrew as *halak* ("smooth") and in Yiddish as *glatt*. Fish do not need to be inspected or killed in a special way.

The Bible does not permit the blood to be eaten because it contains the soul of the animal (Lev. 10–14); therefore every effort is made to remove blood from an animal before it is eaten. After slaughter, the carcass is hung up to allow the blood to drain. The meat is then soaked in cold water, covered with coarse salt that absorbs blood, and then rinsed well in cold water. Another method of removing blood is to roast the meat over an open flame. If any blood remains in the meat after one of these processes has been properly completed it may be eaten with the meat. The blood of fish is permitted. Other parts of a mammal, such as the sciatic nerve and the fat attached to the stomach and intestines, must also be removed before eating.

The Bible forbids the cooking of "a baby goat in its mother's milk" (Ex. 23:19, 34:26; Deut. 14:21). Since the prohibition appears three times in the Torah, the rabbis ruled that its meaning is far wider than may appear from the words themselves. They included in the prohibition any meat cooked in any milk as well as any meat product mixed with any dairy product (*Hul.* 113b). Even though they do not produce milk, the meat of

Ritual slaughter of an ox. The inspector, on the right, makes sure that the dietary laws are observed. Italy, 1435.

birds is included in the prohibition. The rabbis also ruled that it is forbidden to sell such mixtures, even to non-Jews, or to otherwise make any profit from them (*Hul.* 115b). As a way of ensuring that these strict laws of separation of milk and meat are not violated, Jewish law requires separate dishes, pots, pans, and silverware for dairy and meat meals. Fruit, vegetables, eggs, and fish may be eaten with milk or with meat, although the rabbis believed that it was unhealthy to eat fish with meat. All fruits and vegetables are kosher.

The Bible gives no reason for keeping the dietary laws, except to connect them with HOLINESS. Many attempts at explaining them have been made. Some have explained them as a way to develop self-discipline and others that the permitted animals are better for one's health. Some insist that the laws have only to do with spirituality and that, indeed, the Bible is not a "lowly" health manual. Some claim that the laws are a more humane way of eating, since the animal's death is instant; and others that eating vegetarian animals that chew their cud makes human beings gentler, since "you are what you eat."

Until modern times, *kashrut* was observed by nearly all Jews. In the 19th century, the REFORM MOVEMENT rejected the dietary laws, because they felt they were outdated, and they did not agree that observing them made a person more spiritual. CONSERVATIVE JUDAISM still upholds these laws, although with some changes.

Today many Jews ignore the dietary laws. At the same time, there has been an increase in their observance in some Jewish communities, with many new kosher products and restaurants available. In the State of Israel, nearly all food produced is kosher and *kashrut* is observed in all public institutions, including the Israeli army.

See also AGRICULTURAL LAWS; MIXED SPECIES; TITHE; WINE.

DINA DE-MALKHUTA DINA   ("The law of the land is the law"). An idea put forth by the scholar SAMUEL in about 242 CE. It states that the "law of the land" in which Jews live comes before Jewish law and is, in fact, supported by Jewish law. This applies especially to the obligation to pay taxes to the local government and to repay debts under local law. Such a ruling has made it more comfortable for Jews to live in countries throughout the world. *Dina de-malkhuta dina* does not apply to matters of Jewish religious observance.

DIN TORAH   (lit. "judgment according to the Torah"). A court case held before judges (often DAYYANIM) who rule according to Jewish law. Any Jew may bring another Jew for a *din torah* when a dispute arises, but outside of Israel the court has no power to enforce its rulings. A Jewish court usually will take a case only if both parties sign an agreement to accept the court's verdict as binding.

DISPUTATIONS   Term used for public debates between people of different faiths about the merit of the religion of the debaters. In the Middle Ages Jewish scholars were sometimes forced against their will to debate with Christian clergy who were trying to prove that CHRISTIANITY is superior. At the same time, the Jews were not allowed to say anything offensive about the Christian religion.

The most famous of all disputations took place in the 13th century in Barcelona, Spain. NAHMANIDES was forced to debate Pablo Christiani (a Jew who had converted to Christianity) in the presence of King James I of Aragon. Christiani insisted that Jesus was the MESSIAH, that Jesus was both human and Divine, and that the laws of the TORAH had been canceled by the "truth" of Christianity. Nahmanides had to proved that Judaism was correct in rejecting these beliefs.

Nahmanides risked his life by clearly explaining to the king that it was not logical to believe that God would assume human form (i.e. that of Jesus) and that the Torah was therefore still in force. The king listened attentively to his arguments, and in the end gave Nahmanides a purse with 300 gold coins. Even so, Nahmanides had become an enemy of the Church and was forced to flee the country.

DIVINATION   See WITCHCRAFT

DIVINE PRESENCE   See SHEKHINAH

DIVORCE   In the Bible, we read the following about divorce: "When a man takes a wife and possesses her, if she fails to please him because he finds something obnoxious about her, then he writes her a bill of divorce, hands it to her, and sends her away from his house" (Deut. 24:1–4). From this, the rabbis understood two important principles about divorce: (a) the power to call for and bring about a divorce lies completely with the husband; and (b) a written document (called a *get*) must be prepared and delivered by the husband to the wife for divorce

to take place (*Git.* 20a). It is important to understand that without a Jewish divorce, a Jewish couple is considered to still be married in the eyes of Jewish law, even if they have a civil divorce – even to this day.

The rabbis of the Mishnah disagreed over what were valid reasons for divorce, i.e. how to interpret the phrase "finds something obnoxious about her." Such reasons could range from the woman's ADULTERY, to the husband's finding a woman he preferred, to the wife's burning the husband's dinner (*Git.* 9:10)!

Divorce is generally frowned upon in the Bible. The prophet MALACHI wrote "For I hate divorce, says the Lord, the God of Israel" (2:14–16). He goes on to describe it as an act of betrayal of the original agreement between a husband and wife. According to the Talmud, "the altar sheds tears for the man who divorces the bride of his youth" (*Sanh.* 22a).

In Talmud times, some important changes were made to divorce law. The court (BET DIN) was given the right to try to force a man to divorce his wife under certain conditions, such as that (a) she was not able to conceive a child with him after ten years of marriage; (b) the husband developed a repulsive disease; (c) he could not or refused to support her financially; (d) he refused to have sexual relations with her; or (e) he continued to beat her despite being warned by the court to stop. Since the man is still required to grant a divorce of his own free will, the court cannot issue the divorce on its own authority. It can, however, apply pressure and even use physical force until a man says, "I want to divorce my wife." Since the Talmud is not completely clear about precisely when the court should exercise this right, many Jewish courts have hesitated to force a man to issue a divorce, even in cases where the marriage is long over. In the rare cases in which Israeli rabbinic courts decide to force a *get*, they have the authority to put a man in jail until he agrees to grant his wife a divorce.

In the 11th century Rabbenu GERSHOM made an important ruling that was eventually accepted as law by most of the Jewish world: a woman may not be divorced against her will. This greatly increased the rights of Jewish wives. Even so, many problems still remain with Jewish divorce law. Since the man must be the one to give a *get* to his wife, a husband who cannot be located is a terrible obstacle. His wife remains an AGUNAH (an "anchored" woman), and cannot remarry according to Jewish law. Similarly, a husband who refuses to cooperate with the court can withhold a *get* for many years, since Jewish courts in Israel are reluctant to apply their full power in forcing his hand; Jewish courts outside of Israel have no real power to enforce their rulings.

Many attempts have been made to address these problems. In CONSERVATIVE JUDAISM, the bride and groom can add a paragraph to their marriage contract (KETUBBAH) that would require them to follow the decision of the Conservative religious court if the marriage should fall apart. If the husband is unavailable to appear before the *bet din,* this court has the power to annul the marriage. Although annulment of marriage took place on rare occasions in the period after the Talmud was written, Orthodox rabbis do not approve of this procedure today. REFORM JUDAISM does not require a *get* to dissolve a marriage.

DOV BAER OF MEZHIRECH (c. 1710–1772). Leader of the main group of Hasidic Jews after the death of the BA'AL SHEM TOV; organizer of the Hasidic movement and its leading religious thinker (see HASIDISM). He is also known as "the Mezhirecher" or "the Great Maggid."

Dov Baer studied with the leading Talmud scholar Jacob Joshua Falk. He served as the MAGGID (preacher) in Rovno and in Mezhirech, Volhynia. He only came to know the Ba'al Shem Tov in his later years. Thus even though he is considered by many Hasidim to be the leading student of the Ba'al Shem Tov, he really developed all of his own thinking independently throughout his life. The Maggid was accepted as the leader of the Hasidic movement after the death of the Ba'al Shem Tov and had a circle of saintly followers. Many later became Hasidic masters with their own following, and thus the Maggid built the Hasidic movement through his followers.

The Maggid left no writings, but his students often wrote about what he had taught. One of his main beliefs (in the words of the ZOHAR) was that "God fills all worlds and no space is unoccupied by Him." All human emotions – love, fear, etc. – have their source in God, and therefore people should dwell on their feelings as a way of connecting to God. He believed in worshiping God with joy (SIMHAH), and his students were encouraged to engage in playful activity to increase their joy. He also taught that a person must put aside his own ego in order to receive God.

SAYINGS OF DOV BAER OF MEZHIRECH

Man's energy and his soul are not his own. Even when he calls upon himself to worship God, it is God's doing – not his.

Overcoming one's pride demands a lifelong struggle.

What sin have I committed that I should be so popular?

A man should see to it that he spends time alone with God each day. Constant practice will make this second nature to him, and he will then have his mind on God even in the middle of conversation.

DOWRY   The property that a bride brings to a MARRIAGE. In the Bible, for example, Rebekah brought maidservants with her on her journey to marry Isaac (Gen. 24:61). On the other hand, the Jewish custom from Bible times and later of the groom's purchasing the bride by paying the *mohar* ("bride-price") is still a tradition among Jews of the Near East.

In the time of the Talmud, the custom was for the father of the bride to give his daughter a dowry, and a minimum sum was fixed. The husband had various rights to use and profit from

Head-covering with gold ornaments and coins worn by Yemenite brides which was part of their dowry ("bride-price").

the wife's property in those days. This changed in modern Israel, where a husband does not have rights to his wife's property.

The custom of "dowering the bride" (HAKHNASAT KALLAH) was popular in Europe and remains so in the ultra-Orthodox world today. The bride's parents give the young couple the amount needed for them to support themselves while the husband studies in a YESHIVAH for a number of years. If the parents cannot afford this expense, they turn to special charitable funds to help them. "Dowering the bride" – especially one from a poor family – is considered an especially good deed (MITZVAH) in Judaism (*Pe'ah* 1:1; *Shab.* 127a).

DREAMS   A channel for people to receive messages and visions from the supernatural world. In the Bible, we often read of messages from God "spoken in a dream" to a chosen individual (Gen. 15:1; Num. 22:20; Isa. 29:7; Job 33:14–16). Prophets (see PROPHETS AND PROPHECY) usually received their information this way; MOSES was the only person to whom God spoke face to face (Num 12:5–8). While a prophet could easily grasp the dream's message, kings and others usually required the services of an expert interpreter. Joseph and Daniel, the Bible's most outstanding dream interpreters, saw their ability as a gift from God (Gen. 41:16; Dan. 2:1–23).

Dreams in the Bible usually point to future events, or they may serve as a warning. They usually contain symbols that need to be interpreted. Only rarely, as with Jacob at Bethel (Gen. 28:12–16) or Joseph the young shepherd (Gen 27:5–11), is the meaning clear to the dreamer. In later biblical books we find some doubts about the truth of dreams (Isa. 29:8; Job 20:8; Eccl. 5:6).

Later rabbinic writings contain conflicting opinions about the importance of dreams. On the one hand, they were believed to have no effect (*Git.* 52a; *Hor.* 13b) or to reflect only the dreamer's own thoughts (*Ber* 55b). On the other hand, there were rabbis who took dreams quite seriously. They recommended certain ways to avoid the possible effects of a bad dream.

The Talmud gives a list of meanings for certain symbols that appeared in dreams. For example, all animals are a good sign, except for an elephant, monkey, or porcupine (*Ber.* 56b–57b).

In the Middle Ages, a number of rabbis provided guidelines for interpreting dreams. Moses ben Jacob of Coucy, MEIR OF ROTHENBURG, and Isaac ben Moses of Vienna even claimed to receive messages about solving Jewish legal problems through dreams. Rabbi JACOB BEN ASHER, however, warned against trusting in dreams because this showed a lack of faith in God. MAIMONIDES wrote about the connection between dreams and prophecy and advised fasting after a bad dream.

DUALISM   The belief that there are two Divine powers, one that is good and one that is evil. Zoroastrianism, the ancient religion of Persia, and Gnosticism are based on this belief. Judaism absolutely opposes the idea of dualism. As we read in Isaiah (45:1, 7): "Thus says the Lord … I form the light, and create darkness; I make peace and create evil; I the Lord do all these things."

DYBBUK   See DIBBUK

ECCLESIASTES, BOOK OF One of the Five Scrolls in the HAGIOGRAPHA ("Writings") section of the Bible. The Hebrew name of the book is *Kohelet*, which is the name of the author mentioned in the first verse. Ecclesiastes is read in the synagogue by Ashkenazi Jews on the SABBATH of SUKKOT (or on SHEMINI ATSERET if there is no intermediate Sabbath).

BOOK OF ECCLESIASTES	
1:1–3:15	All is vanity: life, wisdom, and earthly pleasures
3:16–3:21	People and animals have the same fate
4:1–4:16	People work for nothing
5:1–6:12	People's wealth is meaningless
7:1–7:29	Various wise sayings
8:1–9:16	The righteous and the wicked have the same fate
9:17–10:20	Various wise sayings
11:1–11:8	The uncertainty of people's labors
11:9–12:8	The joy at birth; the weakness of old age
12:9–12:14	Conclusion

Ecclesiastes, which has 12 chapters, has no organized structure. It is made up of about 15–20 units, and each discusses a specific topic. The book's motto is "Vanity ["nothingness"] of vanities, all is vanity." This conclusion is reached by looking at the cycle of life. All are equal in death, because death wipes out all that people achieve during their lifetime – wealth, wisdom, possessions, honor, pleasure, and labor. *Kohelet* advises that one enjoy life as much as possible. The book ends as it began, reflecting on the life cycle of people from youth to old age.

According to tradition, King SOLOMON is the author of Ecclesiastes (Song R. 1:1). The author describes himself as having been king of Jerusalem (1:12), and the book begins, "The words of *Kohelet* the son of DAVID, king in Jerusalem" (1:1).

The SONG OF SONGS was also said to have been written by Solomon. The Midrash explains that he wrote the Song of Songs in his youth and Ecclesiastes in his old age, which ex-

plains why the book is so pessimistic compared to the Song of Songs (Song R. 1:1, 10). Scholars date Ecclesiastes to the late third century BCE, because its style is similar to Ancient Near Eastern WISDOM LITERATURE of that time.

There was a dispute among the rabbis about whether or not Ecclesiastes should be part of the canon (works included in the Bible; see BIBLE, canon). In the Mishnah (*Yad.* 3:5), the School of HILLEL claimed that Ecclesiastes is a holy book, and therefore it was included in the Bible.

ECCLESIASTES RABBAH MIDRASH on the Book of ECCLESIASTES, known in Hebrew as *Kohelet Rabbah* (see also MIDRASH AGGADAH). It was probably edited sometime in

Opening page of the Book of Ecclesiastes. From the Duke of Sussex Pentateuch. Germany, 14ᵗʰ century.

the geonic era (7th–9th cent.; see GAON), because the editor included sources from the Jerusalem Talmud and some parts of the Babylonian Talmud. It follows the text of Ecclesiastes verse by verse, and the editor borrowed poems from older works of Midrashim, such as GENESIS RABBAH, LEVITICUS RABBAH, Pesikta de-Rav Kahana, and SONG OF SONGS RABBAH.

This Midrash explains the text in a story-like way, turning it into a more positive, optimistic, religious ALLEGORY. For example: on the verse, "I searched in my heart how to pamper my flesh with wine …" (Eccl. 2:3), the Midrash gives the following interpretation: "… to pamper my flesh with the wine of Torah, while my heart behaved itself with Torah wisdom." Likewise, the pessimistic statements in Ecclesiastes are turned into religious optimism. *Kohelet* asks: "What profit does a man have from all his labor under the sun?" The Midrash in the name of Rabbi Judah comments that "under the sun he has no profit, but above the sun [in the world to come] he does have."

ECOLOGY The interaction between creatures and the environment. Judaism has always been concerned with the environment. The Torah teaches that when an army besieges a city, it may not cut down fruit trees (Deut. 20:19–20). Only non-fruit-bearing trees can be cut down. SIFREI extends this rule to include sources of water, which may not be polluted. Rabbi Samson Raphael HIRSCH commented that preserving fruit trees was an example of the basic prohibition against destroying anything without cause (BAL TASHHIT).

When the Israelites built the 48 cities of the LEVITES, they were commanded to leave a "green belt" of a thousand cubits (about 1,500 feet), around each city and another 2,000 cubit belt of farm land (Num 35:2–5). According to RASHI, this belt could not be sold for any reason, and MAIMONIDES taught that the same rule applied to any other city in Israel.

In order to preserve the quality of life in the cities, the Torah teaches that CEMETERIES, slaughter houses, threshing floors, and leather tanneries must be located outside the city limits. Tanneries, and other bad-smelling businesses, must be located downwind from the city. The Talmud states that in Erets Israel, where the wind blows from the west, tanneries must be located to the east of the city.

The rabbis cautioned against raising sheep or goats in Erets Israel, because their close grazing can leave the land without any greenery. Finally, the Bible commands that an army must bury its waste (Deut. 23:13–15), which surely shows extreme concern for the environment.

EDELS, SAMUEL ELIEZER BEN JUDAH HA-LEVI (known by the acronym *Maharsha* 1555–1631). Talmudic scholar. Edels was born in Cracow, Poland, where he studied under his father and married the daughter of Rabbi Moses Ashkenazi of Posen. For 20 years he headed a *yeshivah,* which his mother-in-law, Edel, ran at her own expense. In gratitude to her, he adopted the last name Edels. After her death, he held rabbinical positions in the Polish cities of Chelm, Lublin, and Ostrog.

Edels taught and influenced hundreds of students in Poland. His *Hiddushei Halakhot* ("Original Ideas About Jewish Laws"; see also NOVELLAE) on most books of the Talmud are printed in nearly all Talmud editions. His *Hiddushei Aggadot* ("Original Ideas About Talmudic Legends") are an attempt to interpret the Talmudic *aggadot* (see AGGADAH) in a rational way. His other major work, *Zikhron Devarim* ("Recollection of Words"), is a collection of his writings by scholars of Posen.

Edels attacked wealthy people who tried to control communal offices and rabbis who misused their power. In 1590, he took part in the rabbinic Council of the Four Lands, which imposed a ban on people who had used their money to secure a position in the rabbinate.

EDEN, GARDEN OF (Heb. *Gan Eden*). The garden where God placed ADAM AND EVE immediately after they were created (Gen. 2). Eden contained "every tree that is pleasant to the sight and good for food," as well as "the TREE OF LIFE" and "the tree of knowledge of good and evil." A river flowed from Eden, dividing into four branches: the Pishon; the Gihon; the Tigris; and the Euphrates. After Adam and Eve ate from the "Tree of Knowledge," they were banned from Eden so they would not eat from the "Tree of Life" and live for ever. ANGELS with flaming swords blocked their entrance.

Scholars believe that according to the geographic information in Genesis 2:10–14, Eden is located in the Persian Gulf, in Bahrain.

In Jewish literature, Eden is considered to be the example of perfection. The prophet EZEKIEL writes of "Eden, the Garden of God," with every kind of precious stone within it (Ezek. 28:13), and of the amazing trees growing within the garden (Ezek. 31:8–10). Later, the rabbis talk about two different Gardens of Eden: the earthly one below and the heavenly one above. The heavenly Garden of Eden is Paradise; thus *Avot* 5:20 says, "The brazen is doomed to Gehinnom while the modest will go to the Garden of Eden." *Yalkut Shimoni* describes Eden as a place where four rivers flow: of milk, wine, balsam, and honey. In it, 800,000 kinds of trees grow, and in each corner 600,000 angels sing in praise of God. God Himself sits in the Garden of Eden, explaining the Torah to the righteous people of all times.

EDUCATION Judaism has always considered the study of the TORAH to be extremely important. The Bible commands: "You shall teach them [biblical laws] carefully to your children" (Deut. 6:7). This verse has become part of the first paragraph of SHEMA, which is recited in the daily morning and evening prayers. The Bible mentions in four places the father's responsibility to tell his children about the EXODUS from Egypt (Ex. 10:2; 13:8, 14; Deut. 6:20–21). In biblical times it was the father's duty to teach his children both religious and practical subjects. The Bible also commands the LEVITES to teach the people: "They shall teach your laws to Jacob and your instruction to Israel" (Deut. 33:10). After the return from the Babylonian EXILE, EZRA gathered the people of Israel and read the Torah before them (Neh. 8).

According to tradition, it was Ezra who began the custom of reading the Bible every Monday and Thursday morning, on the days when people came to the markets.

The Mishnah quotes Rabbi Judah ben Tema on the subject of education: "Five years old is the age for the study of the Bible, ten years old for the Mishnah, thirteen for the obligation to keep the commandments, and fifteen years old for the study of the GEMARA" (*Avot* 5:25). According to Jewish law, parents must begin the education of their children at the earliest possible age. According to the Talmud, a father must teach his son Talmud, an occupation, and, according to some, to swim (*Kid.* 29a).

SIMEON BEN SHETAH (1st cent. BCE) established the first schools, and obligated parents to send their sons to them. However it was Rabbi Joshua ben Gamla (1st cent. CE) who really created the first educational system. He had been a HIGH PRIEST before the TEMPLE was destroyed, and he appointed teachers in every town. The Talmud says of him: "May Rabbi Joshua ben Gamla be remembered for the good, for had it not been for him, the Torah would have been forgotten in Israel" (*BB* 21a). The Talmud also gave guidelines for the size of the class. One teacher may teach up to 25 students. If there are between 25 and 40 students, a teacher's assistant should be hired. More than 40 students require two teachers.

In Babylonia, there were ACADEMIES where important scholars gave lectures, but these were often too complicated for common people. However, twice a year, special study sessions known as *kallah*, were held for common people (see KALLAH MONTHS).

It is likely that in the period between the completion of the Talmud (500 CE) and the EMANCIPATION of the Jews in modern times, most Jewish males received some kind of education and could read and write. Usually they studied only holy books; however, there were times when education also included secular subjects. The Spanish Jews in the 12th and 13th centuries, for example, were open to the outside world. Some rabbis felt that there was no contradiction between the need to study Torah and the need to study worldly subjects. Joseph Ibn Aknin (1150–1220), who wrote *Mevo ha-Talmud*, felt that a complete education should include the study of logic, rhetoric, arithmetic, geometry, astronomy, music, the sciences, and metaphysics. However, when the Jews were persecuted, the study of secular subjects was forbidden in many places.

Beginning in the 19th century until the emancipation of the Jews, the typical educational framework in both Ashkenazi and Sephardi communities was the HEDER (Yid. and Heb. word for room). The *heder* was a single classroom, with one teacher and a number of students studying only religious subjects. In certain communities there was an organized TALMUD TORAH, which had different classes, but the studies were also mostly or only religious. Sometimes some secular subjects would be taught, mostly to help pupils understand the religious subjects. Most children would attend these schools for a few years but would then begin to work at a very young age.

In the 19th century, organized *yeshivot* were opened, mostly in Eastern Europe. Great talmudic centers developed, such as Tels, Ponevezh, and Slobodka, as well as different Hasidic centers. These *yeshivot* had official levels, with students moving up from one class to the next. The *yeshivot* usually took students in their teens, and the better students would go on to a lifetime of Torah study. They studied Talmud and HALAKHAH (Jewish law), with no secular studies.

With the emancipation, Jews began to study secular subjects such as mathematics, languages, and sciences, once again. This was the beginning of the HASKALAH ("Enlightenment") movement. In the 19th century, Rabbi Samson Raphael HIRSCH spread the idea of *Torah im Derekh Erets*, a strong Jewish education with secular studies. Many schools were opened along these lines in Western Europe, and they formed the basis for Jewish education today. East European *yeshivot* began to include the study of ethics under the influence of the MUSSAR MOVEMENT. The French organization Alliance Israélite Universelle opened schools in North Africa and the Middle East in which secular and religious subjects were studied in French.

Once Jews began to attend public schools, supplementary schools were opened in order to provide Jewish education to supplement the secular education provided by the public schools. In Western Europe and in the English-speaking world, this was the model during the first half of the 20th century. In certain areas, Jewish day schools were set up, which taught Jewish subjects as well as the public school curriculum.

After World War II, the Jewish community realized that the supplementary schools were not enough. This caused a huge growth in Jewish day schools. In the United States, the *Torah U-Mesorah* network grew from 100 to 600 schools. Later, the CONSERVATIVE movement opened their own Solomon Shechter schools, and even the REFORM movement now sponsors day schools. In other countries, the Zionist movement has opened day school with a strong emphasis on the study of modern Hebrew.

New models of Jewish schools of higher education were developed at the end of the 19th century (see RABBINICAL SEMINARIES), which aimed to study Judaism from a modern point of view. In the United States, the Reform and Conservative rabbinical seminaries, Hebrew Union College and the Jewish Theological Seminary, were modeled after German schools in Berlin and Breslau. The ORTHODOX movement also made changes. It opened New York's Yeshiva University, where a *yeshiva*h education is combined with a Liberal Arts education. These seminaries now have graduate schools in all fields of Jewish studies.

Until as late as the 20th century, Jewish females were mostly uneducated (see WOMEN). Rabbi Eliezer stated: "He who teaches his daughter Torah, teaches her lewdness" (*Sot.* 3:4). While this was always considered a very extreme view, women were usually taught only the laws that affected their daily lives. The statement was interpreted to mean that women could be taught Bible, but not ORAL LAW. The Reform movement did not accept any difference in the education of men and women.

In 1917, Sara Schnirer started the Beth Jacob (*Beis Yakov*) Orthodox school system. These schools offered women a Jewish education, but did not teach Mishnah and Talmud. Today the Stern College for Women of Yeshiva University does offer talmudic study for women, as do many Orthodox day schools. The Reform and Conservative rabbinical schools now both ordain women to be rabbis on a regular basis.

Nowadays, there are many *yeshivot* where post-high school students can spend a few years studying as adults (see KOLLEL). Since World War II, Judaic Studies departments in many universities have grown, and both Jewish and non-Jewish students can take courses in Hebrew and other areas of Judaism.

EDUYYOT ("Testimonies"). Seventh tractate (book) of the Order of NEZIKIN in the Mishnah. Unlike most tractates, *Eduyyot* is made up of a variety of laws on many different subjects. The subjects include menstruation, the priest's share of the dough, the MIKVEH (ritual bath), TITHES, and MARRIAGE. It also contains 30 laws in which the School of Hillel has a stricter opinion than the School of Shammai (see BET SHAMMAI AND BET HILLEL). *Eduyyot* has eight chapters. The purpose of this collection was to record the later rabbis' "testimonies" of the opinions of earlier rabbis.

EHAD MI YODE'A ("Who Knows One?"). Popular table song dating from the 15th century, which ASHKENAZIM sing near the end of the SEDER on PASSOVER. The song is in Hebrew, but a few Aramaic words are used for the sake of rhyme. It is made up of short questions and answers that explain the significance of the numbers 1–13. The Talmud teaches that children should be encouraged to stay awake and ask questions throughout the *Seder* night, and this song is placed at the end to give the children another reason to stay awake.

Ehad Mi Yode'a was first included in the Ashkenazi *haggadot* in the 16th century. It was probably taken from an old

Detail from the page on which Ehad mi Yode'a *appears. From the* Vienna Haggadah. *Austria, 1752.*

German song that the Church used for its own needs. The German-speaking Jews changed the words but kept the phrase "One is our God in heaven and on earth" as the refrain of *Ehad Mi Yode'a*. The original song ended at the number 12, because Christians believe 13 to be an unlucky number. *Ehad Mi Yode'a* was later adopted by many other Jewish communities and used on other occasions in addition to the Passover *Seder*.

EINHORN, DAVID (1809–1879). American REFORM rabbi. Born in Bavaria, Germany, Einhorn was one of the first *yeshivah* students to study in the university as well. From the very beginning, Einhorn was a radical Reform Jew; therefore it was difficult for him to get a position as a rabbi. In 1852 he was appointed rabbi of a Liberal synagogue in Budapest, but the synagogue was closed by the government. In 1855 Einhorn moved to Baltimore and became the rabbi of the Har Sinai Congregation. He was forced to leave Baltimore in 1861 because of his anti-slavery viewpoint. In 1866 he became rabbi of Adath Israel (later Temple Beth El) in New York.

Einhorn believed that the moral and ethical elements of the Bible were the only eternal part of Judaism, and all other details of Jewish law must change with the times. This was considered a very radical opinion at the time, and he was somewhat of an outsider among American Reform rabbis. His main opponent was Isaac Mayer WISE, who gained support in the Midwest. Einhorn was a thinker, not a builder, and Wise understood the needs of American Jewish life more than Einhorn could.

Einhorn published a prayer book called *Olat Tamid* (1856), on which the *Union Prayer Book* (1892) was based. The Pittsburgh Platform (1885), a major convention of Reform rabbis was mostly the work of his son-in-law and student Kaufmann Kohler, and caused Einhorn's opinion to be influential after his death.

EISENDRATH, MAURICE NATHAN (1902–1973). Rabbi and leader of American REFORM JUDAISM. Born in Chicago, he was educated at the University of Cincinnati and at Hebrew Union College. In 1929–1943 he was the rabbi of the Holy Blossom Congregation in Toronto. In 1943, he returned to Cincinnati as the director of the Union of American Hebrew Congregations.

EHAD MI YODE'A – WHO KNOWS ONE?

(last stanza)

Who knows thirteen? I know thirteen!
Thirteen are the attributes of God;
Twelve are the tribes of Israel;
Eleven are the stars in Joseph's dream;
Ten are the Commandments;
Nine are the months of pregnancy;
Eight are the days for circumcision;
Seven are the days of the week;
Six are the Orders of the Mishnah;
Five are the books of the Torah;
Four are the Matriarch mothers of Israel;
Three are the Patriarch fathers;
Two are the Tablets of the Law;
One is our God in heaven and on earth!

People felt at the time that the organization was not adapting itself to changes in American Jewry, and Eisendrath quickly transformed it. He was active in many causes that the synagogue had not been involved in before, such as supporting the State of Israel and social action. When he established a social center in Washington, people feared that it would become a political organization, and they began to oppose him.

Eisendrath was part of a new generation of Reform Jews who were not as anti-traditional as before. Both the HOLOCAUST and the State of Israel caused them to see things differently. Eisendrath guided the Reform community to strive for a better society. He was a follower of Isaac Mayer WISE, but also left his own stamp on Reform Judaism.

EL   See GOD, NAMES OF

EL ADON   ("God, the Lord over all works"). Alphabetical "Hymn of Creation" recited during the Sabbath MORNING SERVICE. It was probably written in the geonic era (8th–9th cent.; see GAON), and it replaces a shorter poem (*El Barukh Gedol De'ah*), which is read during the week. *El Adon* has 22 lines and uses images from the Book of Ezekiel to give praise to God for creating the sun, moon, and planets. There are minor differences in the text in the Ashkenazi, Sephardi, Oriental, and Hasidic prayer books.

ELDERS   (Heb. *zekenim*). In biblical society, persons who had reached a special status because of their age, wisdom, and social position. The earliest mention of the elders in the Bible is when God tells MOSES to gather 70 men already known as elders of the people. They were to experience the SHEKHINAH, God's Presence, and share the leadership with Moses (Num. 11:16, 24).

The Bible also mentions the "elders of the city" when it discusses five laws that appear in Deuteronomy: blood redemption (Deut. 19:12, see BLOOD AVENGER), murder by an unknown attacker (Deut. 21:1–9), REBELLIOUS SON (18–21), rape of a virgin (Deut. 22:13–21), and marriage of a childless widow to her late husband's brother (Deut. 25:5–10; see LEVIRATE MARRIAGE). All of these laws involve serious family matters and therefore the elders are involved. The Mishnah (*Avot,* intro.) teaches that in Bible times the elders were responsible for continuing Jewish tradition after JOSHUA's death, and they then passed this responsibility on to the prophets.

In Talmud times, the title "elder" was given to scholars. The Talmud discusses the case of a ZAKEN MAMREH (rebellious elder), a scholar who goes against a final decision of the Great SANHEDRIN (see Deut. 17:8–12; *Sanh.* 11:2).

After talmudic times, the title "elder" is used both for a leader of the community and for a scholar. From the middle of the 18th century, the term disappeared completely. Modern anti-Semites have used the term to describe an aging Jewish leadership whom they accuse of plotting to control the planet, as in the late 19th century forgery, the "Protocols of the Learned Elders of Zion" (see ANTI-SEMITISM).

ELEAZAR BEN AZARIAH   Palestinian *tanna* (rabbi) of the second generation. Eleazar was born a few years before the destruction of the Second Temple, and fled to the Galilee during the Jewish Revolt of 66–73 CE. He inherited great wealth from his father and studied under Yose he-Gelili. When Rabban GAMALIEL II was removed from the position of president of the SANHEDRIN, Eleazar was chosen to take over the position. He was only 18 years old at the time, and it is said that he miraculously grew 18 rows of gray hair to make him look more mature. It was then that he made his well-known remark, which appears in the Passover HAGGADAH: "I am like a 70-year-old" (*Ber.* 28a).

As *nasi* (president) of the Sanhedrin, Eleazar made a drastic change. He allowed all who wished to study to do so at the academy, as opposed to Rabban Gamaliel's policy of only allowing advanced scholars to study in the *bet midrash*. He also settled all questions of Jewish law that remained unsolved at the time. After Rabban Gamaliel was reappointed *nasi*, he shared the leadership with Eleazar.

Eleazar concentrated on the plain meaning (PESHAT) of the text of the Bible, saying: "The words of the TORAH are written in the language of ordinary people" (*Kid.* 17b). He also taught about the importance of doing good deeds in addition to learning Torah. "If there is no proper behavior, there is no Torah…" (*Avot* 3:17).

ELEAZAR BEN JUDAH BEN KALONYMUS OF WORMS   (known as Eleazar Roke'ah; c. 1165–c. 1230). mystic, scholar, and religious poet; the best-known writer and main spokesman of HASIDEI ASHKENAZ and the best-known student of JUDAH HE-HASID. His wife and daughters were killed by the Crusaders (see ANTI-SEMITISM), and his son was injured. Rabbi Eleazar wrote a memoir in which he described his family's suffering, and he dedicated a poem to his wife and daughters. He felt that the long line of his family was coming to an end. In his book, *Sefer ha-Hokhmah* ("The Book of Wisdom," 1217), he describes his loneliness after his teacher Rabbi Judah He-Hasid's death.

Eleazar's main work was his commentary on the prayer book. It was very detailed and was the first commentary on the prayer book written in the Middle Ages. He also wrote a major book of Jewish law called *Roke'ah*, which had two important prefaces. One was about the "Ways of Hasidism" and the other was about REPENTANCE. He also wrote a major work about Jewish mysticism called *Sodei Razzaya*, "The Secret of Secrets." In this book, he used his teacher's ideas and summarized the traditions of the *Hasidei Ashkenaz*.

Eleazar believed that God's light had once revealed itself to the world, creating a bridge between God above and man below. In order to be able to "see" this situation, a person must always search for God by praying, humility, and loving all people. Many mystics in the following generations made use of his ideas.

ELECTION   See CHOSEN PEOPLE

ELIEZER BEN HYRCANUS   (c. 40–c. 120 BCE). *Tanna* (rabbi) of the second generation of Mishnah times, also known as Rabbi Eliezer the Great; student of Rabbi JOHANAN BEN ZAKKAI. Eliezer had an amazing memory, and Rabbi Johanan compared him to a "plastered cistern [well] that never loses a drop." Over 300 of Eliezer's *halakhot* are recorded in the Mishnah, and 300 more in the *Tosefta* and the *baraitot* (see BARAITA). After the Second Temple was destroyed, he moved from Jerusalem to the new Academy of Yavneh. Later he established his own Academy in Lydda (Lod; see ACADEMIES). He and Rabban Gamaliel II went to Rome (c. 95 CE) to try to improve the Jews' conditions.

Rabbi Eliezer had very strong, conservative opinions, and he tended to explain the Bible quite literally. For example, he insisted that the biblical "eye for an eye; tooth for a tooth" (Ex. 21:23; see RETALIATION) should be taken literally. This caused many disagreements with other rabbis, especially his student Rabbi AKIVA. When Eliezer defied a ruling made by all of the other rabbis, he was excommunicated (see EXCOMMUNICATION; *BM* 59b). Despite the excommunication, Rabbi Eliezer was highly respected throughout the world. When he died, the rabbis lifted the ban and mourned his death. He wrote several books of MIDRASH, including *Pirkei de-Rabbi Eliezer*.

SAYINGS OF ELIEZER BEN HYRCANUS

Work is great, for even Adam tasted nothing until he had labored to produce it (cf. Gen. 2:15).

One who brings no children into the world is like a murderer.

If two men appear in a court before you, one wicked and the other pious, do not prejudice your decision against the wicked one.

Cherish your friend's honor as you do your own; do not be easily provoked to anger; repent one day before your death [i.e., every day].

When you pray, know before Whom you stand.

When a man sincerely wishes to become a non-believer, draw him near rather than keep him at arms length.

ELIJAH   (9th cent. BCE). Prophet who lived during the rule of Ahab, king of ISRAEL, and his son Ahaziah. The story of his life is told in I Kings 17–19, 21 and II Kings 1–2.

Elijah fought to purify the belief of the people of Israel in one God. They had been influenced by Jezebel, Ahab's Phoenician wife, to worship the BAAL. When the priests of Baal gathered on Mount Carmel (I Kings 18:16), Elijah asked the people of Israel: "How long will you waver between two opinions? If the Lord is God follow Him; and if Baal [is a god], follow him!" The prophets of Baal tried, but could not bring down a fire from heaven to burn their sacrifice. Elijah said a prayer, and a fire came down from heaven and burned his sacrifice. The people then said: "The Lord, He is God," and the prophets of Baal were killed.

Elijah was always in conflict with Ahab. He tried to undermine Ahab's rule as king, but was forced instead to wander from place to place. An important moment in Elijah's life was when God's word was revealed to him in the cave on Mount Horeb (traditionally Mount SINAI). God commanded him to do three things in the future: to anoint Hazazel as king of Aram, to anoint Jehu as king of Israel, and to anoint ELISHA to be the next prophet (I Kings 19). When the time came for Elijah to die, he was carried off to heaven in a fiery chariot with fiery horses (II Kings 2).

In rabbinic literature, Elijah is thought to give the final word on problems that cannot be solved. Many of these questions end with the word *teku* in the Talmud, which is said to be an acronym (see ACROSTICS) for "the Tishbite [Elijah] will decide." This is based on the belief that Elijah will bring peace to the world and between parents and children.

Because Elijah never really died, many stories have been told of his reappearance on earth, often to save Jews or Jewish communities. In talmudic times, he "taught" some of the sages, the result being the books *Midrash Eliyahu Rabbah* ("Great Midrash of Elijah") and *Midrash Eliyahu Zuta* ("Small Book of Elijah").

In the GRACE AFTER MEALS, Jews pray for Elijah to bring good news: "The Merciful One [God] will send us Elijah the prophet, may he be remembered for good, and he will bring us good news and consolation." According to legend, Elijah has appeared to great scholars and has also appeared in synagogues when a tenth man was needed for the MINYAN.

Elijah is known as the one who will announce the REDEMPTION and the arrival of the MESSIAH (Mal. 3:23): "Lo I will send the prophet Elijah to you before the coming of the awesome, fearful day of the Lord." For this reason, a fifth cup of wine stands on the Passover SEDER table, known as "Elijah's cup."

Jews leave the door open on Passover eve in the hope that Elijah will come and bring the redemption. Many songs are sung about the longing for the redemption that include Elijah. They are sung mostly after the Sabbath, which is a time when Jews traditionally think about a better future. See also ELIJAH, CHAIR OF.

ELIJAH, CHAIR OF   A chair upon which a baby boy is placed before his CIRCUMCISION. When the baby is placed on the chair, the *mohel* (circumciser) says: "This is the chair of the prophet ELIJAH, blessed be his memory!" Elijah is called the "angel of circumcision," because he tried to cause the Israelites to circumcise their children when they were worshiping BAAL. According to the MIDRASH, God told Elijah that because he believed the Jews had abandoned the covenant, he would be present at every circumcision ("covenant" = berit = circumcision) to see that the Jews had not left their faith.

ELIJAH BEN SOLOMON ZALMAN (Gaon of Vilna; also known by the acronym *ha-Gra*; 1720–1797). Outstanding Talmud scholar. He was born into a family of important rabbis and studied with his father. He was a child prodigy and, at the age of six, gave a learned talk at the Great Synagogue of Vilna. By the age of 13, he had mastered the Talmud and KABBALAH (mystical literature), and he married at the age of 18. He traveled around until the age of 25, when he settled as a hermit on the outskirts of Vilna. A special House of Study was built for him at the edge of the city, and his fame as a scholar spread throughout the Jewish world.

The *Gra* lived as a student-hermit until the age of 40. He was always wearing his prayer shawl and TEFILLIN, seeing no one, sleeping no more than two hours a day, and noting in his diary any wasted minutes. He never held a position in the community or corresponded with other rabbis or the community. Following a talmudic tradition, he came out of seclusion at the age of 40 and took on a small number of students, who were already all scholars. He studied natural sciences in order to understand the Torah, in addition to his study of the Bible, Talmud, and Kabbalah. He was also interested in the study of Hebrew grammar. He was greatly opposed to the study of what he called the "accursed" philosophy. He also opposed the modern HASKALAH movement, even though at the time, its members were still observant Jews.

Elijah attacked the Hasidim, whose influence was quickly spreading throughout Europe. He considered the Kabbalah to be above the *halakhah* and meant to be studied only by very great scholars who had already studied all of the Talmud. He was also worried that the way the Hasidim highly honored their TSADDIK (leader) would lead to more false Messiahs (see SHABBETAI TSEVI). He objected to the fact that the Hasidim taught the Kabbalah as popular literature, and he thought that the joyful style of the Hasidim mocked the seriousness of the Torah. The Hasidic leaders Menaham Mendel of Vitebsk and SHNEUR ZALMAN OF LYADY tried to meet with Elijah, but he put them in *herem* (EXCOMMUNICATION), and refused to

Elijah ben Solomon Zalman, the Gaon of Vilna.

speak to them. The Gaon's opposition turned most Lithuanian Jews into MITNAGGEDIM (oppositionists), but did not stop the Hasidim in the long run.

Toward the end of his life the Gaon set out for the Land of Israel, but for unknown reasons he returned. He encouraged his students to go to Erets Israel, which they did about ten years after his death.

The prayer customs of the Gaon were collected by his student Issachar Baer in his book *Ma'aseh Rav*. It eventually was called *Siddur ha-Gra* ("Prayer Book of the *Gra*"), and is still used. Elijah left 70 books and commentaries, most of which were published after his death. His work was mostly in the form of notes and comments on the Bible, Mishnah, *Tosefta*, Talmud, early mystical works, and Rabbi Joseph CARO's *Shulhan Arukh*. He had strict opinions about Jewish law and tried to bring back traditions and laws that were no longer used.

ELIMELECH OF LYZHANSK (1717–1787). Early leader of HASIDISM, who especially promoted the practice of extreme devotion to the Hasidic *Rebbe* or TSADDIK. Elimelech traveled to DOV BAER OF MAZHIRECH and became one of his followers. After the death of Dov Baer, Elimelech became a Hasidic mas-

---

SAYINGS OF THE VILNA GAON

Desires must be purified and idealized, not removed.

Life is a series of aggravations and pains,
sleepless nights are the common lot.

It is better to pray at home, for in the synagogue it is impossible to escape envy and hearing idle talk.

Like rain, the Torah nourishes useful
plants and poisonous weeds.

The tongue's sin weighs as much as all other sins put together.

Only things acquired by hard labor and
great struggle are of any value.

ter in Lyzhansk, Galicia, and was one of the fathers of Polish Hasidism. His book *No'am Elimelekh* was first published in 1787 and soon became a manual for Hasidic Jews. The book was a running commentary on the Torah, and also contained a great deal about Hasidic beliefs and the Hasidic way of life. Elimelech stressed the *Rebbe*'s position as a kind of religious superman who lives in a higher world and connects God to humanity.

In Elimelech's time, there were many harsh disagreements among different streams of Judaism. The Yiddish anti-Hasidic folksong, *Der Rebbe Elimelech*, portrays Elimelech as a Hasidic "Old King Cole." The song mocks the Hasidic joy in serving God and was probably written by a Lithuanian *Mitnagged* or HASKALAH writer.

Elimelech's two leading students were Jacob Isaac, "the Seer" of Lublin (1745–1815), and Kalonymus Kalman Epstein of Cracow (d. 1823), author of *Ma'or va-Shemesh*.

ELISHA   Prophet and student of ELIJAH. Elijah was commanded to anoint Elisha as a prophet on Mount Horeb (1 Kings 19:19–21). Elisha then followed Elijah until Elijah was taken to heaven.

Elisha was said to have performed many miracles. By striking the water of the Jordan, he caused it to split so that he could cross over on dry land, (II Kings 2:13); a poor widow's jar of oil was miraculously refilled (II Kings 4:1–7); a son was born to a Shunnamite woman after many childless years (II Kings 4:14–17); a dead child was brought back to life (II Kings 4:35); and the leprosy of Naaman, the Aramean captain, was cured (II Kings 5).

Elisha continued Elijah's struggle against the House of King Ahab and against BAAL worship. He had Jehu anointed king and told him to destroy the House of Joram, the son of Ahab.

ELISHA BEN AVUYAH   (c. 70–c. 140 CE). *Tanna* (rabbi) of the third generation of Mishah times; a great scholar who nevertheless gave up the teachings and customs of the rabbis. The Talmud gives several different reasons for Elisha's becoming a non-believer. One source says that he was involved in mysticism, which caused him to go crazy (*Hag.* 14b). Others say he was affected by the collapse of the BAR KOKHBA revolt (132–135 CE), which caused him to believe that God was not involved in the world, nor in reward and punishment. Having lost his belief in basic Jewish ideas, he was attracted to the early Christian sect. The Talmud calls him *Aher* ("Another"), so as not to mention his name. Elisha was not abandoned by his student Rabbi MEIR, who continued to quote him and tried to bring him back to Judaism. Many of Elisha's sayings, which are about doing good deeds and ethics, appear in the Talmud.

In the 19th century, some modern Jewish thinkers identified with Elisha ben Avuyah and said he was treated unfairly by the other rabbis. In 1939 Milton Steinberg wrote a historical novel about his life and career called *As a Driven Leaf*.

ELI TSIYYON VE-AREHA   ("Let Zion and its cities mourn"). Opening words of a prayer that is said at the end of the MORNING SERVICE on the fast of TISHAH BE-AV. The author of the prayer is unknown, but it is traditionally thought to be written by JUDAH HALEVI. *Eli Tsiyyon* is a poem, with the second word of each line beginning with a different Hebrew letter, in alphabetical order (see ACROSTICS). It tells about the horror of the destruction of the Second Temple.

EL MALEI RAHAMIM   ("God, full of compassion"). Prayer for the dead said by ASHKENAZIM; its Sephardi equivalent is the *hashkavah* (see MEMORIAL PRAYERS). Some say it was originally written in the time of the Crusades (11th cent.), when Christian troops marched through Jewish towns in Europe killing and maiming. However it is more likely that it was written during the Chmielnicki massacres in Eastern Europe (1648–49). A person who is observing a YAHRZEIT (anniversary of death) for a parent or other relative, is called to the READING OF THE LAW close to the date, and the *El Malei Rahamim* prayer is recited in memory of the person. *El Male Rahamim* is recited in the synagogue on the three PILGRIM FESTIVALS and on the DAY OF ATONEMENT. It is also said at a funeral, when visiting the graves of close relatives, and when unveiling a tombstone.

Memorial services throughout the world often include a special *El Malei Rahamim* for the victims of the Nazi HOLOCAUST. There is also a special prayer, said mainly in Israel, for those who died fighting for the State. *El Malei Rahamim* is chanted to a solemn melody, and is usually very dramatic and emotional.

EL MALEI RAHAMIM

O God, full of compassion, Who lives above, grant a perfect rest on the wings of Your Holy Presence – in the holy places among the holy and the pure ones who shine like the brightness of the sky – to the soul of …(the name of the deceased is added here), who has gone to his/her eternal rest. May the Compassionate One shelter him/her forever in His protective wings and may his/her soul be tied up in the bond of everlasting life. The Lord is his/her inheritance; may he/she rest in peace, and let us say: Amen.

EL MELEKH NE'EMAN   ("God is a faithful King"). Short prayer said by Ashkenazi Jews before the SHEMA when praying without a MINYAN (quorum of ten men). This phrase is added because the total number of words in the *Shema* should correspond to the 248 "limbs" that according to the rabbis, make up the human body. The *Shema* itself adds up to 245 words, so three words needed to be added. When praying with a *minyan*, the reader adds three words by repeating – *Adonai Elohekhem emet*, "The Lord your God is true." *El Melekh Ne'eman* is a declaration of faith. In addition the first letters of each word spell AMEN (see ACROSTICS).

EL NORA ALILAH   ("God who does amazing deeds"). Opening words and title of the hymn recited by Sephardi and Yemenite Jews before the Concluding (NE'ILAH) Service on the DAY OF

ATONEMENT. It was written by Moses IBN EZRA, and the first letter of each stanza spells out his name (see ACROSTICS). The text of the hymn talks about the worshiper's trust in God's forgiveness. The words and music of the hymn are very emotional, and it has been adopted by some CONSERVATIVE congregations.

ELOHIM   See GOD, NAMES OF

ELUL   (Akkad. *Elulu*). Sixth month of the Jewish religious CALENDAR; twelfth month of the Hebrew civil year, counting from TISHRI. It has 29 days, and coincides with August/ September. Its sign of the zodiac is Virgo. There are no festivals or fast days in the month of Elul; however it is a month in which Jews prepare themselves for the HIGH HOLIDAYS in Tishri. It is known as "the month of repentance, God's mercy, and forgiveness." In ancient times, messengers were sent from Jerusalem to announce the new MOON of Elul, so that the exact dates of the High Holidays could be calculated. The SHOFAR (ram's horn) is blown after the MORNING SERVICE and Psalm 27 is recited every day of Elul. Prayers of forgiveness, SELIHOT, are recited every day by SEPHARDIM and for the last week of the month by ASHKENAZIM.

EMANATION   See MYSTICISM, JEWISH

EMANCIPATION   The granting of civil rights to Jews. For many centuries the Jews lived as second-class citizens in both Christian and Muslim countries. In the Western world, in the 17th century, people began to change their attitudes. These changes increased with the growth of the Enlightenment in the 18th century. The new Protestant countries began to separate Church and State, and they returned to studying the Bible, which caused them to understand the Jews better. Some Christians thought that the Jews were so different that they could never become part of general society, and others thought that given the chance, the Jews could become productive members of society. There were disagreements among the Jews themselves. Moses MENDELSSOHN was a pioneer of Jewish emancipation. He grew up in a ghetto and became one of Prussia's most respected scholars, while remaining an observant Jew. Others believed that emancipation would lead to ASSIMILATION and that living in ghettos had helped preserve Jewish tradition. They pointed out that although Mendelssohn had remained religious, almost every one of his descendants converted to CHRISTIANITY.

In 1776, the new state constitution of Virginia stated that "all men are entitled to free practice of religion according to the dictates of their conscience." In 1786, a law of religious freedom that included Jews was passed in the United States, and the Constitution of the United States provides complete religious freedom.

These freedoms affected only a small number of Jews in America. The more important breakthrough was the French Revolution. In 1789, the Jews of France lost the powers of self-government. In 1791 they received full rights of French citizenship. The Jews became loyal French citizens, but did not change their religious beliefs. In 1806 Napoleon called an Assembly of Notables (important Jews) in order to discuss contradictions

Lionel de Rothschild, the first Jew to be sworn into the House of Commons, in 1858. From a contemporary German newspaper

that might arise between the Jews' loyalty to the State and their religion. For example: Can Jews marry Christians? How does Jewish law see French Christians? The Notables were able to answer all of Napoleon's questions. They said that the law against intermarrying applied to heathens in biblical times, but not to France today. Napoleon called a "Great Sanhedrin," made up mostly of rabbis, to approve the Notables' decisions. It confirmed that French rabbis were spiritual leaders only, and that French Jews would not require separate rabbinical courts for civil matters. The Jews no longer considered themselves a separate nation and did not want to leave France and return to Zion (see CONSISTORY). Napoleon's armies help spread the ideas of equality and civil rights all over Europe. In Italy, for example, Napoleon's armies, the local Christians, and the Jews tore down the gates of the ghettos.

By the 1870s emancipation had reached all of Central and Western Europe. The Jews now faced a new challenge: living amongst the Christians as Jews. Many Jews became completely assimilated and converted to Christianity. REFORM JUDAISM was founded by Jews who thought that traditional Jewish life was outdated. Orthodoxy also changed certain of its elements through the development of NEO-ORTHODOXY.

Emancipation did not reach the Jews of Eastern Europe until the March 1917 Revolution. After the Bolshevik Revolution, the Jews were granted civil rights in Russia, but the new government outlawed all religion, including Judaism.

In Muslim countries, Jews were awarded emancipation only after the breakup of the Ottoman Empire in the first part of the 20th century. In distant lands such as Yemen, Jews were never emancipated. They first received civil rights when they left those countries and arrived in Israel.

EMDEN, JACOB (1697–1776). Talmud scholar, rabbi, son of "Hakham Tsevi" ASHEKANZI, also known by the acronym *Yavets* (Ya'akov ben Tsevi). Emden was born and lived mainly in Altona, Germany. He established his own printing press, which he used to publish criticism of other German rabbis of his time. He wrote about 40 works on Jewish law (including RESPONSA), as well as his *Siddur Bet Ya'akov*, a prayer book with commentary. He was greatly opposed to the messianic movement of SHABBETAI TSEVI, which he saw as a threat to Judaism. This is why he rejected the ZOHAR, a classic work of Jewish mysticism. He constantly struggled against Jonathan EYBESCHÜTZ, the rabbi of Altona, Hamburg, and Wandsbeck, whom he perhaps rightly suspected of following Shabbetai Tsevi. He was on friendly terms with Moses MENDELSSOHN the pioneer of EMANCIPATION. Emden's autobiography, *Megillat Sefer* (1896), contains important religious and historical information about 18th century German Jewry.

EMET VE-EMUNAH ("True and faithful"). Blessing recited daily in the EVENING SERVICE that forms a bridge between the SHEMA and the AMIDAH. The subject of the blessing is God's uniqueness and power to redeem the people of Israel (see REDEMPTION). According to the Mishnah, this blessing is the first and longest of the two blessings that follow the *Shema* (Ber. 1:4), the other being HASHKIVENU. In the MORNING SERVICE, EMET VE-YATSIV is recited instead. Both prayers were originally said in the Temple (*Tam.* 5:1) as a "blessing of redemption" (see GE'ULAH). Psalm 92:3 declares that it is praiseworthy "to declare God's lovingkindness in the morning and His faithfulness every night." For this reason, *Emet ve-Yatsiv* is recited after daybreak and *Emet ve-Emunah* is recited after nightfall (*Ber.* 12a). No interruption may be made between saying the last words of the third paragraph of *Shema* and the first word of *Emet ve-Emunah* (*Ber.* 14a–b).

EMET VE-YATSIV ("True and firm"). Opening words of the GE'ULAH ("redemption") blessing recited daily in the MORNING SERVICE. It is a bridge between the SHEMA and the AMIDAH. It was probably recited in the Temple (*Tam.* 5:1), and according to the Mishnah is the blessing after the *Shema* (*Ber.* 1:4). EMET VE-EMUNAH is the parallel blessing that is recited in the EVENING SERVICE, and the source of both prayers is a verse in Psalms (92:3). No interruption may be made between saying the last words of the third paragraph of *Shema* and the first word of *Emet ve-Yatsiv* (*Ber.* 2:2, 9b, 14a–b). The theme of the prayer is the Jewish people's belief in One God and in the eternal truth of His TORAH.

EMISSARY See SHALI'AH

EN K(E)-ELOHEINU ("There is none like our God"). Opening words and title of a hymn that has been part of the prayers since the ninth century. Ashkenazi congregations outside of Israel sing it only on Sabbaths and festivals at the end of the ADDITIONAL SERVICE. Most other communities, including Israeli ASHKENAZIM, sing it at the end of the weekday MORNING SERVICE. The hymn is made up of five sets of four short phrases that repeat four of God's Names ("God," "Lord," "King," and "Savior"). Jewish mystics claim that these names refer to four of God's powers involved in the process of creation. In Sephardi-Oriental tradition, *En K(e)-Eloheinu* ends with a verse of Psalms (102:14), while the Ashkenazi version connects with PITTUM HA-KETORET, a passage about the spices burned in the TEMPLE.

ENLIGHTENMENT See HASKALAH

ENOCH (Heb. Hanokh). Biblical figure. Enoch was the son of Jared (Gen. 5:18), born the seventh generation after ADAM. Unlike other people of his time, Enoch lived only 365 years (the number of days of the solar year). The Bible says about Enoch that he "walked with God; then he was no more, for God took him" (Gen. 5:23).

The unusual description of Enoch's death has inspired many legends, which were recorded in several books of MIDRASH. Enoch was taken to heaven, where he became a heavenly scribe. He was said to be the inventor of all sciences and knowledge, since he knew the secrets of God. These and other legends can also be found throughout the APOCRYPHA AND PSEUDEPIGRAPHA.

Early Christian sources also contain many legends about Enoch; however, there is no mention of him whatsoever in the Mishnah. The New Testament states that Enoch and ELIJAH were witnesses of Jesus' journey to heaven (Revelations 11:3), which is probably why the rabbis of the Mishnah did not discuss him. An early Midrash declares that Enoch went back and forth between being a righteous man and a sinner, and God took him up to heaven before he could go back to sin.

It was only after early CHRISTIANITY was no longer a threat to Judaism that Jewish authors began to write about Enoch. A late Midrash says that Enoch was taken to heaven in a fiery chariot pulled by a fiery horse. He was one of nine righteous men who did not suffer the pain of death and entered paradise alive. The ZOHAR, as well as other early mystic literature, tells many of the early legends about Enoch.

EN-SOF ("Infinite"). One of God's Names in Jewish mystical literature. It is the highest aspect of God, which human beings cannot understand. The early mystics used this term for the "hidden God" and used the different SEFIROT to discuss those aspects of God that are revealed and active (see MYSTICISM). In the ZOHAR, *En-Sof* originally meant God's never-ending thought. It was later used as a Name for God, signifying the total perfection of God. Because *En-Sof* is beyond understanding, it is discussed very little in the mystical writings; some rabbis even say that we have no hint of it from the Bible. Some Jewish mystics taught that *En-Sof* has to do with the will of God and with the highest of the *Sefirot, Keter Elyon* (the "Supreme Crown").

EPHOD   See PRIESTLY GARMENTS

EPHRAIM   See TRIBES, TWELVE

EPIKOROS (OR APIKOROS)   A non-believer; a person who does not keep all of the commandments. Originally this term was used for the followers of Epicurus, the fourth-century BCE Greek philosopher. He thought that the soul was not immortal, and therefore the most important thing was the body. In the Talmud, a person who did not believe in Jewish tradition was called an *Epikoros*. Later it came to mean anyone who was not respectful of the TORAH or its teachers and students.

According to MAIMONIDES (*Hilkhot Teshuvah* 3:8) three kinds of Jews are labeled *Epikoros*: (1) one who does not believe in prophecy; (2) one who denies that MOSES was a prophet; (3) one who says that God does not know about the daily deeds of human beings.

An *Epikoros* was often considered evil and destined not to enjoy the world to come. Today, among Orthodox Jews, the term is used for people who do not lead a religious way of life.

ERETS ISRAEL   See ISRAEL, LAND OF

EREV ("eve"). In general, the day before a holy day. Friday is referred to as *erev Shabbat* ("SABBATH eve") and the day before a festival is called *erev yom tov* (lit. "eve of the good day"). On the day before Sabbaths and festivals, the TAHANUN prayer is not said. The day before each different holiday usually has its own observances. For example, the day before PASSOVER is the Fast of the Firstborn.

In Judaism, a day is a 24-hour period from sunset until sunset; therefore the Sabbath and all festivals begin at night. The more exact meaning of *erev*, therefore, is the first evening of the holy day.

ERUSIN   See BETROTHAL

ERUV (lit. "mixing," pl. *eruvin*). A legal device used to make the SABBATH and FESTIVALS easier to observe. Because it was developed by the rabbis, it can be used to make rabbinic laws easier to follow, but not laws that are directly from the TORAH. There are several types of *eruvin*.

Eruv Hatserot ("*eruv* of courtyards"). In Torah law, it is forbidden to carry anything between a public area and a private area or for 6 feet in a public area on the SABBATH. The Torah law, however, does not forbid carrying from one private area to another. The rabbis forbade this later in order to prevent people from getting confused and accidentally carrying from a public to a private area. If there are a number of private areas with a public area connecting them (as in a condominium), they may arrange to have all the houses or apartments considered one area by using an *eruv hatserot*.

The best way to make an *eruv hatserot* is to have one of the people take a loaf of bread and hand it to a person living in another one of the houses, with the clear understanding that the bread now belongs to all of the people living in all of the apartments. The first person then takes back the loaf of bread, says a special blessing and then announces that through this *eruv*, everyone will be able to carry objects freely among the apartments and between any apartment and the common area. This only works if the area is surrounded by some kind of fence that separates it from public property.

Eruv Reshuyyot ("*eruv* of domains" or simply *eruv*). It is the most common type of *eruv* and can include an area as large as an entire city. The area is surrounded by a "partition" made of posts at least 40" high linked by string or wire going over the top of each post, which makes it a single domain or area. Once the *eruv reshuyyot* is made, one can carry within the entire area of the *eruv*. Nowadays, every city in Israel has an *eruv* as do many Jewish neighborhoods and cities in North America.

Eruv Tavshilin ("*eruv* of prepared foods"). This type of *eruv* is used when a festival falls on a Friday. It is forbidden to cook on the festival for the next day's Sabbath even though one may cook on the festival for the festival itself. An *eruv tavshilin* is made by taking a piece of bread and something cooked (such as a boiled egg) on the day before the festival, and reciting the proper blessing. This allows the family to cook for the Sabbath during the festival as if it was a continuation of cooking begun the day before.

Eruv Tehumim ("*eruv* of boundaries"). The Bible says (Ex. 16:29) "Let no man go out of his place on the Sabbath day," which means that one must stay within 12 miles of the place where one happens to be when the Sabbath begins. According to rabbinic law, a person must stay within a 2,000 cubit radius of the city on the Sabbath and festivals. A person who wishes to visit a place between 2,000 and 4,000 cubits away from the city, can make an *eruv tehumim*. One must go to a place that is 2,000 cubits away from the city before the Sabbath and leave enough food for two meals in that place. This causes the place to be considered the person's home and he can walk 2,000 cubits in any direction from that place, on the Sabbath or festival. Thus if a person makes an *eruv tehumim* 2,000 cubits to the east of the city, he may walk 4,000 cubits to the east on the Sabbath or festival.

ERUVIN ("Joining of the Sabbath Limits"). Second tractate (book) of the Order of MO'ED in the Mishnah. It is a logical continuation of the tractate SHABBAT, which comes before *Eruvin*, because it deals with travel and carrying of objects on the SABBATH. It has ten chapters that deal with different kinds of *eruvin* (see ERUV) and the activities performed only in the TEMPLE on the Sabbath.

ESCHATOLOGY The idea of a perfect world that will arise in the future, at the end of days (Heb. *aharit ha-yamim*). Eschatology in Judaism deals with the final destiny of the Jewish people and the world and not the destiny of individual people (see AFTERLIFE). It talks about Israel as God's people and the victory of God's truth and justice. When the eschatological era comes, there will be world peace and peace among all the creatures of the universe. During recent years, some Hasidim, especially the Lubavich sect, have claimed that there are signs that the MESSIAH is on its way. Some of the signs are a war between the forces of good and evil (GOG AND MAGOG) and the return of Jews to their homeland.

One of the main ideas in Jewish eschatology is the Day of the Lord, which becomes the DAY OF JUDGMENT. First, it will be the time when God punishes those who have made Him angry, and when the people of Israel have their revenge on their enemies. Second, it will be a time when the righteous receive their reward. According to ISAIAH (11:6), after the great destruction will come a time of peace both for human beings and for the animal world. Then God alone will be King and all nations will come to serve Him.

When the Jewish people returned from the Babylonian EXILE, they assumed that the last step of the REDEMPTION would be to rebuild the TEMPLE. When this did not happen, some religious leaders began to write about how they expected the redemption would come about. The latter part of the Book of DANIEL contains visions of what the redemption would be like. He describes four periods of history in their natural order:

the Babylonian, Median, Persian, and Greek monarchies. After these four periods, God will raise up his CHOSEN PEOPLE and rule the world, which would be an "everlasting kingdom" (Dan. 3:33). Later on rabbis interpreted the expression "son of man," which appears in the Book of Daniel, as the idea of Messiah. The idea of RESURRECTION also came from this prophecy.

The destruction of the Second Temple (70 CE) caused some eschatological ideas to fade away, while others survived and new ideas developed. Some ideas were preserved in the prayer book; others became part of rabbinic literature. Some saw the BAR KOKHBA revolt (132–135 CE), which was successful at first, as the beginning of an eschatological era, because the Jews managed to fight their enemy and win.

In his PRINCIPLES OF FAITH, MAIMONIDES included the belief in the world to come and in the coming of the Messiah as two of the 13 most important ideas in which a Jew must believe.

REFORM JUDAISM rejects the idea of a human Messiah, but has adopted the idea of the world moving toward a final stage of complete peace and justice. The CONSERVATIVE movement recently published its principles of belief called *Emet ve-Emunah*, which describes their idea of eschatology: "For the world community, we dream of a time when warfare will be abolished, when justice and compassion will be the basis of relationships between people and international relationships ... for our people, we dream of the gathering of all Jews to Zion where we can again be the masters of our destiny and express our special ideas in every area of national life ... for the individual human being, we believe that death does not mean extinction."

ESHET HAYIL ("Woman of Valor"). Song in praise of a virtuous wife recited by the husband before the SABBATH evening meal. It is made up of verses from the last chapter of PROVERBS (31:10–31). The first letter of each line is part of an alphabetical ACROSTIC. The poem describes a woman who is familiar with business, responsible, hard-working, charitable, and wise. She brings honor to her family, especially her husband, who, thanks to her support, becomes a leader of the community. Later on, this poem was thought to symbolically describe the TORAH or the SHEKHINAH (God's Presence).

The *Tikkunei Shabbat*, published in Prague in 1641, first suggested that *Eshet Hayil* should be recited in the home before the KIDDUSH on Sabbath eve. This became the accepted custom

---

ESHET HAYIL
(opening)

A woman of valor who can find?
Her value is far above rubies.
The heart of her husband safely trusts in her,
And he lacks nothing.
She does good to him, never evil,
All the days of her life.

in most Jewish communities. REFORM JUDAISM suggests that women read a parallel Psalm, "Happy is the man who fears the Lord ..." (112:1–9) in honor of their husbands.

ESSENES A Jewish sect active during the end of the Second Temple period (2nd cent. BCE to 1st cent. CE) in different parts of the Land of Israel, especially along the shores of the Dead Sea. The exact meaning of the name of the sect – Essenes – is unknown, but Jewish thinkers have suggested "holy ones," "pious ones," or "healers."

Until recently, the only knowledge of the sect was based on ancient historians such as Josephus and Philo. Recent discoveries in the Judean desert have added to this knowledge; however, many details, such as when the sect began, still remain a mystery. The sect may have originated in the days of Antiochus and the anti-Jewish laws in the years before the Maccabee's revolt (167 BCE).

There were over 4,000 Essenes in the early 1st century CE. The members had to be completely obedient to their superiors. A person who wished to become a member had to undergo a three-year probation period. At the end of the probation, he had to take an oath and promise to keep the teachings of the sect a secret from outsiders. Only then was he fully accepted into the sect.

Only adult males could become Essenes, but children were allowed to enter in order to be taught the ways and beliefs of the community. Members worked at agriculture or crafts. All property, money, clothing, and food belonged to the community. Officials were elected to distribute these supplies. The members of the community did not marry. No women were allowed to join, because women were considered incapable of being faithful.

The Esssenes stressed modesty, cleanliness, and ritual PURITY. They wore only white clothing and considered common pleasures to be evil. They ate their meals together, offered only non-animal sacrifices, and observed the Sabbath very strictly.

A member of the Essenes cult who spoke badly of MOSES was punished by death. Other serious crimes were punished by expulsion from the sect. They studied ETHICS very carefully, and read and discussed the TORAH in depth. During the Great Revolt against Rome (66–70 CE) the Essenes fought alongside the other Jews. When the Temple was destroyed in 70 CE, the Essenes disappeared from history.

Nowadays, historians agree that the Essenes were probably part of the Qumran community associated with the DEAD SEA SCROLLS.

ESTHER, BOOK OF One of the five "scrolls" (*megillot*) in the HAGIOGRAPHA ("Writings") section of the Bible. It tells the story of how Esther and her uncle Mordecai ruined the plans of the evil chief minister, Haman, to destroy all the Jews in the kingdom of Ahasuerus (Xerxes I, King of Persia). The story ends with the hanging of Haman, with Mordecai becoming chief minister, and with the Jews taking revenge on their enemies.

BOOK OF ESTHER

1:1–1:22	Ahaseurus' feast and removal of Vashti
2:1–2:23	Esther is chosen as queen
3:1–4:17	Haman's decree to destroy all the Jews
5:1–7:10	Esther reveals Haman's plan to the king at the second feast; he and his sons are hanged.
8:1–10:4	Mordecai is appointed as second to the king. The Jews fight their enemies and the festival of Purim is established.

The book does not mention God's name even once; the only other such book in the Bible is SONG OF SONGS. For this reason, there was a debate in the Talmud about whether or not the Book of Esther should be included in the Bible.

The Book of Esther is read in the synagogue on the festival of PURIM, which is the aniversary of the day the Jews were saved from Haman. It is read at both the EVENING and the MORNING SERVICE. It must be read from a parchment scroll, and a blessing is recited before the reading. Women, too, must hear the reading, because "they too were saved by the miracle" (*Meg.* 4a).

Modern scholars disagree about the historical value of the book. No other sources have been found that confirm the events in the Book of Esther, and sources have even been found that contradict certain parts of it. Some suggested that there is a kernel of truth, but the facts were changed in order to teach religious values, such as God's direction of all events on earth. Jews all over the world took comfort in its message about the downfall of the enemies of the people of Israel.

ESTHER, FAST OF See FASTING AND FAST DAYS

ESTHER RABBAH Midrash on the Scroll of ESTHER (see also MIDRASH AGGADAH). The original version divided the text into six sections, but in later editions there were ten chapters. Esther Rabbah's first half was probably written in the times of the *amoraim* (before 550 CE); its second half was written much later (11th–12th cent.). The sources of Esther Rabbah include: both Talmuds, GENESIS RABBAH and LEVITICUS RABBAH, the Aramaic versions of the Book of Esther, and the TARGUM SHENI. The later sources added various passages, such as the dreams of Esther and Mordecai and a description of Esther's appearance before Ahasuerus.

ETERNAL LIGHT (Heb. *ner tamid*). A lamp that burns constantly, usually found in the SYNAGOGUE. The original Eternal Light was a lamp stand or MENORAH, which was placed in the Tent of Meeting in the SANCTUARY. God commanded the people of Israel to bring clear oil from beaten olives for burning, so there would always be a light (Ex. 27:20–21). AARON and his sons were responsible for the care of the lamp and making sure it was not extinguished (Lev. 24: 3–4).

The synagogue used to have a special niche for the Eternal Light on the western wall, opposite the ARK. Nowadays, the Eternal Light hangs above the Ark in synagogues.

In the past when the Eternal Light was a wick that burned olive oil, it was considered a good deed to give donations for its upkeep. A special MI SHE-BERAKH (blessing) was said in honor of the donors after the READING OF THE LAW in synagogues on SABBATH mornings.

ETHICAL LITERATURE   In Judaism, one of the main themes of the Bible is morality. However, in later times, this subject was not developed as much as other Jewish subjects.

Three books of the Mishnah deal with ethics: AVOT, DEREKH ERETS, and KALLAH, but no Talmud commentary on these books has been preserved. Moral teachings did not often receive the attention of the rabbis who wrote the codes of Jewish law.

The first book written about ethics was *Hovot ha-Levavot* ("Duties of the Heart") by BAHYA IBN PAKUDAH (11th cent.). Bahya criticizes the scholars of his time, who only taught about the physical acts that a Jew must perform and did not pay attention to the importance of faith, love of God, repentance, and humility.

Jonah ben Abraham Leon Gerondi tried to show how people could become closer to God through their attitude and speech in his *Sha'arei Teshuvah* ("Gates of Repentance"). MOSES HAYYIM LUZZATTO wrote a book called *Mesillat Yesharim* ("The Way of the Righteous"), which discusses steps for reaching holiness. It became the most popular work of its kind. These works do not deal with relationships among people. They deal with character traits that a person should try to improve in order to become closer to God.

In the Middle Ages, it became popular for parents to write letters or wills in which they taught their last lessons to their children. They stressed the importance of moral behavior. In some families it became a custom for each generation to pass on such an "ethical will."

In the 13th century, some leaders of the HASIDEI ASHKENAZ wrote ethical books. *Sefer ha-Roke'ah* was written by ELEAZAR OF WORMS and *Sefer ha-Hasidim* was by JUDAH OF WORMS. Jewish mystics also wrote a number of ethical works. Most of the literature produced by the Hasidim in the 18th century was ethical. Among the most important are the *Tanya* by Rabbi SHNEUR ZALMAN OF LYADY and *Sefer ha-Middot*, by Rabbi NAHMAN OF BRATSLAV.

The MUSAR MOVEMENT was founded in the 19th century by ISRAEL SALANTER and continued by his student Isaac Blaser. This movement stressed the importance of ethics in Judaism. Until this time, the trend in Judaism had been to stress the importance of rituals and to neglect moral obligations, such as respect for privacy, refraining from gossip, and willingness to help others. The *Musar* movement came as a reaction to this trend and taught the complete opposite. The *Musar* movement made changes in the educational system of the *yeshivot*, so they began to develop the ethical side of Judaism. They formed a new approach to education based on an understanding of human psychology.

ETHICS   Ethics is the science of morality or the study of moral rules. The term morality refers to rules about the way people should behave toward one another and principles that teach what is good for human beings. In classic Jewish writings there is no term for ethics or morality. The modern Hebrew word *musar*, which is used today for this purpose, literally means "rebuke" or "chastisement." The Bible, however, contains an elaborate moral code.

Morality in the Bible   In the story-like books of Genesis and Exodus, and the books of the early prophets, various moral values are reflected. The Bible has a positive view of gratitude (Gen. 4:3), hospitality (Gen. 18), righteousness (Gen. 18:19), self-restraint (Gen 39–12), humility (Num. 12:3); it clearly disapproves of murder (Gen. 4:11), jealousy (Gen. 37:4), and deception (Gen. 6:11–12). Among the various lists of commandments are moral guidelines for relationships, such as those between family members, old and young, employers and employees, rich and poor, men and women, rulers and ruled. Many moral principles are presented, such as "You shall love your neighbor as yourself" (Lev. 19:18) and "You shall do what is right and good" (Deut. 16–20). We are also told that a person must be careful not to lie, curse, or slander (Lev. 19:11, 14, 16), or to speak badly about one's fellow human (Deut. 19: 16–18).

The moral characteristics used to describe God are particularly important. God's acts of CREATION and judging the world are seen as good and fair. The Bible says that a person should try to imitate God: "You shall walk in His ways" (Deut. 11:22; see IMITATION OF GOD).

In later books of the Bible, morality became an issue to think about and discuss. The Book of JOB deals with the problem of a righteous person who is suffering. The Book of JONAH discusses wicked people who apparently receive no punishment.

Morality in Rabbinic Literature   The rabbis explained the moral commandments in the same way they dealt with any other area of HALAKHAH (Jewish law). One example is a commandment such as "When you build a new house, then you shall make a fence for your roof, that you do not bring blood upon your house, if any man fall from it" (Deut. 22:8). The rabbis saw this as a law about both fences on roofs and as a general principle about responsibility for safety in the home. In discussing this law, the rabbis defined the exact height of a roof that requires a fence. They also discussed the principle of safety and decided that it should also apply to other possibly dangerous areas, such as wells and contaminated drinking water.

Another method the rabbis used was AGGADAH (folklore), which gave them many moral insights. The Mishnah *Avot* presents biblical characters such as Abraham, Aaron, and Moses as models of good character traits. They also developed lessons from different stories in the Bible. From Genesis 18:1–3 they learned that one may bend the truth for the sake of peace in the home; and from Genesis 38:25, they learned that one should prefer to be burned alive than to embarrass one's fellow human bring in public. The rabbis searched for a master principle or supreme value of the morality of Judaism. Rabbi AKIVA said of the command "You shall love your neighbor as yourself" that it is a great principle of the Torah. Rabbis also defined the highest qualities for which a person could aim: *hasidut* (kindliness) and *anavah* (humility).

The rabbis generally referred to morality by the phrase *bein adam le-havero* ("between a person and his fellow human being") or DEREKH ERETS ("ways of the world" or "right conduct"). Morality was considered one of most important aspects of Judaism. Simeon the Just said: "The world stands on three things: Torah, serving God, and acts of lovingkindness" (*Avot* 1:2). Hillel said: "What is hateful to yourself do not do to your fellow person. This is the entire Torah; the rest is commentary. Go and study" (*Shab.* 31a).

The rabbis taught that speech has great power. They condemned the use of flattery, hypocrisy, and impolite speech; they encouraged proper greetings to all and the need to cheer people up with good humor and to comfort with kind words during hard times. They based these ideas on biblical statements, such as "Death and life are in the power of the tongue" (Prov. 18: 21).

The morality of Judaism includes people's relationship with animals. In the ancient world, animals were often used for work and sport and treated with extreme cruelty. According to Jewish law, animals must be allowed to rest on the Sabbath (Ex. 20:8–10). According to the Talmud, people must provide for animals that belong to them and must not cause them unnecessary pain (*BM* 32b). When needed for food, animals may be slaughtered only as painlessly as possible (see DIETARY LAWS). It is permitted to experiment with animals only when this is directly connected to medicine.

Another feature of Jewish morality is concern for a person's dignity. One must respect the privacy of others and be careful no to cause anyone shame or embarrassment.

Sources of Moral Knowledge   From the beginning of time, people were held responsible for their actions (Gen. 4:6–7, 9:5–6). The rabbis developed this idea along with the NOACHIDE LAWS (*Sanh.* 56a–b). The Torah was necessary as a constitution for the Jewish people, but ultimately as a moral code for all people.

The morality of Judaism applies to all humanity. In the Bible, all men and women are created equal, in the image of God. The Jew is told to love his fellow Jew as himself (Lev. 19:18), to love a stranger as himself (Lev. 19:33, 34), and to love all of God's creatures (*Avot.* 1:12).

The morality of Judaism is a system. No moral code can include every possible future situation; therefore it is made up of principles such as "You shall love your neighbor as yourself." The members of each generation added individual rules for themselves, such as visiting the sick and comforting the mourner.

The Jewish moral system, like the rest of the Jewish legal system, has laws that help one decide what to do when two values conflict with each other. Thus, a positive commandment comes before a negative commandment (*Shab.* 133a), all negative commandments are put on hold in order to save a human life (Lev. 18:5), and peace is higher than truth (*Sanh.* 10). Human life, however, is not always the very highest value in Judaism. A Jew must be prepared, under certain circumstances, to sacrifice his life in defense of the Jewish people or in the name of God. These guidelines are the basis of much of Jewish law.

In Judaism, moral actions are part of Jewish law (*halakhah*), but morality is not the same as *halakhah*. Sometimes the law is less strict than a person's conscience. In such situations a person acts *lifnim mi-shurat ha-din* ("beyond the letter of the law"). For example, there may be a situation in which according to the letter of the law one does not have to return a certain object to its owner, yet the finder may feel morally obligated to do so (*BM* 24b). In Judaism, a person receives special recognition for these actions, but he cannot be blamed if he does not perform them.

Human Choice   When humans were created, they were created in the image of God (Gen. 1:27). The Bible never explains what exactly this means. However, it is clear that while animals reach their potential just by being animals, human beings are expected to aim higher. Different rabbis have commented on what it means to be created in God's image. They connected the idea with certain characteristics of human beings, such as the ability to speak, free will, self-consciousness, the ability to invent, and creativity. Humans are told to live and work for God, which will make them ethical beings, or creatures that are able to choose good over evil.

According to Judaism, a human being's potential is to choose good over evil. Thus when people choose the way of God, the moral life, they complete the CREATION of the world.

Later Thinkers   The medieval Jewish philosophers did not pay much attention to morality. MAIMONIDES taught that a person could reach perfection by intellectually knowing God, and that included the moral side of God. However, in Maimonides' opinion, the essence of a human being was not his morality. Most thinkers of the time believed that morality was mostly for the good of the community.

In the 16th century, JUDAH LÖW OF PRAGUE explained that morality was important as a way of knowing God. The only aspect of God that was shown to people was His moral nature. Therefore, the only way a person can be like God is by imitating His ways (e.g., love, kindness, mercy). Acting morally is the best way to become closer to God.

Later Jewish thinkers such as David Luzzatto, Hermann COHEN, and Martin BUBER also taught that the love of human brings is connected to the love of God.

According to Judaism, morality is the bridge between human brings and God. It connects humans with their fellow humans based on the values of God. A person needs morality to build his ethics and fulfill his destiny.

ETHICS OF THE FATHERS   See AVOT

ETHIOPIAN JEWS   Jews have lived in Ethiopia since ancient times. Others call them "Falashas" (in Ge'ez, "strangers" or "outsiders"), but they call themselves "Beta Israel" (in the Ge'ez language, "House of Israel"). They were cut off from mainstream Judaism for many centuries, and there are several theories of their origin: (1) Ethiopian Jews are descendants of King SOLOMON and the Queen of Sheba; (2) they are Hamatic (Cushitic) originally, and converted to Judaism; (3) they are a branch of Yemenite Jews; (4) they migrated from Egypt to Ethiopia; or (5) they are the descendants of the tribe of Dan.

The religion of the Ethiopian Jews is based on the Bible in Ge'ez translation as well as a number of books that were not included in the Bible, such as Judith, Tobit, I & II Maccabees, Baruch, Ben Sira, and the books of Enoch and Jubilees. They do not possess the ORAL LAW.

Their religious leader is called a *kes,* and he is assisted by a *debtara* (musician who chants the prayers). Prayer, in the Ge'ez language, takes place in the *mesgid* (synagogue), which is divided into an inner "holy of holies" and an outer hall.

Religion is observed strictly as written in the *Orit* (Torah). Ethiopian Jews observe the SABBATH very strictly, as well as the laws of PURITY. Menstruating women, as well as women during and after childbirth, live in a special hut outside the village.

On PASSOVER, the Beta Israel sacrifice a lamb and eat unleav-

An Ethiopian family in Jerusalem.

ened bread for seven days. They fast on the DAY OF ATONEMENT but do not sound the SHOFAR. They have many fast days as well as festivals that are not celebrated by other Jews. The most important of these is the SIGD. On this day, sections of the Torah are read. They observe the fast of Esther, but PURIM is unknown.

In the 1970s Ethiopian Jews began to arrive in Israel. In 1973, Sephardi Chief Rabbi Ovadiah Yosef ruled that the Jews of Ethiopia were the descendants of the tribe of Dan. The Israeli government decided that Ethiopian Jews were entitled to full immigration rights as Jews. Up until 1984, some 8,000 Ethiopian Jews had immigrated to Israel. In 1984, an additional 8,000 were airlifted to Israel from the Sudan. In a dramatic, 36-hour airlift in May 1991 (Operation Solomon), 14,000 more were brought to the country.

Nowadays, the Chief Rabbinate of Israel demands that the Beta Israel undergo ritual immersion as a symbolic conversion. They do not doubt their Judaism, but require it because their divorce laws and laws of personal status are different. The Ethiopian community continually demands that this requirement be canceled.

ETIQUETTE   See DEREKH ERETS

ETROG   See FOUR SPECIES

EULOGY   (Heb. *hesped*). Funeral speech delivered at or after a BURIAL, honoring a dead person's memory (see FUNERAL SERVICE). The Hebrew verb *li-spod* or *le-haspid* ("to mourn, lament, eulogize") is used many times throughout the Bible in the context of mourning the dead: ABRAHAM's grief for his wife SARAH (Gen. 23:2), Egypt's official mourning for JACOB (Gen. 50:10–11), the people of Israel's mourning for the prophet SAMUEL (1 Sam. 25:1). In Talmud times, special eulogies were made for great scholars and other important people (TJ, *Ber.* 2:8; *MK* 21b). Rabbis who died were mourned at each KALLAH month gathering (special monthly learning sessions for the general public) of the Babylonian ACADEMIES. Probably as a result of this custom, ASHKENAZIM later chose 7 Adar, the anniversary of MOSES' death, as a day to mourn important rabbis who died in that year.

The first week of mourning (*shivah*) is the best time for a eulogy (*MK* 27b), which should be delivered in a town square or at the cemetery before the burial (*BB* 100b). According to the SHULHAN ARUKH (*YD* 344–5), giving a eulogy is a religious obligation for which the burial itself may be delayed if the speaker must come from far away. A eulogy is not given for a person who has committed SUICIDE or a person who has been excommunicated (see EXCOMMUNICATION).

According to Jewish law, no *hesped* may be said on SABBATHS, FESTIVALS, new MOONS, the day before or after a festival, during the month of NISAN, or on days when the TAHANUN is left out of the prayer service. Nowadays, the eulogy is usually delivered in the cemetery's chapel right before the burial or at

A eulogy of the deceased (hesped) *delivered before burial. From a series of paintings of the Burial Society of Prague, c. 1780.*

the graveside. It is customary for the funeral procession of great rabbis to stop at a synagogue, where the eulogy is given (*YD* 344:20). Additional eulogies are delivered at the end of the first week of mourning, after the 30-day mourning period, and at the unveiling of the TOMBSTONE.

Eulogizing has become very important among Jews. Some people serve as special eulogizers, and collections of eulogies have been published, especially in the United States since World War II. American funeral parlors have rabbis on call who meet with the family of the dead and then deliver the eulogy at the funeral.

EVAR MIN HA-HAI   (lit. "a limb from a living animal"). Rabbinic expression referring to a basic law of Judaism that forbids eating any flesh cut from the body of an animal while it is still alive (Gen. 9:4; Lev. 17:10; Deut. 12:23–25). This type of behavior was popular in ancient times, but the Bible called it an offense against God. It is forbidden to eat all "flesh with the life thereof" or to consume an animal's lifeblood. The *evar min ha-hai* rule applied to non-Jews as well, because it was one of the seven NOACHIDE LAWS (*Sanh.* 56a–57a, 59b).

EVE   See ADAM AND EVE

EVENING SERVICE   Daily prayer service recited after nightfall. It is called *"Ma'ariv"* in Hebrew ("Who brings on the dusk"), based on the first blessing recited; or *Arvit*, from the word *erev* ("evening"). According to tradition, JACOB the patriarch began the custom of the evening service (Gen. 28:11). Unlike the other two daily (MORNING and AFTERNOON) services, *Ma'ariv* does

not replace a sacrifice that was offered in the TEMPLE, since no offerings were brought at night. It is called a *reshut* or voluntary prayer, but over time it became obligatory. It symbolizes the leftover parts of the different sacrifices that were burned at night.

On weekdays, the service begins with Psalms 78:38, 20:10 and BAREKHU, followed by two blessings, SHEMA, and the two blessings that come after *Shema*, EMET VE-EMUNAH and HASHKIVENU. Outside of Israel, ASHKENAZIM add a third blessing. Until about the end of the ninth century, the Evening Service ended here, and no AMIDAH was recited. Later, the *Amidah* was added, but it is recited silently, with no repetition by the reader. Services end with the ALEINU prayer, together with mourner's KADDISH.

On Friday night, the eve of the Sabbath, services begin with KABBALAT SHABBAT. Special prayers are added in the *Amidah*, and the services end with *Kiddush* and either the YIGDAL hymn or ADON OLAM. On Saturday night, Psalms 144 and 67 are chanted at the beginning and the service ends with Psalm 91 and the HAVDALLAH ceremony. On the first eve of PASSOVER, HALLEL is read after the Evening Service, and on the eve of the Day of Atonement, several special hymns are sung after the *Amidah*.

One may recite the Evening Service from 1¼ "variable hours" before sunset. A "variable hour" is defined as one-twelfth of the time between sunrise and sunset on that day. The Evening Service should take place no later than midnight. In order to make it easier for people, many synagogues arrange the afternoon service late in the day so only a short time passes before the evening service begins. A study session takes place in between the two services.

EVIL Jewish thinkers, from the time of the Bible, have asked many questions about the source of evil and its purpose. God is seen as good and the source of all good, but where does evil come from? According to the Bible, God is responsible for both the good and the evil in the world. In the book of ISAIAH, God says: "I form the light and create the darkness. I make peace and create evil" (Isa. 45:7). Evil, like everything else that God created, is part of God's plan. At the same time, it is difficult for a person to understand the purpose of evil. It is only natural for people to protest against suffering and pain in the world.

The greatest difficulty is to understand why good things happen to bad people and bad things happen to good people. The prophet JEREMIAH does not question God's justice, but asks (Jer. 12:1): "Why does the way of the wicked prosper?" The Book of JOB is about a righteous man who suffers without an understandable cause. The Bible does not offer an answer to this problem. It emphasizes that the purpose of evil and what seems like lack of justice cannot be understood by human beings.

The sages of the Talmud also believed that both good and evil are part of God's plan: "Everything that God does, He does for the good" (*Ber.* 60b). In the end, all of creation, even death, is good. Evil is not only expressed in death and suffering, but also in a person's character. Even the "evil inclination" of people, i.e., their strong urges to satisfy themselves, can be aimed at good: "For had it not been for the evil inclination, no man would build a house, or marry a woman, or have children" (Gen. R. 9:7).

The rabbis offered more than one answer to the question of why good things happen to bad people and bad things happen to good people. One is that the good are being punished for the sins of their fathers and the wicked are enjoying their fathers' good deeds. The Talmud offers another explanation: "When evil befalls the just, it is because they are not completely just and when good befalls the wicked it is because they are not completely wicked" (*Ber.* 7a). However, their primary answer was the idea of reward and punishment in the world to come. People may suffer without reason in this world, but they will receive their rewards in the world to come (see AFTERLIFE).

Medieval thinkers taught that evil was the absence of good and that evil did not really exist in its own right. In this way, God was not responsible for evil because it did not really exist. In Maimonides' *Guide for the Perplexed*, he explains that there are several types of evils. The most common type is spiritual or physical evil that a person brings upon himself by giving in to his evil inclination. Since people cause this kind of evil to happen to themselves, only they are responsible.

Jewish mystics (see MYSTICISM) also dealt with the question of evil. They taught that like anything else in the world, God created the world of evil. The book of the BAHIR says: "God has an attribute called Evil." The ZOHAR teaches that evil is a system of powers parallel to the SEFIROT (God's holy powers). According to the mystics, not only is a person responsible for the evil that befalls him, but by doing evil he increases the amount of evil in the world. This happens when the evil that is contained within God is released because of a person's sins.

In the 19th century, Hermann COHEN (1842–1918) taught that "evil exists only in myth." From an early mystical source he develops the idea that suffering, especially Jewish suffering, is God's way of challenging His people. The people of Israel are taught to behave according to the highest moral standards, even though they will always be the "suffering servant."

For Martin BUBER (1878–1965), the source of evil is missing an opportunity to have a relationship with another human being. Evil does not exist on its own. It is a force within people that prevents them from learning about themselves through relationships with other people around them. After the tremendous expression of evil that was the HOLOCAUST, Buber was not sure if he could consider God "kind and merciful"; however, he never gave up hope that human beings could improve the world.

For Abraham Joshua HESCHEL (1907–1972), the Holocaust became possible because modern individuals had blurred the differences between good and evil. Other modern thinkers taught that the Holocaust was created by people alone, like a student who has thrown away everything his teacher had taught him. Some considered the victims of the Holocaust to be sacrificial offerings for the REDEMPTION of the world. Still others considered it to be a punishment for SIN.

EVIL EYE (*ayin ra'ah* or *ein ha-ra*). Idea that certain people have the power to cause harm by directing their gaze at others. According to this ancient belief, anyone possessing the evil eye can cause bad luck, sickness, or even death. Potential victims must think of ways to protect themselves and their property from the evil eye (see DEMONS AND DEMONOLOGY; WITCHCRAFT).

The ancient Canaanites used practical MAGIC, but biblical law forbade the use of magic (see AMULETS). In both the Bible and the Mishnah, the "evil eye" is simply ill will, jealousy, or envy (e.g., Prov. 23:6–7, 28:22; *Avot* 2:9, 11, 5:13).

In the Midrash and Talmud, the evil eye becomes a more serious issue. For example, a *midrash* explains that the evil eye

Amulets, in the form of hands with fingers spread, worn as pendants against the evil eye. North Africa, 19th century.

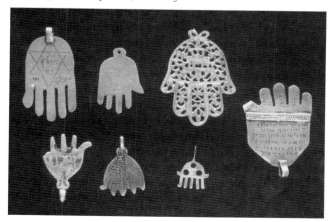

cast spells on JACOB and JOSEPH (*Ber.* 54b), inspired the idolatry of the GOLDEN CALF (Num. R. 12:4), and is responsible for 99 deaths out of 100 (*BM* 107b). The evil could be avoided by taking certain precautions, such as hiding a woman's beauty and giving another name to an infant. Protective charms were worn, and red and blue colors and mirrors were used to keep the evil eye away.

Jews continued to believe in these superstitions, although MAIMONIDES and other rabbis condemned them (*Yad Akkum* 11). Today, there are a number of religious customs and laws that probably were originally superstitions, such as breaking a glass at a wedding and not calling a father and son or two brothers to the READING OF THE LAW one after the other. Sephardi and Oriental Jews often paint a doorpost blue, display amulets with words from the Bible or the KABBALAH, and smear a bride's hands with a reddish-brown henna dye at the *hinna* ceremony that takes place before the wedding. ASHKENAZIM tie a red ribbon to a newborn baby and never give the name of a living father to his son. Ashkenazim also often use the Yiddish expression *keyn ayn-hora* or *keynahora,* "May no one cast an evil eye").

EVOLUTION   The theory, developed by Charles Darwin in the 19th century, that all types of plants and animals developed over a period of millions of years from earlier forms of life. According to his theory, slight changes occurred in them over the years that were passed down from generation to generation. Each generation became closer to what the species looks like today. According to the Bible, all forms of life were created during the six days of CREATION, after which no changes necessarily occurred in them. For this reason, both Jews and Christians considered Darwin's theory a contradiction of the Bible. Rabbi Menahem Mendel SCHNEERSOHN, the rabbi of Lubavich, taught that a Jew should accept what is written in Genesis literally. God's creation was sudden, even if it planted the seed of gradual growth. Other Jewish thinkers taught that Genesis is not to be taken literally, and therefore it is possible to find hints of evolution in the Bible itself.

The rabbis of the Talmud presented many ideas about how exactly the world came to be as it is today. Rabbi ABBAHU said that God created several worlds and destroyed them before deciding on the existing one (Gen. R. 3:7). Rabbi Yose taught that hybridization (mixing two different kinds of plant or animal to create a new species) is one of man's greatest achievements, since it allows the creation of new organisms "like those created by the Creator" (*Pes.* 54a). Rabbi Judah talks about something similar to evolution: "God made man a tail like an animal and then removed it from him for his self-respect" (Gen. R. 14:12).

There are also medieval sources that support the theory of evolution. MAIMONIDES and JUDAH HALEVI both thought that modern scientific ideas did not necessarily contradict the Torah. The British Chief Rabbi, Joseph Hermann Hertz, said "there is nothing un-Jewish about the theory of evolution ... Evolution, far be it from destroying the religious teachings in Genesis 1, is

its proud confirmation" (*Pentateuch and Haftorahs* 1938, p. 194). The first Chief Rabbi of Israel, Abraham Isaac KOOK, accepted the idea of evolution. He believed that the Bible's story of creation is not to be taken literally. He thought that the next step of evolution would be man's becoming moral (see ETHICS).

Many modern Jewish thinkers have tried to explain each day of creation as a symbol of a geological era. These theories did not solve the philosophical problem of God's role in creation. Finding answers to these questions is still a challenge to Jewish thinkers of today.

EXCOMMUNICATION   Punishment given by a rabbinic court of law (BET DIN) to those who violate the most serious commandments or do not accept the decrees of the local rabbinate. The first time this punishment is mentioned in the Bible is in the Book of EZRA 10:8: "Whoever would not come within three days ... would be separated from the congregation." The Talmud (*BM* 59b) tells that after ELIEZER BEN HYRCANUS refused to accept the view of the majority of the sages he was excommunicated.

At the time of the Talmud, there were four types of excommunication:

a) *nezifah* – a "rebuke" – the mildest type. It was used against those who showed disrespect for the head of the community or against a student who showed disrespect for a teacher. The person had to stay at home alone and not come in contact with others. In Babylonia it lasted one day and in Erets Israel a week.

b) *shamta* – a word that possibly means "destruction." Today, rabbis are not sure what exactly this punishment was. Some say it was the same as *niddui* (below).

c) *niddui* – "separation." It lasted 30 days in Erets Israel and seven days in the Diaspora, but could last longer if the person refused to change his ways. A person in *niddui* had to dress as a mourner (see MOURNING) and could enter the synagogue only by a side entrance to hear the Torah read.

d) *herem* – "anathema." This was the most severe type. The person was not allowed to hear or teach Torah and had to observe all the laws of mourning, including not wearing leather shoes and not washing his entire body. All except his immediate family had to shun him, and he could not be included in a MINYAN or a three-person quorum for reciting GRACE AFTER MEALS. If he died while in *herem,* a stone was placed on the coffin, showing that he was worthy of stoning, and his family would not mourn for him. A special ceremony was held when a person was put in *herem.* Black candles were lit, the ARK was opened, and a SHOFAR (ram's horn) was sounded. A rabbinical court would put a curse on him. The *herem* lasted for an unlimited time until it was removed.

After Talmud times, the three lighter forms of excommunication were not used. The *herem* was not used very often, but it was a powerful weapon. Rabbis could add additional punishments if they thought it was necessary. A famous ex-ample is the threat of excommunication by Rabbenu GERSHOM (960 CE–1028) for actions such as reading other people's letters, divorcing one's wife without her agreement, and marrying more than one woman. ELIJAH, the Vilna Gaon, put a *herem* on the Hasidim.

As Jewish communities grew weaker, especially after EMANCIPATION (civil rights for Jews), rabbinic courts used the *herem* more and more in an attempt to keep their power over the people. The result was often the opposite: the *herem* was used so often that it lost its sway over the people.

Recently, the *Edah Haredit* – the extreme ultra-Orthodox community in Israel – has used the *herem* to show its displeasure.

EXEGESIS   See BIBLE COMMENTARY

EXILARCH   (Aram. *Resh Galuta*) Head of the Jewish communities in exile (see GALUT) – a title given to an important Jew who represented the Jewish community of Babylonia to the non-Jewish rulers. The title was passed from father to son, and traditionally it was given to members of the house of DAVID. The Talmud mentions 15–17 exilarchs. The most important was a scholar called Mar Ukba.

The exilarch was responsible for collecting taxes from the Jewish community. He could give fines and put people in prison if they did not cooperate with him.

The religious leaders of the community, the *ge'onim* (see GAON), and the exilarch had many conflicts. Towards the end of the geonic period, the exilarch had to receive the approval of the *ge'onim* before he could be appointed to the position.

EXILE   See GALUT

EXILE, BABYLONIAN   Forcible removal of the population of the kingdom of JUDAH to Babylonia by the Babylonian king, Nebuchadnezzar, in the early part of the sixth century BCE. When King Jehoiachin of Judah surrendered to the armies of Nebuchadnezzar in 598 BCE, the king, the residents of his palace, and 10,000 other captives were forced to leave Israel. Nebuchadnezzar appointed Zedekiah, Jehoiachin's uncle, as king. However, he soon revolted, and again Jerusalem was attacked. At this point the rest of the Jews were exiled. In 538 BCE the Jews were given permission to return to their homeland by the Persian ruler Cyrus, who had conquered Babylonia (Ezra 1:1–4). Many Jews chose to stay in Babylonia, which became the first community of the Jewish Diaspora.

According to tradition, the Babylonian exile lasted 70 years (Jer. 29:10). Because the Jews no longer had a TEMPLE, they began to pray in SYNAGOGUES. They prayed for God to return them to their land and rebuild the Temple. According to the rabbis, this was the time period in which Hebrew writing changed to the square script and the Babylonian names for the months were added to the Jewish CALENDAR.

EXODUS   Departure of the Israelites from slavery in Egypt. The people of Israel were slaves in Egypt for 430 years (Ex. 12:41). After the tenth plague – the killing of the firstborn – they were set free. Later, as they fled, the Red Sea miraculously parted before them and then closed over Pharaoh's soldiers, who drowned (Ex. 14:15–30). The Exodus is a symbol of freedom to the Jews and also to many other people. It led to the formation of the Jewish people as a single nation.

The exact date of the Exodus is not mentioned in the PENTATEUCH, but scholars believe that it occurred in the 13th century BCE.

The Exodus has played a major role in Jewish life throughout

The "dividing" of the Red Sea at the time of the Exodus from Egypt. Illustration from a Haggadah, Trieste, 1864.

the ages. The event is mentioned 160 times in the Pentateuch and is linked to many laws, such as: "The stranger who lives with you shall be to you as one of your citizens ... for you were strangers in the land of Egypt" (Lev. 19:34), and "You shall have an honest balance, honest weights ... I am the Lord your God, Who freed you from the land of Egypt" (Lev. 19:36).

Jews are specifically commanded to remember the Exodus every day: "You shall remember the day of your departure from the land of Egypt as long as you live" (Deut. 16:3). Reciting the third paragraph of the SHEMA prayer fulfills this commandment. There is a separate commandment to remember and discuss the Exodus on Passover: "You shall tell your son on that day, saying 'This is done because of that which the Lord did unto me when I came out of Egypt'" (Ex. 13:8). The HAGGADAH, which is recited at the Passover SEDER, retells the story. The KIDDUSH, said on the SABBATH eve, notes that the Sabbath is "a remembrance of the Exodus from Egypt."

EXODUS, BOOK OF   Second book of the PENTATEUCH, known in Hebrew as *Shemot* ("Names") from the second word of the first sentence. The MIDRASH calls it *Sefer ha-Ge'ulah* ("The Book of Redemption"), and the Greek name is *Exodos,* "Departure from Egypt."

Exodus is divided into 40 chapters and 1,209 verses. It spans a period of 129 years, from the death of JOSEPH to the building of the SANCTUARY. According to Jewish tradition, MOSES wrote Exodus, like the rest of the Pentateuch, under God's inspiration.

Exodus is a direct continuation of the Book of Genesis. Genesis describes the beginning of the people of Israel, first as individuals and later as a family; Exodus describes Israel's becoming a nation. The Book of Genesis tells of God's promise to the patriarchs that they will have descendants and a Promised Land, while Exodus shows how these promises are slowly fulfilled. This happens in three stages: (1) the REDEMPTION of the Israelites from Egypt; (2) the COVENANT (agreement) made by God with His people; and (3) the building of the Sanctuary.

The only historical hint in the book is the mention of the two Egyptian cities, Pithom and Raamses. Raamses was the capital of Egypt under the 19th dynasty, and was built by Ramses II (Usermare Ramses, 1294–1224 BCE). If Ramses II was the "Pharaoh of the Oppression" the Exodus from Egypt took place during the rule of his son Baenre Merneptah (1224–1204 BCE).

EXODUS RABBAH   MIDRASH on the Book of EXODUS, meant to be a continuation of GENESIS RABBAH; in Hebrew it is known as *Shemot Rabbah* (see also MIDRASH AGGADAH). It is divided into 52 sections and made up of two parts that are very different. Part One is the first 14 sections, which are a story-like commentary on each verse of the biblical text, up until Exodus 12:2. The sources of that section are the Midrash, including the TANHUMA and the Talmud. It ends at the point where the Mekhilta de-Rabbi Ishmael begins.

	BOOK OF EXODUS
1:1–2:25	The enslavement of the Israelites and early career of Moses
3:1–7:13	The call and mission of Moses
7:14–11:10	The first nine plagues brought upon Egypt
12:1–13:16	The sacrifice of the paschal lamb and the tenth plague – the slaying of the firstborn
13:17–15:21	The Exodus from Egypt and the Song at the Sea
15:22–17:16	The complaints of the Israelites and the battle with Amalek
18:1–18:27	Jethro's visit and advice
19:1–20:18	The Giving of the Law on Mount Sinai – the Ten Commandments
20:19–23:33	Rules and laws
24:1–24:18	The ceremony of the covenant
25:1–31:18	The commandment to build the Sanctuary and its utensils
32:1–34:35	The Golden Calf, idolatry; replacement of the broken Tablets of the Law
35:1–40:38	The building of the Sanctuary and its utensils

The second half of Exodus Rabbah is a story-like Midrash on chapters 12–40 of the Book of Exodus. Each section is introduced by a poem, sometimes in the name of Rabbi Tanhuma bar Abba. The sources of this section are mostly from the time of the Mishnah, and only occasionally from the Talmud. Since much of the material in chapters 12–40 is also found in *Midrash Tanhuma,* the second part was probably written in the ninth century.

The two sections were combined in the 11th century, and NAHMONIDES is the first medieval author to quote Exodus Rabbah.

EXORCISM   See DIBBUK; WITCHCRAFT

EXPULSIONS   Jews were first expelled from the Land of Israel in the First Temple period by the Assyrians and Babylonians (see EXILE, BABYLONIAN). Later, Jews were expelled from different cities and areas under both Roman and Arab rule. From the Middle Ages on, it was very common for Christian rulers to expel their Jews from entire countries, provinces, and towns. They used many different excuses, such as BLOOD LIBELS, well-poisoning accusations, and charges that Jews spread the Black Death. However the real reason for expulsions of Jews from their homes was pure and simple hatred of the Jews. The Church gave local governments the right to expel Jews from their boundaries (see CHRISTIANITY).

The Jews were expelled from England in 1290, from France in 1306 and 1394, from Spain in 1492, from Portugal in 1497, and from most of Germany and Northern Italy by the end of the Middle Ages. Jews were forced to move to Poland, Lithuania, and the Muslim lands of the Ottoman Empire. In Russia, the Jews had to move to a Pale of Settlement in 1772. The most horrible expulsions were when the Nazis expelled millions to the ghettos, concentration camps, and death camps of Eastern Europe. See also ANTI-SEMITISM.

EYBESCHÜTZ, JONATHAN BEN NATHAN NATA (c. 1690– 1764). Talmud scholar and mystic. Eybeschütz was born in Cracow, where he studied in *yeshivot.* He then traveled to Vienna and Prague, where he became a popular teacher. Members of his family and friends accused him of being a follower of the false MESSIAH, SHABBETAI TSEVI. He swore that this was not true and even signed the rabbinic letter of *herem* (EXCOMMUNICATION) written in Prague against followers of Shabbetai Tsevi.

Rabbi Jonathan Eybeschütz. 19ᵗʰ century oil on canvas.

Eybeschütz later left Prague and became the rabbi of Metz in 1740, where he soon had many followers. In 1750, he became Chief Rabbi of the three neighboring German communities of Altona, Wandesbeck, and Hamburg. His rival had been Rabbi Jacob EMDEN, who accused him of giving out amulets with the name of Shabbetai Tsevi. Once again, Eybeshütz found himself under attack by the community, but this time the greatest rabbis

of Poland and Moravia defended him. Emden was forced to move to Amsterdam. Three years later, Eybeschütz published his *Luhot Edut,* in which he defended himself against his accusers. Some scholars still think that Eybeschütz was a secret follower of Shabbetai Tsevi.

In 1756, the King of Denmark and the Hamburg senate officially appointed Eybeschütz as Chief Rabbi of the Three Communities. The last eight years of his life were peaceful, and when he died, even his enemies mourned a beloved and respected rabbi. He was one of the greatest speakers and Talmud scholars of his time, and he wrote NOVELLAE (original commentaries) on the SHULHAN ARUKH and a mystical work called *Shem Olam.*

EYE FOR AN EYE   See RETALIATION

EZEKIEL   The third of the Major Prophets in the PROPHETS section of the Bible. He was the son of Buzi, probably from the priestly family of Zaddok. In 597 BCE he was taken away to EXILE in Babylonia, along with the royal family of the kingdom of JUDAH. He settled near Tel Abib, a Jewish colony near the Chebar Canal, where he had a vision of the throne-chariot of God. Ezekiel began to prophesy in the fifth year of Jehoiachin's exile and continued for 22 years. According to Jewish tradition, Ezekiel is buried in Babylonia, between the Euphrates River and the Chebar Canal. See EZEKIEL, BOOK OF.

EZEKIEL, BOOK OF   Third book in the PROPHETS section of the Bible. The Book of Ezekiel has 48 chapters and 1,273 verses. According to Jewish tradition, it was edited by the men of the GREAT ASSEMBLY (*BB* 15a).

The Book of Ezekiel may be divided into the following sections: a) Chapters 1–24: Ezekiel draws a very gloomy picture of the entire history of the people of Israel. They sinned and rebelled against God and will now suffer for it. He writes the words "lamentations and mourning and woe" on a scroll and then eats the scroll (2:9–3:3), makes a model of the city of

BOOK OF EZEKIEL	
1:1–3:21	Ezekiel's call
3:22–24:27	Prophecies directed against Judah and Jerusalem before the destruction of Jerusalem.
25:1–32:32	Visions of doom against seven foreign nations
33:1–39:29	Prophecies of Israel's restoration
40:1–43:12	Vision of the future Temple
43:13–46:24	Restored worship in the Temple
47:1–47:23	The river of holiness
48:1–48:35	The holy land

BOOKS OF EZRA AND NEHEMIAH

EZRA

1:1–1:11	Declaration by Cyrus and the first emigration from Babylonia
2:11–2:70	List of those who came to Zion under Zerubbbabel's leadership
3:1–3:13	The building of the altar and the festivities at the laying of the foundation of the Temple.
4:1–4:24	Disturbances of the building by the Samaritans
5:1–6:22	The completion of the building of the Temple after receiving permission from Darius
7:1–7:10	Ezra's lineage and his move to Jerusalem
7:11–7:22	Artaxerxes' letter to Ezra
8:1–8:14	List of those who traveled with Ezra and their lineage
8:15–8:30	The move by the Levites, the Temple servants, and the priests
8:31–8:36	The journey to Jerusalem and the offering of sacrifices
9:1–10:44	The sin of the people of Jerusalem – mixed marriages with foreign wives

NEHEMIAH

1:1–2:10	Nehemiah receives permission from the king to go to Jerusalem
2:11–2:20	Nehemiah decides to rebuild the wall of Jerusalem
3:1–4:17	The building of the wall of Jerusalem, disturbed by members of other nations
5:1–5:14	The freeing of the Hebrew slaves and the lowering of the tax burden
6:1–7:4	Nehemiah completes the wall of Jerusalem
7:5–7:72A	A list of the lineage of those who returned from exile in Zerubbabel's time
7:72B–8:12	The reading of the Torah by Ezra on Rosh ha-Shanah
8:13–8:18	The Sukkot festival
9:1–9:37	Separation from the foreigners and confession
10:1–10:40	Sealing of the covenant
11:3–11:36	List of the residents of Jerusalem and the cities of Judah
12:1–12:26	A list of priests and Levites who went into exile with Zerubbabel
12:27–12:43	The dedication of the Jerusalem wall
12:44–13:13	The appointing of officials in the Temple; Ezra's second trip to Jerusalem
13:14–13:31	Ezra's decrees about the Sabbath and the banishing of foreign wives

Jerusalem and then places a siege around it as a symbol of its fate (4:1–4:8), and performs many other symbolic acts. When Ezekiel's wife dies, he does not mourn her death, which is a symbol of doom (24:15–24:23). The prophet attracted much attention, but many people saw him as a type of entertainer. b) Chapter 25–32: Visions of doom against foreign nations. Tyre and Egypt are the main targets of these visions, because they were the main enemies of Israel. These nations will suffer because of the way they treated Israel, "That they may know that I am the Lord God." c) Chapters 33–48: These chapters are visions of the REDEMPTION. They include the vision of the dry bones (ch. 37) and of the new Jerusalem.

Many of the teachings in the Book of Ezekiel conflict with those in the Torah; therefore the rabbis made Ezekiel part of the Bible only after long discussions. It is not considered a source of Jewish law (HALAKHAH), because prophets do not have the right to add laws or COMMANDMENTS. Instead the book is seen as based on the ORAL LAW, which explains the Pentateuch. The 24th chapter of the Book of Ezekiel is also a source for laws of MOURNING (*MK* 15a–b, 27b).

EZRA   Priest, scribe, and religious leader who led a group of Jews who were in exile in Babylonia back to Jerusalem in 458 BCE (see GALUT). He was joined later on by NEHEMIAH.

Ezra was a descendant of the HIGH PRIEST at the time of the destruction of the TEMPLE in 586 BCE. When Ezra moved from Babylonia back to Jerusalem, the king allowed him to accept gifts for the new Temple, to appoint judges, and to teach the TORAH. On the festival of SUKKOT after his arrival in Jerusalem, he gathered the first GREAT ASSEMBLY. It decided to force all the Jewish men who had married foreign wives to divorce them.

On ROSH HA-SHANAH he gathered another assembly of the people. He read the Torah and convinced the people to keep its commandments. The people confessed their sins and agreed to send away their foreign wives.

According to the Talmud, Ezra knew as much Torah as MOSES (*Sanh.* 21b). The Jews of Judah had forgotten the Torah during the Babylonian EXILE, and Ezra re-taught it to them. Ezra made ten decrees, including the READING OF THE LAW at the Sabbath AFTERNOON SERVICE and at the MONDAY AND THURSDAY MORNING SERVICES. According to Josephus, he was buried in Jerusalem; however, another source says he was buried on the Shatt-el-Arab of the River Tigris. (See also EZRA AND NEHEMIAH, BOOKS OF.)

EZRA AND NEHEMIAH, BOOKS OF   Two books in the HAGIOGRAPHA ("Writings") section of the Bible.

Ezra-Nehemiah is the main source of information for the period of the Return to Zion from the Babylonian EXILE and the rebuilding of Jerusalem and the TEMPLE. It covers a century of history, from Cyrus' decree (538 BCE) to the kingdom of Darius II (c. 420 BCE).

Ezra-Nehemiah is a collection of different sources. Parts of the Book of Ezra are in ARAMAIC.

EZRAT NASHIM   ("women's section"). Separate prayer area for women. The original *ezrat nashim* was in the eastern section of the courtyard of the Second TEMPLE.

Early SYNAGOGUES in the Diaspora did not have a separate women's section. By medieval times, women were definitely separated from men in the synagogue. Sometimes the women sat in a balcony, behind a curtain, or in a little room off the main hall. In Southern France in the late Middle Ages, the women sat in a room under the main prayer hall with a grating in the ceiling that allowed them to hear the service. In Muslim lands, the women sat outside and listened through the windows. In the wooden synagogues of Poland, women even had a separate entrance to the synagogue.

A *mehitsah* – divider – was made of wood, cloth, or metal and used as a barrier between men and women if they sat in the same prayer hall. There are many rabbinic RESPONSA about the exact size and placement of the *mehitsah*.

In the 19th century, the REFORM movement called for family seating in the synagogue. They removed the *mehitsah* and closed down the separate balconies. Nowadays, almost all CONSERVATIVE synagogues have family seating as well.

FAITH Judaism uses not one but two words to refer to faith. *Emunah* means belief in a concept that cannot be proven beyond all doubt. *Bittahon* describes a second aspect – trust or faithfulness. In the biblical use of *emunah*, the term really means "belief in," such as faith that God will fulfill His promises. It is never used to mean belief that God exists; this is taken for granted. Thus faith in God's promises – particularly His promise to the patriarchs – is at the heart of what the Bible requires Jews to believe.

Nowhere does the Bible specifically command a belief in God's existence. At the same time, various laws in the TORAH and the ethical statements of the prophets treat God's existence as a given – something that requires no proof. The laws of IDOLATRY (worship of more than one god) illustrate the point. Idolatry is clearly prohibited: but idolatry is an outrage only if you have accepted God's existence first. For this reason the rabbis said: "For him who denies idolatry it is as if he acknowledged the entire Torah" (*Sif.* Deut. 28). The prophets dealt more with the impact of God's existence in the world. They spoke out against those who acknowledge God but deny that He is aware of human affairs (Ps. 94:7) or that He governs justly (Ezek. 18:23; Mal. 2:17, 3:14). In each case, they assumed that even the individuals they were criticizing accepted God's existence. It is only later in the rabbinic period that lacking faith meant a total denial of God's existence (see *Sanh.* 11:1 and ATHEISTS AND AGNOSTICS).

In the Middle Ages Jews were faced for the first time with atheism (denying the existence of God). In this period the term *emunah* was used to mean a belief in the existence of God. In the philosophical writings of this era there is much more concern with this aspect of faith. Moses MAIMONIDES (1135–1204) compiled his 13 PRINCIPLES OF FAITH, which listed the beliefs that were essential to Judaism. Maimonides devotes the first five of the 13 principles to defining exactly what "perfect faith" in the existence of God actually means. Over the next three centuries great Jewish thinkers debated Maimonides' basic description of Jewish belief. To this day, Maimonides' document serves as the starting point for any discussion of Jewish belief.

Throughout the ages, different grounds for belief in God's existence were stressed. In the biblical period there was no real need to base belief on a particular rational principle. After all,

the people of Israel were eyewitnesses to God's revelation in nature. By the time of the rabbis, direct encounters with God had ceased; therefore there was a need to justify one's faith. For some, the fundamentals of Judaism are true because there is a reliable tradition that supports them. Maimonides added to this rational deductive proofs – philosophy. For him, intellectual reason brings one to a higher religious level. For JUDAH HALEVI, love of God creates a spiritual closeness that is even higher than reason. The intense relationship itself is the basis of belief.

The necessity to explain Jewish belief about God continued as Jews came into contact with other cultures that challenged Jewish faith, for example, CHRISTIANITY, ISLAM, and even the KARAITE sect within Judaism.

FALASHAS See ETHIOPIAN JEWS

FAMILY The Bible serves as the basis for the values of Jewish family life. The Book of Genesis is in many respects a book of family histories. It deals with barren wives, rivalries between brothers, families parting and reuniting, and the constant threat to the process of continuity. Biblical heroes achieve their identity within the context of their families.

In the Bible there is a sharp division between the roles of men and women. Men dominate in the political arena, and women dominate in the home. While the PATRIARCHS were leaders in the community, the MATRIARCHS were clearly not docile women. They argue (Gen. 30:1), give orders (Gen. 16:2), and even deceive their husbands (Gen. 27:5–17) – to insure the formation of the Jewish nation. Their awareness of the important future of their families (Gen. 12:7, 26:2–4) shaped their behavior and their values.

The family in the Bible was called *bet av*, "house of a father" (Gen. 24:38, 46:31). The house was a subdivision of the clan (Heb. *mishpahah*). People who were related by blood, who had legal ties such as by marriage, or who lived closely with the family belonged to that particular family organization. As such, each family had its own religious traditions and its own burial ground (Gen. 23:1–20). It also had its own set of legal responsibilities. For example, if one of the family members was forced to sell his land, the other members were duty bound to redeem it (Lev. 25:25). In the JUBILEE year, land sold outside

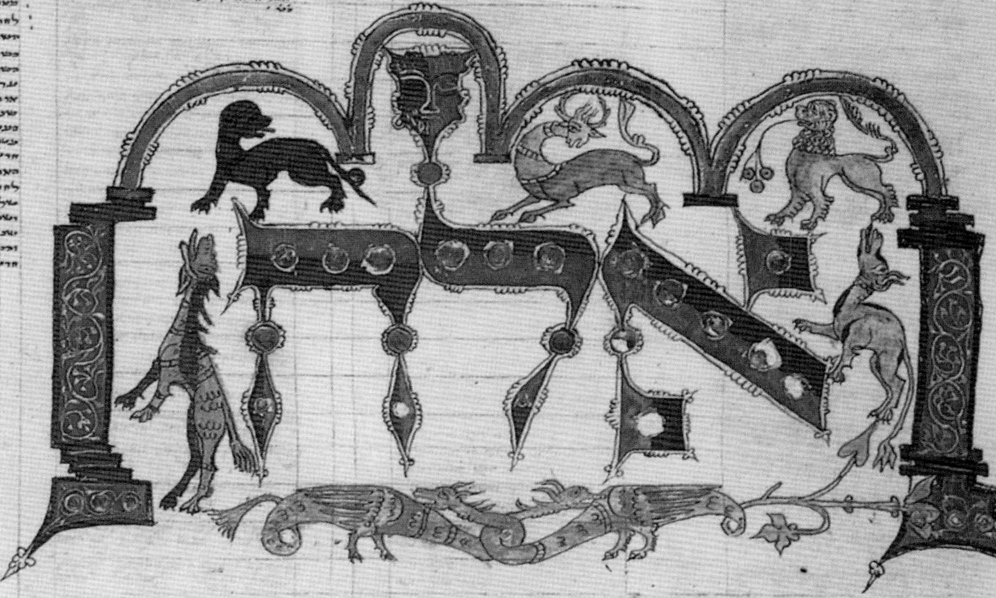

דו שָׁאַן אוֹכְלִיז אַל שִׁיּב

מָה עַל שׁוּם שֶׁלֹּא הִסְפִּיק

בְּצֵקָה שֶׁל אֲבוֹתֵינוּ לְהַחֲמִיץ

עַד שֶׁנִּגְלָה עֲלֵיהֶם מֶלֶךְ

מַלְכֵי הַמְּלָכִים הקב"ה וּגְאָלָם

שֶׁנֶּאֱמַר וַיֹּאפוּ אֶת הַבָּצֵק אֲשֶׁר

הוֹצִיאוּ מִמִּצְרַיִם עֻגֹת

חג פסח מצה ומרור

פסח שהיו אבותינו אוכלים בזמן

לחיי ישראל ירך פרעה וטבע וכל חילו הרכבים ושלישים על כלו

of the family went back to the family. Finally, family members were required to avenge the murder of a kinsman (see BLOOD AVENGER).

The functions of a father and mother are described in the Bible. As the head of the family, the father's authority over his children was almost absolute. ABRAHAM's son Isaac does not protest as his father prepares to sacrifice him (Gen. 22); JEPHTHAH sacrificed his daughter (Judg. 11:39); Judah ordered his daughter-in-law Tamar burned for breaking her marriage vow (Gen. 38:24). While these cases are extreme, they do make sense in light of later developments. In II King 4:10, children were seen as the father's property and could be taken as servants to pay off a father's debt. A father could sell his daughter into marriage (Ex. 21:7–11) but not prostitution (Lev. 19:29). Children who struck or cursed their parents could be put to death (Ex. 21:15, 17).

The mother shared the honor that was due the father. She loved her children (Gen. 25:28) and was more directly involved in their early training (Prov. 1:8). Motherhood was a blessing and barrenness a misfortune (Gen. 30:23; 1 Sam. 1). If a woman were childless, she could employ another woman in order to have children on her behalf (Gen. 16:1, 2, 30:3).

The Talmud introduced a formal pattern of Jewish family life with its laws. Marriage usually took place at 18 (Avot 5:24) or preferably earlier (Kid. 29b). The parents in both families usually arranged the marriages. ADULTERY was punishable by death. Sexual life in marriage was regulated by the laws of FAMILY PURITY. DIVORCE was permitted (Deut. 24:1–4) but frowned upon by the sages. Divorce tended to be rare in Jewish communities and was considered a stigma.

The father bears a number of responsibilities toward the children. He is required to circumcise his son (see CIRCUMCISION), redeem him if he is the firstborn, teach him TORAH, marry him off, and teach him a craft. One authority in the Talmud adds to this teaching him to swim (Kid. 29a). The Talmud also required the father to serve as a teacher and role model and to instill Jewish values and moral behavior in his children. He was to help his sons become self-sufficient by teaching them a trade. Daughters were taught about Judaism and the domestic responsibilities of a Jewish woman at home by their mothers. The child's "honor" for the parent took on practical meaning later in life – honor meant providing food and drink, clothing and transportation for aged parents.

The Talmud places great importance on the value of domestic harmony. It states: "A man should spend less than his means on food; up to his means on clothes; beyond his means in honoring his wife and children, because they are dependent on him" (Hul. 84b).

FAMILY PURITY   (Heb. *tohorat ha-mishpahah*). Jewish law regulates the sexual relationship between a HUSBAND AND WIFE. According to these laws, couples may not engage in sexual relations during the wife's menstrual period and for seven "clean days" following it. During this time, observant Jews abstain from physical contact. When the period of abstention ends, the wife immerses herself in a ritual bath (MIKVEH) and the couple resumes normal relations. The laws of family purity are based on Leviticus 20:18: "If a man shall lie with a woman having her period, and shall uncover her nakedness, he has laid bare her flow, and she has exposed her blood flow; both of them shall be cut off from among their people." Tractate NIDDAH in the Talmud is devoted to family purity.

One reason for the laws of family purity appears in the Talmud: "The husband becomes over familiar with his wife and tired of her, thus the Torah prohibited her to him [each month] so that she might remain as beloved to him as she was on her wedding day" (Nid. 31b). Modern observers note that women are usually most fertile at the time of the cycle when relations may be resumed. Both reasons explain why the system of family purity is at the heart of the observant family.

FASTING AND FAST DAYS   Fasting in Jewish tradition involves refraining from eating and drinking for the purpose of intensifying one's religious experience. It is considered helpful in atoning for sin (see ATONEMENT). Fasting is used as a way to commemorate national tragedies and can also play a part when one is personally seeking God's help.

The Jewish calendar has seven required fasts. First, the DAY OF ATONEMENT (Lev. 16:31) – the most important of all fasts – commands us to "afflict (y)our souls" which is interpreted to mean fasting (Yoma 11a, 73b). Affliction of the soul also prohibits bathing, anointing with oil, wearing leather shoes, and engaging in sexual relations. The second category of fasts commemorates tragic events in Jewish history. There are four fasts of this type: 10 Tevet (ASARAH BE-TEVET), 17 Tammuz (see SHIVAH ASAR BE-TAMMUZ), 9 Av (see TISHAH BE-AV), and 3 Tishri (the Fast of GEDALIAH). All of the events referred to in these fasts are connected with the siege and destruction of the TEMPLE and Jerusalem by the Romans in 70 CE. Of the second category of fasts, only the Ninth of Av is a full 24-hour fast; the others begin at dawn and do not involve additional prohibitions. A third category of fasting – the fast of petition – also forms part of the Jewish calendar. In the Book of Esther, Queen ESTHER calls on her fellow Jews to observe a three-day fast as she prepares to plead with the king for her people (Est. 4:16–17). A one-day fast was added to the calendar immediately before PURIM in honor of Esther's plea. The last obligatory fast is the Fast of the Firstborn. It takes place on 14 Nisan, the day before Passover. It was added as a reminder of the death of the firstborn of Egypt and the miraculous escape of the Jewish firstborn from death. This fast is only symbolic: the firstborn can avoid fasting by participating in a *siyyum* – the celebration of the conclusion of study of a book of the Talmud, which permits the participants to eat and drink.

As a rule, males must observe the required fasts when they are over the age of 13 and females when they are over the age of 12. Youngsters below this age observe partial fasts in order to get used to fasting. Sick people and women in advanced stages of

Opposite page: Illustration of Had Gadya *("Only one kid"), a popular folksong chanted at the end of Passover Seder. Lithograph by E. Lissitzky (1890–1941).*

pregnancy, as well as nursing mothers who have recently given birth, are not required to fast. Whenever there is a danger to health, the rabbis prohibit fasting.

Except for the Day of Atonement, any fast that falls on the SABBATH is postponed to Sunday. The Fast of Esther cannot be postponed to the next day since Purim follows; it also cannot be predated to Friday since fasting the day before the Sabbath is forbidden. Therefore this fast is pushed back to Thursday, when required.

Pious Jews throughout the ages observed various individual fasts – for spiritual reasons and in times of trouble. In the Bible, King DAVID fasted when his child was near death (II Sam. 12:16). Some mourners fast annually on the day of the burial of a parent or on the anniversary of the death (YAHRZEIT). It is a common custom that brides and grooms fast on the day of their wedding before the ceremony. This shows their desire for FORGIVENESS for any past sins as they are about to start a new life together. Historically, the mystics fasted on the day before the New Moon. Other pious Jews have fasted on Mondays and Thursdays throughout the year. Together both the obligatory and non-obligatory fasts show that fasting has always played a role in Jewish spiritual life.

FATALISM   See PREDESTINATION

FATHER   When a married woman gives birth, Jewish law takes it for granted that her husband is the father. This applies even when a rumor exists that the woman was unfaithful. An unmarried woman who claims that a particular man fathered her child does not establish paternity, since the law assumes that she may have had sexual relations with other men as well (*Hul.* 11b). If a man says, "This is my child," he is believed, because he is taking on legal responsibility for the child. In a marriage between Jews, family lineage follows the father; in a relationship between Jew and non-Jew, family lineage goes according to the mother.

In Bible times the father was not legally obliged to support his children when they were young. This duty became law at the Synod of Usha (2nd cent.). The father owns all the income of his minor children. This is given to him because he must support and maintain them. He may not help himself to the income of a son over the age of six who is not dependent upon him (e.g., if the son has an inheritance from the side of the mother). The father may annul the vows of his daughter while she is still a minor. He may also marry off his daughter while still a minor, though this practice was eventually discouraged.

The father bears a number of responsibilities toward his children. He is required to circumcise his son (see CIRCUMCISION), redeem him if he is the FIRSTBORN, teach him TORAH, marry him off, and teach him a craft. One authority in the Talmud adds: teaching him to swim (*Kid.* 29a). For the Talmud, the father was required to serve as a teacher and role model and to instill Jewish values and moral behavior in his children. He was to help the child become self-sufficient by teaching him a trade. When the son reaches BAR MITZVAH, the father recites a special blessing on being relieved of legal responsibility for the son (BARUKH SHE-PETARANI). The father must provide his daughter with the proper clothes and other items needed to prepare her for MARRIAGE.

In the East European SHTETL, the father's activity within the home was mostly spiritual and intellectual; his authority was understood. His position was more distant than that of the MOTHER, and, when home, his time was often devoted to his own affairs rather than to the family circle. Among immigrant families in the Western world and in Oriental communities in Israel, the father's traditional authority diminished. He came to represent the culture of the past.

FATHERHOOD OF GOD   "God as Father" is one of several ways that Jewish tradition relates to the Divine. Fatherhood implies many ideas: producing offspring, providing care, and imposing discipline. The religious theme of fatherhood allows the expression of each of these ideas.

Other ancient religions took the idea of God as producing offspring far more literally than does Judaism. In Egypt, for example, Pharaoh was considered the actual physical son of the god Ra. Some measure of this relationship appears symbolically in the Bible. Psalm 2:7 reads: "The Lord has said to me [David the King], 'You are My son; this day I have begotten you.'" Various names of God – for example, Abijah ("the Lord is my Father") – include the aspect of fatherhood. Yet the overwhelming emphasis in the Bible is on creation and the ongoing parent relationship: God is the Father of the Jewish nation in all its aspects. As the prophet Hosea writes: "When Israel was still a child, I loved him, and ever since Egypt I have called My son…. It was I who taught Ephraim [another name for the people of Israel] to walk, taking them up in My arms I drew them with bands of love …" (11:1–4).

The Bible includes parental discipline in the relationship between God and Israel: "Bear in mind that the Lord your God disciplines you [the entire people], just as a man disciplines his son" (Deut. 8:5). In counterbalance, God's fatherhood also means compassion. This theme is central to prayers of repentance, e.g. AVINU SHE-BA-SHAMAYIM ("Our Father Who is in Heaven") or the *K'rahem Av al-Banim* ("As a Father has Mercy on Children") idea. In short, the parental relationship between God and Israel displays the same complications as human parenthood.

FEAR OF GOD   (Heb. *yirat Elohim*; in rabbinic literature "fear of heaven," *yirat shamayim*). Fear of God is Judaism's most sincere expression of reverence toward God. It is a positive COMMANDMENT that comes from the verse, "Fear only the Lord your God, and worship Him alone …" (Deut. 6:13).

In traditional Jewish wisdom literature, Fear of Heaven was seen as the single most important emotion in shaping proper human behavior. In Proverbs, "Fear of God is the beginning of wisdom" (Prov. 9:10). In the Talmud, JOHANAN BEN ZAKKAI told his disciples before his death, "Let the fear of heaven be upon you as the fear of flesh and blood." When they replied, "Is that all?" he answered them, "If only you could achieve this! For when a man wants to commit a sin, he says, 'I hope no man will see me'" (*Ber.* 28b). For the rabbis, man controls his impulses only by taking the Fear of Heaven to heart.

According to the rabbis, Fear of Heaven is central to man's ethical makeup. Even so, God allows man absolute freedom in developing his own sense of fear (see FREE WILL). The Talmud states, "Everything is in the hands of heaven except the fear of heaven" (*Ber.* 33b). MAIMONIDES writes that in order to have proper fear of heaven, a person should think deeply about God's wondrous creation and thus obtain a glimpse of His infinite wisdom. Man will then become afraid and realize that he is a "small, lowly creature, with limited intelligence, standing in the presence of Him who is perfect in knowledge" (*Yad, Yesodei ha-Torah* 2:2). (See also LOVE OF GOD.)

FEINSTEIN, MOSES (1895–1986). Rabbinical authority and leader of Orthodox Judaism in the United States (see ORTHODOXY). Feinstein was born near Minsk, White Russia, and studied in the *yeshivot* (Talmud academies) of Slutsk and Shklov. In 1921 he became rabbi of Luban; in 1937 he emigrated to the United States. He was appointed *Rosh Yeshivah* (head of the talmudic academy) of Mesivtha Tifereth Jerusalem on Manhattan's Lower East Side, where he remained until his death.

R. Feinstein was best known for his halakhic (Jewish legal) RESPONSA. These answers to religious questions were published in seven volumes entitled *Iggerot Mosheh* (1959–85), arranged according to the order of the SHULHAN ARUKH. His rulings on all matters of Jewish life were accepted throughout the world. Feinstein's rulings touched on questions about advancements in science and medicine in the light of HALAKHAH, including ABORTION, BIRTH CONTROL, ARTIFICIAL INSEMINATION, and transplants. He also dealt with problems of personal status in the areas of CONVERSION TO JUDAISM, MARRIAGE, and DIVORCE that resulted from the breakdown of religious life in Europe and the United States. He served as president of the Union of Orthodox Rabbis and as chairman of the American branch of Agudat Israel's Council of Torah Sages.

FEMINISM The modern Jewish women's movement that stresses increased Jewish learning for women and greater involvement in public Jewish life. It is uniquely modern – in earlier times, women who were able to become Jewish scholars or leaders did so under unusual circumstances and with great difficulty. The modern period marks the first time that such achievement comes with broad popular support.

The women's movement has found important role models in the classical Jewish sources. The Bible and MIDRASH describe a number of women leaders. According to the rabbis, SARAH, the wife of ABRAHAM, converted the women of her area to belief in one God while Abraham converted the men. According to

the Bible, God Himself counseled Abraham to listen to Sarah when they disagreed about sending Hagar and Ishmael away (Gen. 21: 11–12). Other examples of female biblical leaders are the prophetess MIRIAM, sister of MOSES and AARON, who led the women in song at the Sea of Reeds; the five daughters of Zelophehad, who insisted on receiving their inheritance (Num. 27:1–8); DEBORAH, a judge of Israel; the prophetess Hulda, whom the king consulted when the nation faced great danger (II Kings 22:14); and Queen Esther, who saved the Jewish people from destruction in the times of the Persian Empire.

The rabbis recognized that during the period of slavery in Egypt, the women heroically encouraged the men to continue having children. The Midrash relates that in the desert after leaving Egypt (see EXODUS), these same women withheld their jewelry from the making of the GOLDEN CALF. As a reward for their loyalty, the festival of the New MOON was given to women as a day of rest. The Talmud also contains examples of women who took leadership roles as scholars or in community affairs. BERURYAH, daughter of R. Hanina ben Teradyon and wife of R. MEIR, was able to learn 300 laws in one day. Her legal opinions are cited with respect.

From talmudic times to the present, there have been unusually talented women in Jewish communities throughout the world who have broken through the limitations imposed on them. They have run businesses, served the community, and excelled in learning. One exceptional woman – Hanna Rachel Werbermacher (1805–1892) – was known as the Maid of LUDMIR. She is probably the only example of a woman functioning as a Hasidic rebbe (see HASIDISM). These noteworthy exceptions help to inspire today's women's movement.

Following World War II, the rise of feminism in the United States began to influence Jewish women. More and more women studied and began to take on the performance of COMMANDMENTS from which they were technically exempt. Within the REFORM and RECONSTRUCTIONIST movements, some women became rabbis and CANTORS. Much later in the 1980s, women did so within the CONSERVATIVE movement as well.

Within the Orthodox feminist movement, women have formed separate prayer groups that include reading from the Torah and other formal prayer gatherings. In 1988, a group of women led by Rivka Haut, an Orthodox Jewish woman from New York held a women's prayer service at the WESTERN WALL that included reading from a Torah scroll. An uproar broke out among ultra-Orthodox worshipers at the Wall, who used violence to prevent the group from continuing. This marked the beginning of "Women of the Wall," a group that is still fighting in the Israeli courts for women's rights, within the framework of Jewish law, at the Western Wall.

Orthodox Jewish women have found significant opportunities for high-level TORAH learning. Organizations such as the Jewish Orthodox Feminist Alliance and Edah were among the first to provide support and resources to Jewish women who wished to strengthen their Jewish learning without compromising their religious observance. *Kolech* ("Her Voice") is the name of the new and growing Orthodox feminist organization in Israel. In time, major institutions of higher Jewish learning have opened divisions for women. Today it is almost expected that a committed Jewish young woman will spend at least one year after high school in full-time Torah learning. In Israel, there are now *Hesder* programs for girls that intersperse military service with semesters of *yeshivah* attendance. Several decades ago, women's prayer groups were rare. Now, Orthodox women's groups that refrain from reciting those parts of the service for which one needs a MINYAN of men can be found all over the world. More and more mainstream Orthodox synagogues are allowing women to dance with the SCROLL OF THE LAW. Some provide an opportunity for women to be called to the READING OF THE LAW on the SIMHAT TORAH festival and at other times in an all-female gathering. No doubt, these trends are the direct and permanent offspring of the Jewish feminist movement.

FESTIVALS   (Heb. *yom tov* [lit. "a good day"]). The Bible forbids work on seven festival days. They are: ROSH HA-SHANAH (the New Year, 1 Tishri), the DAY OF ATONEMENT (Yom Kippur, 10 Tishri), SUKKOT (the first day of Tabernacles, 15 Tishri), SHEMINI ATSERET (the Eighth Day of Solemn Assembly, 23 Tishri), the first and last days of PASSOVER, *Pesah*, 15 and 22 Nisan), and SHAVU'OT (Feast of Weeks, 5 Sivan). At a later point, because of doubts as to the date on which the New MOON appeared, it was ruled that those living outside the Land of Israel would keep two days rather than one for each of the festivals, except the Day of Atonement. Even in Israel, two days of Rosh ha-Shanah are observed. (See SECOND DAY OF FESTIVALS.)

Work prohibitions on festivals are similar to the SABBATH, with some exceptions. The Day of Atonement is identical to the Sabbath, with the added restrictions of fasting and self-denial. On the other festivals, work related to the preparation of food is allowed. Thus, cooking is allowed on these festivals (unless they fall on the Sabbath). Fire may be transferred, but not created. Carrying from domain to domain is allowed.

Passover, Shavu'ot and Sukkot are the three PILGRIM FESTIVALS. They are unique in that they have both agricultural and national aspects. Passover is the celebration of the EXODUS from Egypt, and it is the biblical "festival of spring"; Shavu'ot honors the giving of the Torah, and it is the biblical "harvest festival"; Sukkot recalls the 40 years of wandering in the desert following the Exodus, and it is the biblical "festival of ingathering," when grain is brought in from the fields. Rosh ha-Shanah and the Day of Atonement are days of PRAYER and REPENTANCE; they have no specific national or agricultural meaning.

In addition to the festivals already mentioned, the Bible commands that each New Moon be celebrated. The rabbis added some major and minor festivals, including PURIM and HANUKKAH, to the calendar. The NEW YEAR FOR TREES (Tu bi-Shevat), Purim Katan (the 14th and 15th days of Adar 1 in leap years; see PURIM), Second Passover (the 14th of Iyyar; see PASSOVER), LAG BA-OMER, and the Fifteenth of AV. In the period of the modern State of Israel, INDEPENDENCE DAY (*Yom ha-Atsma'ut*, 5 Iyyar) and JERUSALEM DAY (*Yom Yerushalayim*, 28 Iyyar) were added.

Festival Prayers   On all the seven major festivals a special AMIDAH is said in the EVENING, MORNING and AFTERNOON services. HALLEL is added to the morning service; the ADDITIONAL SERVICE is also read. On Hanukkah and Purim, there is no Additional Service; there is a READING OF THE LAW, and on Hanukkah *Hallel* is recited. On the Day of Atonement, a fifth service – NE'ILAH – is added just prior to the conclusion of the fast day. The *Amidah* for each service is followed by a long CONFESSION.

The prayers of certain biblical festivals include special ritual objects. The *shofar* must be blown on Rosh ha-Shanah. On Sukkot, the FOUR SPECIES must be taken and waved. During the annual cycle of the festivals, the FIVE SCROLLS (*megillot*) are read: SONG OF SONGS on the Sabbath day of Passover, RUTH on Shavu'ot, LAMENTATIONS on Tishah be-Av, ECCLESIASTES on the Sabbath day of Sukkot, and ESTHER on Purim.

On Israel's Independence Day and Jerusalem Day, *Hallel* is recited in religious Zionist communities.

FIFTEENTH OF SHEVAT   See NEW YEAR FOR TREES

FINKELSTEIN, LOUIS   (1895–1991). Rabbinic scholar and leader of CONSERVATIVE JUDAISM; president (1940–51) and chancellor (1951–72) of the Jewish Theological Seminary of America. Finkelstein was born in Cincinnati, studied at the City College of New York, and received his doctorate from Columbia University (1918). The following year he was ordained at the Seminary. He served as a rabbi and later joined the Seminary faculty, where he was a great scholar. He wrote on Jewish social and religious issues and on rabbinic texts. He published the first critical edition of SIFREI on Deuteronomy (1939) as well as the first volumes of an edition and commentary on the SIFRA. His works on the PHARISEES stressed the social and economic basis of rabbinic Judaism.

As head of the Jewish Theological Seminary, he continued to uphold a high standard of scholarship and religious practice. He also emphasized contact with the non-Jewish community. He founded the Institute for Religious and Social Studies, where thinkers from various fields and religions come together to consider moral problems of the day. Under his leadership, Conservative Judaism became the largest movement in American Jewry.

FIRSTBORN, REDEMPTION OF   (Heb. *pidyon ha-ben*). The practice of redeeming the firstborn male child from a PRIEST. It stems from the importance attached to the firstborn son in Bible times (Gen. 49:3). Firstborn sons were dedicated to serve God and were the original priests in the SANCTUARY until they were replaced by the LEVITES (Num. 3:12). Just as the FIRST FRUITS and the firstborn of animals had to be given to the priests, so the male firstborn belonged to God.

The obligation to redeem a firstborn son is first mentioned in connection with the slaying of the firstborn of the Egyptians (Ex. 13:13, 22:28, 34:20; Num. 3:13) just before the EXODUS: "For every firstborn among the Israelites, man as well as beast, is Mine; I consecrated them to Myself at the time that I killed every firstborn in the land of Egypt" (Num. 8:17). The Book of EXODUS commands fathers to redeem their firstborn son; the Book of NUMBERS clarifies that they do so by paying five shekels to a priest.

The laws of the Redemption of the Firstborn are found in the eighth chapter of the Mishnah, in the tractate (book) of BEKHOROT and in the GEMARA of that chapter. These laws state that the sons of priests and Levites are exempt from redeeming their firstborn sons; those whose mother is the daughter of either a priest or Levite are also not redeemed. If a mother has had a previous miscarriage or stillbirth, the child is not regarded as firstborn.

The ceremony for the Redemption of the Firstborn takes place on the 31st day after the birth of the child – unless this falls on a Sabbath or festival, in which case it is held on the evening after the Sabbath or festival. The father declares to the priest that this is the firstborn son of his mother and that the father is obligated to redeem him. The father quotes Numbers 18:16 and Exodus 13:1. The priest then turns to the father and asks whether he prefers to give his son to the priest or to redeem him for five shekels. The father replies that he wants to redeem his son and hands the priest the five shekels. He then recites two blessings: *al pidyon ha-ben* and SHE-HEHEYANU. The transaction between the priest and the father takes place in the Aramaic language, rather than Hebrew.

FIRST FRUITS   (Heb. *bikkurim*). The earliest-ripening fruits and grains brought each year to the TEMPLE in Jerusalem as an offering. Exodus 23:19 commands: "The choice first fruits of your soil you shall bring to the house of the Lord your God …" (see also Ex. 34:26). This is traditionally interpreted to mean fruits and grains of the seven species native to the Land of Israel: wheat, barley, grapes, figs, pomegranates, olives and dates (*Bik.* 1:3). According to the rabbis, the farmer was required to mark those early fruits that were most developed. The marked fruits – one-sixtieth of the total – were then taken to the Temple in Jerusalem as an offering (see SACRIFICES AND OFFERINGS).

When the farmer brought the first fruits to the Temple, he recited Deuteronomy 26:1–11. These verses recall the ISRAELITE's origins, the slavery in Egypt, and the EXODUS. The passage concludes with the commandment to "set before the Lord" the first fruits. According to Numbers 18:12–13 the first fruits became the property of the PRIESTS and was considered part of their income. The first fruits were brought between SHAVU'OT (*Hag ha-Bikkurim*, Festival of the First Fruits) and HANUKKAH, although it was considered best to bring them before SUKKOT.

An imaginary representation of the First Fruits festival showing a procession carrying produce to the Temple, preceded by a flute player.

First fruits ceremonies of various types have been revived in agricultural settlements in Israel. Celebrations include costumes, folk dancing, fruit baskets, and the participation of young children. They usually coincide with Shavu'ot.

FIVE BOOKS OF MOSES   See Pentateuch

FIVE SCROLLS   (Heb. *Hamesh Megillot*). The biblical books SONG OF SONGS, RUTH, LAMENTATIONS, ECCLESIASTES, and ESTHER. They appear together in this order in the HAGIOGRAPHA ("Writings") section in printed Hebrew Bibles. During the annual cycle of the festivals, the Five Scrolls are read: SONG OF SONGS on the Sabbath day of Passover, RUTH on Shavu'ot, LAMENTATIONS on TISHAH BE-AV, ECCLESIASTES on the Sabbath day of Sukkot, and ESTHER on Purim. Not all of the scrolls are read by all communities: some traditions divide Ruth over both days of Shavu'ot. In the Diaspora, Song of Songs is sometimes read on the last days of Passover. The Book of Esther must be read from a properly written parchment scroll. Generally, the other *megillot* are read today from printed texts. There are certain Ashkenazi congregations in Jerusalem that read all but Lamentations from a handwritten parchment scroll.

FIVE SPECIES   Varieties of cereal, grain, or "corn" (*dagan*) native to the Land of Israel. These species are subject to the biblical and rabbinic AGRICULTURAL LAWS (*Ned.* 7:2). When flour made from any of these five "species" or "kinds" of cereal is kneaded into dough, a portion of CHALLAH must be separated and thrown into the fire. The Mishnah (*Hal.* 1:1) lists the five species: wheat (*hittim*), barley (*se'orim*), emmer (*kusmin*), oats (*shibbolet shu'al*), and rye (*shifon*). All five are also listed as the grains from which unleavened bread (MATZAH) can be prepared for PASSOVER (*Pes.* 2:5).

In addition to separation of *challah*, these grains are subject to other restrictions. When they are used in baking BREAD, one must recite the special blessing for the bread before eating and the GRACE AFTER MEALS following the meal. Their flour is considered leaven (HAMETS) on Passover; anything prepared from it may neither be used nor stored during the festival.

FLOOD   Forty days and nights of rain that, according to the Bible (Gen. 6:9–9:17), covered the earth and destroyed the human race as a punishment for its wickedness. The Bible tells us that NOAH was the only righteous person on earth at the time. God forewarns him about the flood, and Noah builds an ark that will provide shelter for his family and for representatives of every species on earth. The flood lasts for 40 days and, after five months, the ark comes to rest on Mount Ararat. Noah makes four probes to see if the land is dry – once by sending out a raven as a scout and three times using a dove. When the dove does not return from its third flight, Noah knows that it has found dry land. A year after the beginning of the flood, the occupants leave the ark. Noah builds an altar and offers a sacrifice to God in thanksgiving for having been saved. God vows never to destroy the world again on humanity's account. He sets the rainbow in the sky and makes a COVENANT with Noah.

There are many parallels to the biblical flood story in Ancient Near Eastern literature, for example the Babylonian Gilgamesh Epic. The similarities among these accounts lead scholars to believe that they must refer to the same natural disaster.

FOOD, SABBATH AND FESTIVAL   The DIETARY LAWS (*kashrut*) and the special foods of the SABBATH, PILGRIM FESTIVALS, and other holidays make Jewish cuisine unique. The basis for the laws of *kashrut* is the verse: "You shall be holy to Me; for I the Lord am holy, and I have set you apart from other peoples to be Mine" (Lev. 20:26). HOLINESS therefore is the goal of Jewish dietary regulations. Dietary restrictions include refraining from eating foods forbidden by the Torah, keeping separate meat and dairy utensils, ritual slaughtering and preparation of meat, preparation of all cooked foods in accordance with laws of *kashrut*, and many other details. For the rabbis, the dining table was like God's altar in the TEMPLE.

Specific dishes that make up a "Jewish" diet vary from ethnic community to community, from location to location, and from event to event in the Jewish calendar. However, some foods have been traditional from time immemorial. When the Israelites

---

ON FOOD

You shall serve the Lord your God, and He will bless your bread and your water.

The generous man shall be blessed, for he gives of his bread to the poor.

When Rav Huna had a meal, he would open the door wide and say: "Let all who are hungry, come and eat."

If three men have eaten at the same table and have spoken over it words of Torah, it is considered as if they had eaten at the table of God.

The wise man eats to live; the fool lives to eat.

---

were in the wilderness, they complained: "We remember the fish that we used to eat freely in Egypt" (Num. 11:5). It comes as no surprise then that Jews have long eaten fish on Friday night.

The three Sabbath meals – Friday evening, Saturday midday, and late Saturday afternoon – are central to the Day of Rest. Sabbath meals open with KIDDUSH (sanctification) over a cup of wine, followed by the HA-MOTSI blessing recited over two challahs (twisted loaves of bread). A typical Ashkenazi menu includes chopped herring or gefilte fish (fishballs), chicken soup with noodles, roast chicken or meat, *tsimmes* (side dish of carrots and prunes), and a fruit compote. The highlight of the midday meal is usually a steaming hot *tcholent* (called *hammin* by Sephardi Jews), which consists of potatoes, beans, barley, and meat placed in a heated oven before the Sabbath and allowed to stew and thicken overnight. Hasidic Jews consider the third meal (SE'UDAH SHELISHIT) most important, as they eat it in the presence of their *Rebbe* (rabbi). After the conclusion of the Sabbath, many Orthodox Jews enjoy a fourth meal known as MELAVVEH MALKAH ("Escorting the [Sabbath] Queen").

ROSH HA-SHANAH, the New Year, has its own special foods. Challah loaves are usually baked round or into different shapes, each with a symbolic meaning. Following *Kiddush* at the evening meal, the challah is dipped in honey instead of salt as usual. On the second night, an apple is dipped in the honey and the people recite: "May it be Your will … to renew unto us a good and sweet year." Eating the head of a fish symbolizes the hope that one may become "the head [a leader] and not the tail [a follower]" (Deut. 28:1). Sour or bitter foods are not eaten on Rosh ha-Shanah nor are nuts, for symbolic reasons ("nut" and "sin" have the same numerical value in Hebrew).

While the DAY OF ATONEMENT is associated with fasting, it does have two festive meals connected to it: the meal served before the fast and the breaking of the fast that follows. The Talmud states: "If a man eats and drinks on the ninth [of Tishri], Scripture considers it as if he has fasted on both the ninth and tenth [Yom Kippur]" (*Yoma* 81b). Traditionally, the challahs for the meal before the fast are round and braided; soup with *kreplakh* (dough filled with meat) is served. Salty fish and spiced dishes are traditional appetizers after the fast.

SUKKOT has its special dishes as well. In Yemen, a number of families would join together to buy a sheep or an ox for the festival. In Poland and Russia, *holishkes* (stuffed cabbage) was the traditional meal. German Jews ate a type of cabbage known as *Wasserkohl* on HOSHANA RABBAH, because on this day the *Kol Mevasser* hymn is recited. *Teyglakh*, a pastry boiled in honey, is also a traditional Sukkot delicacy.

There are three unique HANUKKAH foods. Among Ashkenazi Jews, latkes – potato pancakes fried in oil – symbolize the miracle of the oil. In the Oriental communities, doughnuts (*sufganiyyot*) boiled in oil remind us of this miracle. It is also customary to eat dairy dishes, in honor of the heroism of Judith. Judith, of the Maccabean family, slew the enemy general Holofernes after feeding him milk, cheese, and wine until he fell into a deep sleep.

PURIM has both unique foods and a special festive meal. Traditionally, on Purim Jews send food portions (*mishlo'ah manot*) to their neighbors and friends. These gifts usually include *hamantashen*, the three-cornered poppyseed cookies associated with the holiday. In Israel, these are called *oznei Haman* ("Haman's ears"). In addition, Purim has a festive meal known as the Purim SE'UDAH, where wine and alcohol are served in greater than normal quantities.

PASSOVER brings with it special foods and its own system of laws that govern the preparation of food for the weeklong holiday. Passover laws forbid HAMETS (leaven); they require the eating of MATZAH (unleavened bread). This is based on the verse: "Seven days you shall eat unleavened bread; on the first day you shall remove leaven from your homes" (Ex. 12:15). Hamets includes the fermented products of the FIVE SPECIES of grain – wheat, barley, emmer, oats, and rye – and all foods containing yeast or leaven. The Passover festive meal is called the SEDER and is the most ritually elaborate meal of the year. During the *Seder*, each person drinks four cups (ARBA KOSOT) of wine to recall God's four promises of REDEMPTION in the Bible (Ex. 6:6–7). In addition, each person must eat matzah and MAROR (bitter herbs). Traditionally, one also eats vegetables dipped in salt water and a sandwich made of *haroset* – a sweet paste made of apples, nuts, cinnamon and wine – that symbolizes the mortar from which the Israelites made bricks for the Egyptians. Among the favorite Passover dishes are: *borsht* (beetroot soup), *kneydlakh* (matzah dumplings), *khreyn* (horseradish), etc.

SHAVU'OT is the holiday for eating dairy foods. This is because the Torah was given on Shavu'ot, and the Torah is compared to milk and honey. Special holiday dishes include: blintzes (rolled pancakes filled with cream cheese), cheese knishes (filled and baked dough), cheesecake, and cheese *kreplakh*. Sephardi housewives often prepare a seven-layer cake called Siete Cielos ("Seven Heavens") that symbolizes the number of heavens that God broke through to reveal the Torah on Mount Sinai. Others made *baklava*, a sweet pastry with many layers of thin dough stuffed with nuts, sugar, and honey.

FORGIVENESS (Heb. *mehilah, selihah*). Forgiving sin is one of the 13 main qualities of God (Ex. 34:6–7); in the sixth blessing of the AMIDAH prayer, God is addressed as "the One who forgives abundantly." The Bible gives example after example of God's mercy. Even in the most extreme case, when the Israelites abandoned Him and worshiped the GOLDEN CALF, God listened to the pleas of Moses and forgave the people (Ex. 32:11–14). The central theme of the PROPHETS is the return to God's ways (*teshuvah*), which is made possible by God's willingness to forgive.

FORGIVENESS

To him who is compassionate toward his fellow creatures, and forgives wrongs done to him, compassion is shown from heaven.

If your fellow has done you some good, let it be great in your eyes; but if he has done you a great wrong, let it be small in your eyes.

If a man has sinned all his life, yet repents on the day of his death, all his sins are forgiven him.

Imitate God by being compassionate and forgiving. He, in turn, will have compassion on you and pardon your offense.

In Jewish tradition, it is the individual's responsibility to seek forgiveness from God and from one's fellow human being. God is viewed as eager to forgive (*Hag.* 5a); human beings are encouraged to "walk in His ways." The rabbis noted the biblical example of ABRAHAM, who not only forgave Abimelech but also prayed to God on his behalf (Gen. 20:17). In the rabbinic view, readiness to forgive is a virtue. One who rejects another person's plea for forgiveness three times is considered to be evil.

The rabbis understood that human beings do not easily forgive. For this reason it is not enough simply to pay someone back for an offense. One must also personally seek the injured party's forgiveness (see *RH* 17b). It is a custom before the DAY OF ATONEMENT to approach people that one may have wronged and to beg forgiveness and offer to make amends. The Talmud advises the injured party to be "soft as a reed and not hard as cedar" (*Ta'an.* 20b) in accepting the apology.

The process of seeking forgiveness from God resembles the process among people. MAIMONIDES identified three stages of repentance: first the individual must confess to the particular sin; next, one must express regret for having transgressed; finally comes the resolve never to sin again if the opportunity should arise.

FOUR CUPS See ARBA KOSOT

FOUR QUESTIONS (Heb. *Arba Kushiyot*). Traditional and most well-know part of the Passover SEDER. The Four Questions are usually asked by the youngest child or *Seder* participant.

They deal with four unique aspects of the Passover ritual. The child asks: why do we eat unleavened bread (MATZAH) and bitter herbs (MAROR), and why do we dip two vegetables in salt water and lean our bodies to one side at the *Seder* table. The questions direct the child's attention – in fact, all participants' attention – to the story of the Exodus from Egypt, which is about to be told.

The Four Questions that appear in the HAGGADAH today are not the original version. Originally, the questions related to eating matzah and *maror*, to dipping the two vegetables, and to the practice of eating only roasted meat (not stewed or cooked) at the *Seder* table. This last question related to the sacrifice of the paschal lamb (see SACRIFICES AND OFFERINGS) and became outdated after the destruction of the TEMPLE. It was replaced by the more relevant question about leaning to one side. The order of questions has been the same as it is today since the time of the *ge'onim* (see GAON).

From the time of the Mishnah until the late Middle Ages, an adult asked the Four Questions. In recent centuries, the original practice of having the youngest child ask the questions has been restored.

FOUR SPECIES   (Heb. *arba'ah minim*). Four different plants used as part of the SUKKOT ritual. The Bible commands: "You shall take on the first day [of Sukkot] the fruit of goodly trees, branches of palm trees, and boughs of thick trees, and willows of the brook, and you shall rejoice before the Lord your God seven days" (Lev. 23:40). According to the accepted interpretation, these plants are the *etrog* (citron), *lulav* (palm branch), *hadas* (myrtle), and *arava* (willow). The palm branch, myrtle and willow are tied together in a small bundle with strips of palm leaves, with the myrtle on the right of the *lulav* and the willow on the left. It is held in the right hand. The *etrog* is held separately in the left hand. A BENEDICTION (blessing) is recited, and then all the plants are brought together and waved in six directions.

In Temple times, the Four Species were taken and waved in the Temple itself on each of the seven days of Sukkot. On the first day it was also waved in other places. When the Temple was destroyed, R. JOHANAN BEN ZAKKAI ruled that in remembrance of the Temple, the plants would be waved on all seven days of the festival in all places. Today (except on the SABBATH), the Four Species are waved throughout Sukkot during the singing of HALLEL. They are also marched around the synagogue during the HAKKAFOT (see also HOSHANOT).

The Bible does not offer a reason for waving the Four Species. However, the rabbis saw the symbolism of the ritual. According to them, the *etrog* has both taste and fragrance. It symbolizes the "model" Jew with both knowledge of Torah and good deeds to his credit. The myrtle has only fragrance, the date palm only taste, and the willow neither. These symbolize Jews who have knowledge but no good deeds, or good deeds but no knowledge, or who have neither knowledge nor good deeds. Taking the Four Species together on Sukkot symbolically unites Jews

A man holding the four species in his sukkah.

of all types, and each type makes up for the shortcomings of the other (Lev. R. 30:12).

FRANKEL, ZACHARIAS   (1801–1875). Founder of the "positive-historical" school of Jewish study, later to be known as CONSERVATIVE JUDAISM; rabbinic scholar and leader of German Jewry. Frankel was born in Prague and received a traditional Jewish education. He later studied philosophy and language development in Budapest. He served from 1836 as the rabbi of Dresden. In 1854 he was appointed director of the Judisch-Theologisches ("Jewish Theological") Seminar in Breslau, where he remained until his death. His outstanding writings include an introduction to the Mishnah (*Darkhei ha-Mishnah*, 1859) and a commentary on sections of the Jerusalem Talmud (*Ahavat Tsiyyon*, 1875). In 1851 he founded (and edited until 1868) a well-respected Jewish scholarly journal in German.

Frankel was involved in the big disagreements of his day between NEO-ORTHODOXY and REFORM JUDAISM. At the Frankfurt rabbinical conference of 1845 he tried to convince the non-Orthodox rabbis to adopt firm guidelines for making changes. When the conference called for using German and other languages instead of Hebrew for prayer, Frankel walked out in protest. The issue of Hebrew for prayer split the non-Orthodox into two different groups – the Reform (who rejected Hebrew) and the Positive-Historical. Frankel's Positive-Historical viewpoint argued that Judaism should continue to develop throughout history. He emphasized the role of the people in developing Jewish law (HALAKHAH). However, changes should be based on a clearly defined way of interpreting biblical laws. His essays also called for Jews to settle in Erets Israel decades before HERZL.

FRANKISTS   Followers of the false MESSIAH Jacob Frank. Frank (1726–1791) was a charismatic and ambitious leader who was influenced by SHABBETAI TSEVI, the 17th century false Messiah. He was born in Podolia, in the Ukraine, and later moved to Turkey. Frank began to see himself as a "reborn" Shabbetai Tsevi. He declared that we would complete Tsevi's mission. He developed a mystical belief system that included elements of Judaism and CHRISTIANITY. His system closely paralleled the Christian trinity (three-part god). It included: the "First One"(Shabbetai Tsevi), the "Holy Lord" (Jacob Frank), and "the Lady," a female Messiah (or, as Frank referred to her, "the Virgin," namely a combination of the aspect of God called SHEKHINAH and the Christian Virgin Mary).

Frank demanded that his followers be prepared at any time to "descend into the depths." This meant abandoning all religious and moral rules and participating in ritual sex orgies. Members were expected to remain silent and to pass from one religion to another. Their final goal was to attain knowledge.

The Frankists were excommunicated (banned from Judaism; see EXCOMMUNICATION) in 1756. They enlisted the support of Nicholas Dembowski, the Catholic bishop of Kamenets-Podolski. He ordered the excommunicating rabbis to defend the Talmud at a public DISPUTATION the following year. When the rabbis were judged to have lost the debate, thousands of copies of the Talmud were seized and burned. In 1759 a second disputation was held, but this time the rabbis won. Shortly afterward, thousands of Frankists converted to Catholicism; Jacob Frank himself converted a second time in Warsaw Cathedral. However, when Polish priests learned that Frank's version of the trinity was not identical with that of Christianity, he was arrested and imprisoned.

The movement continued for some time after Frank's death under "the Queen," his daughter Eva-Emunah. Eventually it ceased to exist, with followers either intermarrying or returning to Judaism.

FREE WILL   It has always bothered the rabbis that God's first command to a person in the Bible is one that he disobeys and for which he is punished (Gen. 2:16–3:24). This places the theme of human responsibility for one's actions – free will – at the head of the Bible's list of concerns. God tells CAIN that although he is subject to powerful emotions and "sin couches at the door; its urge is toward you, yet you can be its master"

(Gen. 4:7). MOSES takes up the theme when he addresses the Israelites in the desert: "I have set before you life and death, the blessing and the curse, therefore choose life" (Deut. 30:19). Humanity has freedom of choice to obey God's commands, both as a community and as individuals. If humanity chooses properly it earns reward; if it chooses poorly, it is subject to punishment. The Bible makes a distinction between sins committed on purpose and unintentional acts (Num. 35:1–34). The rabbis also wrote at length about the limits of legal and moral responsibility and the effect of a person's being forced from the outside to sin (BK 8:4).

The concept of free will was not accepted by everybody in the Jewish world. The ESSENES, a non-rabbinic Jewish sect, held that God decided everything in advance. The SADDUCEES denied that God was directly involved in the world; they believed that everything occurred by chance. The rabbis stressed the biblical concept of man's freedom with the statement: "All is in the hands of heaven except the fear of heaven" (Ber. 33b). However the idea of people's freedom of choice is very difficult to grasp because of conflicting ideas in Jewish belief. If God knows everything, how can people have freedom of choice? If God is all-powerful, what real choice can man exercise? The rabbis struggled with this conflict and arrived at the conclusion: "Everything is seen [by God] in advance, yet permission [to act freely] is given [by God]" (Avot 3:5). Even when God intervenes in history, He does not interfere with human choice.

MAIMONIDES described the idea of free will as a "great principle and pillar of the TORAH and the mitzvot (Yad, Teshuvah 5:3). He pointed out that the entire system of REPENTANCE is based on the idea of freedom of choice. The constant call to people to return to God and receive Divine FORGIVENESS assumes that people have the power to free themselves from past ways. God wishes people to come to Him voluntarily, out of free choice. God does not force people to change, but waits for their response (Ex. 19:8). In making moral choices freely, a person becomes more and more the "likeness of God."

Some modern thinkers have particular difficulty accepting the idea of free will. For modern psychology, a person's behavior can be predicted, based on individual character, background, or circumstances. Because of this, they believe that man's choice is really limited.

FREEWILL OFFERING   See SACRIFICES AND OFFERINGS

FRINGES   See TSITSIT

FUNERAL SERVICE   While the BURIAL service may vary among ASHKENAZIM and SEPHARDIM, certain features are common to all Jews. They are: keri'ah – tearing one's clothes (see RENDING OF GARMENTS); the funeral procession, including ritual stops made on the way to the grave site; a EULOGY speech in honor of the deceased; MEMORIAL PRAYERS and a special mourner's KADDISH. during the return procession, those present formally offer their comfort to the mourners. The burial service

A funeral. From a series of paintings of the Burial Society (Hevrah Kaddisha) *of Prague, c. 1780.*

is sometimes referred to as *Tsidduk ha-Din* (lit. "Justification of [God's] Judgment"). This refers to the central portion of the service in which mourners accept the fact that the death was God's will and confirm their belief in God's justice. In some places, mourners beg forgiveness from the dead for any sins that may accidentally have committed against them.

At Ashkenazi funerals, the eulogy is said in the chapel in the presence of the body before the pallbearers take the coffin into the graveyard. The rabbi recites *Attah Gibbor* ("Your might is boundless"), the second blessing of the daily AMIDAH. This is followed by the *Tsidduk ha-Din*. As the funeral procession moves toward the gravesite, the rabbi chants Psalm 91 and pauses three times on the way. After the body is lowered into the grave, those present, particularly the mourners, shovel earth into the grave until the body is covered. They hold the shovel upside-down, to show that this is not its normal use and are careful not to pass it from hand to hand. After the participants leave the cemetery, all wash their hands.

Sephardi funerals have their own unique customs. Sephardim make seven circles (HAKKAFOT) around the coffin, while reciting a prayer for God's mercy on the deceased. Many Sephardi communities observe the mystical tradition that prohibits sons from accompanying their father's body to the grave. Sephardim often begin the funeral in the synagogue rather than in the chapel, and women do not always attend the actual burial. If a man has left children, Syrian Jews blow a SHOFAR. In Sephardi funerals the procession stops up to seven times. *Tsidduk ha-Din* follows the burial, as does the rending of garments.

GAD See TRIBES, TWELVE

GALUT (Heb. "exile" or "captivity"). Another word for *Galut* is *Golah*. In the Bible, both *Galut* and *Golah* refer only to the group of Jewish exiles in Babylonia, or to their captivity there (see EXILE, BABYLONIAN). Later on, *Golah* came to mean the same as the Greek word *diaspora* ("dispersion"), which is any land outside of Erets Israel in which Jews live (*RH* 1:4).

The idea of exile, or of the Jews living outside of their land, is found early in the Bible. The Book of EXODUS tells about the Israelites' slavery in the land of Egypt, and how God took them out of Egypt. This exile became the model of *Galut* in the minds of the rabbis.

After the Israelites received the TORAH and entered into the COVENANT, they were warned to keep God's commandments. If they fail to keep the commandments, they will be expelled from the land: "The Lord will scatter you among all peoples, from one end of the earth to the other ..." (Deut. 28:64). God also promises that if the people of Israel do REPENTANCE, "the Lord our God will return you from captivity ... and gather you from all the peoples ... and bring you into the land which your fathers possessed" (Deut. 30:3–5).

In the times of the PROPHETS, when the people of Israel sinned, they were punished with EXPULSION and exile. This did not mean that God had left them. He continued to give them opportunities to repent and return to the Land of Israel.

When Cyrus gave permission to the Jews living in Babylonia to return from exile to the Land of Israel, many of them chose to stay in Babylonia. The rabbis criticized them, but they also warned them to obey a lawful Gentile ruler (*Yoma* 9b). They said that God forced the people of Israel and the Gentiles to swear three oaths: "... that the people of Israel would not escape from *Galut* by force of arms, nor rebel against the people of the land of their exile; and that the nations would not treat the people of Israel cruelly" (*Ket.* 111a).

For the rabbis, *Galut* was the worst possible punishment, rightly given to the people of Israel by God for their sins (*Avot* 5:9; *Sif.* to Deut. 11:17). It meant homelessness and experiencing cruelty and discrimination. However, exile was also an unnatural condition and would not last forever. Through the text of the prayers and different *halakhot* (Jewish laws), the rabbis reminded the people of the aspects of religion they could not practice in exile. While they understood that exile was a punishment, the rabbis begged God to return the Jews to their land. According to the MIDRASH, the prophets and PATRIARCHS prayed for the people of Israel to be released from exile. The rabbis knew that because the Gentiles hated Jews, the process of ASSIMILATION (blending in with other nations) would be slowed down. However, if the Jews were accepted by the Gentiles, they might assimilate more quickly. The rabbis had two different approaches to the idea of *Galut*. On the one hand, "the seal-ring of Haman" (used to pass a law of genocide against the Persian Jews) did more to bring Jews back to Judaism than all the preaching of the Hebrew prophets (*Meg.* 14a). On the other hand, "God scattered Israel among the nations only in order that the converts should be numerous among them" (*Pes.* 87b; see also CONVERSION TO JUDAISM).

Since the slavery in Egypt was the model for all exiles, the rabbis compared the first redeemer (MOSES) to the final redeemer (MESSIAH of the house of DAVID) and the first REDEMPTION to the final redemption. God's promise to JACOB applies to every *Galut* experience: "Fear not to go down to Egypt, for I will go down with you and surely bring you up again" (Gen. 46:3–4). The rabbis teach that this means that God Himself accompanies His people into exile. This idea, known as *Shekhinta be-Galuta*, "God's Presence in exile," later became an important subject in the KABBALAH. Just as the Jew is humiliated in *Galut*, so God is humiliated with His exiled people. There are many *mitzvot* (commandments) that cannot be performed outside of Israel, such as AGRICULTURAL LAWS that are connected to the Land of Israel or laws of the TEMPLE. That is why the rabbis declared: "Whoever lives outside the land is regarded like one who has no God" (*Ket.* 110b; *Tosef. AZ* 4:5). The Jews, however, concentrated on the commandments they could perform, such as studying the Torah and prayer.

After the First Temple was destroyed, the prophets promised the people of Israel that their exile would end. Earlier, God promised ABRAHAM that his descendants would be enslaved for 400 years (Gen. 15:13). The rabbis no longer received such promises from God. They knew Israel would be redeemed, but they did not know when.

Each community in exile, from Babylonia to Spain and

Poland, bore the title *Galut*. The Babylonian EXILARCH was called *Resh Galuta* ("Head of Captivity"). When Rabbi GERSHOM BEN JUDAH became a brilliant scholar in medieval Germany, he became known as *Me'or ha-Golah* ("Light of the Exile"). During the Golden Age of Spanish Jewry, Rabbi JUDAH HALEVI wrote poetry about his people's feelings of longing for the Land of Israel.

From the mid-19th century, the age-old Jewish hope for *kibbuts galuyyot*, the INGATHERING OF THE EXILES, was re-awakened, and the Zionist movement was established. Moses Hess, a German socialist, wrote: "In exile, the Jewish people cannot be regenerated" (*Rome and Jerusalem*, 1862). Since the establishment of the State of Israel in 1948, there have been many arguments over the role of ZIONISM in the Diaspora. Many Jews in Israel felt that, given the opportunity, a Zionist Jew was obligated to move to Israel. However, long before the State of Israel came into being, Shmarya Levin (a Russian Zionist leader) said: "It is easier to take a Jew out of *Galut* than to take the *Galut* out of a Jew."

GAMALIEL   Rabbinical dynasty.
Gamaliel I   Known as "the Elder" (1st cent. CE), president (*nasi*) of the SANHEDRIN, grandson of HILLEL. He and his descendants were called *Rabban* ("our master") instead of the usual Rabbi ("my master").

Gamaliel I lived in the times of King Agrippa I, who often consulted with him on halakhic (Jewish legal) problems. He issued proclamations from the TEMPLE to the Jews in Erets Israel and in the Diaspora about tithing, the leap year, and the Jewish CALENDAR. He made a number of rules (see TAKKANAH) about what to ask witnesses who had seen the New MOON. He and the Sanhedrin were able to proclaim the new month according to what the witnesses had seen. He also made a number of important regulations affecting MARRIAGE and DIVORCE (*Git.* 4:2–3).

Gamaliel taught that Gentiles should be treated as charitably as Jews, in areas such as visiting the SICK, burying the dead, and comforting their mourners. Their poor should also be able to gather food from the corners of fields (Lev. 23:22). He even showed tolerance towards the new Judeo-Christian sect, adopting a "wait and see" policy when Peter and the other apostles were brought before the Sanhedrin. The New Testament calls him "a teacher of the law held in high regard by all the people" (Acts 5:34).

Gamaliel's advice to his students was: "Provide yourself with a teacher; rid yourself of doubt; and when giving a tithe do not do so by estimation [i.e., measure carefully]" (*Avot* 1:16).
Simeon ben Gamaliel I   became the *nasi* of the Sanhedrin after his father, Gamaliel I. Like his father, he issued proclamations to the Jewish communities of Erets Israel and the Diaspora informing them of the Sanhedrin's decisions about tithing and leap years (*Sanh.* 11a).

Simeon was very modest and was known for his saying: "All my days I have grown up among the sages, and I have found

no better way than silence; not learning but doing is the main thing; and too many words cause sin" (*Avot* 1:18).

According to the historian Josephus, Simeon directed the war against Rome during the Jewish rebellion of 66 CE.
Gamaliel II   (of Yavneh, mid-1st cent. CE; d. before 132 CE). A son of Simeon ben Gamaliel I, he was also the *nasi* of the Sanhedrin. He ruled just after the Romans destroyed the Temple and Jerusalem (70 CE), and continued the work of JOHANAN BEN ZAKKAI – restoring the Jewish nation and religion. He guided the community of rabbis of Yavneh to begin recording a collection of legal, ritual, and ethical teachings that later formed the basis of the MISHNAH. His grandson, JUDAH HA-NASI, finished editing the Mishnah two generations later. Gamaliel's opinions are quoted in the Mishnah about 70 times.

Gamaliel was an intelligent, deeply religious man of strong character who accomplished many things in his lifetime. However, he was involved in many conflicts. In one clash with JOSHUA BEN HANANIAH, he overstepped the line and humiliated the elderly scholar. This led to a revolt in which the scholars of Yavneh decided to replace him with a new head of the Sanhedrin. He eventually returned to his position, but tension remained between him and the Sanhedrin.

In addition to his duties as president of the High Court and ACADEMY, Gamaliel was a leader of the nation. He often traveled to Rome and represented the Jews before the Roman leaders.

Gamaliel was involved in almost every area of Jewish practice. He made it obligatory to recited the AMIDAH, and standardized its text, including the blessing against heretics (MINIM). He also made the EVENING SERVICE obligatory. He tried to strengthen the observance of the FESTIVALS, and to make sure that the priests and Levites would receive their tithes and offerings after the Temple was destroyed. It is possible that he and his Sanhedrin at Yavneh were responsible for the final Bible canon ("final fixing" of the Bible).
Simeon ben Gamaliel II   (2nd cent. CE). Son of Gamaliel II, head of the Sanhedrin. When he became the *nasi*, the Sanhedrin had moved to Usha (*RH* 32a). His opinions were accepted 100 times and rejected three times in the Mishnah (*Ket.* 78a). He warned against making rules that the public would find too difficult to bear (*AZ* 36a) and called for local CUSTOM to be respected (*Ket.* 6:4).

Simeon was very much concerned with peace. The world, he said, rests on three pillars: Law, Truth, and Peace (*Avot* 1:18). Peace begins in the home and ends in the nation.

GAMBLING   The Bible does not mention gambling. It is first mentioned in the Mishnah, which says: "The following are ineligible to testify in a Jewish court of law: one who plays dice, one who races pigeons …" (*RH* 1:8). Although the rabbis explained that this only applies to professional gamblers, they are nevertheless opposed to all gambling. In fact, they ruled that winning money at gambling is close to robbery, and therefore gambling debts cannot be collected through a Jewish court of law. The rabbis also felt that people should do more productive things with their time.

Although the rabbis tried to prevent all types of gambling, it is permitted on HANUKKAH and PURIM. The RESPONSA literature is full of cases of fines given to people who did not respect the rabbis' rulings against gambling. Leone de Modena, for example, was an important Talmud scholar who lived in Venice at the end of the 16th century. The community was afraid that he would ruin the reputation of the Jews with his gambling. In 1628, they published a decree forbidding all gambling, under the threat of EXCOMMUNICATION.

Some rabbis have tried to forbid all games, including chess, because the time spent playing games should be spent learning TORAH. However, this ruling has not been accepted.

GAON (pl. *ge'onim*). Honorary title given to the heads of the ACADEMIES of Sura and Pumbedita in Babylonia, from the seventh to 11th centuries. They had more power and authority than the heads of the academies in the generations before. Questions on all aspects of Judaism were sent to them from Egypt, North Africa, and Spain, and they had the exclusive right to answer them.

These RESPONSA became a source for the religious, economic, and social history of the time. This has been especially true since the discovery of the Cairo GENIZAH, where many of the geonic responsa were found.

The *ge'onim* had unquestioned authority, which one could see from their responsa: "This is the law and it is forbidden to deviate from it to the right or to the left." They were appointed by the head of the Jewish community, the EXILARCH; however, the position was often passed down from father to son. In Sura, for example, for over almost 200 years, the position of *gaon* was always given to a member of one of three families.

A *gaon* received a fixed salary, as well as a portion of the donations sent to the academies. Babylonia was divided into three districts, two of which were under the rule of the *ge'onim* of the two academies and one under the Exilarch. In each district, the *gaon* or Exilarch appointed judges and other community officers. Because the *ge'onim* were usually more learned than the Exilarch, decisions made in the Exilarch's court had to be approved by a *gaon*. This caused much controversy between them. The most famous conflict was between SAADIAH GAON and the Exilarch David ben Zakkai, who at one point removed Saadiah from the position of *gaon* of Sura. Saadiah, in turn, had Ben Zakkai removed from his position.

Saadiah Gaon, appointed in 928, was the greatest rabbi connected with Sura. After his death, the academy closed for 45 years, reopening when Samuel ben Hophni took over. The Pumbedita Academy's greatest period was under the leadership of SHERIRA GAON (968–998) and his son HAI GAON (998–1038). After the death of Hai Gaon, the two academies joined together for another 150 years.

The *ge'onim* made a lasting contribution to Jewish literature.

They wrote many responsa that explained how a Jew should behave, based on the teachings of the Talmud. They passed on the oral interpretations of the SAVORAIM and began organizing the HALAKHAH (Jewish law) into codes.

The *ge'onim* also wrote many hymns and prayers. Rabbi AMRAM GAON of Sura (853–856) put together the first complete Order of Prayers (see PRAYER BOOK).

Later on, the term Gaon came to mean outstanding scholar, such as the great East European scholar and spiritual leader ELIJAH BEN SOLOMON ZALMAN (1720–1797), who was known as the Vilna Gaon.

GAON OF VILNA See ELIJAH BEN SOLOMON ZALMAN

GARDEN OF EDEN See EDEN, GARDEN OF

GEDALIAH, FAST OF (*Tsom Gedalyah*). A minor fast observed on the third of TISHRI in memory of the tragic fate of Gedaliah, the governor of JUDAH. His story is told in the Book of JEREMIAH (40:5–41:3). After the destruction of the First Temple, most of the Jewish people were exiled to Babylonia (see EXILE). Nebuchadnezzar appointed Gedaliah ben Ahikam as the governor of Judah. The Ammonites hired Ishmael ben Nethaniah to kill Gedaliah. He killed Gedaliah and his bodyguards in Gedaliah's home in Mizpah. Ignoring Jeremiah's advice, the surviving Jewish loyalists fled to Egypt because they thought that Nebuchadnezzar would blame them for the murder. The King did in fact blame the Jews, and sent more of the population into exile. The murder of Gedaliah is therefore associated with Judah's final collapse.

The fast of Gedaliah falls on the third day of Tishri (*RH* 18b), the day after Rosh ha-Shanah. Fasting is from dawn to dusk and SELIHOT are read in the MORNING SERVICE. All the rules of a minor fast apply. Should it fall on a SABBATH, it is put off to the next day.

GEHENNA See AFTERLIFE

GEIGER, ABRAHAM (1810–1874). Reform rabbi and Jewish thinker; main leader of REFORM Judaism in 19th century Germany. Geiger received a formal Jewish education in Frankfurt and studied at a university in Bonn. One of his classmates, Samson Raphael HIRSCH, later became his main opponent. As rabbi in Weisbaden (1832–38), he organized the first of several conferences (or SYNODS) of German Reform rabbis. In Breslau (1838–63) he became the leader of the Reform camp. Geiger announced that Judaism is a "universal mission" and that CIRCUMCISION is "a barbaric and bloody rite." He published a new prayer book in 1854 that left out any mention of ANGELS and RESURRECTION of the dead, as well as all prayers for the INGATHERING OF THE EXILES, the Return to Zion, and the rebuilding of the TEMPLE. He also added choral singing and sermons in German to the Reform prayer service. In 1870, Geiger moved to Berlin, where he became the director of the new Hochshule für die Wissenschaft des Judentums (see RABBINICAL SEMINARIES) in 1872.

Geiger believed that German Jewry should be reformed slowly, and used his research work in the "Science of Judaism" (WISSENSCHAFT DES JUDENTUMS) to justify his opinions. Geiger did not believe that the PENTATEUCH is the word of God and did not consider the commandments an obligation. In his later years, Geiger adapted himself to the trend of German non-Orthodox Jewry and restored some of the prayers and practices he had abandoned. He had a major impact on later Reform rabbis in the United States.

GEMARA   See TALMUD

GEMATRIA   (*gematriyya*, "numerology"; from the Greek *geometria*). A method of revealing deeper or hidden meaning in words or phrases. Each letter of the Hebrew alphabet has a numerical value (see NUMBERS for table), as does any word if one adds up the value of its letters. Thus, when JACOB tells his sons to "*go down*" (Heb. *Redu* = 210) and buy grain in Egypt (Gen. 42:2), this is interpreted to mean that Jacob's descendants will be in Egypt for 210 years (Gen. R. 91:2). *Gematria* is one of the 32 official methods used for interpreting the Torah (see HERMENEUTICS). Mystical literature is full of *gematria*, which is the basis for AMULETS. However, some rabbis (NAHMANIDES, for example) preferred not to use it too much.

Gematria has often been used for less serious matters. Both *yayin* ("wine") and *sod* ("mystery, secret") have the numerical value of 70. We therefore have the saying, "When wine goes in, the secret will go out" (*Er.* 65a). Jews often give charity in multiples of 18 (= *hai*, "alive, life").

Gematria is not a Jewish invention. It was first used by Greeks, Assyrians, and Babylonians. During the Hellenistic period, magicians and dream interpreters used *gematria*. Nowadays, some experts on the subject are trying to prove its scientific value.

GEMILUT HASADIM   ("acts of lovingkindness"). According to the Mishnah, kindly acts, along with TORAH and worship of God, make up the three pillars of the earth (*Avot* 1:2). According to the rabbis, *gemilut hasadim* is one of the special characteristics of the Jewish people (Deut. R. 3:6). Both charity and *gemilut hasadim* are equal to all of the commandments in the Torah.

The rabbis taught that *gemilut hasadim* are kind social acts, for example: visiting the SICK, providing HOSPITALITY, giving a bride a dowry (HAKHNASAT KALLAH), feeding the poor, comforting a mourner, or attending a funeral. According to the rabbis, "lending money without interest is preferable to giving charity, and investing money in a poor man's business is better still" (*Shab.* 63a). This is true because these forms of aide can help the person get back on his own two feet. Today, most Jewish communities have special *gemilut hesed* societies that lend money interest free.

GENESIS, BOOK OF   First book of the PENTATEUCH, known in Hebrew as *Be-Reshit* ("In the Beginning") from its first word. It is also called *Sefer Beri'at ha-Olam* and *Sefer Ma'aseh be-Reshit*

Opening of Genesis. From the Castro Pentateuch *Germany, 1344.*

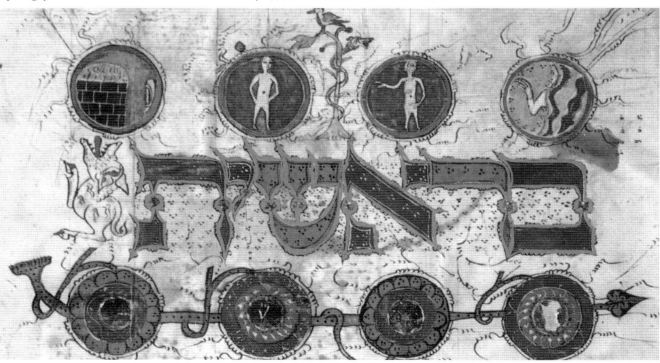

BOOK OF GENESIS

("The Book of Creation"). Genesis is divided into 50 chapters and 1,534 verses.

The Book of Genesis has three sections: (1) a history of the universe and early mankind (chapters 1–11); (2) the history of the Patriarchs, ABRAHAM, ISAAC and JACOB (12–36); (3) the story of JOSEPH (37–50). Its religious lessons include the oneness of God and the creation of the world by God; the origin of evil, the moral law of God, and the unity of mankind; God's choosing of Israel and His promise that the land of Canaan will belong to the people of Israel, who are bound by a COVENANT (agreement with God); and the idea that God directs the course of history.

In Jewish tradition, the Pentateuch is the word of God written by MOSES. Modern scholars believe that Genesis (and the rest of the Pentateuch) is a collection from a number of sources. Similar stories of CREATION and the FLOOD have been found in other Ancient Near East cultures, but the idea of one God and morality are unique to the Hebrew Bible.

GENESIS RABBAH Midrash on the Book of GENESIS, known in Hebrew as *Be-Reshit Rabbah* (see also MIDRASH AGGADAH). This Midrash is a story-like interpretation of Genesis, chapter by chapter, verse by verse. Its text is divided into 101 sections. Each section is introduced by a poem, mostly from PSALMS and PROVERBS. The Midrash is written mainly in Hebrew, but some parts are written in Aramaic, Greek, and Latin.

The language and style of Genesis Rabbah is very similar to that of the Jerusalem Talmud. According to modern scholars, they both were written based on the same ancient source, some time in the fifth century CE. Together with LEVITICUS RABBAH and LAMENTATIONS RABBAH it is the earliest Midrash written by the rabbis of the Talmud.

GENETIC ENGINEERING See MEDICAL ETHICS, JEWISH

GENIZAH A storeroom for worn-out and damaged holy books and ritual objects, such as TEFILLIN or MEZUZOT. According to Jewish law, such objects cannot be thrown out but must be buried in a Jewish CEMETERY. Many synagogues set aside a special area as a Genizah (literally "hiding place"), where people can leave things for later burial.

Nowadays, the term "the Genizah" usually refers to the storeroom of the ancient Ben Ezra synagogue in Cairo. In 1896, two Scottish ladies on a visit to Cairo bought a bundle of fragments of Hebrew manuscripts. The following year, Solomon SCHECHTER, then a reader of Rabbinics at Cambridge University, identified one of the pages as being part of the Hebrew original of *Ecclesiasticus* (or *The Wisdom of Ben Sira*). In 1897, Schechter traveled to Cairo and bought the rest of the contents of the Genizah on behalf of Cambridge University. He took back 140,000 fragments. Another 60,000 that had been sold before he arrived reached other libraries around the world.

Throughout the 20th century, the process of identifying fragments continued. Much was learned about Jewish history that was previously unknown or vague.

Reconstruction of old manuscripts being placed in the Cairo Genizah *in the Ezra Synagogue of Fostat.*

The material discovered includes important fragments of the Jerusalem Talmud; parts of the MIDRASH that were previously unknown; RESPONSA of the *ge'onim*; KARAITE writings; hymns and poetry from the time period after the Talmud; large sections of works of HALAKHAH (Jewish law) from the Academy of Tiberius; letters by MAIMONIDES; and the earliest written examples of the YIDDISH language.

GENTILE A non-Jew; any person neither born of a Jewish mother nor converted to Judaism. Various Hebrew words are used for the gentile, each with a slightly different meaning. The term *goy* is used often, but it actually means "a nation," and the Jewish people is also regularly called *goy* in the Bible (see Ex. 19:6, for example). In ancient Judaism, there are two categories of gentiles, the *ger toshav* (literally "resident alien") and the *akum,* which is an acronym for a Hebrew phrase meaning "worshipers of stars and planets." To be considered a *ger toshav,* a non-Jew must live by the seven NOACHIDE LAWS. These laws require belief in the One God and forbid blasphemy, murder, theft, sexual immorality, and the eating of a limb from a living creature (see EVAR MIN HA-HAI). Anyone who does not accept these laws is considered an *akum,* or pagan. A Christian or Muslim is generally considered a *ger toshav.* According to Jewish law, a gentile who wishes to live in the Land of Israel must take on the laws of a *ger toshav.*

Judaism sees itself as a universal religion. The seven Noachide laws apply to gentiles just as the 613 COMMANDMENTS apply to Jews. According to Jewish tradition, gentiles who keep the Noachide laws are guaranteed a place in the world to come.

The Talmud contains many laws that reflect the tension between Jews and gentiles. Some laws were meant to protect Jews from gentiles who wished to harm them. For example, a Jew was not to walk on the left-hand side of a non-Jew who wore a sword, for fear of being stabbed, and a Jew was not to sell Jewish items, such as TSITSIT, to a non-Jew, for fear that the non-Jew might dress up as a Jew and harm Jews. The Talmud teaches that there is a difference between nations who respect human life, such as the Greeks, and those who do not, such as the Persians (*BK* 117a). Certain laws were meant to prevent the Jews from violating specific Jewish laws. Jews were not permitted to buy milk from a gentile, for fear that it might be mixed with milk from a non-KOSHER animal. Other laws were meant to prevent Jews from socializing with gentiles.

However, some laws showed a very cooperative attitude. The Jerusalem Talmud (*Git.* 5:9) says, "In a city in which both Jews and gentiles live, we appoint Jewish and gentile overseers and we support the gentile poor together with the Jewish poor, we visit their SICK, and comfort their mourners."

Although some of the rabbis' statements about the gentiles are quite harsh, one must remember that Jews were persecuted by Christians and Muslims, and developed negative stereotypes (see ANTI-SEMITISM; DHIMMI LAWS). After the EMANCIPATION of the Jews, most of the barriers between Jews and non-Jews were removed. They began to mingle, which has caused some stereotypes to disappear on both sides, and has led to more mutual understanding.

Many Jews still believe that some or all Christians want to convert Jews to Christianity. Others are worried about ASSIMILATION and INTERMARRIAGE. In the Western world today, Jews have a friendly attitude toward non-Jews, without all or most of the historical tensions.

GER   See CONVERSION TO JUDAISM

GERSHOM BEN JUDAH   (known as *Me'or ha-Golah* ["light

of the Exile"] and Rabbenu Gershom ["our rabbi Gershom"]; 960–1028). Rabbinic authority. Born in Metz, Germany, he established his academy in Mainz and taught there for the rest of his life. His TAKKANOT (new laws) were accepted by all ASHKENAZI communities. Two of his most important *takkanot* dealt with the status of women in Jewish law: the first outlawed marrying more than one woman (see POLYGAMY); the second changed the laws of DIVORCE, so that a man could not divorce his wife without her consent. He also forbade reading letters addressed to others.

One of Rabbenu Gershom's greatest achievements was putting together a complete and authentic text of the Talmud. In those days texts of any kind were very rare and expensive because they had to be copied by hand. Teaching was done orally, and students would write out the texts for themselves. The result was that many versions of the same passages were in circulation. Rabbenu Gershom put together a complete Talmud manuscript with his signature, which is more or less the accepted text of the Talmud today. He also prepared a complete Bible text that was correct to the last detail of the *masorah* (tradition).

His comments on the Talmud are quoted by RASHI. He wrote several SELIHOT (penitential prayers) and PIYYUTIM (hymns), some of which appear in the prayer book.

GET   See DIVORCE

GE'ULAH   ("Redemption"). Term used for a number of prayers that ask God to redeem His people. (For the religious idea, see REDEMPTION.) In the Talmud, *Ge'ulah* usually refers to the two long passages recited between SHEMA and the AMIDAH – EMET VE-YATSIV in the MORNING SERVICE and EMET VE-EMUNAH in the EVENING SERVICE. Both end with the blessing "He who redeemed Israel." The category of *Ge'ulah* also includes some hymns that are recited on the PILGRIM FESTIVALS, a BENEDICTION (blessing) recited before the second cup of wine at the Passover SEDER, and the seventh benediction of the weekday AMIDAH.

GEZERAH   (lit. "decree"; pl. *gezerot*). Hebrew term with several meanings: (1) a commandment from God for which no reason is given, such as the RED HEIFER. (2) A decree from a foreign ruler forbidding the observance of Jewish law. Antiochus IV Epiphanies issued such decrees in the Hasmonean era, as did the Roman Emperor Hadrian in the days of Rabbi AKIVA. (3) Organized forced conversions of Jews to a different religion, religious persecution, massacres, and pogroms. An example of this are *gezerot tah ve-tat* (decrees of the Hebrew year 5048–9 = 1648–49 CE), the viscious massacre of Jews in Poland and the Ukraine during the Cossack uprising led by Bogdan Chmielnicki. (4) A preventive measure given by the rabbis in order to safeguard the law of the Bible, as the men of the GREAT ASSEMBLY taught, and "make a fence around the TORAH" (*Avot.* 1:1). For example, the "18 *gezerot*" of the students of HILLEL and SHAMMAI in the first century CE, which were designed to strengthen the barriers between Jews and non-Jews.

Later on, rabbis limited these restrictions. For example, they believed that "a *gezerah* should not be imposed on the community unless the majority is able to live with it" (*AZ* 36a). However, once the Jews accept a *gezerah*, it is just like a biblical law, and cannot be removed.

Restrictions added to Jewish law after the times of the Talmud are usually called *herem* (EXCOMMUNICATION), because they carry the punishment of being banned from taking part in the community. An example is the Ashkenazi rule that forbids a man to marry more than one woman. This is known as *herem de-Rabbenu Gershom* (see GERSHOM BEN JUDAH; TAKKANAH).

GIRL-NAMING CEREMONY   See SIMHAT BAT

GITTIN   ("Bills of Divorce"). Sixth tractate (book) of the Order of NASHIM in the Mishnah. Its nine chapters deal with Jewish DIVORCE (Deut. 24:1–4). According to Jewish law, a *get* (bill of divorce) is the only way of permanently separating a husband and wife. The *get* must be given by the husband to his wife. The Mishnah discusses the wording of the *get*, the witnesses, divorcing a minor, and the issuing of a *get* by a man not of sound mind.

GIYYUR   See CONVERSION TO JUDAISM

GLATT   See DIETARY LAWS; KOSHER

GLEANINGS   See LEKET, SHIKHEHAH, PE'AH

GOD   The Supreme Being; creator of the world; Lord of the universe. In the Bible and rabbinic sources, knowledge of God comes from observing His actions and His revelations to man.

In the Bible   God rules over everything, and is subject to no laws or limitations. He can do anything and be anything. God is One (Deut. 4:35; see MONOTHEISM). He is the source of everything in the world, including evil (Isa. 45:7). God is above time (Ps. 90:2) and outside space (Isa 66:1; Jer. 23:24). He is infinite, without beginning and end, and unchanging (Mal. 3:6). He is beyond the world, yet He is very much the ground of all being, the "soul of our soul," accessible to human beings at all times (Ps. 145:18). He is the God who reveals Himself to humankind, yet often appears to be a "hidden God" (Isa. 45:15).

In the Bible, God is given human-like qualities. He speaks to people, judges, punishes, and rewards. God plans, decides, and chooses. He is aware of the human condition (Ex. 2:24) and reaches out to people with love.

God is the creator of the universe, He brought all into existence out of nothing. The universe cannot exist without God, who constantly gives it life. If God would cease to exist, the universe would collapse into nothingness.

God is the Lord of the history of the universe, Who guides the course of the affairs of nations, and particularly the history of the people of Israel. After creating the world, God continued to guide its history, but He must deal with humanity's freedom, which often turns into rebelliousness. The prophets teach, however, that in the "end of days," God's Will will be done.

Having given people freedom, God limits Himself in order to allow them freedom of choice (see FREE WILL). God relates to human beings like a loving father rather than a king.

The Bible describes God as having emotions (see ANTHROPOMORPHISM): He is angry (Ex. 22:23), pleased (Gen. 1:31), sad and disappointed (Gen 6:6), has pity (Jonah 4:11), loves (Deut. 23:6), and hates (Amos 5:21). As the rabbis explained, "The Bible speaks in human language" (*Ber.* 31b) so that human beings can understand God's actions. However, God does not actually experience what human beings call "emotions."

In the Bible, God is sometimes described as having a body and sometimes as having none. MAIMONIDES explains that God has no body and the references to His hand or heart are symbolic. He quotes passages such as "The Lord spoke to you out of the fire, you heard the sound of words, but perceived no shape, only a voice" (Deut. 4:12) to prove his point.

The two major REVELATIONS of God take place at Mount SINAI. The first is witnessed by the entire nation of Israel, when they receive the TABLETS OF THE COVENANT and the DECALOGUE (Ten Commandments). MOSES alone experiences the second, before receiving the second set of Tablets.

God and Morality   God commands human beings to behave morally, which is the essence of His covenant with Israel. When God reveals Himself to Moses, he does not promise to perform certain actions, but reveals His character traits: "… God [is] compassionate and gracious, slow to anger, kind and faithful …" (Ex. 34:6). While only the people of Israel received the Ten Commandments, God expects all of humanity to behave morally. Acting morally is humanity's way of imitating God, which is a person's purpose in life (see IMITATION OF GOD).

Divine Attributes   While God is not like humans in any way, when speaking of Him, one has no choice but to speak of human actions and qualities. Therefore, any qualities that God possesses must not be understood literally. According to Maimonides, one can say: "God is the creator of the world, the giver of the Torah, the liberator of Israel from Egypt, and the healer of the sick, etc.," because this does not suggest how these acts are done. When the Bible says: "God was angry with the people of Sodom," it meant that the city could expect from God the kinds of actions that human beings carry out when they are angry.

Is there anything people can know about God? According to Maimonides, the only things people can know about God is what He is *not*. For example, we know that God is not unwise. One cannot call Him wise because wisdom is a human characteristic, but at the same time God is not unwise.

Modern thinkers insist that in order for people to find meaning in religion, they must be able to have a relationship with God. What is important is not the words or ideas one uses to describe God, but the belief that God is involved in nature and history.

In Talmudic Literature   In the Talmud, believing in God is one of the main concepts of Judaism. One who denies the existence of God is called *kofer be-ikkar*, "a denier of the most important thing" (*Ar.* 15b). The Talmud also continued the struggle of the prophets against IDOLATRY (worship of more than one god). The rabbis taught, "Whoever denies idolatry it is as if he acknowledges the entire Torah" (*Sif.* Deut. 28). One of the achievements of history was the fact that by the end of the Second Temple period the people of the civilized world were no longer pagans (*Yoma* 69b).

Two of God's moral traits are JUSTICE and MERCY (Ex. 34:5–6). These are both positive traits, yet they conflict with one another. The rabbis developed these ideas, calling them *middat ha-din*, "His measure of strict justice," and *middat ha-rahamim*, "His measure of mercy." When giving out rewards and punishments, God decides how much strict justice and how much mercy to use. The rabbis described God as praying to Himself that His compassion should overcome His anger (*Ber.* 7a).

In Medieval Jewish Thought   In the Middle Ages, Jewish thought was influenced by Arab and Greek philosophy. According to SAADIAH GAON, God gave human beings the gift of logic, which is just as powerful as revelation (when God appears to a human being). It is therefore a religious obligation to try to understand the ideas in the Torah. Many medieval thinkers agreed that religious belief based on study and thought is better than belief based on faith alone. Thus they explained that such a perfectly designed world is proof that God exists.

According to JUDAH HA-LEVI, a genuine religious experience is communication between a person and God. It is more than just logical. Only a God-given revelation can teach people how to communicate on that level. The God of ABRAHAM is more than what a person can understand by the power of logic.

In Kabbalah   In Jewish MYSTICISM, as in all mysticism, God is directly and closely present. Unlike the logical explanation that a person can never understand what God is, mystics argue that one can experience the many aspects of God.

The Kabbalah teaches that there are two sides to God. The EN-SOF ("the Infinite") is "God in Himself, hidden in the depths of His being," about whom nothing is known except that He exists. The ten SEFIROT represent the revealed God or SHEKHINAH (God's Presence). These can be understood as stages in the process of creation or as powers of the revealing God.

The Kabbalah of Isaac LURIA added the idea of *tsimtsum* ("concentration" or "contraction") as an answer to the question: How can there be a world if God is everywhere? He explains that the infinite God, who fills all space, withdrew into Himself leaving a space in which He created the world. According to Gershom Scholem, this explains why there is a part of God in all beings.

In the Modern Period   Moses MENDELSSOHN (1729–1786) believed that God is a Supreme Being, who is the creator of the world and guarantees the immortality of the human soul. Samson Raphael HIRSCH (1808–1888) taught that God teaches

man to find self-fulfillment and concrete freedom. Mordecai KAPLAN (1881–1983) believed that God is the sum total of forces in nature working for human fulfillment.

Franz ROSENZWEIG (1886–1929) and Martin BUBER (1878–1965) agree with the biblical and rabbinic view that God meets human beings in a personal encounter. According to Rosenzweig, this revelation is God showing his love to humanity. People, in return, are commanded to love God. Buber believed that this meeting with God does not require people to observe any "commandments."

Abraham Joshua HESCHEL (1907–1972) tries to answer the following question: What are the grounds for believing in a living God? His answer is that when a person experiences a moment of awe at the wonders of the world, the joy of being alive, or amazement at the fact that there are facts at all, he is experiencing the Presence of God. In his opinion, God is actually pursuing humankind, and faith comes from being aware that He exists. (See THEOLOGY.)

GOD, NAMES OF   The different names of God that are found in the Bible and the Talmud are also a way of understanding the essence of God. Therefore, in the story of the Burning Bush (Ex. 3), Moses hesitates to accept God's mission because the Egyptians will ask: "What is your God's name?" God answers him using the name of YHWH, the Tetragrammaton.

God's name is part of His being, which explains why the name is treated with such respect. In the TEN COMMANDMENTS (Ex. 20:7), it clearly says that God's name, YHWH, must not be taken in vain. The priests use the name of YHWH to bless the people of Israel (Num. 6:24–26).

God's different names express different aspects of His being.

SOME NAMES OF GOD IN JEWISH TRADITION	
YHWH (The Tetragrammaton)	The Lord (also *Adonai, Yah*)
El, Eloha, Elohim	God
Shaddai	Almighty
Ha-Kadosh Barukh Hu	The Holy One, Blessed be He
Ribono Shel Olam	Master of the Universe
Ha-Makom	The Place
Ha-Rahman	The Merciful
Shekhinah	God's Presence
En-Sof	The Infinite
Gevurah	The All-Strong
Tsur Yisrael	Rock of Israel
Shomer Yisrael	Guardian of Israel
Melekh Malkhei Melakhim	The Supreme King of Kings

Therefore, those who know His name are aware of His identity and His nature.

El *El* is the generic Hebrew name of God. The word probably comes from the word "power." The name *El* is not a personal name of God.

Some names are a combination of *El* and another word. *El Elyon* is the "exalted God," as in Genesis 14:18–20, where Melchizedek is the priest of *El Elyon*. He blessed Abraham with the name of the One who "possesses heaven and earth." This name came to mean One God, as opposed to a god who rules over the other god's. *El Olam* is "God the everlasting." *El Shaddai* may mean "God, the One of the mountains," or "God the All-Powerful."

Elohim Two other well-known names of God are *Eloha* and *Elohim*. *Eloha* appears in the Book of JOB and means "the God of Israel." *Elohim* (translated "God") is the name of God used most often in the Bible. Usually, it refers to the God of Israel, but it can be used for a pagan god and even a goddess. The term *Adonai* is taken from the word *Adon*, best translated as "Lord."

YHWH The most important name of God, YHWH, is the one that is written but never spoken. This name is known as the Tetragrammaton (i.e., four-lettered). During the times of the First Temple, this name was spoken, but by the third century BCE, it was being read out loud as *Adonai*. In the Middle Ages, Christian scholars transformed the word YHWH into Jehovah, and this became the basic name for God in CHRISTIANITY.

In Talmud times the rabbis asked themselves which of God's names may be written, which may be spoken, and which may be erased from documents after they had been written. Seven names of God may be written, but not erased. These are *El, Elohim, Ehyeh Asher Ehyeh, Adonai,* YHWH, *Tseva'ot* ("hosts"), and *Shaddai* (*Shevu.* 35a-b). The rest of the names may be written freely. Orthodox Jews substitute *Elokim* for *Elohim* and *Ha-Shem* ("the Name") for *Adonai* because they believe that one should not say any of God's names.

In the Temple, the HIGH PRIEST said the name YHWH on the DAY OF ATONEMENT as part of the service. Nowadays, in the section about Temple worship in the ADDITIONAL SERVICE AMIDAH, the congregation in the synagogue falls to the floor or bows when God's name is mentioned. The Talmud also mentions names of God with 12 letters and 42 letters.

Hebrew texts containing God's name may not be destroyed when they are damaged or worn out. They must be buried or placed in a GENIZAH (storage).

GOG AND MAGOG King (Gog) and country (Magog, ruled by Gog) mentioned in Ezekiel 38–39. According to traditional belief, after the people of Israel finally return to their land at the time of future REDEMPTION, Gog will lead the forces of evil in an invasion of the Land of Israel. Israel will defeat Gog, which will cause the world to realize that God had not abandoned the people of Israel. There are many opinions as to what historical figure, if any, Ezekiel had in mind when he wrote these chapters of prophecy.

These two chapters were also written in copies of the Book of ENOCH that were discovered among the DEAD SEA SCROLLS, as well as in the New Testament. In the Mishnah and Talmud, the wars of Gog and Magog (it was believed that Magog was also a person) will be a sign that the MESSIAH is coming. For this reason, throughout history, major wars often caused Jews to believe that the Messiah was on his way.

GOLDEN CALF Object worshiped by the Israelites. The golden calf was a statue of a young bull made of wood and plated in gold. The Bible tells of two golden calves: one in the desert when MOSES was on Mount SINAI (Ex. 32) and the second made by King Jeroboam I (1 Kings 12:28). Moses' brother, AARON, made the first calf. When Moses went up to Mount Sinai, the Israelites thought he would not return, so they asked for a god to lead them instead of Moses. Aaron collected gold jewelry from the people and melted it down to form the calf. The people of Israel danced and feasted and worshiped the calf. When Moses returned after 40 days, he broke the tablets of the

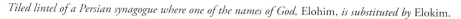

Tiled lintel of a Persian synagogue where one of the names of God, Elohim, *is substituted by* Elokim.

The Israelites dancing around the Golden Calf. Engraving by Peter van der Borcht, 1584.

TEN COMMANDMENTS in anger, destroyed the calf, and forced the people to drink the ashes of the calf mixed with water. The LEVITES killed 3,000 of the people, and God sent a plague upon them for their sin.

Jeroboam made two calves, and put one at Beth El and one at Dan (1 Kings 12:28). These calves were supposed to be a substitute for the TEMPLE in JERUSALEM, so that people would not go to Jerusalem and accept the rule of King Rehoboam, against whom Jeroboam had revolted.

GOLDEN RULE   The statement in the New Testament (Matt. 7:12; Luke 6:31), "As you would want men to do to you, you should also do to them," is generally called the Golden Rule. This is actually a variation of "Love your neighbor as yourself" (Lev. 19:18). When HILLEL (1st cent. BCE) was asked to teach a gentile the entire TORAH "in a nutshell," he answered: "Whatever is hateful to you, do not do to your neighbor" (*Shab.* 31a).

GOLEM   ("shapeless matter"). The word *golem* was used only once in the Bible to describe an "unformed substance" or embryo (Ps. 139:16). In the Mishnah, it was used to mean a stupid, uncultured person (*Avot* 5:9). In the Talmud, *golem* describes an early stage of ADAM's creation (*Sanh.* 38b). In the Kabbalah, it means material with no shape or form.

The idea of a man-made creature first appears in the Talmud, when two rabbis create a calf for their Sabbath meal and RAVA produces a manlike creature, which Rabbi Zera returns to dust (*Sanh.* 65b). In medieval Germany, the HASIDEI ASHKENAZ used the power of Hebrew letters to make a *golem* into a useful servant that could be brought to life and put back to "sleep." Rabbi Tsevi Hirsch ASHKENAZI dealt with the question of whether a *golem* could be counted in a MINYAN (ten men needed for prayer).

The most famous *golem* was the *golem* of Prague. According to legend, Rabbi JUDAH LÖW (*Maharal*) of Prague and two of his students created a *golem* out of clay and breathed life (though not speech) into it, using mystical powers. The *golem* lived in the attic of Prague's Altneuschul Synagogue and often saved the Jews from anti-Semitic plots. One Sabbath eve, it got out of control and Rabbi Judah had to end its career. Some say that the *golem* is still hidden in the attic of the Altneuschul, waiting to be brought to life by a new master.

GOMEL BLESSING   (Heb. *ha-Gomel*). Blessing of thanks to God, recited by a person who has survived a life-threatening experience. In Temple times, such a person brought a thanksgiving offering. According to the rabbis, *ha-gomel* is recited by those who return safely from an oversees journey, who return from a journey in the desert, who have recovered from a serious illness, or who have been released from captivity (*Ber.* 54b). The *gomel* blessing should be recited in a MINYAN (group of ten men who pray together) and within three days of the event. In traditional communities, at the first possible READING OF THE LAW (a Monday, Thursday, or Sabbath), people who need to say the blessing are called to the Torah reading, after which they recite the blessing. Women, especially after childbirth, recite this blessing after the Torah reading or at the end of the service.

In REFORM synagogues, the blessing is recited on Friday evening, when the Torah is read. In both CONSERVATIVE and Reform communities, a woman may recite *ha-gomel* after being called to the Reading of the Law.

GOOD   See EVIL; RIGHTEOUSNESS

GOVERNMENT, PRAYER FOR THE   Blessing recited in many congregations on SABBATHS and FESTIVALS, after the READING OF THE LAW, which blesses the ruler or president and government of the state. SEPHARDIM also recite it on the eve of the DAY OF ATONEMENT. The Bible teaches that one must "seek the peace of the city" where Jews live "and pray unto the Lord for it" (Jer. 29:7). In the Second Temple period, prayers were said for the welfare of the Roman emperor. Rabbi Hanina, the HIGH PRIEST, believed that one should "pray for the welfare of the government, since if not for the fear of it, people would swallow each other alive" (*Avot* 2:3). After the Temple was destroyed, rabbis ruled that one should still pray for, and obey, the government (*Zev.* 102a).

Refugee Spanish Jews spread the *Ha-Noten Teshu'ah* ("He who gives salvation unto kings") prayer to other lands. A version of this prayer is recited in British Commonwealth synagogues until today. In the United States, Orthodox Jews recite *Ha-Noten Teshu'ah* but pray that God may "bless and protect the President and the Vice President, together with all the officials of this country." CONSERVATIVE congregations recite a prayer for the United States, "its government, leaders, and advisors," written by Louis Ginzburg.

When the State of ISRAEL was established in 1948, *Ha-Noten Teshu'ah* was replaced by a new prayer for the Welfare of Israel (*Tefillah li-Shelom ha-Medinah*). It starts with the words AVINU

SHE-BE-SHAMAYIM and talks about Jewish independence in Israel as "the first dawning of our REDEMPTION." It includes prayers for the welfare of Jews living outside Israel and for the INGATHERING OF THE EXILES. It is often recited with a special prayer for the soldiers of the Israel Defense Forces. Most synagogues throughout the Diaspora recite some form of the Prayer for the Welfare of Israel.

GOY See GENTILE

GRACE AFTER MEALS (Heb. *Birkat ha-Mazon*). A series of blessings recited after any meal where BREAD is eaten. The commandment to say Grace comes from the PENTATEUCH: "When you have eaten and are satisfied, you shall bless the Lord your God for the good land which He has given you" (Deut. 8:10). A minimal amount of food must have been eaten ("the size of an olive") in order to say Grace. It is customary to leave some bread on the table, but remove the knives. Some Jews also dip their fingers in water before reciting the blessings (see MAYIM AHARONIM).

When at least three males above the age of 13 have eaten together, an "invitation" to say Grace, known as *Birkat ha-Zimmun,* is first recited by one of them (*Ber.* 7:1–5, 49b–50a). If at least ten males are present (MINYAN), the word *Elohenu*

Part of Grace after Meals, with an illustration of six men at a table. From a manuscript. Germany 1738.

> **GRACE AFTER MEALS**
> **THE FIRST BLESSING**
>
> Blessed are You, O Lord our God, King of the universe, who feeds the whole world with Your goodness, grace, kindness, and mercy. You give food to all flesh, for Your kindness is forever. Through your great goodness, food has never failed us, may it never fail us, for the sake of Your great Name, for You nourish and sustain all beings, and do good to all, and provide food for all Your creatures whom You have created. Blessed are You, O Lord, who gives food to all.

("our God") is included. Three or more women who have eaten together can form a *zimmun* of their own (*Ber.* 46a).

On SABBATHS, FESTIVALS, and other happy occasions, Psalm 126 (SHIR HA-MA'ALOT) is sung before reciting Grace.

Grace after Meals is made up of four blessings, three ancient and one from the Mishnah. The first blessing, written by MOSES, praises God for feeding all of His creatures. The second, written by JOSHUA, thanks God for taking the Israelites out of Egypt, for His COVENANT (agreement) with the people of Israel, and for the land He gave His people; on HANUKKAH and PURIM, the AL HA-NISSIM prayer is recited here. The third blessing, written by DAVID and SOLOMON, begs God to fill the needs of the people of Israel, and to restore Jerusalem. An extra prayer is said here on the Sabbath, while YA'ALEH VE-YAVO is recited on the New MOON, Pilgrim Festivals, and the New Year.

The fourth and last blessing was written after 135 CE by the sages of Yavneh. It thanks God for all of His blessings. This is followed by series of requests, each asking "the All-Merciful" (*Ha-Rahaman*) to grant things, such as Israel's redemption from exile.

Special prayers are added before Grace in a house of MOURNING and at the meal following a CIRCUMCISION or a wedding feast (see MARRIAGE). REFORM JUDAISM in English-speaking countries has substituted Grace with a shorter English text. CONSERVATIVE Judaism keeps the original text and adds special *Ha-Rahaman* prayers for the State of Israel, Jews suffering from persecution, and a BAR MITZVAH or BAT MITZVAH.

GRACE BEFORE MEALS BENEDICTION (blessing) recited before eating BREAD, added by the Men of the GREAT ASSEMBLY. In Hebrew, it is known as *Ha-Motsi* since the text is: "Blessed are You O Lord, who brings forth [*ha-motsi*] bread from the earth." The rabbis taught: "It is forbidden to enjoy the good things of this world without a blessing" (*Ber.* 35a), and that failing to recite a blessing over food is "the same as cheating the Almighty" (*Tosef. Ber.* 4:1).

Before reciting *Ha-Motsi*, a person must wash and dry the hands (see ABLUTIONS). *Ha-Motsi* is recited over bread made from any of the FIVE SPECIES of grain that grow in the Land of Israel.

On the SABBATH, the blessing is made over two special Sabbath loaves (challahs, see CHALLAH). It is customary to sprinkle the bread with a little SALT, in memory of the ancient offerings brought in the TEMPLE, except during the New Year season. The same blessing is recited over unleavened bread (MATZAH) on PASSOVER.

When saying Grace before a meal, one does not recite the blessings over other foods eaten during that meal, aside from the blessing over WINE. If a person eats a piece of bread the size of an olive or larger, he must then say GRACE AFTER MEALS.

GREAT ASSEMBLY, THE   (also known as the Great Synagogue; Heb. *Keneset Gedolah*). An institution from the Persian period, about which little is known. The first paragraph of the Mishnah AVOT teaches that the Torah (ORAL LAW) was passed down from the prophets directly "to the men of the Great Assembly."

EZRA and NEHEMIAH in 444 BCE gathered the first Great Assembly. Eighty-three leaders of the community signed an agreement to keep several important new laws (Neh. 10).

According to the Mishnah *Avot*, the men of the Great Assembly taught the following three things: "Be careful in judgment, teach many students, and put a fence around the Torah" (*Avot* 1:1). Each one of these sayings deals with a different one of the jobs of the Great Assembly. The first deals with the fact that they were judges; the second, with the fact that the SCRIBES (*soferim*) who taught and interpreted the Torah were all members of the Great Assembly; and the third deals with the task of making Jewish laws. The Great Assembly developed into the SANHEDRIN.

According to one source, there were 85 members, including 30 prophets. Another source says there were 120 members, including some prophets. The Great Assembly also developed the *Bet Din ha-Gadol* ("the High Court"), in which for the first time, scholars, PRIESTS, and LEVITES interpreted the law together.

The Great Assembly made two kinds of laws. TAKKANOT were new CUSTOMS to be followed by the people of Israel, such as the public reading of the PENTATEUCH on MONDAYS AND THURSDAYS (market days in ancient Israel), the FESTIVAL of PURIM, fixing the number of blessings and the text of the AMIDAH, the KIDDUSH (the prayer recited over the wine on the SABBATH and festivals), and the HAVDALLAH prayer (recited at the end of Sabbaths and festivals). *Gezerot* were meant to prevent Jews from doing things that were forbidden in the Torah. An example of a *gezerah* is the prohibition against touching things that are not to be used on the Sabbath.

GUR   (Yid. *Ger*). Hasidic group founded in Gura Kalwaria, Poland, in 1859 by Isaac Meir Rothenburg Alter (1789–1866), a student of MENAHEM MENDEL OF KOTSK. The new sect attracted many of the Kotsk Hasidim. The sect flourished under Alter's grandson Judah Aryeh Leib (1847–1905), author of the *Sefat Emet* on the Torah and Talmud and an extreme anti-Zionist. Under his son Abraham Mordecai (1866–1948), the group became one of the largest and most important in Europe (see HASIDISM). In 1940 Abraham Mordecai escaped from German-occupied Poland and moved to Erets Israel, where he established the new world center of Gur. The next "Gerer Rebbe" was Abraham Mordecai's son Israel (1892–1977), who was president of Agudat Israel's Council of Torah Sages. In the United States, Gur Hasidim live mostly in the Boro Park section of Brooklyn, New York, together with BOBOV and BELZ Hasidim.

R. Abraham Mordecai Alter, Gora Kalwaria, Poland.

HABAD   See CHABAD

HABAKKUK   The eighth of the 12 minor PROPHETS. While nothing is known about his life, it appears that Habakkuk lived in Judah in the seventh century BCE. The book of his prophecies contains three chapters and 53 verses. It largely deals with the problem of injustice in the world – how can God allow the wicked to overwhelm the righteous?

Some rabbinic commentators feel that the psalm in the last chapter of the book shows that Habakkuk was a PRIEST, among those who sang in the TEMPLE. His statement, "The just shall live by his faith" (2:4), was described by the rabbis as the essence of Judaism (*Mak.* 24a). A commentary in MIDRASH form on the book was found among the DEAD SEA SCROLLS.

	THE BOOK OF HABAKKUK
1:1–1:4	Complaint against violence and oppression
1:5–1:11	The Chaldeans as instruments of God
1:12–1:17	The prophet's protests concerning the oppressor
2:1–2:5	The righteous shall live by his faith and the wicked shall perish
2:6–2:20	Five woes unto oppressors
3:1–3:19	God will come to save His people

HAD GADYA   ("Only One Kid"). Folksong in the Aramaic language sung at the end of the Passover SEDER. Its author and date of writing are unknown. *Had Gadya* consists of ten stanzas with the refrain "*had gadya.*" Each stanza includes all the previous lines.

It seems that *Had Gadya* was written as a table song to amuse children. Even so, a number of interpretations have been offered about the many symbols in the song. Some suggest that it is actually a religious interpretation of Jewish history. The "kid that father bought for two *zuzim*" represents the Jewish people. The remaining items in the song stand for nations that oppressed Israel, each one giving way to a new tyrant nation. According to this interpretation, Assyria is the cat that fell to

FINAL STANZA OF HAD GADYA
Then came the Holy One, Blessed be He,
And smote the Angel of Death
Who slew the slaughterer
Who slaughtered the ox
That drank the water
That quenched the fire
That burned the stick
That beat the dog
That bit the cat
That ate the kid
That father bought for two zuzim,
An only kid, an only kid!

Persia, the dog; Persia fell to Greece, the stick, which in turn fell to Rome, the fire; Rome fell to the Barbarians, water, who in turn fell to Islam, the ox; they fell to the Crusaders, the slaughterer. Finally, the ANGEL OF DEATH is the last conqueror – and God will bring even him to account. The message of the song is clear: God Himself protects Israel in the end.

HADLAKAT NEROT   See CANDLES

HAFETS HAYYIM   (Israel Meir ha-Kohen Kagan; 1838–1933). Rabbi and author. After studying in Vilna, Lithuania, he settled in Radun, Poland, which was his home for the remainder of his life. He refused to become a rabbi. He was supported by a small grocery store, which his wife managed while he did the bookkeeping. Even so, a group of followers gathered around him that became known as the Hafets Hayyim *yeshivah* of Radun. The *yeshivah* grew until it became one of the leading institutions of European ORTHODOXY.

His first book – *Hafets Hayyim* ("Desires Life") – was published anonymously in 1873. It dealt with the laws against slander, gossip, and tale bearing (see LESHON HA-RA). The author widely became known by the name of the book. He published additional works of ETHICS: *Shemirat ha-Lashon* on the importance of proper speech; *Ahavat Hesed* on acts of loving-kindness;

Mahaneh Yisra'el for Jewish soldiers; and *Niddehei Yisra'el* to inspire Jews who had emigrated to the West. His six-volume commentary on the SHULHAN ARUKH, the *Mishnah Berurah*, is his most widely studied work. It has gained acceptance as the basic guide for daily Jewish observance.

The Hafets Hayyim was central in establishing the ultra-Orthodox Agudat Israel organization in 1912 and was its spiritual leader.

HAFTARAH ("conclusion"). Section from the PROPHETS in the Bible that is recited in the SYNAGOGUE after the READING OF THE LAW at the MORNING SERVICE on the SABBATH and FESTIVALS, during the AFTERNOON SERVICE on fast days (see FASTING AND FAST DAYS), and at both services on TISHAH BE-AV. The custom of reading from the prophets was well-established long before the destruction of the Second Temple. Some historians trace the custom to the anti-Jewish persecutions of the Syrian tyrant Antiochus Epiphanes in 165 BCE. He banned the study and public reading of the Torah. The sages then substituted a passage from the prophets that was connected to the weekly reading instead.

The Talmud lists the *haftarot* for special Sabbaths and the Sabbath of HANUKKAH, for TISHAH BE-AV, the intermediate Sabbath of the festivals, the Sabbath coinciding with the New Moon, and the Sabbath which falls on the eve of the New Moon, as well as the *haftarah* for each major festival (*Meg.* 4:1, 31a). It is likely that all the other *haftarot* that were not mentioned were set in the time after the close of the Talmud.

The *haftarah* is usually at least 21 verses, although some are less. In the time of the Talmud, each verse of the Torah was followed by a translation into Aramaic; each group of three verses from the *haftarah* was translated. Within the annual cycle, all the prophetic books of the Bible are represented except Nahum and Haggai.

In Sephardi and Oriental communities, a child may read from the *haftarah*. It is a universal custom that the BAR MITZVAH boy is given the honor of reading the *haftarah*. In CONSERVATIVE and REFORM congregations, the honor is often given to a BAT MITZVAH girl as well. The *haftarah* is chanted to a melody that is different from the one used for the Torah reading, and the particular melody that is used varies from community to community.

HAGGADAH (lit. "narration, recital"). The name of the text read at the Passover SEDER. The word *haggadah,* and the Jew's obligation to tell the story of the EXODUS, come from the Bible: "You shall tell (*ve-higaddeta*) your son on that day: it is because of what the Lord did for me when I came forth out of Egypt …" (Ex. 13:8). The commandment is repeated three times (Ex. 12:26–27, 13:14; Deut. 6:20ff.). Apart from eating MATZAH (unleavened bread), the central act of Passover is reading the *Haggadah* on the first night of the week-long holiday (in Israel; second night as well in the Diaspora).

The *Haggadah* text includes biblical verses, psalms, and rabbinic commentaries. Much of the content has been in place since early Second Temple times (5th cent. BCE). The framework had already been set by the time of the Mishnah (*Pes.* 10). The *Haggadah* teaches about God's shaping of history, the value of Jewish nationhood, the COVENANT between God and Israel, and the idea that liberty cannot be taken for granted.

Reading the *Haggadah* at the Passover *Seder* is an especially beloved Jewish ritual. There are a vast number of commentaries on it, and it has been translated into many languages. Since each participant in the *Seder* must have his own copy of the *Haggadah*, a huge number of printed and beautifully illustrated editions can be found from all over the world. The first printed *Haggadah* appeared in Spain in 1482; the oldest illustrated edition was printed in Prague in 1526. Since then, more than 2,000 editions of the *Haggadah* have been printed, and new ones are still appearing.

HAGGAI Tenth of the 12 minor PROPHETS. The Book of Haggai is included in the Prophets section of the Bible; it has two chapters and 38 verses. It is built on four revelations experienced by Haggai during the second year of Darius I of Persia, c. 520 BCE. Haggai criticizes the delay in rebuilding the Second TEMPLE. He assures the people that even though it is not as magnificent as the Temple of SOLOMON, it eventually will be so. His final prophecy tells the future fall of the Persian Empire.

According to rabbinic tradition, Haggai was the first of three prophets (Haggai, ZECHARIAH, MALACHI) who prophesied in the time of EZRA. When these three died, "the Divine Spirit departed from Israel" (*Yoma* 9b).

BOOK OF HAGGAI	
1:1–1:11	Exhortation to build the Temple
1:12–1:15	Historical account of beginning of work
2:1–2:9	Encouragement to the builders
2:10–2:19	Promise of prosperity to accompany work of restoration
2:20–2:23	Messianic promise to Zerubbabel.

HAGIGAH ("Sacrifice brought on the first day of the PILGRIM FESTIVALS"). Twelfth tractate (book) of the Order of MO'ED in the Mishnah. *Hagigah* deals with two subjects: 1) the law that every male must appear in Jerusalem for the three Pilgrim Festivals and to bring a "free-will" offering on the first day; and 2) the laws of purity and impurity of TITHES, SACRIFICES, and the vessels that contain them. The connection between the two subjects is that all who entered the TEMPLE had to be in a state of ritual purity.

HAGIOGRAPHA (lit. "Holy Writings"). The third and final section of the Hebrew Bible; Heb. *Ketuvim*. The Hagiographa include: PSALMS, PROVERBS, JOB, the FIVE SCROLLS, DANIEL,

EZRA, NEHEMIAH and CHRONICLES. The Hagiographa were the last part of the Hebrew Bible to be included in the text. The Talmud debates whether or not to include certain books, such as SONG OF SONGS and ESTHER, which were finally included.

HAI GAON (939–1038). Last GAON of the Academy of Pumbedita (see ACADEMIES). Hai belonged to a distinguished rabbinic family; he married the daughter of Samuel ben Hophni, Gaon of Sura. He succeeded his father, SHERIRA GAON, in 998, and served for the next 40 years. R. Hai Gaon was one of the great legal experts of his age. Nearly 1,000 of his RESPONSA have been preserved on religious and philosophical questions. None of his commentaries on the Talmud have survived; however, quotations from these commentaries can be found in medieval writings.

R. Hai Gaon's chief contribution was in the field of creating legal codes, some of which have survived. He also made the rule that the law must follow the Babylonian Talmud rather than the Jerusalem Talmud when the two clash.

HAKHAM ("wise man"). A sage. In Bible times, *hakham* was a general term, but by the time of the Mishnah this was a formal community position. The *hakham* ranked third after the NASI (president) and the head of the BET DIN ("court"; *Hor.* 13b), although it is not altogether clear what the *hakham's* responsibilities were. Sephardi Jews today refer to an ordained rabbi as a *hakham*. In England, the Sephardi Chief Rabbi has the title of *Hakham*.

HAKHAM BASHI Title given to the Chief Rabbi in countries of the Ottoman Empire in the 19th century. It is made up of the Hebrew HAKHAM ("wise man") and the Turkish word *bashi* ("chief"). The *Hakham Bashi* was officially recognized by Turkish rulers as the leader of the Jewish communities.

HAKHEL Religious ceremony performed in Bible times in the year following the SABBATICAL YEAR. The Bible states: "Gather (*hakhel*) the people together, men, and women, and children, and your stranger that is within your gates, so they may hear, and they may learn, and fear the Lord your God, and observe to do all the words of this law" (Deut. 31:12). According to the *hakhel* law, all men, women, and even children were to gather in the TEMPLE courtyard in Jerusalem on the SUKKOT holiday just after the Sabbatical Year. At the gathering, the king read aloud various portions of DEUTERONOMY. The reader stood on a special wooden platform in the women's courtyard in the Temple. As the Talmud explains, the men were there to learn, the women to listen, and the children to reward those who brought them. For the most part the *hakhel* ceremony ended with the destruction of the Temple. Still, there have been attempts in modern times to revive the tradition.

HAKHNASAT KALLAH (lit. "bringing in the bride," i.e. helping the bride enter into marriage). *Hakhnasat kallah* funds

are charities devoted to providing for needy brides. It is one of the basic funds organized by a religious Jewish community (see CHARITY).

The SHULHAN ARUKH states that no cause is greater than enabling a poor young girl to marry. Where only limited funds are available, priority is given to a poor young woman over a poor young man, "for it is more embarrassing for a woman to be unmarried than it is for a man" (*Sh. Ar.*, YD 251:8). The COMMANDMENT of *hakhnasat kallah* also includes helping the bride rejoice at her wedding.

HAKKAFOT (lit. "circles"). Circles made around the SYNAGOGUE and other places by worshipers on various occasions, both joyful and solemn. *Hakkafot* are a symbol of completeness, because they are circular and because they are usually performed seven times (see NUMBERS). Orthodox Ashkenazi brides make three or seven *hakkafot* around the bridegroom under the wedding canopy just before the wedding ceremony. Seven circuits are made around the synagogue with Torah scrolls when a synagogue is dedicated (see CONSECRATION). The same number is made around a CEMETERY when it is opened. Sephardi and Hasidic Jews make seven circuits around the coffin immediately before BURIAL.

The best known of all *hakkafot* are the festive ones held in the synagogue during SUKKOT. The ARK is opened and a SCROLL OF THE LAW is carried to the reader's platform. Congregants make one circuit around the synagogue holding the FOUR SPECIES and reciting HOSHANOT. On the seventh day, HOSHANA RABBAH, seven processions take place. No *hakkafot* take place on the Sabbath.

Hakkafot also take place on SIMHAT TORAH, the Rejoicing of the Law. After EVENING and MORNING SERVICES, all the Torah scrolls are removed from the Ark and carried around the synagogue in seven processions. Hasidic Jews in the Diaspora follow the Israeli practice by holding *hakkafot* on the eighth night (SHEMINI ATSERET), but also do so again on the evening and morning of 23 Tishri (when Diaspora communities observe Simhat Torah). In Israel "second *hakkafot*" are held throughout the country, usually in the open air, on the night after Simhat Torah. These celebrations usually involve bands, singers, dancing, and large enthusiastic crowds.

HA LAHMA ANYA ("This is the bread of affliction"). Opening words of a statement in the Aramaic language recited during the Passover SEDER. MATZAH is called "bread of affliction" because it is a poor man's meal, and because the Israelites baked the bread in haste when they were sent from Egypt (Ex. 21:39). Before *Ha Lahma Anya* is recited, the three matzahs are uncovered, raised, and shown to all present at the *Seder*.

HALAKHAH (rabbinic law). The branch of rabbinic literature that deals with Jewish religious laws. The laws include those between "person and person" and those between "people and God." *Halakhah* encompasses practically all aspects of human behavior: birth and marriage, joy and grief, agriculture and commerce, ethics and theology.

The term *halakhah* comes from the Hebrew word "to walk" or "to go." God tells Moses in the Bible: "Obligate them in the laws and teachings, and make known to them the way they are to go and the practices they are to follow" (Ex. 18:20). *Halakhah* implies a ruling handed down by the religious authorities, or more specifically the accepted or authorized opinion in a legal dispute. The term also is used for the legal parts of Jewish tradition, as opposed to the legendary material of the AGGADAH.

The Commandments　*Halakhah* is first and foremost an outgrowth of the Bible's COMMANDMENTS. The PENTATEUCH includes 613 commandments – the *halakhah* explains how the commandments are to be performed and the penalty for breaking them. The traditional view is that the commandments were given by God to MOSES at SINAI.

The Oral Law　The rabbis understood that it was impossible for the WRITTEN LAW to be passed on without additional explanations. The ORAL LAW is the body of details and commentaries transmitted from master to disciple, from the time of the giving of the Torah on Sinai.

The Oral Law was central to the development of the *halakhah*. First, it placed a great emphasis on TRADITION – laws were traced to their earliest known source. Second, it placed an equally large emphasis on the study and teaching of Torah (TALMUD TORAH). True mastery required a lifetime of study.

The rabbis interpreted the Bible by a method called MIDRASH. The *halakhah* had its own specific methods of interpreting the commandments, called MIDRASH HALAKHAH. As time went on, the Midrashic method became more involved, allowing for more and more halakhic rulings to be found in the basic Torah text. HILLEL used seven methods of Midrash, the best known being *kal va-homer* or reasoning from a less strict case to a more strict case. He also used the *gezerah shavah*, a method that derived law based on similar phrases in unrelated Bible passages. ISHMAEL BEN ELISHA, expanded the list of methods to 13. His contemporary, R. AKIVA, read the text so closely that he was able to derive the law from every mark found in the text. R. Akiva is credited with collecting the halakhic *midrashim*: MEKHILTA on EXODUS, SIFRA on LEVITICUS, and SIFREI on NUMBERS and DEUTERONOMY.

Scholars of the Oral Law hold a range of opinions about the real connection between a *halakhah* and the biblical verse on which it is based. Many *halakhot* seem to have little support from the Bible. Some seem to bypass the simple meaning of a text in order to lay down the law. Some *halakhot* were even transmitted without any reference to the Bible and were designated HALAKHAH LE-MOSHE MI-SINAI ("a ruling received by Moses on Mount Sinai"). This has led some to conclude that the real purpose of the Midrash was not to create new *halakhot* but to find a traditional basis for *halakhot* that already formed part of the Oral Law.

Authority of the Sages　In certain areas of the *halakhah*, the rabbis decided the law largely on their own. For example, about

work on the intermediate days of the festivals (HOL HA-MO'ED), the Talmud states: "Scripture gave it over to the sages to decide which type of work is forbidden and which is permitted" (Hag. 18a). In fact, the authority of the sages was virtually unlimited in deciding the law. "'The Torah is not in heaven' (Deut. 30:12); it has already been given over from Sinai, and in the Torah it is written, 'The law should follow the majority [of the authorities]' (Ex. 23:2)" (*BM* 59b).

The authority of the sages allowed them at times to cancel a law of the Torah if they felt it was necessary for the general upholding of the law. The classic example of violating the law to preserve it came when R. JUDAH HA-NASI (c. 138–217) wrote down the MISHNAH when he was faced with the problem of the Oral Law being forgotten. With the difficulties of Jewish life and the growing numbers of *halakhot*, people simply could not remember the traditions accurately. On the other hand, there was a ban on writing down the oral traditions: "Teachings which were given orally may not be committed to writing; teachings given in writing [i.e., Scripture] may not be transmitted orally" (*Git.* 60b). The rabbis decided: "'[Since] it is time to act for the Lord, they have voided Your Torah' (Ps. 119:126). They said, 'Better that [a single principle in] Torah should be uprooted than the [entire Oral] Torah should be forgotten from Israel'" (*Tem.* 14b).

Ordination　The original source of halakhic authority is Moses, who passed on the authority to decide questions of Jewish law to Joshua (Num. 27:18). This ORDINATION (*semikhah*, or "laying on of hands") also allowed the ordained person to transfer authority to another, thus creating a chain of halakhic tradition that was passed on from generation to generation. By the time of the Talmud, the physical laying on of hands had ceased; instead the title of HAKHAM (sage), DAYYAN (judge) or RABBI was transferred. The sages ruled that ordination could be conferred only in the Land of Israel.

The Sanhedrin　With the exception of Moses, binding decisions of Jewish law were made by bodies of ordained Jewish men, or courts. The council of 70 ELDERS gathered by Moses was the first body of this type (Num. 11:16–17). In the days of Ezra, the supreme governing body was the 120-member GREAT ASSEMBLY. When the Great Assembly was restored in the days of the HASMONEANS (2nd cent. BCE), it consisted of 70 members and was known as the Great SANHEDRIN. It is called by the rabbis the "Great Court of Law."

The Sanhedrin's chief function was to interpret the Torah's teachings for all Israel. Once it proclaimed the law, any scholar who defied its ruling could be punished by death (Deut. 17:12).

Anti-Halakhah Movements　In the early days of the Sanhedrin, some questioned the whole idea of the Oral Law. The SADDUCEES were the first major movement of this type mentioned in the Talmud. In the eighth century, during the geonic period, the KARAITES challenged the authority of rabbinic Judaism. The rabbis – particularly under SAADIAH GAON – fought fiercely against them. By the 12th century the Karaites were no longer considered to be Jews. The modern anti-halakhists were the founders of REFORM JUDAISM in the early 19ᵗʰ century. Orthodox rabbinic leaders responded with the same type of opposition in order to preserve the integrity of the *halakhah*.

Gezerot. The Men of the Great Assembly laid down another principle to guide the sages: "Make a hedge around the Torah" (*Avot* 1:1). A GEZERAH is a restriction that was developed around an accepted law to safeguard it from violation. Over the generations many such rulings of rabbinic origin have become part of Jewish law. No attempt is made to associate these laws with verses from the Bible.

How important is a *gezerah* in the *halakhah*? A *gezerah* can override a positive commandment of the Torah. For example, if the only available SHOFAR on ROSH HA-SHANAH is on a tree, the tree may not be climbed (a *gezerah*) to obtain the *shofar*, even though it means not being able to perform the biblical commandment of sounding the *shofar* (*RH* 4:8). Furthermore, once a *gezerah* has been decreed by competent authorities and accepted by Jewry at large, later authorities cannot cancel it.

Hierarchy of Authority   Jewish tradition assumes that every later group of scholars is inferior to an earlier one. Rabbis are therefore bound by the rulings of those who came before them. Nevertheless, the rule is that where the earlier authorities differ, the *halakhah* (the accepted ruling) is according to the later authority. Since the completion of the Babylonian Talmud was later than that of the Jerusalem Talmud, the *halakhah* follows the Babylonian in the event of a conflict.

The authority of the Talmud is supreme. Maimonides states: "All Israel is obliged to follow all the statements in the Babylonian Talmud. Every city and every province is compelled to conduct itself in keeping with the customs, decrees, and regulations instituted by the sages of the GEMARA, since all Israel agreed to accept them" (Introduction to *Mishneh Torah*). As a result, post-talmudic authorities consider themselves incompetent to make rulings that are more lenient than those of the sages of the Talmud. On the other hand, restrictions have tended to accumulate.

Takkanot   The sages passed regulations that were actually innovations in the *halakhah* in response to new economic and social conditions. The Men of the Great Assembly are credited with creating the structure of the daily prayers (*Meg.* 17b). HILLEL introduced the PROSBUL, a document that prevented the cancelation of debts and extending loans beyond the SABBATICAL YEAR (*Git.* 4:3). Other important *takkanot* included the regulation of marriage contracts (see KETUBBAH) and the distribution of INHERITANCE. The power to enact a TAKKANAH has enabled communities through the ages to regulate their own affairs.

Minhag   Another division of rabbinic law is *minhag* (CUSTOM). *Minhagim* are practices that came about not from a specific ruling but as a result of a community itself adopting a certain ritual. *Minhag* refers to local custom that may not necessarily apply to other communities. The sages stressed that it was important to follow local custom. A traveler is require to follow both the strictures of his hometown and those of the community that he is visiting (*Pes.* 4:1). Local custom also became the norm in fixing employer-employee relations. In the case of *gezerot, takkanot,* and *minhagim,* once they have become part of the *halakhah,* many hold that even if the original reason that they were passed no longer exists, they must still be observed.

Codification   Although the Talmud is the source for the *halakhah,* it does not serve as a concise, well-organized law text for the layman. Beginning in the period of the *ge'onim,* clearly arranged digests of *halakhah* begin to appear. See CODIFICATION.

Responsa   Another branch of rabbinic literature that guides halakhic practice is the RESPONSA (*teshuvot*). Responsa are the answers given by legal authorities to the practical questions they have received from laymen or colleagues. The strength of their halakhic authority depends on the reputation of the author as well as the quality of his reasoning.

Contemporary Issues   Modern technology poses special problems that were never before dealt with in halakhic literature (see HALAKHAH AND TECHNOLOGY). Questions about the nature of electricity, telecommunications, medical practice, definition of death, organ transplants, etc. (see MEDICAL ETHICS), continue to challenge rabbis today. Thanks to the ability of the *halakhah* to be adapted to new cases, rabbis today are responding to these questions, based on similar situations from the past, in the spirit of the law.

The Conservative Approach   While they recognize the central importance of *halakhah,* CONSERVATIVE JUDAISM holds a view of *halakhah* that allows for orderly change. It seeks a greater balance between past practices and the sociological, ethical, political, and technological realities of the present. The Conservative Movement has established the Law Committee of the Conservative Rabbinical Assembly to debate and, if necessary, change the *halakhah.*

The Reform Approach   Reform Judaism is at odds with a single, unified approach to the *halakhah.* For this reason, both in the classical German Reform and the American Reform movements, a variety of views about Jewish practice has existed, and many have changed over the last century. For example, in the Pittsburgh Platform of 1885, Reform Judaism completely rejected the Jewish DIETARY LAWS. Yet the 1976 Centenary Perspective calls on Reform Jews to show greater openness to ritual *halakhah.* The Central Conference of American Rabbis has published a series of guides for home and communal observance, the festivals, Sabbath and daily use.

HALAKHAH AND TECHNOLOGY   In the modern period, advances in technology have affected the HALAKHAH (Jewish law) in two specific ways. First, halakhic decisions are required on questions posed by modern technology in areas not faced by earlier generations. Second, modern technology in some cases may actually make easier the observance of *halakhah.* To be sure, few modern rabbis have the knowledge to make halakhic decisions in these technical areas. However, a number of institutions have been established in Israel to deal with specific challenges of technology.

Advances in technology have given rise to many new halakhic questions. The discovery of electricity and related inventions, for example, require decisions about whether or not and under what conditions electricity may be used on the SABBATH and FESTIVALS. Is the use of electricity a violation of laws against producing a flame, burning, cooking, or building? Most halakhic authorities rule that electrical appliances may not be operated or electric lights turned on or off on the Sabbath or festivals. In this case, however, the practice has evolved of placing them on a timer before the beginning of the Sabbath.

In the area of medical technology, the *halakhah* distinguishes clearly between life and death, when all the vital organs (heart, brain, lungs, etc.) cease to function at the same time. Today, rabbinic authorities have to deal with new definitions of the exact dividing line between life and death, since medicine is now able to separate the functioning of different vital organs (e.g., the heart may beat even though the brain has ceased to function). Determining the moment of death is critical when there is a desire to donate organs for transplant. Doctors today routinely impregnate women by ARTIFICIAL INSEMINATION or by implanting ova in a woman. The *halakha*h must deal with issues of parenthood when the child is not the result of a standard pregnancy.

Centuries ago, many handicaps were considered incurable, and it was expected that the individual would die or never function normally. For example, in former times, the deaf were not considered to have legal responsibility because of their inability to communicate with the outside world. Today, hearing aids make it possible for the deaf to function almost normally. Do laws regarding the deaf still apply?

The ability to see has improved since telescopes and microscopes were invented; through television, people can see things far removed from themselves. They can hear things from far away over the telephone. Where the *halakhah* demands actual seeing (e.g., the new MOON, eyewitness testimony, reading from the Torah, etc.) or hearing (e.g., the sounding of the SHOFAR, the reading of the Scroll of Esther, etc.), does this include seeing or hearing by means of technology?

In civil courts, a person's reliability could be determined only by the testimony of another witness. Since the polygraph was invented, rabbinic authorities have debated to what extent this device can be trusted. In previous generations, time was absolute – it was impossible to be in two time zones at the same time. Today a person can act between two time zones, for example, by sending a fax during daylight hours to a place where night has already fallen. What effect does this have on the timing of transactions?

Technology has made it possible to avoid the need to violate *halakhah*. The electric shaver permits many to shave without violating the prohibition against using a razor on their faces. Women who previously would have been unable to conceive because their fertile period was during the time when sexual relations are forbidden may now find a solution through hor-

mone therapy that regulates their menstrual cycle. In agriculture, crops that were once annuals have now been made perennials through artificial means, thus aiding in the observance of the SABBATICAL YEAR.

Finally, technology has had its most far-reaching impact on the study of TORAH itself. Photo-offset printing has made it easier and cheaper to produce books for study. The various forms of electronic communication deliver Torah to places where it was never heard of before. Digital storage makes complete libraries available on disk, for a tiny fraction of the cost of the originals. Computerized search engines that accompany these electronic libraries make it easier to find relevant *halakhah* texts on any topic.

HALAKHAH LE-MOSHEH MI-SINAI   ("A law [given] to Moses at Sinai"). According to the Talmud, a category of laws that came from MOSES, even though they are not found in the Bible or directly derived from it. The term occurs three times in the Mishnah and is used frequently in the Talmud. It means that the particular law was communicated to Moses by God at SINAI, but Moses was instructed not to record it in the WRITTEN LAW. Laws falling in this category include: a number of details in the design and making of phylacteries (TEFILLIN; see *Er.* 97a, *Men.* 35a); details of specific flaws that cause a slaughtered animal to be TEREFAH (*Hul.* 42a); details of the WATER-DRAWING FESTIVAL (*Suk.* 34a), etc. As a rule, laws called *Halakhah le-Mosheh mi-Sinai* were not subject to further dispute.

HALAKHOT GEDOLOT AND HALAKHOT PESUKOT   The first two major codes of rabbinic law, written in Babylonia during the geonic period. These codes are the earliest systematic digests of the HALAKHAH. Yehudai Gaon was the author of the *Halakhot Pesukot* ("Decided Laws," c. 760). His work dealt with practical rules about the observance of the SABBATH, FESTIVALS, etc. The original Aramaic book was translated into Hebrew as *Halakhot Re'u*.

On the basis of this pioneering work, other summaries of law from the Talmud began to appear. *Halakhot Gedolot* ("Great [Code of] Laws," c. 825) was the best known of these. Scholars believe it was the work of Simeon Kayyara of the Babylonian academy of Sura. The code draws largely from the Babylonian Talmud, though it quotes from the Jerusalem Talmud and geonic RESPONSA (legal questions and answers) as well. It deals with both practical *halakhah* and laws that no longer apply, because of the Temple's destruction. If was the first work of its kind to include a detailed list of the 613 COMMANDMENTS. (See also CODIFICATION.)

HALITSAH   See LEVIRATE MARRIAGE

HALLAH   See CHALLAH

HALLAH   ("Portion of Dough"). Ninth tractate (book) of the Order of ZERA'IM in the Mishnah. It consists of four chapters that deal with the laws of separating the priest's share from the dough, whether the bread is baked at home or at a bakery.

HALLEL ("Praise"). Hymns of thanksgiving and praise to God, taken from the Book of PSALMS; they form part of the prayer service for festive occasions. There are three varieties of *Hallel*: *Hallel ha-Gadol* ("The Great *Hallel*") – Psalm 136 – recited at the beginning of the MORNING SERVICE on the Sabbath and festivals, as an additional psalm for the last day of PASSOVER, and as part of the HAGGADAH; *Hallel* ("Full *Hallel*") – Psalms 113–118 – the standard version of *Hallel*; and *Hatsi Hallel* ("Half-*Hallel*") – *Hallel* minus the first 11 verses of Psalms 115 and 116. The psalms deal with themes of deliverance and God's love for Israel and with Israel's response in praise. It appears that in Temple times the choir of LEVITES sang *Hallel* (*Tosef. Sot.* 6:2, cf. *Tos.* to *Pes.* 95b). Later traditions differed. With the exception of the *Hallel* of the Passover *Seder*, worshipers stand when reciting *Hallel*.

Origin of Hallel According to the rabbis, Kind DAVID is the author of almost all of the psalms, including those of *Hallel*. R. Eleazar ben Yose, however, thought *Hallel* came from MOSES and the Israelites; while R. Judah taught that the prophets had decreed that these psalms be recited to mark national events and deliverance from danger. Other sages say that *Hallel* was recited by various leaders of Israel, such as JOSHUA, DEBORAH, Hezekiah, Mordecai and ESTHER (*Pes.* 117a–118a).

Occasions for Saying Hallel According to the Talmud (*Ta'an.* 28b) "Full *Hallel*" is recited on 18 days each year in the Land of Israel: on the eight days of SUKKOT (including SHEMINI ATSERET and SIMHAT TORAH), the eight days of HANUKKAH, both days of SHAVU'OT, and the first day of PASSOVER. In the Diaspora, because of the additional festival days, the number of occasions rises to 21. It is also recited during the *Seder* on Passover and (according to Sephardi and Israeli Ashkenazi practice) at the conclusion of the Evening Service preceding the *Seder*. "Half-*Hallel*" is recited on the New Moon and on the latter days of Passover.

Israel's Chief Rabbinate has ruled that "Full *Hallel*" with its blessings should be recited on Israel's INDEPENDENCE DAY (5 Iyyar) and on JERUSALEM DAY (28 Iyyar). This practice is followed by most Orthodox as well as CONSERVATIVE and REFORM congregations. Some Orthodox congregations recite *Hallel* without the blessings; non-Zionist congregations do not recite *Hallel* on either date.

Hallel – either full or abbreviated – may be said at any time during the festive day. However, the accepted custom is to recite it between the Morning Service AMIDAH and the READING OF THE LAW.

HALLELUJAH Biblical expression found only in the Book of PSALMS. It means "Praise the Lord!" *Hallelujah* occurs in 15 psalms, either as the opening word or the closing word. It is an exclamation of joy, praise, or thanksgiving. In Temple times, it was a signal that the congregation should respond to the choir of LEVITES.

HALUKKAH ("distribution"). Financial assistance sent to Jews in the Holy Land by their fellow Jews in the Diaspora. In particular, this took place from the end of the 18th century, after groups of Hasidim moved to Erets Israel.

The practice of sending money to Jews in Erets Israel dates back to the Second Temple period (Ezra 1:6, 8:33), and continued through all periods of settlement in the Land. From the 16th century, more organized methods were used to collect contributions in Central Europe. Money was often collected by means of CHARITY boxes named for R. MEIR BA'AL HA-NES.

From the late 18th century, *halukkah* was the major support of new Hasidic immigrants to Erets Israel, as well as the PERUSHIM settlers from the early 19th century. Donations were distributed in the four Holy Cities of Jerusalem, Tiberias, Safed and Hebron.

HA-MAPPIL See NIGHT PRAYERS

HA-MAVDIL See HAVDALAH

HAMETS Leaven; Jews are forbidden to have *hamets* in their homes or possession from just before the first day of PASSOVER until the conclusion of the festival. The Bible explains (Ex. 12:39) that we do not eat *hamets* in order to remember the EXODUS from Egypt, when the Children of Israel left in haste and had no time for the dough they were baking to rise. It warns that any person eating leaven during Passover "shall be cut off from his people" (Ex. 12:15; see KARET). The ban refers to all dough made from the FIVE SPECIES of grain: wheat, emmer, barley, rye, and oats.

Before Passover, *hamets* is gradually removed from the home. On the night before Passover, the head of the household searches for any remaining *hamets* (see LEAVEN, SEARCH FOR). Any *hamets* remaining in the home is burned on the morning before Passover. Leaven was also forbidden in meal-offerings in the Temple.

HA-MOTSI See BREAD; GRACE BEFORE MEALS

HANUKKAH ("Dedication"). Festival celebrated for eight days, beginning on 25 KISLEV. Hanukkah celebrates the military victory of the Maccabees (see HASMONEANS) over the Syrian-Greeks, who attempted to destroy Jewish religion. The Hanukkah events took place between 165 and 163 BCE, although the military struggle with the Syrians continued for a number of years afterwards. The holiday is not a full festival; there are no work prohibitions.

The Syrian-Greeks took various steps against Judaism, including practicing IDOLATRY in the TEMPLE in Jerusalem. After a three-year struggle, the Maccabees under JUDAH MACCABEE conquered Jerusalem and rebuilt and purified the ALTAR. They also produced new holy objects for the Temple service. According to the Talmud (*Shab.* 21b), only a small quantity of the pure, holy oil for use in the candelabrum (MENORAH) –

Lighting the first candle of Hanukkah at the President's residence in Jerusalem.

enough to burn for only one day – was found. Miraculously, the oil lasted for eight days, and the holiday is eight days long because of this miracle.

The main ritual associated with Hanukkah is the lighting of the festival lamp (*hanukkiyyah*) each night of the holiday. "Publicizing the miracle" (*pirsumei nissa*) is the chief reason for the festival lamp (*Shab.* 23b). For this reason, the lighted lamp is placed in the doorway or window or even in the street outside the house. The lighting takes place immediately after dark, except on Friday evenings, when it must be lit before the Sabbath lights. The candles must burn for at least half an hour. An additional candle, the *shammash* ("serving light") is used to kindle all the others.

Hanukkah has its special prayers as well. AL HA-NISSIM is added to the AMIDAH and GRACE AFTER MEALS. HALLEL is added to the MORNING SERVICE, and there is a special READING OF THE LAW each day of the festival. The popular 13th century Hanukkah hymn, MA'OZ TSUR, is sung in the home and synagogue. Other customs include playing the *dreydel* game and eating *latkes* (potato pancakes) and *sufganiyyot* (doughnuts).

In modern Israel, Hanukkah has become an occasion for celebrating national courage. In recognition of the heroism and battlefield skill of the Maccabees, a torch is carried from their traditional burial site in Mode'in to various points throughout the country.

HANUKKAH LAMP (Heb. *hanukkiyyah*, also known as the Hanukkah MENORAH). The *hanukkiyyah* is the eight-branched candelabrum lit during the celebration of HANUKKAH. It has eight separate candles or openings for wicks, such that each light can be seen separately (*Shab.* 23b). The Hanukkah lamp was originally placed outside the entrance of the house to the left of the door, in order to publicize the miracle of the holiday. If danger was involved in placing the lamp outside, rabbis permitted it to be lit inside. Today many also put it in their windows. Candles (or oil and wicks) are placed in the *hanukkiyyah* from right to left. The candles are lit from left

to right – that is, the candle for the new day of the festival is kindled first each night.

Many artistic designs came into use for the *hanukkiyyah*. Among ASHKENAZIM, an eight-spout metal lamp developed; SEPHARDIM used a glazed ceramic lamp. In Spain the lamp was hung from a back-wall. Throughout the Jewish world, the Hanukkah lamp was decorated and embellished to make it an object of beauty.

HANUKKAT HA-BAYIT See CONSECRATION

HAREDIM (lit. "fearful"). Term for ultra-Orthodox Jews. Typically, *Haredim* live in their own neighborhoods, maintain their own schools and community services, conform to a dress code, and separate the sexes quite strictly. The men dress in black, and women wear a wig or a kerchief over their short hair or a shaved head. The greatest number of *Haredim* live in the United States and Israel. There are between 100,000 and 125,000 in the United States (about a quarter of the total Orthodox population) and 250,000 to 300,000 in Israel. In Israel, the main *Haredi* population centers are Jerusalem and Benei Berak.

Haredim see themselves as true believers. They point to a rich heritage that they have created in two thousand years of exile. So far they have succeeded, perhaps more than any other group, in maintaining their traditional culture and deeply devoted religious life.

HAROSET See SEDER

HASHKIVENU ("Cause us to lie down [in peace]"). Opening word of the second blessing after SHEMA in the daily EVENING SERVICE. *Hashkivenu* emphasizes man's helplessness (particularly while asleep) and begs for protection. There are two versions of the prayer, the Babylonian text and the longer Palestinian one (see TJ, *Ber.* 4:5). Since the time of the *ge'onim*, the Babylonian text is recited on weekdays and the Palestinian version on Sabbaths and festivals.

HASIDEI ASHKENAZ ("the pious men of Franco-Germany" or "ASHKENAZI Hasidim"). The term *Hasidei Ashkenaz* refers to several groups of Jewish scholars who lived in Germany in the second half of the 12th century and the first half of the 13th. They created new concepts in Jewish thought, MYSTICISM, and ETHICS. They wrote their books after the massacres of Ashkenazi Jewry by the Crusaders, which started in 1096 and continued throughout the 12th century. Their reaction to these persecutions can be seen in many of their ideas.

In matters of belief, the *Hasidei Ashkenaz* were the first Jews in the Middle Ages to present a concept of God in which several powers together make up the Divine unity. In their thinking, separate layers of God's powers fulfill different functions. This system led the way to the kabbalistic system of *sefirot* (see KABBALAH).

The first important writer of this school was R. Samuel ben Kalonymus he-Hasid (the Pious). He was followed by his son JUDAH HE-HASID. The most important writer of the group was ELEAZAR OF WORMS, who was a disciple of Judah he-Hasid. The last two scholars were the first to write detailed commentaries on the Jewish prayer book.

The *Hasidei Ashkenaz* were interested mainly in two aspects of God's REVELATION: PROPHECY and PRAYER. They tried to understand how a God who is eternal and unchanging could reveal Himself to prophets or make decisions when listening to prayers. Their solution was to describe secondary Divine powers – especially the Divine Glory – that were revealed to the prophets and heard and answered individual prayers.

The single most important work of ethics to emerge from the schools of the *Hasidei Ashkenaz* is the *Sefer Hasidim* ("The Book of the Pious"), written by R. Judah he-Hasid (d. 1217). This is the most detailed work of ethics written in Judaism in the Middle Ages. It covers every aspect of life – family, education, attitude towards non-Jews, prayer, study, social relations, and worship. The book suggests that every ethical and religious deed includes an element of suffering and sacrifice, since one must often triumph over one's nature to perform it. The supreme sacrifice is martyrdom (KIDDUSH HA-SHEM) but every ethical act is a miniature *Kiddush ha-Shem*. Thus the ethics of the *Hasidei Ashkenaz* are designed to help every Jew prepare for the trial of *Kiddush ha-Shem*.

HASIDIM RISHONIM ("the pious men of former generations"). Talmudic term referring to individuals who were especially pious and careful in their observance of the COMMANDMENTS. One sage from the Mishnah declared that the piety of the *hasid* leads to Divine inspiration and ultimately to the REDEMPTION (*Sot.* 9:15). The *Sifrei* to Deuteronomy 11:22 states that just as God is a *hasid*, always doing more than is required, so man should be a *hasid*. Behavior that goes beyond the letter of the law is the ideal of the *hasid*.

The period of the *hasidim rishonim* seems to have ended by the time of HILLEL (late 1st cent. BCE). The Talmud represents the *hasidim rishonim* as individuals dedicated to observing the commandments no matter what the danger or expense; avoiding all acts that could result in sin; and showing extreme concern for the welfare of their fellow humans. There are many examples of their acts of piety. For example, the pious men of former generations always took an hour in preparing for prayer (*Ber.* 5:1). They gave CHARITY beyond their means. They were known to bury thorns and broken glass deep in their fields so they would not be exposed by plowing and become a danger to passersby (*Tos.* to *BK* 32b).

Early rabbinic sources also refer to *hasidim ve-anshei ma'aseh* ("pious men and men of action"). These include Honi the circle-maker, and Hanina ben Dosa, who lived at the end of the Second Temple period and was the last of the "men of action" (*Sot.* 9:15).

HASIDISM (Heb. *Hasidut*). Popular movement founded by Israel ben Eliezer BA'AL SHEM TOV ("Master of the Good Name") in 18th century Podolia.

Two of the disciples of the *Besht*, as the Ba'al Shem Tov was known, were responsible for spreading his teachings after his death in 1760. JACOB JOSEPH OF POLONNOYE was the author of *Toledot Ya'akov Yosef* (1780), which quotes at length from the teachings of the Ba'al Shem Tov. The second disciple, DOV BAER, the "Maggid" of Mezhirech, was really the founder of the Hasidic movement. He gathered around him a remarkable group of disciples who became the Hasidic masters of Poland, Russia, and Lithuania. By the beginning of the 19th century, the movement that sprang from this group had won over half the Jewish population of Eastern Europe.

The Hasidic movement was made up of groups of Hasidim who congregated around a special rabbi, or *Tzaddik*. The *Tzaddik* functioned as a holy man, who taught his followers and prayed on their behalf. The followers believed that the prayers of that particular holy man were most holy and effective. The most important Hasidic leaders of the next generation had a great influence on the movement: ELIMELECH OF LYZHANSK, Israel of Kozienice, LEVI ISAAC OF BERDICHEV, NAHMAN OF BRATSLAV, SCHNEUR ZALMAN OF LYADY, and MENAHEM MENDEL OF KOTSK. Each *Tzaddik* or *Rebbe* (see ADMOR) had his own "court," and his followers traveled there to be near him. In the early years of the movement, the leading disciple succeeded the *Rebbe* when he died. Later on, the sons or close relatives took over the leadership, like a dynasty. In time, fierce struggles over who would be the next *Rebbe* became the norm, so much so that when Mordecai of Chernobyl died in 1837, each of his eight sons founded a new dynasty, as did his sons-in-law.

At the heart of Hasidic practice are several ideas. First, they rejected the dry intellectual approach of mainstream Jewish scholars, who were an elite. Instead, there was a new emphasis on the joy of prayer (SIMHAH) – over the joy of study. Next, religious enthusiasm (*hitlahavut*) for the Hasidim became an end in itself. The *Tzaddik* – the holy *Rebbe* – is the channel

Hasidic family at the Western Wall in Jerusalem.

through which the Hasid gains access to God. The Hasid observes the *Tsaddik*'s conduct, learns how to pray and study, and tries to follow his example. In this way, the ordinary person can achieve holiness.

There was tremendous opposition to the new Hasidic movement. The *Mitnaggedim* (Heb. "the opponents") attacked Hasidism on social and religious grounds. Socially, they objected to the new way of praying and to the fact that the Hasidim separated themselves from the general community, and formed their own groups. In fact, many of the conflicts that raged between the Hasidim and *Mitnaggedim* really had at their core a rebellion against the established COMMUNITY. The *Mitnaggedim* also objected to their devotion to the *Tsaddik*, the Hasidic idea that "all is in God," and the suspicion that the Hasidim were secret Shabbateans (see SHABBETAI TSEVI). More offensive yet, Hasidism taught that *devekut* ("attachment" to God) could be better achieved through prayer than study. The Hasidim were therefore accused of putting down scholars and scholarship. As a result of the conflict with the *Mitnaggedim*, several bans of EXCOMMUNICATION were proclaimed against the Hasidim, such as that of ELIJAH BEN SOLOMON ZALMAN, the Gaon of Vilna. He rejected the attempt at reconciliation made by Menahem Mendel of Vitebsk and Shneur Zalman of Lyady.

Devotees of the HASKALAH (Jewish Enlightenment) movement in 19th century Russia were also outspoken opponents of the Hasidim. They accused the Hasidim of rejecting all secular learning and relying on the prayers of the *Tsaddik* instead of taking practical measures to lessen the suffering of the Jewish masses. However, since radical Haskalah Jews abandoned religious observance, they in time became the common enemy of both the Hasidim and the *Mitnaggedim*.

Hasidism developed its own writings, including many tales of the *Tsaddikim*. From early on the belief took hold that telling stories about Hasidic masters improved the faith of the Hasid and reawakened the mystical powers of the *Tsaddik* in the story. Of course, some of the Hasidim took a skeptical view of the stories. One Hasidic saying sums up the attitude towards the tales: "Whoever believes all these tales is a fool; but anyone who cannot believe them is a heretic." The more important type of Hasidic literature includes the unique systems of ideas advanced by the individual masters. These were written more often by disciples of the *Rebbe*, although many were written by the *Rebbes* themselves.

The Hasidim remained, for the most part, in Eastern Europe. Some did reach Erets Israel in 1777; others later settled in Western Europe and America. Following the HOLOCAUST and the destruction of Europe's Jewish communities, most of the surviving *Rebbes* moved to Israel or the United States. Among the best-known groups active today are BELZ, BOBOV, GUR, Klausenburg, Zanz Lubavich (CHABAD), SATMAR, and Vishnits.

Each Hasidic dynasty has its own unique traditions; however, they have many customs in common. Yiddish is spoken widely; there is a familiar clothing style, including long black coats, fur hats (*shtraymel*), *gartel* (belt) for prayer; the *Rebbe* distributes *shirayim* ("leftovers") from his table following the communal meal; song and dance are considered holy. All Hasidic *Rebbes* receive their followers in private meetings, and the Hasid brings a written petition (*kvitl*), outlining his needs and problems, so that the *Rebbe* can pray on his behalf. The *kvitl* is usually accompanied by a sum of money that goes for the upkeep of the *Rebbe*'s court.

HASKALAH (lit. "enlightenment"). The Haskalah movement began in the late 18th century. It grew out of the EMANCIPATION of the Jews – their "welcome" into general society, which had been closed to them before. It also resulted from the ASSIMILATION of Jews into European culture after the Emancipation. Haskalah Jews began to have a more sympathetic attitude towards the secular world of their Gentile neighbors. Also, as the restrictions against Jews participating in Gentile society were lifted, Jews wanted to play a more active role.

The Haskalah movement was based on several new ideas: (1) Secular studies and the local language should be part of the education of the Jewish child. (2) Judaism and Jewish history should be studied at length. (3) The study of HEBREW should be promoted. (And YIDDISH, the language of Jewish exile, should be abandoned.) (4) Jewish religion must adapt itself to the changing conditions of the modern world. (This led to the development of REFORM JUDAISM.) (5) Like other nations of the world, Jews must have their own homeland and must conduct a national struggle in order to obtain it. (This led to the development of modern ZIONISM.) (6) Jewish society must become more productive, and Jews should begin to work in the areas of agriculture and manual labor.

Haskalah included both paths to assimilation and means for fighting assimilation. There were Jews who drifted from Haskalah to total identification with non-Jewish society. However, there were also those whose identity as Jews was strengthened through the bonding of Judaism and secular ways.

HASMONEANS Or "Maccabees"; name for the Jewish family and the later dynasty in Erets Israel that led the revolt against the Syrian-Greek ruler, Antiochus IV (Epiphanes), in 167 BCE.

In the year 168 BCE, Antiochus declared a series of anti-Jewish decrees and also brought IDOLATRY into the Jerusalem TEMPLE. Mattathias, the elderly head of a leading priestly family, knew that these decrees would destroy Judaism. He started an armed revolt against the Greeks and their Jewish collaborators. Under his son, Judah, the Jews were able to rededicate the Temple in 164 BCE. Judah was succeeded by his brother Jonathan in 160 BCE and then Simon in 142 BCE. Jonathan was the first of the Hasmoneans to serve as HIGH PRIEST.

The Hasmonean kings ruled until the first century BCE. Theirs was an extremely stable and unchallenged reign, with a Jewish presence all over the Land of Israel. They reestablished MONOTHEISM (worship of one God) in a world that was in the process of being taken over by HELLENISM. If the Hasmonean

Coin of Mattathias Antigonus, the last Hasmonean king (40–37 BCE) with the menorah appearing for the first time in Jewish art.

revolt had not been successful, Judaism might have been lost forever and its daughter religions, CHRISTIANITY and ISLAM, would never have been born.

When Erets Israel became the Roman province of Judea in 63 BCE, the Hasmoneans again led the fight against Rome. However, by 37 BCE, King HEROD had seized the throne with support from the Romans. This was the end of the Hasmonean dynasty.

HATE   See VIOLENCE

HAVDALAH   ("separation"). Blessing recited at the close of the SABBATH and FESTIVALS marking the beginning of a regular weekday. A *havdalah* paragraph is inserted in the fourth BENEDICTION of the AMIDAH of the EVENING SERVICE on Saturday nights. The complete *havdalah* ceremony is chanted at home, after the Evening Service. It consists of four blessings: over wine, spices and lights, and the *havdalah* blessing.

Havdalah is a very appealing ceremony that involves special items. A cup of wine is held up and aromatic spices – cinnamon, cloves, etc. – are smelled by all. Among Sephardim, sweet-smelling plants are used. The *havdalah* spices are usually kept in a decorative SPICEBOX. The *havdalah* candle has more than one wick to create a fire that has at least two flames.

The final blessing, the *havdalah* itself, lists a series of contrasts that God has created side by side in nature. God separates "between the holy and the ordinary, between light and darkness, between Israel and the other nations, [and] between the seventh day and the six days of labor." Even the passage from the holy to the ordinary – the opposite of the Sabbath KIDDUSH – is a special Divine act.

There are a number of *havdalah* CUSTOMS that vary among the communities. Some fill the cup to overflowing and extinguish the candle in wine poured from the cup. Some dip their fingers in the wine and place drops on the forehead or in the pockets, to symbolize success in the coming week. Most people extend their fingers and look at the reflection of the candle in their fingernails. In some communities *havdalah* is said standing; in others, *havdalah* is recited while sitting.

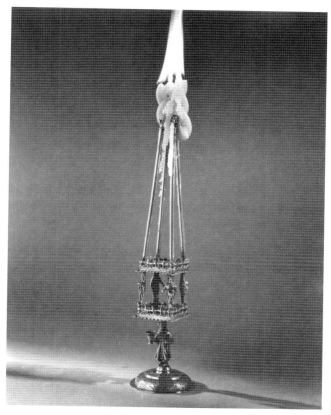

Havdalah candlestick from Frankfurt.

HAVURAH   ("fellowship"). A small group of individuals that seek fellowship and an enriched Jewish communal life together. Modern *havurot* began to form in the United States in the 1960s, because people were disappointed by large, impersonal synagogues that did not serve their spiritual needs.

Most *havurot* fall into one of three categories. The first is a small and Jewishly educated group that wants to set up its own prayer community, such as the Fabrangen founded in Washington DC in 1971. Another kind of *havurah* is much like a commune. *Havurat Shalom*, founded in Somerville, Massachusetts, in 1968 was of this type. Members lived together, studied, observed holidays, and worked daily to improve the quality of their Jewish experience. Similar *havurot* thrived on college campuses during the 1960s and 1970s. The third type of *havurah* exists within a larger synagogue. This allows the members to remain within the formal Jewish community while attending to their special needs.

As more and more people look for warmth and closeness in their religious activity, the number of *havurot* continues to grow. It remains to be seen what their long-term effect on the American Jewish community will be.

HAZON ISH   See KARELITZ, AVRAHAM

HAZZAN   See CANTOR

HEAD COVERING   See COVERING THE HEAD

HEAVEN   See AFTERLIFE; ESCHATOLOGY

HEAVE OFFERING   See SACRIFICES AND OFFERINGS

HEBREW   (Heb. *Ivrit*). A Semitic language, known as "the Holy Tongue" (Heb. *leshon ha-kodesh*). Like all languages, Hebrew as we know it developed over time. The early language of the Bible was not called "Hebrew" until the time of Ben Sira (2nd cent. BCE). The Bible calls the local language of the Land of Israel of its time either the "Canaanite language" or "Judean." The classical literary Hebrew of the Bible probably came into its final form at the time of King SOLOMON. This was when people started coming from all parts of the country to the TEMPLE in JERUSALEM, to meet with PRIESTS and "wise men." This is the language of Biblical poetry and the speeches of the PROPHETS. It marks still another stage in the development of the language.

The later books of the Bible, such as ECCLESIASTES, EZRA, NEHEMIAH, ESTHER, and perhaps CHRONICLES, use a later form of biblical Hebrew. Scholars suggest that the language in these books was the official language of the royal court.

During the Second Temple period, religion was taught by the *tannaim*, who used the spoken Hebrew of the time. Their language had different grammar, language rules, and vocabulary from biblical Hebrew. In this period, when local synagogues came into being, prayers such as the AMIDAH were composed in a Hebrew close to the spoken language. This is Mishnaic Hebrew, named for the MISHNAH. Mishnaic Hebrew was used for religious texts throughout the Middle Ages, although it was influenced by the various languages that Jews spoke in different areas (see JEWISH LANGUAGES).

Although Hebrew ceased to be an everyday language, since Jews spoke the languages of the lands in which they lived, it did not disappear from Jewish life. The prayer services continued mainly in Hebrew, and it continued to be the language of Jewish study. Most important, it was the language in which Jewish scholars wrote. Jewish communities, however small or isolated, hired teachers to instruct boys from the age of three years and up in Hebrew, so they could understand religious books. In this way, the knowledge of the language was preserved throughout the community, even though Hebrew was hardly ever spoken.

Hebrew was never really a dead language. There is evidence that Jewish men spoke Hebrew with other Jews with whom they had no other language in common. In the second half of the 18th century, leaders of the HASKALAH (Jewish Enlightenment) began to publish articles in Hebrew and to call for teaching the Hebrew language in Jewish schools. In the late 19th century, Eliezer Ben-Yehuda, father of Modern Hebrew, began his work in Erets Israel. He insisted that Hebrew be spoken in all situations, and that Jewish immigrants leave behind all of the other languages that they had spoken before they came to Erets Israel.

In reality, Hebrew was a dormant ("sleeping") language, waiting for the right conditions to be reawakened as a spoken language. When immigration to Erets Israel began in the late 19th century, Hebrew was taught in schools there to give immigrants from various lands a common language. With the establishment of the State of Israel in 1948, the revival of Hebrew was completed, and Hebrew was declared the national language. At this time the Sephardi pronunciation of Hebrew became standard.

HEDER   (lit. "room"). A type of school that was especially widespread in Eastern Europe until World War II and is still to be found in many Orthodox communities. Students were generally a small group of young boys – from ages five to 13 – who met at the home of the "*rebbe*" (teacher). The *rebbe* would divide the students into three age groups and work with each in turn. The youngest students learned how to read from the prayer book. The intermediate group generally studied the TORAH with RASHI's commentary; the older group studied the TALMUD. Extremely bright students might go on to YESHIVAH after *heder*. However in poverty-stricken Europe, most had no choice but to go to work.

Traditionally, the course of studies included only holy books. However, beginning in the 19th century, following the HASKALAH ("Enlightenment"), some teachers tried to modify the *heder* to include Hebrew language and other modern Haskalah studies. This curriculum was called *heder metukkan* ("reformed *heder*"), but the experiment did not succeed and was soon discontinued.

The *heder* model was attempted in the United States, without much success. In Britain, the congregational Hebrew school was also known as a *heder*.

HELL   See AFTERLIFE; ESCHATOLOGY

HELLENISM   Term for the social, political, economic, and cultural/religious influences on Europe and the Near East beginning with the end of the fourth century BCE. These influences came mostly from the culture of Classical Greece. Jews in both Erets Israel and the Diaspora were influenced by Hellenism, yet at the same time they struggled against it. Greek literature, philosophy, and architecture were encouraged – the pagan worldview (see IDOLATRY) was rejected.

We know about the impact of Hellenism on Jewish thought

from Jewish books that were written in Greek. They include mostly the APOCRYPHA AND PSEUDEPIGRAPHA, works that were not included in the Jewish Bible. Jewish communities throughout the Middle East were influenced by the political, social, and cultural trends around them. In general, where the basic content of Judaism was concerned, most Jews refused to accept the Hellenistic order of the day. Unlike the pagans, who aimed to prove how Greek their cultural heritage was, the Jews stressed the special nature of Jewish culture. However, particularly among the upper class, many Jews went along with the Hellenistic lifestyle.

HELLER, YOM TOV LIPMANN (1579–1654). Rabbinic scholar and commentator on the Mishnah. He was learned in Kabbalah, mathematics, and astronomy, as well as rabbinics.

Heller's main work is the *Tosefot Yom Tov* ("The Additions of Yom Tov"), which supplies "additions" to the commentary of Obadiah di BERTINORO on the Mishnah. Heller provided linguistic information, explained the text, and added his own legal decisions. His RESPONSA have survived and are printed in three volumes. He also wrote an autobiography – *Megillat Eivah* – that sheds important light on the Jewish communal life and history of his time.

HEREM See EXCOMMUNICATION

HERESY A belief that goes against mainstream religious teaching. While neither the Torah nor Talmud set out a clear system of beliefs for Judaism, there are certain ideas that are central. These include GOD, REVELATION, and REWARD AND PUNISHMENT. The Mishnah (*Sanh.* 10:1) tells us that heresy can cause people to lose their place in the world to come. In the Talmud, a person guilty of heresy is called a *kofer ba-ikkar*, a "denier of a basic principle." This was an individual whose beliefs or actions showed that he did not believe in the Divine origin of the Torah and the HALAKHAH (Jewish law).

MAIMONIDES (12th cent.) was the first to clearly set out a list of Jewish beliefs. His 13 PRINCIPLES OF FAITH not only define the essential beliefs of Judaism but define as a heretic anyone who does not accept them. According to Maimonides, to deny any one of these principles meant that the person lost his share in the world to come. Of course, many who followed Maimonides disagreed with such a short list of principles. Isaac ABRAVANEL and David IBN ZIMRA lived in the generation of the expulsion from Spain. The argued that each and every detail of the Torah was essential, therefore denial of any point counted as heresy. Ibn Zimra stated: "My mind does not agree to say that any particular principle of our perfect Torah is essential, because it is all essential" (*Responsa*, Vol. 1, no. 344; see also AGNOSTICISM AND ATHEISM; APOSTASY).

HERMENEUTICS Rules for interpreting the Bible that were developed by the *tannaim* (see TANNA). They are used to develop halakhic (Jewish legal) rulings out of the biblical text,

particularly when the connections between the law and the text are unclear. The process of determining the law is called MIDRASH – explaining the Scripture.

As time went on, special principles of Midrash known as *middot* ("measures") were developed to determine the law. HILLEL the Elder (end of 1st cent. BCE) identified seven methods of interpretation (*Tosef.* to *Sanh.*, end of ch. 7). R. Ishmael developed 13 rules by which the Bible is interpreted. Rabbi Eliezer ben Yose he-Gelili expanded these rules to 32, although most of the additions are used for explaining the AGGADAH (rabbinic legends). R. AKIVA reached the height of hermeneutics – he was able to learn additional rulings from prefixes, suffixes, and other small words in the Bible.

The rabbis were not completely free to apply hermeneutics to a verse and come up with a legal ruling. In some cases, they had to have a tradition that stated that a given law applied to the verse. For this reason, some have suggested that the purpose of hermeneutics was to connect traditional rulings that were already part of the ORAL LAW (*Torah she-ba'al-peh*) to the written Bible text, rather than to introduce new rulings.

HEROD (73–4 BCE). King of Judea. Descended from Idumean converts, Herod advanced under Roman rule thanks to his father Antipater's high position. He became governor of Galilee in 47 BCE, executing Jewish rebels and ignoring the efforts of the SANHEDRIN to bring him to trial. In 43 he was made tetrarch (local ruler) by Marc Antony and afterwards gained control of the whole country with Roman support. He then married Mariamne, granddaughter of the HASMONEAN Hyrcanus II.

As king, Herod quickly consolidated his power, getting rid of the Hasmoneans and the SADUCCEE aristocracy, including 45 members of the Sanhedrin. Under the emperor Augustus he expanded his kingdom to include Transjordan, the Hauran Mountains, and the Golan Heights. Becoming very rich, he built extensively, refortifying Jerusalem and Masada and repairing the TEMPLE. He followed Jewish practices for political and personal reasons, not placing his portrait on coins nor eating pork, but he was also very cruel (Augustus' joked: "I would rather be Herod's pig than his son").

Herod's atrocities included executing Mariamne's brother Aristobulus III and after him Hyrcanus, Mariamne, his mother-in-law Alexandra, and three of own his sons (in 30–28 BCE). Such ruthlessness and his great skill in maintaining good relations with Rome assured his survival and got him the name "monster" in the later rabbinic literature (*BB* 3b–4a, b; *Ta'an.* 23a, etc.). In all, he had ten wives and 15 children. On his death Augustus approved his last will and testament, dividing the kingdom among three of his sons.

Under Herod's iron-handed rule the authority of the rabbis declined and the seeds of the Jewish revolt against Rome were planted. His achievement was in his monumental building projects. He built cities, palaces, fortresses, theaters, colonnades, and aqueducts. In his restoration of the Temple, started in the 18th year of his rule and continuing for 46 years, he doubled the size of the TEMPLE MOUNT, built retaining walls (including the WESTERN WALL), bridges, and porticos, and rebuilt the sanctuary. In truth, the Second Temple is the Herodian reconstruction.

HERZL, THEODOR (1860–1904). Founder of political ZIONISM, which led to the establishment of the modern Jewish State of Israel. Herzl was born in Budapest and moved to Vienna at the age of 18 to pursue his studies. After a short career as a lawyer, he began writing full-time as a journalist and playwright. As a journalist, he covered the trial of Captain Dreyfus in France in 1894. Dreyfus had been framed for the crime of treason, because he was a Jew. Herzl's exposure to shocking ANTI-SEMITISM among the French elite while covering the trial convinced him that the only solution to the "Jewish problem" was to create an independent Jewish state. In 1896 he published his views in *Der*

Theodor Herzl in front of the synagogue in Basel, during the 1903 Zionist Congress.

Judenstaat ("The Jewish State"). Herzl's essay was enthusiastically read by many. Following the First Zionist Congress in Basel in 1897, he founded the World Zionist Organization. His goal was to found a homeland for the Jewish people in Palestine.

From this point on, Herzl devoted his life to this goal. He served as chairman of five Zionist Congresses. He engaged in diplomatic activity among the leaders of the world. Under his leadership, the Zionist movement became an important force on the world stage. The Zionists were finally able to achieve the Balfour Declaration in 1917, which recognized the right of the Jewish people to establish a homeland in Palestine.

Herzl died of pneumonia in 1904. His body was brought for reburial in Jerusalem, Israel, in 1949 in a state funeral.

HERZOG, ISAAC HA-LEVI (1888–1959). Rabbinic scholar and second Ashkenazi Chief Rabbi of modern Israel. Herzog received a traditional rabbinic education and earned a doctorate from London University. Before immigrating to Israel, he served as Chief Rabbi of Ireland. He settled in Jerusalem in 1937 to succeed Abraham Isaac KOOK as Ashkenazi Chief Rabbi of Palestine.

Herzog worked tirelessly to guide the Orthodox community after the establishment of the State of Israel in 1948. He had to deal with a host of new halakhic (Jewish legal) problems that arose once the Jews had a country of their own in Erets Israel. These included SABBATH observance and DIETARY LAWS within the framework of a modern state and society. Above all, he struggled to secure halakhic standards in matters of MARRIAGE and personal status.

His son **Chaim Herzog** (1918–1997), a former general and diplomat, was elected sixth President of the State of Israel in 1983.

HESCHEL, ABRAHAM JOSHUA (1907–1972). Scholar and philosopher of religion. Heschel was born into a distinguished line of Hasidic rabbis. He received serious training in Talmud as a young man and later added intense study of HASIDISM and KABBALAH. Heschel's books deal with every aspect of classical Jewish thought. He published major works on the prophets of the Bible, medieval Jewish philosophers, the Kabbalah and Hasidism, methods of rabbinic study, and various aspects of the festivals.

Heschel developed his own philosophy of Judaism that combined his scholarship with a warmth and humanism that had not existed before. He saw in the relationship between God and humanity two special features. From God's side there is a particular concern for His creatures and for Israel. From our side, religion is based on the human response to the bond with God. Jewish observance is not a series of technical acts; it is the expression of love and devotion. For Heschel, neither a dry academic approach nor a purely cultural approach tells the whole story. Judaism is all about the living relationship between God and human beings.

Heschel also made an effort to apply Jewish sources to

modern problems. He was a leading activist in the American Civil Rights Movement and in other humanistic causes. He was also active in Jewish-Christian dialogue. He was involved in the high-level discussions that led to the positive Vatican II statement about the Jews. Throughout his career, Heschel influenced generations of rabbis, teachers, Jews, and non-Jews through his writings and lectures.

HESHVAN Eighth month of the Jewish CALENDAR. Heshvan has either 29 or 30 days and falls in October–November in the secular calendar. No Jewish holidays fall in Heshvan. Its sign of the zodiac is Scorpio.

HEVRAH KADDISHA See BURIAL SOCIETY

HIGH HOLIDAYS See ROSH HA-SHANAH, DAY OF ATONEMENT, and TEN DAYS OF REPENTANCE

HIGH PRIEST (Heb. *kohen gadol*). The chief among the PRIESTS; the first was AARON (Ex. 28:1), and all later High Priests (and other priests) descend from him.

The High Priest was unique in several ways. Common priests wore four special garments (coat, girdle, turban, breeches). The High Priest also wore the apron, the breastplate, a robe, and a gold headplate on which the words "Holy to the Lord" were written (see PRIESTLY GARMENTS). He wore these garments while serving in the TEMPLE. The High Priest began his service when he was anointed by having oil poured over his head (see ANOINTING).

The breastplate that the High Priest wore was very special. It contained the URIM AND THUMMIM, which was an oracle (truth teller) that was consulted for difficult questions. If a king or head of the SANHEDRIN wanted to ask God whether or not to start a war or another important national question, he went to the High Priest. The High Priest faced the Divine Presence, wearing the breastplate as the question was asked. The letters written on the stones of the breastplate then spelled out the answer (*Yoma* 73a).

The High Priest had special responsibilities in the Temple. He alone had the privilege of sacrificing the sin-offering on the inner ALTAR. On the DAY OF ATONEMENT, he performed the AVODAH service in the holiest moment of the Jewish year. This was the service of ATONEMENT on behalf of the entire Jewish nation.

According to Jewish law, the High Priest also had extra restrictions place upon him. Common priests could not come in contact with the dead, but they could mourn for close relatives; the High Priest was not even allowed to mourn for his closest relatives. In addition the High Priest had to marry a virgin.

HILLEL (c. 70 BCE–c. 10 CE) Greatest sage of the Second Temple period; known as Hillel the Elder (or "the Babylonian"). Hillel studied first in Babylonia and then in Jerusalem under SHEMAYAH AND AVTALYON. One famous legend describes

One of Hillel's sayings: "If I am not for myself, who is for me?" illustrated by American artist Ben Shahn (1898–1969).

Hillel's efforts to enter the *yeshivah* of these two great masters in Jerusalem. Hillel was a poor man and he was not able to pay to enter the academy. He therefore crawled onto the roof to hear the lesson through a skylight. At daybreak one morning, Shemayah and Avtalyon saw that something was blocking the skylight. When they went up to the roof, they found Hillel buried under a blanket of snow. Although it was the Sabbath, they lit a fire to revive him. They declared that he was worthy of violating the Sabbath (*Yoma* 35b).

Hillel was an important teacher of HALAKHAH (Jewish law). He used the seven principles of interpretation (see HERMENEUTICS), which he had developed, to decide the law in difficult cases. His reputation grew until he was eventually appointed NASI (president) of the SANHEDRIN. His descendants occupied this position for several centuries. Hillel's name is joined in history with that of his colleague and rival, SHAMMAI. Both attracted scores of followers to their methods of learning. Rabbinic literature records numerous arguments between Hillel and Shammai and between their students, BET HILLEL AND BET SHAMMAI.

As head of the Sanhedrin, Hillel presided over the Jewish people's highest religious and legal body. He is responsible for a number of important social reforms. The PROSBUL is possibly the most important of these. This ruling allowed people to get around the biblical law that canceled debts in the SABBATICAL YEAR (see Deut. 15:1–8). In practice, people would not lend money if they knew that the debt would be automatically canceled in the seventh year. The *Prosbul* made it possible to carry on normal business while at the same time respecting the biblical law.

Hillel was known for his piety and his caring about the common people. He himself rose from the lower levels of society to the highest, but he did not forget his origins. He taught Torah to laborers on their way to work and received questioners at his home. He also displayed a great measure of tolerance towards others. The Talmud tells that he was once asked by a would-be convert to teach him the whole Torah while standing on one foot. Shammai had driven the man away when asked the same question. But Hillel finally replied: "What is hateful to you, do not do unto others; this is the whole Torah – the rest is commentary. Now go and learn!" (*Shab.* 31a). For Hillel, this was not only a good introduction to Torah, but its central message.

HILLULA   Aramaic word meaning "festivity," originally a wedding party. Among Jews in Muslim lands, the *hillula* is generally held on the anniversary of the death of a sage. For example, the *hillula* marking the death of SIMEON BAR YOHAI is celebrated on LAG BA-OMER. At this annual celebration, as many as 100,000 people gather in Meron, his burial place. The Lag ba-Omer celebration in the courtyard of the al-Ghariba synagogue in Djerba, Tunisia, is probably the largest *hillula* outside of Israel.

HILLUL HA-SHEM   See KIDDUSH HA-SHEM

HIRSCH, SAMSON RAPHAEL   (1808–1888). German rabbi and founder of NEO-ORTHODOXY. Hirsch was born in Hamburg and attended the University of Bonn. There he met and became friends with his future opponent, Abraham GEIGER. He served as Chief Rabbi of Oldenburg, Aurich, and Osnabrück in Hanover, and finally of Moravia in 1846.

Hirsch taught that Orthodox Judaism should accept and become involved in Western culture while at the same time maintaining strict observance. He convinced many in the relatively assimilated community of Frankfurt on the Main to return to traditional observance while he was the rabbi of that community. This was remarkable at a time when REFORM JUDAISM was starting to take hold in Germany. He was a strong opponent of Reform and worked hard to set up separate Orthodox institutions.

Hirsch's most important writings include *Choreb*, a book about the COMMANDMENTS, and his *Commentary to the Pentateuch*. This later work is a modern classic that has been translated into many languages.

HOL HA-MO'ED   The middle days of the PASSOVER and SUKKOT holidays. On the first and last days of these holidays almost all work is forbidden, except work involved in preparing meals. While the days of *hol ha-mo'ed* have many special observances, work is generally permitted. In Israel, *hol ha-mo'ed* lasts five days during Passover and six days during Sukkot. In the Diaspora it is a day shorter for each holiday, because the second day of each holiday is fully observed as a festival when work is prohibited.

The phrase *hol ha-mo'ed* literally means "the weekdays of the festival," and the days of *hol ha-mo'ed* are indeed a combination of ordinary weekdays and the festival. Some rabbis have ruled that work such as lighting a fire, driving, and writing should not be done on *hol ha-mo'ed* unless a person would lose money by not doing them. Other rabbis hold that these activities may be done during *hol ha-mo'ed*, but that they should be done in a special way, in honor of the holiday. Shaving and haircuts are generally not allowed during *hol ha-mo'ed,* but sometimes exceptions are made.

Weddings may not be held during *hol ha-mo'ed*, because it is Jewish custom not to combine two joyful events (the wedding and the holiday), but to celebrate each separately. There is no official MOURNING during *hol ha-mo'ed* either. In Israel, *hol-ha-mo'ed* is considered a half-day holiday, and many businesses and government offices are open only in the morning (see also FESTIVALS).

HOLINESS   (Heb. *kedushah*). A religious, spiritual quality of special objects, places, times, and people. The literal meaning of *kedushah* is "to be set apart." The source of all holiness is God, "the Holy One, blessed be He," and the people of Israel are commanded to be holy because God is holy (e.g., Lev. 19:2). When speaking about God, holiness means that God is over and above the entire universe and all things in it.

At the same time, objects can also have holiness. The Bible describes the SANCTUARY, its furnishings, and utensils as holy (Ex. 26:33, 28:2–4, 29:1, 30:29 ff., 37). This can be true of places: JERUSALEM is the Holy City and Erets Israel is the Holy Land. The special days of the calendar, starting with the SABBATH and including all the biblical FESTIVALS, are holy days (Ex. 31:12ff.; Lev. 23; Num. 28–29). There is also a certain degree of holiness attached to PRIESTS (Lev. 21).

When the concept of holiness is applied to the people of Israel, holiness means separateness. Israel is supposed to be separate and apart from all other peoples (see Lev. 19, 20). The rabbis helped define the ways in which Jews could express holiness in their behavior. The Talmud says that holiness is achieved by trying to imitate God and by modeling individual and communal life on His ways: "As He is merciful, you be merciful; as He is gracious, you be gracious" (*Shab.* 133b). Elsewhere, holiness is interpreted as: "You shall distance yourself from sexual immoralities" (Rashi on Lev. 19:2). In general, the Jewish concept of holiness is based on separation – one must separate oneself from that which contaminates.

Camp inmates risking death for some bread, Beri Friedlander, 1946.

HOLOCAUST: RELIGIOUS RESPONSES AMONG THE VICTIMS, AND THE RELIGIOUS THINKING THAT FOLLOWED

Six million Jews died in the Holocaust of European Jewry in World War II (1939–1945), murdered at the hands of the German Nazis and their collaborators in a systematic attempt to exterminate the Jewish people. Though they made war against all the civilized world they used special barbaric means against the Jews: ghettoization, deportations, mass executions by firing squads, and gassing in death camps.

Religious responses still have not been fully voiced and studied. In general, the following are true:

1. Jews and non-Jews entered the camps. Of those who survived, some lived again, but never achieved full and meaningful lives.
2. Each of the six million Jews who died was an individual and responded in his or her own way. Believers became non-believers; non-believers became believers; some strengthened their beliefs. Many did not understand and waited for an understanding that never came.
3. Some of the responses of individuals were written down at the time. Some were recorded in diaries or letters or remembered later.
4. Religious responses were not made only by rabbis. Musicians, poets, children, and many others spoke out.
5. Religious resistance to evil took on many forms: active and passive, silent and unspoken, violent and non-violent.

Starting with these general statements, a beginning can be made in charting various religious responses. For Rabbi Nahum Yanchiker of the Slobodka MUSAR movement, our duty after the Holocaust was clear: to remember those who died and the institutions that were destroyed; to surround oneself with the TORAH and try to live by it. Psychologists have drawn their own conclusions: those who believed in anything strongly had a better chance of surviving, in part because they had a support group and in part because they could rally inner strength against the surrounding evil. Philosophers of religion offer many, many responses. Eliezer Berkovits argues that God was in the camps, and many found Him – this was their source of strength. He also contrasts the faith of the suffering Jew against the lack of humanity of the Christian, whose religion contributed to the Holocaust. Emil Fackenheim develops the concept of a new commandment, the 614th Commandment: "The Jew must survive." For him, there must be no final victory for Hitler, the Nazi leader. Jews living in the post-Holocaust era must concern themselves with Jewish survival.

The State of Israel, which rose from the ashes of the Holocaust, is also part of this discussion. Israel has created a number of institutions that ensure that the Holocaust will not be forgotten. These include the Holocaust Memorial Center of Yad Vashem, the museum at Yad Mordekhai, and the museum at Kibbutz Lohamei ha-Getta'ot. Israel itself can be seen as a response to the Holocaust, simply because it exists. It certainly does not provide a solution to the horrors of the Holocaust, but its existence means that the Nazi murderers did not succeed in their aim of destroying the Jewish people. The emphasis on Jewish life is central to Jewish thinking after the Holocaust. No matter how devastating the Holocaust has been, the people of Israel continue to exist as a witness to God and for God.

HOLY CITIES   Term applied to four cities in Erets Israel: JERUSALEM, Hebron, Safed, and Tiberias. These were the four main centers of Jewish life after the Ottoman conquest of 1516. The concept of the holy cities actually dates from the 1640s, when the Jewish communities of Jerusalem, Hebron, and Safed organized an association to raise CHARITY money in the Diaspora. When Tiberias was re-founded in 1740, it joined the association. In truth, going back to ancient times, the only city regarded as holy is Jerusalem.

HOLY LAND   See ISRAEL, LAND OF

HOLY OF HOLIES   The most sacred place in the SANCTUARY, and later the TEMPLE; only the HIGH PRIEST was allowed to enter. The Temple was composed of a series of rooms behind other rooms; the level of holiness increased as one moved from outermost to innermost.

The ARK OF THE COVENANT and two CHERUBIM were found in the Holy of Holies (1 Kings 6:19, 23–28). These objects disappeared when the Temple was destroyed by the Babylonians in 586 BCE. When the Temple was rebuilt some 50 years later, it followed the same plan as the First Temple, including the innermost room. However, throughout the entire Second Temple period, the Holy of Holies was empty.

HOLY PLACES   Term used for shrines in the Land of Israel; for places of pilgrimage; and for graves of famous rabbis and wonderworkers. The classic Jewish source for holy place is in the Mishnah (*Kel.* 1:6ff): "There are ten degrees of holiness.

The Land of Israel is holier than any other ..." The Mishnah continues through all the levels of holiness until it reaches the holiest of all locations: the HOLY OF HOLIES, the inner room of the TEMPLE.

In the course of time, places other than the Temple became more important in Jewish life. Some places were considered better places to pray than others. For example, the Cave of Machpelah in Hebron is identified as the burial cave purchased by ABRAHAM (Gen. 23). According to tradition, Abraham, ISAAC, and JACOB are buried there with their wives (except RACHEL). Religious Jews regularly seek out the opportunity to visit the cave and pray there. Other holy places include Rachel's Tomb in Bethlehem, the Tomb of DAVID on Mount Zion, as well as the gravesites of prophets, sages, and scholars all over Israel.

Every SYNAGOGUE is considered a holy place. This means that the place itself must be treated with respect. Moreover, a synagogue or its contents cannot be sold freely. Special laws must be followed by a community that decides to sell a synagogue, even one not in use, because it is considered holy.

HOLY SPIRIT   (Heb. *Ru'ah ha-Kodesh*). An appearance of God's spirit in the natural world; usually to a PROPHET having a vision. The Bible refers about 80 times to the "Spirit of God" that rests upon a person. In addition, the rabbis held that the Holy Spirit rested upon the HIGH PRIEST when he consulted the URIM AND THUMMIM, upon King DAVID when he wrote the PSALMS, and upon King SOLOMON when he wrote PROVERBS, ECCLESIASTES, and the SONG OF SONGS.

According to the Talmud, when the last of the prophets, HAGGAI, ZECHARIAH, and MALACHI died, the Holy Spirit ceased to appear in Israel (*Yoma* 9b). Even so, the MIDRASH states that the Holy Spirit continues to rest on the especially righteous people (*tzaddikim*) in each generation: "All the righteous do, they do with the power of the Holy Spirit" (*Tanh.*, *Va-Yehi* 13). This gives them the ability to see into the future and to bring blessings upon those in need.

HOME, JEWISH   The SYNAGOGUE and the Jewish home are the two places where the majority of the COMMANDMENTS are performed. The rabbis called both the synagogue and the home *mikdash me'at* (Ezek. 11:16), meaning "minor holy place." But it is the home, perhaps more so than the synagogue, that keeps many of the traditions of the ancient TEMPLE alive.

The home contains many of the symbols of Judaism. These include: the MEZUZAH on each doorpost, ritual objects (SABBATH candles, KIDDUSH cup, SPICEBOX for HAVDALAH, and the MENORAH for HANUKKAH. In addition, one finds a CHARITY box to collect money for the poor, and many Jewish books.

Equally important, the Jewish home has a Jewish kitchen, where food is prepared in keeping with the DIETARY LAWS. Separate utensils are kept for meat and dairy; an entire second set is stored during the year and brought out for PASSOVER.

Meals are accompanied by GRACE BEFORE MEALS and GRACE AFTER MEALS.

In addition, the Jewish home has a Jewish bedroom. The bedroom of a married couple has special holiness. Where possible the bedroom of the mother and father is separated from that of the children. This gives them privacy, in keeping with the laws of modesty. The laws of FAMILY PURITY govern sexual relations between husband and wife.

The home is the "minor holy place" where many of the rituals of the Jewish year are performed. Although FESTIVAL and Sabbath prayers take place in the synagogue, most specific observances are performed at home: lighting CANDLES, the festive meal, studying the weekly Torah portion, singing Sabbath hymns, blessing the children, offering hospitality to guests, etc. Above all, the home is the place where Jewish values are passed from parents to children. Educators today have concluded that even an intensive Jewish EDUCATION could prove meaningless if the child encounters different standards in the home.

HOMILETICS   The art of preaching. In the ancient world, the Torah was taught in two different ways. Scholars actively debated the HALAKHAH (Jewish law) in the academy, day in and day out. By contrast, on the SABBATHS, FESTIVALS, and other special occasions, the rabbis spoke to the general congregation, both the educated and non-educated. Their sermons dealt with matters of FAITH, ETHICS, morality, and social conditions. They were meant to inspire the listener as well as educate him. For this reason the ability of the preacher to capture the attention of the listener – to entertain and to instruct – was as important as the message. Homiletics is the art of this type of public teaching.

The Talmud and *Midrashim* have preserved much of this homiletic material in written form. Although the feeling of hearing a master preacher deliver his sermon is lost, the clever and entertaining way in which ideas were presented to the audience comes through to the reader. The *darshan* (preacher) used legends, examples from the lives of the sages, symbolism, imaginative stories from the Bible, and more to instruct the listener and hold his attention.

Throughout the centuries, up to and including modern times, preaching has become a type of profession. From the *darshan* of the talmudic era to the MAGGID of Europe in the late Middle Ages, able preachers were those who mastered the art of giving emotional and intellectual satisfaction to the listeners. Some were respected community officials; others traveled from community to community is search of a pulpit.

Today, many preachers have published their sermons in collections. This has created a vast literature available to rabbis and others. In fact, Jewish weekly journals usually include a written sermon that relates to the current Sabbath.

HOMOSEXUALITY   The Bible forbids sexual relations between males (Lev. 18:22); the sages extend the prohibition, though not the penalty, to lesbianism (*Yev.* 76a). Homosexual relations of both types fall into the category of the "abhorrent practices" of the Egyptians and the Canaanites (*Sif.* 9:8). The Bible is clear in calling homosexual relations between males an "abomination" punishable by death (Lev. 20:13).

Jewish law rejects the idea that homosexuality is a disease, or an acceptable alternate life style. It is condemned even when two adults mutually consent to live together in this way. There are those who distinguish between the homosexual act and the homosexual person. They believe that every effort should be made to convince people to change homosexual habits.

Today a number of "gay" congregations have formed in the United States and REFORM JUDAISM has officially accepted gay or lesbian marriages, as have fringe rabbis of the CONSERVATIVE movement, taking the more liberal view that people of different sexual orientations should be treated equally.

HORAYOT   ("Legal Decisions"). Tenth tractate (book) of the Order of NEZIKIN in the Mishnah. Its three chapters deal with the laws of accidental sins committed either by the individual or by the community. The Mishnah also discusses mistaken decisions passed by the court, among other subjects.

HOSEA   First of the 12 minor PROPHETS. Hosea prophesied during the reigns of Uzziah (769–733 BCE), Jotham, Ahaz, and Hezekiah (727–698 BCE), kings of JUDAH, and during the reigns of Jeroboam II and Menahem, kings of ISRAEL (784–737 BCE). About his personal life we know only that he is commanded in a vision to marry a prostitute, who symbolizes the Israelite's disloyalty to God. He marries Gomer, who bears him three children.

The Book of Hosea is made up of 14 chapters and 197 verses. The first three chapters compare Israel's flirtation with the Phoenician god, BAAL, to the flirtations of an adulterous wifes. Chapters 4–14 are prophecies of comfort.

BOOK OF HOSEA	
1:1–1:9	Hosea's marriage to an unfaithful wife
2:1–2:3	The restoration of Israel
2:4–2:25	God the spouse of Israel
3:1–3:5	Hosea's marriage
4:1–5:7	Reproaches aimed at corrupt priests, superstitious people, and idolatry
5:8–6:6	Rebuke of Israel and Judah
6:7–9:10	Rebuke of Israel for various sins including idolatry, civil strife, and lack of trust in God
9:11–10:15	Oracles based on historical sins of Israel
11:1–12:1	God's love for Israel
12:2–14:10	Divine judgment and call for repentance

The Talmud (*Pes.* 87a) states that Hosea, ISAIAH, AMOS, and MICAH all prophesied at the same time, and that the greatest of the four was Hosea.

HOSHANA RABBAH   The seventh day of SUKKOT. During each of the earlier days of the festival, a single verse of the HOSHANOT poem is said in the synagogue and the congregation makes a circle around the reader's platform carrying the FOUR SPECIES. On Hoshana Rabbah, the congregation circles the synagogue seven times, with a different stanza of the *hoshanot* recited each time. They then lay down the Four Species and take up a bunch of five willow branches for the remainder of the *hoshanot* prayer. At the end, they beat the willows on the ground three times or until some of the leaves have fallen off. This stands for man's dependence on RAIN.

In Jewish tradition, Hoshana Rabbah is considered the last possible day on which one can seek and obtain FORGIVENESS from God for the sins of the previous year. For this reason, the day is solemn, and the MORNING SERVICE has a similar mood to the HIGH HOLIDAY prayers.

HOSHANOT   Prayers in poetry form that begin with the word *hoshana* ("please save"). They are chanted on the SUKKOT festival. *Hoshana* is also the name given to the willow branches that the worshiper holds and then beats against the ground on HOSHANA RABBAH. In Talmud times, the Four Species were called *hoshanot*.

The *Hoshanot* prayers contain praises of God's ways and express a longing for REDEMPTION. The *hoshanot* that became part of the modern service were composed by Eleazar Kallir, by his teacher R. Yannai, and by later poets.

HOSPITALITY   (Heb. *hakhnasat orehim*). The patriarch ABRAHAM is known for his generous hospitality. We read in Genesis 18 that he welcomed travelers, who turned out to be angels. The Talmud (*Shab.* 127a) lists hospitality as a MITZVAH "whose fruit is eaten in this world, while the benefit remains for the world to come."

The rabbis teach us how to make guests feel comfortable. When they arrive, they should be treated with courtesy. Food should be brought to them as soon as possible, so that if they are poor and hungry they will not have to ask. The host must appear cheerful, even if he is troubled. Like Abraham, the host should attend to the guests himself.

For their part, the guests should express their appreciation to the host. There is a special place in the GRACE AFTER MEALS for guests to ask for God's blessing for the host and his family.

HOZER BI-TESHUVAH   See BA'AL TESHUVAH

HUKKAT HA-GOY   ("Law of the Gentile"). Term for various foreign practices that Jews are forbidden to imitate. Based on Lev. 18:3 and 20:23, Jews are commanded in the Bible not to "copy the practices" of their pagan neighbors (see IDOLATRY).

In the Talmud, such pagan customs are called *darkhei ha-Emori* ("the ways of the Amorites"). The particular customs range from alien beliefs to non-Jewish dress (see *Shab.* 67a–b; *Sanh.* 74a–b).

In the Middle Ages, additional activities were forbidden to Jews under the category of *darkhei ha-Emori*. RASHI forbade non-Jewish forms of public entertainment, such as theaters and horse races. MAIMONIDES included sorcery, ASTROLOGY, and copying Gentile dress and hairstyles (*Yad, Akkum*, 11:1–3). Jewish legal authorities emphasized the prohibitions against CREMATION and embalming, the mutilation and castration of animals, and using WINE made by non-Jews (for their rituals).

In modern times ORTHODOXY considers bareheaded worship, mixed seating for men and women during PRAYER, the playing of an organ in the synagogue, and prayers in languages other than Hebrew – all innovations of REFORM JUDAISM – to be examples of *hukkat ha-Goy*.

HULLIN   ("Unholy Things"). Third tractate (book) of the Order of KODASHIM in the Mishnah. It has 12 chapters that deal mostly with SHEHITAH, the ritual slaughter of animals for ordinary eating and all aspects of the DIETARY LAWS.

HUMANISTIC JUDAISM   (or Secular Humanistic Judaism). A trend that sees Judaism as the civilization of the Jewish people, rather than a religion. Since the EMANCIPATION, more and more Jews identify with the Jewish people but less so its religious ideas. Humanistic movements appeal to those who identity with Judaism in ways other than through FAITH and religious practice.

Followers of Secular Humanistic Judaism hold that the belief in God does not make sense. For them, the Bible and the writings of the sages were the products of a developing civilization and of a people that tried to adapt itself to changing conditions. Judaism – because of its wide range of influences – lacks a consistent moral philosophy. For Secular Humanists, moral values can be found in a general human moral sense that has been influenced by Jewish culture. They place the individual and not a Supreme Being in the center of the human world.

HUMILITY   One of the virtues most admired by Jews since biblical times. The Bible (Num. 12:3) describes MOSES as a "very humble man, more so than any other man on earth." Because of his humility, the rabbis state he was worthy of receiving the Torah. Numerous passages praise humility, including Psalm 37:11: "The humble shall inherit the land" (see also Ps. 147:6; Prov. 11:2). The prophet Micah (Mic. 6:8) writes that man is required "to do justice, and to love goodness, and to walk modestly with God." According to the rabbis (*Mak.* 24a), this verse could stand for the whole Torah and "walking modestly with God" is the highest Jewish ideal.

The Talmud is filled with statements in praise of humility. R. AKIVA advised: "Take your seat a little below the one due

**RABBINIC TEACHINGS
ABOUT HUMILITY**

Why are the words of the Torah likened to water, wine, and milk (Isa. 55:1)? The answer is: Just as these liquids are kept only in the simplest of vessels, so those holy words are preserved only in the men of humble spirit.

Holiness leads to humility and humility to the fear of sin.

Man's prayers are only effective when he regards himself as dust.

Let a man be ever humble in learning Torah and performing good deeds, humble with his parents, teacher, and wife, with his children, with his household, with his kinfolk near and far, humble even with the heathen in the street, so that he may become lovingly regarded on high and deservedly respected on earth.

Good deeds performed modestly are more enduring than those performed with a fanfare of publicity.

Humility displayed for the sake of approval is the worst form of arrogance.

---

to you, for it is better to be told 'Come up!' than 'Go down!' (Lev. R. 1:5). There are, however, times when humility is out of place: "Disciples of the wise should be proud enough to stand up in defense of the Law" (*Sot.* 5a).

HUMMASH   See PENTATEUCH

HUNA   (c. 216–c. 297). Babylonian *amora* (rabbi) of the second generation; student of RAV, whom he succeeded as head of the Sura Academy. Under Huna, the academy grew to include 800 regular students, besides the many hundreds more that came on a temporary basis. He was the leader of Babylonian Jewry for 40 years, and his opinions were highly respected by the scholars of Erets Israel as well.

R. Huna is quoted widely in both the HALAKHAH and the AGGADAH. Literally hundreds of his statements are preserved. He died at an advanced age and was brought from Babylonia to Erets Israel for burial.

HUPPAH   See MARRIAGE

HUSBAND-WIFE RELATIONSHIP   See FAMILY; FAMILY PURITY

HYMN OF GLORY   See AN'IM ZEMIROT

I

IBN EZRA, ABRAHAM (c. 1092–1167). Spanish Bible commentator, poet, Hebrew grammar expert, philosopher, scientific writer, and medical doctor. At the age of about 50, Ibn Ezra left his native Spain and became a traveling scholar. During the next 25 years he wandered among many cities in the Middle East, Italy, France, and England. He suffered from poverty and misfortune. In a poem that described his own bad luck he wrote: "Were I to deal in candles, / The sun would never set: / Were selling shrouds my business, / No one would ever die!"

His scholarship amazed people wherever he roved, and he left a lasting impression. Even so, he always had a bitter sense of exile from his native Spain. He wrote a great amount, both in Arabic and Hebrew, in an effort to spread Jewish knowledge wherever he went. His writings include several books on Hebrew grammar; a wide variety of secular poems; the well-know Sabbath song *Ki Eshmerah Shabbat*; and two short works of religious philosophy.

Ibn Ezra is best known as a Bible commentator. Only RASHI was a more popular commentator than he. His style was to write extremely briefly and to the point, but his observations about the language of the Bible are also often playful and witty. Ibn Ezra's views of Jewish thought are scattered through the many comments that he wrote on the Bible. He believed that the most important duty of man is to pursue the knowledge of God. He disapproved of those who mixed secular learning with Jewish scholarship, those who challenged the authority of the rabbis (see KARAITES), and those whose biblical interpretations were too symbolic. He believed that a straightforward understanding of the grammar of the Hebrew language of the Bible was the key to its meaning. Perhaps his boldest statement was that the last eight verses of the Bible, which describe the death of Moses, were written much later than the rest of the Bible, which we are told was written down by Moses himself.

IBN EZRA, MOSES (c. 1055–after 1135). Spanish Hebrew poet. He was born and raised in Granada, into a wealthy and cultured family. He formed a lasting friendship with the poet JUDAH HALEVI. After Granada was conquered by fanatical Muslim Almoravides, he fled to Christian Spain. There he remained a suffering wanderer for the rest of his life.

Ibn Ezra wrote both secular and religious poetry. His secular poems are mostly found in his *Sefer ha-Anak* ("Necklace Book"), where he writes about love, wine, and nature. He wrote over 200 PIYYUTIM (prayer poems), many of which have become part of the High Holiday service in Sephardi and other congregations. He was so skilled at writing *selihot*, poems that beg for God's FORGIVENESS and for closeness to God, that he became known as *Ha-Salah* ("Writer of *Selihot*").

IBN GABIROL, SOLOMON (c. 1020–c.1057). Spanish Hebrew poet and philosopher. Little is known of his life, except that he was born in Malaga, Spain, and raised in Saragossa. He began to write poetry as a young man and became well known for both his secular and religious poetry. His secular works include poems on the subjects of love, drinking, nature, and ethics. His religious poems show brilliant mastery of the Hebrew language, deep and serious religious feeling, tremendous respect for God, and strong identification with the suffering of the Jewish people as well as hope for future redemption. His holy verses have been included in the PRAYER BOOKS of all Jewish groups. The Sephardi service for the DAY OF ATONEMENT includes his most famous poem, *Keter Malkhut* ("Royal Crown").

Ibn Gabirol's work of ethical behavior, *Tikkun Middot ba-Nefesh* ("Improving Moral Qualities"), was originally written in Arabic and translated into Hebrew. It is a popular work that discusses what benefits and what harms the human soul.

IBN ZIMRA, DAVID BEN SOLOMON (known as the *Radbaz*; 1479–1573). Scholar of Jewish law (HALAKHAH) and MYSTICISM. He was born in Spain but moved to Safed in Israel at the age of 13, after the Jews were expelled from Spain. He later moved to Jerusalem. He spent 40 years of his life in Egypt, where he served as Chief Rabbi. Ibn Zimra settled many legal disputes and brought about important changes in the Jewish community. In 1552 he returned to Israel and served as DAYYAN (rabbinic judge) in Safed for the remainder of his life. By this time he was considered the leading rabbi of his day and received questions on Jewish law from scholars in Israel, Greece, Africa, and Italy. He wrote over 3,000 RESPONSA in answer to these questions. Although he also studied Jewish mysticism, he believed that the proper practice of Jewish law was more important. Even so, he was usually lenient in his interpretation of the law.

His many writings include: a commentary on MAIMONIDES' *Mishneh Torah*, a mystical commentary on the SONG OF SONGS, a work on methods for studying the TALMUD, and an explanation of the 613 COMMANDMENTS.

IDOLATRY (Heb. *avodah zarah*, lit. "foreign worship"). The forbidden practice of worshiping "graven images" made of wood, stone, metal, etc. Worship of such objects, and of many gods, was widely practiced among peoples of the ancient world. The Bible clearly forbids idolatry. Most clear is the warning in the TEN COMMANDMENTS: "You shall have no other gods besides Me … you shall not make for yourself a graven image or any likeness of anything that is in the heaven above or on the earth below … you shall not bow down to them or serve them" (Ex. 20:3–5). The SHEMA prayer, which is said twice daily, further warns: "Beware that your heart not be seduced and you go astray and worship foreign gods and bow down to them" (Deut. 11:16).

Idolatry is one of the three most serious sins in Judaism, along with INCEST and MURDER. A person must allow himself to be killed rather than practice idolatry. A Jew is not permitted to do business with an idolater or to sell land in Erets Israel to one. An entire book of the Talmud, AVODAH ZARAH, deals with laws and statements designed to keep Jews from idolatry. In yet another book of the Talmud we read: "Whoever rejects idolatry, it is as though he accepted the entire Torah" (*Yoma* 69b). One of the best-known stories from the MIDRASH tells how ABRAHAM, the first to believe in one God, smashed the idols in his father's idol shop when he was still a young boy.

Despite the seriousness of the sin of idolatry, the Israelites unfortunately violated it many times during their early history. When MOSES disappeared from the people for 40 days to ascend Mount SINAI and receive the TORAH, the Israelites built a GOLDEN CALF to worship in God's place. The PROPHETS warned both the kings and the people time and again to stop worshiping foreign gods and to return to MONOTHEISM – the belief in only one God.

ILLEGITIMACY The Hebrew term that us usually translated as "illegitimate child" is "*mamzer,*" but its meaning is quite different from the English word "bastard." A *mamzer* is the child of either INCEST or ADULTERY, which are forbidden sexual unions. The child of an unwed mother is not a *mamzer* and has no negative status in Jewish law.

The Bible states that "a *mamzer* shall not be admitted into the congregation of the Lord" (Deut. 23:3). The rabbis understood this to mean that a *mamzer* could not marry another Jew. The rabbis were aware of the problem of punishing a child for the sins of the parents. They held that God promised, "I will comfort them in the future life" (Lev R. 32:7). In addition, the rabbis ruled that the status of *mamzer* would only apply if the forbidden relationship between the parents was clearly proven and not merely suspected. There are rabbis who suggested that we not investigate too closely into whether or not a person is

a *mamzer*, but rather assume the best about everybody. They also found a solution: a *mamzer* may marry either another *mamzer* or a convert to Judaism (*Kid.* 72b; see CONVERSION). The children of such marriages would then be legitimate. Aside for the limitation in marriage, a *mamzer* is a full Jew in all other regards; he or she is expected to follow all other Jewish laws and may participate in all Jewish celebrations and ceremonies.

In most cases today, *mamzer*s are born when a woman remarries who has not first received a legally valid Jewish DIVORCE (*get*). The second marriage is considered a relationship of adultery. A civil divorce is not sufficient to end a marriage between two Jews, even if the first marriage ceremony was not a religious one. Reform Judaism does not require a Jewish divorce before remarriage and does not consider the child of the second marriage to be a *mamzer*. Even so, non-Reform Jews are not permitted to marry such children.

IMITATION OF GOD (Lat. *imitatio Dei*). The belief that a person should try as much as possible to follow in the moral ways of God. It is based on the biblical idea that man is created in the image of God (Gen. 1:26, 27). In speaking about ABRAHAM, God says in the Bible: "For I have known him in order that he may command his children and his household after him, that they may keep the way of the Lord to do righteousness and justice" (Gen 18:19). The Bible commands people to "be holy, for I the Lord your God am holy" (Lev. 19:2). The commandment "… to walk in His ways" (Deut. 11:22, 28:9) became the basis for the Jewish law that requires people to try to imitate God and His caring and righteous ways to the best of their ability. The Talmud gives some specific examples: "as He clothed the naked [Adam and Eve] (Gen. 3:21), so shall you clothe the naked; as he visited the sick [Abraham] (Gen. 18:1), so shall you visit the sick; as He comforts mourners [Aaron] (Lev. 16;1), so shall you comfort those who mourn; as He buried the dead [Moses] (Deut. 34:6), so shall you bury the dead (*Sot.* 14a).

The idea of imitating God has been important to Jewish thinkers throughout the ages. For example, the rabbis of the MUSAR MOVEMENT, which emphasizes proper behavior, wrote a great deal about it.

IMMORTALITY OF THE SOUL   See SOUL

IMPURITY   see PURITY, RITUAL

IM YERTSEH HA-SHEM ("God willing"). Popular Hebrew phrase that expresses the hope that something will take place in the future as planned. Since observant Jews believe that all is in the hands of God, they add this phrase to their announcement of any future plans.

INCENSE (Heb. *ketoret*). The smoke from a SACRIFICE that was burned on the ALTAR in the TEMPLE. There were two types of incense. One came entirely from burning frankincense (Lev. 2:1), a spice that was used together with some of the meal-

Incense burners from Tel Zafit and Tel Amal, two excavation sites in Israel, dating from the 11th–10th century BCE.

offerings. The other was made up of 11 spices that were ground to a powder. They were mixed together according to a secret formula that was known only to one family of PRIESTS. That formula has now been lost to us, and Jewish law forbids anybody else from trying to copy it. Incense was offered twice daily, in the morning and just before the evening, and was burned on a special "incense altar." Only the priests were permitted to offer incense (Num. 17:5).

INCEST Sexual intercourse between two people who are too closely related to marry legally (Lev. 18). The Bible lists the women whom a man is not allowed to marry: mother, stepmother, sister, granddaughter, aunt, daughter-in-law, sister-in-law, stepdaughter, step-granddaughter, and a wife's sister while the wife is still alive (the latter applied when men were allowed to have more than one wife). MAIMONIDES explains that these are the people who generally live together in the family home, which certainly was true in times when extended families tended to live together. Females as well as males are forbidden to commit incest.

Incest is considered a very serious crime in Judaism, and it carries the death penalty (see CAPITAL PUNISHMENT) or the punishment of being "cut off" by God (see KARET). A person

is supposed to allow himself to be killed rather than commit incest.

INDEPENDENCE DAY OF ISRAEL (Heb. *Yom ha-Atsma'ut*). The anniversary of the declaration of the State of Israel on the fifth day of the Hebrew month of IYYAR (April/May) 1948. It was declared a religious holiday by the CHIEF RABBINATE of Israel, which considers the establishment of the Jewish state to be a miracle. Special religious services are held on the day, for which new prayers were written. HALLEL, the series of psalms praising God that are recited on Jewish holidays, is said by most congregations. The Orthodox kibbutz movement added additional prayers, such as the joyful SHE-HEHEYANU blessing and the BENEDICTIONS for HALLEL. A small minority of anti-Zionist Jews, who do not believe that a Jewish state should exist before the MESSIAH comes, either ignore the holiday or consider it a day of mourning.

In Israel, the day just before Independence Day is a national day of remembrance (*Yom ha-Zikkaron*) for those Israeli soldiers who fell in battle and for those who have been killed in terrorist attacks. MEMORIAL PRAYERS are recited, memorial candles are lit in homes, and the next-of-kin visit military cemeteries. Many Israelis participate in memorial ceremonies, and a moment of silence in observed throughout the country while a special siren is sounded.

INGATHERING OF THE EXILES (Heb. *kibbuts galuyyot*). The idea that God will gather together all of the Jews who are scattered throughout the world to Israel at a time of future REDEMPTION. The PROPHETS spoke frequently of these beliefs during the time when the Israelites were in exile (GALUT) in Babylonia in the sixth century BCE. According to Isaiah, the exiles of the Jewish people will be assembled "from the four corners of the earth" (11:11–12). Ezekiel believes the promise of redemption will be fulfilled if the people keep the COMMANDMENTS.

The important idea of *kibbuts galuyyot* made its way into the PRAYER BOOK. In the AHAVAH RABBAH prayer we ask God to "Bring us in peace from the four corners of the earth and lead us proudly to our land." The tenth blessing of the weekday AMIDAH prayer asks God to "sound the great ram's horn for our freedom, raise the banner to assemble our exiles, and gather us together from the four corners of the earth."

In modern Israel, the idea of *kibbuts galuyyot* became part

The Ingathering of the Exiles: the theme chosen to illustrate a leather case for the Book of Ezra. Sketch by Meir Gur-Arie, 1925.

of the state's Declaration of Independence. Many religious Jews believe that the mass immigration of Jews from over 100 countries since the state was founded is a fulfillment of the promise of the prophets.

INHERITANCE   The laws of inheritance were first laid down in the Bible: A firstborn son receives a double portion of the inheritance (Deut. 21:17). If a man dies without a son, then his daughter receives his property. If he has no children at all, the property goes to his brothers. If there are no brothers, it goes to his nearest relative from his own family, since the rabbis ruled that property should remain in the family. Despite these rulings, a person can get around the biblical laws by giving the property as gifts to others. This desire must be written and properly signed in a will, unless it is a deathbed request (*BB* 151b). In the Middle Ages, laws written for various communities modified the biblical laws somewhat.

The rabbis ruled that a husband inherits from his wife but a wife does not inherit from her husband (*BB* 8:1). However, a wife is provided for by her KETUBBAH (marriage contract). Upon the death of her husband, the wife collects the sum mentioned in the *ketubbah*, or may continue to live in the family home and be supported from the estate as long as she remains a widow (*Ket.* 4:13).

In the Diaspora today, inheritance is governed by the laws of the land (see DINA DE-MALKHUTA DINA). In the modern State of Israel, the law allows daughters to inherit equally with sons, and a wife is entitled to half of her husband's estate.

INSANITY   In Jewish law, an insane person (*shoteh*) is considered completely incompetent and without any responsibility. The *shoteh* is not required to follow any commandments, is not permitted to testify in court or to enter into any business agreements, is not held responsible for any damage that he or she causes, and may not marry or divorce.

The rabbis listed symptoms of insanity: wandering out alone at night, remaining overnight in a cemetery, tearing one's clothes (*Hag.* 3b). Maimonides adds: "A *shoteh* not only walks about naked or breaks things or throws stones, but is one whose mind is deranged and is always confused about matters ..." (*Hilkhot Edut* 9:9). The rabbis also wrote about the condition of temporary insanity (*RH* 28a; *Ket.* 20a).

INTERFAITH RELATIONS   Jews have taken part in interfaith activity mostly with Christians (see CHRISTIANITY), largely since World War II. Dialogue with Muslims – or three-way talks among the three religions – has been very limited. This is partly because of the nature of Islam, which does not encourage friendship with members of other religions. It is also connected to political disagreements between Jews and Muslims about Israel and the Palestinians.

Before World War II there was almost no interfaith activity. Although modern Jewish thinkers, such as Moses MENDELSSOHN, Franz ROSENZWEIG, and Martin BUBER were open to Christianity, there were no parallel feelings about Judaism on the Christian side. Churches continued to maintain their anti-Jewish teachings and prayers (see ANTI-SEMITISM).

Only after the horrors of the HOLOCAUST became known did Christian attitudes change. Catholics and mainstream Protestant churches began to take responsibility for their anti-Jewish teachings, which had in many ways led to the Holocaust. Anti-Jewish beliefs and prayers were removed from textbooks and services, and positive Christian-Jewish relations were encouraged. Most, but not all, Christians stopped trying to convert Jews to Christianity. Eastern Orthodox churches have not changed their ideas regarding Jews.

Jews have responded to this new Christian thinking in various ways. Abraham Joshua HESCHEL pointed out that all human beings are connected and should communicate with one another. Many Orthodox leaders are opposed to interfaith activity. Joseph Baer SOLOVEICHIK felt that the complicated inner life of Jewish faith must not be exposed to the beliefs of others. Others are not willing to forgive the Christian world for centuries of oppression and murder. Still others fear that Christians still have a hidden agenda to eventually convert the Jews.

On the practical level, rabbis (usually non-Orthodox ones), priests, and ministers often work together on the community level. The media has also increased people's understanding of Jews and Jewish life and history in the world at large.

INTERMARRIAGE   Marriage between a Jew and a non-Jew. Intermarriage has been either frowned upon or forbidden in Judaism since the time of the Bible. We read about the local Canaanite tribes: "You shall not intermarry with them; do not give your daughters to their sons, nor take their daughters for your sons. For they will turn your children from following Me to worship other gods (Deut. 7:3–4). Intermarriage could lead to the extremely serious sin of IDOLATRY; prohibiting it made the Israelites into a tight-knit community. Despite the Bible's warning, there are numerous examples in the Bible of intermarriage, from MOSES to many of the kings of Israel.

When the Jews returned to Erets Israel from EXILE in Babylonia (5th cent. BCE), many of them began to marry local pagan women. Their leader, EZRA, forced them to divorce their "foreign" wives, and from then on intermarriage was banned by Jewish law. Rabbis were not permitted to perform such marriages, and the children were considered Jewish only if the mother was Jewish. Until recent years, parents would observe the laws and customs of MOURNING for a child who had intermarried.

The rise of non-Orthodox Judaism over the past 150 years has led to a tremendous increase in intermarriage. This has become a matter of grave concern to religious leaders. In the United States, the intermarriage rate has been over 50% since 1985. The majority of American rabbis still refuse to perform such marriages. However, a large number of REFORM rabbis will do so in order to keep the Jewish partner involved in Jewish life. Many Reform leaders accept the idea of PATRILINEAL DESCENT, meaning that they recognize the child of a non-Jewish mother and a Jewish father as a Jew. ORTHODOXY and the CONSERVATIVE movement would not consider such a child to be Jewish.

A marriage between a born Jew and a properly converted Jew (see CONVERSION TO JUDAISM) is not considered intermarriage; it is a Jewish marriage in every sense.

INTERMEDIATE DAYS OF FESTIVALS   See HOL HA-MO'ED

ISAAC   The second of the three PATRIARCHS, son of ABRAHAM, born when his father was 100 and his mother, SARAH, 90 years old (Gen. 21:5). His name (Heb. *Yitshak*) comes from the fact that Sarah laughed (*tsahaka*) when told that she would bear a child at her age (Gen. 18:12). After his elder half-brother, Ishmael, made fun of Isaac, Ishmael and his mother, Hagar, were banished from Abraham's household (Gen. 21:9ff.), although later, when Abraham died, his sons came together to bury him (Gen. 25:9).

When Isaac was a young man, God told Abraham to offer him as a sacrifice (Gen. 19:1–19). Isaac's readiness to permit this is praised by the rabbis, and his readiness to die for God was the model for many Jews who preferred martyrdom to violation of Jewish law (see AKEDAH). The rabbis believed that Isaac was 37 years old at the time (Gen. R. 56:8). They also taught that the news about the intended sacrifice caused Sarah's death (*Pirkei de-Rabbi Eliezer* 32).

When Isaac was 40 years old, Abraham sent his servant, Eliezer, to his family in Mesopotamia, where Eliezer found REBEKAH, whom he brought back to marry Isaac (Gen. 24). As Rebekah had difficulty having children, both she and Isaac prayed to God, who granted them twins, JACOB and Esau. Isaac was 60 years old when his sons were born (Gen. 25:19–26).

In his later years, Isaac's eyesight failed him. It was then that Jacob, at the urging of Rebekah, posed as Esau and received Isaac's blessing as the firstborn (Gen. 27). Isaac died at the age of 180 and was buried by Jacob and Esau in the Cave of Machpelah, where his parents had been buried (Gen. 35:27–29).

According to tradition, Isaac started the afternoon prayer (*Ber.* 26b).

ISAIAH   (Heb. *Yeshayahu*). One of the major PROPHETS of the Bible. He prophesied in the late eighth century BCE in JUDAH, during the reign of four kings: Uzziah, Jotham, Ahaz, and Hezekiah. At the time, the kingdom of Judah was under pressure from the alliance of Syria with the Northern Kingdom of ISRAEL, and from Assyria.

We have only limited information about Isaiah's life. He began prophesying in the year that King Uzziah died (733 BCE; Isa. 6:1). Some scholars believe he was a PRIEST, because of his knowledge of TEMPLE rituals. He may have come from a noble family, because he seemed comfortable in the kings' courts. He is one of the few prophets who had devoted students (Isa. 8:16). According to Jewish tradition, he was killed by King Manasseh (698–642 BCE).

Isaiah bitterly criticized the sinful moral life of the people. He warned them that their sacrifices were meaningless if they were unkind to the weaker members of society. He urged them to trust only in God and not to form political alliances with other nations. The Israelites will be punished for their sins, but a small remnant will keep the COVENANT with God in the Land of Israel. His best-known vision is of a time when the lion shall lie down with the lamb and the sword will be beaten into a plowshare for farming. It has inspired many in the Western world. (See also ISAIAH, BOOK OF.)

ISAIAH, BOOK OF   First book in the PROPHETS section of the Bible. It is traditionally the record of the prophecies of ISAIAH, son of Amoz. The book has 66 chapters and 1,295 verses. Many modern scholars believe that it was actually written by more than one prophet, and that only chapters 1–39 are the work of Isaiah, son of Amoz. However, various attempts have been made to prove that the book is indeed the work of a single author.

BOOK OF ISAIAH	
1:1–6:13	Denouncing the sins of Israel
7:1–11:16	Encouraging people to look to God to save them from Assyrian armies
12:1–12:6	Hymn of thanksgiving
13:1–23:18	Prophecies against Babylon, Philistia, Moab, Syria, Egypt, Arabia, and Tyre
24:1–27:13	Universal prophecies
28:1–35:10	Prophecies of comfort and rebuke
36:1–39:8	Account of Sennacherib's siege of Jerusalem
40:1–41:29	Prophecies of comfort and salvation
42:1–44:28	Passages about the "servant of the Lord"
45:1–48:22	God's power is shown through Cyrus and the fall of Babylon
49:1–55:13	Hymns of Jerusalem and Zion
56:1–59:21	Worship rituals of the restored community
60:1–60:22	Glory of the new Jerusalem
61:1–62:12	Consoling Zion
63:1–64:11	God's revenge and hymn of lamentation
65:1–66:24	God destroys idol worshipers but saves the faithful

According to the "two Isaiah" theory, the first Isaiah lived in the late eighth century BCE. His prophecies focus on warnings and visions of the disaster that will befall JUDAH. They take place at the time that the Northern Kingdom of ISRAEL is plagued by wars and Jerusalem is almost captured by Assyria. The second Isaiah, often called "Deutero-Isaiah," lived during the EXILE in Babylonia or afterwards and made prophecies of hope and comfort.

Like other prophets, Isaiah condemned the moral failings of the people and called upon them to mend their ways. He summarized Jewish moral belief in two brief guidelines: "Observe what is right and do what is just" (56:1). His pleas seem to have fallen on deaf ears. He also talked about a future "Day of the Lord," when sin would be punished. The middle portion of the book contains prophecies against the various nations, when the enemies of Judah will be punished. Chapters 36–39 deal with the siege of Jerusalem by the Assyrians, which ends miraculously when King Hezekiah repents and changes his evil ways.

The second part of the book stresses hope, comfort, and a renewed relationship with God. It speaks about a time when the people recognize that their suffering was a punishment by God for past sins. God is hailed as the only God. Isaiah's message has always been an important one to the Jewish people. No less than 15 of the 54 yearly HAFTARAH portions read in the SYNAGOGUE on the SABBATH come from this book. All seven of the "haftarot of comfort" that follow the fast of TISHA BE-AV come from Isaiah.

ISHMAEL BEN ELISHA   (died c. 130 CE). Rabbi who helped keep Judaism alive, and even strengthened it, in the years following the TEMPLE's destruction (70 CE). As a child, Ishmael was a captive of the Romans and was ransomed by Rabbi Joshua ben Hananiah (see CAPTIVES, RANSOMING OF). His main teachers were Rabbi Joshua and ELIEZER BEN HYRCANUS. He engaged in many debates and discussions about Jewish law and tradition with Rabbi AKIVA, and these are recorded in the Talmud. Rabbi Ishmael's interpretations were as close as possible to the plain meaning (PESHAT) of the Bible. His best-known statement is: "The Torah speaks in the language of human beings" (*Ker.* 11a).

Ishmael is listed among the famous TEN MARTYRS executed by the Romans, about whom we read on the DAY OF ATONEMENT. His list of 13 ways to interpret the Torah was added to the daily MORNING SERVICE at an early date.

ISLAM   Religion of the Muslims, based on the Koran. It was founded by Muhammad in the seventh century and is based on a belief in one God. The word Islam comes from the Arabic word "submit," and Muslims are expected to submit to the will of God and the mission of Muhammed.

The basic belief of the religion is recited everyday: "There is no god but God (*Allah*) and Muhammad is his prophet." Faith is one of the five pillars of Islam. The other four are: praying five times daily, payment of charity, the month-long fast of Ramadan, and the pilgrimage to Mecca. Islam stresses that God is one. It teaches that God reveals Himself to humanity through prophets, beginning with ADAM and including NOAH, ABRAHAM, and others. God gave holy books to three prophets: the Law to MOSES, the Gospel to Jesus, and the Koran to Muhammad. Muhammad, as the last of the prophets, is the one chosen to bring God's final and complete message.

Muhammed was born and raised in Arabia, and both Jews and Christians lived there and influenced his thinking. According to the Koran, at the age of 40, in the year 610, he received a call from God through the angel Gabriel. He was commanded to become a prophet and bring a new Divine message to the world in the Arabic language. He was continually opposed in Mecca, where he lived. He traveled to Medina in 622 with some followers and became a political and religious leader there. In the next ten years, until his death, he conquered all of Arabia, and brought Jews, Christians and others under the rule of Islam.

Islam has borrowed much from Judaism, but with many changes. For example, Abraham (the father of Judaism, according to the Bible) is considered by Islam to be neither Jew nor Christian but the "friend of God." He is the first true believer in God and therefore the first Muslim, who submitted without question to the will of *Allah*. Both Judaism and Islam are based on law, have a central written text with a tradition of ORAL LAW based upon it, and consider study of the holy texts to be like worship. Both religions have laws of PURITY and cleanliness and foods that one is not permitted to eat or drink.

Strictly speaking, as "People of the Book," Jews are not considered nonbelievers, since they believe in the one God. However, Jews are officially treated as second-class citizens at best in most Muslim countries, because they do not accept the mission of Muhammad. At worst, Jews have been violently attacked, driven out of their homes, and murdered throughout their history of living with Muslims. See also DHIMMI LAWS.

ISRAEL   The name given to Jacob after he wrestled with an angel of the Lord all night (Gen. 32:29). It means "you have struggled with God." Later, Jacob's 12 sons were known as the Children of Israel, or the ISRAELITES. The land of CANAAN also became known as the Land of Israel (see ISRAEL, LAND OF).

After the death of King Solomon, when the ten northern tribes formed their own state, it became known as Israel (see ISRAEL, KINGDOM OF). In May 1948, when the modern Jewish state was established, it was given the name Israel. Today, all citizens of the State of Israel are called Israelis, no matter what their religion.

ISRAEL, KINGDOM OF   The northern kingdom in the divided state of the Israelites (928–722). Israel was one country under the first three kings SAUL, DAVID, and SOLOMON. After the death of Solomon, his son Rehoboam took over the throne. Jeroboam led a rebellion against him, and the northern section of the country broke away into a separate kingdom, called Israel. The new kingdom included ten of the Israelite tribes – all except the tribes of Judah and Benjamin. These remaining two tribes became the southern kingdom of JUDAH.

Rehoboam set up central places of worship at Dan and Beth El to challenge the centrality of the Jerusalem TEMPLE in the south. The capital city was at first Shechem, and later Tirzah. The kingdom was almost constantly at war with Judah, as well

KINGS OF ISRAEL	
Jeroboam	928–907 BCE
Nadab	907–906
Baasha	906–883
Elah	883–882
Zimri	882
Timri	882–878
Omri	878–871
Ahab	871–852
Ahaziah	852–851
Jehoram	851–842
Jehu	842–814
Jehoahaz	814–800
Jehoash	800–784
Jeroboam II	784–748
Zachariah	748–747
Shallum	747
Menahem	747–737
Pekahiah	737–735
Pekah	735–733
Hoshea	733–724

as with surrounding peoples. Its kingship was unstable, and kings changed frequently, often through violence. King Omri finally strengthened Israel by establishing friendly relations with the surrounding nations and Judah. This was achieved by marrying his daughters and granddaughters to princes from these countries. Unfortunately, these marriages also brought IDOLATRY to Israel, since the foreign wives wished to build altars to their national gods. Prophets such as AMOS and HOSEA rose up to issue sharp warnings to the people and their kings about the religious and social decay of Israel. They warned that if the idolatry continued, God would destroy the country. They also harshly criticized the wealthy residents of Israel, who took advantage of the weaker members of society and "oppressed" and "crushed" the poor.

During the last years of Israel, King Pekah formed an alliance with other nations against Assyria and also made war against Judah. Assyria fought against Israel for several years until the kingdom fell in 722. The land became a province of Assyria, and its Jewish inhabitants were exiled (II Kings 17:6). See also TRIBES, TEN LOST.

ISRAEL, LAND OF   (Heb. Erets Yisrael). The land that God promised to ABRAHAM for his descendants (Gen. 12:7), also known as the Promised Land. There are several conflicting descriptions in the Bible of the borders of the land. It also varied considerably in size throughout the ages and under different rulers.

In the Bible we read that the grandson (JACOB) and great-grandchildren of Abraham went to Egypt during a drought and remained there for 400 years. After many years of slavery, MOSES

brought the people out of Egypt to return to the Promised Land. Joshua led the people into Canaan, as it was called at the time, and the Israelites conquered much of it from the Canaanite tribes in the 13th century BCE. The territory was divided among the 12 Israelite tribes, and it became known as the Land of Israel. The Israelites lived in Israel continuously until they were sent into EXILE by conquering nations. The northern kingdom of ISRAEL was conquered by Assyria in 722 BCE and the southern kingdom of Judah was conquered in 586 BCE. About 50 years later, the Israelites were permitted to return to the Land of Israel from Babylonia, but many chose to remain there.

For the next six centuries, Jews lived in the Land of Israel under Persian, Syrian, independent, and Roman rule. In 70 CE, the Jerusalem TEMPLE was destroyed and they were sent again into exile by the Romans. The name of the country was changed from Israel to Palestine, after the ancient Philistine people that once lived in the region. Jews continued to live in Israel, mainly in the northern Galilee region, for a few more centuries. However, by the 7th–8th centuries, very few Jews remained, due to economic hardship and Christian persecutions (see ANTI-SEMITISM). However, there were always at least a small number of mostly very religious Jews living in Israel. Toward the end of the 19th century, the modern ZIONIST movement grew, and Jews began to return to their homeland. This led to the creation of the State of Israel in 1948.

According to Jewish law, the Land of Israel is holy. It was first made holy by Joshua when he conquered it. It declined in holiness during times when it was ruled by foreigners, but the holiness returned along with the Jewish people. Jews would therefore often travel great distances and take great risks in order to visit Israel, or at least to die there. Jews living abroad would try to buy a small bag of soil from the Land to be placed in their graves. Special religious AGRICULTURAL LAWS apply to parts of the land that were under Jewish rule during the time of the Second Temple. The great medieval legal expert, NAHMANIDES, believed that all the COMMANDMENTS were really given for the sake of those who live in the Land of Israel. Those living outside the land observe the commandments only so they will know what to do when they finally arrive in Israel. Different opinions exist among the sages about whether one is required by Jewish law to live in Israel.

The Land of Israel is central to Jewish life and prayer all over the world. The three PILGRIM FESTIVALS are celebrated by Jews in all countries according to the agricultural cycle and seasons of Israel. Prayers for Rain and Dew (see RAIN, PRAYERS FOR) are recited in keeping with the rainy season in Israel.

In the 19th century, the REFORM MOVEMENT broke away from the general feeling among all Jews that the Land of Israel is central and holy to Jews. Reform Jews took all mention of it out of their prayers, claiming that it is preferable to concentrate on spreading holiness among the people of the world rather than focusing on a Jewish country. This stand was reversed in recent years, and now the Reform movement supports Zionism. ORTHODOXY and the CONSERVATIVE movement all support

Sightseeing in the north of Israel.

modern Zionism and share in the hope of a Jewish return to the Land. A small minority of ultra-Orthodox Jews believe that the MESSIAH must come before Jews reestablish a Jewish homeland in Israel.

ISRAEL, RELIGION IN THE STATE OF   Ever since the EXILE of the Jewish people from Erets Israel (see ISRAEL, LAND OF) under the Romans, the desire for the INGATHERING OF THE EXILES – a mass return to the land – has been part of Jewish hopes and prayers. Maimonides taught in his code that "The days of the MESSIAH will be the period when the power to rule Israel is restored to the Jewish people, and they return to Erets Israel" (*Melakhim* 11–12). When the modern State of Israel was created in May 1948, the CHIEF RABBINATE ruled that it qualified to be described as "the beginning of the flowering of our redemption." This phrase became part of a prayer for the State that is said in SYNAGOGUES on the SABBATH and FESTIVALS. Rabbi Abraham Isaac KOOK wrote about an ideal Jewish state that would be dedicated to spiritual perfection. He saw this as the goal of ZIONISM. Most religious Jews share these ideas.

The minority that is reluctant to see the State of Israel as a sign of religious REDEMPTION feels this way for several reasons: (1) the belief that the Messiah will come under completely miraculous circumstances, and that human political activity cannot bring him; (2) the tradition from the Talmud that the people of Israel are not meant to reclaim the Land by force; (3) the fact that the leaders of the state may be nonobservant and even anti-religious Jews.

The first Basic Law of the State of Israel, the Law of Return, recognizes that all Jews are potential citizens of the state. A Jew who moves to Israel automatically becomes a citizen, in keeping with the ancient Jewish tradition "every Jew has a portion in Erets Israel" (*Otsar ha-Ge'onim, Kid.* 60–63). When the state was established religious Jews were a minority; however, almost all were Orthodox (see ORTHODOXY). They demanded that a number of laws be enacted to safeguard the religious character of Israel. Their demands were met, mostly to avoid creating a divide between religious and non-religious Jews. As a result, the DIETARY LAWS, the Sabbath, and festivals are officially observed in all areas of public life in Israel. The official observance of these laws does not conform precisely to *halakhah* (Jewish law), but rather is a compromise. Although Israeli government law is separate and different from the *halakhah*, some important principles from Jewish law – such as fair employment practices – have been built into Israeli law.

Rabbinical courts (see BET DIN) have complete authority in the areas of MARRIAGE and DIVORCE for Israel's Jewish population. Religious councils in each area of the country take care of the religious needs of the population, such as synagogues, ritual baths, burial, and cemeteries. A public (Orthodox) religious school system operates throughout the country alongside the secular public school system. Generous state aid is also given to private ultra-Orthodox schools, which teach religious subjects more intensely. Tens of thousands of young adult students from all over the world study in Israel's many *yeshivot* (Talmud academies).

The religious establishment has been in the hands of Orthodoxy since the pre-state British Mandate period. It has actively opposed the introduction and growth of non-Orthodox religious movements in Israel. Even so, beginning in the 1960s, REFORM and CONSERVATIVE Jews began coming to Israel in relatively small numbers and establishing congregations. These movements continue to grow, but are still a small minority of Israel's Jewish religious population. The non-Orthodox movements receive none of the government funding enjoyed by Orthodox religious institutions.

ISRAELITE   The earliest name for a member of the nation formed by the 12 sons of JACOB, the "Children of Israel." It was the name used throughout Bible times.

By the time Jacob's many descendants left Egypt (see EXODUS), they were called *Benei Yisra'el,* the "Children of Israel," or "Israelites." Sometimes they were called just "Israel." When the tribes were divided between the kingdoms of JUDAH and ISRAEL (10th cent. BCE), the word *Yehudi* ("Judahite") began to be used for those living in the Southern Kingdom. Later, after the fall of the Northern Kingdom (722 BCE) people from Judah also became known as Israelites. The name "Yehudi" was eventually shortened to "Jew," which became the common name for members of the nation.

ISRAEL MEIR HA-KOHEN   See HAFETS HAYYIM

ISRU HAG   (lit. "bind the festival offering"; used today to mean "day after the festival"). The day following each of the three PILGRIM FESTIVALS is a minor holiday. While the Temple stood, people who had made a pilgrimage there for PASSOVER, SHAVU'OT, or SUKKOT would be returning home on that day still in a holiday mood. Sometimes people stayed an extra day in Jerusalem to offer a personal sacrifice (see SACRIFICES AND OFFERINGS). Today mourning practices are limited on *isru hag.*

ISSACHAR   See TRIBES, TWELVE

ISSERLEIN, ISRAEL BEN PETAHYAH   (1390–1460). Jewish legal authority in Central Europe; also known as Rabbenu Isserlein. Israel was born in Regensburg, Germany. His father died while he was a child, and he was raised by his mother and her brother, a leading Austrian rabbi. His mother and uncle were among a large group of Jews burned at the stake in Vienna on 12 March 1421. For the next four years he led a wandering life in Italy and Germany. He served as rabbi in two Austrian

cities and achieved wide recognition as a gifted POSEK (Jewish legal authority) who answered the questions of other rabbis.

His greatest work was *Terumat ha-Deshen* ("The Offering of Ashes," 1519). It contained hundreds of RESPONSA to questions of other rabbis about dealing with the many horrible tragedies faced by Ashkenazi Jews of his day (see ANTI-SEMITISM). Subjects included: forced conversion, APOSTASY (denying belief in God), traveling disguised as a non-Jew, relations with non-Jews, and moving to Erets Israel. He based his legal decisions on the earlier rabbis of the Talmud and the *ge'onim* rather than on rabbis who lived in later centuries. He had a tremendous influence on the development of Jewish law among ASHKENAZIM.

ISSERLES, MOSES BEN ISRAEL   (known as the *Rema*; c. 1525–1572). Jewish legal authority and writer of law codes. Isserles came from a wealthy family. He studied in Lublin, Poland, under the famous scholar Shalom Shakhna. Isserles' father built a synagogue in Cracow in honor of his son, known as the Rema Synagogue. It survived the Nazi Holocaust and is still active today.

Isserles founded a *yeshivah* (Talmud academy) in Cracow, where he paid his students' living expenses and tuition out of his own pocket. He became the head of Cracow's rabbinical court (BET DIN) and a well-known POSEK who answered legal questions sent by other rabbis. Joseph CARO, author of the SHULHAN ARUKH, was his friend and colleague.

Isserles' most important work, called *Ha-Mappah* ("The Tablecloth"), set the standard for Jewish practice among ASHKENAZIM. It was a detailed commentary on the *Shulhan Arukh* ("The Set Table"), which focused mainly on laws and CUSTOMS of SEPHARDIM. He also wrote many other important works, some of which were published years after his death. These include: *Torat ha-Hattat* (1569) on the DIETARY LAWS, a volume of RESPONSA with answers to rabbis' questions, commentaries on the law codes of other leading rabbis. He had a broad knowledge of philosophy, history, and astronomy as well as of HALAKHAH (Jewish law) and MYSTICISM. He brought all this knowledge together in deciding matters of *halakhah.*

Isserles was greatly honored and respected by Polish Jewry. On his tombstone, which still stands in the courtyard of the Rema Synagogue, is written: "From Moses [Maimonides] to Moses [Isserles] there has been none like Moses."

IYYAR   Second month of the Jewish religious CALENDAR; eighth month of the Hebrew civil year, counting from TISHRI. It has 29 days and falls either in April or May. In the Bible (1 Kings 6:1, 37), this month was called Ziv ("glory" or "splendor"), since it comes in the spring. Its Babylonian name, Iyyar, means the same thing. King Solomon began the building of the Temple on the second day of Iyyar. The minor festival of LAG BA-OMER falls on the 18th day. Two modern Jewish holidays, Israel's INDEPENDENCE DAY (5 Iyyar) and JERUSALEM DAY (28 Iyyar), which celebrates the liberation of Jerusalem in 1967, are also celebrated in this month.

J

JACOB (Heb. *Ya'akov*; later also called Israel). The third of the PATRIARCHS, son of ISAAC and REBEKAH. At the age of 130, Jacob said to Pharaoh: "Few and evil have been the days of the years of my life" (Gen. 47:9).

The Bible tells the story of Jacob's life, from his birth to his death. He was born holding on to the heel of his twin brother, Esau (*ekev*, hence the name *Ya'akov* = Jacob; Gen. 25:25–26), and from that moment on the brothers were rivals. The brothers developed into very different types of people; Esau was a hunter and Jacob preferred to remain in his tent (Gen. 25:27). The rabbis interpreted this to mean "tents of Torah" (see Rashi on the verse).

Twice Jacob took what should have belonged to his elder brother. The first time Esau sold his birthright to Jacob for a "mess of pottage" (bowl of lentil soup; Gen. 25:29–34), and the second time Rebekah helped Jacob trick Isaac into giving him the blessing of the firstborn (Gen. 27). Fearing Esau's anger, Rebekah sent Jacob to the home of her brother, Laban, in Mesopotamia (Gen. 32:10).

On his way to Mesopotamia, Jacob dreamed of a ladder reaching to the heavens, with angels going down and up. God stood beside him and promised to give the Land of Canaan to him and to his descendants. When Jacob arrived, Laban, who

Jacob dreaming of a ladder with angels ascending and descending. Detail from a prayer book binding. Austria, 18th century.

promised to give his daughter RACHEL to Jacob as a wife at the end of seven years, put him to work. When the time came, Laban tricked Jacob into marrying his daughter LEAH instead of Rachel, which forced him to work an additional seven years to marry Rachel. After he was paid for his work, Jacob returned to Canaan a wealthy man (Gen. 31).

As Jacob approached Esau's territory, he divided his camp in two, hoping that if Esau attacked, at least one group would be saved. On the night before the brothers were reunited, Jacob fought with an angel, who renamed him Israel (Gen. 32:25–30). Jacob's meeting with Esau was peaceful, and Jacob gave his brother many gifts (Gen. 33:1–15).

Jacob had 12 sons and a daughter from his two wives and his concubines, Bilhah and Zilpah. These were the fathers of the Twelve TRIBES. His favorite wife, Rachel, died giving birth to her youngest son, Benjamin, and was buried near Bethlehem (Gen. 35:16–22).

Jacob was not to know peace. He favored his son JOSEPH, whose jealous brothers sold him into slavery in Egypt. The brothers showed Jacob Joseph's coat stained with the blood of an animal. Jacob believed that Joseph had been killed by a wild animal, and could not be comforted (Gen. 37).

Later, Joseph who had become a powerful official in Egypt, forced the brothers to bring Benjamin, the youngest, with them to Egypt. Only afterwards did Jacob learn that Joseph was still alive, and that he ruled Egypt.

Jacob spent the last 17 years of his life in Egypt. He died at the age of 147, but before his death he asked his sons to bury him in the Cave of Machpelah in Hebron, Erets Israel. Jacob died after blessing his sons, who brought his body back to Canaan as he had asked (Gen. 49:29–50:13).

According to the Talmud, Jacob established the evening prayer service (*Ber.* 26b).

JACOB BEN ASHER (known also as *Ba'al ha-Turim*; c. 1270–1340). Codifier (see CODIFICATION) and Bible commentator. He was the son of ASHER BEN JEHIEL, who taught him HALAKHAH (Jewish law) when they were still in Germany. In 1303, they fled to Spain. Jacob preferred to study; therefore he did not accept a position as a rabbi and lived in poverty. His first important work, *Kitsur Piskei ha-Rosh* ("Abridgement of the

Page from the section Orah Hayyim *("The Path of Life") from Jacob ben Asher's* Arba'ah Turim *("Four Rows"). Italy, 1435.*

JACOB JOSEPH OF POLONNOYE   (c. 1710–c. 1784). Student of the BA'AL SHEM TOV and the first Hasidic author to be published (see HASIDISM). Jacob Joseph was already an important rabbi when he met the Ba'al Shem Tov. Once it became known that he was a Hasid, he was force to leave his rabbinical position in Shargorod, Ukraine. Eventually, he became the MAGGID (preacher) of Polonnoye, after Aryeh Leib. Jacob Joseph fought with DOV BAER, the Maggid of Mezhirech (whom he never mentions in his writings), over the right to succeed the Ba'al Shem Tov. He never founded a Hasidic dynasty of his own, but he was the one who passed on the teachings of the Ba'al Shem Tov directly.

His works included *Toledot Yosef* (1780), *Ben Porat Yosef* (1781), and *Tsafenat Pane'ah* (1782).

JEREMIAH   (7th–6th cent. BCE). Second of the three major prophets in the PROPHETS section of the Bible. He was born in Anathoth, a small village of priests. He lived in Jerusalem during the fall of the Assyrian Empire, Babylonia's rise to power in the Ancient Near East, and the destruction of the TEMPLE and the Kingdom of JUDAH by the Babylonians. He received his prophetic call in 626 BCE, which covered the reigns of the last kings of Judah.

His political message was to submit to the Babylonians and make the most of the captivity. This made the rulers and the people of Israel extremely angry. They persecuted him as a traitor, and once he almost lost his life. He accused the people of wickedness and accused the spiritual leaders of falsehood and hypocrisy. He taught "not to glory in wisdom, might, and wealth, but in the service of God, Who is just" (Jer. 9:23–24).

Because he insisted that it was pointless to resist the Babylonians, Jeremiah was not exiled to Babylonia with the rest of the elite (see EXILE, BABYLONIAN). After the assassination of GEDALIAH, the other leading Jews who remained in Jerusalem fled to Egypt, forcing Jeremiah to come with them. He is last heard denouncing the Jews of Egypt for idolatry.

According to Jewish tradition, Jeremiah wrote the Book of LAMENTATIONS and possibly the Book of KINGS. See also JEREMIAH, BOOK OF.

JEREMIAH, BOOK OF   Second book in the PROPHETS section of the Bible. It is made up of 52 chapters and 1,365 verses and tells the story of JEREMIAH and his prophecies, from 626 until 580 BCE. Originally, the prophecies were oral, but were later written down because of King Jehoiakim's hostility towards Jeremiah. Jeremiah dictated 20 years' worth of prophecy to his scribe, Baruch, who wrote them on a scroll. Jehoiakim showed his hatred for Jeremiah by cutting up the scroll and burning it. Jeremiah therefore dictated his prophecies once more, adding to them (see ch. 36).

It is hard to identify the major themes of the book. One message is that the nation of JUDAH had rejected God, who would therefore punish them by sending Babylonia against the kingdom of Judah. Jeremiah urged them not to resist the

Decisions of Rabbi Asher"), was a book on his father's Talmud commentary that included only the halakhic decision and not the discussion.

Jacob Ben Asher is famous mostly for his great code of Jewish law, called the *Arba'ah Turim* ("Four Rows"), popularly known as "the *Tur*." This code is based on the *Mishneh Torah* by MAIMONIDES, but leaves out all laws that apply to worship in the TEMPLE. It is divided into four parts: (1) Orah Hayyim ("The Path of Life") on the day-to-day laws of the Jewish religion, from when a person wakes up in the morning until he goes to sleep at night; (2) *Yoreh De'ah* ("The Teaching of Knowledge") on DIETARY LAWS, family PURITY, oaths (see VOWS), charging interest, and MOURNING; (3) *Even ha-Ezer* ("The Stone of Help") on MARRIAGE and DIVORCE; (4) *Hoshen Mishpat* ("The Breastplate of Judgement") on legal procedures. It was written in a clear simple style and took into account both the Ashkenazi and the Sephardi traditions. Many commentaries were written on the *Arba'ah Turim*, and Joseph CARO used its structure to write his *Bet Yosef* and SHULHAN ARUKH.

Ben Asher's commentary on the Bible is printed in most editions of the PENTATEUCH under the title *Ba'al ha-Turim*.

BOOK OF JEREMIAH

Babylonians to avoid a disastrous siege. The book also contains a number of prophecies that included dramatic actions, such as burial of a linen waistcloth and its retrieval, breaking a potter's vessel, and offering wine to Rechabites, who were forbidden to drink wine.

JERUSALEM (Heb. *Yerushalayim*). Capital city of Israel and holy city of the Jewish people. During King DAVID's time (c. 1000 BCE), the city was called Jebus, after the Jebusites who lived there. Although the name Jerusalem does not appear in the PENTATEUCH, the city of Salem in Genesis (14:18) is probably the same as Jerusalem. Traditionally, Mount Moriah, where the AKEDAH (binding of ISAAC; Gen. 22:2) took place, is the sight where Jerusalem was later built.

Before the time of David, Jerusalem was a small and insignificant settlement far from the main roads of the time. When David conquered the city, he made it into his capital city after ruling in Hebron for six years (II Sam. 5:1–13). He probably did this because the city was in the center of his kingdom and did not belong to any particular tribe. Afterwards, the city is sometimes called the City of David (e.g., II Sam. 6:12) in the Bible.

David soon moved the ARK OF THE COVENANT to Jerusalem (II Sam. 6), his new capital. Later, the prophet Gad told David to build an altar on land near the city. David bought the land from Araunah the Jebusite, although Araunah wanted to give it to him as a gift (II Sam. 24:18–25). This site is believed to be the TEMPLE MOUNT, where SOLOMON, David's son, later built the first TEMPLE and made Jerusalem the city of God (I Kings 7).

The Jerusalem Temple became the only place where Jews were permitted to bring SACRIFICES, and they made PILGRIMAGES to the city three times a year (on the PASSOVER, SHAVU'OT, and SUKKOT holidays) to offer the FESTIVAL sacrifices (Ex. 23:17; Deut. 16:16–17). This became an important part of the national culture during the First and Second Temple periods. During the Second Temple period, pilgrims came from outside of Israel as well, and the pilgrimages continued even after the Temple was destroyed, in 70 CE (*Ned.* 23a). It was customary to tear one's clothing in mourning for the destruction of the Temple when seeing the WESTERN WALL of the Temple Mount. The Jews continued to visit Jerusalem whenever it was permitted.

As the city was chosen by God, Jerusalem symbolizes Judaism's greatest values and hopes. ISAIAH calls Jerusalem

Jerusalem as seen from the Mount of Olives. Fragment of a pictorial map of the Holy Land. Germany, 1483.

"the city of righteousness" and teaches that "from Zion will go forth teaching, and the word of God from Jerusalem" (Isa. 1:26, 2:3). JEREMIAH prophecies that in the future, "Jerusalem will be called 'Throne of the Lord' and all the nations will assemble there" (Jer. 3:17). Jerusalem was also known for its beauty. The Talmud says that one who has not seen Jerusalem in her glory has not seen a beautiful city in his life (*Suk.* 51b). The MIDRASH tells that ADAM was created from the earth at the site of Jerusalem's altar (*Pirkei de-Rabbi Eliezer* chap. 31).

According to HALAKHAH (Jewish law), the entire Land of Israel is holy and the city of Jerusalem is holier still. The holiest place on earth, the Temple's inner chamber (see HOLY OF HOLIES), was in Jerusalem.

After Jerusalem was destroyed in 70 BCE, it remained a symbol of spirituality and religion. It is customary for Jews to leave a small section of their home unfinished or a potion of a wall unpainted in memory of Jerusalem (*Sh. Ar., OH* 560:1). Whenever and wherever Jews pray, they face Jerusalem. The text of GRACE AFTER MEALS includes a prayer for the rebuilding of Jerusalem, and the psalm recited before Grace on weekdays includes the vow, "If I forget thee, O Jerusalem, let my right hand forget her skill" (Ps. 137:5). The AMIDAH, recited three times a day, contains an entire paragraph begging God to return to Jerusalem, rebuild the city, and reestablish the kingdom of David. There are three fast days each year to mourn the different stages of the destruction of Jerusalem, the most important one being on the Ninth of Av (TISHAH BE-AV).

The rabbis taught that one day, God would rebuild Jerusalem and its Temple and never destroy it (*Tanh. Noah* 11). Jews have always wanted to be buried on the Mount of Olives because it was close to the Temple Mount and would save them travel time when Jerusalem was rebuilt and the dead were reborn (see RESURRECTION). The Passover SEDER and the DAY OF ATONEMENT Service both end with the words "Next year in Jerusalem."

Since David conquered Jerusalem, it has changed hands many times. It was probably in ruins just after the first destruction in 586 BCE, until the Return to Zion 40 years later. From the time of EZRA until the second destruction in 70 BCE, it remained the capital of JUDAH. In 70 CE, the Romans burned the Temple and only the outside walls remained. According to Jewish law, Jews could not enter the actual Temple site; therefore a portion of the Western Wall became the closest they could get to the Temple. The Western Wall (*Kotel Ma'aravi*) became a favorite place to pray and mourn. After the BAR KOKHBA revolt against the Romans in 132 CE, the Jews were not permitted to enter Jerusalem. From this point on, Jews could visit Jerusalem only if the rulers allowed it.

Because Jesus spent his last days in Jerusalem, it became CHRISTIANITY's holy city. According to Muslim tradition, Jerusalem was important in the life of Muhammad and it became their third holiest city, its Arabic name being *El-Quds* ("the holy one"). In 1099, the Jews living in Jerusalem were massacred by Crusaders. In 1187, the city was reconquered by

the Muslims and Jews were allowed to return. The city was controlled by the Turks until 1917.

In 1917, Erets Israel was awarded to the British, since Turkey was on the losing side in World War I. By this time Jerusalem had grown beyond the walls of the Old City. During the 1948 War of Independence, the Old City was captured by the Jordanian Arab Legion, and most of the Jews living there were expelled. They moved to the western part of the city, which was controlled by the Jews. The city remained divided for the next 19 years. During this time the Jews were not allowed to visit the Western Wall or the Old City, and many synagogues were destroyed.

When the State of Israel was formed in 1948, it declared Jerusalem its capital, and built its parliament (the Knesset) and government buildings there. On 7 June 1967, the city was reunited during the Six-Day War (see JERUSALEM DAY). Nowadays, there are many archeological excavations, as well as a residential neighborhood, in the Old City of Jerusalem. The State of Israel guarantees access to people of all religions to Jerusalem's holy places.

JERUSALEM DAY   (Heb. *Yom Yerushalayim*). Annual celebration in Israel and Diaspora communities of the reunification of Jerusalem during the Six-Day War (7 June 1967). On that day, the Israel Defense Forces reunited the "Old City" of Jerusalem (which had been under Jordanian rule) with the "New City." All of Jerusalem was ruled by Jews for the first time since Second Temple period.

The 28th of Iyyar (7 June) became an official day of celebration in Israel. In most congregations, the entire HALLEL Service is recited.

JERUSALEM TALMUD   See TALMUD

JEW ("WHO IS A JEW?")   Disagreement over who is a member of the Jewish people. According to traditional Jewish law (HALAKHAH), a Jew is someone who is born of a Jewish mother, or who has converted according to *halakhah*. Halakhic CONVERSION requires CIRCUMCISION for males and ritual immersion for both men and women, as well as accepting Jewish law as a way of life. In the first half of the 19th century, the REFORM movement did not require its converts to be circumcised or to immerse, only to commit themselves to being faithful Jews. Orthodox circles did not accept these Reform converts as Jews. Recently, the Reform movement decided that a child of a Jewish father (and a non-Jewish mother) is also to be considered Jewish (the PATRILINEAL DESCENT ruling). Both CONSERVATIVE and Orthodox communities object to this decision. The Orthodox rabbis also disagree with the way the Conservative rabbis follow the *halakhah*, and therefore question their conversions.

Secular Jews see being Jewish more in terms of belonging to a nation than to a religion. They say that anyone who becomes a part of the Jewish people is to be considered Jewish. The Jewish religion is only part of being Jewish, and not necessarily the most important part.

In Israel, the question of "Who is a Jew?" takes on a political and practical aspect. The Law of Return allows any Jew to immigrate to Israel and automatically receive Israeli citizenship. At first, the law allowed anyone who considered himself a Jew to immigrate under the Law of Return. Later, the law was redefined, and only applied to a person having at least one Jewish grandparent (which had been the Nazis' definition of a Jew; see HOLOCAUST). Two cases then defined the issue more precisely. The first was case of Brother Daniel, who was born Jewish, but converted to Catholicism and became a monk. He demanded the right to receive Israeli citizenship under the Law of Return. The High Court of Israel ruled that any person who chose to give up the history and destiny of the Jewish people, though halakhically Jewish, is not eligible for citizenship under the Law of Return.

A second case eventually led to a change in the wording of the law. Benjamin Shalit, who had married a non-Jewish woman, demanded that his children be registered as Israeli citizens. As the law did not specify differently, the High Court ruled that the children had to be registered as Jews.

As it stands today, any convert to Judaism, whether the rabbi who performed the conversion was Orthodox, Conservative, or Reform, may immigrate to Israel under the Law of Return. As part of the negotiations in the Israeli government, religious parties often try to change the law so that it applies only to those who have converted under an Orthodox rabbi. While such a bill has been submitted many times, it has never won the required majority, so it has never passed.

Many see the attempt to make Conservative and Reform conversions invalid as aimed at making Orthodox Judaism the only legitimate way. As a result, these attempts at changing the law have been opposed by non-Orthodox Jews outside of Israel. Many feel that should the law be changed, it could cause a gap between Israel and the Diaspora.

JEWISH LANGUAGES Those forms of national speech that Jews have used in the course of their history. HEBREW is the holy language in Judaism, because the Bible, Mishnah, and rabbinic literature all use Hebrew. ARAMAIC is also holy, though less so than Hebrew, because the Talmud, some of the MIDRASH, and the ZOHAR are written in Aramaic. Both were spoken languages before the destruction of the Second Temple. Today Hebrew is once again the national language of the Jewish State. Jews in the Diaspora spoke a number of different languages, adapting each language to suit their needs. Hebrew and Aramaic terms were often used, and sometimes they used Hebrew letters instead of other alphabets. This is how new Jewish languages were created.

Judeo-Arabic was originally spoken by warlike Jewish tribes in the sixth century, but became popular after the Muslims conquered Western Asia. The language survived the expulsion of the Jews from Spain in 1492. Many important rabbis, such as SAADIAH GAON, BAHYA IBN PAKUDA, IBN GABIROL, JUDAH HALEVI, and MAIMONIDES wrote in Judeo-Arabic. Judeo-Berber was a language spoken in Algeria, Morocco, and Tunisia, including communities that spoke Judeo-Arabic.

Judeo-Persian was developed in the 13th century in Persia (Iran today), and was revived in the cultural and religious revival around the year 1900. The Jews who settled around the Crimea spoke Krimchak, while the KARAITES (breakaway sect of Judaism) in the same area spoke Judeo-Tatar.

Judeo-Greek probably dates back to Second Temple times, and was a spoken and written language until the Nazi Holocaust.

Judeo-Italian was developed in the Middle ages, and many important Jewish books were translated into this language. It is used until today, mainly within the old "ghetto" of Rome.

Judeo-Spanish, also known as *Ladino,* and Judeo-Portuguese, became the main languages of the Sephardim in the Diaspora, after 1492. It was the mother tongue and religious language of the Jews living in the Ottoman Empire. Textbooks for schools, novels, poetry, newspapers, and dramatic works, as well as religious books such as *Me-Am Lo'ez,* a Bible commentary by Jacob CULI, were written in Judeo-Spanish.

Judeo-Provençal, spoken in the provinces of southern France, was mostly the local language with a Hebrew touch. Judeo-French was also basically the Old French language spoken by Ashkenazim living in Northern France and the Rhineland. Many important works were full of Judeo-French words, such as the commentaries of RASHI and SAMUEL BEN MEIR. When the Jews were expelled from the Valois lands in 1394, the language died out, and was replaced by Judeo-German (see YIDDISH).

JEWISH LAW See HALAKHAH

JOB, BOOK OF The third book of the HAGIOGRAPHA ("Writings"), part of the WISDOM LITERATURE, divided into 42 chapters and 1,070 verses. The theme of the book is the mystery of why righteous people suffer and the question of the correct response to suffering.

The book begins with Job, a righteous man who is wealthy and has a large family. The SATAN suggests that God test Job by making him suffer and then see if Job would continue to be so righteous. Job loses all of his wealth and his family, but his faith remains strong: "Naked I came from my mother's womb, and naked I shall return there; the Lord gave, and the Lord has taken away; blessed be the name of the Lord" (Job 1:21). The Satan is not satisfied, and suggests that God cover Job with boils. Job still remains faithful to God. At the end of the book, Job has a new family, and his wealth is doubled (ch. 41–42).

The book includes several important dialogues about why a person suffers. First, Job and his three friends try to explain why bad things suddenly happened to Job. The friends thought that Job must have sinned. Job insists that he is innocent and should not be suffering. God later enters the discussion and tells Job that he cannot expect to understand the ways of the Lord.

BOOK OF JOB

1:1–1:5	The wealth of Job
1:6–1:12	Satan's challenge
1:13–2:13	The trials of Job; the arrival of the friends
3:1–3:26	Job's lament
4:1–14:22	First round of dialogue between the three friends and Job
15:1–21:34	Second round
22:1–27:23	Third round
28:1–28:28	In praise of wisdom
29:1–31:40	Job's final speech
32:1–37:24	The speeches of Elihu
38:1–42:6	Speeches of God and the submission of Job
42:7–42:17	Job's wealth is restored

The rabbis of the Talmud did not all believe that Job actually existed (*BB* 15a–b). Some thought that the story was a parable, meant to teach a lesson about good and EVIL and REWARD AND PUNISHMENT. Some rabbis thought Job had lived in the time of ABRAHAM; others thought he had lived in the time of MOSES or the Babylonian EXILE. The rabbis also disagreed whether Job was Jewish or whether he was even righteous.

According to the Talmud, the HIGH PRIEST read the Book of Job before the DAY OF ATONEMENT. Sephardim read it on TISHA BE-AV, the fast in memory of the destruction of both TEMPLES. The Book of Job is one of the few books the rabbis allowed people in MOURNING to study.

Opening page of the Book of Job, showing Job with his wife and friends. From an illuminated manuscript. Italy, 15ᵗʰ century.

JOEL   Second of the Minor Prophets in the PROPHETS section of the Bible. Nothing is known about the prophet's life. His prophecies mention JUDAH and JERUSALEM, so it is safe to assume that he preached in Judah. The book begins with a plague of locusts. Joel calls upon the priests and the people to pray and repent. God promises that those who repent will be saved from disaster and those who do not will be punished. The nations who have persecuted the Jews will be punished.

According to Jewish sources, Joel lived at the time of King Menasseh of Judah and the prophets NAHUM and HABAKKUK. Modern scholars, on the other hand, believe that the book was written after the rebuilding of the Second Temple (515 BCE) and before the Persians conquered Sidon (348 BCE).

BOOK OF JOEL

1:1–2:17	The plague of the locusts, calls to repentance
2:18–2:27	Promise of deliverance
3:1–4:15	The Day of the Lord, judgment of the nations
4:16–4:21	Deliverance of Israel

JOHANAN BAR NAPPAHA   (c. 185–279 CE). Rabbi from Talmud times; the main authority in the Jerusalem Talmud, where he is mentioned more than any other rabbi. Born in Sepphoris, he studied under Hanina bar Hama and Hoshaya Rabbah. He established the ACADEMY in Tiberias, which attracted students from Babylonia. Johanan had memorized the sayings of the previous generations, so he was able to identify the authors of anonymous sayings in the Mishnah. He taught that a quote should include its author and made rules for solving conflicts of opinion in the Mishnah.

Rabbi Johanan often spoke of the joys of family life. He said, "One whose first wife dies is grieved as much as if the Temple had been destroyed" (*Sanh.* 22a). He lost ten sons during his lifetime. He taught that a scholar should be a model to others and stressed the importance of being humble, since "wherever God's power is mentioned in the Bible, reference is also made to His humility" (*Meg.* 31a).

JOHANAN BEN ZAKKAI   (1ˢᵗ cent. CE). Rabbi and leader of the PHARISEES in Jerusalem. He was a student of HILLEL. He abolished the ordeal of the wife suspected of adultery (Num. 5) because adultery had become so common. He was given the title *Rabban*, which was a higher title than Rabbi.

As leader of the Pharisees, Johanan was involved in many confrontations with the SADUCEES (the priests, who were members of a different sect). The Saducees thought that priests should have more privileges than regular citizens and that they should not have to pay the yearly TEMPLE tax (*Shek.* 1:4).

The Temple and TEMPLE MOUNT were at the center of religious and community life. Johanan's job was to supervise the Temple services and to make sure they were carried out according to the Pharisaic tradition. Sitting in the shadow of the Temple, he would teach the law all day long.

When the Jews revolted against the Romans (66 CE), Jerusalem was besieged. Johanan pretended to be dead, and had two of his students carry him out of Jerusalem in a coffin. Outside of the city, he was taken to the Roman camp, where he met Vespasian, the commander of the Roman troops. Johanan greeted him as King-Emperor, and Vespasian rebuked Johanan for giving him an undeserved title. While they were talking, a message arrived form Rome, saying that the Emperor Nero had died, and Vespasian was the new emperor. Vespasian was so impressed with Rabbi Johanan's prediction that he allowed him to make a request. Johanan said: "Give me Yavneh and its sages" (*Git.* 56a–b).

The Temple and Jerusalem were destroyed, but Johanan was able to move the SANHEDRIN to Yavneh. Johanan was the head of the court in Yavneh, as he had been in Jerusalem. He tried to discover the ethical ideas of the Jewish law.

JONAH Fifth of the 12 Minor Prophets in the PROPHETS section of the Bible. God told Jonah to tell the people of Nineveh that if they did not repent, the town would be destroyed within 40 days. Jonah did not want to do this because Nineveh was an enemy of the Israelites. Instead, he boarded a ship headed for Tarshish. On the ship a storm threatened to overturn the ship. The travelers drew lots to find out who was to blame for the storm, and the lot fell on Jonah. The men threw Jonah overboard, and the sea was calmed.

Jonah was swallowed by a great fish. He lived inside the fish's belly for three days and three nights, praying to God. Finally the fish spat him out on the shore. Jonah realized he had no choice but to go to Nineveh. The people of Nineveh fasted and repented and were saved. Jonah was not happy about this. God then made a plant grow near Jonah, then He made it shrivel up and die. Jonah was upset about the plant. God used this as a lesson to Jonah, for if he cared for a small plant which he had

BOOK OF JONAH	
1:1–1:3	Jonah flees from his mission and embarks for Tarshish
1:4–1:16	Jonah is blamed for the storm and thrown into the sea
1:17–2:10	He is swallowed by a fish, prays to the Lord from its belly, and is vomited forth on dry land
3:1–3:4	Jonah goes to Nineveh, foretells its destruction
3:5–3:10	The people of Nineveh repent and the Lord relents
4:1–4:5	Jonah calls on the Lord to fulfill His original intention
4:6–4:11	The Lord explains to Jonah why He relented

not even planted, how could God give up on a city of 40,000 people whom He had created?

The entire book is read in the AFTERNOON SERVICE on the DAY OF ATONEMENT, as a reminder of the power of REPENTANCE.

JOSEPH Elder son of JACOB and his beloved wife, RACHEL. Joseph was his father's favorite child (Gen. 37–50), which made his brothers very jealous. He has two dreams in which symbols of his mother, father, and 11 brothers bow down to him. The brothers then sell him into slavery and tell their father that Joseph was killed by a wild animal, bringing his coat dipped in goat's blood as evidence. Joseph is taken to Egypt and sold to Potiphar, the captain of Pharaoh's guard. Potiphar's wife tires to seduce Joseph, but when he rejects her, she accuses him of trying to rape her. Potiphar puts him in prison. In prison, Joseph earns a reputation as an interpreter of dreams. He successfully interprets Pharaoh's dreams, predicting a period of famine. Pharaoh frees him from prison and puts him in charge of preparing the country for the famine. He accomplishes this successfully, and is made second-in-command in Egypt.

The famine also affects Canaan, and Jacob's brothers come down to Egypt to buy food. They bow down to Joseph, not knowing his identity, and therefore his dream comes true. When he reveals himself to his brothers, he tells them to bring Jacob to Egypt to join them, and Jacob settles in the land of Goshen. Before Joseph's death at age 110, he makes his family swear that his bones will be buried in Canaan. MOSES fulfilled the request by taking Joseph's bones out of Egypt. He was buried by JOSHUA near Shechem (Josh. 24:32).

JOSHUA The son of Nun of the tribe of Ephraim; MOSES' successor and leader of the Israelites as they conquered the land of CANAAN. As Moses' assistant, Joshua led the war against AMALEK (Ex. 17:8–16). He was one of the 12 spies that Moses sent to Canaan. Later only he and Caleb were allowed to enter the Land of Israel because they did not bring back bad reports (Num. 13:6, 8, 14:6–8, 30, 38). After Moses' death, Joshua led the people of Israel into the land of Canaan. He crossed the Jordan as Moses had crossed the Red Sea. He set up an altar on Mount Ebal, where he read the blessings and curses as commanded by Moses. Joshua defeated 31 local kings while conquering the land of Canaan. He died at the age of 110.

In the Mishnah, Joshua was also the spiritual successor of Moses: "Moses received the Torah from Sinai and passed it on to Joshua" (*Avot* 1:1). See JOSHUA, BOOK OF.

JOSHUA, BOOK OF First book of the PROPHETS section of the Bible and a direct continuation of DEUTERONOMY. It tells how MOSES' successor, JOSHUA, led the 12 tribes of Israel to conquer the land of CANAAN and settle there. It begins with the preparations for entering Canaan, and tells about the crossing of the Jordan River, the conquering of different areas of the land, and the division of the land among the tribes. It describes the borders of the territories of the tribes, the cities of refuge and

Joshua leading the Israelites. Opening page of the Book of Joshua. From a 13ᵗʰ-century manuscript.

of the LEVITES, the building of the altar in Transjordan by the tribes of Reuven, Gad, and half of the tribe of Menasseh, and Joshua's death and burial.

The real hero of the conquest is the God of the Israelites, Who demonstrates great power. He is determined to evict

BOOK OF JOSHUA	
1:1–5:12	Crossing the Jordan, preparation for the conquest of the land
5:13–8:35	The conquest of the south (Jericho, Ai)
9:1–10:27	The conquest of the center of the country
11:1–12:24	The conquest of the north of the country
13:1–19:51	The division of the land among the tribes
20:1–21:4	The cities of the Levites and the cities of refuge
22:1–22:34	Two and a half tribes receive an inheritance in Transjordan

the Canaanites so that their IDOLATRY does not tempt the Israelites.

JOSHUA BEN HANANIAH   Rabbi of the Mishnah who lived at the time of the destruction of the Second Temple (70 CE) and was still living when Hadrian arrived in Erets Israel (130 CE). Whenever the Talmud mentions "Rabbi Joshua" it is referring to Joshua ben Hananiah. He was one of the five students of Rabbi JOHANAN BEN ZAKKAI and a LEVITE who served in the Temple before it was destroyed. He preached to the people not to rebel against Rome and to mourn the destruction of the Temple moderately (*BB* 60b). He was also against excessive strictness in observing the law (*Shab.* 153b). Rabbi Joshua established a small ACADEMY at Peki'in. He was humble and peace-loving and lived in poverty, making needles for a living.

A famous MIDRASH tells about a time when Rabbi Joshua disagreed with Rabban GAMALIEL, the president of the SANHEDRIN, as to the specific day of ROSH HA-SHANAH (New Year). Rabban Gamaliel ordered Rabbi Joshua to appear before him with his staff and moneybelt on the day that was the DAY OF ATONEMENT according to Joshua's calculations. Rabbi Joshua did so, although it meant desecrating what he insisted was the Day of Atonement. In another dispute between the two, Rabban Gamaliel made Rabbi Joshua stand rather than sit. This disrespectful treatment angered the people, who removed Rabban Gamaliel from his position. Rabbi Joshua took his place.

JUBILEE   (Heb. *yovel*). A special time that occurs every 50 years according to the Bible, in which slaves are released and property is returned to its original owners. The jubilee was observed after every seven cycles of the SABBATICAL YEAR (each cycle was seven years). The jubilee year began on ROSH HA-SHANAH (New Year). As it was written, when the SHOFAR (ram's horn) was blown at the end of the DAY OF ATONEMENT that year, "you shall proclaim the release throughout the land for all its inhabitants" (Lev. 25:9–10).

The laws of jubilee allowed each Jew to begin life anew on an equal basis. All land sold since the previous jubilee was returned to its original owners, the original families to whom the land had been assigned after JOSHUA conquered it from the Canaanites. All Jewish slaves had to be released and given enough money to allow them to begin a new life. These laws ensured that no individual would become excessively wealthy, nor would any Jew be reduced to poverty and slavery.

All of the agricultural laws of the Sabbatical year applied in the jubilee year. The laws of the jubilee year depended on all 12 tribes living in their own land; therefore the Jews who returned to the Land of Israel after the Babylonian EXILE no longer kept these laws.

JUDAH   See TRIBES, TWELVE

JUDAH, KINGDOM OF   The southern kingdom in the divided state of the Israelites (928–586). When king SOLOMON died in 928 BCE, the northern tribes rebelled and Solomon's son Rehoboam ruled in JERUSALEM over a smaller kingdom that included the tribes of Judah and Benjamin. The rest of the Land of Israel became the Kingdom of ISRAEL, which alternated between cooperating and fighting with the kingdom of Judah.

Rehoboam fought against his rival Jeroboam (king of the kingdom of Israel) all his days (I Kings 14:30). Rehoboam's son Abijah captured the southern hills of Ephraim from Jeroboam (II Chr. 13:13–19) and his son Asa (908–867) retook the region of Gerar from the Egyptians. He also uprooted IDOLOTRY and restored traditional TEMPLE worship (I Kings 15:9–24) and allied himself with Ben-Hadad I of Aram-Damascus to force Israel to withdraw from the area of Jerusalem.

Jehoshaphat (867–846) continued his father's ways, sending out priests to teach the book of the law (II Chr. 17:6). He made Judah a middleman of trade between the Arabian Peninsula and the coast and developed the port on the Gulf of Elath. Jehoram of Judah ended the peaceful era by killing off his brothers and a number of ministers in order to give himself more power. He reestablished the High Places and allowed the practice of idolatry in Judah. The prophet ELIJAH condemned him (II Chr. 21:4). While Jehoram was fighting against Shalmaneser, the Philistines and Arabian nomads invaded the kingdom and killed all of his sons except for Ahaziah, the youngest (II Chr. 21:16–17).

Ahaziah was killed by Jehu (king of Israel, II Kings 10:27). Athaliah (mother of Ahaziah) then killed off the entire royal family of the Davidic line in order to strengthen her hold on the kingdom of Judah. After Athaliah was assassinated in a revolt, Jehoash, Ahaziah's one surviving son, became king. During his long reign (836–798) the Temple was purified and the kingdom was saved from Hazael. After Jehoash's murder, his son Amaziah ruled another 30 years, assassinating his father's murderers and fighting against Edom. In a war against the Kingdom of Israel, he was assassinated, and his son Uzziah was crowned in his stead. During his long reign (769–733) the kingdom grew larger. Uzziah developed its agriculture and built public works. When he was struck with leprosy, his two sons Jotham and Ahaz ruled parts of the kingdom.

Jotham and Ahaz both cooperated with the Assyrians, although the prophet ISAIAH opposed this policy. Ahaz was forced to put an Assyrian altar in the Temple and pagan practices started up once again. When Ahaz died, Isaiah supported Hezekiah (727–698) in his effort to restore the worship of the Lord (Isa. 9:1–7). Hezekiah destroyed the idols and restored the Temple (II Kings 18:1; II Chr. 29:3). After fighting Babylon, Senacherib invaded Judah, exiling 200,000 people and putting Jerusalem under siege. Hezekiah had dug the Siloam tunnel from the Gihon spring beforehand; therefore he was able to save the city by providing water throughout the siege (II Kings 19:37; Isa. 36–37).

Hezekiah's son Menasseh served the Assyrians and worshiped idols. His son Josiah (639–609) restored the Temple in Jerusalem and his priest found a "book of the law" (probably the Book of DEUTERONOMY) and carried out a religious reform.

KINGS OF JUDAH	
Rehoboam	928–911
Abijam	911–908
Asa	908–867
Jehoshaphat	867–846
Jehoram	846–843
Ahaziah	843–842
Athaliah	842–836
Jehoash	836–798
Amaziah	798–769
Uzziah	769–733
Jotham	758–743
Ahaz	733–727
Hezekiah	727–698
Manasseh	698–642
Amon	641–640
Josiah	639–609
Jehoahaz	609
Jehoiakim	608–598
Jehoiachin	597
Zedekiah	596–586

Josiah destroyed the High Places, destroyed idols, and killed their priests. He was killed in a battle at Megiddo.

From 609, the kingdom of Judah was ruled by Egypt, then by Nebuhadnezzar of Babylonia (c. 603; II Kings 24:1). Jehoiakim (608–598) rebelled and Jerusalem was besieged in 598. In 597, his son Jehoiachin surrendered and along with the elite of the kingdom of Judah, was taken to Babylonia. He was replaced by his son Zedekiah, who also rebelled. The city was besieged for two years and then captured in 586. The Temple was destroyed and the population of Judah was exiled (see EXILE, BABYLONIAN).

JUDAH BAR ILAI (usually known just as Rabbi Judah; c. 100–c. 180 CE). Rabbi of the fourth generation of the Mishnah; student of Rabbi AKIVA and Rabbi Tarfon. He founded the ACADEMY in Usha and taught Rabbi JUDAH HA-NASI. He also helped reestablish the SANHEDRIN. Because of his many statements in the Mishnah, *Sifra*, and TOSEFTA, he was called *Rosh ha-Medabrim*, "the chief spokesman" (*Ber.* 63b; *Shab.* 33b). From his collection of statement, Rabbi Judah ha-Nassi was able to put together the standard Mishnah.

Rabbi Judah made his living by doing manual labor. Unlike many other sages, he believed that good deeds come before studying the Torah. He would interrupt his own studies to attend a wedding or funeral.

JUDAH HALEVI   (c. 1075–1141). Poet and philosopher. Born in Spain, he lived most of his life there and studied medicine, philosophy, Hebrew, and Arabic. He practiced medicine and did business successfully, and enjoyed a comfortable life. He lived at the time of the First Crusade, when many Jews believed that the MESSIAH was on its way. This may explain why, at the age of 60, Judah decided to leave his home, his wife, and his children to move to Erets Israel. He believed that a Jew could only live a complete life in the Holy Land. Judah remained in Egypt for a long time, and died there before reaching the Holy Land.

Judah Halevi was famous for his poetry. He wrote 800 poems in praise of friends, nature, and, most importantly, the Land of Israel. Some of his poetry became part of the prayer book (PIYYUTIM).

Judah Halevi wrote his religious philosophy in a book called *Sefer ha-Kuzari* ("The Book of the Khazars"). The book is a dramatic conversation between a Jewish scholar and the King of the KHAZAR tribe, which converted to Judaism at the end of the dialogue. He deals with the contradiction between philosophy and religious faith. He believed that philosophy applied to mathematics and logic, but not to psychology and religious belief. Only religious faith can give a person real satisfaction and bring him closer to God. The Torah and its commandments are the laws of human happiness.

The *Kuzari* is the first book that confronts CHRISTIANITY and ISLAM. Judah Halevi explains that prophecy is God choosing a messenger to make His will known. The PATRIARCHS were PROPHETS as were the great biblical prophets. Because of their devotion to God and the Torah, the Jews alone can be prophets, and the Land of Israel is the land of prophecy.

Letter written by Judah Halevi in Arabic (before 1075), addressed to a friend while both were in Spain. From the Cairo Genizah.

The *Kuzari* was very important to the Jews of that time, because it gave them answers to many of the questions that were troubling them.

JUDAH HA-NASI   ("Judah the Patriarch"; c. 138–c. 217 CE). Leader of the Jews in Erets Israel; son of Simeon ben GAMALIEL II, whom he succeeded. His teachers were JUDAH BAR ILAI, YOSE BEN HALAFTA, SIMEON BAR YOHAI, and Eleazar ben Shammua.

SAYINGS OF JUDAH HA-NASI

What is the virtuous path that man should follow? Whatever brings honor to his Maker and honor from his fellow man.

Be as careful in observing a light as a weighty commandment, for you do not know their relative reward.

Think about three things and you will avoid sinning: above you in Heaven is an eye that sees, an ear that hears, and all your deeds are faithfully recorded.

Fulfill God's commandments joyfully, just as Israel accepted the Torah at Sinai with joy.

I have learned much from my teachers, more from my colleagues, but most from my pupils.

Do not be deceived by the outward appearance of age or youth; a new pitcher might be full of good, old wine, while an old one might be empty altogether.

A man should respect his father and mother as he respects God, for all three are partners in creating him.

As NASI and head of the SANHEDRIN, Judah had almost unlimited authority. He appointed rabbinical court judges (see DAYYAN) and teachers. He made laws about the SABBATICAL YEAR and TITHES. He was also extremely wealthy, which strengthened his position. Another one of Judah's tasks was to act as the spokesman of the Jewish community before the Romans. He developed a friendship with the Roman ruler, Antonius.

Judah arranged the huge collection of the ORAL LAW into the MISHNAH. To do so, he collected information about the law, ethics, Jewish thought, and history from the leading rabbis of his time and edited, classified, and organized it. Some of the material that was not included in the Mishnah itself was collected by Judah's students into other collections, such as the TOSEFTA and the BARAITA. Later, the Jerusalem and Babylonian Talmuds were built on the basis of the Mishnah. Many of Judah's quotes appear in the Mishnah and other literature in the name of Rabbi, "The Master," for short.

Judah was extremely humble, although touchy when the dignity of his position was in question. He was jealous of his rival, the EXILARCH in Babylon, who was a more direct descendant of the house of David (TJ, *Kil.* 9:4, 32b). In his dying hour, he lifted both his hands to Heaven and swore that he had studied the Torah with all his strength, but he had not benifited from it even with his little finger. Judah was buried in Bet She'arim.

JUDAH HE-HASID (Judah ben Samuel ben Kalonymus he-Hasid, "the Pious"; c. 1150–1217). The most important thinker in the school of HISDEI ASHKENAZ, of the Kalonymus family. Judah lived first in the Rhineland and later in Regensberg.

Judah believed that a writer should never acknowledge the authorship of his writing, so that he and his descendants do not take too much pride in them. Therefore, none of his works contain his name, which makes it difficult to know what he actually wrote. He apparently wrote a book called *Sefer ha-Kavod* ("The Book of Glory") and a commentary on the prayers. His most important work, however, is the *Sefer Hasidim* ("The Book of the Pious"). He probably wrote the book in sections throughout his life, and it was combined into a book by his students after his death. This work deals with all areas of life and reflects Judah's idea of creating a movement of elite, extremely religious Jews, led by the Wise One (*he-Hakham*), who would separate themselves from the non-Hasidic communities. His students, especially Rabbi ELEAZAR OF WORMS, did not continue in the same direction, tending to stress the individual Jew's, rather than the community's, religious perfection.

JUDAH LÖW BEN BEZALEL OF PRAGUE (c. 1520–1609; known by his acronym as *MaHaRaL – Moreinu ha-Rav Leib*, "our teacher, Rabbi Löw"). Rabbi, mystic, and Jewish thinker. He was the author of many books on Jewish thought and mysticism. He also wrote many interpretations of the AGGADAH (folklore), including a major commentary on the different aggadic passages of the Talmud. He was also a mathematician and a friend of the astronomer Tycho Brahe.

Judah was a gifted teacher, who stressed the need to follow a curriculum suited to the age of the students. He taught that things should be in their natural order, and he saw living outside the Land of Israel as unnatural for the Jewish people.

According to Jewish legend, Judah had special powers which he used to create the GOLEM, a clay figure that came to life after he inserted a slip of paper with God's name into its forehead.

JUDAH MACCABEE (d. 160 BCE). Leader of the HASMONEAN (Maccabean) uprising after the death of his father, Mattathias. When Mattathias was dying, he chose his third son, Judah, to carry on the revolt he had started against the Syrians. Judah was an outstanding military leader. The title "Maccabee" ("hammer") was another name for the Hasmonean dynasty.

In the year 167 or 166 BCE, Judah began to lead the revolt. Despite his poorly prepared and poorly armed fighters, Judah won victory after victory, defeating the stronger Syrian-Greek forces.

By December of the year 164, the polluted, paganized TEMPLE in Jerusalem was purified and rededicated for Jewish use. This event is celebrated by the yearly festival of HANUKKAH. Judah had many more victories, but in 160 BCE, he was killed in battle.

In seven years, Judah had a string of military victories over the far stronger Seleucid empire. He also caused the anti-Jewish decrees to be removed and restored the heart and soul of the nation's religious independence, the Temple.

JUDAISM (Heb. *Yahadut*). The monotheistic faith (believing in one God) of the Jews. Judaism refers both to the religion and nationality of the Jews. It includes not only religious aspects, but is an entire "way of life" or "civilization." It makes even secular parts of life holy and is concerned with every detail of human life.

Judaism began with ABRAHAM, who came to the conclusion that there is one God (MONOTHEISM). From Abraham, the history of the Jewish people can be traced through the PATRIARCHS, to the slavery in Egypt, the EXODUS and the giving of the TORAH, the conquest of Canaan, the JUDGES, the monarchy and the later division into two kingdoms, the Babylonian EXILE and the return to Israel under EZRA and NEHEMIAH, the HASMONEANS, the destruction of the TEMPLE by the Romans, the scattering of the Jews throughout the world for centuries (see GALUT), the persectuion and pogroms, the HOLOCAUST, and the reestablishment of the Jewish state.

The two most important events in Jewish history were the Exodus from Egypt and the giving of the Torah at Mount Sinai. When the Jews were taken out of Egypt, they gained their freedom and became a nation. When they received the Torah at Sinai, they were given the laws that guide the Jewish people.

Judaism was the first purely monotheistic religion. Belief in one God replaced the worship of a group of gods, which was common among the peoples of the ancient world, up to and including the Greeks and Romans. Judaism is the "mother" religion of CHRISTIANITY and ISLAM.

Judaism sees itself as a universal religion, with different sets of rules for Jews and non-Jews. Non-Jews must observe only the seven NOACHIDE LAWS that were given after the FLOOD. These seven laws require belief in one God and setting up courts of law and forbid blasphemy, murder, theft, sexual immorality, and eating the limb of a living creature,. Jews must also observe all of the 613 COMMANDMENTS. A non-Jew who keeps all of the Noachide Laws is considered a righteous person.

Judaism deals mainly with practical laws that apply to this world, rather than THEOLOGY. Jewish belief includes concern for REWARD AND PUNISHMENT in an AFTERLIFE. REDEMPTION is earned through correct behavior, not through perfect FAITH, and man has an active role in the perfection of the world. Within the overall scheme of things, the people of Israel play the role of "light unto the nations" (Isa. 49:6). This is why the Jews see themselves as the CHOSEN PEOPLE, meaning chosen for their mission.

Judaism teaches that "all Jews are responsible for one another," and this led to a strong sense of community. No Jew has the right to look casually at the suffering of another Jew but must try to help in any way he can. Judaism teaches a very special kind of morality (see ETHICS). The BIBLE is full of demands to take care of a stranger's needs and to tend to the WIDOW AND ORPHAN. The Hebrew language has no word for CHARITY. The word that is used, *tsedakah*, is taken from the root meaning "justice." This shows that it is only just and proper for those who are fortunate to share with those who are not. One must give charity to the poor (see POVERTY), including leaving the corner of each field for them. The JUBILEE year, in which all land is returned to its original owner every 50 years, was also a way to make sure that no family was reduced to poverty.

Another important idea in Judaism is to raise the unholy to a state of holiness. For example, one must recite a BENEDICTION (blessing) before and after eating. This raises food to the holy state of the blessing.

Many have tried to divide Jewish law and belief into categories (see CODIFICATION). The Talmud states that the Pentateuch contains 613 commandments, 248 positive and 365 negative (*Mak.* 24a). It also says that DAVID reduced all the demands on the Jews to 11 principles, ISAIAH to six, and MICAH to three ("to do justly, to love mercy, and to walk humbly with your God," Mic. 6:8). The medieval scholar Moses MAIMONIDES taught that there are 13 PRINCIPLES OF FAITH in which a Jew must believe.

According to traditional Judaism, the ORAL LAW accompanies the WRITTEN LAW, and they were both given by God to the Jewish people at Mount Sinai. This principle was what caused sects to break away from mainstream Judaism, including the SAMARITANS, the SADDUCEES, and later the KARAITES. All three of these groups denied the authority of the Oral Law and relied only on the Written Law and their interpretation of it.

Mainstream Judaism, which developed from the PHARISEES, also sprouted different movements, such as MYSTICISM and HASIDISM, but until modern times, all of them accepted both the Written and Oral Laws. With Jewish EMANCIPATION (late 18th century), different Jewish movements arose. Among them was REFORM JUDAISM, which began in Germany and spread to other countries, especially the United States. Reform Judaism considers neither the Oral nor the Written Law to be the word of God. It sees them as a collection of eternal values inspired by God. CONSERVATIVE JUDAISM, which began as a movement in America at the beginning of the 20th century, is sometimes known as historical Judaism. It saw Judaism as a civilization that developed as a result of its history. The RECOSTRUCTIONIST movement sees Judaism as a developing religious civilization and spiritual nationalism. It believes that the basis of Judaism is its changing culture and the life of the group.

ZIONISM is a national Jewish movement rather than one based on religion. It holds that by making the Land of Israel into a Jewish state, the "Jewish problem" (persecution and hatred of the Jews) would be solved.

Some central elements of Judaism have changed over time. At first worship meant offering SACRIFICES at different High Places. Later it meant doing so at the TEMPLE in Jerusalem. After the Second Temple was destroyed, SYNAGOGUES were built as places for Jews to pray (see PRAYER). The BET MIDRASH, a study hall for Torah studies, also became popular from that time. EDUCATION has always been an important value in Judaism.

In Judaism, certain times are considered to be holy. The SABBATH is in memory of God's rest after creating the world. There are three PILGRIM FESTIVALS throughout the year: PASSOVER, SUKKOT, and SHAVU'OT, as well as ROSH HA-SHANAH and the DAY OF ATONEMENT. Later, more FESTIVALS and fasts (see FASTING AND FAST DAYS) were added to the Jewish CALENDAR.

The basic religious statement in Judaism, the SHEMA, is the verse in DEUTERONOMY: "Hear O Israel, the Lord is our God, the Lord is One" (6:4).

JUDEO-SPANISH   See JEWISH LANGUAGES

JUDGES, BOOK OF   Second book of the PROPHETS section of the Bible, named for the judges who judged Israel after the death of JOSHUA and until the Prophet SAMUEL was appointed. The judges' job was usually to lead the nation in war. The only judge who actually judged the people was DEBORAH.

The book begins with the conquest and settlement of the land of Canaan (parallel to the story in the Book of JOSHUA). Next come the stories of the different judges, which follow a certain pattern: Israel sins, God sends enemies who torment

	BOOK OF JUDGES
1:1–2:5	The conquest of the land of Canaan
2:6–3:6	Introduction to the era of the judges
3:7–3:11	Othniel
3:12–3:30	Ehud
3:31	Shamgar
4:1–5:31	Deborah and the Song of Deborah
6:1–8:35	Gideon
9:1–9:57	Abimelech
10:1–10:5	Tola and Jair
10:6–10:16	Preface to the Latter Judges
10:17–12:7	Jephthah
12:8–12:15	Ibzan, Elon, Abdon
13:1–16:31	Samson
17:1–18:31	The statue of Micah and the settling of the tribe of Dan in the north
19:1–21:25	The concubine of Gibeah and the war against the tribe of Benjamin

Opposite page: Engraved silver Hanukkah lamp from Poland, 18th century.
Overleaf: Fragment of the Book of Isaiah, from one of the Dead Sea Scrolls.

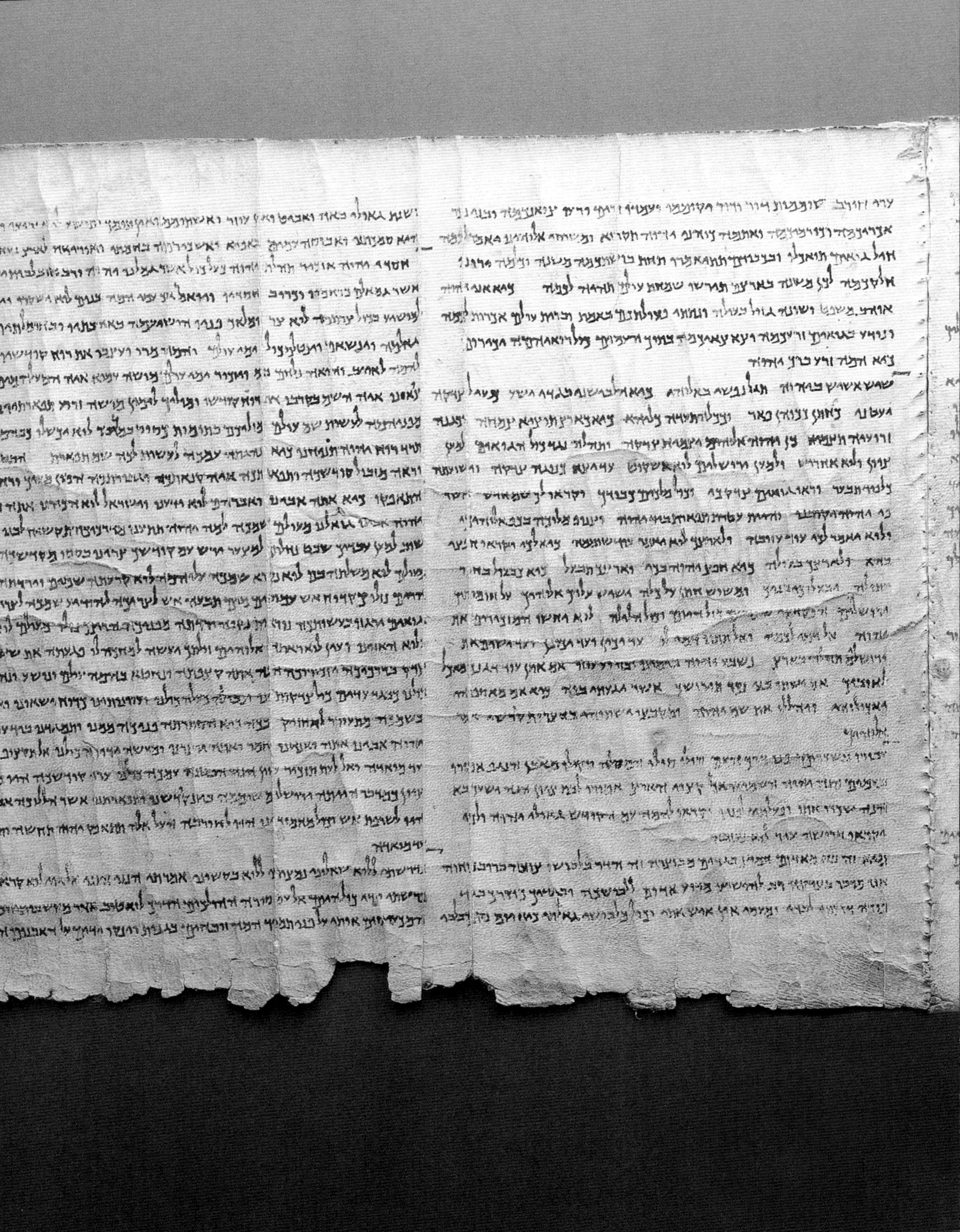

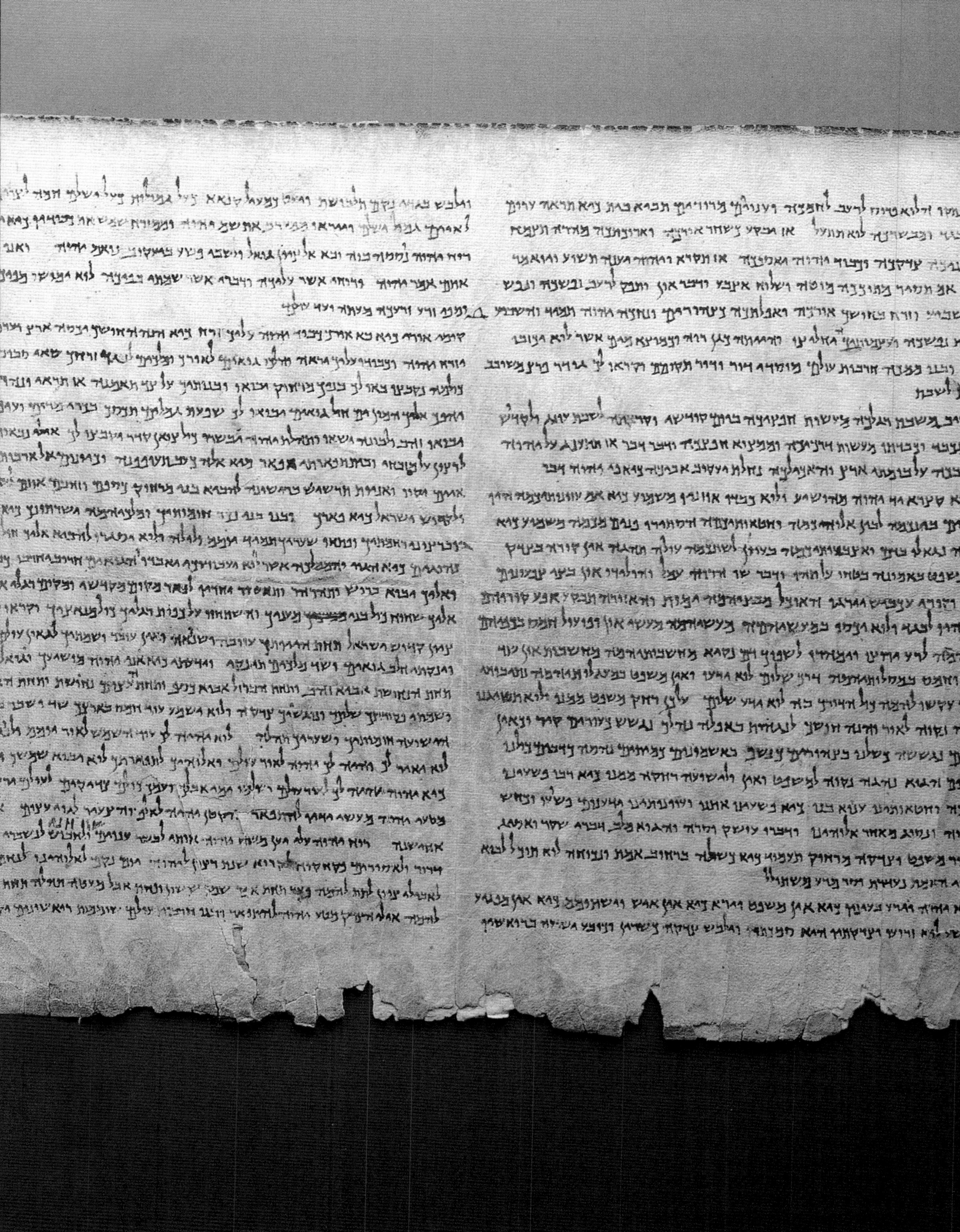

them, the Israelites pray to God, God sends them a judge who saves them, and afterwards the land remains quiet, then the Israelites sin again, and so on.

The Book of Judges contains valuable historical information on a period in the history of Israel that is otherwise unknown. According to Jewish tradition, Samuel wrote the Book of Judges.

JUSTICE   According to JUDAISM, justice is a quality of God that is balanced by His quality of MERCY. In the Book of GENESIS, God is described as using both justice and mercy in His role as Creator of the Universe. God commands the Jewish people to observe the COMMANDMENTS strictly, yet he takes into consideration human weakness and does not judge by the letter of the law; otherwise all human beings would be doomed.

The Bible often shows examples of God using both justice and mercy. ABRAHAM begs God to go beyond the letter of the law and save the cities of Sodom and Gommorah, although they deserve to be destroyed (Gen. 18:16–32). MOSES pleads with God not to destroy the Israelites for the sin of the GOLDEN CALF (Ex. 32).

Many Jewish prayers refer to God's role as the ultimate Judge. In the weekday AMIDAH, God is called "the King who loves charity and justice." When a person dies, Jews bless God as the "true Judge." The special prayers for the HIGH HOLIDAYS refer to God both as King and Judge, because at this time God sits in judgment over the Jewish people.

Jewish thinkers often asked the question, "Why do the innocent suffer and the wicked prosper?" (Psalm 92). The answer often given is that human beings cannot understand the judgments of God and His wisdom and fairness (see REWARD AND PUNISHMENT).

At various times in Jewish history, Jews have asked questions about the justice of God. This happens particularly in times of trouble, such as the destruction of the First and Second TEMPLES, the Inquisition and the expulsion from Spain and Portugal (see EXPULSIONS), and most recently, the HOLOCAUST.

The Jewish people were taught to imitate God (see IMITATION OF GOD), and build a framework of justice in which to live. Moses taught the Israelites, "Justice, justice shall you pursue" (Deut. 16:20), with Jewish law as their guideline.

Opposite page: Ketubbah *(marriage contract) from Casale Monferrato, Italy, 1671.*

KABBALAH   See MYSTICISM, JEWISH; LURIA, ISAAC

KABBALAT SHABBAT   See SABBATH

KADDISH   ("Making holy"). Prayer of praise to God, written in the Aramaic language. At first, it may have been a brief prayer that was said at the end of a lesson in ancient synagogues or houses of study. The *Kaddish* was later expanded and made part of the service. It also came to be used as a mourner's prayer. There are four basic forms of the *Kaddish*: the whole *Kaddish*, the shorter half-*Kaddish*, the rabbis' *Kaddish*, and the mourner's *Kaddish*.

The first two are recited during the service to separate various sections of prayer. The third includes the whole *Kaddish* plus a paragraph praising rabbis and Torah scholars. It is said at the end of a Talmud study session, either during a prayer service or at another time.

The mourner's *Kaddish* contains most of the whole *Kaddish*. It is said by mourners at the grave of close relatives and also during the 11-month mourning period following the death of a parent (and the month-long mourning period after the death of other close relatives; see MOURNING). The tradition is to recite the *Kaddish* at worship services, three times daily, in the presence of a MINYAN (prayer quorum). The practice of reciting mourner's *Kaddish* was established in the 13th century and is connected with the tragic events of the Crusades (see CHRISTIANITY). Originally it was said for 12 months after a death. However, because of the belief that sinners are punished for a full 12 months after death, the period for saying *Kaddish* was shortened to 11 months. This was to show that the person who died had not been a sinner.

The *Kaddish* prayer praises God and calls for the speedy establishment of God's kingdom on earth. Even the mourner's *Kaddish* makes no mention of death. Only the special version of *Kaddish* said at the time of BURIAL mentions the RESURRECTION of the dead.

It was always traditional for male relatives only to recite the mourner's *Kaddish*. In Reform and Conservative Judaism, however, women often say *Kaddish* as well. In recent years in ORTHODOXY, female relatives sometimes take on the responsibility of saying *Kaddish* for a parent who has died. In fact, even

---

> **FROM THE KADDISH**
>
> Glorified and made holy is God's great Name throughout the world which He has created according to His will. May He establish His kingdom in your lifetime and during your days and within the life of the entire house of Israel, speedily and soon. Blessed and praised, glorified and lofty, celebrated and honored, adored and acclaimed be the Name of the Holy One, blessed by He, beyond all blessings and hymns, praises and consolations that are ever spoken in the world, and let us say Amen.

among individuals who have let many other Jewish practices fall by the wayside, there is a tendency to show final respect to one's parents by going to the synagogue daily to recite the mourner's *Kaddish* for 11 months.

KALLAH MONTHS   (Heb. *yarhei kallah*, "months of assembly"). Name given in Babylonia to a month-long intensive study session for working-class Jews from near and far at the Talmud ACADEMIES. The custom lasted from the 3rd to the 11th centuries. The *Kallah* months took place twice a year, in Adar (February/March) and Elul (August/September), since these were not busy months for farmers.

Kallah-month participants would join in large lecture-hall study sessions with 70 sages. The class would be taught by the head of the Academy. Time would also be provided for sages to work with visiting students in smaller groups. At the end of each course, the talmudic book that would be studied six months later was announced.

The *Kallah*-month practice has been revived at Talmud academies in modern Israel (see YESHIVAH). The courses usually last several days and are held during the month of Elul.

KAPLAN, MORDECAI MENAHEM   (1881–1983). Rabbi and educator in the United States; founder and leader of Jewish RECONSTRUCTIONISM. Kaplan was at the center of leadership in Jewish life and thought for nearly 80 years in the United States. He also wrote many important books as well. While he respected the past and its traditions, his eye was more toward modern ways, saying: "The past has a vote but not a veto."

Kaplan was born in Lithuania, and moved to the United States as a child. He studied at the (CONSERVATIVE) Jewish Theological Seminary and graduated at the young age of 21. He became an Orthodox rabbi in New York. Although his personal religious observance remained strict throughout his life, he began to question some of the beliefs of ORTHODOXY. His doubts were increased by his study of modern sociology, biology, psychology, and Bible criticism. He left his position as rabbi to head up the Teachers' Training institute at the Jewish Theological Seminary, where he remained for 50 years. In 1922, his views led him to break with the Conservative movement and found the Jewish Reconstructionist movement. His movement issued its own prayer book, a new HAGGADAH, and the *Reconstructionist Magazine*. It had its own press to encourage the publication of new Jewish ideas.

Kaplan's teachings about God set him apart from other thinkers of his day. He describes God as an impersonal "Power that makes for righteousness" or a "Cosmic Process that makes for life's abundance or salvation." He denied that it is the nature of God to take a deliberate interest in the affairs of mankind.

He believed that ISRAEL is the spiritual center of world Jewry, although living outside of Israel is certainly acceptable. He described Israel as the center of a wheel, the various Diaspora communities as its spokes, and Jewish culture as the rim which holds everything together.

Kaplan's most important book was *Judaism as a Civilization* (1934). In it he argues that Jewish religion and culture have developed in a positive direction throughout the ages. He believed that these changes should continue, allowing for natural development in Jewish practice and creativity.

KAPPAROT ("ridding of sin"). The custom practiced just before the DAY OF ATONEMENT for ridding oneself of sin. A person takes a live chicken (male for a man, female for a woman) and moves it over his or her head three times while saying "This is my atonement, this is my ransom, this is my substitute. This bird shall meet its death, but I shall enjoy a long and pleasant life." The chicken is then slaughtered and given to the poor for their holiday meals. In this way, the sins of the person are symbolically transferred to the bird. Parents may perform *kapparot* for their children as well, by moving a chicken over their heads.

While this custom is still observed in certain Orthodox circles today, many rabbis have opposed it throughout the ages. For example, Nahmanides and Joseph Caro criticized it as superstitious. In modern times, many substitute 18 coins (18 stands for "life" in the system of GEMATRIA) bundled in a cloth for the chicken when they perform *kapparot*.

KARAISM (lit. "Scripturalism"). A sect that split off from Judaism. The Karaites rejected the ORAL LAW, which was developed by the rabbis and recorded in the TALMUD. This led them

Woodcut showing the custom of kapparot *performed with two fowls. Woodcut from the "Book of Customs." Venice, 1593.*

to develop their own form of Jewish practice, which separated them from other Jews.

Most historians agree that the split took place in the eighth century CE, when Anan ben David revolted against the rabbinic leadership. He claimed to the Arab authorities that he represented a new religion that was closer to ISLAM, and that he therefore should have an official leadership position, as the Jews did, which would be recognized by the government (see EXILARCH). The Karaite community grew in Erets Israel, and was at its strongest during the 10th and 11th centuries.

Karaite observance is similar in many ways to Judaism, but the differences are important. The Karaite calendar is always off by a day or so from the Jewish CALENDAR, which means that FESTIVALS are observed on different days. There are also no second days of holidays, no HANUKKAH, different fast days, no blowing of the SHOFAR on the New Year, and no FOUR SPECIES on SUKKOT. Their DIETARY LAWS are similar in that ritual slaughter is observed and animals forbidden in the Bible are not eaten. However, they will eat the meat of one animal with the milk of another, which Jewish law forbids. The order of their prayer service is completely different, and they kneel on the floor in the synagogue after removing their shoes. Men and women pray together. Their laws of MARRIAGE and DIVORCE also differ in important ways, which means that Jews cannot marry them.

Today there are about 30,000 Karaites in the world. Most live in Israel, along with their Chief Rabbi. Small Karaite communities may be found in Poland, the former Soviet Union, California in the United States, France, Switzerland, Turkey, and England.

KARELITZ, AVRAHAM YESHAYAHU (1878–1953). Talmud scholar, also known as the *Hazon Ish*. He was born in Kossovo, a town in Grodno, Russia. At an early age he displayed outstanding ability as a student of Talmud and HALAKHAH (Jewish law). In 1920 he moved to Vilna, where he published an original commentary on the SHULHAN ARUKH. It appeared anonymously under the name *Hazon Ish* ("Vision of Man"). The Hebrew word *Ish* is made up of the letters of his first and middle name. He wrote 23 additional works, all with the same title of *Hazon Ish*.

In 1933, Hazon Ish moved to Erets Israel and settled in Benei Berak. His presence there greatly influenced the community, and it developed as a center of ORTHODOXY and TORAH learning. Although he never occupied a formal leadership position, thousands flocked to his modest home for advice and halakhic decisions. Even David BEN-GURION, Israel's first prime minister, visited him to discuss the problematic issue of drafting religious YESHIVAH students into the army. His many rulings about agriculture and Jewish law set practical guidelines for religious Jewish farmers. For example, he set out permissible ways of milking cows on the SABBATH and methods for growing crops in water rather than on the land, so that the laws of the SABBATICAL YEAR would not be violated.

KARET (lit. "cutting off"). Punishment described in the Bible for several serious sins, such as eating on the DAY OF ATONEMENT or eating bread on PASSOVER. The Bible commands that for such sins, the guilty person "shall be cut off from the people." While this ruling can be explained in a number of ways, all agree that it is a punishment that comes from God and not one that is imposed by a court of law. Some suggestions of what the punishment means include dying before one's time and dying without having children. Unlike punishments that are given by human judges, the punishment of *karet* can be avoided by REPENTANCE and seeking ATONEMENT before God. The Mishnah (*Ker.* 1:1) lists 36 sins for which the punishment is *karet*. More than half of these are forbidden sexual relationships. Maimonides taught that *karet* means "cut off" not only in this world but also in the "world to come."

KARO, JOSEPH See CARO, JOSEPH

KASHER See KOSHER

KAVVANAH ("intention" or "direction" in prayer). State of complete concentration, which Judaism sees as ideal when praying to God. We read in the Bible: "You shall love the Lord your God with all your heart, with all your soul, and with all your might" (Deut. 6:5). Based on this idea, the rabbis stated that prayer needs *kavvanah* (TJ, *Ber.* 4:1). It is required for reading the SHEMA prayer twice daily (*Ber.* 16a). Numerous "warm-up" psalms and readings were added to the beginning of prayer service to help people develop *kavvanah* by the time they reach the central AMIDAH prayer. As Rabbi Eliezer ben Hyrcanus used to warn his students: "When you pray, know before Whom you are standing!" (*Ber.* 28b).

Maimonides spelled out what it means to pray with *kavvanah*: "The first thing you must do is turn your thoughts away from everything else while you recite the *Shema* or *Amidah*… When you have mastered this, try to get used to relieving your mind of all other thoughts as you say each BENEDICTION (blessing). When engaged in performing religious duties (*mitzvot*), have your mind concentrated entirely on what you are doing (*Guide* III, 51). There are differences of opinion about whether certain prayers and other *mitzvot* "count" if one says or does them without *kavvanah*.

The idea of *kavvanah* was most developed in Jewish MYSTICISM and HASIDISM. It was seen as a way of uplifting the soul and bringing it closer to God. By concentrating intensely on prayer and holy activity, it was believed that a person could actually influence the higher spiritual parts of the universe.

KEDUSHAH ("holiness"). Hebrew term for several parts of the prayer service (see KADDISH and KIDDUSH). *Kedushah* quotes expressions of praise for God from the visions of the prophets ISAIAH (6:3) and EZEKIEL (3:12). The prayer presents a scene in which a chorus of angels praises God and then is "answered" by the worshipers, who also stand with their legs tightly together in imitation of angels. The *Kedushah* is recited standing as part of the third benediction of the AMIDAH when the prayer leader repeats the *Amidah* aloud. A second, shorter version of the *Kedushah* is part of the YOTSEROT section of the MORNING SERVICE.

KELAL ISRAEL (lit. "the entire community of Israel"). Term for the Jewish people as a whole that emphasizes that they have a common destiny and responsibility. In Jewish belief, all Jews are responsible for one another, so that the sins of one are considered to be the sins of all (which is why the CONFESSIONS on the DAY OF ATONEMENT are said in the plural). A Jew may also not act in a way that would lead another Jew to sin. What is more, if a Jew sees another Jew sinning, he must criticize him for it to his face, but in a way that he can "hear" it.

KELIM ("Vessels"). First tractate (book) of the Order of TOHOROT in the Mishnah. Its 30 chapters deal with household items – mostly cooking utensils and ovens – that become ritually unclean (see PURITY). Since the destruction of the TEMPLE, these laws no longer have a practical use.

KENESET GEDOLAH See GREAT ASSEMBLY

KERI'AH See RENDING OF GARMENTS

KERITOT ("Being 'cut off'"). Seventh tractate (book) of the Order of KODASHIM in the Mishnah. Its six chapters deal with the sins that bring on the serious punishment of KARET and the sacrifices that are brought to atone for them (see ATONEMENT).

The Mishnah explains *karet* as premature death by the "hand of heaven." It lists 36 sins that are punishable by *karet*. It also lists some of the other SACRIFICES AND OFFERINGS that are brought for various reasons.

KETUBBAH   Marriage contract that is prepared before a MARRIAGE and handed to the bride during the wedding ceremony. It lists the husband's traditional responsibilities toward his wife as understood in the Bible and by the rabbis. The husband's major area of responsibility is in supporting his wife financially and providing for her even if the marriage should end, by divorce or his death. One of the purposes of the *ketubbah* was "that it should not be easy for a husband to divorce his wife" (*Yev.* 89a).

Throughout the centuries, the text of the *ketubbah* has been written in Aramaic, the daily language of Jews during the time of the Mishnah (2nd cent.). In many cases it was embellished with beautiful drawings and decorative lettering, called illuminations, so that it might hang proudly in the couple's home.

The CONSERVATIVE movement has developed an English-language *ketubbah* with a paragraph that requires the husband to grant a Jewish DIVORCE if the marriage should dissolve. REFORM Jews do not use a traditional *ketubbah*. Some use a modern "egalitarian" *ketubbah*, in which both the bride and the groom base their relationship on mutual obligations. Since the 1960s there has been a revival in the use of illuminated, handwritten *ketubbot*.

KETUBBOT   ("Marriage Contracts"). Second tractate (book) of the Order of NASHIM in the Mishnah. Its 13 chapters deal with the laws of the marriage contract (KETUBBAH). The book also discusses the marriage ceremony, the punishments for seduction and rape, grounds for DIVORCE, and the laws of INHERITANCE. The last *mishnah* deals with the greatness of Erets Israel and particularly Jerusalem, saying that a husband may force his wife and children to move there.

KEVER AVOT   (lit. "grave of the fathers"). The practice of visiting the graves of parents or close relatives to pray for the souls of the departed. Another purpose is to pray to God to help the living because of the good deeds of the dead.

Judaism generally discourages too many visits to graves, and one should certainly not visit on joyful days. Visits should be restricted to times like the anniversary of the person's death and around the time of the New Year. It is customary to visit at the end of the week of MOURNING or before a major family event, such as a wedding.

HASIDISM placed a great deal of emphasis on visiting the graves of its holy leaders. In response, their opponents, the MITNAGGEDIM, cut down on visiting even the graves of close relatives.

KHAZARS   Turkic people of south-central Russia who converted to Judaism as a group. After a forced debate about religious

beliefs (see DISPUTATIONS) between representatives of Judaism, CHRISTIANITY, and ISLAM, the Khazar King Bulan (786–809) was so impressed by the Jewish viewpoint that he and his entire people became Jewish. A small Jewish state was even created by the Khazars, and this served as an encouragement to medieval Jews, who were often subject to ANTI-SEMITISM. The Khazar kingdom was destroyed in the 11th century.

KIDDUSH   ("making holy"). Prayer said on the SABBATH and FESTIVALS over a cup of wine at the beginning of the special evening and morning meals of the day. The Bible tells us: "Remember the Sabbath day and keep it holy" (Ex. 20:8). The sages of the Talmud interpreted this to mean "remember it, over wine" (*Pes.* 106a). The man of the household traditionally recites the *Kiddush* on behalf of all who are at the table; however, women are obliged to hear or recite it as well. In non-Orthodox communities, women recite the *Kiddush* interchangeably with men.

The *Kiddush* consists of two sections, the blessing over the wine and the benediction of the day. It is said either standing or sitting, according to various CUSTOMS. Ideas included in the second part are: the people of Israel has been made holy by God's COMMANDMENTS, the Sabbath is a way of remembering the CREATION of the world by God, and the Sabbath is a reminder of the EXODUS from Egypt.

Jewish homes usually have beautiful silver wine cups in with which to make *Kiddush*. Today, in many congregations, a *Kiddush* is held in synagogues, with wine and refreshments, to allow for socializing after the services.

Kiddush *cups. From left to right: one from Bohemia, in red glass; two from Poland; and one from Germany, in silver. 19th century.*

KIDDUSH HA-SHEM AND HILLUL HA-SHEM   (lit. "making the Divine Name holy" and "DESECRATION of the Divine Name"). Two opposite concepts that either shed glory or dishonor on the Jewish people and God. They are based on the Bible's command: "You shall not desecrate My holy name, but

I will be made holy among the Children of Israel" (Lev. 22:32). MAIMONIDES included the obligation to make God's name holy among his list of positive commandments (#297).

Kiddush ha-Shem can include the obligation to remain loyal to one's religious beliefs, even at the cost of one's life. If Jews are faced with the choice between death or being forced to commit one of the three most serious sins – IDOLATRY, murder, or sexual offenses (see SEX) – they must accept death rather than sin. If a person dies under these conditions, or dies for being a Jew, this is considered *kiddush ha-Shem*.

Another use of the terms *kiddush ha-Shem* and *hillul ha-Shem* relates to how a Jew's actions will be viewed by the rest of the world. Actions by Jews that would lead non-Jews to praise Judaism are considered a *kiddush ha-Shem*; when Jews show anti-social behavior this is seen as a *hillul ha-Shem*. It is also considered a *hillul ha-Shem* to erase God's holy name, wherever it may appear.

KIDDUSHIN ("Making Holy"). Seventh tractate (book) of the Order of NASHIM in the Mishnah. Its four chapters deal with the procedure for acquiring a wife through a two part-process: (1) *Erusin* (see MARRIAGE), which takes place 12 months before the actual marriage; (2) *Nissu'in*, which is the conclusion of legal marriage. *Nissu'in* takes place when the groom gives the bride a token of marriage (nowadays a ring) and the couple has sexual relations. Various other laws related to marriage are discussed as well.

KILAYIM ("Mixed Species"). Fourth tractate (book) of the Order of ZERA'IM in the Mishnah. Its nine chapters cover the laws concerning three types of forbidden mixtures: (1) planting seeds of different varieties in the same small area of a garden (see AGRICULTURAL LAWS); (2) mixed animals – harnessing two different species of animals together for work and cross-breeding two different kinds of animals; and (3) mixed garments – wearing a mixture of wool and linen woven together (see SHA'ATNEZ).

KIMHI   Twelfth-century family of Bible commentators and experts in Hebrew grammer. They are of Spanish origin, but lived in Provence.

Joseph Kimhi   (1105–1170; known as *Rikam*). Like Abraham Ibn Ezra, who quoted him, he devoted himself to making Arabic-Jewish books available to the Jews of Europe by translating them into Hebrew. His contribution to Hebrew grammar was very important. His interpretations of texts were plain and straightforward, without the use of stories. He produced one of the earliest anti-Christian arguments (see APOLOGETICS AND POLEMICS) in the form of a fictional debate between a believing Jew and one who favored CHRISTIANITY.

Moses Kimhi   (died c. 1190; known as *Remak*). Joseph's eldest son. He was a pupil of his father and also adopted a "plain" style in his commentaries on PROVERBS, EZRA AND NEHEMIAH, and JOB. He is best known for his Hebrew grammar book,

Mahalakh Shevilei ha-Da'at, which was used by Jewish as well as Christian scholars.

David Kimhi   (c. 1160–1235; known as *Radak*). The youngest son of the family and its most famous member. His Bible commentaries are published in many editions of the Hebrew Bible. They were also translated into Latin and studied widely by Christian scholars. He often referred to events of his day in the course of his commentaries. For example, on the verse "Pray for the peace of Jerusalem" (Ps. 122:6) he refers to the Crusades: "For until now Jerusalem had no peace, because the uncircumcised (Christians) and Ishmaelites are fighting for her possession." He was very supportive of the rational approach of Maimonides and challenged the rabbis of northern France who disapproved of such philosophy.

David Kimhi was very popular as a preacher and teacher. It was very important to him that his works of Hebrew grammar, as well as his commentaries, be written in a clear style that his readers could easily understand. In a play on words on a traditional saying (*Avot* 3:21), it was said about him: "If there is no *kemah* (lit. "flour," i.e. bread to eat – but in this case meaning Kimhi), then there can be no Torah." In other words, one cannot understand the Torah without Kimhi.

KING, KINGSHIP   The supreme king in Jewish tradition is GOD, who is called King of Kings and Lord King of the World. When a Jew takes on the COMMANDMENTS at the time of BAR MITZVAH or BAT MITZVAH, this is called "taking on the yoke of the kingdom of heaven." On ROSH HA-SHANAH, the AMIDAH for the ADDITIONAL SERVICE includes a section of ten verses from the Bible about the Kingship of God.

MOSES commanded the children of Israel to appoint a king after entering the Land of Israel (Deut. 17:14ff.). However, they did not actually do so until centuries later, after the period of the JUDGES. At a time when the Israelites were under threat of being conquered by the Philistines, the prophet SAMUEL bowed to the will of the people and anointed SAUL as the first king of Israel (1 Sam. 10:17ff.).

The choice of the king, as well as his conduct, was limited by Jewish law. He was to keep a copy of the Law of God with him at all times. Kings had the power to charge taxes, draft men into the army or for labor service, and to declare war. They could order executions and take property from rebellious citizens. The people were expected to honor the king, but he was cautioned to be humble, merciful, and kind. He was always bound by the laws of the Torah and would be punished if he sinned.

When David became the second king of Israel, the prophet NATHAN told him: "Your house and your kingdom shall be confirmed forever before you; your throne shall be established forever" (II Sam. 7:16). From this comes the belief that even the MESSIAH shall one day come from the family of David.

KINGS, BOOK OF   The fourth book of the PROPHETS section of the Bible, which has been divided into Kings I and Kings II. It deals with the lives and reigns of kings DAVID and SOLOMON,

---

BOOK OF KINGS

I KINGS

1:1–2:46	The last days of David; Solomon receiving the throne
3:1–11:43	Solomon's reign
12:1–12:24	The division of the united kingdom
12:25–14:20	The reign of Jeroboam
14:21–16:34	Combined history of Judah and Israel
17:1–II KINGS 10:31	The reign of Ahab

II KINGS

10:32–17:41	Combined history of Judah and Israel until the fall of Samaria
18:1–20:21	Reign of Hezekiah
21:1–21:26	Reign of Manasseh and Amon
22:1–23:30	Reign of Josiah and the religious reform
23:31–23:35	Reign of Jehoahaz
23:36–25:30	Last days of Judah and the destruction of Jerusalem

---

and the kings of JUDAH and ISRAEL that followed. It begins with the period of time when Solomon took the throne (c. 970 BCE) until the release of King Jehoaichin from prison in Babylonia (561 BCE).

The history of King Solomon's reign includes a description of the building of the TEMPLE. Also described is the division of the kingdom into two at the time of Rehoboam. The book continues with the stories of the two kingdoms told in a religious light. The relationships of the various kings to God and His laws and the guidance and criticism of the kings by the prophets are important features. According to Jewish tradition, Kings was written by the prophet JEREMIAH.

KINNIM ("Bird Offerings") Eleventh tractate (book) of the Order of KODASHIM in the Mishnah. Its three chapters deal with the laws of SACRIFICES AND OFFERINGS involving birds.

KINOT (sing. *kinah*). Funeral poems that express mourning, pain, and suffering; one of the most ancient types of poetry used in prayer (see PIYYUT).

The Bible mentions various *kinnot*, including: Abraham for Sarah (Gen 23:2), Jacob's sons for their father (Gen. 50:10), and David's famous lament over Saul and Jonathan (I Sam. 25:1). The Book of Lamentations is entirely a *kinah* and is read aloud on TISHAH BE-AV, the day that commemorates the destruction of the Jerusalem TEMPLES.

Other *kinot* were written during the Middle Ages in Europe

and Oriental countries following the Crusades and other attacks and book-burnings in Jewish communities (see ANTI-SEMITISM).

KISLEV Ninth month of the Jewish religious CALENDAR; third month of the Hebrew civil year, counting from TISHRI. It falls in November/December and has 29–30 days. Kislev's sign of the zodiac is Sagittarius, the Archer.

The eight-day festival of HANUKKAH begins of the 25th of Kislev. It celebrates the victory of the Maccabees over the Syrian-Greeks and the purification of the TEMPLE from IDOLATRY.

KITEL Yiddish term for the white robe worn by ASHKENAZIM on serious occasions. It is usually worn in the SYNAGOGUE on the HIGH HOLIDAYS and by the leader of the SEDER on PASSOVER. Its white color is a symbol of ATONEMENT and PURITY, which is why it is worn by bridegrooms under the marriage canopy. Jews are often buried in their *kitel* as well.

KLEZMER See MUSIC AND SONG

KODASHIM ("Holy Things"). Fifth Order of the Mishnah. Its 11 books – ZEVAHIM, MENAHOT, HULLIN, BEKHOROT, ARAKHIM, TEMURAH, KERITOT, ME'ILAH, TAMID, MIDDOT, and KINNIM – deal almost entirely with the laws of SACRIFICES AND OFFERINGS. Most of these are useful today only for study, since there is no longer a TEMPLE in which to offer sacrifices. The most important and relevant book today is *Hullin*, which deals with the ritual slaughter (SHEHITAH) of animals.

KOHANIM See PRIESTS

KOHELET See ECCESLIASTES

KOLEL (lit. "all-inclusive"). Term used to describe a YESHIVAH (Talmud academy) for married students. Students receive a small monthly payment that enables them to support their families while they devote themselves entirely to TORAH studies. R. Israel SALANTER first used the term *kolel* in 1878. A wealthy Berlin man set aside a large amount of money for him to use to support married students at the Great Yeshivah of Kovno. In Israel, since the late 1960s, the number of students studying in the *kolel* has seen striking growth.

KOL NIDREI ("All Vows"). Opening words and title of a key declaration that opens the EVENING SERVICE on the DAY OF ATONEMENT. It solemnly asks that "all vows, obligations, oaths, promises, and undertakings" made by the worshiper during the year be canceled and forgiven. It is chanted three times and with great emotion, since it was first said by Jews who were forced to make vows of allegiance to other religions in the past. *Kol Nidrei* is chanted in the Aramaic language.

SEPHARDIM and Jews in Oriental communities ask to be released from all vows made during the past year, while the

Part of an East European version of Kol Nidrei.

version said by ASHKENAZIM asks for release from vows that might be made under pressure during the coming year.

Three leaders of the congregation become a rabbinical court (BET DIN) during the chanting of *Kol Nidrei*, which officially releases all congregants from their vows. Since a court cannot be convened on the Sabbath or during a festival, *Kol Nidrei* is said just before the Day of Atonement officially begins. Just before *Kol Nidrei*, it is announced that "by the authority of the heavenly court and the court below … we declare it lawful to pray in the presence of sinners." This brief passage, written by Rabbi MEIR OF ROTHENBURG in the 13th century, allowed Jews who had been punished by a ban of EXCOMMUNICATION to join the congregation on the very important Day of Atonement.

From medieval times until the late 19th century many Christians claimed that a Jew's word cannot be trusted, since he says *Kol Nidrei* each year (see ANTI-SEMITISM). However, the declaration applies only to vows and promises of a religious nature (i.e. between people and God); Judaism has no formula for releasing people from vows and promises made to other human beings.

KOOK, ABRAHAM ISAAC (1865–1935).

Rabbi and Jewish scholar and philosopher; first Ashkenazi Chief Rabbi of modern Erets Israek. As a child he received his education from his father and entered the Volozhin Yeshivah (Talmud academy) at age 16. He moved to Erets Israel in 1904 and became Chief Rabbi of Jaffa. He visited new agricultural settlements to encourage and praise the pioneers and to try to persuade them to return to a religious way of life. Even so, he believed that they were doing holy work in farming the Land of Israel, whether or not their personal practice was religious. He helped farmers considerably in the Sabbatical Year of 5670 (1909/1910). He ruled that instead of leaving their fields fallow, as the law required of Jews in Israel, they could symbolically sell them to Muslims and thus continue to work them. This ruling angered some of the other rabbis of Erets Israel, but is still followed by many today. In 1921 Kook was elected Chief Rabbi of pre-State Israel and founded a religious-Zionist *yeshivah* in Jerusalem called *Merkaz ha-Rav* ("the Rabbi's Center").

Kook's teachings were very special, because many different views were combined in his outlook. He was a rabbinic scholar of the old school and a deeply religious mystic (see MYSTICISM, JEWISH) who took an active interest in Jewish affairs and believed in secular study along with Torah study. He wrote a great deal in the fields of Jewish philosophy, religious Zionism, and Jewish law.

Kook, Tsevi Yehudah (1891–1982).

Yeshivah head and spiritual leader of the Gush Emunim ("Bloc of the Faithful") religious-Zionist movement. Gush Emunim led the Jewish return to settlement of lands in Judea and Sameria that were won in the 1967 Six-Day War. Tsevi Yehudah was the only son of Abraham Isaac Kook and came to Erets Israel with his parents in 1904. He assisted his father in running the Merkaz ha-Rav and took

Rabbi Abraham Isaac Kook, in the center, speaking at the laying of the cornerstone of a new quarter in Jerusalem, 1925.

over the *yeshivah* after his death. He emphasized Zionism and the spiritual aspects of the State and influenced thousands from all segments of the Israeli population.

KOSHER (lit. "fit"). Hebrew term for foods that are judged "fit" or "proper" for eating, according to biblical and rabbinic law (see DIETARY LAWS). A symbol on food packages can often be found guaranteeing that a rabbi has supervised the production. Kosher restaurants, hotels, and catering firms also display certificates showing that a rabbi supervises their food preparation. In some cases, particular groups do not accept the general level of rabbinical supervision and require something stricter. It is therefore possible to find foods and restaurants certified as kosher *lemehadderin* ("superfine"). The terms *halak* or *glatt* are used to describe meat slaughtered with extra-strict supervision.

KRANZ, JACOB BEN ZE'EV WOLF (known as the Maggid of Dubno; 1741–1804). Preacher (MAGGID) and Jewish scholar. He became the preacher of the town of Zhetel, Lithuania, at the age of 20. He was such a gifted storyteller that he drew large crowds when he traveled throughout Europe to preach. When somebody once asked how he always managed to find the right story for every situation, he answered with another story!

Based on Kranz's notes and their own recollections, his followers published several volumes of his works years after he died. They have been translated into English, Yiddish and Hebrew.

KROCHMAL, NACHMAN (1785–1840). Historian, philosopher, and leader of the HASKALAH (Jewish Enlightenment) movement and the Science of Judaism (WISSENSCHAFT DES JUDENTUMS). His scholarship attracted the leadership of the Haskalah to Zolkiew, Galicia, where he lived for most of his life.

Krochmal's chief aim was to present Judaism as it developed historically throughout the ages. He was persuaded by his followers to publish his various teaching, which he finally did in his great work, called *Moreh Nevukhei ha-Zeman* ("Guide for the Perplexed of the Time"). He also made many contributions in the study of HALAKHAH (Jewish law). He believed that the *halakhah* had developed naturally from the time of the Bible, and called for new interpretations and laws from the rabbis of his day.

L

LABOR AND LABOR LAWS　In Judaism, physical labor has a positive value. ADAM is placed in the Garden of EDEN "to work it and to guard it" (Gen. 2:15); it is only later that hard toil in agriculture becomes a punishment (Gen. 3:17–19). Some rabbis interpreted the verse "Six days shall you labor" (Ex. 20:9) as a positive commandment. R. Judah the Prince stated, "Just as Israel was commanded to rest on the Sabbath, so were they commanded to work on the other six days" (*Mekhilta* on Ex. 20:9–10). R. Judah ben Betera ruled that a person with no work to do should busy himself with a barren field rather than sit idle (*Avot de-Rabbi Natan* 11). Elsewhere, it is recommended that a man should occupy himself with a trade in addition to learning Torah: "Any study of Torah that is not combined with an occupation will eventually stop and lead a person to sin" (*Avot* 2:2). This advice was clearly taken to heart by the rabbis themselves. The Talmud describes the occupations of various sages, ranging from woodcutting to shoemaking, and from farming to baking.

Jewish law has much to say about the conditions of the worker. According to the HALAKHAH (Jewish law), a day laborer must be paid his wages before sunrise the following day (Lev. 19:13). The Talmud goes on to say that an employer who holds back his worker's wages is like a person who takes the life of another (*BM* 112a). According to the Talmud, an employer may not end a worker's employment without cause in the middle of a contract. However the worker may resign at any time, even in the middle of the day (*BM* 77a). This basically gives the worker the right to strike. However, if the employer loses money as a result of such an action, the court may force him to pay the employer. In addition, an employer may not force his workers to labor beyond their physical ability. He must feed them, and they are allowed to eat from any food items they handle.

On the other hand, the rabbis were also concerned that the employer should receive a fair benefit from the workers they employed. MAIMONIDES (*Mishneh Torah, Hilkhot Sekhirut,* "Laws of Employment" 13:7) insisted that workers must work continuously and to the best of their ability, not wasting time during the working day. The sages ruled that if a worker recites the GRACE AFTER MEALS during working hours, he should shorten it by leaving out the last blessing, so he does not deprive his employer of his services.

LADINO　See LANGUAGES, JEWISH

LAG BA-OMER　("Thirty-third [day] of the Omer"; the Hebrew letters with the sounds "l" and "g" add up numerically to 33 and the "a" has no numerical value; see GEMATRIA). Minor festival in the Jewish CALENDAR; it has been observed since geonic times on 18 Iyyar, during the counting of the OMER between PASSOVER and SHAVU'OT. It helps us remember the end of a terrible plague that killed many thousands of the students of R. AKIVA during the BAR KOKHBA revolt (132–135 CE).

A number of theories have been put forth about why the holiday is celebrated on the 18th of Iyyar. According to some, Bar Kokhba's army suffered many defeats over a long time period; however, on the 33rd day of the Omer, his forces won a victory. Another theory is that during the first Jewish revolt against Rome (66 CE), Jews took up arms on the 18th of Iyyar, which was the 33rd day of the Omer. In order to keep it a secret from the Romans, the day of the uprising was referred to as "*Lag ba-Omer*," which was a numerical code for the actual calendar date.

There are no special laws or celebrations required for Lag ba-Omer. There are, however, many customs. The observance of semi-mourning during the counting of the Omer stops for Lag ba-Omer. Marriages are performed, music is allowed, and people may cut their hair. In Israel, families go on picnics, and on the night of Lag ba-Omer bonfires appear throughout the

Lag ba-Omer celebrated with bonfires.

countryside. It is customary for children to play with bows and arrows, recalling the military origins of the day. In Meron, near Safed, a HILLULA in honor of R. SIMEON BAR YOHAI takes place at his gravesite; R. Simeon died on 18 Iyyar. This event attracts tens of thousands of religious Jews from all over the country. It is also a custom in HASIDISM to give three-year-old boys their first haircut on Lag ba-Omer at R. Simeon's tomb.

LAMED VAV TSADDIKIM The "36 righteous individuals" who live in every generation, according to Jewish tradition. The Talmud tells us that the SHEKHINAH (Divine Presence) rests on these individuals, and their existence in the world prevents its destruction (*Sanh.* 97a–b; *Suk.* 45b). Legend has it that these are simple Jews who earn their living by the sweat of their brow. They are unaware of each other and live in secrecy. At times of great danger, they emerge to rescue their fellow Jews. They then immediately return to their humble lives, usually in a place where they are not known.

LAMENTATIONS, BOOK OF (Heb. *Ekhah*; in the Talmud, *Kinot*). Book in the HAGIOGRAPHA (Writings) section of the Bible; one of the FIVE SCROLLS. The book deals with the de-

Opening page of the Book of Lamentations. From the Castro Pentateuch Germany, 14th century.

	BOOK OF LAMENTATIONS
1:1–1:22	Desolation of Jerusalem
2:1–2:22	God's wrath and Zion's ruin
3:1–3:66	Man's yoke of suffering
4:1–4:22	The agony of the holy city
5:1–5:22	O Lord, remember and save us

struction of JERUSALEM and the TEMPLE (586 BCE). It presents the devastating events of the destruction and the exile that came afterwards as the result of JUDAH's sins. It is the view of the book that the people can blame only themselves for their tragedies.

It also blames the prophets for not instructing the people properly.

According to the Talmud, Jeremiah was the author of Lamentations. This explains the vivid descriptions of the horrors of the destruction that appear in the book, since Jeremiah witnessed the destruction and lived in the period of the first exile.

The Book of Lamentations is read on the evening of TISHAH BE-AV, the fast day commemorating the destruction of the Temple.

LAMENTATIONS RABBAH (Heb. *Ekhah Rabbah*). MIDRASH on the Book of LAMENTATIONS. This is one of the oldest surviving works of Midrash from Erets Israel. It dates from the sixth century CE. The collection begins with 36 introductory essays on the Book of Lamentations. It then continues with commentary in the form of a sermon on the verses of the book in order. It includes ten stories about the cleverness of the people of Jerusalem; a description of the persecution of the Jews by the Romans; and the mocking of Jews in plays performed in the Roman theaters.

LA-SHANAH HA-BA'AH BI-YERUSHALAYIM ("Next Year in Jerusalem!"). Traditional Hebrew phrase recited at the end of the Passover SEDER and at the conclusion of the DAY OF ATONEMENT. It refers to the belief that at the time of the REDEMPTION, Jerusalem will be fully rebuilt and all Jews will go there. In the Talmud (*RH* 11a), R. JOSHUA says that Israel's future redemption will take place in the month of Nisan, when the Exodus from Egypt took place. R. ELIEZER states that it will take place in Tishri, when the Day of Atonement occurs. As a compromise, it became standard practice to call for the coming redemption at both times during the Jewish year.

LAW See HALAKHAH

LAW COURT See BET DIN

LEAH   Elder daughter of Laban. Wife of the patriarch JACOB. In the Bible (Gen. 29–31), Laban promised Jacob his other daughter, RACHEL. However, on the night of their wedding, he substituted Rachel's elder sister, Leah. Leah is the mother of seven of Jacob's 13 children. These include six sons and his only daughter, Dinah. In addition, another two of Jacob's sons were born by Zilpah, Leah's handmaiden. The Bible does not mention Leah's death, although she is buried beside Jacob in the Cave of Machpelah in Hebron, Erets Israel (Gen. 49:30–31).

LEAP YEAR   See CALENDAR

LEAVEN, SEARCH FOR   (Heb. *bedikat hamets*). Ceremony performed on the night before PASSOVER eve (13–14 Nisan). When the first day of Passover falls on Sunday, the search is performed the previous Thursday. The ceremony is the final step in the removal of all *hamets*, leavened foods that are forbidden on Passover, from the house.

After the EVENING SERVICE on the night before Passover eve, the search for leaven is done before eating or doing any other work. The head of the household begins the search by reciting a blessing, "…Who has sanctified us with His commandments and commanded us to remove the leaven." A thorough search of the house takes place, including the odd places where leavened foods may have been left during the course of the year. The search is carried out in silence. The house is darkened, and a candle is carried around for light. The searcher sweeps the leaven he finds into a bag with a feather and wooden spoon. These items and the candle are added to the bag and put aside for burning the following day. At the end of the search the leader recites a legal formula that frees the family from responsibility for any leaven that might still remain. The next morning, the bag containing the leaven, feather, spoon, and candle is burned (*bi'ur hamets*), and a modified version of the formula declaring that all responsibility for *hamets* is gone is said.

In theory, the *hamets* should already have been removed from the house by the time the search takes place. For this reason, ten pieces of bread are wrapped in paper and hidden

Searching for leaven. From Bernard Picart's Ceremonies et Coutumes de tous les Juifs du Monde. *Amsterdam, 1723–43.*

by another family member specifically for the searcher to find. In this way the blessing will not be recited in vain. In many homes this means that although the search is serious and silent, it is also very much enjoyed by the children. They follow their parent around as the search proceeds for the bread that they have hidden.

LEIBOWITZ, NEHAMAH   (1905–1997). Educator and Bible scholar. Leibowitz was born in Riga, Latvia, and educated in Berlin. She moved to Erets Israel in 1930. She devoted her life to teaching and explaining the Bible. She taught at the Mizrachi Women Teachers Seminary and then at Tel Aviv University. In 1957 she was awarded the Israel Prize for her contribution to education.

In 1942, Leibowitz began publishing her "Pages" on the weekly Bible reading (PARASHAH). At first these were circulated informally; however demand soon reached into the thousands weekly. The "Pages" were eventually published in books, one on each of the five books of the PENTATEUCH, which reflect her vast knowledge of both ancient and modern sources.

Leibowitz was a woman who excelled in a field dominated by men. Thus many women in ORTHODOXY who were beginning to enter the world of Jewish learning adopted her as a role model.

LEIBOWITZ, YESHAYAHU   (1903–1994). Rabbi, biologist, and philosopher. Leibowitz was born in Riga, Latvia, and educated in Berlin and Switzerland. He immigrated to Erets Israel in 1935, five years after his sister Nehamah LEIBOWITZ, and taught at the Hebrew University of Jerusalem. After he reached retirement age, he embarked on a new career, lecturing in Jewish philosophy and also giving weekly Torah classes in a Jerusalem synagogue and lecturing on the Torah portion on radio and television. He wrote many scientific articles as well as books and essays on Jewish subjects.

Leibowitz saw people's relationship to God as requiring total submission for its own sake, without any thought of reward. He did not believe that God's promises to the Jewish people were unconditional, regardless of their acts. Thus, unlike the Religious Zionists, he could imagine a situation where even the State of Israel might cease to exist. Shortly after the Six-Day War and from that time on, Leibowitz strongly opposed Israel's staying in the captured "territories," claiming that by remaining an occupying power Israel was eating away at its very soul. His views made him very popular among the left wing in Israeli politics. In 1992, he was awarded the Israel Prize, but following protests, mostly from the right wing, he decided not to accept it.

LEKET, SHIKHEHAH, PE'AH   (known together as *mattanot aniyyim*, "gifts to the poor"). These are the portions of the farmer's crops that must be left over for the poor. (1) *Leket* ("gleaning") is an individual stalk (e.g., of wheat) dropped by the reapers. According to the Bible (Lev. 19:9–10), these must be left for the poor. If three or more stalks fall, the reaper may take them. (2) *Shikhehah* ("forgotten") is a quantity of grain left accidentally in the field. Once they have completed bringing the grain to the storage area, workers may not return to the field to gather it (see Deut. 24:19). This must be left for the poor. (3) *Pe'ah* ("corner") is the grain in the corner of the field that must be left unharvested (see Lev. 23:22). This amount is also left for the poor to gather.

In addition, the farmer also must give a TITHE to the poor. As these gifts show, the Bible called for helping the poor and weaker members of society. While some societies are based on survival of the fittest, the Bible demands of the fit to support the survival of the weak.

LEKHAH DODI   ("Come, my Beloved"). Opening words and chorus of the central SABBATH eve hymn; written by Solomon ben Moses ha-Levi Alkabets. His Hebrew name, Shelomoh ha-Levi, appears as an ACROSTIC in the first eight stanzas. Alkabets lived in Safed, where the KABBALAH developed in the 16th century. He and his fellow mystics were inspired by the theme from the MIDRASH that the Sabbath is Israel's bride (see Gen. R. 11:9). They used to go out into the fields each week, chanting psalms and verses from SONG OF SONGS to welcome the Sabbath Queen and Bride. Around 1540, Alkabets composed *Lekhah Dodi*, which was adopted soon after by most communities. It was already recited by the German ASHKENAZIM by the early 17th century.

FROM LEKHAH DODI

Come, my Beloved, with chorus of praise;
Welcome Sabbath the Bride, Queen of our days.

Come, let us all greet Queen Sabbath sublime,
Fountain of blessings in every clime.
Anointed and regal since earliest time,
In thought she preceded Creation's six days.

One particular ritual of *Lekhah Dodi* reminds us of its connection with the Sabbath Bride. Before singing the final stanza, worshipers turn to face west, toward the entrance of the synagogue. They bow symbolically to the entering Sabbath Queen as she makes her appearance.

How popular is *Lekhah Dodi*? There have been at least 2,000 different melodies used for the hymn over the past 350 years, and others are still being composed.

LESHON HA-RA   ("evil speech"). Talebearing and slander are considered serious offenses in Jewish law. Leviticus 19:6 states: "You shall not spread slanderous tales among your people." *Leshon ha-ra* includes all forms of talebearing, ranging from gossip (Heb. *rehilut*) to deliberately speaking falsely with the intention of injuring the other party. The most extreme ex-

---

LESHON HA-RA

There are three sins that men encounter daily and cannot avoid: impure thoughts, lack of devotion in prayer, and slander.

Keep you mouth from evil talk and live a life of peace.

What is spoken in Rome may kill in Syria.

Silence is good for the wise. How much more so for the foolish.

The punishment of the liar is that he is not believed even when he speaks the truth.

---

ample of *leshon ha-ra* is the informer who makes accusations about his fellow Jew to the government with the intention of harming him.

How serious did the rabbis take *leshon ha-ra*? In Numbers 12, MIRIAM was stricken with leprosy for speaking ill of her brother MOSES. The Talmud went even further. Slander is worse than the capital sins of MURDER, IDOLATRY, and INCEST. Why? Because the murderer kills only one person, while the slanderer kills three. He kills himself, the one who listens, and the person being slandered. Furthermore, the slanderer is listed among four categories of people who lose their place in the world to come (*Sot.* 42a; see AFTERLIFE).

LEVIATHAN   (Heb. *livyatan*). Name for various types of sea monsters in the Bible and the Talmud. In Psalm 104:26 and Job 40:25–41:26 the animal seems to be either a whale or a crocodile. In Psalm 74:14, Job 3:8, and Isaiah 27:1, it is a mythic monster at war with the Creator and doomed to destruction. In rabbinic sources, *livyatan* is a great sea monster that will be served at a banquet for the righteous in the AFTERLIFE (see Lev. R. 13:3; BB 74b–75a). At this time, God will slaughter both Leviathan and the Wild Ox, serve their meat at the feast for the righteous, and make a tent from Leviathan's skin.

LEVI BEN GERSHOM   (1288–1344; known as *Ralbag* or Gersonides). Philosopher, Talmud scholar, mathematician, astronomer, and Bible commentator. Gersonides was born and lived in Provence, France. He was on close terms with leading Church figures of his time. He lectured on astronomy at the Christian university and medical school.

Gersonides is best known for his major commentary on the PENTATEUCH and most of the remaining books of the Hebrew Bible. He also wrote a commentary on *Berakhot*, the first book of the Babylonian Talmud. His other major contribution is *Sefer Milhamot Adonai* ("The Book of the Wars of the Lord"). This is a philosophical work dealing with six major subjects, including the nature of the soul and God's interaction with the world. He wrote this book to deal with subjects that he believed were not explained fully by earlier Jewish philosophers, especially Maimonides.

LEVI ISAAC OF BERDICHEV   (c. 1740–1810). Rabbi and Hasidic leader. Levi Isaac is perhaps the most beloved figure in HASIDISM after the BA'AL SHEM TOV. He is known as the "Berdichever *Rov*," since unlike most Hasidic masters, he was both a TSADDIK (holy Hasidic master) and a communal rabbi. He was a disciple of DOV BAER, the Maggid of Mezhirech.

One should keep in mind that it was almost unheard of for a Hasid to be appointed community rabbi in 18th century Europe. The bitter controversy surrounding the Hasidim was raging, because traditional rabbis were opposed to the Hasidic movement. Yet Levi Isaac was appointed to community posts more than once, first in Zhelechow in Poland and then in Pinsk in Belorussia. He left both of these posts before settling in Berdichev, where he served until his death.

Levi Isaac was an untiring advocate for the Jewish people before God. Once he protested before God: "You always make demands of Your people Israel. Why not help them with their troubles?" Once he noticed a Jew in a prayer shawl (TALLIT) and PHYLACTERIES interrupting his prayers to grease the wheels of his cart. He turned to heaven and said: "Lord, what a wonderful people You have! Even when they grease their cartwheels, they do not forget to wear their *tallit* and phylacteries!"

His major written work is the two-part *Kedushat Levi*. This is an account of Hasidic beliefs in the form of a commentary on the Torah and rabbinic legends. He gives special attention to the theme of HUMILITY.

LEVIRATE MARRIAGE   (Heb. *yibbum*). According to the Bible (Deut. 25:5–6), a woman whose husband has died without children must marry the brother of her dead husband. The "first son that she bears shall be accounted to the dead brother, so that his name will not be blotted out in Israel." The story of Judah and Tamar, in Genesis 38, is the earliest record of levirate marriage. It does not, however, mention there the all-important ceremony of *halitsah*. *Halitsah* was used to release the widow to marry whomever she wishes if the brother (or family member) refuses to marry her. As described in the Bible, the widow calls the surviving brother before the ELDERS. He announces that he refuses to perform *yibbum*, and she removes his shoe and "spits in front of him." She then declares: "Thus shall be done to the man who will not build up his brother's house" (Deut. 25:7–9). According to Jewish law, until the widow undergoes either levirate marriage or *halitsah*, she is not permitted to marry another man.

The laws of levirate marriage are found in the Talmud in the book of YEVAMOT. It explains that if the dead brother had either a daughter or a son, the widow is exempt from levirate marriage. Also, if the widow is pregnant at the time of her husband's death and gives birth only later, she is also exempt. Furthermore, the obligation applies only if the widow is capable of having children. If she is sterile or past childbearing age, she is exempt.

In the period after the Talmud, the rabbis debated whether levirate marriage or *halitsah* was preferable. Among the

Engraving showing the ceremony performed by a widow exempting her from a levirate marriage. Nuremberg, 1724.

Sephardim, levirate marriage was preferred; among Ashkenazi scholars, *halitsah* was encouraged.

In 1944 the CHIEF RABBINATE in Erets Israel issued a ruling that required the surviving brother to support the widow financially until he releases her by *halitsah*. A later ruling by the Israeli Rabbinate (1950) forced the surviving brother to perform *halitsah* in order to release the widow to marry whomever she wished. In other words, he may not marry her even if he wants to. This law was applied especially to SEPHARDIM, who for centuries had practiced levirate marriage. In 1953 Israel's parliament gave the rabbinical courts complete authority over *halitsah*, including the power to imprison the surviving brother if he has not given *halitsah* within three months.

REFORM JUDAISM has eliminated levirate marriage, including *halitsah*. CONSERVATIVE JUDAISM has also invalidated levirate marriage, though there is still some discussion about requiring *halitsah*.

LEVITES   The tribe descended from Levi, third son of the patriarch JACOB. The *kohanim* – PRIESTS – are Levite males who descend directly from AARON, the first HIGH PRIEST, who belonged to the tribe of Levi.

According to the Bible, the roles assigned to this tribe were originally intended for the firstborn of each family. However, after the sin of the GOLDEN CALF – in which the firstborn participated but the Levites did not – the Levites were given a special role in the SANCTUARY and later in the TEMPLE. The Levites were responsible for carrying the different parts of the mobile Sanctuary and its vessels as the Israelites journeyed through the desert. There were three families within the tribe (Gershon, Kehat, and Merari) who were assigned to carry special items. When the tribes camped around the Sanctuary, the

Levites were in the inner area, while the other tribes camped around them.

The Levites were responsible for teaching the people the TORAH (Deut. 33:10). They had no land, but were instead supported by a TITHE given to them by the other tribes. The Levites in turn gave a tithe to the priests.

In the Temple, the Levites functioned as Temple singers and musicians and served as the Temple administration and gatekeepers. They assisted the priests as well, by washing their hands before the PRIESTLY BLESSING. Today their descendants are given the special honor of being called up second (after a descendant of the priests) to the READING OF THE LAW in the SYNAGOGUE.

LEVITICAL CITIES   See ASYLUM

LEVITICUS, BOOK OF   Third book of the PENTATEUCH, known in Hebrew as VA-YIKRA. It has 27 chapters and 859 verses. The Talmud calls Leviticus *Torat Kohanim*, "The Priest's Manual," because the contents of the book describe the ritual activities of the PRIESTS.

Leviticus deals with the following subjects: laws of the SACRIFICES, anointing of priests, DIETARY LAWS, laws of PURITY, the DAY OF ATONEMENT, laws of ritual slaughter (see SHEHITAH), laws of HOLINESS, ritual impurity of priests, the FESTIVALS, laws concerning the tools of the SANCTUARY, the SABBATICAL and JUBILEE years, the BLESSING AND CURSING of the Jewish people, and pledges to the sanctuary.

Modern Bible scholars reject the idea that God is the author of the Pentateuch and particularly wonder who wrote Leviticus. They claim that the style of Leviticus does not match any of the other books of the Bible. Opinions differ: some see it as the latest book of the Pentateuch; Yehezkel Kaufmann identifies it as the most ancient of sources; the scholar Moses David Cassuto sees it as coming from the time of Moses.

LEVITICUS RABBAH   MIDRASH on the Book of LEVITICUS. Leviticus Rabbah is a collection of 37 independent units, each with a specific theme. Each unit begins with one or more introductions that quotes from verses in the biblical HAGIOGRAPHA ("Writings") and then lead into a central sermon.

The sages quoted in the book all lived in Erets Israel during the third and fourth century. The language is a mixture of

BOOK OF LEVITICUS	
1:1–7:38	Laws of the sacrifices
8:1–10:20	Consecration of the priests to work in the tabernacle
11:1–15:33	Forbidden foods and laws of ritual impurity
16:1–16:34	The Day of Atonement
17:1–17:16	Laws of ritual slaughter
18:1–20:27	Laws of holiness
21.1–22:33	Ritual impurity of priests
23:1–23:44	The festivals
24:1–24:23	Laws concerning the *menorah,* the showbread, and the blasphemer
25:1–25:55	The sabbatical and jubilee years
26:1–26:46	The Blessing and the Admonition
27:1–27:34	Pledges to the Sanctuary

Hebrew and Aramaic, with some Greek. It is most likely that the collection was edited some time in the fifth century, probably in Tiberias, Israel.

LEX TALIONIS   See RETALIATION

LIBERAL JUDAISM   See REFORM JUDAISM

LIFE   Judaism places supreme value on human life. According to the Bible, after creating the world and all its creatures, God "breathed into man's nostrils the breath of life" (Gen. 2:7). Life is a gift that was given to man at that moment when all of creation was prepared and ready for him. It is also a gift that can be taken from him if he fails to choose the path of good and obedience to the COMMANDMENTS (see Deut. 30:20; 30:15–19).

Human beings are expected to try to improve their quality of life, both physically and spiritually. The destruction of a single life is equal to destroying the whole world (*Sanh.* 4:5). Saving a life is so important that it pushes aside the SABBATH commandments. Similarly, safeguarding the health of the mother

Part of the Book of Leviticus found at Qumran.

and infant during childbirth or feeding a sick person on the DAY OF ATONEMENT is more important than the observance of any of the commandments associated with that day. (See PIKU'AH NEFESH.)

LILITH   The main female DEMON in Jewish tradition. Originally Lilith referred to a certain type of evil spirit; in the Middle Ages she was identified as a specific demon, the first wife of ADAM before Eve was created.

Lilith is described in the Talmud as a winged creature with long hair (*Er.* 100b; *Nid.* 24b) who haunts people sleeping alone in their homes (*Shab.* 151b). The Talmud relates that during the time that Adam lived separated from Eve, he gave birth to spirits, demons, and liliths (*Er.* 18b). According to later traditions, Lilith seduced Adam and bore from him spirits and demons. According to Jewish folklore, Lilith is particularly threatening for newborn children. It therefore became customary to write AMULETS to protect children from her.

LITURGY   In First Temple times, PRAYER did not yet have the set format that it has today. There were some public religious readings, for example the ceremony of the FIRST FRUITS, the confessions of the High Priest on the DAY OF ATONEMENT, and the recitation of Psalms by the Levites. However, it was not until the Second TEMPLE period that public prayer at fixed times became central to Jewish worship.

According to the Talmud, the Men of the Great Assembly created the order of prayers that the congregation recited at various times during the day (*Ber.* 33a; *Meg.* 17b, 25a). Regular weekday services were held four times daily by the delegations sent to the Temple from the 24 districts of the country, while the rest of the people met to pray in their home towns. These services were given the names *Shaharit* (morning), *Musaf* (additional), *Minhah* (afternoon), and *Ne'ilat She'arim* (evening, lit. "closing of the [Temple] gates"). In this era, prayer existed side by side with the SACRIFICES. Even in the outlying areas, the services matched those performed at the Temple.

After the destruction of the Second Temple (70 CE) prayer replaced the sacrifices, which could no longer be offered (*Ber.* 26b). Prayer became common in synagogues wherever Jews lived. In addition, those who led the prayers did not have to be PRIESTS. The core elements of the prayer service have remained constant until today: formal blessings (BENEDICTIONS), the requirement to recite the *Shema* twice daily, the daily AMIDAH (known as the *Tefillah*), and the ADDITIONAL SERVICE on occasions when an additional service had been offered in the Temple (e.g., SABBATH and FESTIVALS.). Later developments included the EVENING SERVICE, the ALEINU prayer, and the KADDISH. Traditionally, prayers were recited by a quorum of ten adult male worshipers (MINYAN).

Jewish prayer also allows for individual self-expression. The Talmud records many examples of private devotions (see *Ber.* 16b–17a). Likewise, TORAH study was incorporated into the fixed prayer as a form of worship. Portions of the Torah and the PROPHETS were read publicly during the prayer service. By the end of the time of the Talmud, PIYYUTIM entered the fixed prayer service. These were religious poems composed by individuals, rather than passages taken from the Bible. The first *siddur* (PRAYER BOOK) for the ordinary worshiper was edited by SAADIAH GAON (tenth cent.), who arranged the prayers in a logical order.

Two separate prayer traditions developed, that of Erets Israel and that of Babylonia. The Erets Israel variation (see NUSAH) led to the Roman traditions of Italian Jewry, that of northern France, and those of the ASHKENAZIM of Western and Central Europe. The Babylonian variation gave rise to the Yemenite traditions and the Provencal rite of southern France, as well as those of the SEPHARDIM. Hasidic prayer of the 18th century borrowed widely from the Sephardi tradition, yet included *piyyutim* that are Ashkenazi.

New religious movements introduced changes to the prayer book and to synagogue ritual. These have included prayer in the local language (as opposed to Hebrew), the use of western melodies in the service, counting women in the *minyan*, and the removal of prayers that no longer seemed relevant. Each movement printed its own prayer book, which became a statement of where the movement stood on the subject of the important religious issues connected to liturgy. Even in ORTHODOXY, the liturgy has changed in response to important events in the modern world, such as Israel's INDEPENDENCE DAY, JERUSALEM DAY, and HOLOCAUST Remembrance Day.

LOVE OF GOD   Israel is commanded to "love the Lord your God with all your heart and with all your soul and with all your might" (Deut. 6:5). While "fear of God" is also a COMMANDMENT, it seems that love of God is the highest form of religious relationship. Why? Because it is preferable to act out of love. The SIFREI to Deuteronomy 32 states: "Act out of love, for the TORAH makes a distinction between one who acts out of love and one who acts out of fear.... In the former case, the reward is doubled and redoubled." For MAIMONIDES, fear is a stage in the development of love of God, but love of God is the highest level that one should try to reach (*Yad, Teshuvah* 10).

Great Jewish thinkers have debated the best way to achieve love of God. Maimonides says that when a person looks at the world and clearly sees its wonder and the creatures that have been created in Divine wisdom, "he will right away love Him, praise Him … and long to know His great Name" (*Yesodei Torah* 1:1, 2). Others say that love of God is the ecstatic joy of the mystic (see ALBO, JOSEPH; BAHYA IBN PAKUDA; MYSTICISM, JEWISH). There is still another approach, based on the words of the *Sifrei* to Deuteronomy 6:5: "Take these words of the Torah to your heart – and in this way learn to recognize Him at Whose word the world came into being – and cleave to His paths." These actions – the study and performance of the commandments – are identical with love of God.

LOVE OF ISRAEL   (Heb. *ahavat Yisra'el*). Term for the love of one's fellow Jew and a loving regard for the Jewish people. Judaism stresses love of one's neighbor; but at the same, time the idea of Israel as God's CHOSEN PEOPLE leads one to think of a nation of fellow Jews.

The term *ahavat Yisra'el* does not appear in the classic literature. In fact, it did not enter popular Hebrew until the 19th century. It is given a specific meaning by Abraham Isaac KOOK. As opposed to the "blind hatred" (*sinat hinnam*) that led to the Second Temple's destruction (*Yoma* 9b), Kook maintained that Israel's REDEMPTION and the building of the Third Temple would be brought about through *ahavat hinnam* – "blind love" of fellow Jews.

LOVE OF NEIGHBOR   The command to love one's neighbor as oneself. In Leviticus 19:18 we read: "You shall not take vengeance nor bear any grudge against the children of your people, but you shall love your neighbor as yourself: I am the Lord." While the Bible seems to be issuing a command concerning the emotion of love, the sages saw the command as calling for actions. HILLEL (1st cent. CE), at the request of a non-Jew, summarized the message of Judaism as: "That which is hateful to you, do not do unto others" (*Shab.* 31a). MAIMONIDES, interpreted it as follows: "Be loving to your fellow man … speak of him positively and have compassion upon his possessions" (*Yad, De'ot* 6:3).

NAHMANIDES notes an interesting contradiction. R. AKIVA (*Sif.* on Lev. 19:18) refers to love of neighbor "as yourself" as a "great principle of the Torah." Yet elsewhere, R. Akiva rules that one is not required to sacrifice one's life for the sake of another (*BM* 62a). Nevertheless, says Nahmanides, all envy must be removed from one's heart, to the extent that one can wish all kinds of blessings far greater than one's own on one's neighbor.

It is not clear from the sources whether the word "neighbor" means "all people" or "fellow Jews" only. On the basis of the Bible alone, fellow Jews is probably closer to the plain meaning. Elsewhere, however, love of the stranger is commanded: "If a stranger sojourns with you in your land … you shall love him as yourself … for you were strangers in the Land of Egypt" (Lev. 19:33–34). Thus, "neighbor" takes on a more universal meaning.

In actual practice, Jewish attitudes towards their neighbors have been shaped as much by historical experience as they have by the Bible's commandments.

LUBAVICH   See CHABAD

LUBAVICHER REBBE   See SCHNEERSOHN, MENAHEM MENDEL

LUDMIR, MAID OF   (Hanna Rachel Werbermacher; 1805–1892). Hasidic *tsaddika* ("female holy master"; see HASIDISM). She was born in Ludmir, Poland. She prayed with great religious fervor and studied religious texts. After receiving "a new and awe-inspiring soul" in a vision during an illness, she became a charismatic preacher and attracted a large following. She wore a TALLIT and TEFILLIN during prayer and recited KADDISH for her father, all traditionally COMMANDMENTS that apply to males. She had her own synagogue and gave lectures to her Hasidim at the third SABBATH meal, SE'UDAH SHELISHIT, as was the custom of the Hasidic rebbe. At the age of 40 she married and moved to Erets Israel.

LURIA, ISAAC AND LURIANIC KABBALAH   Isaac Luria (1534–1572; known as the *Ari*, acronym for "Divine Rabbi Isaac"). The *Ari* was the founder of a system of Kabbalah named for him. His early history is largely unknown. He was raised in Egypt, before arriving in Safed in 1570. In Safed, he had a small group of disciples. The most important was R. Hayyim VITAL, who later wrote down the main works of the Lurianic Kabbalah. Luria and Vital tried to keep the new system a secret. In fact, after Luria's death Vital collected the notes written by the other disciples and forbade them to study the Kabbalah except in his presence. Two of the disciples did not follow his instructions. This resulted in versions of the Lurianic Kabbalah that differ from that taught by Vital.

Legend has it that when Vital was ill, his manuscripts were stolen from his home and copied. In this way Luria's ideas began to spread in the last decade of the 16th century. Interestingly, Luria himself never put his system into writing. His Kabbalah is based on dynamic mental/emotional pictures that could not translate easily into writing. For this reason those who have tried to explain Luria's system rely on diagrams.

Luria introduced three new terms into Jewish mystical literature: *tsimtsum* (contraction), *shevirah* (breaking [of the vessels]), and *tikkun* (mending or correcting). In his mystical scheme, God – who took up the entire universe – began CREATION by first withdrawing into Himself. This was necessary to provide an empty space in the universe in which to create. At this point God began giving off Divine light (see SEFIROT). However, in the Lurianic system, this was a disaster: the world could not hold the pure Divine light, and the holy vessels that were supposed to contain it shattered. This is *shevirah*, the breaking of the vessels. As a result, the Divine light returned to God, leaving behind a broken world. How did this happen? Could God have meant it this way? The disciples of Luria offer a number of interesting and very complicated explanations, the main one having to do with the existence of evil powers together with good, a bold idea when attached to God.

The most meaningful idea that Luria gave to the world of the Kabbalah is *tikkun*, the "mending" or "correcting" of the disaster of the *shevirah*. Luria's concept of correction is truly revolutionary, because it suggests that true Divine unity did not exist in the past, i.e., "in the beginning." Rather it will come to be when the process of *tikkun* is complete in the universe. Of course, the question must be asked: if the world was "broken"

Emanation of the Sefirot *depicted as vessels, as described in Lurianic Kabbalah. Manuscript. Lithuania, 1749.*

from the beginning and the final "mending" will occur only in the future, what do the events of our history mean? For Luria, history is the story of repeated attempts by God to bring about

tikkun and to free the captured sparks of creation. First with ADAM and the GARDEN OF EDEN, then with ABRAHAM and the people of Israel, then with MOSES and Mount Sinai, etc. He believed final REDEMPTION was always very close, but in each case, another *shevirah* (involving SIN) occurred to delay it.

How then will the great drama of Luria's system play out? The task of *tikkun* has been given to the human race, and especially to the people of Israel. Humans decide the fate of the world with their deeds. The proper performance of the COMMANDMENTS, ethical deeds (see ETHICS), and even proper thoughts and good intentions all contribute to the final repair of the world. Unworthy actions, on the other hand, stand in the way of redemption.

Luria died in a plague at the age of 38. The impact of his system on the entire Jewish world is felt to this day.

LURIA, SOLOMON (BEN JEHIEL) (known as *Maharshal*; 1510–1573). Luria was born in Brest-Litovsk, Lithuania, where he became the leading rabbi and founded a YESHIVAH. In 1555 he became the rabbi of Lublin, Poland.

The *Maharshal*'s approach to the Talmud was rational, strict, and completely unique. He insisted on identifying the actual meaning of the text. He differs from those commentators who attempted to show that various versions of the text could all be correct. His major work is a collection of Jewish law, *Yam shel Shelomo* ("Solomon's Sea"). His shorter work, *Hokhmat Shelomo* ("Solomon's Wisdom"), is about different books of the Talmud. It is printed in most Talmud editions.

LUZZATTO, MOSES HAYYIM (known by the acronym *Ramhal*; 1707–1747). Poet and mystic. He was born in Padua, Italy. As a youth he began to study KABBALAH. He was so carried away by this study that he attempted to take concrete steps to bring about the coming of the MESSIAH. He often went into a trance, in which he believed that he received messages from God. He attracted a circle of followers, but as a result of his actions, he was forced to flee. He eventually settled in Amsterdam and had trouble there as well. He was threatened with EXCOMMUNICATION if he did not stop studying the Kabbalah. It was here that he wrote his *Mesillat Yesharim* ("The Path of the Upright"), one of Judaism's most beloved and widely studied books of ETHICS.

Luzzatto eventually settled in Safed, Erets Israel, in 1743. Following a plague in 1746, which claimed his wife and son, he fled to Acre. He died a year later and was buried in Tiberias.

MA'AMAD (MAHAMAD) (lit. "stand"). Sephardi community leadership body. The *ma'amad* was appointed by the previous one and ruled over all community matters.

MA'ARIV See EVENING SERVICE

MA'ASEROT ("Tithes"). Seventh tractate (book) of the Order of ZERA'IM in the Mishnah. Its five chapters discuss all aspects of the tithes that farmers must separate from the rest of their crop for donations . The laws in this tractate include all categories of tithes: the heave offering, first tithe, second tithe, and poor man's tithe (see TITHE).

MA'ASER SHENI ("Second Tithe"). Eighth tractate (book) of the Order of ZERA'IM in the Mishnah. Its five chapters deal with the laws of separating and eating the second TITHE (one-tenth of the remaining produce after the first tithe; Deut. 14:22–29, 26:12–15). In the last chapter, Johanan the HIGH PRIEST abolishes the declaration made when taking the tithes.

MACCABEES See HASMONEANS

MACHPELAH, CAVE OF See HOLY PLACES

MAFTIR ("One who concludes"). Honor given to the last person called to the READING OF THE LAW in the SYNAGOGUE. This person reads the last verses (at least three) of the portion read from the Torah scroll on that particular SABBATH, FESTIVAL or fast day. On a regular Sabbath, after seven people have been called to the TORAH, the *maftir* repeats the last few verses. On a Sabbath that is also on a New MOON, HIGH HOLIDAY, or PILGRIM FESTIVAL, a special *maftir* is read from an additional Torah scroll. The special *maftir* tells about the TEMPLE sacrifices for that day.

A boy celebrating his BAR MITZVAH usually reads both the *maftir* and *haftarah* (section of the Prophets). If he can, he reads the entire Torah portion for that Sabbath. In many non-Orthodox synagogues, girls read these texts as well on the occasion of their BAT MITZVAH.

MAGEN DAVID (lit. "shield of David"). Six-pointed star, which in recent centuries has become a Jewish symbol. It was

Magen David *("Shield of David") carved on a stone frieze of the synagogue of Capernaum, 2nd–3rd century CE.*

often used in Europe and the Near East for decoration as early as the Bronze Age. It first appeared on a Jewish seal found at Sidon from the seventh century BCE. During Second Temple times, it appears on Jewish and non-Jewish objects, having no special Jewish meaning. It appeared on some synagogues in the 13th and 14th centuries in Germany and on many amulets, *mezuzot*, and magical Hebrew texts of the Middle Ages.

Between the 14th and 18th centuries the symbol was used by Jewish and non-Jewish printers and even found its way into some coats-of-arms. It appeared on the flag of the Jewish community of Prague and on their official seal. In Eastern Europe it was used as a decoration for ritual objects.

The mystical Jews, and especially the followers of SHABBETAI TSEVI, saw the "shield of David" as a symbol of the REDEMPTION. The Jews of the ENLIGHTENMENT (19th century) chose the

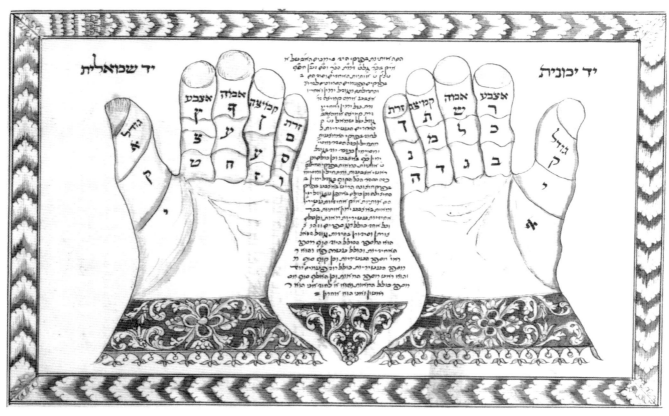

Use of the letters of the Hebrew alphabet in the context of chiromantic mysteries. Manuscript. Lithuania, 1754.

magen david as their identifying symbol. From Central and Western Europe, the "Jewish star" went out to become an identifying symbol in the Jewish world.

The *magen david* was chosen by the Zionist movement during the First Zionist Congress (1897) and later became the central figure on the blue and white flag of the State of Israel. The Nazis used the Jewish star on the yellow "badge of shame" that the Jews were forced to wear during the HOLOCAUST. The Red *Magen David* ambulance service in Israel is like the Red Cross in Western countries.

MAGGID   (lit. "narrator"). Hebrew term meaning "one who brings a message" (II Sam. 15:13). To the mystics (see MYSTICISM, JEWISH), a *maggid* was a mysterious voice that gave secret knowledge to special people through DREAMS or daytime revelations. Rabbi Joseph CARO, SHABBETAI TSEVI, and Moses Hayyim LUZZATTO heard these special voices.

From the times of the Mishnah, the word *maggid* meant preacher (see also DERASH; HOMILETICS) who delivered sermons based on the Bible portion of the week. In Ashkenazi communities of the Middle Ages, preachers would wander from town to town, bringing encouragement to the Jews. From the late 17th century on, there were preachers who received a salary and led the community together with the rabbi. HASIDISM spread through Eastern Europe thanks to Hasidic *maggidim* like DOV

BAER OF MEZHIRECH. The MITNAGGEDIM, who opposed the Hasidim, had *maggidim* of their own who spread their philosophy. One example is Jacob KRANZ, the famous *Maggid* of Dubno. Using dramatic touches, these preachers could move their audiences to tears.

Both the ethical MUSAR movement and the Zionist (see ZIONISM) movement had their own style of preachers.

MAGIC   The Bible shows much interest in magic. Three types of magicians are mentioned in Deuteronomy 18:10–11: those who predict the future using various signs; those who engage in actual magic; and those who make predictions and also perform magic, using the dead as a source of information.

The Bible forbids any type of sorcery. Belief in magical powers contradicts belief in God, the All-powerful. Certain types of magicians are even sentenced to death (Ex. 22:17; Lev. 20:27; see WITCHCRAFT). Despite this, ASTROLOGY and other forms of sorcery were practiced by the Israelites. The PROPHETS spoke out against all forms of magic. According to the Mishnah, magic is like IDOLATRY. Witches and male sorcerers must be executed (*Sanh.* 67a).

In the Middle Ages, God's name was used in *segullot* (charms or remedies), amulets, etc. (see SUPERSTITION). This practice developed under the influence of the KABBALAH and the Jewish mystics. NAHMANIDES, Moses Hayyim LUZZATTO, and Menasseh ben Israel used magic in their work. The EXCOMMUNICATION (*herem*) ceremony used a certain type of magic that apparently was permitted. In the 17th and 18th centuries in East European communities, the *ba'alei shem* (wonderworkers) began to practice magic and popular medicine. They used amulets to drive away demons (see BA'AL SHEM). They used secret names to unmask thieves, find lost items, and purify houses from evil spirits. A magical ceremony removed spirits of the dead believed to be lodged in the body of a living person (see DIBBUK). Another form of magic was believed to create living creatures (see GOLEM).

Still, magic was never an important part of Jewish society. Nonetheless, the medieval Christians believed that the Jews had special powers and that they were the devil's people (see ANTI-SEMITISM).

MAH NISHTANAH   See FOUR QUESTIONS

MAH TOVU   ("How lovely"). Opening words of a prayer recited by ASHKENAZIM on entering the synagogue, just before the MORNING BENEDICTIONS. The first sentence is from the Book of Numbers and the rest is from Psalms. According to the Talmud (*Sanh.* 105b), the "tents" and "dwellings" mentioned in the prayer, which was taken from the story of the heathen prophet Balaam (Num. 24:5), refer to Israel's synagogues and houses of study. The prayer expresses a Jew's love for the synagogue and for the prayer service.

MAHZOR   (pl. *mahzorim*, "cycle"). Prayer book for FESTIVALS. Originally, the term *mahzor* was the same as the *siddur* (PRAYER BOOK). It was a book of prayers arranged according to the cycle of the year. The 11th century *Mahzor Vitry* was a prayer book from Northern France that contained the prayers for Sabbaths, and festivals throughout the year.

In the 13th century, Ashkenazi Jews began to call the daily and Sabbath prayer book a *siddur* and the prayer book for the festivals and special Sabbaths a *mahzor*. These *mahzorim* were mainly used by the CANTOR (prayer leader) and were beautifully decorated. At this time, most of the *mahzorim* were divided into two volumes. The first volume contained prayers for the four special Sabbaths before PASSOVER (see SABBATHS, SPECIAL) and prayers for Passover and SHAVU'OT. The scrolls of SONG OF SONGS, RUTH, LAMENTATIONS, and ECCLESIASTES were usually included as well. The second volume contained the complete prayer services for ROSH HA-SHANAH and the DAY OF ATONEMENT.

Sephardim had a special prayer book for the three PILGRIM FESTIVALS called *Mo'adim* and had separate volumes for the New Year and Day of Atonement. The Hasidim added the Sephardi *piyyutim* (hymns) and adopted Isaac LURIA's version of the prayers. The Jews of Yemen pray from an all-inclusive book called a *Tikhlal*, which was handwritten until the 19th century.

The REFORM, CONSERVATIVE, and RECONSTRUCTIONIST

Piyyut *(liturgical poem) associated with the Torah portion* Shekalim *(Ex. 30:11–16). From a* Mahzor. *Germany, 13th–14th century.*

movements each have their own version of the *mahzor*, which they adapted to fit their ideas and beliefs. Nowadays there are many editions of many versions, some with commentaries and translations to various languages.

MAID OF LUDMIR   See LUDMIR, MAID OF

MAIMONIDES, MOSES   (known by the acronym *Rambam* – Rabbi Moses ben Maimon; 1135 or 1138–1204). Jewish legal expert and philosopher; the leading intellectual figure of medieval Judaism. Maimonides was a successful physician who also wrote important works of HALAKHAH (Jewish law) and Jewish thought. His major halakhic work, the *Mishneh Torah* ("The Second Torah"), is the most important book of Jewish law of all times. His *Moreh Nevukhim* (*The Guide for the Perplexed*) is the most important work of medieval Jewish philosophy.

Moses ben Maimon was born in Córdoba, Spain, to a leading family of rabbis. In 1148, his family was forced to flee to the city of Fez in North Africa, where Maimonides trained as a physician. In 1177, he was appointed head of the Jewish community of Fostat, and in 1185, he became court physician of Saladin's chief minister, al-Fadil. He was buried in Tiberias, Israel, where many still visit his grave.

Halakhic Writings   Maimonides' halakhic writings are written

The Mishneh Torah *the summary of the Oral and Written Torah written by Maimonides.*

Traditional likeness of Maimonides with a reproduction of his signature. Woodcut.

in a clear style and are systematically arranged according to subject. They include:

The Commentary to the Mishnah (the *Siraj*), which was written for both popular and learned audiences. It includes several essays that are each important in their own right. In one of these essays, the Introduction to the Tenth Chapter of *Sanhedrin*, Maimonides talks about ESCHATOLOGY (the "End of Days"), the RESURRECTION of the dead, and his famous 13 PRINCIPLES OF FAITH.

Pastoral Letters or *Epistles.* Maimonides was considered a spiritual leader and guide by many Jewish communities in the Mediterranean region. His pastoral letters (rabbinic advice) and RESPONSA (answers to Jewish legal questions) show sensitivity and reflect serious Jewish thought. These letters are mainly addressed to communities in trouble, such as the Jews of Morocco, who were forced to convert to Islam.

Sefer ha-Mitzvot ("The Book of the Commandments"), the introduction to the *Mishneh Torah*, lists the 613 COMMANDMENTS. It also explains how Maimonides decided which of the commandments should be included in the 613.

The *Mishneh Torah* or *Yad ha-Hazakah* ("Mighty Hand") was Maimonides' major halakhic work. It is a CODIFICATION of all of Jewish law, organized in a clear and logical system. It presents the basic principles behind each group of laws, which are arranged within a framework according to subject rather than in the order of their appearance in the PENTATEUCH. He did not include the sources for his rulings. Unlike other similar works of Jewish law, Maimonides' work includes every commandment, even laws that were no longer in use, such as those of the TEMPLE sacrifices.

Philosophical Views   Maimonides' main philosophical work, *The Guide for the Perplexed*, influenced Jewish thought for hundreds of years. It attempts to answer the questions of the Jews of the time, who were confused by the contradiction between Greek philosophy and Judaism. The book gives philosophical proof of the existence of God. It also interprets the commandments and explains how they help a person become more complete.

Maimonides taught that the world is run by the laws of nature. God intervenes very rarely, and there are very few miracles. Everything else has a natural explanation. He did not feel the need go into the details of complicated ideas, such as the MESSIAH and the Messianic Age, but taught that it is enough to believe in these ideas in general.

He taught that the commandments are a result of the wisdom of God. They are meant for the well-being of human beings, who must try to understand their meaning but observe them even if they do not understand. Maimonides believed that people should love God by studying TORAH and developing their intellect.

Many rabbis disagreed with Maimonides' ideas during his lifetime and afterwards. The controversy continued in one form or another throughout the Middle Ages.

MAIMUNA A joyous celebration held by the Jews of North Africa to mark the end of PASSOVER. The origins of this custom are unknown. The name comes from the Arabic word for "good fortune." After sunset, on the last day of Passover, the *Maimuna* table is set with festive dishes and decorated with flowers. There is also a dish of flour with gold coins (for prosperity) and a bowl of yeast (for making the first loaf of bread after eating unleavened bread for a whole week). An uncooked fish is also set on the table, symbolizing fertility. Friends and relatives visit until late into the night. The host gives each guest a leaf of lettuce dipped in honey and pastries made with honey, symbolizing sweetness. The next morning, families go on picnics. In modern Israel, the *Maimuna* is celebrated by organized communal picnics, with the main gathering held in Jerusalem.

MAJOR PROPHETS See ISAIAH, JEREMIAH, EZEKIEL

MAKKOT ("Lashes"). Fifth tractate (book) of the Order of NEZIKIN in the Mishnah. Its three chapters deal with the trial and punishment of false witnesses, cases of manslaughter, escape to a city of refuge (see ASYLUM), and the 59 sins that are punishable by lashes.

MALACHI Last book of the PROPHETS section of the Bible. The title of the book, Malachi, was either the name of the

BOOK OF MALACHI

1:1–1:5	Introduction
1:6–2:9	Priests held responsible for spiritual downfall
2:10–2:16	Denunciation of mixed marriages and of divorces
2:17–3:5	The approach of the Day of the Lord
3:6–3:12	Denunciation of the Jews for failing to pay tithes to the Temple
3:13–3:21	Condemnation of those who do not believe in God's justice
3:22–3:24	The coming of Elijah before the Day of the Lord

prophet who wrote the book or from the Hebrew word meaning "my messenger." If the second is the case, the author of the book is unknown. According to the Talmud, Malachi lived at the time of HAGGAI and ZECHARIAH, and preached in the second year of the reign of King Darius of Persia. Once these three prophets died, prophecy came to an end. Malachi was the first to suggest that ELIJAH the Prophet would play a role in the coming of the MESSIAH (3:23–24).

MALKHUYYOT ("Kingships"). The first of the three middle blessings of the AMIDAH prayer of the ADDITIONAL SERVICE of ROSH HA-SHANAH (the New Year). This section mentions the additional SACRIFICES in the TEMPLE on Rosh ha-Shanah and has ten verses that talk about God as king. The Talmud says: "Recite *Malkhuyyot* before Me so as to accept Me as King over you" (*RH* 4:6). This section also includes the ALEINU LE-SHABBE'AH prayer.

MAMZER See ILLEGITIMACY

MAN According to the Bible, man was created by God as part of the world. He is the climax and the purpose of CREATION. Abraham Joshua HESCHEL commented that the Bible is not a book about God, but a book about man. Once the world was created, its entire focus became man and his history. Man is created last and is blessed to rule all of the creatures of the earth (Gen. 1:28–29). Man is created in the image of God, "Let us make man in our image …" (Gen. 1:26). The second chapter of Genesis goes into greater detail about the creation of man: "And the Lord formed man of the dust of the ground and breathed into his nostrils the breath of life, and man became a living soul" (Gen. 2:7).

The rabbis taught that unlike other creatures, man is not complete until he develops his own personality and becomes a moral "self." The "image of God" is interpreted as man's freedom of choice, his ability to invent and to learn and use language, his intelligence, and his ability to understand the idea of being created in the image of God (*Avot* 3:4).

The fact that all people are descendants of a common human ancestor means that all men and women are equal and were created in the "image of God." At the same time each person is a unique individual.

According to Jewish tradition, each person has a *yetser ha-tov* (good inclination) and a *yetser ha-ra* (evil inclination; impulses). The ability, to choose between good and evil, right and wrong, existed even before ADAM AND EVE ate from the tree of knowledge. A person can serve God with both his good and evil inclination, by using self-discipline to channel his impulses (see FREE WILL).

In the Bible, the words *nefesh* (soul) and *ru'ah* (spirit) meant the living being that is man and not a separate part of man. The rabbis, however, developed two different aspects of man: "All creatures from heaven have their bodies and souls from heaven. All creatures created from earth have their bodies and souls from earth. Man alone has the body from earth and the soul from heaven. Thus, if he does the will of his Father in heaven, he becomes like a heavenly creature. If he does not, he becomes a totally earthly creature" (*Sif.* 30b).

Since the Bible deals mostly with Israel as a nation, it does not discuss the destiny of man as an individual. The rabbis taught that the life of man does not end with physical death. They spoke of a "world to come" including the "RESURRECTION of the dead," where man is rewarded and punished according to his actions. (See REWARD AND PUNISHMENT; AFTERLIFE).

MANASSEH   See TRIBES, TWELVE

MANNA   The food miraculously given to the Israelites in the wilderness (Ex. 16:14–35). The Israelites ate manna until the day after the first PASSOVER in Canaan (Josh. 5:12). It is called "bread" and described as "a fine, flaky substance" or like "coriander seed, white and tasting like wafers in honey" (Ex. 16:31). It was gathered, ground, boiled and made into cakes (Num. 11:8). Moses told the Israelites to gather one portion per person per day and not to leave any over for the next day. Any manna that was left over stank and became infested with maggots. On Friday each person gathered an extra portion for the Sabbath, when no manna fell (Ex. 16:22–25). The MIDRASH describes the manna in amazing ways: It tasted like different foods according to the needs and wants of the person eating it; it was the food of the ANGELS.

Recently, a food was discovered in the Sinai desert that strongly resembles descriptions of manna. Roaming Bedouin use it for food. It must be gathered in the morning, otherwise it is devoured by ants.

MANSLAUGHTER   In Judaism, there are two kinds of manslaughter. In the first, a person causes death accidentally through an act of negligence. In the second, a person causes the death of another person accidentally but without any negligence. In the second case, the person has not committed any crime and is not punished in any way, but must repent for the rest of his life because he caused the death of another human being.

The Bible gives an example of a person killed through negligence. A man was chopping wood and the head of the ax flew off and killed someone. The negligence was chopping wood with people close by. The killer had to take ASYLUM in one of the cities of refuge set up throughout Canaan, and stay there until the death of the HIGH PRIEST. If he left the city before that time, the relatives of the person he killed had the right to kill him (see BLOOD AVENGER).

When the killing was an act of intentional MURDER, the person was not allowed to enter the city of refuge. He would have to remain a fugitive from the relatives of the person he had killed.

The rabbis of the Talmud taught that there are two ways to tell if the case was manslaughter or murder: a) if the instrument that caused the death was one likely to cause death; and

b) according to the relations between the killer and the victim (Maim. *Hilkhot Rotse'ah* 3).

MA'OZ TSUR   ("O Fortress, Rock of my salvation"; Isa. 17:10). Opening words and title of a hymn sung on the HANUKKAH festival after lighting the candles and reciting the blessings. Written in 13th century Germany, the first letter of each stanza spells the name of the author Mordecai, who is otherwise unknown (see ACROSTICS). Each of the six stanzas describes a different period in Jewish history.

MA'OZ TSUR

Rock of Ages, let our song praise Your saving power;
You amid our raging foes were our sheltering tower.
Furious, they assailed us, but Your help availed us;
And Your word broke their sword when
our own strength failed us.

MARHESHVAN   See HESHVAN

MAROR   The "bitter herb" eaten with unleavened bread (MATZAH) and the PASSOVER sacrifice (*pesah*) as part of the meal before the Israelite's EXODUS from Egypt. The Jews were commanded to observe this traditional meal "throughout the ages" (Ex. 12:7; Num. 9:10–11), and it became a part of the Passover SEDER. The bitter herbs symbolize the Israelites' slavery in Egypt.

According to the Talmud (*Pes.* 2:5), plants that can be used for *maror* must have a "bitter sap and faded leaves." The Mishnah (*Pes.* 2:5) lists five such types of plants: "lettuce, chervil, succory, endives, and *maror.*" In Eastern Europe it became customary to use horseradish root for the bitter herb.

A man holding horseradish roots used by Ashkenazim as maror *("bitter herb") at the Passover Seder. From the* Copenhagen Haggadah.

Maror is eaten twice during the *Seder*: once on its own and once with the *haroset* (nut-apple mixture), in sandwich form.

MARRANOS (Sp. "swine"). A purposely offensive term used in Spain and Portugal for Jews who were forced to convert to CHRISTIANITY and their descendants from the early 15th century on. Since ancient times, Jews forced to take on a different religion were called *anusim* (forced converts) in Hebrew. It was assumed that they would return to Judaism as soon as they could (see APOSTASY).

In Spain in 1391, there was an outbreak of violence against the Jews, who were forced to choose between conversion, exile, or death. Some 100,000 Jews were converted at the time. This process continued over the next few decades. Meanwhile, a number of wealthy converted Jews had begun to take on high positions in the church and government. This caused much resentment and jealousy and led to suspicion that many were only pretending to be Christians. The Spanish Inquisition was established in 1480 to investigate all "New Christians." The first Marranos convicted of practicing Judaism secretly were burned at the stake in Seville. In July 1492 the remaining Jews of Spain were exiled. This caused many more Jews to convert to Christianity. Some were sincere "New Christians," but many remained members of a secret underground Jewish community.

Less than five years later, the entire Jewish community of Portugal was forced to convert to Christianity, with no option of leaving the country. They were genuine *anusim,* who made no secret of their true religious loyalty. From 1540 the new Portuguese Inquisition began to execute them.

The Marranos practiced some Jewish customs in secret, such as fasting on the DAY OF ATONEMENT and lighting the SABBATH candles. Leading this kind of double life was extremely dangerous. They could be betrayed by neighbors or servants. Spies for the Inquisition received huge rewards to turn in secret Jews. The Inquisition tortured them to make them reveal the names of other secret Jews, and many were burned at the stake.

Marranos condemned to be burned at the stake for relapsing into Jewish practices. Engraving by Maurice Picart, 1722.

Whenever escape was possible, Marranos fled to more tolerant places. Many settled in Amsterdam, where they returned to Judaism.

There were no more secret Jews in Spain by 1700 and the Spanish Inquisition was abolished in 1834. The total number of convicted Marranos in Spain and Portugal was 387,000, many of whom were burned alive. Since 1917, various groups have been discovered that practice semi-Jewish customs, and a number of secret Marrano prayer houses have been discovered in Spain.

MARRIAGE   The Concept From the time of CREATION, marriage has been part of God's plan, as we see in the story of ADAM AND EVE (Gen. 1:27–28, 2:18–24). In Judaism, marriage is the natural and desirable state of every adult. Marriage between a man and a woman can be compared to the relationship between God and the Jewish people (Hos. 2:21–22; Song of Songs) and between the Sabbath and the Jewish people (see LEKHAH DODI). According to the ZOHAR, the soul is made up of two parts – one male and one female – that become separated and enter different bodies. If they prove worthy, they are reunited in marriage.

Marriage is the norm and the ideal way of life. The HIGH PRIEST could not perform the DAY OF ATONEMENT rituals unless he was married. It was forbidden for a rabbi in the time of the Talmud to be unmarried (see CELIBACY). One of a father's obligations towards his son is to find him a wife. Marriage is called *kiddushin* (sanctification), because it is considered holy.

The idea of *kiddushin* means that the wife is no longer available to anyone else for the purpose of marriage (*Kid.* 2b). The main purposes of marriage are to build a home (Gen. 2:18) and FAMILY and to continue society. According to the Bible, a man may take more than one wife, but this custom was banned in Ashkenazi communities by Rabbenu GERSHOM in the 11th century. Today almost all Jewish communities follow the ban (see MONOGAMY AND POLYGAMY).

In ancient times, a father arranged the marriages of his sons and daughters. The husband "purchased" his wife for the agreed *mohar* (DOWRY) and she became his property. In Jewish law, the husband "acquires" the wife and not visa versa. By Second Temple times, some husbands would choose their wives from among the girls dancing in the vineyard on the minor festival of Tu be-Av (see AV, FIFTEENTH OF). The marriage ceremony itself was a contract between the groom and bride. The ceremony was followed by a great feast that normally lasted seven days.

In the times of the Talmud, two important developments took place. The *mohar* became a KETUBBAH, which meant that instead of the dowry going to the father of the bride, it was to be given to the bride herself if she would be divorced or become a widow. The small civil wedding service also became a public religious ceremony.

Eligibility for Marriage   In order to get married, a person has to be of age and physically and mentally fit for marriage. A person must be capable of expressing FREE WILL to get married and make a legal contract. This excludes minors and the mentally ill. A 13-year-old boy and a 12½-year-old girl are old enough to marry. The Mishnah teaches that 18 is the proper age for a male to marry, though many married younger.

Days and Periods when Weddings Are Not Celebrated   No weddings are held on the SABBATH or FESTIVALS. In the period of counting the OMER, from PASSOVER through SHAVU'OT, weddings are not conducted, except for the New MOON, LAG BA-OMER, and the three days before Shavu'ot (among SEPHARDIM they are permitted from Lag ba-Omer on). They are also not permitted during the three weeks before TISHAH BE-AV. It is customary to avoid holding weddings during the TEN DAYS OF REPENTANCE, from ROSH HA-SHANAH to the DAY OF ATONEMENT.

The Marriage Process   In the times of the Bible and the Talmud, marriage was a two-step process. It began with the betrothal – *kiddushin* (or *erusin*) – and ended with *nissu'in* – marriage.

Betrothal   The English term "betrothal" refers to the couple's commitment to marry in the future. Today it is the common term for an engagement, which is an agreement between two people to marry that has no legal status. In Bible and Talmud times, it was the first stage of the marriage process and also included *shiddukhin*. In Talmud times, this was when the parents of the bride and groom would agree on how much money each party was giving the couple. The terms were written in a document called a *shetar pesikta*.

From the late medieval period until the present, the prenuptial agreement included the agreement to get married and the date and place of the ceremony. The mothers of the bride and groom would break a dish, symbolizing that "just as a broken dish cannot be repaired, so it is better to proceed with the wedding and get a divorce than to break a prenuptial agreement."

In the times of the Talmud, *kiddushin* or *erusin* made the bride forbidden to all other men. The Mishnah says: "A woman is acquired (in marriage) in three ways: by money, by legal document, or by sexual intercourse." Over the centuries, the traditional act of *kiddushin* became the placing of a ring on the bride's finger by the groom. The groom also says, "Behold, you are consecrated (*mekuddeshet*) unto me with this ring according to the law of Moses and of Israel." This was followed by a blessing over the wine and a special blessing over the *kiddushin*. Up until the Middle Ages, the bride continued to live in her father's house even after this ceremony.

Nissu'in   This was the last stage in the marriage process, when the bride moved into the groom's home. It was accompanied by seven blessings. An important part of this stage of the wedding is that two witnesses must be present and follow the ceremony.

In the Middle Ages, because of the persecution of the Jewish communities, Ashkenazi Jews preferred to postpone the betrothal ceremony until just before the *nissu'in*. This is the custom in most communities today.

The Modern Wedding Ceremony   Many different customs exist. The following is an example of an Orthodox wedding ceremony:

The groom signs the wedding contract (*ketubbah*) before the wedding. The groom is led to the bride and lowers her veil over her face. The couple is then led to the *huppah* (marriage canopy), where the marriage takes place, accompanied by their parents. It is a custom for those leading the couple to carry lit candles.

Under the canopy, the rabbi recites the blessing over the wine and the *erusin* blessing. The bride and groom drink from the cup of wine. The groom then recites the appropriate phrase (see above, "Behold, you are consecrated…") and places the ring on the bride's right index finger. This is in fact the *kiddushin* ceremony.

Before the *nissu'in* ceremony, the *ketubbah* is read out loud. This is what separates the two ceremonies. Then the Seven Blessings are recited over a second cup of wine. The ceremony ends with the breaking of a glass in memory of the destruction of the Temple in Jerusalem. After the ceremony, the bride and groom are led to a private room for *yihud*, "seclusion," which symbolizes the *nissu'in* ceremony and entering their home together. After the wedding meal, the GRACE AFTER MEALS is followed by another round of the Seven Blessings.

Throughout the ages, a wedding has been an occasion for rejoicing. The ceremony is followed by a huge feast with music, dancing, and entertainment. During the week following the wedding, and in some communities for longer periods, the festivities continue. Today many couples are honored by special meals during that week, which each end with the Seven Blessings.

CONSERVATIVE and REFORM weddings follow the traditional pattern with some changes. They often leave out the custom of the groom's veiling the face of the bride before the ceremony, the walk to the *huppah* with candles, and the *yihud*. They have added a double ring ceremony, in which the bride also gives the groom a ring. The Reform service often includes poetry and songs that the rabbi and the couple choose.

Preparations and Customs   Traditionally, a bride must immerse herself in the MIKVEH (ritual bath) before the wedding. The wedding date is carefully fixed so that it does not fall during the period of menstruation or the week after (see NIDDAH). In some Sephardi and Oriental communities, the visit to the *mikveh* is a public celebration for women.

Most Sephardi communities hold a special celebration for the bride on the eve of the wedding called the *hinnah*. Women friends and family come to the home of the bride, whose hands are painted with red henna. In Yemen, women dressed the bride in colorful clothes and jewelry. The purpose of the ceremony was to drive away the EVIL EYE.

On the Sabbath before the wedding, among Ashkenazi communities, the groom is called to the READING OF THE LAW and is showered with candies. In Sephardi communities, it is usually the Sabbath after the wedding.

According to Jewish law, it is not necessary for a rabbi to perform a wedding ceremony, but from the 15th century, weddings were usually conducted by rabbis. In Israel, only the Orthodox Rabbinate is officially authorized to conduct weddings.

MARRIAGE CONTRACT   See KETUBBAH

MARRIAGES, PROHIBITED   Marriages that are prohibited by Jewish law can be divided into two categories: permanent and temporary.

Permanent Prohibitions   Marriages between close relatives as listed in Leviticus 18 and 20. These include a man's mother, stepmother, sister, granddaughter, aunt, daughter-in-law, sister-in-law, stepdaughter, and step-granddaughter, and his wife's sister during the wife's lifetime. Both the man and the woman, if adults, are considered guilty in the case of these sins. In addition:

a. If a husband divorces his wife, and she remarries and is divorced or widowed, her first husband cannot remarry her.

b. a wife who has willingly committed adultery cannot return to her husband or to the adulterer, even after divorce from her first husband (*Sot.* 27b).

c. A woman cannot marry anyone who represented her during her divorce proceedings or who witnessed her husband's death, to avoid suspicion of collusion (*Sh. Ar., EH* 12:1).

d. A PRIEST may not marry a divorcee (Lev. 21:14), widow, or harlot (Lev. 21:7).

e. A *mamzer* (offspring of an adulterous or incestuous relationship; see ILLEGITIMACY) may not marry a Jewish man or woman. Maimonides explains that this shows "the horror of forbidden marriages ... the [parents] were thus taught that by their act they bring upon their child irreparable injury" (*Guide* III, 49).

f. INTERMARRIAGE is forbidden. However, where the non-Jewish partner converts to Judaism before the marriage, it is permitted (see CONVERSION TO JUDAISM).

g. A man may not take a second wife, according to the decree of Rabennu GERSHOM (see MARRIAGE). This ban originally applied only to Ashkenazi Jewry, but was later accepted by most other Jewish communities as well.

Temporary Prohibitions   Certain marriages are prohibited only for a certain amount of time, after which they are permitted:

a. A widow or divorcee may not remarry for 90 days after the death of her first husband or receiving her *get* (bill of DIVORCE). This is to avoid confusion over the father of any child born soon afterwards.

b. A person may not marry in the 30-day period of MOURNING, and a widower must wait until three festivals have passed. If he has no children or has young children that need a mother's care, he need not wait that long to remarry (*Sh. Ar., YD* 392:2).

c. It is forbidden to marry a pregnant woman or nursing mother until the child is 24 months old (*Yed.* 42a).

d. If a woman's first two husbands died, she may not remarry a third time because the fate of her former husbands may bring bad luck to the third marriage.

e. A married woman may not take a second husband. In order for a divorce to be valid, the husband must give his wife a *get*. If he refuses, or if he is missing and cannot be found, the wife is left in a problematic situation. She has the status of an AGUNAH – an "anchored" woman, still attached to her husband and not free to remarry. Rabbis throughout the centuries have in many cases made great efforts to solve this problem in situations involving missing husbands.

MARTYRDOM   See KIDDUSH HA-SHEM

MASHGI'AH   ("supervisor"). a) The spiritual mentor in a rabbinical academy (YESHIVAH). It is his responsibility to supervise the studies and other activities of the students and to give lecturess on proper moral behavior. Ideally, the students feel under the influence of the *mashgi'ah* even when he is not physically present.

b) A person who supervises the DIETARY LAWS in a factory, restaurant, or any other place that food is prepared. He makes sure that the food is prepared according to Jewish law. The *mashgi'ah* reports to the rabbi, who endorses the product as being "kosher."

MASSEKHET   (lit. "web" or "woven fabric"; also called "tractate"). A book of the MISHNAH or TALMUD, more commonly called *Masekhta* (Aramaic). Each deals with a specific subject or area of law. It is customary for people who finish studying a *Massekhet* to hold a SIYYUM ("conclusion") ceremony – a festive meal at which they speak to the others present about the book's final idea.

MATRIARCHS   (Heb. *immahot*). SARAH, REBEKAH, RACHEL, and LEAH, the wives of the Patriarchs and ancestors of the Jewish people. Each of these women played a role at the dawn of Israel's history. Just as ABRAHAM, ISAAC, and JACOB were chosen by God to participate in the COVENANT (agreement), so were the matriarchs chosen rather than accidentals wives. Execpt for Sarah, the Bible tells in great detail how each wife was chosen. Each matriarch tried to ensure their sons' position in God's plan. They sometimes used deception and manipulation to achieve their aims as well as love and support.

Although the matriarchs have an honored place in Jewish folk life, they are not included in the prayers where God is called "God of our Fathers." In recent years, under the influence of Jewish FEMINISM, some groups have added the matriarchs' names to these prayers. Traditionally, Jewish girls are blessed by their parents on Friday nights in the names of the matriarchs (see PARENTAL BLESSING).

MATTAN TORAH   See REVELATION

MATZAH   Unleavened bread made from dough with no yeast or leavening and baked before it begins to rise. The oppsite of matzah is HAMETS (regular leavened bread). Both are made of

Child eating a Matzah.

one of the FIVE SPECIES of grain: wheat, emmer, rye, barley, and oats. According to Jewish law grains begin to ferment, causing the dough to rise, 18 minutes after they are mixed with water. Therefore, in order for dough to qualify as matzah, it must be baked no more than 18 minutes after the water was added to the flour.

According to the Bible, one may not eat or posess *hamets* for the seven days of PASSOVER. On the SEDER night, each person must eat one olive's weight (*ka-zayit*) of matzah (Ex. 12:15–20, 13:7; see also *Pes.* 28b, 120a). At the *Seder,* a special blessing is said over the matzah. It is customary to refrain from eating matzah in the days leading up to Passover, so that the matzah will be special at the *Seder.*

The matzah is a symbol of both slavery and REDEMPTION. On the one hand, the matzah stands for the Egyptian slavery. Deuteronomy 16:3 calls it the "bread of affliction" (*lehem oni*), and the Haggadah says: "This is the bread of affliction that our fathers ate in the land of Egypt." On the other hand, matzah is a symbol of freedom. The Passover Haggadah explains: "It is because there was not time for the dough to rise, before the Ruler of All revealed Himself and redeemed them."

MAYIM AHARONIM   ("Latter Waters"). Symbolic washing of the fingers before reciting GRACE AFTER MEALS. In ancient times, only a knife and the fingers were used to eat, therefore Grace could not be recited until each diner had cleaned his hands (*Ber.* 46b). Another explanation was that a food accompaniment known as "salt of Sodom" could lead to blindness if rubbed in the eyes (*Er.* 17b; *Hul.* 105a–106b). Nowadays, there are some rabbis who believe that this custom is no longer necessary.

MEAL OFFERINGS   See SACRIFICES AND OFFERINGS

ME-AM LO'EZ   See CULI, JACOB

MEAT AND MILK   See DIETARY LAWS

MEDICAL ETHICS, JEWISH   Guiding principles and standards of behavior based on traditional Jewish norms. The subject became an important one only recently and is now beginning to develop its own experts and literature. The main form of this literature is rabbinic RESPONSA.

Issues   The moral problems in medicine usually have to do with birth (e.g., BIRTH CONTROL, ABORTION, ARTIFICIAL INSEMINATION and fertilization, genetic engineering, etc.) or DEATH (e.g., resuscitation, ending treatment, definition of death, removal of donor organs, etc.). Other issues include experimentation on animals and humans and doctor-patient relationships. Some questions are directly connected to Judaism, such as medical practice on the SABBATH; medications that contain non-kosher substances; fasting on the DAY OF ATONEMENT; visiting and praying for the SICK; or health hazards, such as smoking.

Trends   Traditional Jewish law is quite liberal, when compared with other religious systems. For example, in Jewish law, there is no absolute ban on birth control or abortion. The physical and mental health of the mother is one of the main considerations in deciding when these are allowed.

There have been some changes of opinion over the years, usually in the more lenient direction. In the past, the only abortions that were permitted were those that clearly saved the mother's life. Today, there are quite a few judgments that permit abortions even though the mother's life is not in danger.

Some Major Principles   The guidelines for cases of Jewish medical ethics are usually principles found in the Bible or Talmud.

1. *The sanctity of life*, the infinite value of every innocent human life. This rule affects decisions concerning mercy killings, experimentation on human beings, and breaking religious laws, such as keeping the Sabbath, in order to save a human life.

2. *The commandment to save life and preserve health*. It is not optional but mandatory to do anything possible to save a human life. A doctor may not refuse to treat a patient, and a patient may not refuse to be treated.

3. *The obligation to reproduce.* This affects the attitude towards abortion and birth control as well as sterilization, which is allowed only for pure medical reasons and never on economic or social grounds.

4. *Holiness of the marriage bond.* This affects issues such as donor insemination, INCEST, active HOMOSEXUALITY, and sexual relations during the menstrual period (see NIDDAH).

5. *The duty to relieve pain and suffering.* In Judaism, a person does not have to perform certain commandments if it will cause physical pain. One is not allowed to inflict pain on an innocent person, including oneself. A person does not own his body, but is its caretaker; therefore one is not allowed to damage his body in any way.

6. *Respect for the dead.* Because a person is created in the Image of God, the body is considered holy even after death. BURIAL must take place as soon as possible, and CREMATION and unnecessary autopsies are forbidden. However PIKKU'AH NEFESH (saving human life) is the most important principle of all; therefore autopsies may be performed in order to study the effects of a new drug, or study a family's medical history. Likewise, donating organs for transplant is permitted.

Gray Areas and Some Summary Conclusions   A few examples are listed here:

The beginning of life. In Judaism, a person is considered alive from the moment of birth. Therefore, all rabbis agree that abortion is permitted if the mother's life is in danger. There are different opinions about what to do if her health is in danger or the fetus suffers from a defect. Many questions arise on the subjects of experimentation with embryos, cloning, and surrogate motherhood.

The terminal stage of life. It is never permitted to relieve a patient's suffering by deliberately hurrying death (e.g., by "pulling the plug"). Some rabbis permit not performing "heroic methods" to preserve life that would prolong the patient's suffering.

Miscellaneous   Possibly dangerous medical experiments may be performed only on people who would directly benefit from the success of the test. A healthy person may not endanger himself even if it could save millions of others.

Medical experiments may be conducted on animals, but every effort must be made to reduce the animal's suffering to a minimum.

MEGILLAH   ("Scroll"). Tenth tractate (book) of the Order of MO'ED in the Mishnah. Its four chapters deal with the times, places, and way of reading the Scroll of ESTHER on PURIM, the laws of the four special Sabbaths (see SABBATHS, SPECIAL), and the way of reading from a SCROLL OF THE LAW and the HAFTARAH (portion of the PROPHETS).

MEGILLAT TA'ANIT   ("Fast Scroll"). Ancient Aramaic text that lists the days of the year on which fasting is not permitted, since on these days joyful things happened. The scroll is an important source of information for the history of the Second Temple period, since it was written before the Mishnah.

MEHITZAH   See EZRAT NASHIM

ME'ILAH   ("unlawful use of holy property"). Eighth tractate (book) of the Order of KODASHIM in the Mishnah. Its six chapters deal with the sin of accidentally benefiting from anything that was set aside for a donation the TEMPLE.

MEIR   (c. 110–c. 175 CE). Rabbi of the fourth generation of the Mishnah, outstanding scholar. His teachers were Rabbi AKIVA, Rabbi ISHMAEL BEN ELISHA, and Rabbi ELISHA BEN AVUYA. He was secretly ordained as a rabbi during the time of the persecutions led by Emperor Hadrian. After Hadrian's death, Meir moved with the Yavneh ACADEMY to Usha in the Galilee. He was a traditional SCRIBE, and once wrote a scroll of ESTHER from memory. He and Rabbi Nathan ha-Bavli tried to remove the *Nasi* (president of the SANHEDRIN), Rabbi Simeon ben GAMALIEL, from his position and were exiled. He died in exile.

Meir's name appears more than 330 times in the Mishnah and 452 times in the TOSEFTA. Most of the anonymous statements in the Mishnah were made either by Meir or by Rabbi Nathan. Their names were removed from these statements because they tried to remove the *nasi*. Meir gave public Torah talks for women and men, and his own wife was a Torah scholar (see BERURYAH).

MEIR, GOLDA   (Myerson; 1898–1978). Zionist leader and prime minister of Israel. Golda Meir grew up in Kiev and Pinsk and settled with her family in Milwaukee in 1906. In 1921, she left for Erets Israel and began her career on the Women's Labor Council of the Histadrut trade union federation. She later became a member of the Histadrut's executive committee. In 1930, she was among the founders of the Mapai Party, which ruled the country's politics for nearly 50 years. During the War of Independence, she raised over $50 million for Israel in the United States.

In the new State of Israel, Meir served as ambassador to the Soviet Union and then minister of labor in BEN-GURION's government. Ben-Gurion called her "the only man in my cabinet." In 1965, she was diagnosed with cancer and left the government. In 1969, she became Israel's prime minister and led the country in its quest for peace with the Arabs. After the Yom Kippur war (1973) Golda Meir retired, her spirit broken because the country had not been prepared for the war. For over 50 years she had struggled to revive Jewish national life in the State of Israel, becoming one of the world's most admired women.

MEIR BA'AL HA-NES   ("Meir the Miracle Worker"). Name used for Rabbi Meir, who had the reputation in Jewish folklore of performing miracles. Traditionally, his tomb is in Tiberias, but it is not certain which Rabbi Meir is buried there. Some

FROM THE SAYINGS OF RABBI MEIR

When speaking to the Holy One, blessed be He, a man should keep his words to a minimum.

Reduce your business engagements and study Torah.

Whoever lives permanently in the Land of Israel, eats its fruits in ritual purity, speaks Hebrew, and recites the *Shema* each morning and evening is assured a place in the world to come.

For the sake of true penitence, the whole world is forgiven.

The dust used for creating Adam was gathered from every corner of the world.

All mankind is judged on Rosh ha-Shanah and the verdict is sealed on the Day of Atonement.

Don't look at a flask, but rather at its contents; a new flask may be filled with old wine, yet there may not even be new wine in an old container.

A man should recite 100 benedictions daily.

As God returns good for evil, so should you.

say it is Rabbi MEIR of the Mishnah (2nd cent. CE); some a Rabbi Meir ben Jacob, who went to the Land of Israel in the 13th century; and there are other views as well. There is an annual pilgrimage to the tomb on *Pesah Sheni* (see PASSOVER, SECOND). From the 18th century on, charity was collected in the name of Rabbi Meir Ba'al ha-Nes, and to this day many Jewish homes have a charity box with his name on it. Some believe that giving to these charities will protect them from evil.

MEIR (BEN BARUCH) OF ROTHENBURG (known by the acronym of *Maharam*; c. 1215–1293). Leading German Tosafist (see TOSAFOT) and author of PIYYUTIM (hymns). Meir answered many letters with questions of HALAKHAH, and about 1,000 of his RESPONSA have survived. He was the leading Talmud scholar of his day. His opinions appear in many places in the *Tosafot*, and he wrote commentaries on 18 of the books of the Talmud.

He witnessed the burning of the Talmud in Paris in 1242, after which he wrote the hymn *Sha'ali Serufah be-Esh* ("Ask You Who Burned by Fire") which is recited by Ashkenazi Jews on the fast of TISHAH BE-AV. In 1286, Rabbi Meir was put in a prison tower by Emperor Rudolf I. The emperor was willing to release him for a huge ransom, but Rabbi Meir would not allow the Jews to pay it, fearing it would encourage the emperor to arrest more Jews. Meir died in 1293, but his body was only returned to the Jews in 1306, after a high ransom was paid. He was buried in the cemetery in Worms. He passed his TORAH legacy on to his students, mainly Rabbi ASHER BEN JEHIEL.

MELAVVEH MALKAH ("Escorting the [Sabbath] Queen"). Festive gathering and meal arranged on Saturday night after HAVDALLAH has been recited at the end of the SABBATH. The custom probably began in the time of the Talmud, when the rabbis could not agree on the number of meals that had to be eaten on the Sabbath (*Shab.* 117b). One opinion was that a light meal should be eaten after the Sabbath (*Shab.* 119b; see also SE'UDAH). There is an obvious parallel between the *Kaballat Shabbat* service, welcoming the Sabbath, and the *Melavveh Malkah* ceremony at the end of the Sabbath. Another name for this meal is *Se'udat David* ("King David's Banquet). God told David that he would die on a Sabbath, but He did not tell him the precise date (*Shab.* 30a). Therefore, the end of each Sabbath became a reason to celebrate.

Unlike the three Sabbath meals, the *Melavveh Malkah* is a custom and not an obligation of Jewish law. Its mystical importance was stressed by the mystics and the Hasidim (see HASIDISM).

The custom today is to have a gathering with light refreshments and to sing Hebrew and Yiddish melodies. According to an old legend, ELIJAH will bring the MESSIAH just after the Sabbath ends; therefore *Eliyahu ha-Navi* ("Elijah the Prophet) is one of the songs (ZEMIROT) usually sung.

MEMORIAL LIGHT (Heb. *ner neshamah* or *ner zikkaron*). A special lamp lighted in memory of a departed relative. This custom is based on the idea that "the soul of a man is a lamp

Woman lighting memorial lights inside the cave of Honi Hamaagel near Hatzor Haglilit in Israel.

for the Lord" (Prov. 20–27). The practice came from medieval Germany, but soon spread to other Jewish communities (see YAHRZEIT). A memorial light is lit on four occasions: during the first seven days of MOURNING (*shivah*) in the home of a family in mourning; on the anniversary or *yahrzeit* of a close relative's death; on the eve of the DAY OF ATONEMENT; and on the eve of the final day of the PILGRIM FESTIVALS, when MEMORIAL PRAYERS are said in the synagogue. The memory light burns for 24 hours. It is also customary to light a memory light on those festivals when *Yizkor* MEMORIAL PRAYERS are read in synagogue. In Israel, memorial candles are lit on Yom ha-Sho'ah (HOLOCAUST Memorial Day) and Yom ha-Zikkaron (Remembrance Day for Israel's fallen soldiers).

MEMORIAL PRAYERS AND SERVICES

(Heb. *hazkarat neshamot*, "commemorating souls"; often shortened to *hazkarah*, *azkarah*, or *mazkir*). Traditional prayers in memory of the dead and expressing the hope that their souls will be granted eternal rest. This is an ancient custom that was already in practice at the time of JUDAH MACCABEE. After his victory over Gorgias he sent people to Jerusalem "to pray for the dead and make atonement for them, so that they might be cleared of their sin" (II Macc. 12:43). By the time of the Talmud, prayers in memory of the dead had become an accepted custom.

Memorial prayers are recited at a FUNERAL, during the week of MOURNING after burial, when the TOMBSTONE is put on the grave, and on the YARZHEIT, the anniversary of a close relative's death.

The best-known memorial prayer is the KADDISH, recited during the mourning period and on the *yarzheit*. In fact this is not really a memorial prayer, but a prayer in praise of God's name that is also recited after studying TORAH. The general custom is to recite it for 11 months for parents who have died and 30 days for other relatives.

Among Sephardi, Italian, and Oriental Jews, the standard memorial prayer is known as *hashkavah* ("laying down to rest"). The *hashkavah* is read on the Sabbath before or after a death anniversary when it is customary to give a donation in memory of the deceased. In many Sephardi communities, a *hashkavah* is recited every Sabbath morning for those who died in the past 11 months. A special *hashkavah* is read on the Day of Atonement in honor of rabbis and leaders of the community.

Ashkenazi Jews replace the *hashkavah* with the *hazkarat neshamot* service. The main part of this service is the EL MALEI RAHAMIM prayer, which is recited after the Torah reading on weekdays (never on a regular Sabbath), on the Monday or Thursday closest to the anniversary of death. A memorial service is held four times a year in Ashkenazi synagogues after the READING OF THE LAW: on the last day of PASSOVER and SHAVU'OT, the Day of Atonement, and SHEMINI ATSERET. This service is known as *Yizkor* and is made up of special prayers in memory of parents and other close relatives, as well as *El Malei Rahamim* prayers for the six million HOLOCAUST martyrs, and those who fell in defense of the State of Israel. It is customary for those who have two living parents to leave the synagogue while *Yizkor* is recited.

Yom ha-Sho'ah (HOLOCAUST Memorial Day) is now observed throughout the Jewish world (on 27 Nisan in Israel; on 19 April in the Diaspora). In Israel, Yom ha-Zikkaron (Remembrance Day) is observed on 4 Iyyar in honor of those who fell in the defense of the State of Israel. MEMORIAL LIGHTS are also lit on each of these occasions.

MENAHEM MENDEL OF KOTSK

(known as "the Kotsker"; 1787–1859). Polish Hasidic leader. His teachings were different from those of mainstream HASIDISM. Menahem Mendel was a famous Talmud scholar who devoted his life to challenging those who were not sincere. He searched for *emet* ("truth") and rebuked anyone, including other Hasidic masters, whom he found insincere. He once said that all he needed was a company of 200 young devotees prepared to shout from the rooftops: "The Lord, He is God!"

He studied under Jacob Isaac, "the Seer of Lublin," but followed his student, Jacob Isaac, "the Holy Jew" of Przysucha (1766–1814). After his death, Menahem Mendel became the outstanding student of Simhah Bunem. Members of this branch of Hasidism fought hypocrisy and prided themselves on doing good in private and, when they sinned, doing so openly.

After Simhah Bunem's death in 1827, Menahem Mendel became the head of the Przysucha school. For reasons unclear, he spent the last 20 years of his life shut away in his room, refusing to see the Hasidim who came to see him. Although the Rebbe's son David was appointed after his death, many of the Hasidim preferred to follow his brother-in-law Isaac Meir Alter (1789–1866), who founded the GUR dynasty.

Menahem Mendel left no writings, but his ideas can be found in the works of his followers and in a number of collections published after his death.

MENAHOT

("Meal Offerings"). Second tractate (book) of the Order of KODASHIM in the Mishnah. Its 13 chapters deal with the laws of the different meal (grain) offerings brought to the TEMPLE (cf. Lev. 2:5–1:6, 6:7–1, 23:13–17). It also includes the laws of drink offerings. The *minhah* (lit. "gift" or "present") was also called the poor man's offering, because those too poor to bring an animal sacrifice were allowed to bring a meal offering instead (see SACRIFICES AND OFFERINGS).

MENDELSSOHN, MOSES

(1729–1786). German-Jewish pioneer of EMANCIPATION and community leader, philosopher, scholar, and translator. Born in Dessau, son of a Torah scribe, he received a traditional Jewish education from the local rabbi, David Frankel. When Frankel became the Chief Rabbi of Berlin (1743), Mendelssohn followed him there.

Mendelssohn studied many languages and wrote philosophical works on subjects such as immortality and the existence of God. He quickly became one of the leading thinkers of the European Enlightenment. His book *Jerusalem* took on a more Jewish point

Moses Mendelssohn, on the left, playing chess with the Lutheran theologian J.C. Lavater. Looking on, Gotthold Lessing. 1866.

of view, discussing the separation of Religion and State, religious freedom, and other aspects of Jewish philosophy.

The Swiss pastor J.C. Lavater publicly challenged Mendelssohn to either disprove the truth of CHRISTIANITY or convert. He was forced to publish a reply, in which he declared himself a proud Jew. This event caused Mendelssohn to concentrate on Jewish issues and fight for civil rights for Jews in Europe. He also wrote a very influential German translation (in Hebrew letters) and commentary (*Bi'ur*) on the PENTATEUCH. He believed that the Jews needed to find ways to integrate their religion into the general society. He established a Jewish Free School, in which modern textbooks were used to teach Jewish subjects.

Mendelssohn wrote in Hebrew and contributed to several Hebrew journals. When asked what he thought about plans to settle the Jews in their own state, he said that a major European war would have to take place first. He also worked towards understanding between Christians and Jews, writing: "What a world of happiness we would live in if all men adopted the true principles that the best of the Christians and the best of the Jews hold in common."

Mendelssohn was the most admired Jew of his time. He guided the Jews of Germany out of the ghetto and into the environment of Emancipation and Enlightenment.

MENORAH   Candelabrum (lamp), especially one with seven branches like the one in the SANCTUARY and TEMPLE, which became a main Jewish symbol. It is described for the first time in Exodus 25:31–38, where God tells Moses how to build it. "You shall make a candelabrum of pure gold … Its base and its shaft, its branches, bowls, knobs, and flowers shall be of one piece. Six branches shall come out of its sides …"

The *menorah* was placed in the Sanctuary and later a similar one was placed in the Temple. SOLOMON's Temple had ten gold candelabra. When the Jews were exiled into Babylonia, they took one of these candelabra with them, and when they returned to Jerusalem, they placed it in the Second Temple. In the second century BCE, Antiochus Epiphanes and the Syrian army looted the Temple and stole the gold *menorah*. After the HASMONEANS defeated the Syrian army, JUDAH MACCABEE made a new seven-branched *menorah*.

After the Romans conquered and destroyed Jerusalem in the year 70 CE, all traces of the *menorah* disappeared. The Romans displayed it in their victory parade in Rome. There are many legends about the fate of the *menorah*.

The *menorah* became a main Jewish symbol. It has been discovered on mosaic floors, walls, and latticework in ancient synagogues. It was carved and painted in Jewish cemeteries and used to decorate utensils of glass, ceramics, and metal. Drawings of the *menorah* were also found in the caves and hiding places of Jewish rebels and ZEALOTS. The symbol of the

Earliest known representation of the Temple menorah, *found in Jerusalem, dating from the reign of Herod (c. 37–4 BCE).*

menorah expressed the great myth of the exile and the hope for redemption.

The seven-branch *menorah* was hardly ever fashioned in three dimensions, because the Talmud teaches that one may not make a *menorah* identical to the one that stood in the Temple.

When the Jews of Central and Western Europe began to integrate into society, they gradually stopped using the *menorah* as a symbol because it stood for Temple worship and mysticism. They looked for a symbol that would express the message that Judaism brought to all of humanity. They adopted the Shield of David (MAGEN DAVID), which became the most popular Jewish symbol, or the two TABLETS OF THE COVENANT.

In the beginning of the 20th century, many Zionist organizations chose the *menorah* as their symbol. The Bezalel Academy for fine arts, founded in Jerusalem in 1906, encouraged the use of traditional Jewish symbols, including the *menorah*. After the establishment of the State of Israel, the official symbol of the state was based on the seven-branched *menorah*.

MENSTRUATION   See NIDDAH

MERCY

(Heb. *rahamim*). A quality of God that man, particularly Jews, should be inspired to imitate. The Hebrew word for mercy or compassion, *rahamim*, is taken from the same root as *rehem*, "womb," so that mercy is related to a mother's feeling for her child. In Judaism, mercy is extremely important. Ideally, the three characteristics of the Jewish people are that they be "merciful, modest, and perform deeds of lovingkindness" (*Yev.* 79a). One of God's names is *Ha-Rahaman* – the Merciful One – therefore people too must be merciful: "Just as God is merciful, so must you be merciful" (*Sifrei Ekev* 89; see IMITATION OF GOD). However, God quality of mercy is balanced by His quality of JUSTICE.

Many laws of the PENTATEUCH are based on the quality of mercy. These laws include mercy towards ANIMALS. Unlimited mercy is not appropriate, however, so that "He that spares his rod hates his son" (Prov. 13:24).

The Bible teaches: "He will show you mercy and have compassion (Deut. 13:18)." Rabban GAMALIEL comments on this verse: "He who shows mercy to his fellow creatures will be dealt with in a merciful fashion from Heaven, whereas he who is not merciful to his fellow creatures will not be dealt with in a merciful fashion from Heaven."

MERIT

(Heb. *zekhut*). A virtue that is earned by freely choosing to obey God's commandments and performing good deeds (see GEMILUT HASADIM). The term *zekhut* is also used in the sense of giving someone the benefit of the doubt: "Judge every man favorably since one who judges his fellow man favorably is likewise judged favorably by others" (*Shab.* 127b).

This idea gave birth to the idea of *zekhut avot* ("the merits of one's fathers"), which means that the merit of past generations – including the PATRIARCHS of Israel – may benefit their descendants. This explains why the "good deeds of our ancestors"

are mentioned so often in the prayers. The "merits of the fathers" are one of the five things that will bring Israel's REDEMPTION more quickly; however, they are no substitute for good behavior, and do not outweigh the sin of abandoning the Land of Israel. This idea inspired many folktales of "hidden saints" (LAMED VAV TSADDIKIM), and led to the saying that "for the sake of even one righteous man the world would have been created … and for the sake of only one it will survive" (*Yoma* 38b). By observing one single commandment, "a man can tip the scales in favor of himself and the entire world" (*Kid.* 40b).

MESSIAH

(from the Hebrew *mashi'ah*, "anointed [one]"). The savior and redeemer at the End of Days. The term was originally used for anyone with a mission from God. After God's promise to DAVID (II Sam. 7:12–13), the family of David was considered specially chosen. ISAIAH and JEREMIAH predicted a king from the House of David whose rule would be particularly glorious. In the time of the Babylonian EXILE, this idea became associated with the "end of days."

Messianism and the Messianic Era

The messianic era will restore the kingdom of the House of David and will bring back all Jewish exiles to the Land of Israel. It will bring about a perfect society in which all of humanity will live in peace and harmony and worship one God.

The Book of Isaiah describes the messianic era as beginning with the DAY OF THE LORD, a day of utter chaos. Its end is the End of Days, when the House of the Lord will be built on a mountaintop and all the people of the earth will gather there. Both Judaism and CHRISTIANITY have interpreted the four evil beasts in the Book of DANIEL as the rise and fall of four empires that will come before the messianic era.

Messianism was an important idea in the times of the Second Temple. As the situation under the Romans grew more difficult, the Jews' belief in the Messiah grew (see ESCHATOLOGY). The Messiah was seen as an ideal human being who would save the Jewish people. Many believe that human nature would not be changed, nor would this be a miraculous event. God would be accepted by all, and justice would flourish. Many people were considered possible messiahs, from Zerubbabel at the time of the return from Babylonia, to BAR KOKHBA, leader of the second century CE revolt against the Romans.

After the Second Temple was destroyed and the Romans conquered the kingdom of Judea, the belief in a Messiah helped the Jews deal with their powerless situation in the Diaspora. Throughout the times of persecution, the dream of the return to the Land of Israel helped keep the spirit of the people of Israel alive.

According to Jewish tradition, before the Messiah comes, there will be a period of exile from the Holy Land, called the "birth pangs of the Messiah" (*hevlei mashi'ah*). The exact conditions necessary for the arrival of the Messiah are unknown. The Talmud states that the Messiah will come when the world is either all evil or all good.

Before the Messiah arrives, a leader from the house of JOSEPH will do battle with the forces of evil in order to redeem the people of Israel. After the Messiah of the house of Joseph is defeated, the Messiah of the House of David will arrive.

There are many prayers for the coming of the Messiah. The daily AMIDAH contains five BENEDICTIONS that mention the Messiah. (See also LITURGY.)

According to MAIMONIDES, belief in the Messiah is one of the 13 PRINCIPLES OF FAITH that every Jew must follow. He taught that the Messiah King would be a PROPHET with extraordinary intellectual gifts, who would be devoted to Judaism. He will serve as a model for all Jews and will found a dynasty to rule after him. Maimonides believed that the messianic era would be a "natural" time in which nearly all the physical laws of nature would remain the same. There would be some supernatural events; the most important is the RESURRECTION of the dead. Israel would no longer be ruled by other nations, and it would be a time of complete social justice. The Messiah would concentrate on the INGATHERING OF THE EXILES from the four corners of the earth to the Holy Land, world peace, and the acceptance of God as the one true king of the universe.

According to the ZOHAR (13th century), the main Jewish mystical book, the Messiah will start out by living in a palace (its symbol is a "Bird's Nest") in the Garden of EDEN. He will then appear on earth, in the Upper Galilee. Some mystics believe that the soul of the Messiah was that of the mystical first man, *Adam Kadmon*, which was transferred into the body of King David. The Messiah would have supernatural powers and bring on a period of a thousand years in which time would move more slowly and the nature of the universe would change.

During times of trouble, various false MESSIANIC MOVEMENTS have arisen, claiming that they would bring better times. Scholars and mystics have used numerical calculations to try to figure out when the Messiah would arrive.

Modern Orthodox Judaism sees the messianic era as a time when Jews are gathered together in the Land of Israel and are able to fulfill all of their religious obligations, including those that can be fulfilled only in the Land of Israel. The Temple and its sacrifices will be restored.

REFORM JUDAISM (19th century) taught that the Messiah was not a person but a state of moral perfection towards which the world was moving. Their goal for a messianic movement is to cooperate with all people in the world in establishing the Kingdom of God: universal brotherhood, justice, truth, and peace on earth.

CONSERVATIVE JUDAISM also teaches that the Messiah is a period of time rather than a human being. It will be a time of world peace, social justice, and the solution of all problems of disease and all forms of evil. This will happen in a natural way, and the world will be redeemed by the efforts of good people. The Jew is responsible to live and work toward a messianic age.

Modern ZIONISM can be seen as a secular messianic idea. Instead of waiting and praying, the Jewish people brought about an important change through human effort, by establishing a Jewish State. According to the first Ashkenazi Chief Rabbi of Israel, Rabbi Abraham Isaac KOOK, modern-day Jewish resettlement in the Land of Israel is the first stage in the process of REDEMPTION. It will eventually bring the messianic era.

The power of belief in the Messiah was courageously displayed during the time of the HOLOCAUST. Jews who were being taken to their deaths in the gas chambers sang the words of Maimonides' Principle of Faith: "I believe with complete faith that the Messiah will come, and even though he delays, I continue to believe."

MESSIANIC MOVEMENTS Organized attempts by leaders to present themselves as the MESSIAH and to restore the Kingdom of DAVID and Jewish independence in Erets Israel. From the Babylonian EXILE until the 18th century, such movements were inspired by: the age-old belief in the Messiah, feelings of homelessness and exile (GALUT), persecution and ANTI-SEMITISM, and a desire to prove God's justice in the world. As long as the Jews lived peacefully in exile, they were satisfied with praying for the Messiah. As soon as they faced massacre, EXPULSIONS, or other threats, a "prophet" would begin to preach about the Messiah. These "Messiahs" enjoyed varying amounts of popularity, but eventually, they were proven to be false.

In the Bible, some believed that Hezekiah (Isa. 11) and later Zerubbabel (Hag. 2:21–23) were possible Messiahs. Many believed that the HASMONEANS would bring the Messiah, even though they were not descendants of King David. The rabbis taught that before the REDEMPTION would come a time of great wars, which would be the "birth pangs of the Messiah" (*hevlei mashia'h*). "When you see great empires at war with one another," said the rabbis, "look for the Messiah" (Gen. R. 4:7).

In the time of the Romans, many "prophets" promised to end the Roman rule over Erets Israel. The most famous was Jesus of Nazareth. The DEAD SEA SCROLLS talk about the powerful messianic feelings of the Dead Sea sect. During the first revolt, which led to the destruction of the Temple, both Simeon bar Giora and Eleazar ben Yair claimed to be the Messiah. Simeon BAR KOKHBA, who headed the second revolt (132–135 CE) and died fighting the Romans, was more influential. Rabbi AKIVA called him "King Messiah" but was later told that "grass will grow in your cheeks before the Messiah will come" (TJ, *Ta'an.* 4:8).

The rise of ISLAM caused the Jewish messianic movements of the Near East to become violent. In the eighth century, Abu Isa al-Isafani and Yughdan of Persia set out to fight the Muslims. David Alroy founded another messianic movement in Kurdistan. At that time (the Second Crusade, c. 1146–1147) the Muslims and Christians were at war, and he took advantage of the conflict to gain the support of the warlike mountain Jews. He set out to defeat the Muslims and prepare for the Kingdom of the Messiah in Jerusalem, with his followers, the "Menahemites." The plan was ruined when Alroy was murdered.

Among the Sephardi communities of Spain and Portugal, there was much messianic activity. Abraham Abulafia was the first of many Sephardi "prophets." He tried to bring the redemption through mystical powers and appeals to popes and emperors. Two other factors encouraged the many false Messiahs over the next 300 years: traveler's stories of the Ten Lost TRIBES of Israel, who were rumored to be living beyond the River Sambatyon; and the ZOHAR (c. 1300), the major mystical work that had a powerful affect on the Jews of Spain and Portugal.

Events such as the forced conversions to CHRISTIANITY in Spain (1391), the fall of Constantinople to the Turks (1453), and the EXPULSION of the Jews from Spain (1492) were seen as signs of the arrival of the Messiah. The mystics of Safed (see LURIA, Isaac) and the sudden appearance of David Reuveni in Europe in 1524 also caused the Jews to expect the Messiah.

Reuveni was a mysterious adventurer who claimed to be the son of King SOLOMON and the brother of a King Joseph, who ruled the lost tribes of Reuven, Gad, and Manasseh in the Arabian province of Khaibar. His mission was to gain Christian support and conquer Jerusalem from the Muslims. Reuveni's story impressed Jews and non-Jews alike, and he gained many MARRANO followers. A Portuguese Marrano named Diego Pines returned to Judaism and escaped from Portugal to become a mystic and pseudo-Messiah under the name Solomon Molcho. He and Reuveni appealed to the Holy Roman Emperor, but were unsuccessful. Molcho was burned at the stake and Reuveni died in prison. Before his death Molcho attracted many followers, paving the way for the most famous false Messiah, SHABBETAI TSEVI.

The Thirty Years War and the Chmielnicki massacres of 1648–9 led to a new messianic movement led by Shabbetai Tsevi. Mystics believed that 1648 was the "messianic year." In the early 1650s Shabbetai Tsevi first claimed to be the Messiah. Nathan of Gaza, supported him, claiming that the Messiah had arrived and would overthrow the sultan of Turkey in 1666. Tsevi was the most charismatic (attractive) false messiah of all times. He had huge numbers of "believers" everywhere. Even after he was arrested by the Turks, converted to Islam when they threatened his life, and died, many continued to believe in him.

Most recently, many members of the CHABAD movement believe that the Lubavicher Rebbe, Menahem Mendel SCHNEERSOHN, is the Messiah. Even after his death in 1994, many of his followers still believe he is the Messiah and that he will return in the flesh to bring the redemption. Most non-Lubavich rabbis feel that this view is HERESY.

MEZUMMAN   See GRACE AFTER MEALS

MEZUZAH   ("doorpost"). The small scroll of parchment that contains passages from the Bible and is traditionally attached to the doorpost of every Jewish home. The custom comes from the COMMANDMENT in the Bible: "Write [these word of TORAH] upon the doorposts of your house and in your gates" (Deut. 6:9). The first passage in the *mezuzah* contains the opening paragraph of the SHEMA. It includes the commandments

Engraved silver mezuzah *affixed to the doorpost of the Great Synagogue in Jerusalem.*

to: 1) love God; 2) study the Torah; 3) read the *Shema* prayer; 4) wear TEFILLIN; and 5) put up a *mezuzah*. The second passage is also part of the *Shema* and talks about observing the above commandments.

The *mezuzah* must be written by a SCRIBE on parchment made from the skin of a KOSHER animal. The scroll is rolled and placed in a protective case and attached to the upper part of every right-hand doorpost in the home. The case is often beautifully decorated

When putting up the *mezuzah* the blessing "Who has commanded us to affix the *mezuzah*" is recited. *Mezuzot* should be checked twice in every seven years by an expert to make certain they are still valid.

Traditional Jews sometimes touch the *mezuzah* with their hand when entering and leaving their home to show that they are aware of fulfilling the commandment and that they rely on God's protection.

MICAH   Sixth of the 12 minor PROPHETS. He probably lived during the reigns of Jotham, Ahaz, and Hezekiah (c. 745–700 BCE), kings of JUDAH (Jer. 26:18; Mic. 1:1), and AMOS, the prophet. He preached both to the northern kingdom of ISRAEL and to the southern kingdom of Judah.

According to the Talmud (*BB* 14b), Micah also lived in the times of the prophets HOSEA and ISAIAH. He was the first prophet to predict that Jerusalem would be destroyed as a punishment for the city's sins against God. As a result, King Hezekiah prayed to God, and the city was not destroyed. Micah taught that God requires of man "only to do justice, to love mercy, and to walk humbly with your God" (Micah 6:8).

The Book of Micah is divided into three major parts. The

BOOK OF MICAH

1:1–3:12	Threatening prophecies: the sins of Israel and Judah; condemning of rich enemies, tyrannical rulers, and false prophets
4:1–5:15	Promise to restore Zion, rebuild the Temple, ingather the Jewish exiles, and bring the Messiah
6:1–6:16	God's charges against Israel; the city is threatened
7:1–7:20	Conquest of enemies and return of the exiles

---

first (ch. 1–3) predicts the destruction of Samaria and Jerusalem for their sins. The second (ch. 4–5) talks about the destruction of the state of Judah and rebuilding it to be greater than before. In the last part (ch. 6–7), Micah talks about dishonesty in the marketplace and corruption in the government of Samaria.

MIDDOT ("Measurements"). Tenth tractate (book) of the Order of KODASHIM in the Mishnah. Its five chapters describe the Second TEMPLE, give the measurements of each of its parts, the meeting hall of the Great SANHEDRIN, and where the PRIESTS stood watch.

MIDRASH ("exposition"). Rabbinic commentary on the Bible using stories, parables, and legends. The word comes from the Hebrew root meaning "to inquire, study, investigate," and "to preach." In the days of EZRA, those who wanted to understand God's law (Ezra 7:10) were already interpreting the ORAL LAW in order to explain it fully to the people (see DERASH).

During the times of the MISHNAH, the Midrash began to serve two purposes. The first, based on teachings of the ACADEMIES, helped to explain Jewish law as it appears in the Bible. The second, based on preaching in the synagogues, was a collection of tales (see AGGADAH) woven around biblical figures or rabbis used to teach lessons from the Bible (see MIDRASH AGGADAH).

The aggadic kind of Midrash has been a source of inspiration for Jewish preachers and has also influenced Christians and Muslims.

MIDRASH AGGADAH Homiletical MIDRASH teaching lessons through stories, parables, and other illustrations, often linked with biblical figures. The rabbis believed that the Bible was not only a book about the past, but also a book that speaks to the present generation, with its problems and concerns. The method of the Midrash is to uncover and find meaning in certain events and commandments in the Bible.

For the authors of the Midrash, a word or phrase in the Bible could be interpreted without considering its context. For example, it is clear that in Psalm 22:7 ("But I am a worm, less than a human, scorned by men, despised by people"), the Psalmist is referring to himself. The Midrash, however, explains

that it refers to Israel's position among the nations: "Just as the worm is the most despised of all creatures, so Israel is the most despised among nations. But just as the only visible organ of the worm is its mouth, so by its mouth [through prayers] does Israel cancel the evil decrees planned against them by the nations" (Midr. Ps. 22:18).

The text of the Bible is somewhat repetitive. The authors of the Midrash tried to interpret these repetitions. Rabbi AKIVA also taught that "the fact that two sections of the Torah are next to each other is meant to teach us some lesson" (Sif. Num. Balak 139). The Midrash asks why the story of the death of AARON follows the story of the breaking of the two Tablets of the Covenant (Deut. 10:6–7). It answers, "The order is meant to teach us that the death of the righteous is as sad in the eyes of the Lord as the breaking of the two tablets" (Lev. R. 20:7).

The Bible rarely states the reason or the background of the commandments or events. The Midrash often adds the reasons and motives. When ABRAHAM goes to war against the five kings (Gen. 14), the Bible says that the word of God came to Abraham in a vision, saying: "Do not fear, Abraham …" (Gen 15:1). Why, the Midrash asks, was Abraham afraid? And it answers: "Abraham feared and said to himself, 'Perhaps there was a righteous man among those whom I killed'" (Gen. R. 44:4).

The Midrash uses metaphor and allegory to interpret the text of the Bible. The rabbis of the Midrash often rejected the simple meaning of the text (PESHAT), for a number of different reasons. For example, the plain meaning of the sensuousness of SONG OF SONGS offended the rabbis' modesty. They therefore interpreted Song of Songs as a dialogue between God, the lover, and Israel, his beloved.

The Midrash often offers an explanation for sins committed by biblical figures. DAVID's affair with Bathsheba is explained by the theory that she had already been divorced by her husband, Uriah (Shab. 56a). Before going into battle, David's soldiers gave their wives a divorce that would be valid if they should go missing in action.

Another type of Midrash is barely even related to the text of the Bible. These legends are very similar to general folk tales. An example is the legend of King SOLOMON and Ashmedai, prince of the DEMONS (Git. 68a).

The Talmud says that one should not draw conclusions about the law (halakhah) from the aggadah. Nevertheless, later rabbis did so in the RESPONSA literature.

See also GENESIS RABBAH; EXODUS RABBAH; LEVITICUS RABBAH; NUMBERS RABBAH; DEUTERONOMY RABAH; LAMENTATIONS RABBAH; ESTHER RABBAH; SONG OF SONGS RABBAH; RUTH RABBAH; ECCLESIASTES RABBAH (this collection of ten works is known as the Midrash Rabbah).

MIDRASH HA-GADOL ("The Great Midrash"). Collection of midrashim from the entire range of rabbinic literature, put together by Rabbi David ben Aaron of Aden, Yemen, in the 13th century. It is based on the PENTATEUCH and is written according to the weekly readings. Before each weekly reading, there is a rhymed introduction written by the editor. He uses many ancient sources that are now lost, such as SAADIAH GAON's Arabic translation of the Pentateuch (*Tafsir*), which otherwise is almost unknown. Works that were lost over time have been reconstructed based on quotations in *Midrash ha-Gadol*.

MIDRASH HALAKHAH   MIDRASH that clarifies legal issues. This term is usually used for the *midrashim* on the last four books of the PENTATEUCH.

It is likely that the editors of these *midrashim* all used a common ancient source. This source was taught in the different schools and each school left its mark on the material. The *midrashim* of the school of Rabbi ISHMAEL make legal decisions using HERMENEUTICS while those of the school of Rabbi AKIVA prefer to learn the law by interpreting the text of the Bible. Both the Talmud and the TOSEFTA quote the *Midrash Halakhah* quite often.

MIDRASH TANHUMA   See TANHUMA

MIKRA   See BIBLE

MIKVA'OT   ("Ritual Baths"). Sixth tractate (book) of the Order of TOHOROT in the Mishnah. Its ten chapters deal with the laws of building a ritual bath (MIKVEH) and of immersion (Lev. 11:36, 15:16). It includes the measurements of the ritual bath, proper immersion, the use of springs, rivers, and seas as ritual baths, and the utensils that must be immersed in a ritual bath.

MIKVEH   (pl. *mikva'ot*; lit. a "collection" or "gathering" of water). Ritual bath. From ancient times, the *mikveh*, along with the synagogue and religious school, was an important part of Jewish COMMUNITY life. According to the PENTATEUCH (Lev. 11:36), it is the only way to purify people or utensils from the different sources of impurity mentioned there: "Only a spring, cistern, or collection of waters (*mikveh*) shall be cleansing." These sources include contact with a dead body, childbirth, menstruation, and seminal emissions. Many pious Jews visit the *mikveh* as a matter of CUSTOM before the DAY OF ATONEMENT and Hasidim do so before the SABBATH.

A whole book of the Mishnah, MIKVA'OT, is dedicated to the laws of the ritual bath. Archeological excavations have uncovered *mikva'ot* that were built according to its rules. Many were discovered near public bathing houses since before immersing in the *mikveh* a person has to first scrub away every possible bit of dirt. Such dirt is considered a barrier (*hatsitsah*) to the cleansing power of the ritual bath.

The source of the ritual bath must either be underground water (such as a spring), rainwater, or melted snow or ice. Spring water, seas, and rivers purify when flowing or moving, but rainwater purifies only when gathered in a natural pool. The pipes through which the water passes on its way to the pool must be made of earthenware, stone, concrete, cement, asbestos, or plastic and not of any material that can become impure.

The minimum amount of water is 40 *se'ah*. Today the standard amount in most communities is 762 liters (201 gallons). Once the bath contains this minimum amount, any amount of ordinary water can be added. Nowadays rainwater is collected on the roof and flows into a built-in cistern.

In Israel, the Ministry of Religious Affairs supervises and pays for the building of ritual baths. Today there are over 1,200 ritual baths in Israel. The CONSERVATIVE movement uses the *mikveh* for the immersion of converts. The REFORM movement considers the ritual bath unnecessary, although communities outside the United States insist on immersion for converts.

MILAH   See CIRCUMCISION

MINHAG   See CUSTOM

MINHAH   See AFTERNOON SERVICE

MINIM   ("sectarians"; sing. *min*). Term used by rabbis to mean Jewish groups that broke away from mainstream Judaism, such as the SADUCEES and Boethusians, KARAITES, SAMARITANS, and Nazarenes (Judeo-Christians or Ebionites). In the Talmud, a *min* is often closely associated with EPIKOROS or *kofer* (one who openly rejects the rabbis and the ORAL LAW).

When the Temple was destroyed in 70 CE there were more than two dozen sects within the Jewish camp. Many were seen as a threat to Judaism. Around 80–90 CE, BIRKAT HA-MINIM, a prayer against heretics, was added to the daily AMIDAH. This removed Judeo-Christians from the synagogue and the Jewish community and made them into a sect that was eventually destroyed by the Gentile Church. During the early talmudic period, the term *min* was used for pagan philosophers, Gnostics, or Christians. By the Middle Ages, it had come to mean those who supported ATHEISM or IDOLATRY. See APOSTASY and HERESY.

MINYAN   ("number," pl. *minyanim*). Traditionally, a prayer group of at least ten males over the age of 13. The Bible teaches that "God stands in the Divine assembly" (Ps. 82:1). The rabbis understood that this meant that if ten men pray together the SHEKHINAH – God's presence – is with them (*Avot* 3:6; *Ber.* 6a). The rabbis taught that it is very important to pray with a *minyan*. According to the Talmud (*Ber.* 6b), "When the Holy One enters a synagogue and does not find ten worshipers there, His anger is immediately kindled, as is written in the Bible: 'Why, when I came was no one there; why when I called, was there no answer?'" (Isa. 50:2). The idea of the *minyan* reflects the importance of COMMUNITY. REFORM JUDAISM, RECONSTRUCTIONISM, and many CONSERVATIVE congregations have accepted women in the *minyan*.

A *minyan* is required for:

Reciting the BAREKHU and the SHEMA in public worship.

Repetition of the AMIDAH with the KEDUSHAH prayer included.

Chanting of the PRIESTLY BLESSING.

The READING OF THE LAW and the appropriate section of the PROPHETS (HAFTARAH).

Reciting the KADDISH in public worship, at a funeral, or in a house of mourning.

The Seven Benedictions recited at a wedding and for seven days afterwards (see MARRIAGE).

Reciting the special GRACE AFTER MEALS for a CIRCUMCISION, a Redemption of the FIRSTBORN (*pidyon ha-ben*) ceremony, or a banquet in honor of a newlywed couple.

MIRACLES (Heb. "*nes*"). Extraordinary events that appear to violate the laws of nature, and are caused by God. The Bible describes many of these events, including the parting of the Red Sea, the falling of the MANNA, and ELIJAH's journey to heaven.

In the Bible, the activity of God is often described, and His "mighty deeds" are the main subject of the Bible. God destroys the cities of Sodom and Gomorrah, allows SARAH to have a baby at the age of 90, and causes a well of water to appear in the wilderness for Hagar (Gen. 21:29). These are not considered miracles, although they violate the laws of nature. In the Bible, in order for an event to be "miraculous," it had to have a psychological effect on those who witnessed it. The classic "sign and wonder" that Israel must never forget was the EXODUS from Egypt, which involved the Ten Plagues and the Parting of the Red Sea. Those who witnessed these events saw them as the "hand of God."

There is a pattern to the miracles in the Bible. Until MOSES appeared, "miracles" happened to people but no person was described as performing a miracle. From Moses until ELIJAH, miracles are performed by people, but only for a large crowd. In the times of Elijah and ELISHA, miracles are performed for individuals by individuals.

According to MAIMONIDES' (*Yesodei ha-Torah* 7), the miracles in the Bible were not meant to prove that God exists. The relationship of the Jewish people with God was based on their meeting with Him at Mount SINAI. The miracles in the Bible achieved concrete results: to save the Israelites, to provide food in the wilderness. In the Talmud, the rabbis taught that performing a miracle does not prove that one's opinions are correct (*BM* 29b).

Since God created the world, He would not need miracles to complete His handiwork. The rabbis taught that "at the time of creation, God set aside a condition for the sea, that it should part before the Children of Israel upon their leaving Egypt …" (Gen. R. 5:45). In this way, the "miracle" is part of nature.

NAHMANIDES wrote that the purpose of obvious miracles is to draw attention to the "hidden miracles" that are all around every day. The greatest miracle of all is life itself. In fact, says Nahmanides, there is no such thing as "nature." It is all miracle!

In the HALAKHAH (Jewish law) it says that a person must recite a special blessing when visiting a place where miracles occurred for the benefit of the Jewish people (*Ber.* 9:1).

MIRIAM Elder sister of MOSES and AARON. Miriam waited by the river to see what would become of the infant Moses after he was hidden among the reeds (Ex. 2:3–4). When the Israelites were taken out of Egypt, she led the women in song and dance (Ex. 15:20). Miriam was struck with leprosy for speaking badly about Moses' relationship with his wife, but was later healed (Num. 12:1ff). She died in Kadesh and was buried there (Num. 20:1).

In modern times, Miriam has become a symbol for feminists. Some have even added a "Cup of Miriam" to the Passover SEDER. The cup contains water, in memory of "Miriam's well" that accompanied the Israelites in their journey through the desert. Some dance in celebration of Miriam after the "Cup of ELIJAH." Miriam lived among the people, with lovingkindness for all.

MI SHE-BERAKH ("He who blessed [our fathers]"). Opening words and title of various blessings recited at the time of the READING OF THE LAW. A *Mi she-Berakh* prayer is usually said on behalf of each person called to the Reading of the Law, a sick person, the mother of a newborn baby, a BAR MITZVAH boy, or a groom before his wedding.

A separate and longer *Mi she-Berakh*, the Prayer for the Community, is recited on SABBATHS after the Reading of the Law. In Israeli synagogues, an additional *Mi she-Berakh* is recited for the protection of the soldiers of the Israel Defense Forces.

MISHKAN   See SANCTUARY

MISHMAROT AND MA'AMADOT (lit. "watches and stands"). Divisions of PRIESTS, LEVITES, and Israelites. At the time of the TEMPLE, all priests, Levites, and Israelites were divided into 24 groups, each group serving in the Temple for one week each half year. During the remaining four weeks of the festivals, all were divided into seven groups, each group serving one day a week. The shift of the Levites was called *mishmar* and the shift of the Israelites was called *ma'amad*.

After the Temple was destroyed, the rabbis assigned certain verses to be recited instead of the sacrifices. It became customary to recite special prayers, called *ma'amadot,* after the morning prayers. The *ma'amadot* are not a central part of the prayers and are only recited by people who wish to do so.

MISHNAH First written collection of the ORAL LAW, including nearly five centuries of Jewish legal traditions, from the time of the SCRIBES to the time of the *tannaim* (c. 20–200 CE; see TANNA and AMORA). The Mishnah (lit. "teaching" or "instruction") was handed down by word of mouth. It is the most important Jewish religious document after the Bible and was the basis of the TALMUD. It is the first collection of HALAKHAH (Jewish law) and was edited by Rabbi JUDAH HA-NASI in Erets Israel in the years 200–220 CE. Its purpose was to supply judges and teachers of religion with a guide to Jewish law. The Mishnah remains today as Judah ha-Nasi and his partners arranged it.

Before the Mishnah was written, various collections of

TRACTATES OF THE MISHNAH AND TALMUD

Order	Number of Mishnaic chapters	Babylonian Talmud	Jerusalem Talmud	Tosefta
ZERAIM				
Berakhat	9	•	•	•
Pe'ah	8		•	•
Demai	7		•	•
Kilayim	9		•	•
Shevi'it	10		•	•
Terumot	11		•	•
Ma'aserot	5		•	•
Ma'aser Sheni	5		•	•
Hallah	4		•	•
Orlah	3		•	•
Bikkurim	3		•	•
MO'ED				
Shabbat	24	•	•	•
Eruvin	10	•	•	•
Pesahim	10	•	•	•
Shekalim	8		•	•
Yoma	8	•	•	•
Sukkah	5	•	•	•
Bétsah	5	•	•	•
Rosh Ha-Shanah	4	•	•	•
Ta'anit	4	•	•	•
Megillah	4	•	•	•
Mo'ed Katan	3	•	•	•
Hagigah	3	•	•	•
NASHIM				
Yevamot	16	•	•	•
Kettubot	13	•	•	•
Nedarim	11	•	•	•
Nazir	9	•	•	•
Sotah	9	•	•	•
Gittin	9	•	•	•
Kiddushin	4	•	•	•

Order	Number of Mishnaic chapters	Babylonian Talmud	Jerusalem Talmud	Tosefta
NEZIKIN				
Bava Kamma	10	•	•	•
Bava Metsi'a	10	•	•	•
Bava Batra	10	•	•	•
Sanhedrin	11	•	•	•
Makkot	3	•	•	•
Shevu'ot	8	•	•	•
Eduyyot	8			•
Avodah Zarah	5	•	•	•
Avot	5			•
Horayot	3	•	•	•
KODASHIM				
Zevahim	14	•		•
Menahot	13	•		•
Hullin	12	•		•
Bekhorot	9	•		•
Arakhin	9	•		•
Temurah	7	•		•
Keritot	6	•		•
Me'ilah	6	•		•
Tamid	7	•		
Middot	5			
Kinnim	3			
TOROROT				
Kelim	30			•
Oholot	18			•
Nega'im	14			•
Parah	12			•
Tohorot	10			•
Mikva'ot	10			•
Niddah	10	•	•	•
Makhshirin	6			•
Zavim	5			•
Tevul Yom	4			•
Yadayim	4			•
Uktsin	3			•

Detail from the title page of a Hebrew-Latin Mishnah. Illustration by Michael Richey. Amsterdam, 1700–1704.

halakhot were used in the ACADEMIES. The collection of Rabbi AKIVA was arranged by his student Rabbi MEIR and taught orally in the Academies in Erets Israel. The material was not arranged according to subject. Several *halakhot* would be grouped together following the name of the *tanna* who gave them, or they might be arranged according to similar phrases. This made it easier to remember, but harder to study and discuss a certain topic.

Judah ha-Nasi and his partners arranged legal opinions in the Mishnah mainly according to subject. In some cases, however, he preserved entire blocks of material as they appeared in the older sources. For example, chapter 13 of KETUBBOT includes a number of *halakhot* arranged by author.

Nearly 150 different rabbis are named in the Mishnah, from HILLEL and SHAMMAI to Rabbi Judah himself. When there is a difference of opinion, the view that was not accepted is mentioned first, to show that it was taken into consideration. The accepted view is placed last.

There are six "Orders" of the Mishnah, which together make up the *Shishah Sidrei Mishnah* ("Six Orders of the Mishnah"

or SHAS, for short). These Orders are divided into 63 tractates (books; see MASSEKHET), which are made up of chapters (*perakim*). Each chapter is divided into paragraphs of *halakhah*. Each paragraph is known as a Mishnah (pl. *mishnayot*). The six Orders are:

1. ZERA'IM ("Seeds"), dealing first with BENEDICTIONS and daily prayers, then with AGRICULTURAL LAWS;
2. MO'ED ("Appointed Time"), on laws of observing the SABBATH, FESTIVALS, and fast days;
3. NASHIM ("Women"), dealing with MARRIAGE and DIVORCE, as well as VOWS and other issues;
4. NEZIKIN ("Damages"), on civil and criminal law, PUNISHMENT, IDOLATRY, and the ethical teachings of *Avot*;
5. KODASHIM ("Holy Things"), on ritual slaughter (SHEHITAH), SACRIFICES AND OFFERINGS, the TEMPLE and its services;
6. TOHOROT ("Cleanness"), on the laws of ritual PURITY and impurity.

A statement about the *halakhah* not included in the Mishnah but later quoted in the Talmud is known as a BARAITA. Additional material, collected later and published parallel to the Mishnah, is called the TOSEFTA. In the Talmud, passages from the Mishnah are followed by a discussion, which is called the GEMARA.

Many commentaries were written on the Mishnah. Some of the more important ones are those of MAIMONIDES, Obadiah di BERTINORO, and Yom Tov Lipmann HELLER (*Tosafot Yom Tov*). Two outstanding modern commentaries are also widely read, by Hanokh Albeck and Pinhas Kehati.

MITNAGGEDIM ("opponents"). Originally, this was a negative term that Hasidim used for their opponents in Eastern Europe (see HASIDISM). Towards the end of the 18th century, HASIDISM became popular. The Hasidim adopted the prayer customs of the Sephardim, built their own synagogues, and devoted very little time to Torah and Talmud study. These changes and especially the Hasidic practice of showing extreme devotion to the *Rebbe* or TSADDIK caused great protest on the part of the *Mitnaggedim*, who believed that the traditional way of life was unchangeable.

When Hasidism reached Vilna, ELIJAH BEN SOLOMON, the Gaon of Vilna, led an attack against the Hasidim. In 1772, the Hasidic movement was outlawed on the penalty of EXCOMMUNICATION. After the Vilna Gaon died, the two camps were less hostile, but each side denounced leaders of the other camp to the Russian authorities. This continued well into the 19th century until both groups united to oppose the modern ways of the EMANCIPATION and Enlightenment (HASKALAH).

Lithuanian Jewry produced many YESHIVOT, where generations of scholars and the MUSAR movement flourished. An entire *Litvak* culture developed. The *Litvak* Jew spoke Hebrew and Yiddish with a particular accent and proudly called himself a "*Misnagged.*"

From 1770 onward, followers of the Vilna Gaon immigrated to the Land of Israel and formed the largest Ashkenazi community in Jerusalem (see PERUSHIM). Many also moved to English-speaking countries such as the United States and England (see HAREDIM).

MITZVAH (pl. *mitzvot*; lit. "commandment"). A religious duty commanded by the TORAH and defined by Jewish law. Some commandments are originally from the Bible (*de-oraita*) and other were added by the rabbis (*de-rabbanan*; see COMMANDMENTS, THE 613). RAV (early 3rd cent.) taught that "the *mitzvot* were given only in order to improve human beings" (Gen. R. 44:1). Some believed that this meant that the commandments were to teach obedience to God, without asking questions. MAIMONIDES taught that the *mitzvot* were given for the benefit of people (*Guide* III, 27). Over the years rabbis have been divided between those who seek the reasons for the commandments (*ta'amei ha-mitzvah*) and those who do not search for reasons. The second group feared that once the reason is found, people might think they could achieve the purpose of the *mitzvah* without doing the *mitzvah* itself.

Saadiah Gaon believed that the *mitzvot* are a gift from God to people "enabling them to reach constant happiness. For a person who achieves the good life as a reward for doing *mitzvot* receives double the benefit gained by one who receives the good life only as a result of God's kindness" (*Emunot ve-De'ot*).

The rabbis taught that it is not enough to perform the commandment. A person must be aware that he is obeying God's word. This awareness is called KAVVANAH. This is why one must recite a blessing before performing many of the positive commandments.

According to the Talmud, a girl must observe the *mitzvot* from the age of 12 (BAT MITZVAH) and a boy from the age of 13 (BAR MITZVAH). However, a father must teach his children to perform the *mitzvot* when they are younger, so they will be able to observe them properly when they come of age (*Suk.* 42a).

The rabbis taught that a *mitzvah* should be done with beauty (*hiddur mitzvah*). "Make a beautiful SUKKAH, a beautiful SHOFAR, a beautiful SCROLL OF THE LAW" (*Shab.* 133b), but one should not spend more than a third above the normal cost for the sake of beauty (*BK* 9b). They also taught that a *mitzvah* performed by committing a sin is invalid (*Suk.* 30a). One who is busy performing one *mitzvah* is exempt from performing another at the same time (*Ber.* 11a, 17b). A person should not delay in performing a *mitzvah* (*Mekhilta* to Ex. 12:17).

The Torah promises blessings of peace and prosperity as a reward for keeping the *mitzvot*. The rabbis taught that "he who performs one *mitzvah* receives good things: his days are lengthened and he inherits the land" (*Kid.* 39b; see REWARD AND PUNISHMENT). The *mitzvot* a person does are balanced against the sins he commits; one additional *mitzvah* can tip the scales in his favor so that he is considered a righteous person (*Kid.* 39b; *RH* 17b).

MIXED SPECIES   See AGRICULTURAL LAWS

MIZRAH ("east") Point on the horizon where the sun rises. This is emphasized in the Bible's phrase, *mizrah-shemesh*, "rising of the sun" (Deut. 4:47; Mal. 1:1; Ps. 113:3).

From ancient times, the synagogue has been arranged so that the congregation faces JERUSALEM and the TEMPLE MOUNT while praying (see PRAYER). For many communities outside of Israel, in Europe and the Americas, this means facing east. The ARK with the Torah scrolls and the rabbis' seats were placed along the eastern wall. A decorative plaque with the word *mizrah* is usually placed on the eastern wall of the synagogue and BET MIDRASH, facing Jerusalem. This shows worshipers the direction in which they should face when praying.

MODEH ANI ("I give thanks"). A short prayer thanking God for his protection, which Jews recite every morning when they wake up. It is usually said even before leaving the bedroom. Because it is so simple a prayer, *Modeh Ani* is one of the first prayers that a child learns.

MO'ED ("Appointed Time"). Second Order of the Mishnah, dealing with laws of the Jewish FESTIVALS. Its 12 books (SHABBAT, ERUVIN, PESAHIM, SHEKALIM, YOMA, SUKKAH, BETSAH, ROSH HA-SHANAH, TA'ANIT, MEGILLAH, MO'ED KATAN, and HAGIGAH) are arranged according to the number of chapters, with the longest first. Every book in the Order is interpreted in both the Jerusalem and Babylonian Talmuds (except for *Shekalim*, which is covered only in the Jerusalem Talmud) and the TOSEFTA.

MO'ED KATAN ("Minor Festival"). Eleventh tractate (book) of the Order of MO'ED in the Mishnah. Its three chapters deal with the types of work permitted or forbidden on the intermediate days (HOL HA-MO'ED) of PASSOVER and SUKKOT (Lev. 23:37). It also discusses the rules of MOURNING on SABBATHS and FESTIVALS.

MOHEL   See CIRCUMCISION

MOLCHO, SOLOMON   See MESSIANIC MOVEMENTS

MÖLLN, JACOB BEN MOSES HA-LEVI (known as the *Maharil*; c. 1360–1427). Rabbi and spiritual leader of Jewish communities in Germany, Austria, and Bohemia. Born in Mainz, he studied under his father, then traveled to Vienna, where he continued his studies. After his father's death, he became he rabbi of Mainz and founded a YESHIVAH there. Some of his students went on to become distinguished rabbis in Central Europe. When the Crusaders attacked the Jewish communities of Austria, those in Bavaria and the Rhineland begged Mölln to intervene on their behalf. He proclaimed a three day fast and used his influence with the rulers to avoid a massacre.

Questions of Jewish law were sent to the *Maharil* from many parts of Europe. He believed in taking local conditions into consideration when answering the questions. He also wrote many hymns and was an excellent *hazzan* (cantor). His Jewish legal decisions were written down by his student, Zalman of St. Goar, and later published as *Minhagei Maharil* (1556). This work was quoted by Rabbi Moses ISSERLES in his *Mappah*.

MONDAYS AND THURSDAYS   On Mondays and Thursdays there are special additions to the prayers of the MORNING SERVICE. Since the times of the Talmud, these two weekdays were special because they were market days, when all the people of the area would gather in the market place. These were also the days when the court (BET DIN) convened. According to the Talmud, EZRA began the custom of special Torah teachings on those days in the fifth cent. BCE. Later the READING OF THE LAW was introduced in the synagogues every Monday and Thursday. Special prayers are added to the Morning Service.

MONOGAMY AND POLYGAMY   At the very beginning of biblical history, MARRIAGE was monogamous (a man married only one woman). Lamech is the first to marry two wives (Gen. 4:19). It is only because Sarah is barren that Abraham takes Hagar as a second wife (Gen. 16:1–3). Esau has three wives, and JACOB marries two sisters, LEAH and RACHEL, who also give him their handmaids as concubines (secondary wives). According to the Book of Deuteronomy, it is legal to marry more than one woman, as was the custom in the Ancient Near East. A woman, however, is never permitted to be married to more than one husband at the same time.

After the period of the JUDGES, it became the norm to have one wife, except for kings, who had many. King DAVID already had six wives when he moved to Jerusalem. King SOLOMON had 700 wives and 300 concubines. The Talmud declared that 18 was the maximum number of wives for a king and warned against "multiplication of wives."

In the time of the Talmud, there were different attitudes towards polygamy. RAVA had no problem with polygamy, as long as the husband could provide for each of his wives. Rav Ammi taught that a man could only take a second wife if his first wife agreed (*Yev.* 65a). The rabbis agreed that a man could take a second wife if his first wife did not have a child after ten years of marriage. Jewish law eventually insisted that in such a case, the first wife must be divorced, so that she could also remarry.

Although it is rare, polygamy is still permissible in the Sephardi-Oriental world. In the West, polygamy disappeared entirely by the 13th century. Rabennu GERSHOM (*Me'or ha-Golah*) made a special TAKKANAH (regulation) in the 11th century that outlawed polygamy throughout the Ashkenazi world.

Nowadays, in Israel, it is illegal to have more than one wife unless a person arrived in Israel with more than one wife. In rare cases, courts allow additional marriage if the first wife refuses to accept a bill of divorce or has been committed to a mental institution.

MONOTHEISM   The belief in one GOD. This is a basic principle of Jewish faith and is listed second in MAIMONIDES' 13 PRINCIPLES OF FAITH. The most famous Jewish prayer, SHEMA, expresses a Jew's belief in one God: *Shema Yisrael Adonai Elohenu Adonai Ehad* ("Hear O Israel, the Lord is our God, the Lord is One"; Deut. 6:4).

ABRAHAM was the first Hebrew, because he was the first to believe in one God. In the Bible, the people of Israel went back and forth between belief in one God and worshiping many gods. MOSES and the PROPHETS preached about the dangers of worshiping many gods, and the people of Israel were punished for this sin many times. After the EXILE, monotheism became the norm of the Israelite religion.

Monotheism leads to belief in two main ideas. The first is that God created the universe. Thus He cares about each individual that He created and is the Lord of the history of the world that He created. Secondly, since one God created all people, all men and women in the world are brothers and sisters, equal in the eyes of God.

MONTHS OF THE YEAR   See CALENDAR

MOON   The Jewish months begin with the New Moon (*Rosh Hodesh*). The Jewish calendar is based on the cycle of the moon, each month lasting a little more than 29 days. The SANHEDRIN decided which months had 29 days and which had 30. If the outgoing month had 29 days, then the next day would be the only day of *Rosh Hodesh*. When a month had 30 days, then the last day of the month and the first day of the new month would both be *Rosh Hodesh*.

In ancient times, the Sanhedrin in Jerusalem set the day of the New Moon according to the testimony of eyewitnesses, who had seen the New Moon. Hillel II fixed the permanent calendar in 325 CE, based on calculations of astronomy and mathematics.

In the period of the First Temple, the New Moon was a FESTIVAL, with special sacrifices and feasts. Around the time the Jews returned from exile (see EXILE, BABYLONIAN), the New Moon lost its special observances. It is not clear exactly when or how this happened. At this point it became a semi-holiday, like HOL HA-MO'ED. Only necessary work was done, and the women did not sew or weave. Over time, the New Moon became a regular working day.

On *Rosh Hodesh* a special prayer, YA'ALEH VE-YAVO, is added to the AMIDAH and GRACE AFTER MEALS. A shortened version of HALLEL is read in the MORNING SERVICE. A special Bible reading that describes the Temple sacrifice for the New Moon and an ADDITIONAL SERVICE are included. FASTING and MOURNING are forbidden on the New Moon.

The Sabbath before the New Moon is called *Shabbat Mevarkhim*, meaning the Sabbath on which God blesses the new month. The new month is announced in the synagogue, and the day in the following week when it will occur is mentioned. A prayer is recited, asking that the coming month be blessed

The moon, showing its different phases (when turned), on a pedestal bearing the benediction for the New Moon. Sculpture by Menahem Berman, 1984.

is to recite them all together just before the MORNING SERVICE. The traditional blessings include thanks to God for not having been created a Gentile or a slave or a woman (by men). In the 13th century, the rabbis added a blessing for women to say, thanking God for "having created me according to His will." Non-Orthodox Jews have rewritten these three blessings, the only ones that are in a negative form (i.e., "for *not* having created"). They changed them into a positive form, praising God "Who made me a Jew, Who made me free" (Conservative *Sim Shalom* Prayer Book).

The *Birkhot ha-Shahar* are part of the PESUKEI DE-ZIMRA, which are said just before the Morning Service to spiritually prepare the person for the main prayers.

MORNING SERVICE   (Heb. *Shaharit*; from *shahar*, "dawn"). The longest of the three daily prayer services. According to Jewish tradition, Abraham was the first to pray *Shaharit*, and it replaces the morning sacrifice. It is recited in the first third of the day.

The Morning Service is made up of (1) the MORNING BENEDICTIONS (*Birkot ha-Shahar*); (2) PESUKEI DE-ZIMRA ("passages of song"), taken mostly from PSALMS; (3) BAREKHU, the reader's call to prayer; (4) SHEMA and its blessings; and (5) the AMIDAH and its repetition by the reader. On weekdays, the *Amidah* is followed by TAHANUN, confessional prayers.

On the New Moon, HANUKKAH, the PILGRIM FESTIVALS (including their intermediate days), and, in many communities, on Israel's INDEPENDENCE DAY, the *Amidah* is followed by HALLEL, after which the READING OF THE LAW takes place. On regular Sabbaths, as well as the HIGH HOLIDAYS, only the prescribed Torah portion (no *Hallel*) is read. This is also the case on non-festive MONDAYS AND THURSDAYS, when the passage chanted is the first section of the following Sabbath's Torah reading, to which three worshipers only (a priest, a Levite, and an Israelite) are called. The weekday service then concludes (apart from minor variations between the different rites) with ASHREI, *U-Va le-Tsiyyon* (a sequence of mainly biblical verses headed by Isa. 59:20–21), ALEINU, and the daily psalm (Sunday, Ps. 24; Monday, Ps. 48; Tuesday, Ps. 82; Wednesday, Ps. 94:1–95:3; Thursday, Ps. 81; Friday Ps. 93). The mourner's KADDISH is recited after the latter two sections.

On Sabbaths and festivals, when the ADDITIONAL SERVICE (*Musaf*) is recited following the Morning Service, the congregation may be addressed by the rabbi either before or immediately after the Torah reading.

At every Morning Service, except on TISHAH BE-AV, the TALLIT (prayer shawl) is worn. On all days apart from Sabbaths, the Pilgrim Festivals, High Holidays, and Tishah be-Av, men wear TEFILLIN (phylacteries) during the morning prayers, removing them before the Additional Service on those days when *Musaf* is recited.

with health, prosperity, and religious faith. This blessing is not recited on the Sabbath before ROSH HA-SHANAH.

Another custom, known as *Kiddush Levanah,* focuses on the holiness of the New Moon. When the New Moon is at least three days old and before the 15th day, it is blessed with rejoicing and prayer. Ideally this ceremony is performed on Saturday night before the special atmosphere of the Sabbath has worn off. It is usually recited by a MINYAN (group of ten) in the courtyard of the synagogue.

MORIAH   The place to which God sent ABRAHAM: "Take your son, your favorite son, ISAAC, whom you love, and go to the Land of Moriah, and offer him there as a burnt offering" (Gen. 22:2). Later, Moriah became the site of the Jerusalem TEMPLE.

MORNING BENEDICTIONS   (Heb. *Birkhot ha-Shahar*). Fifteen blessings said upon arising in the morning. Originally, each blessing was said at the time of a given action. For example "Who gives sight to the blind" was said upon opening one's eyes; "Who dresses the naked," upon getting dressed. The custom now

MOSES   PROPHET, lawgiver, leader of the Jewish people out of Egypt and to the borders of the Promised Land, and outstanding figure in the Jewish religion. According to the Bible, the name Moses (*Mosheh* in Hebrew) comes from the phrase "From the water I drew him" (*meshitihu*; Ex. 2:10).

Moses was born in Egypt, the son of Amram and Jochebed, both of the tribe of LEVI. At the time of his birth, Pharaoh had made the decree for the Hebrews: "Every boy that is born you shall throw into the river" (Ex. 1:22). For the first three months of his life, Moses was hidden in his parents' home. Then Jochebed placed him in a basket on the Nile River. He was found there by Pharaoh's daughter, who adopted him as her son. Moses grew up as an Egyptian prince. However, when he killed an Egyptian taskmaster who was beating an Israelite slave, Moses was forced to flee from Egypt and reached Midian. There he married Zipporah, the daughter of Jethro, priest of Midian. Moses tended Jethro's sheep and arrived at Mount Horeb. God appeared to him there from inside a BURNING BUSH that was not consumed by the flames. God commanded Moses to return to Egypt and redeem his people from slavery. At the age of 80 Moses appeared before Pharaoh, but Pharaoh refused to release the Israelites. God then struck Pharaoh and the people of Egypt with ten plagues. Only after the last plague, when all the Egyptian firstborn were killed, did Pharaoh agree to release the Israelites (see EXODUS). When the Israelites arrived at the shores of the Red Sea, Moses split the

The finding of Moses in the Nile. From a Judeo-Persian commentary on the Book of Exodus. Iran, 1686.

sea so the Israelites passed over on dry land. The sea then came crashing down on the Egyptians, who drowned. Moses and the Israelites then sang a song of praise to God. After a short period of wandering in the Sinai desert, the Israelites reached Mount SINAI, where God gave them the TEN COMMANDMENTS (Ex. 20:1–17). Moses went up to Mount Sinai for 40 days and nights, and received the TABLETS OF THE COVENANT. While Moses was on the mountain, the Israelites persuaded AARON to make a GOLDEN CALF to serve them as a god. When Moses came down the mountain and saw the calf, he broke the tablets, burned the calf and mixed the gold of the calf with water for the Israelites to drink. God wanted to destroy the Israelites because of the sin of the golden calf, but Moses begged Him not to. Moses went up the mountain for another 40 days and brought down a new set of tablets. According to Jewish tradition, he also received the WRITTEN and ORAL LAW at that time.

Moses and Aaron were punished for disobeying God at Marah. Instead of speaking to a rock, as God commanded, they hit the rock to bring forth water for the thirsty people. Moses was therefore not allowed to enter the Promised Land. Moses died at the age of 120 on Mount Nebo, just before the Israelites entered Erets ISRAEL. According to the Bible, Moses was the greatest prophet who ever lived. "Never again did there arise in Israel a prophet like Moses, whom the Lord singled out, face to face" (Deut. 34:10).

As a leader, Moses faced many problems. At first, he was the only judge in the entire nation. Later, he appointed other judges to help him (Ex. 18:13–23). Moses was also a military leader. He fought against AMALEK (Ex. 17:8–13) and other Canaanite nations. Moses was the "servant of God and a very humble man, more humble than any other man on the face of this earth" (Deut. 34:5; Num. 12:3).

According to the rabbis, Moses was like a king, although his sons did not inherit his position. The ZOHAR says that "50 levels of wisdom were created in the world, and all but one were given to Moses." There was a difference between Moses and all the other prophets; "All the prophets saw through hazy, unclear glass, but Moses saw through clear glass" (Lev. R. 1:14). According to legend, Moses was born holy. He was born circumcised and began to speak at birth, saying prophecies from the age of three months. He was chosen as the Israelites' leader after God saw how he treated his sheep with compassion (Ex. R. 2:12). He received the Torah and passed it on to JOSHUA, starting the "chain of tradition" (*Avot* 1:1).

According to Maimonides, the seventh PRINCIPLE OF FAITH is to believe that Moses was the supreme prophet: "I believe with perfect faith that the prophecy of Moses our master is true, and that he was the chief of all prophets."

MOSES BEN SHEM TOV DE LEON (c. 1240–1305). Main author of the ZOHAR and one of the greatest Jewish mystics. Born in Leon, Castille, he studied both KABBALAH and Jewish philosophy, especially MAIMONIDES' *Guide for the Perplexed*.

Moses de Leon wrote four types of books: (1) Hebrew books written before the *Zohar*; (2) Works written before the *Zohar* that were later woven into the *Zohar*; (3) the *Zohar*; (4) Hebrew works written after the *Zohar*. In addition, he wrote many RESPONSA (answers to Jewish legal questions).

By the time Moses de Leon died in Arevalo, several portions of the *Zohar* were already circulating among the mystics of the time. Rabbi Isaac of Acre believed that the *Zohar* was originally written by Rabbi SIMEON BAR YOHAI. After Moses de Leon died, Rabbi Isaac began to search for the original copy of the *Zohar*. Moses' widow denied that such a copy existed and claimed that her husband wrote the *Zohar* himself. Ever since then, scholars have disagreed about who wrote the *Zohar*.

MOTHER   In cases of MARRIAGE between a Jew and non-Jew, the children are Jewish if the mother is Jewish. When two Jews marry, the FAMILY lineage is according to the father (*Kid.* 3:12).

In the event of a DIVORCE, the mother has custody of her sons until the age of six and her daughters until they marry. In

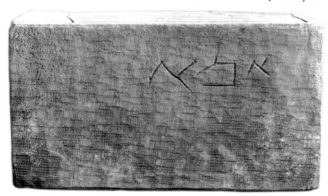

The word Imma *("Mother") inscribed on a stone ossuary found in the Kidron Valley, Jerusalem. 1st century BCE–1st century CE.*

Jewish law, both parents were seen as equally responsible for bringing up the children (*Kid.* 28a), and the child must give equal honor and respect to both parents (*Kid.* 30b–31a; see PARENT–CHILD RELATIONS).

The mother was traditionally the main figure in the Jewish household, leaving her stamp on her children through her constant contact with them. The father was usually more distant.

Jewish tradition has great respect for its mothers. Rabbi Joseph said when he heard his mother approaching: "I must stand up, for the Divine Presence is entering." There is a Jewish proverb that says "God could not be everywhere, so he created mothers."

MOURNERS OF ZION   See AVELEI ZION

MOURNING   Jewish law and tradition includes a specific framework to guide mourners through their grief. The laws of

mourning apply to a male over the age of 13 or a female over the age of 12 who has lost a father or mother, husband or wife, son or daughter, and brother or sister.

The Jewish mourning laws allow a person to grieve, but not in a very extreme manner. A mourner is expected to cry, tear one's clothing, and participate in the BURIAL ceremony, but not to injure oneself or die, as in certain other cultures. During the mourning period, a person is supposed to concentrate on recovering from the loss and getting back to the business of living.

Death is seen as a natural and positive thing. The rabbis suggested that one should say *Barukh ha-tov ve-ha-metiv* ("Blessed is God Who is good and Who does good) in a house of mourning. Rabbi AKIVA called for the blessing *Barukh dayan ha-emet* ("Blessed is the True Judge"). Both of these BENEDICTIONS are included in the blessings following the meal after the funeral.

The mourning process has several stages. From the moment of death until the burial takes place, the mourners come under the category of ANINUT. During this time, the mourners do not perform positive *mitzvot* (commandments), such as praying, wearing TEFILLIN, and reciting the GRACE AFTER MEALS. An *onen* may not have a festive meal or participate in enjoyable activities. Mourners must tear their garments (*keri'ah*; see RENDING OF GARMENTS). This is done when a person receives the news of death, just before the funeral, or at the funeral.

After the burial, the mourners return to the home of the deceased and eat a meal of bread and hardboiled eggs. This meal is prepared by others, as a sign of kindness to the mourners.

The most intense part of the mourning period, *shivah*, lasts for seven days, starting with the day of the burial. Mourners sit on the floor, on cushions, or on low benches. They do not shave, bathe, go to work, study Torah, have sexual relations, wear leather shoes, greet each other, have their hair cut, or wear freshly laundered clothes. It is a custom to cover the mirrors in a house of mourning. During the *shivah*, people visit the mourners and offer their condolences. In many communities, it is customary for people to bring or prepare food for the mourners. Visitors do not greet the mourners, but speak to them softly.

Public mourning is not allowed on the Sabbath, but some customs are still privately observed. The *shivah* ends on the morning of the seventh day. A less strict period of mourning continues for 30 days, called the *sheloshim*. During this time mourners should not cut their hair, shave, wear new clothes, or attend parties. Mourning for all relatives other than parents ends here. The mourning period for a parent lasts for a year. Mourners recite KADDISH daily throughout the period of mourning.

The laws of mourning do not apply if the person who died was a serious sinner or a suicide (unless there is reason to believe that the suicide was a result of insanity).

It is customary to mark the anniversary of the death of a relative each year. Most light a memorial light and recite *Kaddish*. Some also hold a session of Torah study or chant the HAFTARAH (see YARZHEIT).

MUKTSEH ("set apart," "excluded"). Hebrew term used for objects that may not be touched or moved on the SABBATH or FESTIVALS. The reason is that touching these items may lead a person to break the Sabbath by using them to do something forbidden.

The rules of *muktseh* are written in the Babylonian Talmud and explained by MAIMONIDES, the SHULHAN ARUKH, and other books. Some of the objects that are considered *muktseh* are: (1) wood, earth, rocks, etc., which serve no purpose on a holy day; (2) tools, money, pens, and computers, which may not be used on the Sabbath; (3) objects such as matches and candles (because fires may not be lit on the Sabbath). On festivals, when cooking is permitted, items such as candles and matches may be handled.

MURDER "You shall not murder" is the sixth of the TEN COMMANDMENTS. It is also one of the seven NOACHIDE LAWS: "Whoever sheds a man's blood, by man shall his blood be shed" (Gen. 9:6). According to the Bible, the punishment for murder is death. However, the ORAL LAW added so many conditions for actually executing the murderer that the death penalty was almost never carried out. In order to execute a murderer for his crime in a Jewish court (BET DIN), two witnesses must first warn the murderer that murder is forbidden and remind him of the punishment for murder; the person must then say that he is aware of these facts; the witnesses must see the actual killing, no amount of other types of evidence is acceptable; the murderer must be tried before 23 judges (in TEMPLE times) and a majority of two is necessary to convict the murderer; if all of the judges voted to convict the murderer, he is still not executed, because no judge spoke in his favor (It was as if had no lawyer among the judges). Although the courts were very rarely able to execute a murderer, they could imprison a guilty person for a long time.

One may kill a person in self-defense or to prevent a person who is chasing another (*rodef*) from killing or raping. Killing, even in these cases, is allowed only if there is no other option. In Israel, CAPITAL PUNISHMENT for murder is used only in the case of genocide, and Adolf Eichmann (a Nazi leader who killed many Jews during the HOLOCAUST) is the only murderer to have been executed on Israeli soil.

MUSAF See ADDITIONAL SERVICE

MUSAR MOVEMENT Movement that developed around the YESHIVAHs of Lithuania, that taught ETHICS (*musar*) in the spirit of the HALAKHAH (Jewish law). The movement was founded in the 19th century by Israel Lipkin SALANTER (1810–1883). Today, its influence is felt in most non-Hasidic *yeshivot*.

In the second half of the 19th century, traditional Jews were suffering from poverty, on the one hand, and from the modern ways of the HASKALAH (Enlightenment) on the other. The community's goal was to keep to the letter and spirit of the law, based on serious Jewish learning. Salanter was bothered by the fact that many devoted themselves to the ritual details of Jewish law rather than the moral side of Judaism. He and two followers, Isaac Blaser and Simhah Zissel Broida, began to teach ethics in the *yeshivot*. The *Musar* movement, which grew out of these teachings, aimed to strengthen traditional Jewish values. It taught that learning should lead to more proper behavior.

Many in the *yeshivot* began studying an ethical text for half an hour each day, usually at twilight, chanting it to a special melody. A MASHGI'AH, or spiritual supervisor, was added to the *yeshivah's* staff. The *mashgi'ah* gave regular talks on morals and character development and took a personal interest in each student. Nowadays, *Musar*, is an important part of nearly every Lithuanian-style *yeshivah*.

MUSIC AND SONG Musical ideas and styles that have always been important in Jewish life.

In the Bible Yuval, the father of music, was said to have invented the *kinnor* (lyre) and *ugav* (pipe organ), which were ancient musical instruments (Gen 4:21). Another instrument mentioned in the Bible is the *tof* (tambourine) that MIRIAM played after the splitting of the Red Sea (Ex. 15:20).

Some of the poems in the Bible were probably sung or chanted. Women welcomed leaders of war with song and dance (Judg. 5, 11:34). A "company of prophets" were accompanied by a *nevel* (harp), *tof, halil* (pipe), and *kinnor*. DAVID played the *kinnor* to cheer up King SAUL (1 Sam. 16:23).

David was the first to use holy music. He accompanied the ARK to Jerusalem with instruments and singing (11 Sam. 6). Although King David did not build the TEMPLE, he was the father of music of the first Temple. He established groups of musicians and invented musical instruments.

The instruments played in the Temple were the *kinnor, nevel*, and *metsiltayim* (cymbals). The SHOFAR (ram's horn) was also blown. Psalms written by David and his chief musician were sung by two groups of singers, or by the soloist and the congregation. Temple soloists were usually LEVITES.

In the Second Temple According to the Mishnah, the choir in the Second Temple was made up of at least 12 Levites (*Ar.* 2:3). The orchestra had two to 12 *halilim*, two to six *nevalim*, *kinnorot*, and one cymbal. The priest blew at least two trumpets and used a loud instrument called *magrefah* to announce the beginning of the service. The *halil* was used at weddings and funerals.

By the first century BCE, synagogues had been built in many towns in Israel and in the Diaspora. No musical instruments were used in the synagogue, but psalms and prayers were chanted. The Bible was chanted to a special melody called the cantillation (see READING OF THE LAW).

After 70 CE After the Second Temple was destroyed, HALAKHAH (Jewish law) prohibited playing and singing in certain cases, for three reasons: (a) rules of observing the SABBATH; (b) to prevent an atmosphere that was too social; and (c) mourning the destruction of the Temple.

The mourning over the destruction of the Second Temple

led the rabbis to ban all instrumental music in the society. They later agreed that music could be performed for the sake of a *mitzvah*, such as a wedding. No musical instruments were played during the services in the synagogue, except for the *shofar* on ROSH HA-SHANAH.

After the fourth century CE, poetic prayers (PIYYUTIM) were added to the already existing prayers. Some had refrains for the congregations to sing and others were probably sung by a small choir.

In Muslim Lands   Arab culture had a deep influence on Jewish poetry and music. After the EXPULSION from Spain in 1492, the Jews continued to write music and poetry in the Spanish style. In the late 16th century, poets who were influenced by the mystical school of Safed (see LURIA, ISAAC), tried to revive Hebrew poetry according to medieval Spanish ideas. They wrote Hebrew poems that were sung to the original Arabic or Turkish tunes.

In Spain, many songs were written in the Judeo-Spanish ("Ladino") language. These songs were kept alive in the different countries where SEPHARDIM lived after their expulsion from Spain. Many more songs were created in the new countries. Some of these melodies were adapted to the texts of prayers and are sung to this day in synagogue services and at Sabbath meals.

Ashkenazi Prayer Chants   Ashkenazi Jews wrote their own synagogue songs. The communities of Germany and northern France tried to unify the melodies of the prayers. Special melodies were singled out as *niggunim mi-sinai* (tunes from Sinai) and were considered holy. The most famous of these is the KOL NIDREI melody. During the Middle Ages, these tunes spread to Eastern Europe.

The first printed collection of music for the synagogue was *Ha-Shirim Asher le-Shelomoh* ("Solomon's Songs," Venice, 1622) by Salomone di Rossi. This music was written in the style of the Renaissance. Fifty years later, Jews began to perform Baroque-style Hebrew operettas at special synagogue or family parties. Synagogues, such as the famous Altneuschul in Prague, used the ORGAN and other musical instruments to welcome the Sabbath on Friday afternoons.

The REFORM movement composed new music for old Hebrew hymns in a European style. Some musicians tried to preserve the syles of ancient music while bringing it up to European standards. See CANTOR AND CANTORIAL MUSIC.

Kabbalah and Hasidism   According to the Kabbalah of Isaac Luria, all music is inspired by God. However, because of the sins of mankind, many melodies are caught in unholy forms. Righteous people must find a TIKKUN, a type of purification, for these unholy melodies by singing them to holy texts or in prayer, Torah study, or at the Sabbath meal.

Many melodies were written for the *Kabbalat Shabbat* ceremonies, welcoming in the Sabbath, and the Friday night meal. Some examples are the poem LEKHAH DODI and ZEMIROT (songs) that are sung at the Sabbath table.

The founders of HASIDISM, Rabbi Israel BA'AL SHEM TOV and his students, saw music and dance as the most important way to lift the soul. The TSADDIKIM (holy leaders) wrote NIGGUNIM (melodies) that were considered extremely holy. These *niggunim* did not have words and were sung as a type of meditation. Different melodies are associated with different Hasidic groups.

Instrumental music was played at weddings and other celebrations and during the festivals of HANUKKAH and PURIM. Bands of Jewish musicians developed from the Middle Ages in many countries. Most famous were the Eastern European musicians, called *klezmorim*. Since most of their music was not written down, it was lost over time. Lately, however, there has been a revival of *klezmer*-style music in Israel and the United States.

MYSTICISM, JEWISH   Since the second century CE, there have been various attempts to create a closer, more intimate relationship with God than might be possible through standard Jewish religious practice and thought. These efforts, and the abstract systems on which they are based, form the subject matter of Jewish mysticism. The best known and most important of the Jewish mystical movements is the KABBALAH, dating from the end of the 12th century. But this movement was preceded in ancient times by Hekhalot and Merkavah Mysticism and by the HASIDEI ASHKENAZ in the Middle Ages.

What is unique about Jewish mysticism? On the one hand, it teaches that mystical truths can be discovered in visions, dreams, revelations of heavenly powers, and meditation. However, it also allows that mystical truths can be discovered in the holy texts that make up mainstream Judaism. If one can only apply the correct interpretation to verses from the Bible or passages from the Talmud, the deeper, hidden meaning opens up to the mystic. The mystics did not reject mainstream tradition; Jewish mysticism has an extremely respectful relationship to mainstream Judaism.

The core of Jewish mysticism is a set of symbols that can be found in the Kabbalah. According to the kabbalists, God gave the Bible to the mystics as a kind of dictionary of symbols, which only a mystic can understand. The symbols used by the earliest kabbalistic sources – *Sefer ha-*BAHIR and the works of R. Isaac the Blind in the late 12th century – became the standard language of the kabbalists. The various schools and each individual mystic added their own terms and their own specific meanings, but the concept of "emanations" (levels of divine powers; see SEFIROT) was already in place at an early stage.

The really systematic writings that reveal the inner workings of mystical structures do not begin to appear until the 16th century. Before that time, the mystics tended to keep their mystical speculations to themselves. In fact, both the *Hasidei Ashkenaz* and the Spanish kabbalists (see NAHMANIDES) were responsible for the most influential ethical works of the Middle Ages. These include R. JUDAH HE-HASID's *Sefer Hasidim* ("Book of the Hasidim") and R. Jonah Gerondi's *Sha'arei Teshuvah* ("Gates of Repentence"). This probably reflects their belief that mystical systems were for the elite minority, but ETHICS was for the masses. This type of thinking changed with the spread of the Kabbalah of R. Isaac Luria (see LURIA, ISAAC AND LURIANIC KABBALAH).

History The history of Jewish mysticism is divided into five main periods. Each period represents a different mystical attitude and a different place of the mystics within Jewish culture. The five periods are: (1) Ancient Jewish mysticism, the mystical schools that developed in late antiquity, during the time of the Talmud. (2) The early Jewish mystical schools in medieval Europe in the 12th and 13th centuries. (3) The Kabbalah in Spain in the 13th to 15th centuries and its spread to other countries in Europe and the East. (4) The Kabbalah after the expulsion from Spain, the center in Safed, the spread of Lurianic Kabbalah, the Shabbatean movement, in the 16th to 18th centuries. (5) The emergence of Hasidism, modern and contemporary Hasidic, anti-Hasidic, and non-Hasidic schools of Kabbalah.

In the first three periods, until the late 15th century, Jewish mysticism was not a central part of Jewish religious culture. It was studied and/or practiced in closed elite circles – even when the practitioners had roots in the mainstream scholarly community, as was the case with R. AKIVA, R. ISHMAEL, and R. Nehuniah ben ha-Kanah.

One contribution of the medieval mystical movement must be mentioned. The *Hasidei Ashkenaz* groups in the late 12th century developed the revolutionary idea that God was in fact the unity of several different forces. The biblical and rabbinic concepts that God as a single unity was replaced with a complex system. This system described Divine unity as the result of the harmony of between three and 13 Divine powers. From this period on, until the present day, the main concern of Jewish mystics has been the description of the relationship between the various Divine powers that make up God. This includes their division into "masculine" and "feminine" elements; their relation to evil; and their role in CREATION, in the Divine guidance of world affairs, in the fate of the Jewish people, and in the future REDEMPTION.

Another major event in the development of Jewish mysticism came in the final years of the 13th century. At this time, the ZOHAR, the central text of the Kabbalah, first appeared. Most scholars agree that the main part of the *Zohar* was compiled by R. MOSES (BEN SHEM TOV) DE LEON, the great Spanish kabbalist. The *Zohar* emerged at a time when a large group of kabbalists were active in northern Spain. They made their contribution to the language and symbolism of the Kabbalah. Their most important contribution was to gain a central place for the *Zohar* in Jewish mysticism.

The fourth historical period in the development of Jewish mysticism is the richest of all. As a result of the EXPULSION of the Jews from Spain in 1492, new centers of Jewish learning were established in Italy, Turkey, and Safed (in Erets Israel). By the 16th century, the mystical *Zohar* had actually become

Man holding a tree with the ten sefirot. *Title page of Latin translation of work by the Spanish kabbalist Joseph Gikatilla.*

a mainstream document, referred to and quoted by scholars everywhere. It is in this period in Safed that R. Isaac Luria began to teach his revolutionary Kabbalah. Based on the *Zohar*, Lurianic Kabbalah developed a new idea system. It teaches that the problems of the earthly condition are a reflection of a flaw in the Divine world which allows evil to flourish. It is the purpose of Jewish religious life to correct this flaw and to bring salvation first to the Divine world. This paves the way for Redemption on earth. Lurianic Kabbalah transformed mysticism into an belief system that applies to the everyday Jewish problem of evil in the world. As for the practitioners of Jewish mysticism, it brought them into the mainstream.

The fifth and last stage in the development of Jewish mysticism began in the 18th century. The central event of this period is the appearance of the modern Hasidic movement, founded by R. Israel BA'AL SHEM TOV. In a curious way this period makes way for the complete entry of Jewish mysticism into the mainstream. The Hasidim were forcefully opposed by the MITNAGGEDIM, and there was a clear divide in East European Jewry between the two camps. Ironically, however, both sides were kabbalists! In various ways, the leaders of the Hasidim and the *Mitnaggedim* both accepted the basic ideas of the Kabbalah. Even though the Hasidim and the *Mitnaggedim* were very often devoted to Lurianic concepts in different forms, the acceptance of Jewish mysticism by both groups paved the way for its important role in all branches of Judaism today.

NAHMANIDES (Moses ben Nahman, known as *Ramban*; 1194–1270) Spanish Bible commentator, leading rabbinic authority, Talmud scholar, communal leader, and doctor by profession. He was born in Gerona in the district of Catalonia and later in his life he became a favored person at the court of King James I of Aragon. Nahmanides influenced Jewish life in Spain and throughout the Jewish Diaspora. He wrote great halakhic (Jewish legal) works that were influenced by both French and Spanish cultures. Because of his wide knowledge of HALAKHAH, rabbis in Spain referred to him simply as "the Rabbi."

When Nahmanides was young, French Jewish scholars, such as the authors of the TOSAFOT, influenced his writing. His Bible commentary brings together conservative philosophy, AGGADAH, and Jewish MYSTICISM. Nahmanides believed that

Personal seal of Nahmanides inscribed: Mosheh (Moses) ben Nahman of Gerona (his native town); hazzak *(be strong).*

the source of the Bible text is a miraculous one, and he was against the purely rational approach to the Bible. He also found hidden meanings in the MIDRASHIM of the ancient sages. In his opinion, there is meaning to the order of chapters and portions in the Bible. Unlike other commentators (including RASHI), he claims that there is a chronological order throughout the Bible, except for when the text tells us otherwise.

Unlike MAIMONIDES, who thought that philosophy is the basis of religious truth, Nahmanides believed that religious authority lay in the Bible and in rabbinic tradition. Furthermore, he strongly objected to some of Maimonides' commentaries on the Bible. Nevertheless, when French rabbis declared Maimonides' philosophical works dangerous and illegitimate, Nahmanides tried to convince them to change their minds.

In 1263 a convert to CHRISTIANITY challenged Nahmanides to a public DISPUTATION, which he won. His victory caused some of the surrounding Christians to hate him, and he was forced to leave Spain (See ANTI-SEMITISM). When he was 70 years old, he arrived in Erets Israel, the love for which he expresses in all his writings. There he devoted himself to reviving Jewish religious and community life, which was destroyed by the Crusaders.

Nahmanides spent the end of his life in Acre, where he completed his commentary on the Bible. There are various traditions about the location of his grave.

NAHMAN OF BRATSLAV (c. 1772–1811) Hasidic leader, great-grandson of Israel BA'AL SHEM TOV and founder of a separate branch of the Hasidic movement (see HASIDISM). As a young man, while he was in the Ukraine, he established his position as a TSADDIK (holy leader). He believed that one must seek God through simple faith and doing good deeds.

In 1798–1799 he visited Erets Israel. This visit made such an impression on him that he used to say: "No matter where I go, it is always to Erets Israel." Soon after he returned to the Ukraine, Nahman became involved in a dispute with other Hasidic leaders. They thought he was arrogant because he wanted to change Hasidism as it stood. Some claimed that Nahman's soul had come into the world before its time; his response was that their soul had come into the world too late. The dispute continued while he lived in Bratslav (1802–1810).

SAYINGS OF NAHMAN OF BRATSLAV

Man must lose himself in prayer and forget his own existence.

Solitude is a good quality. One should set aside an hour every day to be alone with God, especially in the forest or the desert.

Humility for the sake of approval is
the worst kind of arrogance.

Better a superstitious believer than a rationalistic unbeliever.

One who keeps silent when abused is a true Hasid

Melody and song lead the heart of man to God.

Nine *Tsaddikim* (righteous men) cannot pray together, but one common man who joins them can complete their *minyan*.

The whole world is [like] a very narrow bridge,
and the main thing is not to be afraid.

God is present whenever a peace treaty is signed.

Since God is Infinite and man finite, a man is bound to have religious doubts; but like Moses, he should go into the darkness where he will find God.

BOOK OF NAHUM

1:1–1:10	God's vengeance and punishment
1:11–2:3	Threats against Assyria and promises to Judah
2:4–2:14	Attack on Nineveh
3:1–3:19	Sack of Nineveh

Nahman left Bratslav for Uman, and at the age of 39 he died there of illness. His grave has been visited by many generations of Hasidim who follow his instruction and dance around the grave on his YAHRZEIT.

Since Nahman promised to lead his Hasidim also after his death, a successor was not declared for him. This is why Bratslavers are known as "the dead Hasidim," because they do not have a living *Rebbe*. The Braztslavers' strong religious devotion to Nahman caused some branches of the Hasidic movement and other movements to oppose them, especially the MITNAGGEDIM.

Nahman's teachings were gathered and published after his death by his devoted follower Nathan Sternhartz. The best known works are *Likkutei Moharan* (1806), *Likkutei Moharan Tinyana* (1811), *Sefer ha-Middot* (1811) and *Sippurei Ma'asiyyot* (1815).

NAHUM Tenth book of the PROPHETS section of the Bible. It has three chapters and 47 verses. According to Jewish tradition, Nahum's prophecy came after that of JONAH.

The only specific information known about Nahum is that he was from Elkosh in the kingdom of JUDAH. The background of the Book of Nahum is the destruction of Nineveh by the Medes and the Babylonians (612 BCE). The phrase in the first verse, "the burden of Nineveh," is an example of how the prophets used to announce the doomed fate of the nations of the world.

The Hebrew text of Nahum in 1:2–10 contains a partially preserved alphabetical ACROSTIC.

NAMES The importance of names is known early in the Jewish tradition, since ADAM gave names to all creatures (Gen. 2:19–20). He named his wife Eve (Gen. 3:20), and a reason is given for the choice of this particular name. Thus, we see that the name of an individual represents his or her being and nature. Therefore if the individual changed in some way, the name had to change too. In the Bible, for example, the names Abram, Sarai, JACOB, and Hoshea became ABRAHAM, SARAH, ISRAEL, and JOSHUA.

In ancient times some names included the name of a god. When the Israelites worshiped BAAL, they had names like Ishbaal. But when they started believing in God, their names changed and included various forms of God's name – El, Eli, Yeho. Even today some modern Hebrew names contain God's name.

R. Eleazar explains in the Talmud (*Ber.* 7b) that when God gives a name, it determines a person's future. The sages of the Talmud also explain the names of people, places, and animals in the Bible.

According to Jewish law, if names are misspelled in legal documents, specifically those that deal with MARRIAGE and DIVORCE, the agreements are considered invalid.

A new baby is named on one of two occasions. In the case of a boy, he is named at the CIRCUMCISION ceremony. If the newborn is a girl, she is named in the synagogue at the READING OF THE LAW. A baby's name is often kept secret until the public announcement.

A Hebrew name is traditionally made up of the given name, the word "son" (*ben*) or "daughter" (*bat*), and the name of the father (e.g., Avraham ben Ya'akov or Dinah bat Ya'akov). This name is used when one is called to the reading of the law. The mother's name is used when praying for the recovery of a sick person (e.g., Avraham ben Sarah). The Talmud introduces the custom of changing the name of a seriously ill person as a way to mislead the ANGEL OF DEATH. Another custom, still practiced in Orthodox circles, is to add an additional name to the name of the sick person. Usually, the new name is either Hayyim or Hayyah, which both come from the word "life." From then on, the person goes by both the original and the added name.

For many centuries children have been given names that are common in the non-Jewish environment. Some of these names have become accepted Jewish names. Hebrew names were often translated into other languages; for example, the name "Baruch" became "Benedict."

NAPHTALI See TRIBES, TWELVE

NASHIM ("Women"). Third Order of the Mishnah. Its seven tractates (books) deal with betrothal, the marriage contract (KETUBBAH), the faithless wife, DIVORCE, and relations between men and women. It also examines the legal obligations of vows, the freeing of slaves, and the laws of the NAZIRITE.

All its tractates are discussed in both the Babylonian and Jerusalem Talmuds and in the TOSEFTA.

NASI ("prince," "ruler"). Title used in different time periods with a meaning that changed. In the Bible, this title belonged to the head of a tribe or a king. When the Israelites wandered in the desert and during the conquering of the land of Canaan, it referred to the head of an Israelite tribe. The names of the *Nesi'im* (pl. of *Nasi*) are given in Numbers 1:5–16. Moses sent the *Nesi'im* to spy out the Holy Land (Num. 13:1–15) and told them how to divide the land after it was conquered (Num. 34:16ff). In the book of EZEKIEL, the title Nasi referred to the king of JUDAH (Ezek. 12:10, 19:1, 32:29, etc.).

In 132–135 CE, during the BAR KOKHBA revolt against the Romans, coins were minted with Bar Kokhba's title on them: "Simeon *Nasi* of Israel."

In the Mishnah (*Avot* 1), five pairs of scholars (ZUGOT) are mentioned as the legal authority of the Jewish community. According to the Talmud, the first person in each pair served as the *Nasi* (President) of the SANHEDRIN. Some scholars think that the use of the title *Nasi* only started at a later date, during the time of HILLEL or R. JUDAH HA-NASI. All those who held the title after that were HILLEL's descendants. The office continued until 425 CE, when the authorities abolished it.

Starting with R. Simeon ben GAMALIEL II, the Romans recognized the *Nasi* (Patriarch) as the leader of the Jews in Erets Israel.

As head of the Sanhedrin, the *Nasi* had many responsibilities. He arranged and fixed the Jewish CALENDAR and appointed scholars (see ORDINATION). The *Nasi* also established courts in the Diaspora and collected money for the ACADEMIES and scholars of Erets Israel. The Diaspora communities recognized his religious authority.

Most of the special laws (TAKKANOT) found in the Talmud are attributed to different *Nesi'im*. A *Nasi* was addressed as *Rabban* (our Master).

The title *Nasi* continued to be used throughout the Middle Ages, when it was used to describe the head of the local Jewish community. Since 1948, the title *Nasi* has been used for the President of the State of Israel.

NATHAN Prophet at the time of kings DAVID and SOLOMON. Nathan was involved in three events in the life of David. In the first, God tells David, through Nathan the prophet, not to build the TEMPLE. He adds that His favor will always be upon the House of David (II Sam. 7; II Chr. 17).

In the second, Nathan reprimands David after he sins with Bathsheba, which leads to the death of her husband, Uriah the Hittite. This includes the famous parable of Nathan's of the poor man whose lamb is stolen (II Sam. 12).

The third event takes place when David is old and weak. Nathan, together with Bathsheba, urges David to fulfill his promise and appoint Solomon as his rightful heir. This happens at a time when David's eldest son, Adonijah, has claimed his father's throne. David appoints Solomon to take his place (I Kings 1).

NAZIR ("Nazirite") Fourth tractate (book) of the Order of NASHIM in the Mishnah. Its nine chapters deal with the laws of taking a NAZIRITE vow (cf. Num. 6:1–21). Some of the subjects discussed are the minimum duration of the Nazirite vow, the three things forbidden to a Nazirite, and what a Nazirite should do if he breaks his vow. The last *mishnah* says that both SAMUEL and SAMSON were dedicated as Nazirites before birth and therefore were Nazirites for life.

NAZIRITE (from Heb. *nazar*, "to dedicate"). A person who vows to stay pure and dedicate himself to God for a certain period of time. The Nazirite vow was taken voluntarily by both men and women. The vow was often taken to express thanks or simply for spiritual purification. It had to be taken for at least 30 days. During this time, the Nazirite was not allowed to drink or enjoy anything that comes from the grape, have a haircut, or go near a dead body. If Nazirites did any of these, they had to purify themselves according to the Bible's instructions, and then restart the vow. When the days of the vow were over, Nazirites had to bring an offering to the TEMPLE, shave their hair, and burn it on the alter. The Nazirite now returned to normal ways and could drink wine (Num. 6:1–21). The prohibition of going near a dead body did not apply to lifelong Nazirites.

Like other acts of abstinence, the Nazirite vow was discouraged by the rabbis (*Naz.* 19a). Ideally, the laws of the Nazirite apply only in Erets Israel when PRIESTS serve in the Temple, although there have been some cases of Nazirites in the Diaspora.

The Bible speaks about two people who were lifelong Nazirites: Samson (Judg. 13:3–7) and Samuel (I Sam. 1:11).

NEDARIM ("Vows") Third tractate (book) of the Order of NASHIM in the Mishnah. Its 11 chapters deal with the laws of voluntary promises to dedicate an object to serve God, or to express thanks to Him (cf. Num. 30:2–17; Deut. 23:22–24). The book mentions the different ways of wording a vow, invalid vows, vows of abstinence from certain foods or drink, and the cancelation of vows.

NEGA'IM ("Marks of Leprosy"). Third tractate (book) of the Order of TOHOROT in the Mishnah. Its 14 chapters deal with the laws of infection from leprosy and its treatment by the PRIEST (cf. Lev. 13–14). Other subjects discussed in the book are the different kinds of leprosy and their signs, inspection by the priest, the spread of leprosy, the separation of the leper from the community, and the cleansing of the leper by the priest.

NEHEMIAH (5th cent. BCE; see EZRA AND NEHEMIAH, BOOKS OF). Jewish governor of Judah, appointed by the Persian king Artaxerxes I (464–424 BCE). Nehemiah was responsible for the king's beverages, but when he heard about the bad state of Jerusalem, he asked for and received the king's permission to visit the city. He arrived in Jerusalem as the governor of Judah in 444 BCE.

The first thing Nehemiah did when he arrived was to rebuild the wall around the city, with the help of the residents. Despite the objection of Jerusalem's neighbors, the building continued and the wall was finished in 52 days. Nehemiah also initiated social changes. He canceled the debts of the poor people and rearranged the population of Judah so that more people lived in Jerusalem. Nehemiah and EZRA changed the Jewish community by making the people agree to separate themselves from the other nations.

In 432 BCE Nehemiah returned to Jerusalem after he had been away for some years. He removed foreign wives, reorganized the guard duties of the PRIESTS and LEVITES in the TEMPLE, and ensured that the Sabbath was kept in Jerusalem.

NEHEMIAH, BOOK OF   See EZRA AND NEHEMIAH, BOOKS OF

NE'ILAH (short for *Ne'ilat She'arim*, "the closing of the [heavenly] gates"). Fifth and last prayer service on the DAY OF ATONEMENT. It is considered the last chance on that holy day to pray for forgiveness. *Ne'ilah* is said as the sun starts to set. It has its own melodies. The cantor's repetition of the AMIDAH includes a few *piyyutim* (liturgical poems), and during this repetition the ARK is left open. Unlike the ten days before the DAY OF ATTONEMENT, when one prays to God to "be written" in the BOOK OF LIFE, in the *Ne'ilah* one asks to be "sealed" by God for a good fate. In Israel, the PRIESTS (*kohanim*) also bless the congregation. The service ends with the public "acceptance of the Kingdom of Heaven." The congregation recites the verse "Hear O Israel, the Lord is our God, the Lord is One," recites "Blessed be the name of His glorious kingdom for ever" three times, and then recites "the Lord is God" seven times. The SHOFAR (ram's horn) is sounded and all exclaim, LE-SHANA HA-BA'AH BI-YERUSHALAYIM, "next year in Jerusalem!"

NEOLOGY (lit. "new doctrine"). Term originally used to describe the Hungarian version of Reform Judaism. Like Aaron CHORIN in the early 1800s, some modern Hungarian rabbis were very active in trying to change education, religion, and the Jewish community. They wanted to open a modern rabbinical seminary in Budapest and to assemble conventions that would reorganize Hungarian Jewish life. The Orthodox community, which followed the rulings of Moses SOFER, was against Neology. It claimed that changes and new elements are not allowed according to Jewish law. After the Emancipation (entrance into

the national culture) of the Hungarian Jews in 1867, the government supported the Neologists and helped them organize the Hungarian National Jewish Congress (1868–1869). Because the Orthodox representatives were a minority at the Congress, they were not able to get the SHULHAN ARUKH (i.e., mainstream rabbinic law) declared the highest Jewish legal authority, and their objection to the Neologists' suggested changes was disregarded. Most of the Orthodox representatives then left the Congress and the Neologists were able to run it as they chose.

In 1871, a new law was passed in Hungary causing Hungarian Jewry to split into Neologist, Orthodox, and "Status Quo Ante" (nonaligned traditionalist) communities. In order to prevent the gap that was now forming among Jews from different communities, the Neologists adjusted their movement and became more traditional than before. For example, an ORGAN was allowed to be played during synagogue services but men and women had to sit separately, and no further changes were made in the prayer book. Neology also kept the laws of SHEHITAH (ritual slaughter) and KOSHER food supervision. Neologist rabbis became similar to the West European Orthodox rabbis in their learning, their views, and their clothes. There were still ideological differences between Neology and Hungarian ultra-Orthodoxy, but after the Holocaust the two movements became closer. Today, only in Eastern Europe do both of these movements exist within one central organization.

NEO-ORTHODOXY   An branch within ORTHODOXY that combines observance of rabbinic law and Jewish tradition with a positive attitude toward modern society and Western culture. The first promoters of Neo-Orthodoxy were Isaac BERNAYS and Jacob Ettlinger of Hamburg, Germany. Both had a strong influence on young, German-speaking Jews. At first, it was hard for them to find their place within the Orthodox community – they were considered "modernists." However, by the mid-19th century, because of the declining appeal of the REFORM movement, they had gained supporters and were more socially accepted.

From then on, the main leader of the Neo-Orthodox movement was Samson Raphael HIRSCH, who wrote *Torah im Derekh Erets* ("Torah and the Way of the World"). The branch of Neo-Orthodoxy that Hirsch created was not only strict about following traditional Jewish law, it also tried to distance its members from the non-Orthodox Jewish community. Yet Hirsch was quite liberal in other ways: he promoted German culture, adopted Western dress, improved the status of women, and preached that living in exile from Erets Israel is a positive reality. Some of these ideas were challenged within his own branch of Judaism.

The Neo-Orthodox movement introduced sermons in the local language and translations of the prayer book into those languages; synagogue services with a cantor and a choir; participation in civil, professional, and political life; and the establishment of RABBINICAL SEMINARIES in Italy (1829), France (1830), England (1855), and Germany (1873). Nathan Marcus

Adler (1803–1890), the first Chief Rabbi of the British Empire, was part of the Neo-Orthodox movement.

After the Prussian Law of Secession was passed in 1876, Hirsch and his supporters broke away from the Neo-Orthodox community and established a separate congregation. Azriel Hildesheimer, a fellow Neo-Orthodox Jew, thought that Hirsch's separation from the communal framework would cause the Jewish community to fall apart. Hirsch and Hildesheimer also had different opinions about political ZIONISM. Hirsch led the anti-Zionist, ultra-Orthodox Agudat Israel organization, while Hildesheimer and his followers supported the Zionist camp, and their ideas helped build modern Orthodoxy.

NESHAMAH YETERAH   ("additional soul"). Talmudic concept of an additional soul that God gives each Jew on the SABBATH (*Bets.* 16a). This "extra soul" gives a feeling of well-being and delight throughout the Sabbath. The *neshamah yeterah* was described in the writings of Jewish MYSTICISM. During the HAVDALAH ceremony at the Sabbath's end, one smells spices in order to "revive" the weekday soul, which returns when the *neshamah yeterah* departs with the Sabbath.

NETILAT YADAYIM   See ABLUTIONS

NEVELAH   See TEREFAH AND NEVELAH

NEW MONTH, ANNOUNCEMENT OF   See MOON

NEW MOON   See MOON

NEW YEAR   See ROSH HA-SHANAH

NEW YEAR FOR TREES   (also known as Tu bi-Shevat or Hamishah Asar Bi-Shevat, i.e., 15 Shevat, its Hebrew date, or *Rosh ha-Shanah la-Ilanot*, the New Year for Trees). A minor festival day in the Jewish calendar that is not mentioned in the Bible. It first appears in the Second Temple period as the cut-off date for measuring the TITHE (tenth part) that needs to be taken from all fruit trees and brought as an offering (see SACRIFICES AND OFFERINGS). Fruit grown before this day was included in the calculation of the year before, while fruit grown after this day was taxed the next year.

The Mishnah records a debate between the schools of HILLEL and SHAMMAI about the date of this festival. The rabbis ruled according to the opinion of the school of Hillel: the festival would take place on 15 Shevat, just like Passover and Sukkot – other festivals connected to nature – which are also celebrated in the middle of the month. After the destruction of the Second Temple and the exile of the Jews, the laws of tithing did not apply any more. Nevertheless, the festival was still celebrated, strengthening the connection of Jews everywhere with Erets Israel. FASTING is not allowed on 15 Shevat and sorrowful TAHANUN prayers are not recited.

In the 15th century, Isaac LURIA and the mystics of Safed

Two young boys planting a tree in Jerusalem to celebrate the New Year for Trees.

established new customs for the New Year for Trees. The festival was celebrated with gatherings at which certain fruits were eaten, and special songs and Bible passages were recited to praise the Holy Land and its fruit. This ceremony included drinking four cups of wine, as at the Passover SEDER. Among the fruits traditionally eaten on Tu bi-Shevat is the carob, which grows all over Erets Israel. The almond, which is the first fruit tree to blossom in Israel after the winter and is usually in full bloom on 15 Shevat, is another favorite. In modern Israel, thousands of new saplings are planted on Tu bi-Shevat, many of them by young schoolchildren.

NEXT YEAR IN JERUSALEM   See LE-SHANAH HA-BA'AH BI-YERUSHALAYIM

NEZIKIN   Fourth Order of the Mishnah. Its ten books deal with the laws of damage to public and private property or money, capital crimes, homicide, setting up courts, and testimony by witnesses. One of the books in this Order deals with the laws of IDOLATRY (*Avodah Zarah*), and another is a collection of moral and ethical sayings of the sages of the Mishnah (*Avot*). Most of the books in this Order are discussed further in both Talmuds and in the TOSEFTA.

NIDDAH   ("Menstral Uncleanness"). Seventh tractate (book) of the Order of TOHOROT in the Mishnah. Its ten chapters deal with a woman's halakhic (Jewish legal) status during and after her menstrual cycle (cf. Lev. 15:19–30). Some of the topics discussed are the period of menstruation and the resulting ritual uncleanness (NIDDAH), the status of a virgin, the transmission of uncleanness, self-examination, miscarriage and abortion, the signs of puberty in girls, and the status of a woman who has a discharge not during her usual menstrual period. This is the only book in the Order of TOHOROT that is discussed further in both Talmuds and in the TOSEFTA.

NIDDAH   Term that describes separation due to menstrual impurity. It first appears in the Book of Leviticus. It refers to a woman who has not yet been ritually cleansed from her menstrual period and therefore cannot have any contact with her husband, the TEMPLE, and certain objects and foods that require ritual PURITY. Throughout the Bible the term is also used symbolically to refer to impurity and sin in general.

Leviticus 15 deals with normal and abnormal genital discharges, different levels of ritual impurity, and the conditions of purification. Although Leviticus 15 warns of contaminating the SANCTUARY, being in a state of impurity is not considered a sin. Purification of a woman or man who have had a normal discharge includes bathing and a waiting period: a woman must wait seven days before immersing herself in the MIKVEH (natural gathering of water of a specified minimum size), whereas a man must wait until sunset after his bathing and then he is considered purified. Abnormal discharges cause impurity both in a man (*zav*) and in a woman (*zavah*). They must each wait until their discharge stops, count seven "clean" days, purify themselves, and bring a sacrifice.

Having sexual relations with a menstruating woman is forbidden by the Bible. According to Leviticus 18:19 sexual contact with a menstruating woman is a sin punishable by KARET (being "cut off" from the people of Israel).

The rabbis further discussed and clarified issues surrounding *niddah* in the Mishnah, TOSEFTA, and SIFRA. During that time, a new way of distinguishing between normal and abnormal bleeding was introduced. The minimum number of days between the end of one period and the beginning of the next (11 days) was set and defined as a "law of Moses from Sinai" (HALAKHAH LE-MOSHE MI-SINAI). After the destruction of the Temple, the rabbis created even more rules so that the biblical laws would not be broken. For example, all women were placed in the stricter category of *zavah* and not *niddah*. These rules were accepted into Jewish law and are the accepted Orthodox practice today. In the 19th century, REFORM JUDAISM dismissed the *niddah* laws as outdated. In CONSERVATIVE JUDAISM the subject is not a main issue within the movement. The laws of *niddah* are known today as the FAMILY PURITY laws.

NIGGUN   See MUSIC AND SONG

NIGHT PRAYERS   Series of blessings, prayers, and verses from the Bible that are said before going to sleep. They ask God for protection during the night. The first paragraph of the SHEMA ("Hear, O Israel") is an important part of these prayers. The Hebrew name for Night Prayers is therefore *Keri'at Shema (she-) al ha-Mittah* ("the reading of the *Shema* in bed"). The rabbis prescribed these prayers for protection against demons of the night (*Ber.* 4b–5a). Two parts of the Night Prayers mentioned in the Talmud (*Ber.* 60b) are the *Shema*'s opening section (Deut. 6:4–9), and the blessing that begins "Who casts the bonds of sleep on my eyes." Today, the Night Prayers include medieval additions: the short prayer HASHKIVENU followed by quotes from the EVENING SERVICE; the PRIESTLY BLESSING; verses from

the Book of Psalms (90:17, 91, 3:2–9, 121:4, 128: 4–5); and the ADON OLAM song at the end. Young children recite a shorter version of the Night Prayers.

NINE DAYS   Final stage of public mourning for the TEMPLE's destruction. The public mourning lasts for THREE WEEKS: it begins on the fast of SHIVAH ASAR BE-TAMMUZ (17 Tammuz), and ends the day after TISHAH BE-AV (9 Av). During the Three Weeks, observant Jews practice various MOURNING customs, places of entertainment are avoided, and marriage ceremonies do not take place. During the nine days between the first (New Moon) of Av until the afternoon of the tenth, more restrictions are added: eating meat and drinking wine are prohibited except on the Sabbath. Some Orthodox Jews do not wash their clothes or wear new clothes as a sign of mourning. It is also customary not to shave or have a haircut during this time. In general, similar customs are practiced in Ashkenazi, Sephardi, and Oriental communities.

NISAN   First month of the Jewish CALENDAR; seventh month of the Hebrew civil year, which starts in TISHRI. It is a "full" month of 30 days and usually falls during March–April. Its zodiac sign is Aries, the Ram. The rabbis connect this sign with the lamb offering brought on PASSOVER. In the Pentateuch (Ex. 13:4, 23:15, 34:18; Deut. 16:1) Nisan is known as Abib (Heb. *Hodesh ha-Aviv*, "the month of spring").

Many historic events took place during the month of Nisan: the exodus from Egypt in mid-Nisan, the building of the TABERNACLE (EX. 40:17) on the first (New Moon) of Nisan, and the Israelites' crossing of the Jordan river into the Holy Land on the tenth of Nisan, one generation later. Fasting, funeral eulogies, and public acts of mourning are prohibited during Nisan because it is *zeman herutenu* ("the Season of our Freedom"), when Israel was redeemed from slavery.

Passover is celebrated on 15–21 Nisan in Israel (15–22 Nisan in the Diaspora), and the counting of the OMER begins on the second night of Passover. In ancient times the SANHEDRIN sent messengers to Jewish communities in the Diaspora to announce the exact time of Passover. Traditionally, 15 Nisan marks the beginning of the harvest season in Israel (*BM* 106b). HOLOCAUST Memorial Day (*Yom ha-Sho'ah*) is observed on 27 Nisan.

NISHMAT KOL HAI   ("The soul of everything that lives"). First words of the prayer of thanksgiving that is said in the MORNING SERVICE for the SABBATH and FESTIVALS before the end of PESUKEI DE-ZIMRA, the "verses of praise" that come before the SHEMA and its blessings.

The prayer, which is mentioned in the Talmud and includes verses from the Bible, praises God's greatness in comparison to humans. It mentions some of God's great deeds, and ends with a poetic description of these deeds and of the Jew's promise to praise Him forever.

Although neither the Sabbath nor the festivals are mentioned in the prayer, it is said on these days because they are days of rest, which allow more time to think about God's actions. The prayer is also recited as part of the Passover SEDER.

NOACHIDE LAWS   Seven basic rules of morality which, according to Jewish law, all people must obey. These laws existed before the TORAH and the HALAKHAH (rabbinic law), and were originally given to NOAH. According to MAIMONIDES, a Gentile who accepts these seven rules is considered one of "the pious ones among the nations of the world (*Hasidei Ummot ha-Olam*) who deserves a share in the world to come" (*Tosef.* to *Sanh.* 13:2). Christians and Muslims are considered by most rabbinic (Jewish legal) authorities as having accepted the Noachide laws.

NOACHIDE LAWS

1.   civil justice (the duty to establish a legal system)

2.   the prohibition against taking God's name in vain (which includes the bearing of false witness)

3.   the abandonment of idolatry

4.   the prohibition against incest (including adultery and other sexual offenses);

5.   the prohibition against murder

6.   the prohibition against theft

7.   the law against eating flesh ("a limb") cut from a living animal (i.e., cruelty in any shape or form)

(TB, *Sanh.* 56a)

NOAH   Hero of the FLOOD story, father of Shem, Ham, and Japheth. At a time that the rest of the world was corrupt (Gen. 6:12), Noah was the only person who "walked with God" (Gen. 5:9). God instructed Noah to build an ark and to bring into it seven of every type of clean beast, two of every other kind of living creature, and his family. Once he had done this, God made it rain for 40 days and 40 nights, causing a flood that destroyed all the living creatures in the word except for those in the ark. The water stayed at the same level for 150 days before it started to settle. Forty days later, Noah sent out a raven and later a dove. The second time he sent the dove it returned with an olive leaf in its beak, as a sign that the treetops were no longer under water. When the dove did not return the third time it was sent, Noah knew it was safe to leave the ark. After leaving the ark, Noah built an alter and offered a sacrifice to God. God then gave the rainbow as a sign that a flood would never again destroy the earth. God also gave Noah a series of COMMANDMENTS, the NOACHIDE LAWS. Later, after planting a vineyard and drinking its wine, Noah became drunk and his son Ham "uncovered his nakedness." When Noah became sober again, he cursed Ham and his son Canaan. It has been suggested that Ham's sin was homosexuality, or that he had committed incest with his mother.

Noah's Ark on the mosaic floor of a Byzantine period in a church near Medeba.

Commentators are divided about the meaning of Genesis 6:9: "Noah was a just man and perfect in his generations." Some say that this shows that Noah was great in spite of the bad people around him. Others say that he was only great compared to his generation, but that there were greater people than him in other generations.

NOVELLAE   (Heb. *hiddushim*). Original interpretations of passages in the Talmud. Unlike commentators such as RASHI and others, the writers of the novellae tried to solve problems and explain the logic in the Talmud, or in the interpretations of the commentators (e.g., the TOSAFOT explain Rashi's commentary). Some novellae were written in order to explain previous novellae. Famous novellae were written by R. Yom Tov ben Abraham Ishbili (late 13th–early 14th cent.), who commented on the writings of NAHMANIDES (1194–1270); by R. Solomon ben Abraham ADRET (1235–1310); and by R. Bezalel Ashkenazi (Egyptian talmudist, 16th cent.), whose collected novellae, *Shittah Mekubbetset* ("Collected System"), discuss five books of the Talmud. Since these works present different readings, they are being used as the basis for a scientific edition of the Talmud.

NUMBERS   Certain numbers appear often in the Bible and in Jewish tradition. The number seven is most common: every seven days is the SABBATH, the SABBATICAL YEAR occurs every seven years, and the JUBILEE year is celebrated after seven Sabbatical years. Both PASSOVER and SUKKOT are seven-day celebrations. On the Sabbath, seven people are called up to the READING OF THE LAW, and on HOSHANA RABBAH and SIMHAT TORAH, the synagogue is encircled seven times (see HAKKAFOT). Ten is another important number. It appears in ABRAHAM's last appeal to God to save Sodom, in the TEN COMMANDMENTS, and in the TITHE (tenth part of produce) that was given to the LEVITES and to the poor. Ten people are needed for a MINYAN (prayer quorum) and for special additions to the GRACE AFTER MEALS. The numbers 12 and 40 are also mentioned often in the Bible. There are 12 months in the year,

JACOB had 12 sons, and there are 12 TRIBES. The FLOOD was 40 days long, MOSES spent 40 days on Mount SINAI (twice), and in the time of the Judges "the land was quiet for 40 years" (Judg. 3:11, 5:31, 8:28).

Every letter in the Hebrew alphabet also has a numerical value. This number system is called GEMATRIA, and is often referred to in Jewish MYSTICISM. It assigns many interpretations to the numerical value of certain words and phrases.

According to the Bible, Jews are not to be counted directly. In ancient times every person had to give a half-shekel coin as a donation. When a census of the Israelites was taken, these coins were counted and the number of people was determined according to the number of coins. When David counted his people directly, they were struck by a plague that killed 70,000 (II Sam. 24). To this day, some observant Jews recite a ten-word verse from the Bible, assigning a word to each person, to see if a ten-person prayer quorum is present in order to avoid counting the people directly.

NUMBER VALUES OF HEBREW LETTERS

א–1   ב–2   ג–3   ד–4   ה–5   ו–6   ז–7   ח–8   ט–9   י–10   כ–20   ל–30

מ–40   נ–50   ס–60   ע–70   פ–80   צ–90   ק–100   ר–200   ש–300   ת–400

NUMBERS, BOOK OF Fourth book of the PENTATEUCH, *Be-Midbar* in Hebrew ("In the [Sinai] Wilderness"). It contains 36 chapters and 1,288 verses. The sages call it the "*Hummash* (i.e., Pentateuchal volume) of the Numbered," because a census of the Israelites was taken in it on two occasions. Numbers describes the events of a period of about 38½ years, from the second year of the Exodus until after the death of AARON.

Well-known verses that come from Numbers are the PRIESTLY BLESSING (6:24–26) and the third paragraph of the central SHEMA prayer.

NUMBERS RABBAH A MIDRASH (commentary) on the book of NUMBERS, which includes many sages' sermons on themes from the Bible text. It is divided into 23 sections. The Midrash's language is basically the Hebrew of the Mishnah. Hebrew from the Middle Ages has also influenced the text. There is evidence to suggest that the printed text of Numbers Rabbah is made up of two different *midrashim* (one on Numbers 1–8 and one on Numbers 9–36), and that an editor joined the two parts in the 13ᵗʰ century.

NUSAH (or *nosah*; "arrangement, version, style"). Hebrew term which indicates (a) the liturgical or prayer tradition of a major Jewish community, and (b) the traditional way of reciting a specific prayer or biblical passage. The word *minhag* is often used as another word for "*nusah*" (see CUSTOM).

By the early Middle Ages, different kinds of ritual had developed from the old Babylonian and Erets Israel prayer traditions. Each one adopted different types of prayer po-

---

BOOK OF NUMBERS

1:1–4:49	The first census; the order of camping and traveling in the desert
5:1–7:89	Various laws and offerings
8:1–8:26	Purification of the Levites
9:1–9:23	Passover and the fire cloud
10:1–12:16	The order of travel; complaints
13:1–14:45	The 12 spies and the punishment that followed
15:1–15:41	Additional laws of offerings, Sabbath observance, and the fringed garment
16:1–17:28	The Korah rebellion
18:1–19:22	Duties of the Priests and Levites; laws of ritual purification
20:1–21:35	The Israelites at Kadesh: the sins of Moses and Aaron, defeat of enemy kings
22:1–24:25	The story of Balaam
25:1–25:18	Phinehas, the zealous priest
26:1–26:65	The second census
27:1–27:11	The daughters of Zelophehad
27:12–27:23	Joshua to succeed Moses
28:1–30:17	Sacrifices, the laws of oaths
31:1–31:54	The war against Midian
32:1–32:42	Tribal settlement east of the Jordan river
33:1–35:34	The long journey of the Israelites, the borders of the Holy Land, the Levitical cities and cities of refuge
36:1–36:13	Laws of inheritance by daughters

---

etry – KINOT, PIYYUT, and SELIHOT – and was influenced by other communities.

The Babylonian tradition was the basis for rituals in Spain, Portugal, Southern France, parts of North Africa, and the Near East. Its most important branch was *nusah Sefarad*, the Spanish form, which is used by SEPHARDIM in Israel, England, Holland, the United States, and other countries. This type of prayer has unique elements that can be found in the MORNING SERVICE, KADDISH and KEDUSHAH, GRACE AFTER MEALS, and the order of the READING OF THE LAW. *Nusah edot ha-Mizrah*, the "Oriental" communities' form of worship, is similar to the Sephardi one. It is used in North Africa, Syria, Turkey, Iraq, and Israel. The Yemenite style, *minhag Teiman*, is based on SAADIAH GAON's and MAIMONIDES' prayer books.

The Erets Israel tradition influenced fewer prayer customs.

The Romaniot or Byzantine rite (*nusah Romania*) was used in Turkey, Greece, and Sicily until the 16th century. The Italian or Roman rite (*minhag Italyani*), possibly the oldest *nusah* in Europe, is still practiced by Italian Jews, both in Italy and in Jerusalem. *Nusah Ashkenaz*, the version that developed in central Europe, spread to Poland, Lithuania, and Russia, when the ASHKENAZIM were driven out of their homes and forced to move east. This rite, also known as *minhag ha-Gera*, is widely used in Israel and has the largest following in the Jewish world. Ashkenazi Jews who accept HASIDISM use a changed version of the Sephardi *nusah*, based on that of Isaac LURIA (*Ari*), which is called *nusah ha-Ari*. Since 1948, some attempts have been made in Israel to form a "unified rite" (*nusah ahid*), which would suit Jews from different communities.

Except for minor modifications (e.g., changing the words of prayers that have to do with the Temple sacrifices), CONSERVATIVE JUDAISM has kept the traditional Ashkenazi form of prayer. REFORM JUDAISM, however, has made wide-ranging changes in the traditional rite over the years.

The term *nusah* also relates to the musical tunes used for certain prayers on particular occasions. One who is familiar with these tunes and uses them in his prayers is said to "know" or "have" a good *nusah*. See also CANTOR AND CANTORIAL MUSIC; LITURGY; MAHZOR; MUSIC AND SONG; PRAYER; and PRAYER BOOK.

OATHS See VOWS AND VOWING

OBADIAH Fourth of the Minor Prophets in the PROPHETS section of the Bible. It is the shortest book in the Bible: one chapter with 21 verses. Nothing is known about the prophet himself. The MIDRASH says that he was related to Eliphaz, JOB's friend, and that he converted to Judaism (*Yal. Shimoni* 2:549). According to another tradition, he was the same Obadiah who hid the prophets in the time of Ahab and Jezebel (1 Kings 18:3–7).

Obadia's DAY OF JUDGMENT prophecy is against Edom, the nation that helped the Babylonians conquer JUDAH and destroy the First TEMPLE in 586 BCE. Verses 15–21 describe the Day of the Lord, when the house of JACOB will take over Edom.

	THE BOOK OF OBADIAH
1–16	The guilt of Edom and its punishment
17–21	The future restoration of Israel

OFFERINGS See SACRIFICES AND OFFERINGS

OHOLOT ("Tents"). Second tractate (book) of the Order of TOHOROT in the Mishnah. Its 18 chapters mainly deal with two kinds of impurity: impurity caused by coming in physical contact with a corpse and impurity caused by entering a tent or house where a corpse is lying (cf. Num. 19:11, 14–16). Purification from these impurities and others is accomplished by immersing in a ritual bath (MIKVEH) and sprinkling with "living waters" mixed with the ashes of the RED HEIFER.

OLAM HA-BA AND OLAM HA-ZEH See AFTERLIFE

OLD AGE See AGE AND THE AGED

OMER ("sheaf") The offering of the first grains of the new barley harvest, which was brought to the TEMPLE on the second day of PASSOVER. The Omer is a measure equal to one-tenth of an *ephah* (i.e. about 2 quarts). It is a relatively small amount to offer (see Lev. 23:9ff); however, until the Omer had been brought to the priest in the Temple, none of the food from the new harvest could be eaten.

When the Temple was destroyed, the practice of bringing offerings ended (see SACRIFICES AND OFFERINGS). Even so, the counting of the Omer continued. From the night of the 16th of Nisan until the end of the seven-week period between Passover and SHAVU'OT every day is counted separately. The number of days and the number of weeks that passed are both mentioned. The Omer is counted at night during the EVENING SERVICE. Many synagogues have an Omer calendar on the wall to announce which day had been reached in counting the Omer. The "Omer counter" has therefore become a new form of Jewish art.

The practice of counting the Omer comes originally from the Bible; however, many rabbis hold that it was important for all times. MAIMONIDES explained that by counting the days from Passover until Shavu'ot people show how eager they are to welcome Shavu'ot, which is the anniversary of the giving of the Torah. Others have said that the freedom festival of Passover is incomplete without the Torah festival of Shavu'ot, because freedom without Torah law can be dangerous. Counting the Omer serves as a bridge between freedom and Torah law.

As time went on, sadness and semi-mourning became part of the Omer period. The reasons for this are unclear, and scholars disagree about them. In Jewish practice today, several activities are avoided during the Omer by religious Jews as a sign of semi-mourning – shaving, haircuts, weddings, and public parties – except on special days, such as the New Moon and Lag Ba-Omer (the 33rd day of the Omer). However, customs vary among different groups of Jews. Religious Zionists, for example, fully celebrate Israel's INDEPENDENCE DAY (5 Iyyar) and JERUSALEM Day (28 Iyyar), even though these fall during the Omer period.

ONEG SHABBAT (lit. "Sabbath Delight"). The obligation to be happy on the SABBATH, as suggested in Isaiah 58:13: "You shall call the Sabbath a delight." This includes having three meals during the Sabbath, making each of them a festive occasion by serving special dishes (see SE'UDAH), and by singing ZEMIROT (table hymns), especially during SE'UDAH SHELISHIT, the third meal of the day.

The poet Hayyim Nahman Bialik (1873–1934) established an *Oneg Shabbat* program on Sabbath afternoons, which included singing Sabbath songs, Bible study, and refreshments. In this way, non-observant Jews could enjoy the Sabbath too. Bialik's program was adopted in many synagogues and communities.

ORAL LAW   (Heb. *Torah she-be'al-peh*). Judaism's code of law, which is based on rabbinic interpretations of the WRITTEN LAW and appears in rabbinic literature. According to Jewish belief, God gave MOSES the Oral Law at Mount SINAI, together with the Written Law. This principle is based on R. SIMEON BEN LAKISH's explanation of the verse: "The Lord said to Moses, Come up to Me to the mountain and I will give you the stone tablets and the TORAH and the Commandments which I have inscribed to instruct them" (Ex. 24:12). He explains that the phrase "the Commandments which I have inscribed to instruct them" refers to the MISHNAH, the Prophets, the Writings, and the GEMARA (TALMUD). These are therefore considered part of the Oral Law.

The SAGES have continued to interpret the Written Law over the centuries. Because of the ongoing changes in Jewish life over the years, they have had to make rulings on the specific matters of their day. They always explained how their decisions were based on the core of the Written Law. These rulings (HALAKHAH) became a binding part of the Oral Law, which continued to grow. This growth began in the mid-fifth century, in the days of EZRA the SCRIBE, who started to interpret the Torah. Rulings of his time were called *divrei soferim*, "the pronouncements of the Scribes," and were considered to have the authority of biblical law.

Not all rabbinic rulings are based on Scriptures, such as the sages' commands to observe the PURIM and HANUKKAH holidays, the lighting of CANDLES on Sabbath and festival eves, and GEZERAH and TAKKANAH rulings. The Oral Law also includes the issue of community CUSTOM. Because there were disagreements among the sages, a *halakhah* was established only after it was discussed and debated thoroughly (see HERMENEUTICS).

In the period of the *tannaim* (c. 2nd cent. CE), rulings that came from specific verses in the Bible were collected (MIDRASH HALAKHAH). In the third century, R. JUDAH HA-NASI gathered halakhic opinions and arranged them, according to subject in six divisions or "orders." The result was the Mishnah, the basic text of the Oral Law. Some of R. Judah's students gathered opinions that were not included in the Mishnah into a collection called the TOSEFTA. The Mishnah and the Tosefta were discussed by the *amoraim* in the ACADEMIES of Erets Israel and Babylonia. By the sixth century, these discussions were collected and edited into the Jerusalem and the Babylonian Talmuds. The Talmuds were studied in the centuries that followed and continue to be widely studied today.

The later Oral Law literature can be divided into NOVELLAE (*hiddushim)* and TALMUDIC COMMENTARIES; books of rulings, such as the *Mishneh Torah* of MAIMONIDES and the SHULHAN ARUKH with their commentaries (see CODIFICATION); RESPONSA (answers to Jewish legal questions); and works arranged according to the 613 COMMANDMENTS of the Written Law.

Throughout Jewish history, various groups have refused to accept the Oral Law. The SAMARITANS only recognized the Pentateuch. The SADDUCEES and the ESSENES did not accept the Pharisaic (rabbinic) tradition but had their own interpretation of the Written Law. The KARITES (from the eighth century) relied only on the Written Law and rejected all interpretations. REFORM JUDAISM sees the Oral Law as a guide that offers tradition and general direction but not as an authority that must be followed. The CONSERVATIVE movement tries to base its Jewish legal decisions on the Written Law, and its understanding of the Oral Law is often different from that of ORTHODOXY.

ORDINATION   (*semikhah*). The transmission of ritual authority. Traditionally, God gave authority to MOSES, who passed it on to JOSHUA. The Mishnah (*Avot* 1:1) tells about the passing of this authority, through Joshua, to the Men of the GREAT ASSEMBLY. Later, a teacher who was appointed by the Patriarch (see NASI) performed the ordination ceremony in the presence of the SANHEDRIN. The person ordained was given the title RABBI and had full Jewish legal authority. *Semikhah* could only be awarded in Erets Israel.

Even though the Sanhedrin disappeared with the destruction of the Second Temple (70 CE), R. JOHANAN BEN ZAKKAI continued to perform ordination ceremonies. After the BAR KOKHBA revolt failed (135 CE), ordination was forbidden by the Roman emperor. Even so, it continued to exist for many years before disappearing. Over the years, as Jewish communities developed, there was a growing need for qualified teachers and judges. A candidate for either of these jobs had to present a document signed by at least one TORAH scholar, known as *Hattarat Hora'ah*, "permission to teach." This recognition is often referred to as *semikhah*, but it does not have the authority of ancient *semikhah*.

In the 19th century, because of the EMANCIPATION of the Jews in Western and Central Europe and their entry into modern society, there was a need for a new kind of rabbi. Thus RABBINICAL SEMINARIES were founded. They taught certain leadership skills as well as religious subjects and presented their students with the title of rabbi. In Eastern Europe, the Muslim world, and Israel, individual ordination within the YESHIVAH continued.

In 1538 R. Jacob Berav of Safed tried to reestablish ancient *semikhah*, but he did not succeed. In 1948, after the establishment of the State of Israel, reassembling the Sanhedrin was suggested so that *semikhah* could be officially reestablished. This suggestion received very little support and was rejected.

Today, in the American Jewish community, all types of ordination can be found, including ordination of WOMEN among the non-Orthodox.

ORGAN   Musical instrument that became part of Christian worship around the 17th century. Before 1700, there were a few rabbis in northern Italy who allowed the use of an organ on special occasions. Israel Jacobson, a supporter of REFORM JUDAISM, was the first to encourage playing the organ on SABBATHS and FESTIVALS in Westphalia and Berlin, Germany. The Hamburg Temple (1818) followed his example. Akiva Eger and Moses SOFER, representatives of the Orthodox community, were against using an organ. They claimed that not only is playing the organ on the Sabbath a violation of Jewish law, but playing it at all is a non-Jewish custom (HUKKAT HA-GOY).

By 1850, organs were used in Reform synagogues in Hungary, England, the United States, and other countries. Today, many Conservative synagogues in the United States allow an organ to be played on Sabbaths and festivals, but by a non-Jew. ORTHODOXY still objects to using an organ, but some modern Orthodox communities allow it to be played at weddings and weekday services.

ORLAH (lit. "uncircumcised" – the fruit of a tree during its first three years). Tenth tractate (book) of the Order of ZERA'IM in the Mishnah. Its three chapters discuss the laws that forbid one to have any benefit from fruit trees in Erets Israel during the first three years of their growth (cf. Lev. 19:23–25). This prohibition includes using *orlah*-fruit peels to fuel a cooking fire and using *orlah*-fruit essence to make fabric dye. The law against using *orlah* applies also outside of Israel.

ORPHAN See WIDOW AND ORPHAN

ORTHODOXY Classical rabbinic Judaism, as developed by the rabbis throughout the ages. The word "Orthodox" refers to Jews from Central and Western Europe, from the 18th century on, who were against the changes brought about by the EMANCIPATION (when Jews were given entrance to national society), the Jewish Enlightenment movement (HASKALAH), and REFORM JUDAISM. According to the Orthodox view, the WRITTEN LAW (PENTATEUCH) was given to man by God, along with the ORAL LAW. Orthodoxy stresses the importance of observing the laws in the Jewish law code, SHULHAN ARUKH. Orthodoxy sees itself as the rightful holder of Jewish tradition.

Trends in Orthodoxy (1800–1939) As a result of the Emancipation, Jews began to take part in general, non-Jewish society. They were paid better salaries and became active for the first time in the social and political world outside of the Jewish COMMUNITY. For many Jews, the new approach of the Haskalah began to replace religious authority with modern ways of thinking. This new age also caused changes in the traditional Jewish way of life. In addition, mainstream Jewish leadership was threatened by the growth of the Reform movement. Its main promoters, Abraham GEIGER and Samuel Holdheim, challenged the halakhic (rabbinic legal) basis of Judaism.

The traditionalists, who now called themselves "Orthodox" Jews, could not agree about how to deal with these challenges. R. Moses SOFER of Pressburg, Bratislava, and his followers totally rejected the values of the Haskalah, announced a ban

The head of a traditional yeshivah with his disciples.

of EXCOMMUNICATION against the Reformers, and appealed to all believers to separate themselves even further from the would around them. Others, while aware of the dangers, understood the importance of modern world values and tried to include them in traditional Judaism. Rabbinical leaders of this kind, who included Samson Raphael HIRSCH and Azriel Hildesheimer, created NEO-ORTHODOXY, which was the basis for modern Orthodoxy in the West. A similar movement developed in Eastern Europe. It's leaders included ELIJAH the Gaon of Vilna; the BERLIN and SOLOVEICHIK families; R. Isaac Jacob Reines; and Abraham Isaac KOOK, who pioneered modern religious ZIONISM.

The HOLOCAUST did tremendous damage especially to Orthodoxy. Most of the Orthodox communities in the world had been in Europe, and the Nazis destroyed them. During and after World War II, some important Orthodox leaders of HASIDISM and heads of YESHIVAHS (academies) escaped from Europe to North America and Erets Israel, where they rebuilt their organizations.

Orthodoxy remains loyal to Jewish law and to the traditional Hebrew prayer service, rejects much of modern Bible criticism, bans ORGAN music at SABBATH and FESTIVAL prayer services, and separates men and women in the synagogue.

American Orthodoxy By 1880, the religious observance of the American Jewish community (numbering about 250,000) was weakening. Of the estimated 200 major congregations, maybe a dozen were still Orthodox; the rest were Reform. From 1880 to 1920 around two million Jews, mostly from Eastern Europe, arrived in the United States. Most of them had lived traditional Jewish lives. They settled in New York and in other big cities, where they tried to make a living and adjust to American life. Jewish learning, Sabbath observance, and Jewish values, gave way to public school education, financial obligations, and American social values. By the late 1930s, most Jews had left their immigrant neighborhoods and moved to other communities. The process of assimilation was already in progress.

However, Orthodoxy recovered as a result of the arrival of Orthodox scholars and Hasidic leaders from Europe. An American-born Orthodox group appeared that understood the importance of keeping old Jewish traditions. From 1944, many Hebrew day schools and post-high school *yeshivot* were built throughout the United States and Canada.

The most important institutes for the training of Orthodox rabbis and scholars are New York's Yeshiva University and the Hebrew Technical College in Chicago. The largest Orthodox synagogue body is the Union of Orthodox Jewish Congregations of America. It is responsible for the international "OU" certification for KOSHER food.

Unlike the extremely traditional groups (known as the "Ultra-Orthodox"), Modern Orthodoxy follows these main practices: taking part in general cultural activities, such as studying at universities and attending museums and performances; cooperating with all Jews – Conservative, Reform, and secular – in community issues (but not in religious ones); recognizing the State of Israel and taking part in the World Zionist Organization; and a more open view towards Jewish law than before. Modern Orthodoxy's religious leadership is found in the Rabbinic Council of America (RCA).

Ultra-Orthodox institutions include the Union of Orthodox Rabbis; the Rabbinical Alliance; Agudat Israel; all Hasidic communities, from Lubavich (HABAD) to the anti-Zionist SATMAR group; and the traditional *yeshivot*. Most large Ultra-Orthodox communities have their own schools and social organizations. Since they have very large families, their numbers are constantly growing. See HAREDIM.

Other Diaspora Communities   The number of Orthodox Jews in the remainder of the Diaspora is potentially higher than in the United States; it sometimes reaches 80 percent of the general Jewish population. In Sephardi-Oriental communities, Latin America, and some Eastern European communities, the Orthodox make up the greater part of religious Jews, but in these countries most Jews are not connected to any religious group. France has the third largest Orthodox Jewish community in the world, after the United States and Israel. In England, most of the synagogues are part of the Modern Orthodox movement. For the State of Israel, see ISRAEL, RELIGION IN THE STATE OF.

PAGANISM   See IDOLATRY

PALESTINIAN TALMUD   See TALMUD

PARADISE   See EDEN, GARDEN OF

PARAH   ("Cow"). Fourth tractate (book) of the Order of TOHOROT in the Mishnah. It consists of 12 chapters dealing with the laws of choosing, slaughtering, and burning the RED HEIFER (see Num. 19:1–22). The animal's ashes, mixed with pure spring water, were used to purify those who came in contact with the dead. The Mishnah discusses the age of the Red Heifer, being sure it has no hairs that are not red, the manner of slaughter and burning, how to mix the ashes, and purifying those who were unclean

PARASHAH   A section of the PENTATEUCH. The Pentateuch is divided into 54 sections, with one read each week of the year in synagogue. SEPHARDIM use the term to refer both to the 54 weekly portions and the four special sections (*Shekalim, Zakhar, Parah,* and *Ha-Hodesh*) read on special occasions (see SABBATHS, SPECIAL). ASHKENAZIM use the term *sidrah* or *parashah* to refer to the weekly portion.

The weekly portions are known by the first or most important word of the opening verse. Each portion is sub-divided into shorter sections to be read by each person called to the READING OF THE LAW of that day. The printed text of the Torah is marked to indicate the beginning of each portion and sub-section. At the AFTERNOON SERVICE on Sabbaths, the first portion of the coming Sabbath is read; this is also true on MONDAY AND THURSDAY mornings (unless these coincide with a New MOON or fast day).

PARDES   Word from the Persian language, meaning an area surrounded by a fence. In one of the earliest Jewish mystical passages (*Hag.* 14b), it refers to secret Divine wisdom. In the Middle Ages, it was used as an ACROSTIC for four kinds of Bible interpretation: P = *peshat* (literal interpretation), R = *remez* (allusions), D = *derash* (homiletical, based on stories with hidden meanings), and S = *sod* (mystical interpretation).

PARENTAL BLESSING   (Heb. *Birkat Banim*). Blessing usually recited by the father for his children of all ages, usually on the SABBATH eve after services. The text for male children is taken from the blessing of JACOB (Gen. 48:20): "So he blessed them by saying … may God make you like Ephraim and Manasseh." The text for daughters is: "May God make you like Sarah, Rebekah, Rachel and Leah" – the four MATRIARCHS. The PRIESTLY BLESSING (Num. 6:22–27) is then recited for both sons and daughters.

PARENT AND CHILD   Jewish law describes the relationship between parents and children in terms of a system of obligations. The Fifth Commandment states: "Honor your father and your mother, that your days may be long in the land which the Lord your God gives you" (Ex. 20:12). Elsewhere, "You shall each fear his mother and his father" (Lev. 19:3). Together, the two verses teach that both parents should be equally honored and equally feared (*Kid.* 30b–31a). "Honor" is understood by the Talmud to mean feeding, washing, dressing, and helping one's elderly parents. Feeding and caring for parents is to be at the parent's expense. If the parent cannot pay, the children must pay for the care. The children may deduct this expense from their normal donations to CHARITY (*Sh.* Ar., *YD* 240:5). "Fear" was understood as not sitting in a parent's chair nor contradicting them in conversation (*Kid.* 31b). The parent has the right to waive any and all of the child's obligations toward him; parents are called upon not to impose too great a burden upon their children (*Kid.* 30b). In the Bible, injuring and cursing a parent are punishable by death (Ex. 21:15, 17).

The Talmud praises children who honor their parents. Honor for parents is considered to be like honoring God Himself, since the parents have the status of partners in the creation of the child. Jewish law assumes that parents love their children; it does not assume that children love their parents.

In Jewish law, a father bears the primary responsibility for supporting his children. These obligations include providing for daily needs and education, teaching a male a trade, redeeming him if he is the firstborn (see FIRSTBORN, REDEMPTION OF), having him circumcised, and seeing to his marriage (*Kid.* 29a). He is not obliged to see to his daughter's marriage. He is, however, required to provide her with sufficient clothing, etc., so she will be considered marriageable (*Ket.* 52b).

The obligation to honor and revere parents extends beyond the parent's lifetime. Reciting KADDISH for a deceased parent or observing the anniversary of death (YAHRZEIT) falls into the category of honoring the parent. It is also a mark of respect for a child to assume the debts of their deceased parents.

PAREVEH   See DIETARY LAWS

PAROKHET

The finely woven "curtain" that separated the "holy place" in the SANCTUARY from the HOLY OF HOLIES. Exodus 26:31–33 states: "You shall make a curtain of blue, purple, and scarlet yarns and fine twisted linen; with CHERUBS it shall be designed, the work of a skilled craftsman … and it shall serve as a partition between the holy place and the Holy of Holies." A similar curtain was made for Solomon's TEMPLE (II Chr. 3:14). The curtain covered the cherubs and, when worshipers came to the Temple on the PILGRIM FESTIVALS, the curtain was rolled aside so that they could see the cherubs (*Yoma* 54a).

In the synagogue, the ARK that holds the Scrolls of the Law is covered by a *parokhet*. In both Ashkenazi and Sephardi congregations, an embroidered curtain, a symbol of the biblical one, hangs in front of the doors of the Ark. The curtain is made of rich material, such as velvet, brocade, or Italian silk. It is usually decorated with embroidery. Traditional symbols that appear on the curtain include the crown (*keter*) and winged "lions of Judah," which represent the majesty of God. As in the Temple, the curtain is usually made by women.

In place of the normal colored curtain, a white satin or velvet curtain is used on ROSH HA-SHANAH, the DAY OF ATONEMENT, HOSHANA RABBAH, and SHEMINI ATSERET. As a sign of mourning, Ashkenazim remove the curtain from the Ark on TISHAH BE-AV; Oriental Jews hang a black curtain.

PARTICULARISM   See UNIVERSALISM AND PARTICULARISM

PASSOVER

(Heb. *Pesah*). One of the PILGRIM FESTIVALS (with SHAVU'OT and SUKKOT) when Jews were commanded to appear at the TEMPLE in Jerusalem (Ex. 23:14). Passover is celebrated for eight days (seven days in Israel and by REFORM Jews), beginning on 15 Nisan. Outside Israel, the first two and last two days are holy days, while the middle four are HOL HA-MO'ED, the intermediate working days. In Israel, only the first day and the last day are holy, while the middle five days are *Hol ha-Mo'ed.*

Passover has both historical and agricultural meaning. It reminds us of the EXODUS of the Israelites from Egypt. In addition, it celebrates the beginning of the barley harvest in the spring. Passover has four different names, which each relate to its different aspects. It is called *Hag ha-Matzot*, the Festival of Unleavened Bread (Ex. 12:15), which refers to the commandment to eat unleavened bread. It is also called *Pesah* – Passover –

relating to the ANGEL OF DEATH who "passed over" the houses of the Israelites when he killed all the firstborn of the Egyptians (Ex. 12:27). It is called in the prayers *Zeman Herutenu* – the Season of Our Freedom. These three names relate to the historical celebration. The Bible also calls Passover *Hag ha-Aviv*, the Festival of Spring. This refers to the agricultural events that take place at this time of year.

Preparations for Passover   No other festival calls for such extensive preparation. Jews are forbidden to have *hamets*, leavened substances, in their homes or possession from just before the first day of Passover until the conclusion of the festival. The Bible explains (Ex. 12:39) that we do not eat *hamets* in order to recall the Exodus from Egypt, when the Children of Israel left in haste and had no time for the dough they were baking to rise. It warns that any person eating leaven during Passover "shall be cut off from his people" (Ex. 12:15; see KARET). The ban refers to all dough made from the FIVE SPECIES of grain: wheat, emmer, barley, rye, and oats.

Before Passover, *hamets* is gradually removed from the home. On the night before Passover, the head of the household searches for any remaining *hamets* (see LEAVEN, SEARCH FOR). Any *hamets* remaining in the home is burned on the morning before Passover. In addition, unleavened food and the utensils used to prepare it are sold to a non-Jew for the duration of the festival. *Mekhirat Hamets*, the sale of *hamets*, legally removes any leaven remaining in the house from the ownership of the Jew. He thereby avoids violating the very serious law against the possession of *hamets*.

The SEDER is the order of the home ritual performed on the first two nights of Passover (in Israel and among Reform Jews, on the first night only). This is the most important observance of the festival. At the *Seder*, the story of the Exodus is recited from the HAGGADAH.

Liturgy   The special prayers for Passover includes the HALLEL and ADDITIONAL SERVICE, as in all festivals. It is unusual that Hallel is recited in the EVENING SERVICE and at the *Seder* as

Preparation of utensils to be used at Passover by immersion in boiling water.

Houses of Israelites marked with blood of the paschal lamb so the Angel of Death will "pass over" them. 15ᵗʰ-century Haggadah.

well. On the morning of the first day, immediately before the Additional Service, the special prayer for DEW is recited. In Ashkenazi synagogues, *Yizkor*, the MEMORIAL SERVICE, is read. Beginning on the second night of Passover, the OMER is counted (see Lev. 23:15ff.).

Pesah Sheni (Second Passover) When the Temple still stood, people who were unable to participate in the SACRIFICE of the paschal lamb were permitted to do so one month later, i.e. on 14 Iyyar (see PASSOVER, SECOND).

Some Passover Customs The SAMARITANS in Erets Israel observe the Passover rites on Mount Gerizim near Shechem (Nablus). To this day, the slaughter of the paschal lamb is the high point of their ceremony. They set aside a number of sheep on 10 Nisan. On the eve of the 14ᵗʰ they are slaughtered, roasted for six hours in ovens dug in the earth, and distributed to the families to be eaten in their homes with bitter herbs.

The ETHIOPIAN JEWS (Beta Israel) stop eating leaven three days before the festival. They eat only dried peas and beans until Passover eve. Then they fast until their high priest slaughters the paschal lamb on an altar in the courtyard of the synagogue.

The blood is sprinkled around the entrance to the building, and the lamb is roasted and eaten.

In the Caucasus, Jews wear clothes of "freedom" with wide, loose sleeves. They enact a play during their *Seder* in which one participant goes outside, knocks on the door, and pretends that he has just arrived from Jerusalem. All the others ask him for news of the Holy City and whether he has a message of liberation and redemption.

The MARRANOS, the secret Jews of Spain and Portugal, observed Passover on 16 Nisan in order to avoid suspicion on the previous day.

PASSOVER, SECOND Observance of Passover on 14 Iyyar by those prevented from keeping it on its regular date a month earlier. The Bible (Num. 9) relates that a number of Israelites approached MOSES and told him that they were unable to observe the Passover because they had been ritually impure. After Moses brought the question before God, the Second Passover was enacted. There is one reference in the Bible to a mass offering on the Second Passover in the time of King Hezekiah, when the paschal lamb had not been brought because "the priests had not sanctified themselves sufficiently, neither had the people gathered themselves together to Jerusalem" (II Chr. 30:3). Today, TAHANUN is omitted on Second Passover.

PATERNITY See FATHER

PATRIARCHS, THE The three founding fathers (Heb. *avot*) of the Jewish people: ABRAHAM, ISAAC, and JACOB. All three patriarchs communicated with God and established an eternal COVENANT (agreement) with Him. As part of the covenant, God promised that they would have very many descendants. He promised all three patriarchs the land of CANAAN as the eternal inheritance of their people.

The patriarchs are mentioned in many places in the PRAYERS. The opening blessing of the AMIDAH is known as *Avot*. It begins with the words, "… God of Abraham, God of Isaac, and God of Jacob." Elsewhere, prayers appeal to God to be generous and gracious with His people because of the merits of the patriarchs. The sacrifice of Isaac (see AKEDAH) is usually mentioned in these appeals.

According to tradition, each of the patriarchs introduced one of the daily prayer services: Abraham introduced the MORNING SERVICE (*Shaharit*); Isaac the AFTERNOON SERVICE (*Minhah*); and Jacob the EVENING SERVICE (*Ma'ariv*).

PATRILINEAL DESCENT CONTROVERSY Dispute over whether a child born of a Jewish father and a non-Jewish mother is Jewish, or whether the child must be converted. According to Jewish law, "Your son by an Israelite woman is called your son, but your son by a heathen woman is not called your son" (*Kid.* 68b). This means that only a child born of a Jewish mother is automatically considered to be Jewish.

Opposite page: Jewish wedding. Painting by Moritz Oppenheim. Germany, 19ᵗʰ century.
Overleaf: Menorah depicted in the Regensburg Pentateuch: lighting the Menorah amid Temple implements. From Bavaria, Germany, c. 1300.

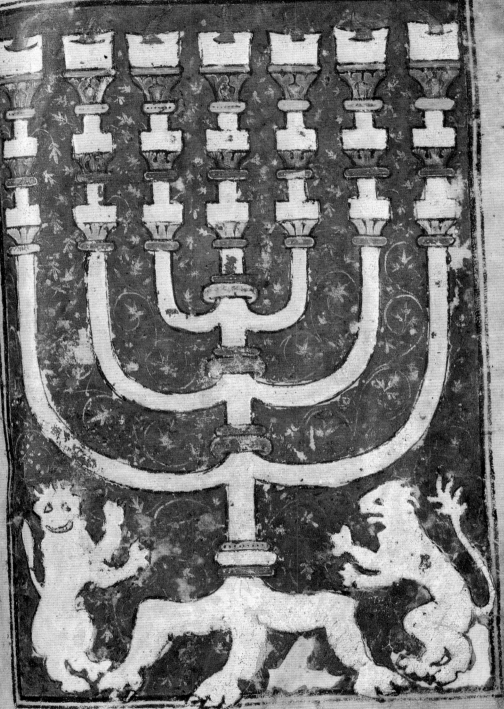

In recent years, the REFORM and RECONSTRUCTIONIST movements have challenged the traditional definition of who is a Jew. In 1982, the Reform movement adopted patrilineal descent as a way of being "born Jewish." According to their decision, a child of an INTERMARRIAGE who is raised as a Jew and observes the duties of the Jewish life cycle is considered Jewish without undergoing a conversion. A child of a Jewish mother, no matter what the father's religion, is also Jewish. The Reconstructionist movement recognized patrilineal descent in 1983. Those who support the idea of patrilineal descent feel that the high intermarriage rate among American Jews makes it unwise to say that the children of such marriages are not Jews. The CONSERVATIVE and Orthodox movements recognize the traditional matrilineal (born to a Jewish mother) descent only.

PEACE   (Heb. *shalom*). The Hebrew root for peace, wholeness, or perfection. In the Bible, the word *shalom* describes a state of harmony, tranquility, and prosperity. It is a blessing from God. It can also be understood as the absence of war.

In rabbinic texts, *shalom* takes on a larger meaning in the area of ETHICS. It is used to mean overcoming strife in family, communal, and national life, and the prevention of war. For the rabbis, peace is the highest purpose of the Torah; it is at the heart of the promise of REDEMPTION. According to the Talmud, one may tell a small lie for the sake of preserving peace (*Yev.* 65b). Furthermore, according to R. Joshua b. Korha, strict justice does not usually allow for peace; therefore, a judge should apply the values of peace to his sense of justice and rule in favor of compromise (TJ, *Sanh.* 1:5; TB, *Sanh.* 6b).

Peace and War   In contrast to the ideal of peace, Jewish sources from the Bible and later recognize that war is a part of human existence. At the same time, throughout history Jews were not

Fragment of the mosaic floor of a synagogue bearing the inscription "Peace to Israel" found at Usafiya, 6th century.

Opposite page: "The Song of Miriam." Oil on canvas by Paulo Malteis, Italy, 18th century.

PEACE IN THE JEWISH TRADITION

Peace is the greatest of all blessings.

The whole Torah exists solely for the sake of peace.

Great is peace, for it is to the world what leaven is to dough. If God had not placed peace in the world, all mankind would have been destroyed by the sword and wild beasts.

Be among the disciples of Aaron: love peace and strive for peace, love people and acquaint them with the teachings of the Torah.

R. Simeon ben Gamaliel said, "The world rests on three things: justice, truth, and peace." R. Mona said, "These three are one and the same, for if there is justice, there is truth, and if there is truth, there is peace."

Peacemaking, like charity, brings benefit in this world and in the world to come.

Jerusalem will be rebuilt only through peace.

---

really central players in matters of war and peace between nations. Jewish political powerlessness, without a country of their own for thousands of years, therefore shaped the rabbis' views of war and peace. It may be thought of this way: the non-Jew waged war for territory and political gains; the Jew waged war against his evil inclination. For the Jew, peace was an ideal concept, not a political reality.

The rabbis discussed three different models of peace. According to the first model, peace will come about when individuals have changed. MAIMONIDES suggested that to bring peace people must replace their attachment to material goods and destructive ways with the universal knowledge of God (see *Yad, Melakhim* 12:5). A second model suggests that all people will one day live in peace under a single framework that will be imposed on them. For example, David KIMHI (see Commentary to Isa. 2:4; Mic. 4:3) presents the MESSIAH as a supreme judge who will make peace between nations. People do not have to perfect themselves; peace is imposed on them from above. The third model looks forward to major changes in the socio-political order. In the teachings of Isaac Arama, the closer that laws and the political order come to a universal sense of justice, the more peace will tend to overcome war (*Akedat Yitshak*, 46, 91, 105a). In this model, man's role is to gradually adjust society and to build a better world in order to come closer to the ideal.

How important is peace in Judaism? All the major prayers – AMIDAH, KADDISH, GRACE AFTER MEALS, and the PRIESTLY BLESSING – conclude with a prayer for peace.

PE'AH   ("Corner [of the field]"). Second tractate (book) of the Order of ZERA'IM in the Mishnah. It has eight chapters that list the "dues" which a farmer must give to the poor (Lev.

19:9–10, 23:22; Deut. 24:19–22). (See AGRICULTURAL LAWS; LEKET, SHIKHEHAH, PE'AH).

PENITENCE   See REPENTANCE

PENITENTIAL PRAYERS   See SELIHOT

PENTATEUCH   Heb. *Humash*; first five books of the Hebrew BIBLE. The books are: GENESIS (*Be-Reshit*), EXODUS (*Shemot*), LEVITICUS (*Va-Yikra*), NUMBERS (*Be-Midbar*), and DEUTERONOMY (*Devarim*). The Hebrew names are taken from the opening words of each book. In Jewish tradition, each book also has another name that relates to its content. In order, they are: *Sefer ha-Yetsirah* ("Book of Creation"), *Sefer ha-Ge'ulah* ("Book of Redemption"), *Torat Kohanim* ("Law of the Priests"), *Humash ha-Pekudim* ("Book of the Censuses"), and *Mishneh Torah* ("Repetition of the Torah").

The historical account of the Pentateuch opens with the CREATION of the world. It then tells the story of Abraham's family growing into a nation, their REDEMPTION from Egypt, and the giving of the Torah in the desert on Mount SINAI. It ends with Moses' death, just before the Israelites enter the Promised Land.

The Pentateuch is read in the synagogue from the SCROLL OF THE LAW. The Babylonian custom, which is accepted today throughout the Jewish world, is to complete the reading of the Pentateuch in the synagogue in a single year. The last section is read on SIMHAT TORAH. The cycle of the reading is divided into 54 *parashiyyot* (see PARASHAH; READING OF THE LAW).

Traditional View   According to Jewish tradition (*BB* 15a), the entire Pentateuch is a single unit that was given by God through Moses to the Israelites. Moses wrote the words of God, except for the last eight verses of Deuteronomy, which were written by JOSHUA. The sages of the Talmud discuss whether the Pentateuch was given scroll by scroll or as a complete, sealed TORAH. The disagreement is over whether Moses wrote down the content as it was dictated to him on Mount Sinai, and then joined the sections together before his death; or whether Moses memorized the content and committed it to writing before he died (*Git.* 60a).

To this day, a SCRIBE writes the Torah by hand on specially made parchment. The text is checked carefully, and if even a single letter is missing or added, the scroll is invalid. This is because the content and the form of the Torah are held in the highest degree of holiness. The rabbis stated that if a certain word or sentence seems unimportant, the reason is human ignorance, and not a problem in the Torah.

Bible Criticism   Bible criticism rejects the traditional view of the origin of the Pentateuch. It holds that the Pentateuch does not come from God and that Moses did not write it down. It is, according to the Bible critics, a collection of documents written at different times and assembled by an editor into a single work.

The German scholar, Julius Wellhausen (1878), was among the first to suggest that the Torah was a combination of various documents. He identified four sources, which he gave the names J, E, P, and D. This analysis makes up the "documentary hypothesis." Martin de Wette (1805) suggested that King Josiah did not discover but wrote Deuteronomy in 622 BCE (see II Kings 23).

In the light of modern Jewish scholarship, including archeological finds, some of the more radical ideas of earlier Bible criticism have been modified. Today, somewhat more conservative views are favored.

PENTECOST   See SHAVU'OT

PERJURY   The Ninth Commandment (Ex. 20:13; Deut. 5:17) forbids bearing false witness in a court of law (BET DIN). In Jewish law, perjury – bearing false witness – applies to a group of witnesses and not to an individual. This is because a Jewish court does not convict based on the testimony of a single witness. At least two witnesses are required for testimony to be considered valid.

What then is the punishment for a group of witnesses who commit perjury? If a group testifies, for example, that it had seen one man kill another in a certain place on a certain day, and a second group of witnesses testifies that the first group was in an entirely different place, the first witnesses are considered perjurers. The punishment is set out in Deuteronomy 19:19: "You shall do to him as he schemed to do to his fellow." The false witnesses are called *edim zommemim*, or scheming witnesses. According to the letter of the law, they are liable for the death penalty, though in practice they would have been flogged (see *Yad, Edut* 18:1, 20:8). If the testimony of the second group was that the accused was somewhere else at the time of the murder or that no murder took place at all, the testimony is contradictory and the court disregards the testimony of both groups of witnesses.

A convicted perjurer loses the right to testify in court forever.

PESAH   See PASSOVER

PESAHIM   ("Paschal Sacrifices"). Third book of the Order of MO'ED in the Mishnah. *Pesahim* consists of ten chapters that deal with the laws of MATZAH and the prohibition against eating leaven (HAMETS) on PASSOVER. It also covers the SACRIFICE of the paschal lamb during the period of the TEMPLE, and the holding of the SEDER on the first night of Passover.

PESHAT   The plain, literal meaning of a text. Bible commentaries generally fall into either the literal or interpretive categories. The literal commentaries try to explain the plain, straightforward meaning of the text – i.e., precisely what the text says. The others interpret the text using MIDRASH, allegory (symbolic stories), MYSTICISM, philosophy – i.e., what the text means beyond the level of the words. The commentaries of RASHI, Abraham IBN EZRA, SAMUEL BEN MEIR, and David KIMHI are the best examples of the *peshat* approach to Bible commentary.

PESUKEI DE-ZIMRA ("Passages of Song"). The sequence of Bible verses and selections from PSALMS read in the daily MORNING SERVICE following the MORNING BENEDICTIONS and coming before BAREKHU. The Talmud states: "one should first give praise to God and then approach Him in worship" (*Ber.* 32a). *Pesukei de-Zimra* were incorporated into the standard prayer service to prepare spiritually for the central worship that followed. The text of *Pesukei de-Zimra* as we know it first appeared in geonic times in the *siddur* of Rav Amram Gaon, in the ninth century.

PETIHAH ("opening"). Ceremony for opening the ARK in the synagogue. From ancient times, this honor was given to a worshiper who removed the SCROLL(s) OF THE LAW from the

Man carrying a Scroll of the Law to illustrate the prayer recited at the opening (petihah) of the Ark for the Reading of the Law.

Ark before the READING OF THE LAW. The same worshiper returned the Scrolls to the Ark after the reading. It is customary for congregants to stand from the moment the Ark is opened until the Ark is closed. The Ark is also opened when ANIM ZEMIROT is chanted and when solemn prayers are recited during the TEN DAYS OF REPENTANCE.

PHARISEES The spiritual leaders of the Jewish people in Erets Israel during the Second Temple period. The name comes from the Hebrew *perushim* ("to be separate, holy"). Unlike the Sadducees, who belonged to the Jewish aristocracy, they were firmly rooted in the common folk.

The Pharisees were a party with a clear belief system in the days of John Hyrcanus (135–104 BCE). They had strong political influence during the reign of Salome Alexandra (76–67 BCE), under the leadership of SIMEON BEN SHETAH. When the Romans took control of Erets Israel (63 BCE), the Pharisees returned to their original role as teachers of the law and judges of the community's internal disputes. They did, at times, take political positions: they supported the revolt against Rome, both in the 1st century CE and again in the time of BAR KOKHBA.

The ACADEMIES of religious learning were central to the world of the Pharisees. The great schools of HILLEL and SHAMMAI were already flourishing in the 1st century BCE, and the town of Yavneh had become a center of learning before the destruction of the Temple in 70 CE. The *bet midrash* (house of learning) in Yavneh had a central role in preserving Judaism after the destruction of the Temple. R. JOHANAN BEN ZAKKAI, the great sage of the Pharisees, moved to Yavneh. Under his leadership and that of his successor, R. GAMALIEL II, the academy in Yavneh made far-reaching decisions that applied to all aspects of Jewish life. The New Testament's view of the Pharisees as being concerned with only the dry details of Jewish law is not accurate. The vast body of talmudic law – essentially the output of the Pharisees – shows their variety of interests and their passionate concern for the religious life and feelings of the people.

The Sadducees and the Pharisees differed on a number of issues. These include the date of SHAVU'OT; the punishment of false witnesses; the belief in the AFTERLIFE, RESURRECTION, and the MESSIAH (which were basic to the Pharisees). What of these two groups today? The Sadducees disappeared as a force in Jewish life after the destruction of the Temple. The Pharisees created the groundwork for mainstream Judaism.

PHILO Hellenistic Jewish philosopher (c. 20 BCE–50 CE). In his writings, Philo attempts to bring together the world-view of Plato's philosophy with the ideas of the Bible. This mix of Greek philosophy and Judaism formed the basis for medieval Jewish philosophy.

Philo belonged to a rich and influential Jewish family in Alexandria. He visited Jerusalem, and he headed a Jewish delegation to the Roman emperor, Caligula, in the year 40 CE. Little more is known about his life. In contrast, many of his works have survived. These include: *On the Life of Moses*, *On the Decalogue*, and *On the Special Laws*. In these books, Philo emphasizes the moral and philosophical side of the PENTATEUCH, which he views as an ideal framework of laws. In his *Questions and Answers on Genesis* and *Questions and Answers on Exodus*, he interprets individual words and verses of the Bible using symbolic stories (see ALLEGORY). His approach can be summed up as follows: philosophical truths are concealed in the Bible; Philo uses allegorical interpretation to reveal them.

Philo commented on the Bible in its Greek translation, the SEPTUAGINT. It appears that he had little knowledge of Hebrew. Furthermore, he does not seem to have had contact with the sages of Israel of his day. His thinking comes out of the Jewish climate of Alexandria: Hellenistic but Jewish, with very little input from Erets Israel. The sages of Erets Israel also do not seem to have been aware of Philo. Azariah dei Rossi, who lived during the Renaissance, was the first Jewish thinker to revive interest in Philo.

PHILOSOPHY   The religion of Judaism relates to philosophy in two ways. First, the "analytical" method of philosophy can be used to study Judaism. This has been done in different ages by Jews who have studied Jewish ideas from a religious point of view – the study of Jewish THEOLOGY. When the study is carried out by individuals from "outside" of the circle of believers, it falls under the subject area of the philosophy of religion.

A second, "synthetic" method of philosophy looks for answers to important questions for the purpose of bringing those answers into their set of religious beliefs. Believers may wish to compare and even integrate their religious beliefs with the teachings of other systems of philosophy. PHILO of Alexandria, for example, was the first to combine Jewish ideas with those of Greek philosophy.

PHYLACTERIES   See TEFILLIN

PIDYON HA-BEN   See FIRSTBORN, REDEMPTION OF

PIDYON SHEVUYIM   See CAPTIVES, RANSOMING OF

PIETY   Word meaning deep love and respect for God; special emphasis on performance of the COMMANDMENTS. Various Hebrew words describe the pious person, such as *Hasid*, *yerei shamayim* ("one who fears Heaven"), or TSADDIK. Through pious behavior, one tries to be godly (see IMITATION OF GOD).

Exactly what is piety? RASHI (on Lev. 19:1) writes that a person who does not violate the commandments is considered pious. By contrast, NAHMANIDES believed that one may follow the Torah completely and still be a terrible person. For him, piety means going beyond the letter of the law. The sages of the Talmud had still a different idea. For them, correct actions, rather than belief, bring piety. They quote God as saying: "Would that they [i.e., the Jewish people] forget Me but observe My Torah, for the light within it will bring them back to the

proper path" (*Yad Shimoni* to Jer., 282). Elsewhere they state that a person should study (or perform commandments) even without the proper intention, because "from deeds not for their own sake will come deeds for their own sake" (*Pes.* 50b). For them, a commandment performed for its own sake is the true expression of piety. The performance of the commandments, even if one at first does so out of self-interest, will eventually bring the individual to a higher state of piety.

PIKKU'AH NEFESH   ("consideration for human life"). Hebrew term for the supreme obligation to ignore most religious laws when someone's life is in danger. There are two sources for this law. Leviticus 19:16 states: "You shall not stand idly by the blood of your neighbor." Leviticus 18:5 directs people to "live by them" [i.e., the commandments]. The rabbis interpreted this to mean to live by the COMMANDMENTS and not die through their observance (*Yoma* 85a).

The law of *pikku'ah nefesh* lists the emergency situations for which the SABBATH, FESTIVALS and other laws are set aside. Examples include: a sick person who needs medical attention or an expectant mother being driven to the hospital on the Sabbath; a sick person eating on fast days; or eating forbidden food if required to save a life (see DIETARY LAWS). The law of *pikku'ah nefesh* does not apply to cases involving the three most serious sins: IDOLATRY, MURDER, and sexual crimes (see INCEST). In these cases Jews must allow themselves to be killed rather than transgress (*Sanh.* 74a–b).

PILGRIMAGE   The obligation to go to the "place which the Lord your God will choose" (Deut. 16:16) on the three PILGRIM FESTIVALS. During the period of the JUDGES, the site to which all came was Shiloh, north of Jerusalem (1 Sam. 1:3); once the TEMPLE had been built, all came to JERUSALEM. During the time of King Rehoboam and the revolt of King Jeroboam, the tribes were split into two nations. Jeroboam established pilgrimage sites for sacrifices at Dan and Beth El in his kingdom.

The Bible requires all adult males to make the pilgrimage three times a year. It furthermore says: "They shall not appear before the Lord empty [-handed]. Every man shall give as he is able" (Deut. 16:16–17). The sages understood this to refer to the SACRIFICE that they would offer in Jerusalem. The Second TITHE of the farmer's crops was also sold, and its value in money was spent in Jerusalem.

How many pilgrims actually came to Jerusalem for a festival? In the Second Temple period, the historian Josephus (*War* VI, 9) writes that in the Passover celebration in the year 66 CE, no fewer than 256,500 lambs were sacrificed. It should be kept in mind that each lamb was consumed by an entire family.

After the Temple was destroyed, pilgrimages to Erets Israel continued. However, they were sad voyages, made in order to mourn Jerusalem's destruction. The term "Wailing Wall" was given by non-Jews to the WESTERN WALL when they saw how the Jews who came there wept. Jewish law says that people who see either Jerusalem in its destruction, or the site of the Temple which had been destroyed, must tear their clothes in MOURNING.

Jews also make pilgrimages to sites other than Jerusalem. Pious visitors come to the graves of ancient sages throughout the Galilee. The graves of the Jewish PATRIARCHS and MATRIARCHS at the Cave of Machpelah in Hebron is another popular pilgrimage site. On LAG BE-OMER in modern-day Israel, as many as 100,000 people visit the tomb of R. SIMEON BAR YOHAI in Meron. Another custom is to visit the tomb of R. MEIR BA'AL HA-NES in Tiberias on *Pesah Sheni* (see PASSOVER, SECOND), 14 Iyyar.

PILGRIM FESTIVALS   The three FESTIVALS that the Bible commanded the Israelites to celebrate in the "place which the Lord your God will choose" (Deut. 16:16). These are PASSOVER, SHAVU'OT, and SUKKOT. Together they are referred to as the *shalosh regalim* – the three (foot) pilgrimages. Until the TEMPLE was destroyed, three commandments had to be observed by adult males on the festivals: going to Jerusalem; bringing individual SACRIFICES ("pilgrimage offerings"), in addition to those brought on behalf of the nation; and rejoicing on the festival.

All three festivals have both agricultural and national aspects. Passover is the "festival of the spring," in which the new barley crop (OMER) is brought. It also celebrates the EXODUS from Egypt. Shavu'ot is the "harvest festival," celebrating the end of the barley harvest and the beginning of the wheat harvest. It also marks the giving of the TORAH at Mount SINAI. Sukkot is the "festival of the gathering" of the crops. It commemorates the 40 years that the Israelites wandered in the desert before entering Erets Israel.

The MORNING SERVICE on each day of these festivals includes the HALLEL prayer, the READING OF THE LAW, and the ADDITIONAL SERVICE. Outside Israel, an extra day is added to each festival (see SECOND DAY OF FESTIVALS). All work except that needed for preparing food is prohibited on the first and last days of the festival.

PILPUL   (from Heb. *pilpel*, "pepper"). A systematic approach to studying rabbinic texts. Its aim is to clarify difficult passages, by using very complicated reasoning. The Mishnah (*Avot* 6:5) lists *pilpul* as one of the 48 ways for knowing and understanding the TORAH. However, when carried to extremes, it could be an exercise in hairsplitting. For example, the rabbis criticized R. MEIR, the outstanding scholar of his generation, when his approach was excessive in *pilpul*.

In the 16th century *pilpul* became widely used in the European YESHIVAH as a tool for sharpening the mind of students and for developing their powers of logic. As a teaching method, unrelated texts were artificially forced into relationship with each other. The resulting *pilpul* discussions became a source of intellectual stimulation in the study halls of Eastern Europe. However, many condemned the practice. R. JUDAH LÖW BEN

BEZALEL OF PRAGUE wrote: "Those who see the essence of study in sharp-witted *pilpul* show disrespect to the Torah ... and would do better to learn carpentry."

PIRKEI AVOT   See AVOT

PIRKEI DE-RABBI ELIEZER   ("Chapters of Rabbi Eliezer"). MIDRASH (story-like commentary) composed in the early decades of the ninth century; believed written by Rabbi ELIEZER BEN HYRCANUS. The work is quite popular. It has appeared in more than two dozen editions, including a 17th century Latin translation.

The book consists of three sections. One describes the occasions when God descended to the earth. Another gives a detailed account of early rabbinic MYSTICISM as well as the calculation of the CALENDAR. The third section is an incomplete Midrash on the AMIDAH prayer. The book was quoted by the Babylonian *ge'onim* and the tosafists (see TOSAFOT); some of its teachings have parallels in the mystical work the ZOHAR.

PIYYUT   (from the Greek word for "poet"; pl. *piyyutim*). Poems used in prayer that were composed from the first centuries CE to the Enlightenment period (18th cent.). At first, the *piyyutim* were meant to replace required prayers, perhaps to add variety to the service. Later, when the content and form of the prayers were set, *piyyutim* were added to the fixed prayer text.

Most of the *piyyutim* were meant to be said during the main FESTIVALS; however, in time they were composed for regular and special Sabbaths, fast days, and even ordinary weekdays. *Piyyutim* were also written for events such as weddings (see MARRIAGE), CIRCUMCISIONS, and days of MOURNING.

The history of the *piyyutim* is divided into three eras. Up until the sixth century, poems were written with meter, but without rhyme, and we usually do not know their authors. Poems from the classical period, sixth to eighth centuries, had rhymed verse. Eleazar ha-Kallir and Haduta ben Abraham are among the best-known liturgical poets of this era. The third period, the late era of the Oriental poets, featured two major schools: one Central European and the other Spanish. The poets of Italy and Provence were influenced by Spanish culture. They represent the high point of Jewish religious poetry. They include: Solomon IBN GABIROL, Moses IBN EZRA, and JUDAH HALEVI. The most familiar *piyyutim* are the SELIHOT (penitential prayers) recited on fast days, the KINOT (elegies) recited on TISHAH BE-AV, and the HOSHANOT recited on SUKKOT.

The style and vocabulary of the *piyyutim* developed over the centuries. Originally, they drew mostly from the Hebrew of the Bible, with some language from the Talmud as well. The style was clear and simple. In time, their vocabulary became more difficult to understand; some *paytanim* even invented their own words. The poets of the school of Kallir used a complex system of terms and material from the MIDRASH. At times, the writers were purposely mysterious, creating poetry that encouraged more than one interpretation. Later religious

Part of the piyyut *"Open the Gates of Mercy," from the Day of Atonement* liturgy. *From a* Mahzor. *Germany, 1345.*

poetry, particularly in Spain, returned to a simpler and clearer type of verse. Solomon Ibn Gabirol played a large role in this process of change.

PLAGUES, TEN   The punishments that were brought upon Pharaoh and Egypt by God at the time of the EXODUS. Their purpose was to persuade the Egyptian leader to set the Israelites free and to show God's might. The plagues were: (1) the Nile waters turning to blood; (2) the swarming of frogs; (3) lice; (4) wild animals (perhaps flies); (5) animal diseases, afflicting Egyptian cattle; (6) a skin rash; (7) heavy hailstorm; (8) locusts; (9) three days of complete darkness; (10) death of the Egyptian firstborn. In addition to the story of the plagues in the Book of Exodus (7–9) in the Bible, there are poetic accounts in PSALMS 78:44–51 and 105:28–36. The MIDRASH offers various interpretations of the plagues, and some of these appear in the HAGGADAH for PASSOVER.

POLEMICS   See APOLOGETICS AND POLEMICS

POLYGAMY   See MONOGAMY AND POLYGAMY

POSEKIM   (sing. *posek*). Rabbinic scholars who decide Jewish law in specific cases; respected legal authorities. The Babylonian TALMUD is the most important source of Jewish law. However, in most cases it does not give a definite legal ruling. From the seventh century on, requests were sent to *posekim* for decisions on points of law. The decisions of each *posek* were usually collected. The first such collection is the *She'iltot* of R. AHAI OF SHABHA (8th century). HALAKHOT GEDOLOT AND HALAKHOT PESUKOT were the forerunners of the later literature of the *posekim*.

Collections of legal decisions took various forms over the centuries. The decisions of MAIMONIDES, ABRAHAM BEN DAVID OF POSQUIÈRES, ASHER BEN JEHIEL, JACOB BEN ASHER, Joseph CARO, and Moses ISSERLES can be found in their codes (see CODIFICATION). In addition, volumes of decisions by various rabbis were edited by SHNEUR ZALMAN OF LYADY, Solomon Ganzfried (*Kitsur Shulhan Arukh*), and R. Abraham Danzig (*Hayyei Adam*). Collections have also appeared on specific subjects. The best known of the modern *posekim* is R. Moses FEINSTEIN, whose decisions are followed by most in ORTHODOXY today.

POSTMORTEM   See MEDICAL ETHICS

POVERTY AND THE POOR   Since Bible times Jewish writings have dealt with the treatment of the poor and disadvantaged. The Bible assumes that the poor and disadvantaged have a right to community support. God provides for the more fortunate; it is therefore the responsibility of the more fortunate to provide for those less so. Also, since God has a special concern for the poor, so must the Jewish community. Deuteronomy 15:11 states: "Open your hand to the poor and the kinsman in your land."

The Bible commands the minimum support that landowners must provide to the poor. When farmers reap, they must leave the edges of their fields to the needy as well as the olives, grapes, and sheaves of grain that fall during the harvest. They are only allowed to beat the olive trees once; the fruit that falls after beating the tree a second time is left to the needy. During the SABBATICAL YEAR, when the fields may not be cultivated, the needy are allowed to come and eat from them. Finally, the poor are entitled to TITHES, which are called by the same name as the tithes for the LEVITES or those dedicated to God's service. From this we learn that the Jewish community has an equal responsibility to the Levites and to the poor.

Why dos one man prosper while another is forced to rely on the charity of others? The rabbis did not see poverty as a reflection of a person's character or efforts. They called upon the people to consider the feelings of the poor. They reminded them that "God stands together with the poor man at the door [when he comes to beg] and one should therefore consider whom one is confronting" (Lev. R. 34:9). Giving without the poor person's knowing the source of the money was viewed as the proper and considerate way to give; the recipient was not to be embarrassed by seeing the donor.

To this day, modern forms of the ancient institution of providing for the poor can be found in almost every Jewish COMMUNITY. Community funds include: a fund for food and clothing; a soup kitchen; a burial fund that was available to rich and poor alike; a dowry society to provide for poor brides; and the HEKDESH that served as a haven for the old, the sick, and the stranger. (See also CHARITY.)

PRACTICAL KABBALAH Term for activities that are like "white" magic, with little or no connection to KABBALAH itself. These activities include the use of God's names and the names of angels to achieve various purposes, the use of AMULETS or charms containing magical letter combinations, the protective services of a GOLEM, etc. One who engaged in these practices was known as a BA'AL SHEM, or "master of [God's] Name."

PRAYER (Heb. *tefillah*). Prayer expresses many aspects of the relationship between human beings and God. These include praise, thanksgiving, requests, petitions, and CONFESSION. Jewish prayer assumes that people are able to communicate with God, both individually and as part of the nation. It is

Rabbi wrapped in a prayer shawl (tallit) *leading the service in the Bucharest synagogue, Rumania.*

SAYINGS ABOUT PRAYER

When praying, cast down your eyes and lift up your hearts.

Do not change the sages' formulations of the prayers.

Let those who are ignorant of Hebrew learn the prayers in their own daily languages, since prayer must be understood.

If the heart does not know what the lips utter, it is no prayer.

Man must lose himself in prayer and forget his own existence.

A poor man's prayer breaks through every barrier and storms its way into the presence of the Almighty.

The gates of prayer are never closed.

Prayer is conversation with God.

---

based on the idea that God hears prayer and responds to man's approach.

Within the Jewish tradition, prayer may be formally set or spontaneous. The Bible contains about 80 examples of prayer, none of which were used as formal worship. In biblical Judaism, the SACRIFICES served as formal worship. There are just two examples of verbal formal worship in the Bible: the pilgrim's declaration on bringing the FIRST FRUITS to the TEMPLE (Deut. 26:5–10) and the priestly confession on the DAY OF ATONEMENT (Lev. 16:21–34).

During the Babylonian Exile (see EXILE, BABYLONIAN), communal prayer in the SYNAGOGUE developed as a replacement for sacrifices. After the destruction of the Second Temple in 70 CE, the rabbis adopted prayer as the official form of worship. They called it *avodah she-ba-lev*, the "service of the heart" (*Ta'an.* 2a). They fixed three daily prayer services, tracing their origin to the PATRIARCHS (see LITURGY). At the same time they tried to preserve the spontaneous quality of biblical prayer (see *Ber.* 26b).

Congregational prayer services expanded to include the MORNING BENEDICTIONS, the SHEMA and its blessings, the AMIDAH or *Tefillah* (a central "prayer" of 18 blessings), and the READING OF THE LAW. Special patterns were adopted for daily, SABBATH, and FESTIVAL services. To this order of prayer, a number of non-obligatory prayers were added (see KINOT; PIYYUT; SELIHOT). Other forms of occasional prayer for the home were added, including GRACE AFTER MEALS, HAVDALAH, and KIDDUSH.

The rabbis stressed the need for praying in the right frame of mind (KAVVANAH) and with devotion (*Shab.* 127a). Advice appeared about the best way to pray: one should form the words with one's lips without shouting (*Ber.* 24b, 31a); one should keep private prayer short (*Ber.* 61a), but prayer on behalf of others has greater significance; one should try to pray with a MINYAN, or prayer quorum.

Direction of Prayer Since ancient times, Jews have turned toward JERUSALEM when praying. At the dedication of the First Temple (c. 950 BCE), King Solomon already knew that the prayers of Israel would be directed "toward this place" (1 Kings 8:30, 35; 11 Chr. 6:21, 26). He foresaw that the exiles in distant countries would "pray to You in the direction of their land which You gave to their fathers, of the city which You have chosen, and of the House which I have built to Your name" (1 Kings 8:48; 11 Chr. 6:38). The Mishnah states that all Jews "should direct their hearts to one place in worship" (*Ber.* 30a). This means that a Jew praying in the Diaspora should face the Holy Land; in Erets Israel, he should turn to Jerusalem; in Jerusalem he should face the Temple, and on the TEMPLE MOUNT he should direct his prayers to the HOLY OF HOLIES (*Ber.* 30a). For the Jewish communities of southern Europe and North Africa, turning to Jerusalem meant facing east (see MIZRAH).

PRAYER BEFORE A JOURNEY (Heb. *Tefillat ha-Derekh*). Prayer recited by a traveler when setting out on an out-of-town journey. The prayer asks for God's protection against "enemy, ambush, bandits, or wild animals on the way." It is recited whether or not danger seems likely. The traveler recites it when he has gone beyond the last houses on the outskirts of the city. When a number of people are traveling together, it is customary for one person to say the prayer aloud, and for the others to answer "amen" at the end.

The Prayer on Setting Out on a Journey illustrated by travelers on horseback and on foot. From a Book of Benedictions. Germany, 1345.

PRAYER BOOK The Jewish prayer book (*seder tefillot, siddur,* or MAHZOR) contains the set LITURGY that is said in the SYNAGOGUE and at home at certain times. Many editions of the prayer book also include the Book of PSALMS, religious laws of prayer, SELIHOT (penitential prayers), and various passages

from the Bible and Talmud for study. At first, the terms *siddur* and *mahzor* were used interchangeably. From the Middle Ages, Ashkenazi Jews began to distinguish between the two terms. From this period on, "*mahzor*" referred to the High Holiday prayer book.

The first formal order of service is found in the book *Soferim*, a work of the eighth century. A century later, AMRAM GAON, a leading Babylonian scholar, compiled the first prayer book, *Seder Rav Amram Gaon*. He did so at the request of Spanish Jewry. In the tenth century, the *Siddur* of SAADIAH GAON appeared containing notes (in Arabic) for actual use by the synagogue worshiper. It was relatively popular until MAIMONIDES' Mishneh Torah was published with its "Order of Prayers for the Whole Year." The 11th century *Mahzor Vitry* is another early prayer book that reflects the practices of northern France. It was compiled by R. Simhah ben Samuel, a student of RASHI, and includes commentary as well. From that time on, it was customary to include rabbis' comments in the margins of prayer books. The first printed prayer books come from the Iberian Peninsula and date from around 1475. The first Ashkenazi *siddur* was printed in Prague in 1512.

Over the centuries, various Jewish communities have produced prayer books that address their specific needs. ASHKENAZIM and SEPHARDIM have their own, unique prayer book traditions. Followers of HASIDISM changed the Ashkenazi prayer book to include elements of the Sephardi liturgy and Rabbi Isaac LURIA's mystical approach. The Arabic-speaking Jews of Yemen have their own *Tikhlal*, a complete prayer book that remained handwritten until it was published in Jerusalem at the end of the 19th century. The first REFORM prayer book was published in 1819, in Germany. As early as 1855, the first American Reform prayer books began to appear. CONSERVATIVE JUDAISM began publishing such texts in 1927. These included *The Festival Prayer Book*, followed by a prayer book for the Sabbath and festivals, and later by a prayer book for weekdays. As time went on, they introduced changes in the traditional words of the prayer service. As early as 1945, RECONSTRUCTIONISM published its own *siddur*. The additional readings added to their prayer book reflect the ideas of the movement. The Orthodox community also has its own editions of the prayer book published in America. Recently, the Rabbinical Council of America has endorsed David de Sola Pool's *Traditional Prayer Book for Sabbath and Festivals* and the Art Scroll *Siddur*. De Sola Pool has also published prayer books for the use of Sephardi Orthodox congregations.

Modern prayer books – either by inclusion or by omission – respond to the two most important Jewish events of the modern era. These are the HOLOCAUST and the reestablishment of the State of Israel. Many have added services for commemorating these events.

PRAYER SHAWL   See TALLIT

PREACHING   See HOMILETICS

PREDESTINATION   The theory that human destiny is set by forces outside the individual will. Carried to the extreme, this belief holds that everything that happens to an individual or to a people is the will and plan of God. (See PROVIDENCE.)

Jewish tradition sees two sides to the issue of predestination. On the one hand, from the earliest stages of biblical thought, people are seen to have FREE WILL to act as they wish. In the story of ADAM AND EVE in the Garden of EDEN, the first couple is given a single law to obey, and they reject it. MOSES continually places before the people the two paths of good and evil or life and death, from which they can choose (see Deut. 11:2ff, 30:15). In fact, without freedom of choice, reward and punishment have no real meaning. On the other hand, the rabbis state: "Everything is in the hands of God except the fear of God" (*Ber.* 33b), though God's absolute power to do anything is not compatible with the idea of absolute freedom of choice.

Another text that hints about the Jewish attitude towards predestination is the U-NETANNEH TOKEF prayer of ROSH HA-SHANAH and the DAY OF ATONEMENT. The phrase, "On the New Year it is decreed and on the Day of Atonement it is sealed who shall live and who shall die …," suggests that everything is predetermined. On the other hand, at the heart and soul of the prayers for the High Holidays is the idea that "repentance, prayer, and charity can lighten [God's] harsh decree." If so, even a predetermined outcome can be changed.

In Judaism, the conflict between predetermination and freedom of choice creates the religious tension in which people live.

PRIESTLY BLESSING   (Heb. *Birkat Kohanim*). The biblical BENEDICTION that includes three short verses. It was recited only by the PRIESTS (Num. 6:22–27) as part of the regular TEMPLE service. It was pronounced each morning and evening after the daily SACRIFICE. Within the Temple itself, the priests combined the three verses (24–26) into a single blessing and pronounced the holiest Name of God from a special podium. Outside Jerusalem, the three blessings were recited separately and a Divine Name of lesser holiness was used (*Sot.* 7:6; *Tam.* 7:2).

All prayer services include the Priestly Blessing during the reader's repetition of the AMIDAH. It is customary for descendants of the priests to recite the blessing today in Erets Israel at all services and during the ADDITIONAL SERVICE for FESTIVALS in the Diaspora. Before reciting it, priests remove their shoes and walk to the rear of the synagogue. LEVITES in the congregation wash their hands ritually (see Ex. 30:17–21). The priests then assemble before the ARK, cover their heads and hands with the prayer shawl, and after they are formally called upon by the reader, they recite the blessing: "… Who has hallowed us with the sanctity of Aaron and commanded us to bless His people Israel with love." On reaching the last word of the blessing, they turn to face the congregation with their hands stretched out. They hold their hands so that the thumbs are touching and their fingers are spread in a special symbolic pattern under the

The kohanim *(priests), their heads covered with prayer shawls, recite the Priestly Blessing at the Western Wall, Jerusalem.*

prayer shawl. Congregants avoid looking at them. They repeat their blessing after the reader, word by word. At the end of each of the three verses, the congregation answers AMEN. The priests then turn back to the Ark and lower their hands and the prayer shawl.

PRIESTLY GARMENTS   Special robes worn by the PRIESTS in the SANCTUARY and TEMPLE. The HIGH PRIEST wore eight garments, four undergarments and four outer garments. Ordinary priests wore the special undergarments, but not the outer garments.

The High Priest's four undergarments were a tunic, a sash, a headdress, and breeches (see Ex. 28:39 ff.). The tunic was woven from linen and wool and, unlike that of the regular priest, was fringed. The sash went around the tunic: that of the High Priest was woven from fine linen and dyed wools, while those of the regular priests were made from fine twined linen only. The turban of the High Priest was like a hat; ordinary priests wore "decorated turbans for headgear." The breeches were the same for both the High Priest and ordinary priests (see Ex. 28:42).

The High Priest also wore four outer garments: the *ephod*, the breastplate, the robe of the *ephod*, and the plate (crown)

אהרן

כל אדם לא יהיה באהל מועד
בבאו לכפר בקדש עד צאתו וכפר
בעדו ובעד ביתו ובעד כל קהל ישראל.

The priestly garments: comprising: a) the tunic; b) sash of the tunic; c) turban; d) bells of gold and pomegranates of tehelet *(sky-blue) linen and wool; e) robe of the ephod; f) band of the ephod; g) breastplate; h) crown around the turban; i) onyx stones with the names of the tribes.*

PRIESTS   (Heb. *kohanim*, sing. *kohen*). Male descendants of the first HIGH PRIEST, AARON, of the tribe of Levi. Originally, the priests had particular tasks and obligations that were different from those of other Israelites. For example, they were assigned to serve in the TEMPLE; they offered the different SACRIFICES brought by the people. They were also meant to be teachers of the people (see Num. 18:20).

At the time of the First Temple; the High Priest was anointed with oil when he took office. This was not the case in the Second Temple. Ordinary priests wore four special garments; the High Priest wore eight such garments. Priests did not own land, rather they lived on "24 gifts to the priests" that were provided by the other Jews. Priests also received parts of the meat of certain sacrifices, meal offerings that had been brought to the Temple, the first shearing of the wool, the firstborn of the flock, and CHALLAH (part of any dough that had been kneaded).

In the Temple service, priests were organized into 24 MISHMAROT, groups that took their turn to serve for a week at a time. During the week, all the priest's portions of the sacrifices were given to those in service. Their responsibilities included offering the daily sacrifices and caring for the MENORAH and INCENSE burned in the Temple. They also stood guard.

The priests were also responsible for examining certain types of growths for leprosy. A growth that appeared on a person's body, in a building, or on fabric could be declared unclean. If so, the person or object was placed in quarantine.

To this day, priests are limited in terms of whom they may marry. According to the Bible, a priest may not marry a divorcee or a "harlot," nor may he marry a woman who has undergone *halitsah* (see LEVIRATE MARRIAGE). The rabbis added to this that he may only marry a woman who was born Jewish.

Priests are prohibited from coming in contact with the dead, because contact with the dead brings ritual impurity (see PURITY, RITUAL). He may, however, become ritually impure to bury his father, mother, brother, unmarried sister, son, daughter, and wife. The priest may not enter a cemetery, except at the FUNERALS of the seven relatives mentioned. One other interesting exception: if a priest encounters a dead body and there is no one else to see to the burial, he is obliged to bury the body, even though he becomes impure.

In Israel today, many hospitals have taken steps to separate their morgues from the rest of the hospital by two sets of doors, only one of which can be open at a time. This separation makes it possible for priests to visit relatives in the hospital.

Even today, priests enjoy a special degree of respect. A priest is called first to the READING OF THE LAW. Similarly, he is the first one invited to lead the GRACE AFTER MEALS.

PRINCIPLES OF FAITH   List of basic beliefs of Judaism. The Bible makes no attempt to set out a basic list of religious beliefs. It is much more concerned with the practices of Judaism than the principles of Judaism.

In time, however, it became important to the sages to define the ideas that formed the basis of Jewish belief. They spoke of

hanging in front of the turban. The *ephod* was worn over the blue tunic. The shoulder straps that held it closed had two onyx stones that had the names of the 12 sons of JACOB written on them, six on each stone. The front of the *ephod* carried the breastplate, which had placed upon it the magical URIM AND THUMMIM. The robe of the *ephod* was worn under the *ephod*. The garment was made of blue wool and had bells of gold and pomegranate shapes hanging from its hem. The plate, sometimes known as a crown, was made of gold and hung on a blue thread. It had written on it the words *kodesh l-Adonai* ("holy to the Lord").

On the DAY OF ATONEMENT, the High Priest wore garments made of ordinary linen (see Lev. 16:4).

> ## SOME FORMULATIONS OF THE PRINCIPLES OF JUDAISM
>
> *Maimonides*
>
> 1. God exists
> 2. God's unity
> 3. God's incorporeality
> 4. God's eternity
> 5. God alone is to be worshiped
> 6. Belief in prophecy
> 7. Moses was the greatest of the prophets
> 8. God revealed the Torah to Moses
> 9. The Torah is unchangeable
> 10. God's omniscience
> 11. Reward and punishment
> 12. Messiah
> 13. Resurrection of the dead
>
> *Hasdai Crescas*
>
> 1. God's omniscience
> 2. Providence
> 3. God's omnipotence
> 4. Prophecy
> 5. Human free will
> 6. The purposefulness of the Torah
>
> *Simeon ben Tsemah Duran – Joseph Albo*
>
> 1. God exists
> 2. Divinity of the Torah – Providence
> 3. Reward and punishment

a person who denies the existence of God as a *kofer be-ikkar,* "one who denies the root," i.e., belief in God is the basis of the entire TORAH (*Ar.* 15b). They defined the heretic (see HERESY) as "he who denies RESURRECTION, the Divine origin of the Torah, and the EPIKOROS" (i.e., he who denies PROVIDENCE and REWARD AND PUNISHMENT; *Sanh.* 10:1). These are all negative forms of principles that, when stated positively, begin to give shape to a basic belief system.

In the Middle Ages, the intellectual climate demanded that mainstream Judaism make a clear statement of its basic beliefs. KARAISM challenged the rabbinic tradition; CHRISTIANITY and ISLAM had clear statements of dogma and often challenged

Jewish thinkers to DISPUTATIONS on the subject of faith. Jewish thinkers were forced to respond.

The best-known list of the principles of Judaism is the "13 Principles of Faith" of MAIMONIDES. It was originally part of his commentary to the MISHNAH (see *Sanh.* 10:1), where he defines the belief requirements for a member of the community of Israel. This list is also printed as part of the prayer book, and it is recited daily. It appears as well in poetic form, in the PIYYUT ("prayer song") YIGDAL.

In the centuries that followed, Maimonides' list was discussed and challenged. Hasdai CRESCAS limited his list of absolute principles of faith to six; Joseph ALBO reduced the list to three. While neither denies the importance of any of Maimonides' 13 principles, they did question whether accepting some of them is an absolute requirement. The discussion of fundamental principles of Jewish faith continues to the present day.

PROFANATION   See DESECRATION

PROMISED LAND   See ISRAEL, LAND OF

PROPHETS AND PROPHECY   The prophets were individuals with a Divine gift for receiving and reporting messages from God. The prophet was a go-between between God and the people. The first person to be called a prophet in the Bible was ABRAHAM (Gen. 21:7); MOSES was the greatest of the prophets (Deut. 34:10).

Once a prophet felt that he had been commanded by God to speak, he had to do so (Amos 3:8). He had to convey the message whether or not the people wished to hear it (Ezek. 3:11). Some of the prophets hesitated at first about serving, as was the case with Moses, JEREMIAH and JONAH. However, they had no choice. Once he prophesies, the prophet is set apart from other people and carries the responsibility of having been chosen.

The second section of the Hebrew Bible is called *Nevi'im* – Prophets. It has two sections, "Former Prophets" and "Latter Prophets." The historical books of JOSHUA, JUDGES, SAMUEL and KINGS contain the stories of the early prophets, including Nathan, ELIJAH, and ELISHA. The "Latter Prophets" include the works of the literary prophets, including ISAIAH, JEREMIAH, EZEKIEL, and the twelve minor prophets, whose books are shorter: HOSEA, JOEL, AMOS, OBADIAH, JONAH, MICAH, NAHUM, HABAKKUK, ZEPHANIAH, HAGGAI, ZECHARIAH, and MALACHI.

The early prophets are sometimes called "seers." Some of them, especially Elijah and Elisha, were miracle-workers. In the early prophetic period (up to the eighth century BCE), there were groups or schools of prophets, who would gather together and train for their role (see 1 Sam. 10:5, 10). These early prophets fearlessly criticized the sins of the king, such as adultery and murder in the case of DAVID (II Sam. 12) and Ahab's unjustly taking Naboth's vineyard and then murdering him (1 Kings 21).

The period of classical or literary prophecy lasted for 300 years, until the mid-fifth century BCE. This period saw the rise of three great empires: Assyria, Babylonia, and Persia. It also included the destruction of the Northern Kingdom by Assyria (722 BCE), and the destruction of the Southern Kingdom and the Temple by the Babylonians (586 BCE), the Babylonian Exile, and the early years of the Return to Zion.

The books of the prophets focus on their message and not on the biographical details of their lives. The prophets would often warn the people about what would happen to them and the kingdom if they did not change their ways. They taught that the sins of the people would lead to national disaster. They also were aware of larger, international events and interpreted them in terms of God's plan. They used symbolic acts to make their message clear. For example, Ezekiel engraved the names Ephraim and Judah on two separate sticks and held them together – a symbol that the scattered tribes of Israel would reunite.

Classical prophecy emphasizes several elements of ETHICS. On the one hand, all the prophets accepted the rituals of the Temple. Yet they harshly criticized those who carefully performed the rituals while being uncaring and unjust towards others in their daily lives. The threat of punishment is often contrasted with the promise of redemption; the sinner is reprimanded, but the prophet reminds us of God's enduring love.

Jewish scholars have long debated the real nature of the biblical prophet. Some argue that the prophet was a person supernaturally chosen by God. All depends on God's choice – any qualifications that the prophet might have are not important. JUDAH HALEVI adopts this view in his *Kuzari*. A second school of thought argues that prophets are people who are perfect in their intellectual and moral life, and therefore are chosen because they are worthy. Maimonides adopts this view in his *Guide for the Perplexed*.

Nearly all Jewish writers on the subject of prophecy agree that prophecy ended with the close of the Bible, and that the last prophet was MALACHI.

PROSBUL   (*Prozbol*). A word from the Talmud, originally from Greek, for a legal document that prevents the cancelation of debts every seven years. According to the Bible, all outstanding debts were forgiven during each SABBATICAL YEAR. It therefore became almost impossible for people to borrow money as the Sabbatical year approached (see Deut. 15:9). HILLEL ruled that the cancelation of debts applied only to debts owed to individuals. He arranged for a *prosbul,* which allowed lenders to turn over all their outstanding debts to a court of law (BET DIN) at the beginning of the Sabbatical year. The debt, now owed to the *bet din* and not an individual, could be collected at any time.

PROSELYTES   See CONVERSION TO JUDAISM

PROVERBS, BOOK OF   Second book in the HAGIOGRAPHA ("Writings") section of the Bible. Along with ECCLESIASTES and

---

BOOK OF PROVERBS

1:1–1:6	Preface
1:7–9:18	The proverbs of Solomon; the value of wisdom
10:1–22:16	Further collection of Solomon's proverbs
22:17–24:22	The study of wisdom
25:1–29:27	Wise sayings ascribed to Solomon
30:1–30:33	The words of Agur, son of Jakeh
31:1–31:9	The words of King Lemuel
31:10–31:31	An alphabetic acrostic in praise of the virtuous wife.

JOB, Proverbs belongs to the category of WISDOM LITERATURE. Literature of this type was popular throughout the Ancient Near East. It was made up of advice and wise sayings about proper behavior in everyday life. The book has 31 chapters and 915 verses. In Jewish tradition, King SOLOMON is the author of Proverbs. According to the Talmud, Solomon wrote the SONG OF SONGS in his youth, Proverbs in his middle age, and ECCLESIASTES in his old age (*BB* 15a). Modern Bible scholars do not believe that Solomon is the author.

The tone of Proverbs is optimistic and universal. Some favorite subjects are the contrast between wise persons and fools; the importance of discipline; the value of expressive speech; the dangers of drunkenness, laziness, and gossip; and the threat posed by "foreign women." The last section of the book, "A Woman of Valor" (31:10–31), is read at home on Friday nights before KIDDUSH.

PROVIDENCE   (Heb. *hashgahah*). The idea that God has total knowledge and command over all life, which He created. Not only does He know and control all things, but He loves all His creatures, and cares for them. In the Bible, providence constantly affects the fate of the people of Israel.

This belief is related to other issues, such as FREE WILL and REWARD AND PUNISHMENT. It raises a number of important questions. First, if God knows all, He also knows what each person will do. How then can there be human free will, which is central to Jewish belief? Next, if providence affects the fate of each person, then the future of that person is also pre-known and pre-determined by God. Thus people's behavior would have little impact on the direction their life would take (see PREDESTINATION). Finally, if all things are a result of Divine providence, how can we explain that the wicked often seem to be rewarded in life, while the righteous suffer?

MAIMONIDES offers an interesting answer to the first question above. He suggests that God knows everything about people's actions – past, present, and future – in a single glance. At the same time, He does not control a person's choice of action. Freedom of choice is left to the individual (see *Guide* III, 30; *Yad, Hilkhot Teshuvah* 5:5). For the second question, there seems to be agreement that Divine providence somehow exists together with human responsibility. From the Bible to the Talmud and beyond, Jewish thinkers agree that the most important factor in deciding people's fate is their own conduct. There are a number of theories about the difficult question of why the wicked prosper and the righteous suffer. For example, some suggest that we simply do not understand the real purpose of suffering. Even a painful experience can lead to a greater good. Others believe that the nature of real good and evil is known to God alone.

All of these explanations satisfy on one level and disappoint on another. For this reason the idea of Divine providence in Jewish belief is open enough to allow for both human freedom and for reward and punishment.

PSALMS, BOOK OF (Heb. *Tehillim*). The first book of the HAGIOGRAPHA ("Writings") section of the Bible; it includes 150 psalms and 2,527 verses. The first two psalms serve as a general introduction to the entire collection and the final psalm is a conclusion. Of the 150 psalms, the majority mention specific authors: one by MOSES, 72 by DAVID, two by SOLOMON, 12 by Asaph, one by Heman, and one by Ethan. According to Jewish tradition, King David composed or edited the Book of Psalms.

THE BOOK OF PSALMS

1–41	Book I: Psalms of David (except 1, 2, 10, 33)
42–72	Book II: 18 ascribed to David, seven to the sons of Korah, 50 to Asaph, 72 to Solomon, and four anonymous
73–89	Book III: 73–83 attributed to Asaph; 84, 85, 87 to the sons of Korah; 86 to David; 88 to Heman the Ezrahite; and 89 to Ethan the Ezrahite
90–106	Book IV: 90 attributed to Moses; 101, 103 to David; the rest are anonymous
107–150	Book V: 15 psalms attributed to David and one to Solomon. Most of the others have no inscription. 120–134 are called "Songs of Ascent"

There are three basic categories of psalms: hymns of praise, mournful laments, and those that teach. Some add a fourth type: songs of trust (e.g., Ps. 23, 129). The hymns usually celebrate God's role as Creator of the world and Redeemer of the Jewish people. Laments are both individual and communal, and mourn God's absence or anger. The teaching psalms retell

Israel's history, offer an idea about the TORAH, or examine the problem of evil.

In the Temple Various psalms were used in the service in the TEMPLE. There was a separate psalm for each day of the week (*Tam.* 7:4). Pilgrims probably sang the "songs of ascent" as they went up the TEMPLE MOUNT. The Levites sang certain psalms to accompany the offering of the SACRIFICES (*Suk.* 4:5).

In the Liturgy More than any other part of the Bible, the Book of Psalms is suitable for use in prayer. The traditional PRAYER BOOK now contains more than 70 complete psalms as well as over 200 additional verses that have been woven into other passages. For example, HALLEL, which is recited on FESTIVALS, is made up entirely of psalms. ASHREI (Ps. 145) is said three times each day, twice during the MORNING SERVICE, and at the beginning of the AFTERNOON SERVICE. Psalm 47 is repeated seven times before the sounding of the SHOFAR (ram's horn) on ROSH HA-SHANAH. There are many more examples.

Pious Jews throughout the Jewish world read from the Book of Psalms daily. All 150 psalms are still printed for this purpose in many editions of the traditional prayer book.

PSEUDEPIGRAPHA See APOCRYPHA AND PSEUDEPIGRAPHA

PUNISHMENT The Bible calls for various penalties for those who violate the COMMANDMENTS. They include: death (see CAPITAL PUNISHMENT); being "cut off" (see KARET); and EXCOMMUNICATION (*herem*). Various other punishments are described below.

Flogging (see Deut. 25:1–3), up to 40 lashes, is the punishment for violating a negative commandment from the Bible, or for refusing to fulfill a positive commandment

Retaliation ("eye-for-an-eye") – in cases of assault and battery

Fines and payment of money were imposed in cases of rape, robbery, and selling a neighbor's property. The Talmud called for fines in additional cases, when the Bible's punishment could not be imposed because of a technicality (*BK* 84b).

Taking away property was used by the court (*hefker bet-din*) to force people to follow the law. This was based on the Book of EZRA (10:8): anyone who did not come [to the assembly summoned by Ezra] would, by decision of the officers and the elders, have his property taken away.

Imprisonment was actually not a Jewish penalty. In the Bible (see Num. 15:34), it was used to hold a person until the court could decide his punishment. In the Middle Ages, some Jewish communities imprisoned those who failed to pay their debts.

For all capital punishment or flogging sentences, the crime had to be committed in front of two eyewitnesses and after the criminal had been warned of the punishment involved.

PURIM ("lots"). FESTIVAL on 14 Adar (February/March; Second Adar in a leap year) to celebrate the saving of Persian Jewry from destruction in the mid-fifth century BCE. The Book of ESTHER tells the story: Haman, the grand vizier of King Ahasuerus, tried

A boy and girl delivering gifts of food to friends and relatives.

to kill all the Jews living in the empire. He cast lots – like tossing dice – in order to set a lucky date for the planned massacre. Esther, the Jewish Queen, uses her wit and her beauty to foil Haman's plot, have him killed, and save her people.

The days surrounding the 14th of Adar are special. The 13th of Adar is a minor fast day, called the Fast of Esther. It is in memory of the public fast declared by Queen Esther before she begged the King to save the Jews. The 15th of Adar is known as *Shushan Purim,* because the fighting between the Jews and Haman's supporters in Persia's capital (ancient Susa) did not end until the 15th. Ahasuerus granted the Jews an extra day to destroy their enemies, which meant the holiday could only be celebrated a day later. The rabbis ruled that in Jerusalem and other cities that had walls surrounding them in the days of Joshua, Purim would always be celebrated on the 15th.

The laws of Purim are discussed in the talmudic tractate MEGILLAH. It calls for the reading of the Esther scroll at both the EVENING and MORNING SERVICE in the synagogue. As part of the joyful atmosphere, whenever the name of Haman is read aloud, congregants stamp their feet or whirl noisemakers to blot out his name. This comes from the biblical command

"Adloyada" – Purim Carnival in Tel Aviv.

to "blot out the memory of AMALEK" (Deut. 25:19), who was an ancestor of Haman's. In addition, it is customary to send gifts of food delicacies to friends and neighbors, to distribute CHARITY to the poor, and to enjoy a festive meal.

A joyful mood surrounds the holiday. Children and adults dress in costume. The rabbis declared that on Purim one should drink so much wine that one "can no longer tell the difference between 'blessed is Mordeccai (Esther's pious uncle)' and 'cursed is Haman'" (*Meg.* 7b).

PURIMS, SPECIAL   Just as Jews throughout the world celebrate the festival of PURIM to mark the saving of the Jews of Persia, certain communities have instituted their own Purims to celebrate their deliverance from disaster. For example, the Padua (Italy) Purim is celebrated on 11 Sivan and celebrates the Jews' deliverance from a major fire in 1795. The Florence (Italy) Purim (27 Sivan) marks the rescue of the Jews from a mob in 1790, thanks to a local bishop. The Baghdad (Iraq) Purim (11 Av) celebrates the conquest of the city by the Arabs and the defeat of the Persians, who were persecuting the Jews. The "Hitler Purim" of Casablanca, Morocco, was celebrated on 2 Kislev (11 November 1943), when the city was saved from falling into German hands. A "Hitler Scroll" was composed that included the words "cursed be Hitler, cursed be Mussolini."

PURITY, RITUAL   (Heb. *tohorah*). A category in Jewish law that describes the fitness of a person to participate in TEMPLE ritual or of an object to be used. Its opposite is *tumah* ("ritual impurity"). One who has become ritually impure must undergo a purification ritual with multiple stages: waiting a certain length of time, bathing in a ritual bath (MIKVEH), and offering SACRIFICES.

According to the Bible, impurity comes from contact with dead bodies, leprosy, or a discharge from the sexual organs. Contact with the dead is the most powerful source of impurity. Purification from this type of *tumah* involved being quarantined for seven days, bathing in the *mikveh*, and then being sprinkled by a PRIEST with the ashes of the RED HEIFER. After the destruction of the Second Temple, sprinkling with the ashes of the Red Heifer was no longer possible, and now all Jews have the status of *tamei met* ("corpse uncleanness").

Impurity caused by a discharge from the sexual organs is the one case in which many of the laws of purification still apply. Following menstruation and a waiting period of seven days, a woman immerses herself in the *mikveh*. This is still a fully observed purification ritual in ORTHODOXY (see NIDDAH). In HASIDISM, men still observe the custom of immersing in the *mikveh* every morning, in case there had been a sexual discharge during the night.

Objects may become unclean as well. Most objects that come into contact with a corpse must be passed through either fire or water; but pottery cannot be purified and must be broken.

Food may become unclean after it is harvested and it becomes wet. Once it comes in contact with a source of impurity, it cannot be purified and therefore cannot be used in the Temple. The custom of washing the hands before eating bread comes from the laws of purity. The hands are considered unclean because they come in contact with unclean objects or parts of the body. Purifying the hands makes it possible to touch food without transferring impurity to it.

RABBAH BAR NAHMANI (known simply as Rabbah in the Talmud; c. 270–331 CE). Babylonian rabbi of the third generation, descendant of a family of priests from the Galilee. Rabbah was a brilliant Talmud scholar, and was nicknamed *Oker Harim* ("Uprooter of Mountains"). His partner and rival, Joseph ben Hiyya, was called *Sinai* (*Ber.* 64a). When the two disagreed about a law, the decision nearly always followed Rabbah's opinion. In 309, Rabbah was appointed head of the Academy in Pumbedita. Thousands came to hear him lecture during the KALLAH months (times when the study house was open to all). The success of these gathering caused the local authorities to accuse him of helping his students avoid tax payments during the *kallah* months. Rabbah was forced to flee to the countryside, where he died.

RABBANITES   See KARAITES

RABBI   ("my master"). Title of Jewish religious authority and teacher. Originally it was an expression of respect. In the first century CE, it became an official title given to members of the SANHEDRIN who were experts in Jewish law. The title was given at a special ceremony called ORDINATION (*semikhah*). Ordination stopped in the fourth century, but the term rabbi continued to be used for any person who was qualified to make decisions in Jewish law.

The Jews settled far and wide, yet they remained a community held together by the laws of the Talmud. They needed rabbis to interpret the text of the Talmud. At first the most learned people of the community volunteered for this duty. Eventually, when religious leaders could not make a living in other ways, the rabbinate became a paid profession. The rabbi's duties were to make decisions according to Jewish law (HALAKHAH) and to supervise religious activities, such as ritual slaughter (SHEHITAH) and the ritual bath (MIKVEH). In large cities, he was also the head of the YESHIVAH. He usually gave a sermon twice a year.

With the EMANCIPATION of the Jews of Europe, the role of the rabbi changed. The rabbis no longer served as judges, because Jews could go to secular courts. Both Reform and Orthodox communities felt that rabbis should get a secular edu-

cation as well as a religious one, and RABBINICAL SEMINARIES were established to train rabbis from the 19th century on.

The large Jewish communities of Eastern Europe were not affected by these changes, and the yeshivahs continued to flourish there. The Russian Czar forced the Jews to appoint certain people as rabbis.

Jews lived in the United States starting in 1654, but it was almost 200 years before the first rabbi arrived. Later on, there were many synagogues, and each one had its own rabbi. The different movements that emerged (REFORM, CONSERVATIVE, ORTHODOXY, and RECONSTRUCTIONISM) each had their own rabbis and rabbinical seminaries.

In the Sephardi and Oriental communities the rabbi's role remained similar to the ancient tradition. In the Ottoman Empire, the rabbi was a judge of religious matters. This system was kept in Israel when the British took over. This means that in Israel there is an official rabbinate that has legal control over areas such as marriage, divorce, and conversion. The rabbis receive a salary from the State. The official rabbinate is Orthodox; non-Orthodox rabbis are not recognized. Israel has both a Sephardi and Ashkenazi CHIEF RABBINATE that confirms every rabbi's appointment.

RABBINICAL AUTHORITY   See AUTHORITY, RABBINIC

RABBINICAL COURT   See BET DIN

RABBINICAL SEMINARIES   In the early 19th century, as part of the movement for Jewish EMANCIPATION, the need for modern-style schools to train rabbis arose. Up to that time, the rabbis had studied Torah in yeshivahs (see YESHIVAH) and their main job was to interpret the law and judge according to the law. With the Emancipation, many Jewish communities needed rabbis who had a modern education.

In 1829 a Collego Rabbinico opened in Padua, then part of the Austrian Empire. It closed and reopened many times. Also in 1829, the French Ecole Rabbinique opened in Merz, France.

In 1854, the Judische-Theologisches Seminar was opened in Breslau. The first director was Zacharias FRANKEL (1801–1875), and he saw the spirit of the seminary as "positive historical Judaism." The students studied a broader range of subjects than did those at traditional yeshivahs, and WISENSCHAFT DES JUDENTUMS, the "science of Judaism," was the key idea in its program.

Under the influence of the REFORM leader Abraham GEIGER (1810–1874), the College for the Science of Judaism was founded in Berlin in 1872. In 1873, the Orthodox Rabbinical Seminary was opened in Berlin under the influence of Azriel Hildesheimer (1820–1899). This school had the same approach as the *Torah im derekh erets* (Torah and the Ways of the World) school of Samson Raphael HIRSCH. Other Orthodox Jews, by contrast, thought that combining TORAH study with secular studies damaged the purity of Jewish teachings.

Although many Jews of Hungary opposed the new rabbinical school, the NEOLOGY movement opened a Seminary in Budapest in 1877. It attracted many scholars and survived both World War II and the Communist regime. Additional rabbinical colleges were opened in Vienna, London, and other European cities. The Russian czarist government tried to modernize the rabbinate by opening seminaries. The Jewish community of Russia was not interested in becoming more modern and ignored the graduates of these schools.

In the United States, rabbinical seminaries came before yeshivahs. The American Jewish communities needed educated, English-speaking rabbis. The first successful school was opened by Isaac Meyer WISE (1819–1900). He became president of the Hebrew Union College when it opened in Cincinnati in 1875. The school was meant to be for all streams of Judaism in the American community, but it became a Reform movement college.

A CONSERVATIVE group established the Jewish Theological Seminary in New York in 1886. Its ideology was similar to that of the Breslau Seminary. In 1922 the Jewish Institute of Religion, which was Reform, was opened in New York by Rabbi Stephen S. Wise.

At the end of the 19th century, many immigrants arrived form Eastern Europe. In 1886 the Orthodox Isaac Elchanan Yeshiva was opened (see ORTHODOXY). Today, it is the Yeshiva University, which includes a medical school as well as a rabbinical training college.

The different American institutions have expanded over the years, opening branches in Los Angeles, New York, and Jerusalem. They include many secular departments, such as social work, archeology, and education.

RACHEL Wife of JACOB; one of the MATRIARCHS of Israel. She was the younger daughter of Jacob's uncle Laban. Jacob met her by a well and wished to marry her, agreeing to work for her father for seven years, but on the wedding night, Laban tricked him into marrying his elder daughter, LEAH. Jacob was forced to work for another seven years to marry Rachel.

Rachel is described as being, "of comely appearance and beautiful" (Gen. 29:17) and she was Jacob's favorite wife. Rachel's children were JOSEPH and Benjamin. She died giving birth to Benjamin.

According to Jewish tradition, Rachel was buried near Bethlehem. Since the Byzantine era, many have made pilgrimages to her tomb. Women, especially those who cannot have children, come to pray for a child at her tomb because she was barren for a long time before giving birth to her children. (See also BARRENNESS.)

RAIN, PRAYERS FOR Various hymns and prayers for rain read in the synagogue, mainly on SHEMINI ATSERET, the last day of SUKKOT. According to the Bible, rain is very important in the Land of Israel. It may be granted to the farmer as a blessing from God (Lev. 26:4) or taken away as a punishment (Deut. 11:16–17). It was customary for the HIGH PRIESTS to say a short prayer for a "rainy year" on the DAY OF ATONEMENT (*Yoma* 53b). Prayers were also added whenever crops might be lost because of a drought. Jewish communities from Yemen and SEPHARDIM in Israel read special prayers and fast when normal rainfall is delayed.

According to the Talmud, Sukkot is the time when the "world is judged for water" (*RH* 1:2). From Shemini Atseret onwards, one request for rain is added to the AMIDAH and a more specific request is added after 7 Heshvan (early winter). The first passage is *Mashiv ha-ru'ah u-morid ha-geshem* ("You cause the wind to blow and the rain to fall"), and it is recited from the ADDITIONAL SERVICE of Shemini Atseret until PASSOVER. Throughout this time, *Mashiv ha-ru'ah* is recited in the second blessing of every *Amidah*. The second addition, *Ve-ten tal u-matar li-verakhah* ("Grant dew and rain for a blessing") is added to the ninth blessing.

In the Middle Ages, hymns were sung at the beginning of the *Amidah* on Shemini Atseret. Known as *Tefillat Geshem*, "the Prayer for Rain," they were similar to the Prayers for Dew that are read on Passover (see DEW, PRAYERS FOR). This prayer is made up of different poems about rain and miracles performed with water. This ritual is followed in CONSERVATIVE synagogues, and REFORM congregations have a shorter version.

RAMBAM See MAIMONIDES, MOSES

RAMBAN See NAHMANIDES

RANSOM See CAPTIVES, RANSOMING OF

RASHI (acronym of Rabbi Shelomo Yitshaki; 1040–1105). Writer of commentaries on the Bible and Talmud. Rashi was born in Troyes, France, where for most of his life, the Jews enjoyed good conditions. At an early age, Rashi went to study in Worms, then in Mainz. His teachers were Jacob ben Yakar and Isaac ben Judah, who were the outstanding students of Rabbenu GERSHOM, *Me'or ha-Golah*.

Rashi had two daughters, Miriam and Jochebed, who married students of their father. His grandchildren were some of the greatest scholars of the next generation. The most famous ones were SAMUEL BEN MEIR (*Rashbam*) and his brother, Jacob (TAM).

The First Crusade of 1096 saddened the last years of Rashi's life. The Crusaders destroyed the Jewish communities of the Rhineland. Some of his comments on the Psalms and other books reflect his sadness (see Rashi on Ps. 38:1, 38:18, 39:2–5; Isa. 53:9).

Rashi's most important accomplishments were his commentaries on the Bible and Talmud. His commentary on the PENTATEUCH is taught to every student from childhood on, and was the first Hebrew book to be printed (1475, Reggio, Italy). In his work on the Bible, Rashi aims to give the plain meaning – PESHAT – of the text. He often gave the Old French translation of difficult words in the text of the Bible. He also paid special attention to the grammar of the Hebrew words and phrases.

In addition to *peshat*, for the simple meaning, Rashi used the method of DERASH in his commentaries to get at the deeper meaning. He claimed to use *derash* mostly when the *peshat* was too difficult. Sometimes he used *derash* because many people found the folktales of the AGGADAH more interesting than the plain meaning of the text.

Rashi's commentary on the Talmud is the clearest, most elementary commentary provided for students of the Talmud. Without his commentary, the Talmud would have remained a closed book. Modern-day students of the Talmud study his commentary as a basic key to understanding the text.

Rashi's work on the Talmud was continued by a school of commentators called the Tosafists (see TOSAFOT). It was founded by his own grandchildren and students and continued for about 200 years. In all standard editions of the Talmud the comments of the Tosafists appear on the outside column of each page, opposite Rashi's commentary printed on the inside column.

SAYINGS OF RASHI

All the 613 commandments are included in the Ten Commandments.

Any plan made in a hurry is foolish

Be sure to ask your teacher his reasons and his sources.

Teachers learn from their students' discussions.

A student of Jewish law who does not understand its meaning or cannot explain its contradictions is just a basket full of books.

Do not rebuke your fellow man so as to shame him in public.

To obey out of love is better than to obey out of fear.

RAV (or Abba Arikha, i.e., Abba the Tall; c. 175–247 CE). Babylonian rabbi of the first generation of Talmud times; founder of the Academy of Sura. Born to a well-established family in Babylonia, Rav went to Erets Israel to study in the Academy of Rabbi JUDAH HA-NASI. He spent many years studying and received limited ORDINATION.

He returned to Babylonia, to the Academy at Nehardea, but soon founded his own Academy at Sura in 219 CE, which attracted many students and scholars. His partner, SAMUEL, who was the head of the Nehardea Academy, was the expert on civil law, and Rav was the expert in ritual matters. There are many discussions between Rav and Samuel in the Talmud, and Rav's opinion is generally accepted. Rav is also known for writing the prayer for the New MOON and for his preaching.

SAYINGS OF RAV

Arrogance is equal to all the other sins.

God Himself prays, "May My mercy overcome My anger."

When your mind is not at ease, do not pray.

In the future world there will be no eating, drinking, propagation, business, jealousy, hatred, or competition, but the righteous will sit with crowns on their head enjoying the brilliance of the Presence of God.

He who refuses to pray for his fellow is a sinner.

What is improper in public is forbidden in secret.

Each person will be called to account in the future for every enjoyment he declined in this world without sufficient cause.

RAVA (Abba bar Joseph bar Hama; c. 280–352 CE). Important Babylonian rabbi of the fourth generation of Talmud times. His teachers were Nahman ben Jacob, Joseph ben Hiyya, and Rav Hisda. When his great rival, ABBAYE, became head of the Pumbedita Academy in 323 CE, Rava settled in his hometown, Mahoza, and began teaching there. When Abbaye died (338 CE), Mahoza became the only academy in Babylonia. The Talmud contains many debates between Rava and Abbaye, which were decided in Rava's favor in all but six cases.

Rava would speak to large crowds on SABBATH afternoons. TORAH study was an important value for him. He also stressed the ethical side of Judaism. He taught that whoever puts someone to shame in public loses his share in the world to come (*BM* 59a).

READING OF THE LAW (Heb. *Keri'at ha-Torah*). The chanting of sections of the PENTATEUCH in the SYNAGOGUE; these must be read from a SCROLL OF THE LAW (*Sefer Torah*) only when a MINYAN (prayer group of ten) is present. According to tradition, MOSES began the custom of reading the Torah on Sabbaths, festivals, and New Moons, while EZRA added shorter Torah readings on MONDAYS AND THURSDAYS (market days in ancient times) and on Sabbath afternoons (when people had time to study) (*Meg.* 31a; *BK* 82a).

The texts for the regular weekly portion were set around the third century CE (*sidrah* or PARASHAH). At least three verses had to be read at a time, so that a minimum of 21 verses were read each week. Eventually two different cycles were adopted. The ancient Erets Israel tradition divided the Pentateuch into 175 portions, so that the Pentateuch would be completed over a period of three years (see TRIENNIAL CYCLE). The Babylonian tradition divided it into 54 portions, so that over the course of a leap year the cycle would be completed. In a regular year, two portions were read on some weeks so that the cycle would still be completed in one year. This system is now traditional throughout the world. The twelve-month cycle of weekly readings begins and ends on the festival of SIMHAT TORAH.

When the ceremony of the Reading of the Law takes place, the congregation stands while the Torah scroll is taken out of the ARK and carried to the BIMAH (reading desk). Verses from the Bible are sung as the Torah scroll is carried from the Ark and returned to the Ark after the reading. After the Reading of the Law, the scroll is raised and displayed to the congregation then rolled up, bound, and covered with its mantle.

On Mondays and Thursdays, fast days, HANUKKAH, PURIM, Sabbath afternoons, and the afternoon of the DAY OF ATONEMENT, three people are called to the Reading of the Law; on New Moons and the middle days of PASSOVER and SUKKOT, four are called; on the PILGRIM FESTIVALS there are five sections; on the morning of the Day of Atonement six, and on a regular Sabbath morning, seven people are called. An additional MAFTIR portion is read on Sabbaths, major festivals, intermediate Sabbaths, or Sabbaths that are on the same days as the New Moon. The person who reads *maftir* is usually honored with reading the HAFTARAH from the PROPHETS. On Mondays and Thursdays, the portion read is the first section of the next Sabbath's reading.

In Hebrew, the honor of being called to the Reading of the Law is called *aliyah la-Torah* ("going up to the Torah"). Until the Middle Ages, each person chanted his own portion, having memorized the pronunciation, vowels, and musical accents, which are not written in the Torah scroll. When most people no longer had the skills to do this, an expert BA'AL KERI'AH or "Torah reader" was hired to chant all of the portions for those called to the Reading of the Law. The person up for the reading recites the Torah BLESSINGS before and after the reading of the portion. A prayer shawl, TALLIT, must be worn.

A special order for the Torah honors was developed by the rabbis (*Git.* 5:8, 60a). A *kohen* (priest) should be called first, a *Levi* (Levite) second, and only then a *yisra'el* (any other Jew). Certain honors are reserved for important scholars and the rabbi of the congregation, such as the third *aliyah*, or the *maftir*. Until modern times, and in Orthodox synagogues to this day, only men are called up to the Reading of the Law.

The Reading of the Law at a bar mitzvah ceremony. Painting by J. Brandon. France, 19th century.

A bridegroom on the Sabbath immediately following his MARRIAGE is called to the Torah, as is a BAR MITZVAH boy, a father naming his daughter or whose son is being circumcised, someone observing a YAHRZEIT; a person who has just finished his week of MOURNING; and anyone who must recite the GOMEL blessing on being saved from danger.

Most REFORM Temples have a shortened version of the Reading of the Law. Some American CONSERVATIVE synagogues have adopted the long-abandoned three-year cycle of readings. In most non-Orthodox synagogues today, women also receive an *aliyah la-Torah,* and in this way a girl may celebrate her BAT MITZVAH in the same way as a boy. Some Orthodox rabbis have permitted women to have their own Torah reading when they form a separate women's prayer group of their own.

REBBE   See ADMOR; HASIDISM; TSADDIK

REBEKAH   Wife of ISAAC and one of the MATRIARCHS of the Jewish people. She was the daughter of Bethuel, who was ABRAHAM's nephew. Abraham sent his servant, Eliezer, to his family to select a wife for his son Isaac. Eliezer prayed that he would be given a sign that would help him choose the right girl. At the well, he would ask a young woman for water for himself, and if she offered to water his ten camels as well, he would know she was the right one. Rebekah appeared and fulfilled his condition. He then went to Bethuel's house and with his and Rebekah's agreement, Eliezer took her back with him.

Isaac was 40 years old when he married, but Rebekah's age is not mentioned. Their twin sons, JACOB and Esau, were born 20 years later.

Rebekah's favorite son was Jacob. She helped him trick Isaac into giving him the blessing of the firstborn. When Esau planned to kill Jacob in revenge, Rebekah sent Jacob to her brother Laban in Haran to find a wife. She died without seeing him again.

Rebekah was buried in the Cave of Machpelah in Hebron, Erets Israel, with Isaac.

REBELLIOUS SON   (Heb. *ben sorer u-moreh*). Term used for a son who purposely rebels against the authority of his parents: "If a man has a stubborn and rebellious son who will not listen to his father's and his mother's voice …" (Deut. 21:18–21).

The rebellious son is brought to the BET DIN (rabbinical court) only after he has stolen money from his father in order to buy a certain amount of meat and wine. He must have been convicted in the past, whipped, and warned by his parents in front of three witnesses to stop his rebellious ways. He is tried in front of a court of 23 judges, and if found guilty, stoned to death by the men of the city.

This law was not included in the 613 commandments that were taken from the PENTATEUCH. This is probably because of what the Talmud says: "A stubborn and rebellious child never was and never will be. Then why was the law stated? For the reward of studying it" (*Sanh.* 71a).

RECONSTRUCTIONISM   An American Jewish movement and philosophy created by Mordecai KAPLAN with the aim of reviving Judaism. He believed that Judaism was not meeting the needs of the modern Jew, and that the ORTHODOX, CONSERVATIVE, and REFORM movements were not offering solutions to problems. Kaplan therefore began to form a program for the reconstruction of Judaism. He held that because the modern Jew no longer believed in the afterlife, Judaism needed to offer a way of achieving salvation in this world.

Reconstructionism is based on the idea that Judaism is a developing religious civilization. It has a special language, history, culture, customs, social organization, and attachment to the Land of ISRAEL. During each period of Jewish history, Judaism has developed, changed, and adapted to its environment without losing its identity.

GOD, TORAH, and Israel form a triangle, where each one is equally important in Judaism. God is the combination of forces within each person and the universe that makes "salvation" possible. Torah, which includes both the Bible and rabbinic literature, is the creation of the Jewish people. It is the record of their experience. The COMMANDMENTS (*mitzvot*) are actually the customs of the Jewish people. They can be changed according to the ideas and values of each generation.

Israel, which is both a Land and People, is extremely important in Judaism. For Judaism to reach its ultimate heights, Israel and the Diaspora must be in constant interaction.

When the Society for the Advancement of Judaism was founded in 1922, Reconstructionism officially became a movement. Nowadays, the headquarters of the Reconstructionist movement are on the campus of the Reconstructionist Rabbinical College in Wyncote, Pennsylvania, in the United States. The college was founded in 1967, and from the very beginning it opened its doors to men and women alike. Synagogues and congregations are organized in the Federation of Reconstructionist Congregations and *Havurot* (see HAVURAH).

REDEMPTION   The Hebrew roots of the word "redemption" are *padah, ga'al,* and *yeshu'ah.* They originally meant deliverance from difficulties, and have come to mean triumph over all troubles and the deliverance of the individual from sin. They also refer to the redemption of the nation and the ideal state of the world.

In the Bible, *padah* and *ga'al* meant the financial "redemption" of land that was sold or a person who was sold into slavery. In the case of a murder, the *go'el* (redeemer) was the BLOOD AVENGER. The word *yeshu'ah* means victory over one's enemies (as in Judg. 25:12; 1 Sam. 2:1, 14:54).

God is seen as the Redeemer who saves people such as widows and orphans from their troubles. He also redeems from sin (Ps. 130:8) although a person must repent (see REPENTANCE). Above all, God redeemed the Jews in the EXODUS from Egypt. This is seen as the blueprint for final redemption.

After the destruction of the TEMPLE and the EXILE, a main focus of Judaism became the longing for the redemption of the

People of Israel by God. These historical tragedies were seen as punishment for not keeping the COVENANT with God; therefore the only way Israel could bring about the redemption was by repenting. The prophets taught that the redemption would come as a combination of the Jews' repentance and God's will. According to JEREMIAH, the Jews must start the process by repenting, but the redemption can only be fully brought about by God Himself. God is seen as the Redeemer Who gathers the exiles to Erets Israel and restores the Jewish people. A time of human perfection and world harmony will follow (Isa. 11:10, 52:10; Zech. 14:9,16).

The rabbis of the Mishnah and Talmud taught that the *ge'ulah* was a religious-national-political redemption that would happen as a natural part of history. The kingdom of Israel would be reestablished, the Temple rebuilt, and the Jews would return to the Land of Israel. This would lead to a spiritual redemption of the whole world. The Presence of God (SHEKHINAH) was in exile along with the Jewish people; therefore when the redemption would happen, God would redeem a part of Himself as well (*Mekh. Bo* 14: *Sif.* Num. 161).

The rabbis of the Middle Ages had two separate views of the idea of redemption. SAADIAH GAON, JUDAH HALEVI, NAHMANIDES, Hasdai CRESCAS, and Joseph ALBO believed that the national redemption would be supernatural, and the natural ways of the world would change. MAIMONIDES, IBN GABIROL, Abraham IBN EZRA, and LEVI BEN GERSHON, believed that the redemption would be brought about by the raising of human intelligence and spirit, but that the course of nature would not be affected (cf. Maimonides, *Guide* III, 11).

The Spanish mystics saw the redemption as a miracle that was not dependent on human behavior. By contrast, the followers of Isaac LURIA believed that the MESSIAH would arrive because of human action. HASIDISM adopted this view, but taught that a person could only redeem his own soul. God, however, would bring about the redemption of the entire Jewish people.

Modern thinkers, such as Martin BUBER, Hermann COHEN, and Franz ROSENZWEIG, taught that personal redemption was the first step leading to national and universal redemption.

According to REFORM JUDAISM, redemption is the advancement of modern society. During the late 19th and early 20th centuries, the Zionist movement (see ZIONISM) aimed to cause the Jewish national redemption by rebuilding the Land of Israel. Religious Zionism saw this as a way that man could initiate the redemption, which would eventually be brought about by God's will.

REDEMPTION OF THE FIRSTBORN   See FIRSTBORN, REDEMPTION OF THE

RED HEIFER   (Heb. *parah adumah*). A cow with a purely red coat whose ashes, mixed with spring water, were used for the ritual cleansing of people or objects that had become impure (Num. 19:1–22). The animal had to be without physical blemish,

The Red Heifer from the portion Parah *read on one of the four special Sabbaths. From an Italian Mahzor, 1441.*

such as cuts or bruises, and must never have been placed under a yoke. According to the PARAH tractate in the Mishnah, only the HIGH PRIEST could slaughter the Red Heifer and then had to sprinkle its blood seven times in the direction of the HOLY OF HOLIES. It was burned whole, together with cedar wood and other spices. Its ashes were placed in a container, mixed with fresh spring water, and set aside for purifying impure people or objects. Anyone who prepared or touched the ashes was contaminated and had to wash their clothes and bathe, remaining unclean until nightfall.

Most of the rabbis believed that the law of the Red Heifer was one of the biblical COMMANDMENTS for which there is no rational explanation. "A corpse does not really defile nor does water really purify; but the Holy One issued a decree and no one has the right to transgress it" (Num. R. 19:4).

Chapter three of the book of *Parah* describes the preparation of the ashes of the Red Heifer. Clearly, a perfect Red Heifer must have been extremely rare and expensive. The Mishnah states that only seven Red Heifers were slaughtered from the time of MOSES until the destruction of the Second Temple. The supply of ritual water lasted until the third century CE (see also PURITY, RITUAL).

On *Shabbat Parah*, the Sabbath about a week after the PURIM festival, the section about the Red Heifer is read in the synagogue. This custom dates from Second Temple times, when it was a reminder to those who were impure that they should be sprinkled with the special water, so that they would be able to enter the Temple on PASSOVER.

REFORM JUDAISM   Stream of Judaism that believes that both the WRITTEN LAW and the ORAL LAW can be changed. Reform Judaism has adapted Jewish thought and custom to the modern world. It is also known as Liberal or Progressive Judaism. Moses MENDELSSOHN, although he always remained an Orthodox Jew, helped to create the climate in which Reform emerged. He taught that the ideas of Judaism were relevant to the whole world. This meant that Judaism could live and develop within the modern world. Jews could live as free and equal citizens and should be educated in the secular world as well as in the Jewish world.

The Reform movement began in Germany, and each synagogue or congregation made some changes in the traditional customs. There were changes in the text of the prayers; some played the ORGAN; ancient melodies were replaced with European-style music; WOMEN were allowed to participate more in the services; etc.

A few years after Mendelssohn's death, EMANCIPATION welcomed the Jews into general society after the French Revolution. The Jews of Germany began moving out of the ghettos and began comparing their synagogues to Christian churches. In 1810, Israel Jacobson built a new-style Temple at Seesen in Westphalia. It was later transferred to Berlin (1815). Orthodox rabbis were opposed to this new synagogue, and in 1823 a decree forbade the slightest change in language, ceremonies, PRAYERS, or songs in Jewish worship (see ORTHODOXY).

In the meantime, a Reform temple was established in Hamburg in 1818, with its own revised prayer book. SERMONS were given in German, although many Orthodox rabbis protested.

A new trend developed in the education of rabbis. They began a scientific study of Judaism (WISSENSCHAFT DES JUDENTUMS) in addition to secular subjects and the traditional study of TALMUD and Jewish law. In 1938, the Jewish community of Breslau decided they needed a rabbi of the new school, and they hired Abraham GEIGER.

Geiger was a scholar who aimed to develop Reform Judaism. He was not satisfied with changing the style of worship. He

The Reform Central Synagogue in New York.

believed that the body of laws and traditions that had come down from the past were no longer relevant. The Jewish people were no longer a closed and separated COMMUNITY, but had become part of the modern world. Therefore prayers for the return to ZION or the restoration of the TEMPLE and SACRIFICES had no place in Jewish worship. He also believed that Hebrew should not be the language of prayer, because German had become the mother tongue of German Jews.

Samuel Holdheim, the first rabbi of the Berlin Reform Congregation, made more drastic changes. He removed Hebrew from the prayer book and transferred the Sabbath to Sunday. The Brunswick Conference (1844) declared that mixed marriages were not forbidden as long as the children were brought up as Jews. It also declared that a Jew must consider the land in which he was born his homeland, as opposed to Erets Israel.

The Sabbath was a subject of much controversy. At first, Reform Judaism emphasized the importance of the spirit of the Sabbath day. However, new attitudes were also approved that laid the foundation for putting aside Sabbath observances in the future. For example, it was noted that "a Jewish official may perform the duties of his office in so far as he is obliged to do so on the Sabbath." Zacharias FRANKEL strongly objected to these changes and withdrew from the conference. He believed that while some changes could be allowed, the "needs of today" were not a good enough reason for change. Change must come from the demands of the people as a whole, under the guidance of scholars. This viewpoint, which he called Positive Historical Judaism, was to form the basis for American CONSERVATIVE JUDAISM.

Reform Judaism spread throughout Europe. In Hungary in 1867, a mild reform position known as NEOLOGY was adopted, and it has remained until today.

Reform in the United States   In the meantime, Reform Judaism had become extremely popular in the United States. The constitution already included the separation of church and state and freedom of religion. When German-Jewish immigrants began to arrive in the United States, the movement began to spread. The Reform congregations of Har Sinai in Baltimore (1842) and Temple Emanuel in New York (1845) were established. In 1846 Isaac Meyer WISE arrived from Bohemia. He wanted to establish a rabbinical seminary, authorize a single American PRAYER BOOK, and unify the different customs of Jews who had arrived from different parts of Europe. In 1855 he gained the support of a conference of rabbis that met in Cleveland to work towards a form of Judaism suited to American Jews. German-trained rabbis, such as David EINHORN (1809–1879) were opposed to his activities. They believed that Reform, as a movement, should come first.

Wise produced his prayer book, *Minhag America* ("American Rite"), a modified version of the Orthodox prayer book, and Einhorn produced his *Olat Tamid* ("Perpetual Offering"), which was mostly in German with a few Hebrew paragraphs.

In 1875, Hebrew Union College was opened, with Wise as president. He hoped that it would train rabbis from all sectors of the American Jewish community. Non-kosher food was served at the banquet celebrating the first ordination (1883), after which many of the more traditional Jews withdrew their support. Two years later, Wise was president of a rabbinical conference at Pittsburgh, where it was decided that the laws of Moses (TORAH) were no longer binding and that the views and habits of modern civilization were part of spirituality. This was the breaking point between the Reform movement and the more traditional communities.

The Pittsburgh Platform was accepted as the position of American Reform Judaism. It rejected the whole idea of personal worship and concentrated on the weekly public service in which the rabbi's sermon was an essential part. A Sunday school was enough for religious education.

In 1937, the position of the Columbus Platform was adopted by the Central Conference of American Rabbis. The Reform movement's new position was that "Judaism is the historical religious experience of the Jewish people ... Judaism is the soul of which Israel is the body ..." It began to support the idea of creating a Jewish homeland in the Land of Israel.

Reform continued to develop in other parts of the world, on a smaller scale. After World War II, Reform leaders realized that the movement had not responded to the challenges facing it. They began to make changes in the program of the Union of American Hebrew Congregations. They moved the headquarters from Cincinnati to New York and began to take an interest in matters of social action.

The years between 1940 and 1980 saw a huge leap in the number of Reform congregations and rabbis. Hebrew Union College opened branches in New York, Los Angeles, and Jerusalem. In the year 2001, the Reform movement could boast 900 congregations, and over 40% of America's synagogue-going Jews belonged to a Reform synagogue.

Today, there are Reform congregations in communities throughout the world. In 1970, the World Union moved its headquarters to Jerusalem. Reform Judaism has had to wage a constant struggle to gain a foothold in Israel, where it is not recognized by the Orthodox CHIEF RABBINATE. Its institutions include 15 congregations, two kibbutzim, and several kindergartens throughout the country.

REJOICING OF THE LAW   See SIMHAT TORAH

REMNANT OF ISRAEL   (Heb. *she'erit yisrael*). The idea that after the mass punishment of the Jewish people for their sins sometime in the future, a faithful few will survive to maintain the COVENANT of God with His people. This remnant would return from exile and then live in security and peace. The idea of the righteous remnant is hinted at in Leviticus 26:36–45, but is developed fully in the prophets. Isaiah speaks to the "remnant of the House of Israel" (46:3) and even named his son *Shear-Jashub*, which means a "remnant shall return" (7:3). The idea appears in Jeremiah (31:6–7), Ezekiel (11:13), and Micah (5:5–7). It seems that the Jews returning from the Babylonian

Exile saw themselves as the righteous remnant (see Hag. 1:12–14; Ezra 9:8; Neh. 1:2–3).

RENDING OF GARMENTS   (Heb. *keri'ah*). The MOURNING ritual in which close relatives of the person who died tear their clothing. The practice comes from a statement by God to AARON and his surviving sons after the death of his other sons, Nadab and Abihu. Leviticus 10:6 states: "Do not uncover your heads; do not rend your clothes ..." The rabbis ruled that if the High Priest had to be specifically told not to tear his garments, this means that other Jews must do so. According to Jewish law, one tears one's clothing at the death of a father, mother, brother, sister, son, daughter, and spouse (*Shab.* 105b). The tear is usually made in the mourner's shirt, near the shoulder. In the Bible, a number of figures tear their garments as a sign of mourning, including ELISHA for ELIJAH and JACOB for his son JOSEPH, whom he thought was killed by a wild animal.

MAIMONIDES mentions other occasions when garments are torn. These include the death of one's teacher of TORAH, the NASI (patriarch), or the head of the law court; seeing a burnt SCROLL OF THE LAW; seeing Jerusalem and the cities of Judah in their destruction; and seeing the site of the destroyed TEMPLE. The BENEDICTION said when the clothing is torn is: "Blessed is the Judge of truth."

REPENTANCE   (Heb. *teshuvah*). The belief that God accepts the repentance of sinners is central to Judaism. The sages refer to two types of repentance: repentance out of fear of punishment for one's sins and repentance out of a deep love of God. Repentance of the first kind causes all sins committed on purpose to be viewed as sins committed through oversight or ignorance. Repentance out of love for God goes further: it changes even sins committed on purpose into merits.

The word *teshuvah*, repentance, comes from the Hebrew word for "return." When the Bible says (Deut. 4:30), "When you return to the Lord your God," the sages understood this to mean repentance. This idea is developed in the PROPHETS, who preach constantly about the need to return to God, to turn away from evil, and to act righteously (see Isa. 44:22; Mal. 3:7; Ezek. 33:11).

The theme of repentance appears frequently in Jewish life. Ten days are set aside each year – the TEN DAYS OF REPENTANCE – especially for repenting. These days begin with ROSH HA-SHANAH and conclude with the DAY OF ATONEMENT, and include the days in between. The Sabbath that falls during the Ten Days of Penitence is called *Shabbat Shuvah*, or the Sabbath of Repentance. Traditionally, whenever a disaster befalls the Jewish community, it is a cause for soul-searching and repentance. If there is a drought, a fast day may be declared (see FASTING) with the goal of moving the people to repent. In fact, all the fast days of the Hebrew calendar are meant to cause people to think about their actions – not merely to avoid eating and drinking. In addition, repentance is the theme of the fifth blessing of the AMIDAH ("Forgive us ... for we have sinned"), which is recited three times daily.

How do the rabbis define repentance? In any sin between human beings, the person must show regret for the misdeed and make good. In every crime, whether between human beings or between humans and God, the person must confess the sin and express regret before God. Finally, one must resolve never to repeat the sin. The mark of complete repentance is when someone has the means and opportunity to commit the same sin as before, but this time acts properly.

See also ATONEMENT; CONFESSION.

RESH LAKISH   See SIMEON BEN LAKISH

RESPECT FOR PARENTS AND TEACHERS   The fifth of the TEN COMMANDMENTS states: "Honor your father and your mother in order that your days may be long upon the land which the Lord your God gives to you" (Ex. 20:12). The rabbis understood that since the reward for fulfilling this commandment is great, so were its responsibilities. Honoring one's parents is in fact a COMMANDMENT that applies during their lives and after their deaths.

According to traditional Jewish law, children must honor their parents by supporting them with food and drink, clothing and shelter if they are in need, not insulting them in public, and not displaying anger towards them. A child must not sit in a parent's chair, contradict them, oppose them publicly in a debate, or call them by their first name. A married daughter should also respect her parents and do as much as she can for them, as long as it does not conflict with her husband's wishes. Even after their deaths, a child honors parents by reciting KADDISH for 11 months. Beyond this period, when speaking of a parent one should say, "May his or her memory be for a blessing" (*Kid.* 31b).

In Jewish tradition, one must also show honor and fear for one's main teacher of TORAH. The rabbis point out that even though the biological parents give one life in this world, one's teacher prepares a person for life in the world to come.

RESPONSA   (Heb. *she'elot u-teshuvot*, "questions and answers"). Written answers about issues of Jewish learning that respond to questions from colleagues and lay people or communities. This form of communication began in the period of the Talmud.

There is more to the responsa than the simple exchange of legal questions and answers. Responsa were really an attempt to preserve unified standards for Jewish practice when the nation was becoming more scattered. Local rabbis sent their halakhic (Jewish legal) questions to central, internationally recognized authorities. In this way spiritual leadership could be extended to far away communities to prevent the splintering of the Jewish world

To the present day, responsa continue to be an important source for deciding religious issues. Rabbis who offer opinions on modern issues such as organ transplants, technology, etc., consult the classical responsa for guidance (see MEDICAL ETHICS). Even during the HOLOCAUST, Jews consulted rabbis to decide the law on matters arising from conditions in the ghettos and concentration camps.

RESPONSES, LITURGICAL   Words or phrases that are said by the congregation in the synagogue as an "answer" to portions of the service that are recited by the reader. Customs vary among the different prayer styles; however, the major responses are common to all. Most of these words and phrases can be traced to the Bible. Three in particular have been used since the era of the Temple: AMEN, BARUKH SHEM KEVOD MALKHUTO LE-OLAM VA-ED, and SELAH.

The Aramaic KADDISH prayer is actually a dialogue between the reader and the other members of the congregation. The central response is: "May His great Name be praised forever and for all eternity" (see *Shab.* 119b). After the words "the Holy One, Blessed be He," Ashkenazim answer "Blessed be He" while in all other communities the congregation answers *amen*. There are many other examples of congregational responses in prayer. HALLEL, the GRACE AFTER MEALS, the READING OF THE LAW, and the PRIESTLY BLESSING all have their own special call-and-response patterns.

What makes the liturgical response such necessary part of Jewish prayer? The prayer or the blessing is really only half of the prayer experience. When the congregation answers in force, it proclaims the truth of what the reader has said. When a congregation says, e.g. *ken yehi ratson* ("May this be God's Will"), it provides the second half of the prayer experience.

RESURRECTION   The belief that the dead will come back to life – that the bodies of the dead will be reunited with their souls – at some point in the future. Not all scholars agree that the belief in resurrection was originally part of Judaism. However, certainly by the time of the Second Temple this idea had become widely accepted. Resurrection was one of the main issues that separated the PHARISEES and the SADDUCEES. The Pharisees stated that one who does not believe in the resurrection of the dead has no place in the world to come (*Sanh.* 10:1). The second prayer of the AMIDAH addresses God as "He Who resurrects the dead." MAIMONIDES included belief in the resurrection of the dead as one of his 13 PRINCIPLES OF FAITH.

Resurrection is actually combined with several ideas. Resurrection, a belief in the immortality of the soul, and a belief in the MESSIAH together create the picture of what happens to the soul after death. Generally, after the coming of the Messiah, the body is to be resurrected and combined with the soul on earth. SAADIAH GAON and other philosophers wrote about two resurrections, one for the righteous Jews and the second for all others. From medieval times on, philosophers and mystics have wondered and written about the details of these processes.

In modern times, REFORM JUDAISM and RECONSTRUCTIONISM have removed all references to the resurrection of the dead from their prayer books.

RETALIATION Leviticus 24:20 declares: "Break for break, eye for eye, tooth for tooth: as he has caused a blemish in a man, so shall it be done to him." At first glance, the law seems to be that if people cause physical injury to others, that same injury is inflicted upon them. The ORAL LAW rules that this verse is not to be taken literally. It creates instead a system of financial compensation, where a person is paid an amount of money that the court decides is equivalent to the loss. The injured party is to be compensated for several categories of losses: pain, the actual damage, medical costs, lost income, and any embarrassment that may have been caused. Within Jewish law, murder is the only case where real "eye-for-eye" retaliation applies.

RETURN TO ZION   See ZION, RETURN TO

REUBEN   See TRIBES, TWELVE

REVELATION   Term referring to the act of God showing Himself to human beings.

In the Bible   A main message of the Bible is that God wishes to be known by human beings. He therefore reveals Himself through His actions in nature and in history. God's concern for people caused Him to intervene in human history long before Israel became a nation. The stories of the FLOOD and the Tower of BABEL show the concerns of a universal God rather than a national one. He has a plan for the people of Israel and a plan for all people.

Revelation is initiated by God. In the Bible, it is not Abraham or Moses who seek out God but God who confronts these individuals with specific tasks. The important acts of God in the history of Israel are the EXODUS from Egypt, the Giving of the Law at Mount SINAI, God's caring for Israel in the Wilderness, and Israel's inheritance of the Promised Land. Each "mighty act" reveals something about the nature of God, His plan for history, and His expectations from human beings.

Throughout the Bible, God appears to people. Sometimes He appears in dreams and visions (see Gen. 15:1, 18:1, 2; Ex. 3:2; Ezek.1). Most often He speaks to human beings, whose role it is to listen and understand. The Bible states, "Man may not see My face and live" (Ex. 33:20), which limits direct physical contact. It seems that God reveals His presence to people by demonstrating His deeds. God's deeds and words are shown to human beings so that they can understand God' purposes.

In the Talmud   The Talmud uses the terms *nevu'ah* ("prophecy"), *ru'ah ha-kodesh* (HOLY SPIRIT), or "coming to rest of the SHEKHINAH" ("God's Presence") for revelation. The rabbis maintained that God reveals Himself directly to those who have developed certain spiritual qualities (see *Shab.* 92a). The Talmud notes that prophecy ceased with the destruction of the First Temple, and that "with the death of Haggai, Zechariah, and Malachi the Holy Spirit departed from Israel" (*Sanh.* 11a; *BB* 12a).

During the Middle Ages   Medieval Jewish philosophers argued that God's revelation to the Jews was superior to the claims of other religions. SAADIAH GAON, MAIMONIDES, and JUDAH HALEVI all cite as proof the fact that the revelation at Sinai took place before the entire nation, while other religions have claimed that God appeared to individuals.

The philosophers of this era tried to understand the special contribution of revelation to Jewish life. What is the purpose of revelation, they asked, if human reason could discover these truths on its own? Saadiah Gaon suggested that revelation provides man with important truths at the beginning of their lives and helps them to avoid the possibility of error. Judah Halevi argued that the goal of Judaism is not knowledge of God but life with God in a highly emotional communion. Human intellect is not enough – man must rely on God to initiate communication with him.

In Modern Jewish Thought   In the modern era, movements and individual thinkers have questioned whether or not God actually speaks to people. The liberal American movements have rejected supernatural communication outright. Martin BUBER and Franz ROSENZWEIG, two modern Jewish philosophers, accept the idea of Divine revelation but challenge the traditional view of its specific content. Abraham Joshua HESCHEL focuses on the consequences of belief in revelation: the meaning of revelation for the religious Jew is the ability to see the Bible as a reflection of the will of God and as relevant to their lives (*God in Search of Man*, sect. 11).

REWARD AND PUNISHMENT   The belief that God will reward the righteous and punish the wicked. The Bible describes God as a moral being Who rules according to principles of JUSTICE. Justice applies to individuals and to nations.

As part of a COVENANT with God, the Jewish people are promised the Land of ISRAEL and prosperity in exchange for following God's laws. They are also threatened with punishment for disobedience (see Deut. 11:13–21). There are also promises of rewards for the performance of individual positive COMMANDMENTS (see Ex. 20:12; Deut. 15:10). Most importantly, the theme of reward and punishment forms part of the basic layer of Jewish religion.

The PROPHETS question the nature of Divine justice in the world. JEREMIAH (12:1) asks: "Why does the way of the wicked prosper?" HABAKKUK states: "For the wicked beset the righteous, therefore judgment emerges perverted" (see 1:2–4). The problem that the righteous suffer is taken up in ECCLESIASTES, PSALMS, and most dramatically in the Book of JOB. These are reactions to what looks like the failure of the principle of reward and punishment.

On the national level, the prophets must explain why Israel's punishment seems to be more severe than the punishment of other nations. Amos answers: "You alone have I known of all the families of the earth; therefore I will visit upon you all of your iniquities" (3:2). Thus, because God has a special relationship with Israel He expects more from His nation. Job offers another explanation: suffering is not necessarily a punishment – it is sometimes a test (see Job 38–41). The test is really for the benefit of the individual, although often in mysterious ways. Job concludes with the idea that man cannot always understand the Divine plan, yet the plan is just.

In Rabbinic Literature The rabbis added a new element to the concept of reward and punishment. They taught that the real arena for Divine justice is in the AFTERLIFE. Two ideas led the rabbis to this conclusion. First, the Bible's promise of material rewards for the performance of the commandments does not seem to come true in this world. Secondly, the rabbis interpreted the biblical promise "that your days may be long" (Ex. 20:12) to refer to the eternal life of the SOUL in the afterlife. The concept of a "two-stage" human existence – "This World" and the "World to Come" – helped to deal with the problem of "the righteous who suffer and the wicked who prosper." The rabbis also developed the idea of "afflictions of love" (*Ber.* 5a), i.e., that suffering is an opportunity for spiritual growth.

For the rabbis, material reward was not a proper motivation for the worship of God. They stated: "Be not like the servants who serve a master for the sake of a reward, but like servants who serve the master without thought of reward, and fear God" (*Avot* 1:3).

Another related idea that appears in the Talmud is RESURRECTION of the dead, which, according to one view (*Ta'an* 7a) will be granted only to the righteous. What happens to everyone else? Some suffer punishment in *gehenom* ("Hell"; see *Er.* 19a) for 12 months. However, some believe that the punishment is eternal for the unrepentant wicked (*RH* 16b).

In Medieval Jewish Thought The medieval philosophers tried to describe all the issues of reward and punishment in a single clear system. According to SAADIAH GAON, after death, the souls of the righteous and the wicked are kept in separate "places" until the resurrection of the dead. The resurrection will take place after the REDEMPTION and the coming of the MESSIAH, which come before the sorting out of the truly righteous and wicked of the Jewish people. Once the body and soul are re-united, judgment will take place. The World to Come follows this judgment and consists of a "new heaven and new earth." At this time, the righteous enjoy eternal happiness and the unrepentant wicked suffer eternal punishment. NAHMANIDES describes a similar chain of events.

MAIMONIDES takes a different approach. He holds that only the rational soul – man's capacity for reason – can be immortal. Therefore, the ultimate "reward" for the individual is a completely spiritual existence in the presence of God. This is the "World to Come." The ultimate punishment of the wicked is the failure to achieve this state.

Almost all of the medieval thinkers believed in the idea of natural rewards and punishments. The rabbis taught: "The reward of a MITZVAH is the *mitzvah*" (*Avot* 4:2). Reward and punishment are the outgrowth of the actual deeds themselves.

In Modern Thought The principle of reward and punishment has been intensely studied and challenged in the years since the HOLOCAUST and the establishment of the State of Israel. There are those who see the rise of the State of Israel as the "beginning of Redemption" and the fulfillment of biblical prophecy. Age-old questions about the suffering of the righteous and the degree of suffering inflicted on the Jews are currently being reexamined

RIGHTEOUSNESS (Heb. *tsedakah* or *tsedek*). The value of JUSTICE and right. Righteousness as justice is one of God's qualities. The Bible describes Him as "a God of faithfulness, and without iniquity, righteous and right is He" (Deut. 16:20). In the Bible, righteousness means following moral teachings. By the time of the PROPHETS, righteousness took on the added meaning of ethical behavior (see ETHICS). The later books of the Bible see the future perfect world as one of "righteousness" (see AFTERLIFE).

For the rabbis, the quality of righteousness means even more than following the COMMANDMENTS. It involves extremely devoted religious behavior, expressed in acts of CHARITY.

RISHONIM (lit. "early" or "former" ones; as opposed to AHARONIM). The term generally refers to the great Talmud scholars who lived between the end of the geonic period (11th cent. CE) and the publication of the SHULHAN ARUKH by Joseph CARO in 1564–5. The commentaries of the *rishonim* are very important for the study of the Talmud in a classical YESHIVAH.

RISHON LE-TSIYYON ("First in Zion"). Title given to the Sephardi Chief Rabbi of Israel. The term dates from the 17th century, when the title belonged to the leading Sephardi rabbi in Jerusalem.

RITUAL BATH See MIKVEH

RITUAL SLAUGHTER See SHEHITAH

ROSENZWEIG, FRANZ (1886–1929). German Jewish philosopher. He was born in Kassel into an assimilated family. Several members of his family converted to Christianity. Eugen Rosenstock-Huessy, a relative, had a profound influence on Rosenzweig, and almost convinced him to convert. However, Rosenzweig changed his mind after attending DAY OF ATONEMENT services in an Orthodox house of prayer. He recognized that he had no need to seek God in CHRISTIANITY, since he had already found Him in Judaism.

After his decision to remain loyal to Judaism, Rosenzweig devoted all his intellectual efforts to Jewish and religious studies, teaching, and writing. He came under the influence of Hermann COHEN and Martin BUBER. In 1920, he helped found the *Freies Judisches Lehrhaus* (Free Jewish House of Learning) in Frankfurt. This institution became one of the most important centers for Jewish studies. It attracted the most distinguished Jewish scholars in Germany.

The Star of Redemption was Rosenzweig's major philosophical work. He developed a system based on three elements of existence: God, the Universe, and Humanity. Each of them is interrelated through the processes of CREATION, REVELATION, and REDEMPTION. For Rosenzweig, the Bible is not the last word in a one-time revelation. Revelation is the ongoing process of God's identifying Himself to the individual who is seeking.

Rosenzweig's other works include a translation into German of JUDAH HALEVI's liturgical poems and his joint translation of the Bible into German with Martin Buber. They reached the Book of ISAIAH before Rosenzweig's death and the project was completed by Buber.

ROSH HA-SHANAH   The Jewish New Year; observed on the 1st and 2nd of TISHRI (September/October) in both Israel and the Diaspora. It marks the beginning of the TEN DAYS OF REPENTANCE. In the Bible, this festival has three names: *Shabbaton*, a day of "solemn rest" to be observed on the 1st of the seventh month; *Zikhron Teru'ah*, "a memorial [proclaimed] with the blast of the SHOFAR" (Lev. 23:24); and *Yom Teru'ah*, "a day of blowing the *shofar*" (Num. 29:1). Later, the rabbis gave the festival two additional names: *Yom ha-Din*, the DAY OF JUDGMENT, and *Yom ha-Zikkaron*, "the Day of Remembrance," when God remembers His creatures.

The name "Judgment Day" stresses that the New Year is an occasion for self-examination. Each person stands symbolically before the throne of God. God enters the decision about the person's fate for the coming year in one of three ledgers: the BOOK OF LIFE, the Book of Death, and a third book for those whose fate hangs in the balance until the DAY OF ATONEMENT.

Rosh ha-Shanah customs reflect the seriousness of the day. Worshipers wear white and the synagogue is decorated in white. On both days of Rosh ha-Shanah, except when the first coincides with a Sabbath, the blowing of the *shofar* is the high point of the service. The *shofar* blasts serve as a rousing call to REPENTANCE (see Maimonides, *Yad, Teshuvah* 3:4). The prayer service is chanted to traditional High Holiday melodies. During the ALEINU LE-SHABBE'AH prayer, worshipers kneel and prostrate themselves. Special prayers that make up the service deal with the theme of judgment and the idea that "Repentance, PRAYER, and CHARITY" can avert God's harsh decree. Worshipers bless each other with the greeting: "May you be inscribed for a good year."

Customs in the home include dipping the special CHALLAH bread of the festival in honey rather than salt. It is also customary to dip pieces of apple in honey, and to eat after reciting a prayer for a "good and sweet year." The challah for Rosh ha-Shanah is usually baked into round loaves, to signify hopes for a "good, complete year."

ROSH HA-SHANAH   ("New Year"). Eighth tractate (book) of the Order of MO'ED in the Mishnah. Its four chapters deal with the laws for fixing the new month and laws about blowing the SHOFAR on ROSH HA-SHANAH. It also deal with differences between the celebration of the New Year during and after the Temple period.

ROSH HODESH   See MOON

RU'AH HA-KODESH   See HOLY SPIRIT

RUTH, BOOK OF   Biblical book in the HAGIOGRAPHA ("Writings") section of the Bible. It tells the story of Ruth, from whom King DAVID was descended. The book contains 85 verses, divided into four chapters. It is one of the FIVE SCROLLS read in the synagogue on special days. Ruth is read on the festival of SHAVU'OT.

The story of Ruth has three main characters: Naomi; her Moabite daughter-in-law Ruth, whose husband has died; and Boaz, Naomi's kinsman, who eventually marries Ruth. Naomi, with her husband Elimelech and two sons, moves to Moab because of famine in Canaan. All three men die, leaving Naomi and her two Moabite daughters-in-law without support. Naomi decides to return home and asks her daughters-in-law to remain in their own land. Ruth insists on accompanying Naomi. She says: "Your people shall be my people, and your God my God." On their return, Ruth goes to glean leftover grain in the fields of Boaz (see LEKET, SHIKHEHAH, PE'AH). Boaz sees Ruth and later marries her in keeping with the law of the LEVIRATE MARRIAGE.

According to rabbinic tradition, the Book of Ruth was written by the SAMUEL the Prophet (*BB* 14b).

BOOK OF RUTH	
1:1–1:5	Elimelech's family goes to Moab; his two sons marry Moabite women; the three men die
1:5–1:22	Ruth insists on returning with her mother-in-law, Naomi, to Bethlehem.
2:1–2:23	Ruth gleans in the fields of Boaz.
3:1–3:18	Following Naomi's advice, Ruth claims kinship with Boaz.
4:1–4:12	Boaz gets the next-of-kin to renounce his duties.
4:13–4:22	Boaz marries Ruth and their descendant is David.

RUTH RABBAH   A MIDRASH on the Book of RUTH. Almost all the material is drawn from the Jerusalem Talmud, GENESIS RABBAH, LAMENTATIONS RABBAH, and LEVITICUS RABBAH. The Midrash begins with an ancient message that states that whenever the phrase "and it came to pass" appears, it indicates sorrow for Israel. A list of many cases in which the phrase occurs follows, accompanied by an explanation of the sorrow connected to it.

SAADIAH GAON (882–942). Outstanding scholar of the geonic period and communal leader. R. Saadiah was born in Upper Egypt, but moved to Erets Israel as a young man. He settled in Tiberias, which was then the center for *masorah* (Bible text) studies. From there he moved to Babylonia and was given the title of *Aluf* (Prince), because of his achievements in Jewish learning.

Both in Erets Israel and in Babylonia, Saadiah found himself embroiled in controversy. In Israel, he argued publicly with the Palestinian *Gaon*, Aaron ben Meir, over who had the right to set the Jewish CALENDAR each month. Control over the calendar had long been the responsibility of the Babylonian academies, and Saadiah tried to keep it that way. In the end he succeeded, and Babylonian rabbis continued to set the calendar. In Babylonia, he clashed with the EXILARCH, David ben Zakkai. The Exilarch put Saadiah under a ban and removed him as *Gaon* of Sura. Saadiah responded with a counter-ban on Ben Zakkai. For seven years Babylonian Jewry was divided until the dispute was settled.

Saadiah continued writing scholarly books, despite the controversy. He produced major works on the grammar of the Bible, a list and explanation of words that appear only once in the Bible, and a Hebrew rhyming dictionary (*Sefer ha-Agron*). He is responsible for commentaries on a number of books of the Bible as well as an Arabic translation of the Bible that is still in use today. His edition of the PRAYER BOOK includes laws, customs, and a number of original prayers. He is also the author of philosophical works, including *Sefer ha-Emunot ve-ha-De'ot* ("The Book of Beliefs and Opinions"), which started medieval Jewish philosphy, offering rational arguments for the truth of Judaism. This book argues persuasively against the KARAITES, who challenged mainstream Judaism. Only one halakhic work, the *Book of Documents*, has survived intact.

MAIMONIDES said of Saadiah Gaon: "If it were not for Saadiah, the Torah could well have disappeared from among the Jewish people."

SABBATH (Heb. *Shabbat*). The seventh day of the week; the day of rest. The Sabbath is one of the central features of Judaism. The Bible itself gives the reasons for the Sabbath: it reminds us of the CREATION (Gen. 1; Ex. 20); it offers an op-

portunity for servants to rest (Deut. 5); and it serves as a sign of the COVENANT of God with the people of Israel and a reminder that He made them holy (Ex. 31). Deuteronomy 5 also connects the EXODUS to the Sabbath. It is the only holy day mentioned in the TEN COMMANDMENTS.

In the Bible From the first week of creation, the Sabbath has been part of biblical religion. Genesis 2:1–3 reports that God completed His work and "rested on the seventh day." While the Bible does not specifically mention that the PATRIARCHS observed the Sabbath, the sages claim that they did (see Gen. R. 11:17, 64:4). For the rabbis, it was unthinkable that something so basic as the Sabbath would have been ignored by the founding fathers of Judaism. Later, in the travels of the Israelites through the wilderness, they were commanded to collect an extra portion of MANNA on the sixth day, because "tomorrow is a day of rest, a holy Sabbath of the Lord" (Ex. 16:23).

The commandment to observe the Sabbath for all times is part of the Ten Commandments. Exodus 20:8–11 reads: "Remember the Sabbath day and keep it holy. Six days you shall labor and do all your work, but the seventh day is a Sabbath of the Lord your God: you shall not do any work, you, your son or daughter, your male or female slave, or your cattle, or the stranger who is within your settlements. For in six days the Lord made heaven and earth and sea, and all that is in them, and he rested on the seventh day; therefore the Lord blessed the Sabbath day and made it holy."

The Sabbath is also a covenant between Israel and God. Exodus 31:13–17 reads: "Keep My Sabbaths, for this is a sign between Me and you throughout the generations, that you may know that I … have made you holy … a covenant for all time: it shall be a sign for all time between Me and the people of Israel."

The Bible records one instance of the death penalty for breaking the Sabbath, in Numbers 15:32–36. In general, a person who violated the Sabbath accidentally had to bring a sacrifice. The book of NEHEMIAH (Neh. 10; 13:15–22) mentions specific efforts to strengthen the observance of the Sabbath, including limiting business on the holy day.

The men of the GREAT ASSEMBLY and the SCRIBES called for strict observance of the Sabbath. The residents of Jerusalem would not defend themselves on the Sabbath when attacked by

Mother and daughter blessing the candles on the eve of the Sabbath.

which served as a "fence around the law." For example, a tailor may not go out just before sunset on Friday carrying a needle, lest he forget about it and carry it on the Sabbath (*Shab.* 1:3). Certain things should not even be touched on the Sabbath (see MUKTSEH), since actually using them is forbidden.

Observances that Override Sabbath Laws   Witnesses of the New MOON, who had to travel to inform the Sanhedrin or BET DIN of what they saw, were allowed to do so on the Sabbath. CIRCUMCISION is performed on the Sabbath and all the required preparations are permitted; dangerous animals may be killed; one may fight in self-defense; anything necessary to save someone's life may be done (see PIKKU'AH NEFESH) as well as any action to assist a woman in childbirth. R. AKIVA established this guideline: whatever can be done before the Sabbath may not be performed on the Sabbath (*Pes.* 66b).

The Sabbath Day   The Sabbath is to be a day of joy: relaxation, spiritual activities, and a change of pace from workdays. In the home, the family shares festive meals and time is devoted to study and rest. It is a tradition to host guests.

The Sabbath begins on Friday at sunset. Approximately 20 minutes before sunset, the woman of the house traditionally lights the Sabbath candles. She recites the blessing: "…Who has hallowed us by Your commandments, and commanded us to kindle the Sabbath light." In some families, one candle is lit for each member. The kabbalists (Jewish mystics) lit seven candles, one for each day of the week.

Kabbalat Shabbat   ("welcoming the Sabbath"). This is the service that comes before the Friday EVENING SERVICE. It takes place at twilight, generally not later than half an hour after sunset. *Kabbalat Shabbat* dates back to the 16th century mystics of Safed, who would go out to the fields on Friday afternoon to "greet the Sabbath Queen." This practice in turn recalls the custom of R. Hanina, who would ready himself for the Sabbath and stand outside at sunset, calling "Come let us go forth to welcome the Sabbath Queen." R. Yannai had a similar custom, though he would say: "Come, Bride! Come, Bride!" (*Shab.* 119a). This theme inspired the LEKHAH DODI hymn that is the central prayer of *Kabbalat Shabbat*.

Evening Service   A special AMIDAH is recited on Sabbath eve, followed by Genesis 2:1–4. The reader then repeats the *Amidah* in a short form: the *Magen Avot* prayer. When a Sabbath falls on a FESTIVAL, the festival *Amidah* is recited, with additions that refer to the Sabbath.

Sabbath Evening in the Home   In the late afternoon, the table is prepared for the festive Sabbath meal. In traditional homes, the father blesses the children when he returns from the synagogue. He places both hands on the head of each child in turn. To boys, he says: "May God make you like Ephraim and Manasseh" (see TRIBES, TWELVE). To girls, he says: "May God make you like SARAH, REBEKAH, RACHEL, and LEAH." He then adds the PRIESTLY BLESSING.

The family then sings *Shalom Aleikhem*. This hymn welcomes the Sabbath angels who, according to the Talmud, accompany the worshiper home from the synagogue (*Shab.* 119b). They then

Ptolemy I. Some 150 years later, however, during the Maccabean wars, Mattathias, the Hasmonean, ruled that the laws of the Sabbath could be transgressed to save lives. Therefore, the Jews could defend themselves on the Sabbath (1 Macc. 2:20–41). After the SANHEDRIN began to operate, many details of Sabbath practices became an important part of the HALAKHAH (Jewish law). These rabbinic laws became the touchstone for all further development of Sabbath laws until modern times.

Work Forbidden on the Sabbath   The basic feature of the Sabbath is not doing "work." The Bible specifically mentions only a few specific types of prohibited work: lighting a fire, plowing, and harvesting. Exodus 16:19 prohibits carrying things from one domain to another.

The early rabbis developed 39 main categories of prohibited work from the activities involved in building the SANCTUARY (see Mish. *Shab.* 7). They called each category heading an *av melakhah* (lit. "father of work"). The rabbis broadened these categories to include secondary types of work. For example, a secondary level of harvesting would be to cut flowers or pick fruit. These sub-categories were to be observed as strictly as the main category.

The rabbis made further rulings called *gezerot*, or decrees, sing Proverbs 31:10–31, the verses of ESHET HAYIL that praise the righteous woman.

The KIDDUSH prayer is recited, followed by the washing of the hands and the blessing over the Sabbath CHALLAH bread. Two loaves are used, to symbolize the double portion of MANNA that was gathered on Fridays when the Israelites wandered in the desert. The singing of table hymns (ZEMIROT) and the GRACE AFTER MEALS follow the meal.

Sabbath Morning   The prayers consist of the special MORNING SERVICE, the READING OF THE LAW, a selection from the PROPHETS, and the ADDITIONAL SERVICE.

On returning home, a festive Sabbath lunch is eaten: the morning *Kiddush* and the blessing over the bread are recited. The meal follows the pattern of the evening meal from the night before.

Afternoon Service   The Sabbath AFTERNOON SERVICE is special in that there is a Reading of the Law before the *Amidah*. It is customary to eat a third Sabbath meal known as SE'UDAH SHELISHIT after this service. This is a lighter meal and one does not say the *Kiddush* prayer. It is accompanied by the singing of *zemirot*. The meal takes place late in the afternoon and usually ends just in time for the Evening Service.

End of the Sabbath   The Evening Service is held well after sunset. When worshipers return home, they recite HAVDALAH. *Havdalah* is the ceremony that marks the passage from the holiness of the Sabbath day to the days of the workweek. Like the *Kiddush*, it is recited over wine.

In Today's World   All streams in Judaism have stressed the centrality of the Sabbath. Exactly what this means and how much of traditional observance is maintained varies with each movement. (See CONSERVATIVE JUDAISM, ORTHODOXY, RECONSTRUCTIONISM, and REFORM JUDAISM.)

SABBATHS, SPECIAL   During the course of the year, certain Sabbaths are special because they have unique Bible, HAFTARAH (reading from the PROPHETS), and prayer readings. Some Sabbaths are considered special because of when they occur in the Jewish religious CALENDAR.

Shabbat Mevarekhim   ("Sabbath of Blessing [the New MOON]"). It takes its name from the prayer for a good month that is recited after the READING OF THE LAW. *Shabbat Mevarekhim* is celebrated when the New Moon occurs during the following week.

Shabbat Mahar Hodesh   ("Sabbath [when] tomorrow [begins the] month") This is the name given to a Sabbath that falls on the eve of the New Moon (cf. 1 Sam. 20:18). Its name comes from the special *haftarah* that is read, 1 Sam. 20:18–42, on this Sabbath. The *haftarah* describes the agreement that Jonathan and DAVID made on the eve of the New Moon (*Rosh Hodesh*).

Shabbat Rosh Hodesh   ("Sabbath [of the] new month") This is the name given to a Sabbath that falls on the New Moon. A special additional reading, Num. 28:9–15, is added to the weekly Torah reading. The *haftarah* is Isaiah 66:1–24, which concludes with a repetition of the final verse.

Shabbat Shuvah   ("Sabbath of Return"). This is the Sabbath that occurs just before the DAY OF ATONEMENT, i.e. the Sabbath that falls during the TEN DAYS OF REPENTANCE. It takes its name from the opening word of the special *haftarah*, "Return, O Israel, to the Lord your God." The *haftarah* is Hos. 14:2–10; Joel 2:15–27 (Ashkenazim) or Hos. 14:2–10; Mic. 7:18–20 (SEPHARDIM). ASHKENAZIM in the Diaspora read Mic. 7:18–20 before the passage from Joel. The community rabbi usually speaks about the importance of REPENTANCE.

Shabbat Hol ha-Mo'ed Sukkot   This is the Sabbath that falls during the intermediate days (HOL HA-MO'ED) of the SUKKOT festival. Following the Morning Service, the Book of ECCLESIASTES is read. The Torah reading is Ex. 33:12–34:26; a selection from Num. 29 is read as the additional reading.

Shabbat be-Reshit   ("Sabbath of Genesis") This is the first Sabbath after the SIMHAT TORAH festival. It takes its name from the Bible reading for that Sabbath, which is the first portion in the annual cycle of readings. Among those called to the Torah on this Sabbath is the *Hatan be-Reshit* ("Bridegroom of Genesis"). Each year the congregation selects a *Hatan be-Reshit* on Simhat Torah, who is then called to the Torah on *Shabbat be-Reshit*. Usually, he provides a festive meal for the congregation.

Shabbat Hanukkah   This is the name given to the Sabbath that falls during the HANUKKAH festival. (Two may occur, when the first and eighth days of Hanukkah fall on the Sabbath). The Torah reading consists of the weekly portion and Num. 7:1–17. If the Sabbath also falls on the eighth day of Hanukkah, the weekly portion is Gen. 41:1–44:17 and Num. 7:54–8:4. If *Shabbat Hanukkah* coincides with the New Moon, Num. 28:9–15 is also read from a second scroll. The *haftarah* is Zech. 2:14–4:7 (for a second Sabbath, 1 Kings 7:40–50); if a New Moon, Isa. 66:1–24 is substituted.

Shabbat Shirah   ("Sabbath of the Song [at the Sea]") This is the name given to the Sabbath when the Torah portion of *Be-Shallah* is read. This portion includes the song that Moses and the Israelites sang after they crossed the Red Sea (Ex. 15:1–18). The actual ritual surrounding the reading of the Song at the Sea varies from community to community.

The *Arba Parashiyyot* ("Four Portions") are read on four special Sabbaths, two before PURIM and two after it. Each of these Sabbaths has a special additional Torah reading that is read from a separate scroll.

Shabbat Shekalim   ("Sabbath of the Shekel Tax") This Sabbath comes just before or on the New Moon of the month of Adar (Adar II in a leap year). The Mishnah (*Shab.* 1:1) states: "On the first day of Adar they gave warning of the shekel dues" which had to be paid before the first day of Nisan. The additional reading (Ex. 30:11–16) describes the half-shekel tax, which in TEMPLE times went to the upkeep of the SANCTUARY. The *haftarah* is II Kings 12:1–17 (Ashkenazim) or II Kings 11:17–12:17 (Sephardim).

Shabbat Zakhor   ("Sabbath of Remembrance") This Sabbath comes immediately before Purim. The additional reading (Deut.

25:17–19) gives the commandment to "remember what Amalek did to you" (i.e., a cowardly attack on Israel's weak and unprotected rear in the Wilderness). Haman, the arch villain of the Purim story, was a descendant of Amalek. The *haftarah* is 1 Sam. 15:2–34; Sephardim begin one verse earlier.

Shabbat Parah   ("Sabbath of the [Red] Heifer") This Sabbath comes before *Shabbat ha-Hodesh* (see below). The additional reading (Num. 19:1–22) deals with the RED HEIFER, whose ashes were used for ritual PURITY. In Temple times, as PASSOVER drew near, anyone not in a state of ritual purity had to be cleansed in order to offer the Passover sacrifice. The *haftarah* is Ezek. 36:16–38 (Ashkenazim) or Ezek. 36:16–36 (Sephardim).

Shabbat ha-Hodesh   ("Sabbath of the Month") This Sabbath comes before or on the New Moon of Nisan, the month in which Passover occurs. The name derives from the opening line of the additional reading: "This month shall mark for you the beginning of the months." The additional Torah reading (Ex. 12:1–20) is about the laws of Passover. The *haftarah* is Ezek. 45:16–46:18 (Ashkenazim) or Ezek. 45:18–46:15 (Sephardim).

Shabbat ha-Gadol   ("Great Sabbath") This Sabbath comes immediately before Passover. It has no special additional reading. The *haftarah* (Mal. 3:4–24) mentions Elijah the prophet, who is supposed to announce the Messiah. According to tradition, the Messiah will bring REDEMPTION in the month of Nisan, the same month as the EXODUS from Egypt (*RH* 11a). The community rabbi usually speaks on the theme of Passover and preparations for the holiday.

Shabbat Hol ha-Mo'ed Pesah   This is the Sabbath that occurs during the intermediate days of the Passover festival. Following the Morning Service, the SONG OF SONGS is read from the Bible. The Torah reading is Ex. 33:12–34:26; a selection from Num. 28:19–25 is the additional reading. The *haftarah* is Ezek. 37:1–14.

Shabbat Hazon   ("Sabbath of Visions") This Sabbath comes just before TISHAH BE-AV (Ninth of Av), during a mourning period in the Jewish year. Its name comes from the *haftarah* that speaks of Isaiah's prophecy about the punishments that will come to the sinful Israelites. The *haftarah* (Isa. 1:1–27) is sung to the special, sad melody of LAMENTATIONS. Many Ashkenazim sing LEKHAH DODI to the mournful tune of ELI TSIYYON on Friday night.

Shabbat Nahamu   ("Sabbath of Comfort") This Sabbath comes immediately after the Ninth of Av. The *haftarah* (Isa. 40:1–26) presents the prophet's message of comfort to the people and the promise of Israel's final redemption.

SABBATICAL YEAR   (Heb. *shemittah*). Seventh year of rest for the land. The Bible declares that every seventh year is "a Sabbath of the Lord" (Lev. 25:1–7, 18–22). During this year the soil of Erets Israel must rest and lie fallow. Farmers are forbidden to plant, sow, prune, or plow. They have to rely on the bounty of God to provide them with a threefold harvest in the sixth year to cover them until the harvest of the eighth year becomes available (Lev. 25:22). Produce that grows in the seventh year

becomes the common property of all – rich and poor, stranger and slave. When all have helped themselves to their fill, what remains is left for domestic and wild animals. In addition, all debts are canceled in that year (see Deut. 15:1–11).

The Sabbatical year forms part of a 50-year cycle (Lev. 25:8–17) that ends with the JUBILEE year. In the 50th year, all land was returned to its original owners and Hebrew slaves were released (Ex. 21:1–6). Following the return from the Babylonian EXILE, it appears that the Jubilee was no longer observed. It was seen as binding only when the majority of the Jewish people were settled in Erets Israel on their tribal lands. The Sabbatical year, by contrast, continued to be an important feature of life in the land.

Over the centuries, changes were made in the observance of the Sabbatical year. HILLEL enacted the PROSBUL, which dealt with the problem of people not wanting to lend money as the Sabbatical year approached. He allowed lenders to sign their debts over to the courts, so the debt did not have to be canceled. Alexander the Great and other kind rulers put aside the royal tax during the Sabbatical year. After the destruction of the TEMPLE, rabbinic authorities relaxed Sabbatical year observances when hostile rulers threatened to punish those who could not pay their tax during these years.

In the modern period, the religious Zionist Mizrachi movement in Erets Israel struggled with the hardships of the *shemittah* year in impoverished new farm communities. Its rabbis created a legal fiction called the *hetter mekhirah* ("leniency of selling"), which involved selling farmlands to a non-Jew during the Sabbatical year. This allowed them to cultivate the lands "so as not to endanger the whole Zionist enterprise." Many opposed this legal maneuver. However, today Israel's Ministry of Religious Affairs relies on this device and arranges the ritual sale of lands to a non-Jew.

The Sabbatical year runs from one ROSH HA-SHANAH to the next.

SACRIFICES AND OFFERINGS   The first sacrifices mentioned in the Bible were brought by CAIN AND ABEL. In the Book of GENESIS, NOAH and all the PATRIARCHS offered sacrifices, and the EXODUS from Egypt was accompanied by the sacrifice of the paschal lamb. It is clear that the sacrifice of animals was basic to biblical religion from the very beginning.

Various explanations have been given for the bringing of sacrifices. The Hebrew word for sacrifice, *korban*, literally means "bringing closer." The sacrifices draw people closer to God and God closer to people. MAIMONIDES, in the *Guide for the Perplexed*, suggests that the sacrifices served as an intermediate step to a more pure form of worship. They were different from the sacrifices of the pagans, because they were brought according to God's strict instructions and not as a human attempt to influence or manipulate God. Indeed the story of the sacrifice of Isaac (see AKEDAH), which was dramatically canceled before it could take place, was meant to denounce the idolaters' practice of sacrificing human beings (see IDOLATRY).

NAHMANIDES and many other medieval rabbis disagree with Maimonides. They see real spiritual and symbolic value in the system of sacrifices. For example, the guilt offering helps the person bringing the sacrifice to understand the weight of the sin: whatever is happening to the sacrificial animal should by rights be happening to him.

Some have claimed that many of the PROPHETS rejected the sacrifices and wished to replace them with a code of superior moral behavior. Others have argued that a careful reading of the verses shows that the prophets did not reject the practice itself, but rather the attitude people had when they brought the sacrifices. They objected to the people taking them lightly, as if the sacrifices themselves were enough to atone for sins. The prophets wanted to teach that the essence of ATONEMENT is one's heartfelt penitence and soul-searching. A sacrifice should never be brought without the proper feelings of REPENTANCE in one's heart.

There are three categories of sacrifices: (1) those brought as a sign of obeying God; (2) those brought as thanks; (3) those brought as a part of the process of repentance for a sin committed by accident. This third offering could not be brought for a sin committed on purpose – in such a case, the sacrifice does not atone for the sin. Thus a person could not commit a sin with the plan of bringing a sacrifice later to atone for it. Most important, the sacrifices addressed the full range of spiritual needs of the Jewish people, exactly parallel to prayer.

Here are some of the general rules that applied to sacrifices. Animals sacrificed had to be free of any physical blemish; birds did not have this restriction. Animals that could be brought as sacrifices included bulls, cows, sheep, and goats; turtledoves and pigeons could be used for an offering of fowl. Certain sacrifices required animals of a particular sex, and there were also age limitations. Animals were slaughtered with a slaughtering knife; birds were killed by a priest pinching their necks with a specially sharpened thumbnail. Except for the burnt offering, all animal sacrifices required the laying of two hands with all one's strength on the animal's head before the slaughter. In all cases, the blood of the slaughtered animal was sprinkled on the altar.

In the case of sacrifices brought by individuals, the person sacrificing the animal could perform all the actions up to the sprinkling or pouring of blood by himself, including laying his hands on the animal, lifting it, slaughtering it, flaying the hide, cutting the animal into pieces, and washing the parts. All actions that followed, including sprinkling or pouring the blood on or near the altar, arranging the wood on the altar, and burning those parts that were to be burned, were carried out by a PRIEST.

There were four types of animal sacrifices: the *olah*, "burnt offering"; the *shelamim*, "peace offering"; the *hatat*, "sin offering"; and the *asham*, "guilt offering."

Olah ("burnt offering"). Only male animals (bulls, rams, or he-goats) could be used for the burnt offering; a fowl might be of either sex. In the case of an animal, the hide belonged to the priest, while the rest of the animal was burned on the altar. In the case of a fowl, the entire bird was burned.

There were 14 types of sacrifices that fall into this category. Some examples are: the daily morning and afternoon sacrifices; the ram brought by the HIGH PRIEST on the DAY OF ATONEMENT; and the sacrifice of the NAZIRITE who was at the end of his term or whose term was interrupted by contact with the dead.

Shelamim ("peace offering"). The animal used for a peace offering could be of either sex. Certain portions of the animal's internal organs were burned on the altar. The meat of the animal was eaten by the person who brought it.

There were four kinds of peace offerings: a) the "community peace offering" brought on SHAVU'OT; b) the "festival peace offering" and the "festive peace offering," brought by an individual to celebrate the festival or as an expression of thanks to God, respectively; c) the *shelamim* that had been pledged, either in the form of "I will bring a sacrifice" or "I will bring this particular animal"; d) the peace offering brought by a Nazirite at the end of his term. In the first sacrifice listed above the meat and the hide of the animal belonged to the priests, while in the other three cases, the person bringing the sacrifice ate the meat and could keep the hide.

Hatat ("sin offering"). This sacrifice was brought when a person or an entire community accidentally violated a commandment where the punishment would have been KARET (being "cut off") if the sin were done on purpose. Depending on the specific *hatat*, a bull aged two or three years, a year-old he-goat, a year-old female sheep or goat, or a fowl was offered. Where the *hatat* was to atone for a sin committed by the High Priest of the entire community, the animal was burned outside the TEMPLE. In all other cases, the priest ate the meat.

Asham ("guilt offering"). There were six types of guilt offerings: a) "guilt offering of theft," where a person denied falsely under oath that he owed another person money; b) "the guilt of desecration," where a person benefited illegally from something belonging to the Temple; c) when a person had sexual relations with a woman who was half slave and half free and who was betrothed to a Jewish slave; d) when a Nazirite became ritually impure by contact with the dead when the vow was in force; e) the guilt offering of a leper on the day of ritual purification; f) "the doubtful guilt offering," brought by a person who was not sure he had committed a sin for which he would have had to bring a *hatat*. In each case, the animal had to be male, and its meat belonged to the priests.

Offerings This category includes all the different grain offerings. Six of the nine grain offerings were known as *minhah*. Of the nine, all except two were made with fine wheat flour. Some of these offerings had to be MATZAH, or unleavened, while others were leavened. As a rule, the offerings were composed of grain, oil, and frankincense. The offerings included: a) "the OMER grain offering, consisting of barley harvested on the second day of Passover; b) "the two loaves" brought on Shavu'ot; c) "the SHOWBREAD," 12 loaves that were placed on a special table in the Temple each Friday; d) *minhat havittin*, a type of matzah brought daily by the High Priest; e) "the grain offering of dedication," brought by a priest on the first day he entered the Temple service; f) "the libation grain offering," which might be brought by an individual or on behalf of the entire community; g) "the grain offering of the [suspected] unfaithful wife"; h) "the grain offering of the sinner"; i) "the freewill grain offering," brought by an individual.

The sacrifice of animals was always accompanied by a libation of wine (*nesekh*) and a meal offering. The wine was poured at the corner of the altar. A handful of the meal offering was placed on the altar and the rest was consumed by the priest.

A twice-daily INCENSE offering was also burned on a special incense altar in the Temple.

The FIRST FRUITS had their own special sacrifice. This particular offering consisted of the SEVEN SPECIES of Erets Israel: wheat, barley, grapes, pomegranates, figs, olives, and dates. These seven grains and fruits were carried in a procession to Jerusalem for Shavu'ot. Each person who brought his first fruits to the Temple had to make a declaration before a priest (see Deut. 26:5–10).

Although PRAYER had become part of the ritual even during the Temple period, once the Temple was destroyed prayer services replaced the sacrifices entirely. Comparison of the names of the sacrifices and the times in which they were offered with the various prayer services and their times make it clear just how closely connected these two systems of Jewish ritual are (see LITURGY).

SACRILEGE   See BLASPHEMY; DESECRATION; KIDDUSH HA-SHEM AND HILLUL HA-SHEM

SADDUCEES   (Heb. *Tsadokim*) A political and religious group in Erets Israel during the second half of the Second Temple period (2nd cent. BCE to 1st cent. CE). Their name comes from a connection with the line of the High Priest Zadok (from the time of King DAVID).

The Sadducees were the main opponents of the PHARISEES. They came from the aristocracy, while the Pharisees tended to be of the common folk. At times, they controlled the highest level of the people's spiritual government – the office of the HIGH PRIEST. According to the historian Josephus, the Sadducees (in contrast to the Pharisees) did not believe in the immortality of the SOUL and the final RESURRECTION of the dead. They accepted the WRITTEN LAW but not the ORAL LAW (or at least the Pharisee's interpretation of it), that is, the vast body of rabbinic legislation and commentary. In matters of Jewish law, they tended to be more severe than their counterparts.

Josephus argued that most Jews rejected the Sadducees and that it was the Pharisees whom they esteemed and turned to for guidance. While this may have been true, the Sadducees were part of the general political scene for a very long time. They were powerful, especially with their strong links to the Temple and the priesthood. In a sense, their connection with the Temple may have been their undoing. The destruction of the Temple forced the people to shift their focus away from the Temple as a daily spiritual center. The Pharisees were ready to step in with new institutions – the SYNAGOGUE and the ACADEMIES – which gave them greater influence with the people. A short time afterwards, the Sadducees disappeared.

SAGES   (Heb. *Hazal*, "Our sages of blessed memory"). Title given mainly to the scholars of Erets Israel and Babylonia in the pre-Mishnah, Mishnah, and Talmud periods. Most importantly, the sages provided the spiritual leadership of the Jewish people after the destruction of the TEMPLE. It was at this time, because of the loss of this spiritual center, that the sages provided a new focus that allowed Judaism to survive.

The sages of the Mishnah period (to 200 CE) who taught in Erets Israel are known as *tannaim* (see TANNA); those of the Talmud period (to 500 CE) are known as *amoraim* (see AMORA). The *amoraim* of Erets Israel created the Jerusalem Talmud; those of Babylonia created the Babylonian Talmud. The sages followed the tradition of the PHARISEES. They believed that the ORAL LAW, which they passed down from generation to generation, had been given at Sinai along with the WRITTEN LAW. Their writings became the basis of the HALAKHAH (Jewish law).

SALANTER (LIPKIN), ISRAEL BEN ZE'EV WOLF   (1810–1883). Lithuanian rabbi and founder of the MUSAR MOVEMENT. He attended the YESHIVAH of Tsevi Hirsch Broida in Salant. There he came under the influence of R. Sundel of Salant, whom he called the "light that he followed all his days." At the age of 30, he became head of the *yeshivah* of Vilna, but he soon resigned to set up his own center for the study of Jewish religious ETHICS. The lectures on ethics that he gave became the standard of the Salant school of *musar* (ethics).

In 1848 Salanter moved to Kovno, where he established a *musar yeshivah*. In 1857 he went to Germany, where he published a Hebrew periodical, *Tevunah*, which featured the contributions of the outstanding rabbis of the day. Towards the end of his life, he spent two years in Paris to strengthen Jewish institutions there. He died in Koenigsberg.

Salanter was a man of saintly character and selflessness. In Vilna, during the cholera epidemic of 1848, he feared that fasting would weaken the health of the Jewish population, so he ordered the congregation to eat and drink on the DAY OF ATONEMENT. He set a personal example during the MORNING SERVICE that year, by reciting the BENEDICTIONS and then eating of cake and drinking wine. His system of *musar* was eventually followed by all the Lithuanian *yeshivot*.

SALT   Mineral used in biblical times for a variety of purposes: for the SACRIFICES, in medicine, and as a preservative for food. Every sacrifice had to be sprinkled with salt (Lev. 2:13), and the TEMPLE had a salt chamber. Newborn infants were rubbed with salt, apparently as a health measure (Ezek. 16:4). Because it is a preservative, salt is a symbol for permanence: a "covenant of salt" (Num. 18:19) is an everlasting covenant.

Salt is important in the DIETARY LAWS. The blood is drained from meat by salting the meat thoroughly and then rinsing it with water. Jewish law requires that a little salt be sprinkled on the bread eaten at the beginning of a meal as a reminder of the sacrifices, which were salted.

SAMARITANS People originally formed by the mixture of Israelites remaining in the northern kingdom of ISRAEL with other peoples settled there by the Assyrian conquerors (after 722 BCE). The center of the region was Samaria. The Samaritans accept the laws of the PENTATEUCH but reject the other books of the Bible and the entire ORAL LAW. They have their own traditions regarding biblical practices.

The Talmud refers to the Samaritans as *Kutim*. It sees them as descended from various non-Jewish tribes that converted to Judaism. One of the minor books of the Talmud, *Kutim*, deals with laws governing the relations between Samaritans and Jews. The opening statement of the book notes that the Samaritans in some ways resemble Jews and in others, non-Jews. It stresses that in most ways they resemble Jews. The Talmud states that with those laws that the Samaritans do observe, they are more careful than Jews (*Hul.* 4a).

The Samaritan Pentateuch is written in its own alphabet. It differs from the Jewish text in a number of places. For example, the last of their TEN COMMANDMENTS declares that "Mount

Samaritan priest displays Torah.

Gerizim," their holy mountain, is the site where the ALTAR is to be built.

Samaritan interpretations of the SABBATH laws are particularly strict. They do not eat any warm food on the Sabbath day itself. They also remain in the area of their homes throughout the Sabbath.

The Samaritan interpretation of the CALENDAR is also unique. They observe the seven biblical FESTIVALS, but they use their own method for adding a leap month when required. As a result, Jewish and Samaritan observance of the same holiday sometimes varies by a month. The Samaritan observance of PASSOVER is special, because they still offer the paschal sacrifice. The Samaritan calendar always begins the count of the 49 days of the OMER on the first Sunday following the first day of Passover, so that their SHAVU'OT always occurs on a Sunday. In Jewish observance, Shavu'ot falls on the 50th day after the second day of Passover. There are other differences as well.

Upon the return of the exiles from Babylonia, the Jews rejected the Samaritan's claim that they were Jewish. They refused to let the Samaritans take part in rebuilding the TEMPLE in Jerusalem. They were barred from bringing sacrifices to the Temple, and they were not allowed to intermarry with Jews. They then built their own temple on Mount Gerizim.

Two communities of Samaritans have survived until today. The main community continues to live in and around Shechem (Nablus), in Erets Israel. There is also a smaller group in Holon, near Tel Aviv. Together, there are about 500 surviving members of the ancient Samaritan community.

SAMBATYON See TRIBES, TEN LOST

SAMSON (c. 12th cent. BCE). Judge in ancient Israel. Samson came from the tribe of Dan. He was known for his super-human strength. His parents were commanded by God to raise

Samson bound to the pillars causing the building to come crashing down on top of the Philistines with his last ounce of strength.

him as a NAZIRITE, which prohibited him from drinking wine, eating unclean food, and using a razor (Judg. 12:5ff.). He performed many heroic deeds and judged Israel for 20 years (see Judg. 14 and 15).

Samson had one unfortunate character flaw that led to his downfall: he preferred Philistine women. Rather than marry in his own tribe, he married a Timnite woman. Later he took up with a prostitute from Gaza and barely escaped disaster (see 16:1–3). Finally, he fell in love with Delilah, a temptress hired by the Philistines to get Samson to reveal the secret of his amazing strength (see 16:4). When he finally told her, the Philistines were able to capture Samson by cutting his hair. They dragged him to a feast for the god Dagon where he was put on display in chains before the Philistine crowd. But by this time his hair had grown back, and with it his strength was restored. He seized the pillars of the temple to which he was chained and pulled the structure down. This act killed 3,000 Philistines and Samson as well (16:23–30).

SAMUEL   (11th cent. BCE). Prophet and last of the biblical judges. He led Israel during the period between the time of the judges and the beginning of the monarchy.

Samuel's father, Elkanah, came from a noble family in Mount Ephraim. His mother, Hannah, was barren for many years. She prayed at the SANCTUARY in Shiloh, in the presence of Eli the priest. She begged God for a son and vowed to dedicate him as a NAZIRITE in the Sanctuary for his entire life. After Samuel was weaned, he was given over to Eli to serve in the Sanctuary.

God appeared to Samuel with a vision of the future destruction of Shiloh and the fall of the House of Eli. When these events came to pass, Samuel was appointed as a judge and prophet of God. Eventually, as the institution of the judges decayed, the people called on Samuel to appoint a king. In accordance with God's command, he anointed SAUL of the tribe of Benjamin as the first king of Israel.

Saul proved to be a disappointing king. First, he offered sacrifices without waiting for Samuel. Then, in the war against AMALEK, he allowed the Amalekite king to survive against God's command. After this, Samuel told Saul of God's prophecy that the kingship would be torn from him and given to another. Samuel then went to Bethlehem and secretly anointed DAVID king in Saul's place.

According to the Talmud, Samuel was just as important a leader as MOSES and AARON. His tomb is located in Nebi Samwil, a few miles northwest of Jerusalem.

SAMUEL, BOOK(S) OF   The third volume of the PROPHETS section of the Bible. The book starts with the birth of the prophet SAMUEL and continues well into the reign of DAVID. It includes stories, prophecies, poems, and lists. According to *Bava Batra* 14b, the book was written by the Prophet Samuel and completed by Gad the Seer and Nathan the Prophet after Samuel's death. Modern scholars prefer a later date for the Book

BOOKS OF SAMUEL	
I SAMUEL	
1:1–3:21	The birth of Samuel and his consecration as a prophet
4:1–6:21	The destruction of Shiloh, the capture of the Holy Ark, and its return
7:1–7:17	Samuel the Judge
8:1–10:27	Saul is anointed as king
11:1–11:15	The victory of Saul over Ammon
12:1–12:25	Samuel's farewell speech
13:1–15:35	Saul's wars against the Philistines and Amalek
16:1–16:23	The anointing of David as king
17:1–17:58	David fights Goliath
18:1–19:10	David in Saul's court
19:11–27:12	Saul pursues David
28:1–28:25	The witch of En-dor
29:1–30:31	David in the camp of Achish and his battle against Amalek
31:1–II SAM.	
1:27	The battle against the Philistines on Gilboa, the death of Saul and his sons, David's lament
II SAMUEL	
2:1–4:12	The civil war of David against the house of Saul. David is made king of Judah in Hebron
5:1–5:25	David becomes king of all of Israel; the conquest of Jerusalem
6:1–6:23	David brings the Ark of the Covenant to Jerusalem
7:1–7:29	God does not permit David to build the Temple
8:1–8:18	David's battles against the Philistines, Moab, Zobah, and Aram of Damascus
9:1–9:13	David and Mephibosheth, son of Jonathan
10:1–10:19	David's battles against Ammon and Aram
11:1–12:31	David and Bathsheba
13:1–19:1	The revolt by Absalom
19:2–19:44	David returns to Jerusalem
20:1–20:26	The revolt by Sheba, son of Bichri
21:1–21:14	David, the Gibeonites, and Saul's descendants
21:15–21:22	List of David's warriors
22:1–22:51	The song of David
23:1–23:39	David's last words, list of David's warriors
24:1–24:25	The census

of Samuel, most likely the sixth century BCE. They suggest that part of the book may be based on the court chronicles of David and Solomon.

SAMUEL, MAR (3ʳᵈ cent. CE). Leading Babylonian sage of the first generation, together with RAV. The Mar (prefix) in his name is a title of honor. In addition to his vast rabbinic knowledge, Samuel mastered the sciences of his day, including medicine. He was once called to Erets Israel to cure R. JUDAH HA-NASI of an eye disease. His knowledge of astronomy was so vast that he was prepared to fix the first day of each festival based on astronomical calculations. This would have abolished the SECOND DAY OF FESTIVALS observed in the Diaspora. However, the rabbis of Erets Israel rejected his offer.

Samuel followed his father as head of the Academy of Nehardea. His legal arguments with Rav, head of the Academy of Sura, form the basis of the Babylonian Talmud. In Jewish law, the rule is: in matters of civil law, the decision is always according to Samuel's view.

SAMUEL BEN MEIR (known as *Rashbam*; c. 1085–1174). Bible commentator and Talmud scholar; grandson of RASHI and elder brother of Rabbenu TAM. He was born in Ramerupt near Troyes, France. He studied mainly under Rashi, but also under his father, one of the first Tosafists (see TOSAFOT).

It is likely that Samuel wrote commentaries on all the books of the Bible. However, only his commentary on the PENTATEUCH has survived intact. His uses an extremely literal interpretation of the text (PESHAT), even when it contradicted the HALAKHAH (Jewish law). For example, he held that, according to the literal meaning of the text, it is not necessary to wear TEFILLIN and the Hebrew day goes from morning to evening. Samuel clearly kept the *halakhah* in his life – he simply felt that the plain meaning of the Torah and the legal meaning operated according to different principles. According to Samuel, his grandfather Rashi told him that if he had the time he would have written another commentary on the Torah more in keeping with the literal meaning.

Samuel is also the author of commentaries on a number of books of the Talmud.

SAMUEL HA-NAGID (SAMUEL HA-LEVI BEN JOSEPH IBN NAGDELA) (993–1055). Spanish statesman, Hebrew grammar expert, poet, and Talmud scholar. He was born in Córdoba and died in Granada. Samuel was a gifted speaker, linguist, and calligrapher. He was appointed the personal secretary of the vizier. The vizier noticed Samuel's natural gift for statesmanship and sent him on a number of important missions. In 1027 the Jews of Spain gave him the title of *nagid*, head of the community. When the vizier died, King Habbus appointed Samuel to take his place.

When Samuel had not yet reached the height of his career, King Habbus died, leaving two sons to struggle for his throne. Samuel backed the elder son, Badis, against the more popular younger son. Eventually Badis came to power and put Samuel in charge of all matters of state. Samuel even led the Spanish army into battle.

Samuel's most important book was *Sefer Hilkheta Gavrata*, a commentary on the two Talmuds and various works of the *ge'onim*. He also produced RESPONSA (answers to Jewish legal questions) and a work on Hebrew grammar.

SANCTIFICATION   See HOLINESS; KEDUSHAH

SANCTUARY ("tabernacle" or "tent of congregation"; Heb. *mishkan*). Portable holy tent, made by MOSES, which traveled with the Israelites in the desert. The Sanctuary was placed in the center of the camp, with the LEVITES camped around it and the other tribes on the outer edges of the encampment. The Sanctuary and all its holy objects were carried from place to place by the Levites.

The Sanctuary stood in an open courtyard and was located in the eastern half of the courtyard. At the end of the sanctuary stood the HOLY OF HOLIES, which was separated from the rest of the sanctuary by a curtain (see PAROKHET). The ARK OF THE COVENANT was kept in the Holy of Holies. The Ark contained the two TABLETS OF THE COVENANT with the TEN COMMANDMENTS. According to rabbinic tradition, both the tablets that Moses had broken and the second, complete set were placed in the Ark. A decorative cloth covering draped the entire Sanctuary. On top this covering was a roof of twelve goatskin sections. Above this was another layer made of ram skins and the skin of *tehashim* (usually translated as badgers).

Inside, before the Holy of Holies, stood the table for the SHOWBREAD, the INCENSE altar, and the MENORAH. Outside in the courtyard stood the outer ALTAR and a brass laver for the priests to wash their hands and feet.

The Sanctuary was the central religious institution of Judaism until SOLOMON built the TEMPLE in JERUSALEM.

SANDAK (or *sandek*; "godfather"). The man honored with holding the infant boy on his knees during the CIRCUMCISION ceremony. Traditionally, a person who had a great scholar as a *sandak* was seen as privileged. The honor is often given a grandparent.

SANHEDRIN (from *synedrion*, Greek for "sitting council"). Higher courts of Jewish law during the later Second Temple period and following it. The Talmud traces the origins of the Sanhedrin to the 70 ELDERS chosen by MOSES. It is known in rabbinic sources by various names: Sanhedrin, the Great Court in Jerusalem, or the Court of Seventy. In non-Jewish sources it is called Council of Elders, *Gerousia* (Council), or Sanhedrin. Smaller courts of 23 members met in each city or region and had responsibility for lesser cases.

The Sanhedrin was composed of SAGES and was headed by a president (NASI). It was the leading institution of the Jewish community in Erets Israel, and its influence extended to the Diaspora. Disputes in matters of Jewish law that arose in local courts were referred to the Sanhedrin for a final, deciding opinion. The Sanhedrin served as the legislative body issuing decrees (GEZEROT) and rulings (TAKKANOT). While individual decisions are recorded in the Talmud in the name of the *Nasi*, the entire Sanhedrin undoubtedly voted on them. This means that the Sanhedrin functioned as both a court and a parliament.

What were the major issues that could be undertaken by the Sanhedrin and the Sanhedrin alone? The Sanhedrin was responsible for fixing the monthly and yearly CALENDAR. It had the right to authorize or veto a war of aggression. It was also the body that took steps against rebellious sects (see MINIM). The Talmud notes that while the Sanhedrin was responsible for trying cases that carried the death penalty, this authority ended 40 years before the destruction of the Second Temple.

After the destruction of the Second Temple, Rabban GAMALIEL reestablished the Sanhedrin in Yavneh. The new court was as powerful as the one that had come before it. However, in the early fifth century CE, the Roman authorities abolished the office of the Nasi (Patriarch), which brought the Sanhedrin to an end.

SANHEDRIN Fourth tractate (book) of the Order of NEZIKIN in the Mishnah. Its 11 chapters deal with setting up courts of law. Courts of three, 23, and 71 judges were set up in Erets Israel depending on the size of the city and the seriousness of the case. The Supreme Court was called the Great SANHEDRIN. The tractate discusses lawsuits and criminal cases, including crimes liable to the death penalty and even the rights of kings and high priests.

SANHEDRIN, "GREAT" See CONSISTORY

SARAH Wife of Abraham, mother of ISAAC, MATRIARCH of the Jewish people. Originally her name was Sarai, but it was changed by God at the same time that Abram's name was changed to Abraham. She originally came from the same family as Abraham (Gen. 11:29–31) and accompanied her husband from Mesopotamia to Canaan.

According to the Bible, Sarah was barren. She gave her maidservant, Hagar, to Abraham as a concubine (secondary wife), and Hagar gave birth to Ishmael when Abraham was 86 years old. Only 14 years later, at the age of 90, did Sarah give birth to Isaac (see Gen. 21). Later, when Sarah observed the way Ishmael mocked Isaac, she requested that Abraham send away both the boy and his mother. God told Abraham, "Whatever Sarah says to you, listen to her voice" (Gen. 21:12). About this verse, the MIDRASH notes that Sarah's powers as a PROPHET were greater than those of Abraham.

The Midrash claims that Sarah died when she received word that Isaac was almost sacrificed (see AKEDAH). After Sarah died, Abraham bought the Cave of Machpelah to use as her burial site.

SATAN Originally the Hebrew word *satan* in the Bible meant "enemy," "someone hostile" (see 1 Kings 11:14). In later books of the Bible, it came to mean a supernatural being who accuses man before God. The role of the Satan is described most clearly in the opening section of the Book of JOB (1–2), where Satan questions Job's sincerity. Both here and in ZECHARIAH (3:1, 2) Satan is not independent – he can act only within the limits set by God.

In the APOCRYPHA AND PSEUDEPIGRAPHA, as well as in the Talmud and MIDRASH, the role of Satan is expanded. He is able to tempt people to disobey the will of God. He is called by various additional names – *Mastemah* (Hatred), Belial, and Angel of Darkness – that hint at his growing independence. He is the subject of many folk beliefs and is mentioned in the PRAYER BOOK.

SATMAR Hasidic group founded by Moses ben Tsevi Teitelbaum (1759–1841), a student of the Seer of Lublin. Through Moses, HASIDISM spread throughout Hungary. Joel Teitelbaum (1888–1979), the great-grandson of Moses, was the most influential of the Teitelbaum dynasty. He became rabbi of Satu Mare in 1929 and set up a large YESHIVAH there. He was saved from the HOLOCAUST on one of the two rescue trains from Bergen-Belsen. He reached Erets Israel and then settled permanently in Williamsburg, New York. Under his leadership, the anti-Zionist philosophy of Satmar was established and strengthened.

Satmar has experienced astounding growth, with around 45,000 members in New York alone. It is the largest Hasidic group in New York City.

SAUL First king of Israel (c. 1029–1005 BCE). Saul, son of Kish of the tribe of Benjamin, was anointed king at Mizpah by SAMUEL the Prophet. Samuel was at first against appointing a king and had warned the people about the possible dangers of having one. However, popular demand for a king was strong, particularly in light of the growing threat of attacks by the Philistines.

The kingship of Saul does not seem to have had the central administration that we see in later kings. He collected taxes, maintained an army, and conducted wars on behalf of the people. He defeated the Ammonites at Jabesh-Gilead, the Philistines at Gibeah and Michmash, campaigned successfully against the Moabites, Edomites, and Arameans, and defeated the AMALEKITES.

The war against the Amalekites was commanded by God, with the goal of destroying Amalek altogether. Saul, however, took the Amalekite king captive and saved alive the best of their cattle (see 1 Sam. 14:48–15:33). This sin cost Saul the kingship. Samuel criticized him harshly and then went to Bethlehem to secretly anoint DAVID in Saul's place. David's popularity drove Saul nearly to madness.

Saul's death came at Mount Gilboa after a new Philistine invasion. His decapitated body was displayed by the Philistines on the wall of Beth Shean until it was buried by the men of Jabesh-Gilead.

Saul being anointed by Samuel. Etching by Enrico Glicenstein (1880–1943), Poland.

SAVORA (Aram. "explainer"; pl. *savoraim*). Term for the Babylonian scholars who came after the *amoraim* (see AMORA) and were responsible for the final contributions to the Talmud. Jewish historians have estimated that the *savoraim* were active for about 50 years (c. 500–550 CE); recent scholars believe they were active into the period of the *ge'onim* (see GAON) or until around 690 CE. Gaonic sources identify about a dozen of the *savoraim* by name, including Simuna and Rabbai of Rov.

The difference between the scholarship of the *savoraim* and the *amoraim* is generally this: the *amora* was a lawmaker; the *savora* offered a reasoned explanation of an existing law. In the Talmud, the *savoraim* supplied brief connecting phrases that clarified the meaning of the laws that appeared there. They also added explanations that helped scholars decide the HALAKHAH (Jewish law). Their brief explanations and notes often appear in the text in such a way that they seem to be part of the original Talmud. But with close reading, scholars of the Talmud are able to recognize the unmistakable contribution of the *savoraim* to the final form of the Talmud.

Later *savoraim* went even further. They inserted long passages into the Talmud's discussions, usually at the beginning of a book or chapter. For example, the *ge'onim* believe that the first few pages of KIDDUSHIN was written by the *savoraim*.

SCAPEGOAT   See AZAZEL

SCHECHTER, SOLOMON (1847–1915). Rabbinic scholar and leader of CONSERVATIVE JUDAISM; founder of its basic institutions. Born in Rumania, Schechter studied in Vienna and then in Berlin. He moved to England in 1882 to lecture in Talmud and Rabbinics at Cambridge University and then at University College, London. His edition of AVOT DE-RABBI NATAN was published in 1887, but his international reputation resulted from his work on the Cairo GENIZAH. Beginning in 1896, he unearthed some 100,000 pages of medieval manuscripts that proved a treasure and changed rabbinic scholarship forever.

From 1902, Schechter headed the Jewish Theological Seminary in New York. He made the Seminary an international center of Jewish learning with one of the world's greatest Jewish libraries. His vision for the Conservative movement was that the Seminary and its associated institutions would serve all traditional Jewish communities in the United States, including modern ORTHODOXY and the "positive-historical" school. This dream was not realized, and the Seminary became identified with Conservative Judaism only.

Schechter published widely. He excelled at presenting the beliefs of traditional Judaism to lay readers in terms they could understand. He took stands on controversial issues. He actively supported ZIONISM, which the Seminary's leadership opposed. He was an opponent of REFORM JUDAISM, specifically its openness to assimilation.

SCHNEERSOHN, MENAHEM MENDEL (1902–1994). The seventh Lubavicher Rebbe; head of the CHABAD Hasidic dynasty. He was a descendant of the first Menahem Mendel of the Chabad dynasty (the *Tsemah Tsedek*), who was the son-in-law and nephew of Dov Baer, who was in turn the son of Chabad founder SCHNEUR ZALMAN OF LYADY. He was born in Nikolaev in the Ukraine and recognized for his great brilliance while still a child. In 1923, he became associated with Joseph Isaac Schneersohn, the Lubavicher Rebbe at the time. In 1928 he married Joseph Isaac's daughter. He then studied philosophy and mathematics at the University of Berlin and then at the Sorbonne. In 1941, he fled from the Nazis and finally joined his father-in-law in the United States. During World War II he served as an electrical engineer in the United States Navy. In 1950, he succeeded his father-in-law as the Lubavicher Rebbe.

Under Schneersohn's leadership, Chabad became a worldwide outreach movement with a following of more than 200,000 Jews. He sent out thousands of emissaries to establish Chabad centers, schools, libraries, mikvehs, often in remote areas where no one else served the needs of local Jews. He inspired Chabad to use all means available to bring Jews back to the fold, including radio, television, and the Internet. He became the best-known religious leader in the Jewish world.

The Rebbe's main means of teaching was the *fahrbrengen*, or Hasidic gathering. In time, the talks he gave at these gatherings were transmitted by cable and satellite hookup. The talks

Rabbi Menahem Mendel Schneersohn. Head of of the Lubavich Hasidim.

were edited and published in the 39 volumes of *Likkutei Sichot* ("Collections of Teachings").

The mystique and charisma of the Rebbe inspired a deep longing for the MESSIAH in his followers. Many believed he was the Messiah, and there are many who still hold this belief even after his death.

SCIENCE   For the most part, the rise of science during the 16th and 17th centuries did not cause the bitter controversy in Judaism that it did in the Catholic Church. However some subjects, like the Copernican theory and EVOLUTION, did create challenges for Jewish THEOLOGY (belief system).

Throughout the ages, knowledge of Torah also involved knowledge of worldly matters (see *Avot* 2:2). The calculation of the CALENDAR required knowledge of astronomy; many laws demanded knowledge of biology and medicine to arrive at a proper decision. The dietary laws are meaningless without a mastery of animal anatomy and the classifications of birds and reptiles. In the Middle Ages, Jews, some of them rabbis and scholars in Jewish subjects, were leaders in science (astronomy, mathematics, medicine, etc.) and also in making Arab science available to the Christian world. According to

MAIMONIDES, himself a leading medical authority, the only way to observe the central commandment of loving God is to study His works – the various aspects of nature.

The Jew has an obligation and even a religious benefit in studying science. But this is not the same thing as accepting all of the conclusions of science, especially when they conflict with the Bible. Sometimes, in Orthodox Judaism, scientific views are reconciled with the Bible; sometimes they are rejected.

SCRIBES   (Heb. *soferim*) Scholars of the early Second Temple period who explained the ORAL LAW, made regulations (TAKKANOT), and wrote holy documents. The scribes also assumed leadership of the Jewish nation in the period between the PROPHETS and the PHARISEES. The time of the scribes began with EZRA ("the scribe"), who led the Jews back from Babylonia in the fifth century BCE, and ended with Simeon the Just, the last surviving member of the GREAT ASSEMBLY (*Avot* 1:2).

In its original meaning, the word *sofer* means "to count." The scribes counted the letters of the Bible and were careful about the spelling and pronunciation of each word. They made sure that the correct text was passed down to the next generation. In Jewish law, the rulings of the scribes are called *divrei soferim* (words of the scribes), *tikkunei soferim* (corrections of the scribes), or *dikdukei soferim* (details of the scribes). The Talmud emphasizes the scribes' importance as authorities on the Oral Law: "Be more careful with the words of the scribes than with the words of the Bible" (*Er.* 21b). The scribes wrote laws about PRAYER and BENEDICTIONS and introduced the festival of PURIM. They also changed the text of the Torah in 18 places, mainly to avoid physical descriptions of God.

The more modern meaning of "scribe" is one who writes MEZUZOT, TEFILLIN, Scrolls of ESTHER, and SCROLLS OF THE LAW. He also writes DIVORCE documents and, occasionally, *ketubbot* (MARRIAGE documents). Laws relating to the scribes are compiled in SOFERIM, a minor book that was added to the Talmud.

SCROLL OF THE LAW   (Heb. *Sefer Torah*). Handwritten copy of the Five Books of MOSES (or PENTATEUCH), kept in the ARK of the SYNAGOGUE and taken out whenever the Law is read (see READING OF THE LAW).

The laws for properly preparing a scroll for ritual use are very demanding. The scroll must be written on parchment (animal skin) by a SCRIBE (*sofer*) who is familiar with all the laws involved. The parchment may come only from a ritually clean species of animal. The parchment has to be embossed with lines before the scribe begins writing. The ink must be black and prepared by a traditional formula. Jewish law defines the shape of each letter. The Torah scroll contains no vowels or cantillation marks; punctuation may not be used to divide sentences or phrases. The sections of the parchment are sewn together, using tendons from a ritually clean animal. These are just a few of the laws and customs that apply to the scroll itself.

If an error of any kind is found in a Torah scroll, the scroll

Raising the Scroll of the Law (hagbahah) *in the synagogue. Painting, Holland, 1780.*

may not be used again until a scribe corrects the error. If correcting the error involves erasing the name of God, the entire segment of parchment containing the error must be replaced. If three errors or more are found in a Torah scroll, it must be checked from beginning to end and corrected before it can be used.

The Torah scroll is the most important Jewish ritual object. There are many ways in which people show their respect for the Torah. For example, whenever the Ark containing the Torah is opened and the scrolls become visible, people stand. Also, when the scroll is opened and raised (*hagbahah*) as part of the service, all rise. If fire breaks out in the synagogue, the Torah scrolls must be the first objects rescued. If a scroll is burned in a fire, the ashes or remaining parts of the scroll are buried in a cemetery.

The last of the 613 COMMANDMENTS states that each Jew should write a Torah scroll for himself. While not every Jew is capable of performing this commandment, there is a view that buying a Torah scroll or even paying for the writing of a single letter in a Torah scroll is enough to fulfill the law.

SCROLLS, FIVE   See FIVE SCROLLS

SECOND DAY OF FESTIVALS   An extra day added to each of the festivals of PASSOVER, SHAVU'OT, and SUKKOT for Jews living in the Diaspora. It comes from Second Temple times, when it was difficult to fix the correct date of the New MOON, which was also the first day of the new Hebrew month. At that time, witnesses testified before the SANHEDRIN that they had seen the New Moon. A chain of beacons was then lit on mountaintops to let people know in the outlying areas that the new month had begun. People could then count the days to know when to celebrate the FESTIVAL that would fall in that month. This system of communication broke down in the last days of the Temple. In order to make sure that they did not miss the correct date for the festivals, Jews in the Diaspora began keeping two holy days (instead of one) at the beginning and end of Passover and Sukkot, and on Shavu'ot. Once a fixed CALENDAR was introduced in the fourth century CE, the date of each New Moon and the festivals was known in advance. By that time, the observance of the second day of festivals had been in place for centuries, and the sages ruled that it had to continue even if the reason for its observance no longer applied (see CUSTOM, GEZERAH).

The Talmud (TJ, *Er.* 3:9) considers the observance of the "second festive days" to be a religious penalty for choosing to live in exile (GALUT). REFORM Jews do not observe the second day of festivals; the CONSERVATIVE movement allows its rabbis to decide whether or not to observe it. Israelis visiting abroad are expected to observe the second day in public. Most rabbis today rule that Jews visiting Israel from overseas during a festival must still observe the second day while in Israel.

SECTARIANS   See MINIM

SEDER   ("order"). The home ceremony observed on the first night (in the Diaspora on the first two nights) of the PASSOVER festival.

In ancient times, the main observance of the eve of Passover was the sacrifice of the paschal lamb, which was then eaten by the family. Following the destruction of the Second Temple in 70 CE, SACRIFICES were no longer possible. The rabbis were forced to redesign the observance of Passover without its main ritual. The ceremony of the Passover *Seder* that resulted maintains strong connections with the ancient observance.

The post-Temple *Seder* developed over time. It became an ordered ceremony with symbols, special foods, thanksgiving, and rejoicing. The following are central to the *Seder*:

i.   HAGGADAH. The special book containing the text of the ceremony.
ii. *Seder* plate. The special plate placed on the table that contains the following items: (1) a roasted egg – a symbol of the festival sacrifice in the Temple; (2) roasted bone (*zero'a*) – a symbol of the paschal lamb eaten at ancient Passover feasts; (3) bitter herbs (MAROR) – a symbol of the bitterness of slavery in Egypt; (4) *haroset*, a mixture of apples, nuts, wine, and cinnamon – a symbol of the mortar used by the Israelite slaves in making bricks in Egypt; (5) *karpas*, parsley or some other green vegetable – a symbol of springtime, when the holiday occurs (6) salt water, representing the tears shed by the Israelites in Egypt.
iii. Three pieces of MATZAH. Two of these take the place of the two loaves of bread used on the Sabbath and festivals (see CHALLAH). The third is part of the *Seder* ritual. The matzah symbolizes both the poverty of slavery and the freedom of the EXODUS from Egypt.
iv. Four cups of wine (ARBA KOSOT). These are drunk in remembrance of God's four promises of REDEMPTION in the Bible (Ex. 6:6–7).
v.   The cup of ELIJAH. A cup filled in honor of Elijah the prophet, who is to announce the MESSIAH.
vi. *Afikoman*. A special piece of matzah that is put away at the beginning of the *Seder* and eaten at the end.

The order of the *Seder* ritual is clearly set out. The participants recite the list of fourteen steps at the beginning of the *Seder*, and then follow the order throughout the evening. The steps are: (1) *Kadesh*, the *Kiddush* blessings; (2) *Rehats*, washing of hands without a blessing; (3) *Karpas*, eating a vegetable dipped in salt water; (4) *Yahats*, breaking the middle matzah; (5) *Maggid*, reciting the story of the Exodus from the *Haggadah*; (6) *Rahtsah*, washing hands with a blessing; (7) *Motsi Matzah*, eating unleavened bread; (8) *Maror*, eating the bitter herb; (9) *Korekh*, eating HILLEL's sandwich; (10) *Shulhan Orekh*, eating the festive meal; (11) *Tsafun*, eating from the *afikoman*; (12) *Barekh*, reciting the Grace After Meals; (13) HALLEL, reciting psalms of praise; (14) *Nirtsah*, reciting the declaration that the celebration is "accepted." The *Seder* concludes joyously with the *La-Shanah ha-Ba'ah bi-Yerushalayim* (Next Year in Jerusalem).

SEFER TORAH   See SCROLL OF THE LAW

SEFIROT   ("Emanations"). Term from the KABBALAH; the ten emanations (heavenly levels) of the Godhead (see MYSTICISM). The mystical idea of the *sefirot* first appeared in *Sefer* YETSIRAH (3rd–4th cent.). The early kabbalists used the term to describe their idea of what made up the Divine world. They suggested that there are ten Divine powers that originate from the EN-SOF, or Godhead. *Sefer* BAHIR (late 12th cent.) presents a system based on ten Divine emanations, and this became the main system of symbols used by kabbalists.

Each of the *sefirot* has a name, and they are arranged according to groupings (from the highest to the lowest): (1) *Keter* (Crown), *Hokhmah* (Wisdom), and *Binah* (Intelligence); (2) *Hesed* (Grace), *Gevurah* (Power), *Tiferet* (Beauty), *Netsah* (Eternity), *Hod* (Glory), and *Yesod* (Foundation); (3) *Malkhut* (Kingdom) or SHEKHINAH (God's Indwelling Presence).

In the symbolism of the Kabbalah, the emanations are often combined into a diagram of a human form. The first grouping of three *sefirot* forms the head of the Divine figure. The next grouping of six powers forms the body. Finally, *Malkhut* is a separate, feminine figure that includes aspects of all the nine *sefirot* above it. *Malkhut* governs the created world.

SELIHOT   (sing. *selihah*). Prayers that ask God for forgiveness and mercy for sins that have been committed. According to tradition, God taught MOSES His 13 attributes, which Moses could always recite in order to plead for mercy (see Ex. 34:6–7).

Selihot were originally recited on the Day of Atonement

A Passover Seder *meal in Rishon le-Zion, Israel.*

and on other fast days. In time, they were said on other days as well. Beginning in the geonic period, *selihot* were read on MONDAYS AND THURSDAYS after the Morning Service AMIDAH. The SHULHAN ARUKH mentions the Sephardi custom of rising each morning for five and a half weeks before the Day of Atonement to recite *selihot*. Ashkenazim begin this practice on the Sunday before ROSH HA-SHANAH.

Many of the *selihot* are based on alphabetical ACROSTICS. Acrostics are code poems in which the first letters of the verses combine to spell something. In many cases, the letters form the Hebrew alphabet, which is as if to say that our pleas for mercy go "from A to Z." In many cases, the name of the author appears in an acrostic after the alphabetical verses.

SEMAHOT Minor tractate (book) of the Talmud that was added to the Order of NEZIKIN. *Semahot* deals with the laws of MOURNING. The work is also known as *Evel Rabbati*, the "Great [Work on] Mourning."

SEMIKHAH See ORDINATION

SEPHARDIM Jews who trace their origin to medieval Spain (*Sefarad* in Hebrew). Today, the term refers to Jews who follow Sephardi prayer traditions, interpretations of the COMMANDMENTS, and CUSTOMS, even if their ancestors did not live in Spain. Thus, in common speech in Israel, Jews originally from Arab lands are referred to as Sephardim or Mizrahim (Easterners) regardless of the historical, cultural, or social differences among them. They are distinguished from ASHKENAZIM, who originally came from Central or Eastern Europe.

The Sephardi community produced many outstanding personalities in philosophy, literature, and the natural sciences as well as in Jewish scholarship. These include: JUDAH HALEVI, Solomon IBN GABIROL, Abraham IBN EZRA, Moses MAIMONIDES, Moses NAHMANIDES, Solomon ben ADRET, and Isaac ABRAVANEL, to name a few.

After the expulsion of Jews from Spain in 1492 and the decree forbidding Judaism in Portugal in 1496, Sephardi Jews were forced to resettle. Communities were established in the Ottoman Empire, Erets Israel, and North Africa. During the 16th and 17th centuries, many MARRANOS – secret Jews who were forced to convert to Christianity in the Iberian Peninsula – found their way to places where they could practice Judaism openly. Some moved to Western Europe and the New World.

Customs varied among the various Sephardi communities. Sephardim of Turkey, the Balkans, Israel, and the north of Morocco spoke Judeo-Spanish (Ladino), in some Greek cities they spoke Greek. Those in Arab countries spoke Arabic. Those in Western Europe and the New World adopted the language of the lands in which they settled (see JEWISH LANGUAGES).

Sephardim have made major contributions to Jewish religion and culture. For example, the mystics of Safed in the 16th century created the foundation for the KABBALAH. R. Joseph CARO gave the Jewish world the great Jewish law code,

the SHULHAN ARUKH. Various Bible commentators, authors of legal RESPONSA, and authors of works on ETHICS come from the Sephardi community. R. Jacob CULI's *Me'am Lo'ez*, an encyclopedia of Judeo-Spanish Bible commentary, is popular to this day.

One of the main differences between Sephardim and Ashkenazim is their styles of prayer (see NUSAH). The prayer customs of the Sephardim go back to Babylonian Jewry; those of the Ashkenazim come from the Jews of Erets Israel. The Sephardi order of prayer is different, and certain PIYYUTIM are omitted. For example, Sephardim do not recite KOL NIDREI on the eve of the DAY OF ATONEMENT. Their melody used for chanting the Torah is unique. Their pronunciation of Hebrew differs from the traditional Ashkenazi pronunciation. Many differences can be noted in the customs of their life cycle events.

Israel has both a Sephardi and Ashkenazi Chief Rabbi serving the needs of the two ethnic communities.

SEPTUAGINT (lit. "seventy"). Oldest surviving Greek translation of the Bible, prepared by the 70 ELDERS. It was composed in Alexandria. According to tradition, Ptolemy II Philadelphus (285–246 BCE) heard from his librarian, Demetrius, that the Jewish Bible was worth translating for the king's archives. The king wrote to the HIGH PRIEST in Jerusalem asking him to send scholars who would be able to translate the PENTATEUCH into Greek. The High Priest sent 72 wise men, whom the king housed in a building on the island of Pharos, near Alexandria. The Talmud (*Meg.* 9a) says that all the elders translated the entire Bible. According to legend, each worked separately and made his own translation, and when these were compared they were found to be identical. Modern scholars believe that the project was started by the Egyptian Jewish community and not by the king, because they needed a Greek Bible translation for their own use. By 100 BCE, the entire Bible had been translated into Greek.

Originally, "Septuagint" meant the Pentateuch only. It was later applied to the other books as well. The Septuagint does not follow the order of the books in the Hebrew version. In addition, it includes a number of works of APOCRYPHA that are not part of the Bible.

The language of the Septuagint is relatively simple, which made it popular. Perhaps for this reason the SAGES of Erets Israel saw the translation as a real danger to the Hebrew language, which they feared would be replaced by Greek. In addition, the translation began to be used as the basis for speeches by Hellenistic Jews. Christians began to use it in their polemics against Judaism (see APOLOGETICS AND POLEMICS). The sages therefore announced: "The day that the Torah was translated was as terrible as the day that the [golden] calf was made" (*Sof.* 1).

SERMONS See HOMILETICS

SE'UDAH ("a meal"). A festive meal served either because of a special day or a special occasion. It is also known as a *se'udat* *mitzvah*, "an obligatory meal." Included are the three SABBATH meals, two meals on festivals, the PURIM afternoon feast, and the Passover SEDER.

The idea of a festive meal celebrating a special occasion is already found in GENESIS, where ABRAHAM made a great meal to celebrate the weaning of his son ISAAC (Gen. 21:8). Occasions that call for a *se'udat mitzvah* are: a CIRCUMCISION, a BAR MITZVAH or BAT MITZVAH, a betrothal, a wedding reception, the *sheva berakhot* (see MARRIAGE), and the completion of the study of a book of the Talmud.

SE'UDAH SHELISHIT ("third meal"; also known as "*shalosh se'udot*"). The third of the three required SABBATH meals. It is generally eaten after the AFTERNOON SERVICE on Saturday. There is no KIDDUSH prayer said at this meal. The melodies sung at the table are solemn, since the holy Sabbath is coming to an end.

SEVEN SPECIES (Heb. *shiv'at ha-minim*). The seven crops that are associated with Erets Israel: wheat, barley, grapes, figs, pomegranates, olives, and dates. These types of produce are mentioned in Deuteronomy 8:8–9. In this verse, God promises that Erets Israel will be "a land where you may eat food without scarceness, where you will lack nothing …"

SEVENTEENTH OF TAMMUZ   See SHIVAH ASAR BE-TAMMUZ

SEX   The Bible views sex as an essential part of MARRIAGE. With the creation of woman, man is told to "leave his father and mother and cling to his wife, so that they become one flesh" (Gen. 2:24). The purpose of marriage, then, is twofold: procreation and companionship. To marry and have children is a religious act – the first MITZVAH.

According to Jewish law, marital relations are the wife's right and the husband's duty. He must fulfill this obligation at specific intervals, based on his occupation and ability (*Ket.* 61b). For this reason, if the husband wishes to change his occupation to one that will keep him away from home for longer periods, the wife must approve. The Talmud notes: A woman prefers a smaller income and a close relationship with her husband (*ibid.*).

The laws about conduct between a husband and wife state that the husband may not force his wife to have intercourse with him. The law also forbids intercourse when either spouse is drunk or when the woman is asleep. The law demands mutual consent. The sages also ruled that a person may not have intercourse with his or her spouse while thinking of someone else. Intimacy means a total relationship between the two parties.

A second aspect of married life is that the relationship should be ongoing. A marriage may not be entered into with the intention of ending it. Sensitivity to physical needs is very important. According to Jewish law, a husband and wife cannot agree to maintain a sexless marriage. In contrast, the wife can agree to give up financial support by her husband.

The Talmud mentions Friday night, the holiest night of the week, as an especially good time for sexual relations between husband and wife (*Kit.* 62b). The law also provides for regular periods of separation. Marital intercourse is prohibited during the woman's menstrual period and at least a week thereafter (Lev. 15:19–28; see NIDDAH).

Sexual Offenses   In Judaism, sexual activity within marriage is considered holy. Sexual acts outside of the framework of marriage are to be shunned. Premarital sex, masturbation, HOMOSEXUALITY, and ADULTERY are all discussed in Jewish law and forbidden.

According to Jewish law, rape is a serious SIN. If a man rapes a betrothed woman, he is put to death. If she is single, he must marry her and he can never divorce her (see Deut. 22:22–29).

SFORNO, OBADIAH BEN JACOB   (c. 1470–c. 1550). Bible commentator, philosopher, and physician. He was born in Cesna, Italy, and educated in Rome. He excelled in the study of Talmud and HALAKHAH (Jewish law) and was considered one of the most important TORAH scholars in the city. In 1525 he left Rome and eventually made his way to Bologna. There he set up a school (BET MIDRASH), which he headed until his death.

Sforno's major contribution to Jewish scholarship was his commentary on the PENTATEUCH and other books of the Bible. He emphasized the plain meaning of the text (PESHAT) and developed its ethical teachings (see ETHICS). His introduction to the Pentateuch, *Kavvanot ha-Torah* ("The Inner Meaning of the Torah"), deals with the structure of the Torah and the reasons for the COMMANDMENTS. He also wrote a commentary on AVOT.

SHA'ATNEZ   ("mingled things"). Term for any woven material that contains a mixture of wool and linen, which Jews are forbidden to wear (see Lev. 19:19; Deut. 22:11). The Torah offers no reason for the prohibition of *sha'atnez*. MAIMONIDES suggests that the use of a forbidden mixture was associated with pagan worship. Nowadays, observant Jews purchase their clothing from reliable tailors and manufacturers who open their premises to inspection. Some send their clothing for inspection after purchase to a "*sha'atnez* laboratory," to ensure the replacement of any cloth, sewing thread, or stiffening material that violates the law. Synthetic fabrics and clothing made entirely from cotton need not be checked.

SHABBAT   ("Sabbath"). First tractate (book) of the Order of MO'ED in the Mishnah. Its 24 chapters deal with the kinds of work forbidden on the Sabbath, the prohibition against certain types of work on the eve of the Sabbath, the lighting of the Sabbath candles, and other laws about Sabbath observance.

SHABBAT   See SABBATH

SHABBETAI TSEVI   (1626–1676). False MESSIAH in Turkey; creator of the most powerful and widespread of all Jewish

MESSIANIC MOVEMENTS in the Diaspora. A number of factors help explain the rise of the Shabbatean movement: the Wars of Religion in Europe (1618–1648); the spread of the KABBALAH (mysticism) of Isaac LURIA; the traumatic effect of the Chmielnicki massacres of East European Jewry (1648–1649). Their combined effect made Jews everywhere open to the idea that a messianic redeemer would emerge from the chaos.

Shabbetai Tsevi was ordained as a rabbi at the age of 18. He devoted himself to the study of the mystical ZOHAR and practices of self-denial. He attracted numerous followers. His personal behavior was inconsistent: he had radical mood swings and sometimes acted in irreligious ways. The fact that he was born on TISHAH BE-AV, the traditional birthday of the Messiah, helped to convince him that he was the Messiah. In 1648, he began pronouncing the holy Tetragrammaton (see GOD, NAMES OF), which is forbidden by Jewish law. The rabbis of his native Smyrna tolerated this behavior for a while, but in 1651 they expelled him. He wandered through Greece and Europe, passed through Jerusalem, and eventually made his way to Cairo. There, he married a woman of doubtful reputation named Sarah, whom he called "the bride of the Messiah."

Around this time, Shabbetai Tsevi met a brilliant young rabbi, Nathan of Gaza (1643–1680), who declared him to be the Messiah. Nathan cast himself in the role of ELIJAH the Prophet (who is traditionally meant to announce the arrival of the Messiah). He was able to create great enthusiasm for Shabbetai Tsevi throughout the Jewish world. The list of leading rabbis who were swept along in the movement is shocking. In many communities, those who resisted were intimidated into silence. The date of the long-awaited REDEMPTION was set for 18 June 1666. Jews, rich and poor, sold everything they had in time for the expected redemption.

Shabbetai Tsevi sailed to Constantinople. However, he was arrested by the Turks and imprisoned in February 1666. The Turks did not want to turn him into a martyr. They offered him a choice between death and Islam. On 16 September 1666 Shabbetai Tsevi converted to Islam, though it seems that he, his wife, and others who followed him led a secret Jewish life. Thousands of his followers returned to traditional Judaism; others remained faithful to him even after his death as an exile in Albania (1676).

The Shabbatean Movement Following the APOSTASY of Shabbetai Tsevi, his followers faced violent opposition from the rabbinical authorities and went underground. Here and there, during the 18th century, secret Shabbateans could be discovered, even in the rabbinate. Many were accused of secretly being part Shabbateans. The well-known rabbinical authority Jonathan EYBESHCHÜTZ was thought by some to be a follower. In Turkey, hundreds of "believers" formally converted to Islam and (between 1683 and 1924) their sect of the *Dönmeh* (Turkish for "apostates") could be found chiefly in Salonika. By 1850, except for the *Dönmeh*, Shabbateanism had practically vanished. Until recently, a small *Dönmeh* community existed in Istanbul.

SHADKHAN ("matchmaker"). A person who arranges marriages, usually for payment. *Shiddukhin* (arranged marriages) were the usual and preferred method of marrying off young people throughout much of Jewish history (see Gen. 24). The Talmud stresses the importance of arranging marriages when it says that although all kinds of business transactions are forbidden on the Sabbath, arrangements may be made for the betrothal of young girls on the day (*Shab.* 150a).

Traditionally, the *shadkhan*'s profession was highly respected. A rabbi was the natural go-between, because he knew the families and his judgment was trusted. The great scholar of the 15th century, R. Jacob MÖLLN, worked as a *shadkhan*. The sages discussed the amount to be paid for a match. The fee was based on the dowry – two percent in most cases, three percent if the couple lived more than ten miles apart.

To this day, in ultra-Orthodox communities, marriages are still arranged by parents or rabbis, and in many cases the introductions are arranged by a professional *shadkhan*. Following the initial introduction, the young people usually meet three or four times before deciding to marry. They are free to refuse the match if it is not to their liking.

SHAHARIT See MORNING SERVICE

SHALI'AH ("messenger," emissary"). A person sent to perform a specific task, an agent who can act on someone else's behalf; an emissary from the Land of Israel to Jewish communities in the Diaspora.

In Jewish law, a bill of DIVORCE may be handed over or received by an agent (*Git.* 4:1, 62b) and HAMETS (leaven) may be sold to a non-Jew through an agent. Goods and property may similarly be bought and sold and even a MARRIAGE contract may be drawn up on behalf of the groom. The principle is "a man's agent is like himself" (*Ber.* 5:5), meaning that acts performed by an agent are binding on the one who has appointed him.

The *sheli'ah mitzvah* is another form of agency in Jewish law. This is someone who is sent to perform a religious function on behalf of another. The *sheli'ah tsibbur*, "messenger of the congregation" or prayer leader sent up to the front of the SYNAGOGUE to conduct the service, is an example. Also in this category is one who is sent abroad to collect money for religious institutions and for the poor in the Land of Israel. Agents of this kind have included some well-known scholars, including Moses Alshekh and Hayyim Yosef David Azulai.

SHALOM ZAKHAR ("peace to the male child"). Friday night festive gathering in Ashkenazi communities just after the birth of a son. The Talmud states: "A boy is born – peace comes to the world" (*Nid.* 31b). It is customary to eat lentils, typically associated with mourning, at a *Shalom Zakhar*. This relates to the traditional belief that when the child was in the womb, he had been taught the entire TORAH, but as he entered the world, an angel struck him on the upper lip and he forgot everything.

SHALOSH REGALIM   See PILGRIM FESTIVALS

SHAMMAI   (c. 50 BCE–c. 30 CE). SAGE in Erets Israel and leader of the SANHEDRIN. He and HILLEL were the last of the five "pairs" (ZUGOT) who transmitted the ORAL LAW. In legal matters, Shammai – a builder by trade – had a more severe approach than Hillel.

Shammai and Hillel founded competing schools (see BET SHAMMAI AND BET HILLEL). There were basic differences in the orientation of the two schools. Bet Shammai tended to oppose contact with non-Jews. They seemed to favor a more conservative approach, based on a more literal interpretation of the Bible.

SHAMMASH   (lit. "servant"). Community or synagogue official; paid sexton in the synagogue. The *shammash* played various roles depending on the institution he served: tax collector, bailiff, process server, secretary, messenger, and even gravedigger. In Eastern Europe, he called people to morning prayers by knocking on their window shutters.

In the 20th century, the *shammash* filled a number of roles in the synagogue. Often he was responsible for running the services in an orderly way; in some cases he read the Torah.

The term *shammash* also applies to the extra light on the HANUKKAH *menorah* from which the other candles are lit.

SHAS   Hebrew acronym of *Shishah Sedarim*, "Six Orders" (of the MISHNAH or TALMUD). Common name for the Babylonian Talmud.

SHAVING   The Bible states, "You shall not round the corners of your head, neither shall you destroy the corners of your beard" (Lev. 19:27). As the ORAL LAW explains, this verse talks about more than one prohibition: removing one's sideburns (known as *pe'ot*), "rounding the corners" of the head, and "destroying" one of the five corners on one's face (two on each cheek and one on the chin). In addition, sideburns must be left to grow until they reach the beginning of the cheekbone, and must be long enough to be held between two fingers. Many ultra-Orthodox Jews do not cut their sideburns at all but let them grow and curl them behind their ears. According to the Oral Law, hair is considered "destroyed" if it is closely shaven. Since using a razor blade touches the skin directly, many Orthodox Jews use an electric razor, because the blades do not come in direct contact with the skin. Other observant Jews wear beards, since they consider this part of the Jewish heritage.

There are specific periods when one is not allowed to shave or get a haircut, for example, on the SABBATH and FESTIVALS. Observant Jews also do not shave in the OMER period between PASSOVER and SHAVU'OT. However, some rabbis permit shaving on intermediate days of festivals, and on Fridays (in honor of the Sabbath) throughout this period. Shaving is also forbidden during the THREE WEEKS between 17 Tammuz and 9 Av, although there are differences in the Ashkenazi and Sephardi

customs during this time. A person in MOURING does not shave for 30 days.

SHAVU'OT   ("Weeks"). Second of the three PILGRIM FESTIVALS, which is observed in Israel and by REFORM Jews for one day (6 Sivan) and in the Diaspora for two days (6–7 Sivan). The only festival not given an exact date in the Bible.

Shavu'ot is known in English as the Feast of Weeks, Pentecost, and the Festival of the Giving of the Law. The name "Feast of Weeks" comes from the Bible's instruction to count seven weeks from the PASSOVER harvest festival until the second harvest festival (Ex. 34:22, Lev. 23:15ff., Deut. 16:9–10). The rabbis identify this second harvest festival with Shavu'ot. The seven-week period between Passover and Shavu'ot is known as the OMER. The word "Pentecost," which means "fiftieth" in Greek, refers to the fact that the festival is celebrated on the fiftieth day of the Omer. The name "Festival of the Giving of the Law" comes from the tradition that the TORAH was given at mount SINAI on 6 Sivan. Shavu'ot is also called *Hag ha-Katsir* ("Harvest Festival"; Ex.23:16) and *Yom ha-Bikkurim* ("Day of the First Ripe Fruits"; Num. 28:26). The three days before Shavu'ot are known as *sheloshet yemei ha-hagbalah* ("Three Days of Preparation"; see Ex. 19:11–12). During these days the MOURNING customs of the OMER period do not apply.

In ancient times, there was a huge farmers' parade to Jerusalem. The farmers would gather all their FIRST FRUITS (*bikkurim*) and march to the TEMPLE, where they would bring a thanksgiving offering. The Mishnah gives a very detailed description of the farmers' preparations, their offerings, and the ceremonies that took place in the Temple (*Bik.* 3). After the Temple was destroyed, Shavu'ot was mostly identified as the anniversary of the giving of the Torah and the TEN COMMANDMENTS at Sinai.

In many communities it is customary to stay awake dur-

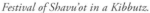

Festival of Shavu'ot in a Kibbutz.

ing Shavu'ot night and study the Torah and the Oral Law. R. Solomon Alkabets and other Sephardi kabbalists established the custom of TIKKUN *Leil Shavu'ot* ("Spiritual Study Session for Shavu'ot Eve") in the 16th century, which included reading verses from the Bible and chapters from the Mishnah. In honor of the festival, synagogues are decorated with flowers or plants. This is a symbol of the summer harvest, which starts after Shavu'ot. Another reason for this custom is the MIDRASH that a miracle happened and Mount Sinai, which is in the desert, was covered with plants when God gave the Torah.

Dairy foods are usually eaten on Shavu'ot. The traditional explanation for this is that on the day of the Giving of the Torah, the Israelites did not have enough time to prepare a meat meal. Other explanations are that light dairy dishes are appropriate for a summer festival, and that dairy foods are a symbol for Erets Israel, the Land of Milk and Honey.

The Book of RUTH is read as part of the service. Its story takes place in the harvest season and is therefore suitable for Shavu'ot. In addition, Ruth's commitment to the Jewish faith is similar to the Israelites' acceptance of the Torah.

Since the Middle Ages, there has been a custom of starting the formal Jewish education of young children on Shavu'ot. Today, in many communities (particularly in America), the festival marks the graduation of teenagers from the formal synagogue education system, or CONFIRMATION in Reform synagogues. In Israel, many kibbutzim hold a "First Fruits" (*Hag ha-Bikkurim*) celebration on Shavu'ot, where the fruits and industrial products of the kibbutz are displayed. Israeli kindergartens hold special pre-Shavu'ot celebrations to which the children carry baskets of fruit and wear wreaths on their heads.

SHE-HEHEYANU ("Who has kept us alive"). Name given to the BENEDICTION said over something new. It is said when moving into a new home, wearing a new item of clothing, or eating a new season's fruit. This blessing is also said on the first evening of festivals; before the blowing of the SHOFAR (ram's horn) on ROSH HA-SHANAH; when taking the FOUR SPECIES before HALLEL on SUKKOT; when lighting the first HANUKKAH candle; before the Scroll of ESTHER is read in the synagogue on PURIM; at the Redemption of the FIRSTBORN ceremony. In Israel, a father also recites *She-heheyanu at the* CIRCUMCISION ceremony. The text of the blessing reads: "Blessed are You, Lord our God, King of the universe, Who has kept us alive [*she-heheyanu*], sustained us, and brought us to this season."

SHEHITAH ("ritual slaughter"). The halakhic (Jewish legal) way of slaughtering a KOSHER animal. The details of the exact method of *shehitah* do not appear in the WRITTEN LAW. They are discussed in the Mishnah and the Talmud in the book of HULLIN.

The ritual slaughterer (*shohet*) must be certified by a qualified rabbinical authority. He has to perform *shehitah* at least three times in front of a supervisor before he is certified. The knife used by the *shohet*, the *hallaf*, must be sharpened to a perfect edge. If even a small defect is found on the blade, either before or after slaughtering, the slaughter is considered invalid.

One purpose of *shehitah* is to prevent cruelty to animals (another commandment of the Bible). Experts say that it is a fast and comparatively painless way of killing an animal. According to the MIDRASH, the commandment to slaughter in a specific way makes the Jew more caring and sensitive (Gen. R. 44:1).

In the 19th and 20th centuries, a number of anti-*shehitah* movements appeared. In Germany, in the middle of the 19th century *shehitah* was officially banned. Switzerland (1893), Norway (1930), and Sweden (1937) followed this example. The banning of *shehitah* was sometimes a hidden expression of ANTI-SEMITISM.

Today, *shehitah* is performed mainly in central slaughterhouses that are owned by big meatpacking companies. When *shehitah* is done, there is usually a *mashgiah* (*kashrut* supervisor) present. All meat is then stamped to make sure that shoppers know that it is kosher. In Israel, the Chief Rabbinate, together with some private organizations, supervises the *shehitah*.

SHEKALIM ("annual half-shekel tax"). Fourth tractate (book) of the Order of MO'ED in the Mishnah. Its eight chapters deal with the half-shekel that every male over the age of 20 had to give for the maintenance of the TEMPLE each year (cf. Ex. 30:11–16, II Kings 12:5–17).

SHEKHINAH A term for the presence of God in a specific place or in the world. It does not appear in the Bible, but it does in the Talmud, the AGGADAH, and the TARGUM. The SAGES use the term *Shekhinah* to describe the relationship between God and Israel. Also, if harmony exists between a man and his wife, the *Shekhinah* is said to be with them.

In the Middle Ages, Jewish philosophers like SAADIAH GAON and MAIMONIDES thought about God and the *Shekhinah* as two different concepts. They thought of the *Shekhinah* as God's first creation. According to Maimonides, the *Shekhinah*, and not God Himself, was reveled to the prophets (*ibid.* I, 21). The separation of God and the *Shekhinah* also appears in Jewish MYSTICISM. The kabbalists did not see the *Shekhinah* as a creation, like the philosophers. They saw it as part of the Divine world, as the lowest of the SEFIROT (heavenly Divine levels). The *Shekhinah* was considered the feminine part of God's nature. In *Sefer* BAHIR, the *Shekhinah* is referred to as a mother or daughter. The ZOHAR sees the *Shekhinah* as a bride. When she is far from her "mate," the *sefirot* above her, she is controlled by dark powers that turn her into an evil force. The *Zohar* further explains that only good deeds can reunite the *Shekhinah* with the other *sefirot*. At the same time, bad deeds can separate them even more. These ideas are main concepts in HASIDISM.

SHELOSHIM See MOURNING

SHEMA Basic statement of the Jewish faith: "Hear O Israel, the Lord is our God, the Lord is one" (Deut. 6:4). The *Shema*

THE SHEMA

Hear O Israel, the Lord is our God, the Lord is one. You shall love the Lord your God with all your heart and with all your soul and with all your might. These words which I command you this day you shall take to heart. You shall teach them diligently to your children. You shall recite them when you are at home and when you are away, when you lie down and when you rise up. You shall bind them as a sign on your hand, they shall be a reminder above your eyes, and you shall inscribe them on the doorposts of your home and upon your gates.

is part of the MORNING and EVENING SERVICE. It includes three paragraphs: (a) *Shema* (Deut. 6:4–9), which is the acceptance of God as the God of the Jewish people; (b) *Ve-haya im shamo'a* (Deut. 11:13–21), which adds the concept of REWARD AND PUNISHMENT; (c) TSITSIT (Num. 15:37–41), which describes the law of putting *tsitsit* (fringes) on clothes that have four corners, and mentions God's rescue of Israel from Egypt.

After the first verse of *Shema* is recited, the sentence BARUKH SHEM KEVOD …, "Blessed be the name of His glorious kingdom for ever" is added. In general it is said quietly, but on the DAY OF ATONEMENT it is said aloud by the whole community. Two blessings come before the *Shema* both times. In the evening there are two blessings after the *Shema* but in the morning there is only one. This blessing, *Ga'al Yisrael* – "Who redeemed Israel" – must be followed immediately by the silent AMIDAH.

According to Jewish law, all adult Jewish males must say the *Shema* twice a day, once in the morning and once in the evening. It is usually the first prayer that Jewish parents teach their very small children. In the Ashkenazi SYNAGOGUE, each person says the *Shema* on his own, whereas among SEPHARDIM, the congregation says the *Shema* together with the cantor.

When reciting the *Shema* it is very important to pronounce the words correctly and to concentrate on their meaning. Many Jews cover their eyes to improve their concentration. Parts of the *Shema* are written in the MEZUZAH on the doorpost, and in both the hand and the head TEFILLIN boxes. The *Shema* is also part of the NIGHT PRAYERS, which are called *keri'at Shema [she] al ha-mittah* ("reading of the *Shema* in bed"); and part of the deathbed prayer. Throughout history, whenever Jews have been put to death, they have recited the *Shema* in their last living moments, confirming their belief in the One God.

The first verse of the *Shema* is part of the daily morning blessings. On Sabbaths and festivals, it is recited aloud by the cantor and the congregation, before the READING OF THE LAW, and in the KEDUSHAH section of the ADDITIONAL SERVICE *Amidah*. At the end of NE'ILAH, the last service of the DAY OF ATONEMENT, the whole congregation recites this verse aloud, in order to show their communal acceptance of God.

SHEMAYAH AND AVTALYON (1st cent. BCE). The fourth of the five ZUGOT, the pairs of sages who connected the periods of the Maccabees and the *tannaim*. According to tradition, they were either converts or children of converts. Shemayah was president of the SANHEDRIN (*Nasi*), and Avtalyon was the head of the law court (*av bet din*). Both are quoted in the Mishnah (*Avot* 1:10–11).

SHEMINI ATSERET ("Eighth Day of Solemn Assembly"). Festival observed immediately after SUKKOT (Tabernacles). The term *Atseret* (lit. "concluding festival") is also used for the last day of PASSOVER (Deut. 16:8). The rabbis also use it for SHAVU'OT, which ends the OMER period (*RH* 1:2; *Shev.* 1:1).

Since Shemini Atseret is a festival of its own, special additions are recited in the AMIDAH and the KIDDUSH. The SHE-HE-HEYANU blessing, which can only be said for a new festival, is recited at the end of *Kiddush*. According to rabbinic law, the yearly cycle of PENTATEUCH readings ends and begins again on this day. Because of this, the festival is also called SIMHAT TORAH, the Rejoicing of the Law. In the Diaspora, where there are two days of Shemini Atseret, Simhat Torah is celebrated on the second day. Whenever there is no Sabbath between the first and last day of Sukkot, the Book of ECCLESIASTES is read on Shemini Atseret.

There are two important additions to the Shemini Atseret prayers. The one is the Prayer for RAIN, which is recited during the ADDITIONAL SERVICE *Amidah*. The second is the *Yizkor* MEMORIAL SERVICE after the READING OF THE LAW in Ashkenazi synagogues.

SHEMONEH ESREH   See AMIDAH

SHERIRA GAON (c. 906–1006). Head of the Academy of Pumbedita in Babylonia; appointed in 968. Sherira came from a long line of *ge'onim* (see GAON). He strengthened the Babylonian ACADEMIES, encouraged contact with Jews in other lands, and wrote many RESPONSA in answer to Jewish legal questions. He is best known for *Iggeret ha-Rav Sherira*, his letter to Jacob bar Nissim of Kairouan, North Africa, in 987. In the letter, Sherira answers R. Jacob's questions on the history and development of the ORAL LAW. Because the answer is long and very detailed, it is an important source about the history of that period. The letter became very famous in Europe because of its "French" version and its "Spanish" version. Scholars today think that the "Spanish" version is closer to the original letter. Sherira's Bible and Talmud commentaries are known only because other writers, later in history, quote them. In 998, after being thrown into jail by his enemies, Sherira resigned from his position, which his son, HAI GAON, took over.

SHEVA BERAKHOT   See MARRIAGE

SHEVAT (Akkad. *Shabatu*). Eleventh month of the Jewish religious CALENDAR; fifth month of the Hebrew civil year.

It has 30 days and usually falls during January–Febuary. Its zodiac sign is Aquarius, the Water Carrier. On the first day of Shevat, MOSES started to read the last book of the TORAH to the Israelites (Duet. 1:3). The NEW YEAR FOR TREES, also known as Tu bi-Shevat, falls on 15 Shevat.

SHEVI'IT ("Sabbatical Year"). Fifth tractate (book) of the Order of ZERA'IM in the Mishnah. Its ten chapters discuss the laws prohibiting any development of agricultural land in Erets Israel in the seventh year (cf. Ex. 23:10–11, Lev. 25:2–7; Deut. 15:1–3). The book also deals with the laws of the "release of debts" during the seventh year.

SHEVU'OT ("Oaths"). Sixth tractate (book) of the Order of NEZIKIN in the Mishnah. Its eight chapters deal with two main issues: the laws of oaths taken in court and in private life, and the rules of ritual defilement (cf. Lev. 5:1–13, 20:26; Ex. 22:6; Num. 30:3). The book also deals with the laws of deposits and four types of trustees.

SHIDDUKHIN See MARRIAGE; SHADKHAN

SHIR HA-KAVOD See ANIM ZEMIROT

SHIR HA-MA'ALOT ("Song of Ascents"). The opening words of each of PSALMS 120–134. The Mishnah recalls (*Mid.* 2:5) that there were 15 steps (*ma'alot*) in the TEMPLE, between the Israelites' and the women's courts. The LEVITES used to play music and sing one of the 15 *Ma'alot* psalms on each step. This was also the custom during the WATER-DRAWING FESTIVAL (*Suk.* 5:4). The basis of these psalms are the songs that used to be sung on the way to Jerusalem on the three PILGRIM FESTIVALS.

In the Ashkenazi rite, Psalms 120–134 are recited at the end of the Sabbath AFTERNOON SERVICE on every Sabbath between SUKKOT and PASSOVER. ASHKENAZIM also recite Psalm 126 – a remembrance of Zion and its promised restoration – before GRACE AFTER MEALS on Sabbaths and festivals.

SHIR HA-SHIRIM See SONG OF SONGS

SHIVAH See MOURNING

SHIVAH ASAR BE-TAMMUZ ("17th of [the month of] Tammuz"). Fast day established to commemorate the beginning of the Babylonians' destruction of the defense wall surrounding Jerusalem in 586 BCE. Three weeks later the city was captured and the First Temple was destroyed.

According to the Bible (II Kings 25, Jer. 53), the Babylonian armies breached the walls of Jerusalem on the ninth day of Tammuz. Therefore, it is possible that the fast was originally observed on the ninth and not on the 17th of the month, but was canceled when the Temple was rebuilt (cf. Zech. 8:19). With regard to the last days of the Second Temple in 70 CE, Josephus mentions that the Romans breached Jerusalem's walls on the 17th of Tammuz. After the Second Temple was destroyed on TISHAH BE-AV (the Ninth of Av), the rabbis decided that one fast, on the 17th of Tammuz, would link the historical events of both the First and Second Temple periods.

Other sad events also happened on this day: MOSES broke the first Tablets of the Law when he came down from Mount SINAI and found the Israelites worshiping the GOLDEN CALF; the Greeks burned a SCROLL OF THE LAW and put an idol in the SANCTUARY (*Ta'an.* 4:6); and the daily ritual of bringing sacrifices to the Temple came to an end.

The THREE WEEKS between this fast and the Ninth of Av are a time of public mourning. The fast of 17 Tammuz starts at sunrise on the day itself and not on the night before (see FASTING AND FAST DAYS). Special Torah passages are read in the MORNING and the AFTERNOON SERVICES. In the afternoon, the passages are followed by a HAFTARAH taken from Isaiah (55:6–56:8).

SHNEUR ZALMAN OF LYADY (known as *Ba'al ha-Tanya*, "author of the *Tanya*"; 1745–1813). Founder of the CHABAD movement in HASIDISM. Already at a young age he was very knowledgeable in Talmud and HALAKHAH (Jewish law), and also in mathematics and astronomy. In 1764 he left home to study under DOV BAER, the Maggid of Mezhirech, who was a great Hasidic prayer master. The Maggid was very impressed with him and asked him to prepare an up-to-date code of Jewish law. Part of it was lost in a fire, but the remaining sections were published as *Shulhan Arukh ha-Rav* (1814). This book is considered a major halakhic achievement.

After the Maggid's death in 1772, Shneur Zalman began to attract followers in Belorrusia and Lithuania. In 1777 he became the official leader of Hasidism in northern Russia, where he established the Chabad movement. He wrote a book of spiritual guidance for his Hasidim called *Likkutei Amarim* ("Collected

---

SHNEUR ZALMAN'S SAYINGS

Good qualities that are based on logic are better than good qualities that are not based on logic

Study of Halakhah should not be interrupted for prayer

Just like salt adds flavor to food, Kabbalah adds flavor to the Torah.

Some of the doors of the holy places in heaven can only be opened through song.

Lord of the universe: I want neither Your Garden of Eden nor Your rewards in the hereafter. What I desire is You alone!

The only way of turning darkness into light is by giving to the poor.

Every act of kindness that God does for man should make him feel humble, not proud.

Opposite page: Opening page of the Book of Numbers. From the Lisbon Bible, 1483.
Overleaf left: Man blowing shofar near The Tower of David in Jerusalem.
Overleaf right: Facade of the Herodian Temple. Part of a scale-model of the Holy City in Second Temple times, Jerusalem.

117

לרע׳ ד׳ פת׳ וסימנהון לא יבקר בין טוב לרע׳ הוי האמרים לרע טוב׳ רגליהם לרע ירוצו׳ ט׳ וג׳ קמ׳ וסימ׳
על׳ כל מחשבתם לרע׳ כי לא תהיה אחרית לרע׳ כי מסלף רשעים לרע׳ וכל למרע דכו פת׳ במב קמ׳ וסימ׳ ולא דבר אבשלום ושניהם המלכים לבבם למרע׳ ט׳

אחזתו לא ימכר ולא יגאל כל
חרם קדש קדשים הוא ליהוה׃
כל חרם אשר יחרם מן האדם
לא יפדה מות יומת׃ וכל מעשר
הארץ מזרע הארץ מפרי העץ
ליהוה הוא קדש ליהוה׃ ואם
גאל יגאל איש ממעשרו ח
חמשיתו יסף עליו׃ וכל מעשר
בקר וצאן כל אשר יעבר תחת
השבט העשירי יהיה קדש
ליהוה׃ לא יבקר בין טוב לרע
ולא ימירנו ואם המר ימירנו
והיה הוא ותמורתו יהיה קדש
לא יגאל׃ אלה המצות אשר
צוה יהוה את משה אל בני
ישראל בהר סיני׃

וידבר

יהוה אל משה במדבר סיני
באהל מועד באחד לחדש
השני בשנה השנית לצאתם
מארץ מצרים לאמר׃ שאו

את ראש כל עדת בני ישראל
למשפחתם לבית אבתם במספר
שמות כל זכר לגלגלתם׃ מבן
עשרים שנה ומעלה כל יצא
צבא בישראל תפקדו אתם
לצבאתם אתה ואהרן׃ ואתכם
יהיו איש איש למטה איש ראש
לבית אבתיו הוא׃ ואלה שמות
האנשים אשר יעמדו אתכם
לראובן אליצור בן שדיאור׃
לשמעון שלמיאל בן צורישדי׃
ליהודה נחשון בן עמינדב׃
ליששכר נתנאל בן צוער׃ לזבולן
אליאב בן חלן׃ לבני יוסף לאפרים
אלישמע בן עמיהוד למנשה
גמליאל בן פדהצור׃ לבנימן
אבידן בן גדעני׃ לדן אחיעזר
בן עמישדי׃ לאשר פגעיאל
בן עכרן׃ לגד אליסף בן דעואל׃
לנפתלי אחירע בן עינן׃ אלה
קריאי העדה נשיאי מטות
אבותם ראשי אלפי ישראל הם׃
ויקח משה ואהרן את האנשים
האלה אשר נקבו בשמות׃ ואת
כל העדה הקהילו באחד לחדש
השני ויתילדו על משפחתם

שמות ט׳ מל׳ בתו׳ וסימנהון ויקרא האדם שמות׳ ויקרא להן שמות׳ שאו את ראש מל עדת׳ ואת כל העדה הקהילו׳ ב׳ בו׳
ויהיו בני ראובן בכר ישראל׳ לבני שמעון לבני גד לבני מנשה׳ לאלה תחלק הארץ׳ ואתכם ג׳ וסימ׳ ואתכם יהיו ואתכם עבדי אדעכם
אבותם ב׳ מל בתו׳ וסימ׳ אלה קרואי העדה ואת שם אהרן וכל נבי וכתו דכו כלה הם וסימ׳ וכלם בשמות להגיד בית אבתם וחב׳ גם בנעהם וכני בנעהם
גם יהודה
לא שמרו ט׳

מ֗ש֗נה

לכל לראש בחר׳ כאום דלת ראש׳ כביכורה תאֵנה בראש׳ ביטה
ואותה דרוש מכל אום לפרוש׳ לנשאה על כל ראש גועלה תשיה
למצר ראש׳ והיא תתריס ראש׳ בכסא כבוד מראש׳

Sayings"). This book was republished in its complete form as the *Tanya*.

In 1798 Shneur Zalman was accused of being a political danger to the state and was put in prison. He was soon cleared of all charges and released on the 19ᵗʰ of Kislev. The Chabad Hasidim celebrate a special festival on this day. After this incident, Shneur Zalman moved to Lyady, Belorussia, but was forced to leave when Napoleon attacked Moscow; he died in the Ukraine

SHO'AH   See HOLOCAUST

SHOFAR   (ram's horn). A kind of trumpet that is blown ritually during the season of REPENTANCE. It is first mentioned as being heard at the REVELATION on Mount SINAI (Ex. 19:16, 19). The *shofar* was also blown to announce the JUBILEE YEAR (Lev. 25:9–10), to call the Israelites to war (Josh. 6:4ff.; Judg. 3:27, 6:34, 7:18–22), and to mark the appointment of a new king (1 Kings 1:34). In TEMPLE days, the *shofar* was used in Temple services and announced the beginning of the SABBATH. Since the Temple's destruction, *shofar* blasts are heard mainly on ROSH HA-SHANAH, the Jewish New Year, which the Bible refers to as "a day of sounding the horn" (*Yom Teru'ah*; Num. 29:1). The Mishnah says (*RH* 3:2–2) that a *shofar* can be made from the horn of any ritually fit animal (sheep, goat, antelope, or gazelle), but not from the horn of a cow or an ox, because these animals are a reminder of the IDOLATRY of the GOLDEN CALF.

It is the traditional custom to blow the *shofar* throughout the month of Elul (except on the eve of Rosh ha-Shanah), towards the end of the morning prayers. It is sounded on both days of Rosh ha-Shanah and at the end of the Concluding Service (NE'ILAH) on the DAY OF ATONEMENT. SEPHARDIM often blow it during HOSHANA RABBAH morning prayers. Orthodox and CONSERVATIVE Jews do not sound the *shofar* on the Sabbath.

According to Jewish law, 100 notes are sounded on each day of Rosh ha-Shanah in a specific order. There are different kinds of *shofar* notes: *teki'ah*, a continuous rising note; *shevarim*, three sobbing sounds; *teru'ah*, nine short blasts; and *teki'ah gedolah*,

Blowing the Shofar.

a long drawn-out *teki'ah*. Since 1949, whenever an Israeli president is sworn in, the *shofar* is sounded.

SHOFAROT   Last of the three middle blessings in the ADDITIONAL SERVICE (*Musaf*) recited on ROSH HA-SHANAH (the Jewish New Year). The blessing's introduction describes the use of the ram's horn at the giving of the TORAH at Mount SINAI. Ten verses from the Bible are then recited: three each from the PENTATEUCH, the HAGIOGRAPHA ("Writings"), and the PROPHETS; and one additional verse from the PENTATEUCH. The section ends with a blessing addressing God as "He Who hears with mercy the sound of the blowing of the *shofar* by His people Israel."

SHOHET   See SHEHITAH

SHOWBREAD   (Heb. *lehem ha-panim*; shew bread; "bread of display"). The 12 loaves of bread placed on a golden table in the SANCTUARY in the desert, and in the TEMPLE, as commanded in the PENTATEUCH (Ex. 25:30; Lev. 24:5–9; Num. 4:7). The 12 loaves are a symbol of the 12 TRIBES of Israel. The showbread was switched every week, on the Sabbath: the fresh showbread was put on the golden table, and the loaves from the previous week, which were still fresh, were given to the PRIESTS to eat. The sages criticized the members of the Avtinas (Garmu) family, who were responsible for baking the showbread, because they refused to teach others how to bake this bread.

SHTETL   (from the Yiddish *shtot*, "town") Smalltown East European Jewish community. The *shtetl* was established in the 16ᵗʰ century, when Jews were invited by the Polish nobility to settle on their lands and become an urban commercial class. Over the next few centuries, the *shtetl* developed into a unique social and cultural institution. In the *shtetl* life revolved around the Jewish CALENDAR, the home, the SYNAGOGUE, and the market place. Religious men prayed and studied, women worked in the home, and most people tried very hard to make a living from small dealings and traditional Jewish crafts. The synagogue was a place where great scholars and important men came in contact with drifters and beggars. The COMMUNITY was involved in all aspect of Jewish life – happy and sad occasions, both public and private. The spoken language in the *shtetl* was Yiddish.

In the 19ᵗʰ century, the *shtetl* way of life spread to Jewish settlements in Russia and the Austro-Hungarian Empire; in the 20ᵗʰ century it weakened because of modernization; and in the Nazi HOLOCAUST it was destroyed. The *shtetl* is described in the stories of Shalom Aleichem and is portrayed in the paintings of Marc Chagall.

SHTIBL   ("little room"). Yiddish term used by Hasidic Jews for their own type of SYNAGOGUE, which combines a prayer, study, and social center. Because of the conflict with the MITNAGGEDIM in the late 18ᵗʰ century, Hasidim could not

Opposite page: Initial-word panel from a festival prayer book, the Worms Mahzor. *Germany, 1272.*

take part in many aspects of religious and communal Jewish life in Eastern Europe. As a result, they established informal houses of worship, where prayers were held according to their special style. The *shtibl* was very simple; sometimes it only had a few tables and chairs in it. This was all the Hasidim needed for joyful prayer, for learning with their spiritual leader (*Rebbe*), and for communal meals.

SHUL   (lit. "school"). Yiddish term used by Ashkenazi Jews for a SYNAGOGUE. The term developed from the ancient Roman word *schola,* a house of prayer. In classical German the term for synagogue is *Judenschule*. When the Jews settled in Poland they shortened this term and used the word *shul* to describe the synagogue. This became the Yiddish term too. The *shul* has a special section for women, above or in the back of the main section of the synagogue. It is known in Yiddish as the *Vaybershul* ("woman's synagogue").

SHULHAN ARUKH   (lit. "set table"). The standard code of Jewish law (HALAKHAH), written by Joseph CARO of Safed in the 16ᵗʰ century, with additional notes (*Mappah*) by Moses ISSERLES of Cracow.

The *Shulhan Arukh* is a summary of Caro's *Bet Yosef*, a commentary on the *Arba'ah Turim* written by JACOB BEN ASHER, which divided Jewish law into four main areas. In his introduction, Caro writes that he was guided mainly by the opinions of Isaac ALFASI, MAIMONIDES, and ASHER BEN JEHIEL. The KABBALAH also influenced him. As a Sephardi Jew, he ruled according to customs of the SEPHARDIM.

While Caro was writing his commentary, Moses Isserles started to write his own commentary to the *Tur*, which he called *Darkei Moshe*. When Caro's *Bet Yosef* reached Poland, Isserles was surprised that the work had already been done by Caro, but he decided to continue writing his commentary because the *Bet Yosef* left out many of the rulings and customs of the ASHKENAZIM. Isserles added his notes (*haggahot*) to the *Shulhan Arukh* once it was published; he called these notes *Mappah*, "a tablecloth" to cover Caro's "table." Together they formed the official code of Jewish law: the Sephardim follow Caro's rulings and the ASHKENAZIM follow Isserles' rulings. The differences between the two have to do with the fact that the Ashkenazi rabbis usually had a more strict approach to *halakhah*.

When the *Shulhan Arukh* was first published, many scholars did not accept it as a legal authority because Caro did not specify his exact halakhic (Jewish legal) sources. Despite these objections, over the years the *Shulhan Arukh* and the *Mappah* became the main text used regularly by religious leaders as a halakhic reference. In the 19ᵗʰ century, Solomon Ganzfried of Hungary published a shortened version of the book, *Kitsur* ("shortened") *Shulhan Arukh*.

SHUSHAN PURIM   See PURIM

SIDDUR   See PRAYER BOOK

SIFRA   Halakhic (Jewish legal) MIDRASH on LEVITICUS. In sources from Erets Israel, the book is known as *Torat Kohanim* ("The Law of the Priests"). Babylonian sources refer to it as *Sifra* ("The Book") or as *Sifra de-Vei Rav* ("the Book of [the Academy] of Rav"). Because of this name, some scholars think this Midrash was gathered by RAV, the Babylonian AMORA.

The *Sifra* is often quoted in both Talmuds; the quotes in the Jerusalem Talmud are almost word for word. The book is divided into sections that deal with different subjects, and each section is divided into smaller chapters. Generally, each chapter starts with the first word of a verse from the Bible, followed by an explanation.

SIFREI DEUTERONOMY   (Aram. "books"). MIDRASH (commentary) on the Book of DEUTERONOMY from the time of the Mishnah. It includes both stories and explanations of laws. Most of the Midrash comes from the school of R. AKIVA, but some of it is from the schools of R. ISHMAEL and R. SIMEON BAR YOHAI.

SIFREI NUMBERS   (Aram. "books"). MIDRASH (commentary) on the Book of NUMBERS from the time of the Mishnah. It includes both stories and explanations of laws. The explanations in it are very similar to those that appear in the *Mekhilta de-Rabbi Ishmael*. Most of the Midrash comes from the school of R. ISHMAEL, but some of it is from the school of R. AKIVA. Today the text is divided according to the weekly TORAH readings and matches the annual cycle of the READING OF THE LAW, but the original document was divided differently.

SIGD   Ethiopian Jewish festival celebrating the giving of the TORAH on Mount SINAI. It is held on the 29ᵗʰ day on the Hebrew month of Heshvan (October/November). In Ethiopia, the Jews would go to the highest mountain in the area; there they would pray and have a festive meal. The festival is also celebrated by Israeli Ethiopian Jews in JERUSALEM. They wear white clothes, look out at the Old City and the TEMPLE

Ethiopian women and children assembling in Jerusalem to celebrate the traditional Sigd festival of the Ethiopian Jews.

MOUNT from the promenade in the Talpiyot neighborhood, and recite special prayers.

SIMEON   See TRIBES, TWELVE

SIMEON BAR YOHAI   Fourth generation *tanna*, one of the great students of R. AKIVA, and traditional author of the ZOHAR. Bar Yohai studied at R. Akiva's academy in Benei Berak, Erets Israel, for 13 years. His own school was in Tekoa, in the Upper Galilee, where he developed the method of HERMENEUTICS (interpreting texts). The basic text of the *Mekhilta de-Rabbi Simeon bar Yohai* on the book of EXODUS and much of the MIDRASH from SIFREI DEUTERONOMY came from his school and were influenced by R. Akiva's teachings. JUDAH HA-NASI was one of his students.

R. Simeon challenged Roman rule all the time. After the BAR KOKHBA revolt, the Roman authorities sentenced him to death, so he and his son R. Eleazar went into hiding. According to the Talmud, they hid for 13 years in a cave, where they continued to study TORAH. The story of the miracles he performed while in the cave is the basis of the belief that he was the author of the *Zohar*, even though many of them have been proven impossible. After the threat on his life was withdrawn, he became the leader of the people and was part of a delegation to the new Roman emperor.

On LAG BA-OMER, believed to be the anniversary of his death, thousands of people in Israel travel to Meron to pray at his grave, bonfires are lit, and special poems are recited about him.

SAYINGS OF SIMEON BAR YOHAI

Hatred upsets the social order.

Throw yourself into a blazing furnace rather than shame a neighbor in public.

Honoring parents is more important than honoring God.

God is angry at one who does not leave a son to be his heir.

It is a duty to save a woman from rape, even at the cost of the attacker's life.

Observing a commandment by performing a transgression is forbidden.

A liar's punishment is that he is not believed even when he tells the truth.

Work is great because it honors him who performs it.

SIMEON BEN GAMALIEL   See GAMALIEL

SIMEON BEN LAKISH   (known in the Babylonian Talmud as Resh Lakish; c. 200–275 CE). Second generation *amora* in Erets Israel. When he was young, Resh Lakish could not find work, so he became a Roman gladiator. After he became friends with

JOHANAN BEN NAPPAHA, he studied under him in Sepphoris and married his sister. Resh Lakish became one of the leading SAGES in Erets Israel. When R. Johanan established an academy in Tiberias, Simeon joined him there, even though they often disagreed on halakhic (Jewish legal) issues. After Simeon's death, R. Johanan was devastated and cried, "Where are you, Bar Lakish?" until he died as well (*BM* 84a).

SAYINGS OF SIMEON BEN LAKISH

Anger robs a sage of his wisdom, a prophet of his vision.

God lends a man an extra soul on the eve of the Sabbath and removes it at the end of the Sabbath.

Synagogues and houses of study are Israel's fortresses.

Great is repentance: it turns sins into motivation to do good.

Correct yourself before correcting others.

He who has mercy on the cruel will end up being cruel to the merciful.

SIMEON BEN SHETAH   (1st cent. BCE). One of the ZUGOT (pairs of scholars who headed the SANHEDRIN between the Maccabean era and the time of Herod). He served as the president (NASI) of the Sanhedrin during the reign of King Alexander Yannai and Queen Salome Alexandra. (Some sources say that the queen was Simeon's sister.) Simeon, leader of the PHARISEE party, had many disagreements with Alexander Yannai, who supported the SADDUCEES.

Simeon established two very important laws. The first had to do with education. In the past, the only children to be educated were those whose parents had money to pay a private tutor. Simeon declared that community schools must be established in order to make sure that all boys would have an elementary education (TJ, *Kit.* 8:11, 32c). The second law had to do with Jewish MARRIAGE customs. Simeon ruled that at the time of marriage, the groom must present the bride with a written promise that if he should divorce her or die before she does, all his belongings will be sold in order to make sure that she is financially secure (see KETUBBAH). This is still the common practice today.

SIMHAH   ("joy" or "rejoicing"). A basic element in Jewish religious life. When the Bible refers to the festival of SUKKOT, it declares, "You shall rejoice in your festival … and be only joyful" (Deut. 16:14–15). One must also be joyful on the Sabbath (Isa. 58:13; see also ONEG SHABBAT), on PASSOVER and SHAVU'OT, on HANUKKAH and PURIM, on the WATER-DRAWING FESTIVAL, and on SIMHAT TORAH (the "Rejoicing of the Law"). According to rabbinic teachings, God's presence rests upon one who "fulfills the commandments with a joyful heart" (Shab. 30b). This is called *simhah shel mitzvah*, "joy in the performance of a commandment." There is *simhah shel mitzvah* in all happy events in the Jewish life cycle: CIRCUMCISION, BAR MITZVAH, BAT MITZVAH, and MARRIAGE. The person being celebrated is named *ba'al simhah* ("host of the joyful festivity"). The concept of joy inspired HASIDISM. Its founder, Israel BA'AL SHEM TOV, said that "he who lives in joy performs the will of the Creator."

SIMHAT BAT   Naming ceremony for girls; also known as *britah*, "her covenant" (a parallel to "*brit*," the CIRCUMCISION ceremony for a boy). Until recently, the birth of a girl was marked only by a prayer for the health of the mother and child and announcing the baby's name, recited by the father in the synagogue on Sabbath morning. In recent times, most naming ceremonies for girls still take place in the synagogue, but the family will also often invite the community for a festive meal. Some families write poems or conduct special, creative ceremonies for their newborn daughters.

SIMHAT BET HA-SHO'EVAH   See WATER-DRAWING FESTIVAL

SIMHAT TORAH   ("Rejoicing of the Law"). Joyful FESTIVAL observed when the annual cycle of the PENTATEUCH reading in the synagogue ends and a new cycle begins. In the Diaspora, Simhat Torah is celebrated the day after the festival of SHEMINI ATSERET, but in Israel both festivals occur on the same day. There are no sources in the Bible or Talmud for Simhat Torah. Scholars believe that this festival was unknown before the ninth century CE. Until then, a TRIENNIAL CYCLE was customary, which meant that the cycle of the READING OF THE LAW was three years long.

The Simhat Torah celebration in the synagogue has to do with the joy of TORAH reading. In the EVENING SERVICE, all of the SCROLLS OF THE LAW are taken out of the ARK and carried around the reader's platform seven times (see HAKKAFOT), special prayers are recited, and the members of the congregation sing and dance. Children also take part in this celebration, carrying Simhat Torah flags and small Torah scrolls. In some communities the Torah is read after the *Hakkafot*. This is the only time when the Reading of the Law takes place at night. *Hakkafot* are also part of the MORNING SERVICE the next day. After the *Hakkafot*, the last chapters of the Pentateuch (Deut. 33–34) are read. It is customary for all males in the synagogue to be called to the Reading of the Law. In many CONSERVATIVE synagogues, women are also called up to the Torah on Simhat Torah. In REFORM Temples men and women participate equally in all parts of the ceremony. Today in ORTHODOXY, some congregations have special Torah services for women in which they read from the Torah.

A special Torah reading is held for children under BAR MITZVAH age; in both modern Orthodox and Conservative synagogues, girls under 12 (BAT MITZVAH) also take part in this ceremony. A prayer shawl is held over the children while they say the Torah blessings. After their section is read, the

Carrying the Torah Scroll on Simhat Torah.

children are blessed with the same blessing that JACOB blessed his grandchildren with (Gen. 48:16). This ceremony is called "*Kol ha-Ne'arim*" ("All the youngsters").

The last section of the Pentateuch is kept for an honored member of the congregation, the BRIDEGROOM OF THE LAW (*Hatan Torah*). Next, the first section of the Pentateuch is read from a different scroll (Gen. 1:1–2:3). The person honored with this reading is called the "Bridegroom of the Beginning" (or Genesis; *Hatan be-Reshit*). The first chapter of the Book of JOSHUA is the HAFTARAH reading for the day.

In the 1960s, Simhat Torah became a major event for the Jews in the Soviet Union. They celebrated their connection with the rest of the Jewish people, from whom they had been separated for years.

In Israel, it is customary to have joyful "second *hakkafot*" celebrations outdoors, the night after Simhat Torah.

SIN   An action that breaks a law, or when a positive COMMANDMENT is not observed. In Judaism, actions that go against the Divine law are more important than the religious idea of sin.

Almost 30 words appear in the Bible to describe different kinds of sins. The word used the most is *het*; its root means, "to miss the mark." It describes many kinds of sins, but it is the only word that describes the least offensive sin: an accidental action that is against the ritual law. The second most commonly used word is *avon*, which means "injustice." It describes a crime committed on purpose, usually against social and ethical laws. The third word is *pesha*, which is translated "to rebel against." This is a more serious crime than *avon*. *Pesha* describes the intentional action of one who wants to rebel against God. In rabbinic writings the three terms are used to describe the complete nature of sin (*Yoma* 36b), because every sin includes part of each kind. The rabbis also use the word *averah* ("transgression") to describe a sin. In ancient times, bringing a sin offering and compensation would achieve ATONEMENT.

In general, sins that go against the laws of the Torah are worse than sins that violate rabbinic law. The most serious sins in Judaism are IDOLATRY, MURDER, and INCEST; a person should rather die than commit any of these.

Judaism does not believe that ADAM's sin affected his descendants. In fact, Judaism rejects any connection between the potential sinfulness of human nature and Adam's "original sin." The principle that all people are responsible for their own actions is central in Judaism (Deut. 24:16, Ezek. 18:1–4).

The Rabbis connect the origin of sin to the *yetser ha-ra*, the "evil inclination" that is part of human nature. However, people can fight the *yetser ha-ra* with the *yetser ha-tov*, the "good inclination" (see EVIL). In addition, the principle of FREE WILL is one of Judaism's basic teachings. This means that humans are free to obey or disobey, to fulfill or reject, God's commandments. The challenge is to choose the right and moral living path. Jewish philosophers claim that when people sin, they cannot reach their full potential because they are separated from God. This situation can be repaired by REPENTANCE, which brings people closer to God. (See also CONFESSION.)

SINAI, MOUNT   (Heb. *Har Sinai*). The location where God revealed Himself to MOSES and the people of Israel; identified in the Bible as Horeb, "the mountain of God," where Moses met God at the BURNING BUSH (Ex. 3). Almost two months after the EXODUS from Egypt, the people of Israel gathered at the foot of Mount Sinai while Moses went to the top of the mountain to receive the TEN COMMANDMENTS and other laws (Ex. 19–20). In Hebrew, this REVELATION is known as *Ma'amad Har Sinai* ("the revelation at Mount Sinai"). When ELIJAH the prophet ran away from Queen Jezebel, he arrived at Horeb and God revealed Himself to him there (1 Kings 19:1–14).

Most modern scholars think that Mount Sinai is located between Egypt and Israel, but they do not agree on one specific location. According to CHRISTIANITY, Jabel Musa (the "Mount of Moses") in southern Sinai is the place of the Revelation, and the place where Moses came across the burning bush when he was young. Jewish tradition concentrates more on the meaning of the Revelation than on its exact location. Traditionally, both the WRITTEN LAW and the ORAL LAW were given at Mount Sinai. According to the MIDRASH, all souls of the future generations of Israel were present at the Mount Sinai Revelation. Many halakhic (Jewish legal) rulings are considered ancient "received traditions" and are known as HALAKHAH LE-MOSHEH MI-SINAI ("the law of Moses from Sinai").

SIN OFFERING   See SACRIFICES AND OFFERINGS

SIVAN   Third month of the Jewish religious CALENDAR; ninth month of the Hebrew civil year counting from TISHRI. It is 30 days long and normally falls during May–June. Its sign of the zodiac is Gemini, the Twins. The rabbis connect this sign with MOSES and AARON, who led the Israelites after the EXODUS.

On the first (New Moon) of Sivan, the Israelites' entered the SINAI wilderness, and on 6–7 Sivan (in Israel only on 6 Sivan), the SHAVU'OT festival is celebrated, celebrating the Giving of the Law on Mount SINAI. According to Jewish tradition, 6 Sivan is also the day of King DAVID's death. The Talmud says that 15 Sivan marks the first day of summer in the Land of Israel (*BM* 106b).

SIYYUM   ("finish"). The celebration of the completion of the study of a book of the MISHNAH or TALMUD. The *siyyum* is made when there is a MINYAN (ten adults) present. It is followed by a special prayer called *hadran,* and then KADDISH is said. It also usually includes a festive meal.

A *siyyum* is usually held in the synagogue on the day before PASSOVER, which is a day on which all male firstborns fast. This fast is a day or remembrance for the miracle that saved the Israelites' firstborns from the tenth plague in Egypt (see FASTING AND FAST DAYS). However, the firstborns do not have to fast if they go to a *siyyum* on this day, because a *siyyum* is considered a *se'udat mitzvah* (festive meal that marks the completion of a COMMANDMENT). A *siyyum* is also held when the writing of a new SCROLL OF THE LAW is completed (called *siyyum ha-sefer,* "conclusion of the book"). At this *siyyum*, the last few letters of the last verse in the scroll are written, and the entire community then joyfully escorts the new scroll into the synagogue.

SLANDER   See LESHON HA-RA

SLAVERY   When a person volunteers to serve another person, or when he is forced to do so. In Jewish law, slavery is limited to a specific period of time. In ancient times, slavery was very common, and society did not try to change this. Judaism did not put an end to slavery, but limited the right of slave owners so much that slaves used to get paid and were considered paid labor. The Bible explains that there is a difference between a Hebrew slave and a Canaanite slave. An Israelite became a slave in one of two ways: he was either sold into slavery by a law court (BET DIN), because he was a thief unable to return what he had stolen; or he sold himself into slavery because he was poor and could not provide for his family. A person sold by the court could serve as a slave for no more than six years. After six years, if he did not wish to go free, his ear was pierced and he continued his slavery until the JUBILEE year.

In his book *Mishneh Torah,* MAIMONIDES lists the master's obligation towards his Hebrew slave: The sale of a man is not done in public. A master cannot make his slave do unlimited work, work of no value, or work that is humiliating. The owner has to give Jewish slaves, male or female, the same quality of food, drink, clothing, and living accommodations as his own. When a Hebrew slave finishes his slavery period, his former owner has to give him a grant so that he can reestablish himself (Deut. 15:13–15).

A female Jew can only become a slave if her father sells her into slavery while she is still a minor. A father may not sell his daughter as a slave unless he has absolutely no land, possessions, or even clothing to sell in order to repay his debts. Even after he sells his daughter, the father must buy her back as soon as he is able to. Either way, a female is freed automatically as soon as she reaches puberty. The Torah commands the master to either marry the grownup female Jewish slave, or give her to his son to marry; if not, she goes free without having to pay for her liberty (Ex. 21:11). In this way, the female slave's honor is protected. Unlike a male slave, a female slave cannot extend her slavery by having her ear pierced.

The law court is forbidden to sell a Jew as a slave to a non-Jew, and one who sells himself to a non-Jew must do everything he can to free himself as soon as possible. If he does not have the money, his relatives must try to free him. If they do not have the money, it is a positive COMMANDMENT for every Jew to free him.

A Canaanite slave is the property of his master for all time. However, his life is not completely controlled by his master. If the slave is circumcised, he is considered part of the master's family and takes part in the paschal sacrifice during the festival of PASSOVER with everyone else. He must also rest on the Sabbath and observe certain Torah commandments. He can be released from slavery if he is redeemed, or if his master gives him a document freeing him. If a master injures his slave, the slave is automatically freed. It is forbidden to return a runaway slave to his master (Deut. 23:16). Even though a Canaanite slave is formally the property of his master, one should not mistreat him or humiliate him. A freed Canaanite slave can become Jewish through CIRCUMCISION and immersion in a MIKVEH and can then marry a Jew.

SOCIAL ETHICS   The Bible matches its ethical demands to social life, without ASCETICISM (self-denial) or removal from day-to-day life. It also stresses the importance of social ETHICS and JUSTICE. The Bible is very specific about these issues. It discusses defending the widow and orphan (Ex. 22:21–23); forbids cruelty towards a (non-Jewish) stranger (Ex. 22:20); requires slaves to be treated well (Ex. 21:1–11, 26, 27; see SLAVERY); prohibits lying under oath, BRIBERY, bias on the part of judges (Ex. 23:1–3; Deut. 16:18–20; 19:16–17); and demands care for the poor (Deut. 15:7–11). These rules and others prevent the harming of one's fellow human being, and protect the weak members of the society (see also LOVE OF NEIGHBOR).

On a number of occasions, the Bible makes clear that observing the COMMANDMENTS is meaningless if society is unethical (e.g. Amos. 5:22–24). The sages of the Talmud also discuss social ethics. When HILLEL was asked to summarize all of Judaism, he said, "What is hateful to you, do not do unto your fellow human being" (*Shab.* 31a). R. AKIVA said that the commandment to love one's neighbor as oneself is a central principle of the Torah. Ben Azzai's response was that creation in the image of God (an expression of the worth of every human being) is an even more important principle (*Sif.* to Lev. 19:18). The Talmud SAGES also wrote more social rules. They introduced the KETUBBAH (marriage document), which protects the rights of divorced women and widows, instituted the PROSBUL to help the poor receive loans, and decreed that a woman cannot be forced to be divorced if she does not want to. They referred to CHARITY by the Hebrew term *tsedakah,* which comes from the word "justice," in order to emphasize the importance of helping the poor. They also ruled that at least two well-known and honest people in every town should collect money every Sabbath eve and give it to the poor. As a result of this, many charity organizations were founded and have operated from the Middle Ages until today (see COMMUNITY).

The Talmud explains that when it comes to social issues, it is important to go beyond the letter of the law. The rabbis say that Jerusalem was destroyed because its people were not willing to go beyond the letter of the law to help others (*BM* 30b).

The Jewish ethical laws are based on the way things should be. The Bible often presents laws of specific cases together with the demand for ethical behavior (such as Lev. 19:18; Deut. 16:20; Jer. 9:22–23). In this way, everyday problems can be dealt with as they come up, while every person and society in general are constantly trying to improve their social ethics.

See also BITTUL HA-TAMID; BUSINESS ETHICS; LABOR AND LABOR LAWS.

SOFER   See SCRIBE

SOFER (or SCHREIBER), MOSES   (1762–1839). Rabbi, Jewish legal expert, and defender of Orthodox Judaism; best known as Hatam Sofer. He was the rabbi of Pressburg (Bratislava) from 1806 until his death and an outstanding leader of ORTHODOXY. Because of his tremendous knowledge of talmudic and rabbinic literature, Sofer was sent halakhic (Jewish legal) questions from many rabbis all over the world. He opposed the NEOLOGY movement and claimed that new elements in Jewish tradition are prohibited.

His seven-volume RESPONSA is called *Hiddushei Teshuvot Mosheh Sofer* ("New Legal Responsa of Moses Sofer"), but is known by its initials as *Hatam Sofer.* He also published two volumes of sermons, NOVELLAE (new ideas) on the Talmud, commentaries on the Bible, and kabbalistic poems (see KABBALAH).

SOLOMON   (10th cent. BCE). King of Israel after his father King DAVID, fourth of David's sons, son of Bathsheba; also known as Jedidiah (II Sam. 12:24, 25). Solomon was appointed king when David was on his deathbed. He was chosen over his elder brother Adonijah, who wanted to be king (I Kings 1) and was later killed because he planned a rebellion against Solomon (I Kings 2).

Solomon inherited a very large kingdom, from the Euphrates River to Philistine Gaza. The Bible describes the 40 years of Solomon's reign as years of peace and harmony throughout the kingdom. He secured his kingdom by marrying the daughters of nearby kings (I Kings 11:1). Altogether he had 700 wives and 300 concubines (secondary wives; I Kings 10:3). His most important wife was the daughter of Pharaoh, king of Egypt (I Kings 3:1). Solomon divided the kingdom into 12 districts

King Solomon, author of Proverbs, teaching his students. Rothschild Miscellany Northern Italy, c. 1450–1480.

run by governors. Each district had to support the royal court for one month of the year.

Solomon had close and friendly ties with Hiram, king of Tyre (980–946 BCE). Hiram helped Solomon with the building of the TEMPLE. He gave Solomon gold and cedar and cypress wood in exchange for wheat, oil, and wine, and sent him craftsmen and artisans to help build the Temple. Solomon and Hiram also operated a fleet of ships together; Solomon supplied the ships and Hiram supplied the crews (1 Kings 10:11).

Solomon was a great builder. His biggest project was the building of the Temple, which took seven years to finish. The House of the Forest of Lebanon, the porch for the throne (of judgment), and the king's palace were built near the Temple and took 20 years to complete. Solomon strengthened the walls of Jerusalem and expanded the city to the north (1 Kings 11:27). He also built and strengthened many cities throughout his kingdom.

These large building projects required heavy taxes and a lot of forced labor. This caused unrest in the kingdom. Jeroboam of the tribe of Ephraim, in charge of the forced laborers from the tribes of Ephraim and Manasseh, tried to revolt against Solomon. The rebellion failed and Jeroboam ran away to Egypt, where he was taken in by the new king of Egypt, Pharaoh Shishak Bel I (Shoshenq; 945–924 BCE). After Solomon's death, the tribes of the north asked the new king, Solomon's son Rehoboam, to ease the taxes. When Rehoboam refused, Jeroboam rebelled again, successfully this time, and established the northern kingdom of Israel (see ISRAEL, KINGDOM OF).

Solomon was famous for the tremendous wisdom that God gave him. His wisdom is described as being greater than that of all the wise men in his time (1 Kings 5:9–11). He is especially known for his judgment of the two women who each claimed to be the mother of the same child (1 Kings 3:16–28). His "solution" was to threaten to cut the child in two, thereby causing the real mother to give up her claim and proving that the child was

hers. When the Queen of Sheba came to visit him and tested his wisdom, he was able to answer her "difficult questions" (1 Kings 10:1–13). Solomon was also known for his parables and his poetry (1 Kings 5:12).

The SAGES claim that Solomon wrote the biblical books of PROVERBS, SONG OF SONGS, and ECCLESIASTES (Song R. 1:11). According to one MIDRASH, he was also one of the ten authors of PSALMS (*Shoher Tov* 1:6). Another Midrash says that he knew the language of the animals and birds (*Targum Sheni* on the Scroll of Esther).

SOLOVEICHIK   Rabbinic family from Lithuania whose members have been among the leading YESHIVAH heads and TORAH scholars since the mid-19th century.

Joseph Baer   (1820–1892) studied at the Volozhin *yeshivah*. He left the *yeshivah* after an argument broke out among the students about who should be the head of the *yeshivah*. He later served as the rabbi of Slutsk (1865–1878) and then as rabbi of Brisk (Brest-Litovsk). His writings, called *Bet ha-Levi* (1863–1891), include his NOVELLAE ("new ideas") on the Talmud, RESPONSA, and sermons on GENESIS and EXODUS.

Rabbi Joseph Baer (Dov-Yosef) Soloveichik.

Hayyim (1853–1918), the son of Joseph Baer, was born and studied in Volozhin. In 1880, he started teaching in the *yeshivah*. He taught there until the Russian czarist government closed it in January 1892. After his father's death, Hayyim became the rabbi of Brisk and was known as "Rav Hayyim Brisker." Many *yeshivah* graduates came to study with him in Brisk.

Hayyim Soloveichik took a new approach towards the Talmud, and stressed the importance of MAIMONIDES' *Mishneh Torah*. His students spread his method of learning all over the world. R. Hayyim did not think that his novellae were ready for publication, but his sons published some of them in 1936. Many of his talmudic novellae have been published since then.

Moses (1876–1941), the eldest son of R. Hayyim, studied under his father and was a rabbi in many White Russian towns. After World War I, he was the head of the Talmud department at the Tahkemoni Seminary in Warsaw. From 1929 he was the head of the Talmud faculty at Yeshiva College in New York. His scholarship and lectures helped raise the level of Talmud studies in the American Orthodox community.

Isaac Ze'ev (1886–1960), the youngest son of R. Hayyim, who also studied under his father. Isaac Ze'ev, known also as "Rav Velvel," became the rabbi of Brisk after his father. Many students from all over Europe went to study under him and learn the "Brisker method" of Talmud study. He was active in the community and was against ZIONISM.

Isaac Ze'ev and seven of his children escaped from the Nazis, but his wife and three other children died in the HOLOCAUST. In 1941, he settled in Jerusalem, devoted himself to his studies, and influenced many Israeli Torah circles. He published his novellae on the Torah and Maimonides, but his sons edited and published his talmudic novellae.

Joseph Baer (1903–1993) was the eldest son of R. Moses. In his youth, he studied rabbinic literature through the "Brisker method" and received a high school education from private tutors. In 1925 he entered the University of Berlin, where he majored in philosophy and received his doctorate (1931). A year later, he moved to the United States and became rabbi of the Orthodox community in Boston. After his father died in 1941, Joseph Baer took his father's place as head of the Talmud faculty at Yeshiva University. He was also president of the Religious Zionists of America (Mizrachi) from 1946 and became chairman of the Halakhah Commission of the Rabbinical Council of America in 1952. He was the spiritual leader of most American-trained Orthodox rabbis for many years.

Joseph Baer Soloveichik's Talmud studies and philosophical thoughts were very unique. He developed his grandfather's methods, and connected HALAKHAH (Jewish law) and philosophy. Many of his published writings discuss "the philosophy of the *halakhah*." He influenced people mostly through his public lectures and his ability to explain difficult religious ideas very simply. At the beginning he did not want to publish his works, but later in his life he did and also let others edit and publish them. He was also known as "the Rav."

Aaron (1918–), the youngest son of R. Moses, immigrated to the United Stats in 1929. He studied at Yeshiva College in New York, lectured in Talmud at different New York *yeshivot*, and also trained to be a lawyer. In 1966 he became dean of the faculty at the Hebrew Theological Seminar in Skokie, Illinois. He then opened his own *yeshivah*, "Yeshivas Brisk," in Chicago. In 1986, Aaron returned to New York and took his brother's place as the head of the Talmud faculty at Yeshiva University.

SONG OF MOSES   Song praising God sung by MOSES and the Israelites after they escaped from Egypt and crossed the Red Sea (Ex. 14:30–15:18); known in Hebrew as *Shirat ha-Yam*. This song ends the PESUKEI DE-ZIMRA section of the MORNING PRAYERS. In addition, it is read on the Sabbath when the TORAH portion *Be-Shallah* is read during the READING OF THE LAW in the synagogue, and on the last (seventh) day of PASSOVER (see SABBATHS, SPECIAL). Various communities have different melodies for the Song of Moses. In Israel, many worshipers gather at the beach on the last day of Passover and sing the Song together.

SONG OF SONGS   (also known in English as Canticles and the Song of Solomon). Biblical book in the HAGIOGRAPHA ("Writings") section of the Bible; one of the FIVE SCROLLS read in the synagogue on the Sabbath of PASSOVER. Sephardim also recite it after the Passover SEDER, and on Friday afternoon

The Song of Songs illuminated by Zev Raban, 1925.

SONG OF SONGS	
1:1–1:8	Songs of the bride
1:9–2:7	The lovers' dialogue
2:8–3:5	The bride's memories
3:6–3:11	The wedding parade
4:1–5:1	Songs of the youth
5:2–6:3	Search for the lost bridegroom
6:4–7:10	The bride's beauty
7:11–7:14	Love in the vineyard
8:1–8:4	Brother and sister
8:5–8:14	Various songs and fragments

before the Sabbath service. The book has eight chapters and 117 verses. The rabbis of the Talmud discussed whether to include Song of Songs in the Bible. In the end, it was included in the Bible because R. AKIVA's interpreted the book as a love song not just between a bride and groom but between God and Israel.

According to Jewish tradition king SOLOMON wrote Song of Songs, but today many scholars think it was written in a much later period. The Song of Songs has many interpretations.

SONG OF SONGS RABBAH   Story-like MIDRASH (commentary) on the SONG OF SONGS, also known as *Midrash Hazitah*. The Midrash presents sermons on the Song of Songs that follow the order of the biblical text. The Midrash is divided into eight sections; each section relates to one of the book's chapters. Sources for Song of Songs Rabbah include the Jerusalem and Babylonian Talmuds, GENESIS RABBAH, LEVITICUS RABBAH and *Pesikta de-Rav Kahana,* and other sources. The main idea discussed in this Midrash is the relationship between God, represented by the groom, and the People of Israel, represented by the bride. The Midrash is written in the Hebrew of the Mishnah mixed with Galilean Aramaic and some Greek words. It was written in the sixth century CE.

SORCERY   See MAGIC; WITCHCRAFT

SOTAH   ("wife suspected of adultery"). Fifth tractate (book) of the Order of NASHIM in the Mishnah. Its nine chapters discuss the laws that deal with a wife suspected of having sexual relations with a man who is not her husband, and her trial by the SANHEDRIN (cf. Num. 5:11–31; Deut. 20:1–9, 21:1–9). Other subjects discussed in this book are laws dealing with blessings and oaths in Hebrew and other languages; the people who are relieved from military service; and the "breaking the heifer's neck" ceremony, which takes place if a man is found dead outside the city with no witnesses to his murder (Deut. 21:1–9).

SOUL, IMMORTALITY OF   The Bible describes the "breath of life" as coming directly from God and representing "God's image" (Gen. 1:27). The words *nefesh, ru'ah,* and *neshamah,* which mean "soul" or "spirit," are used in the Bible to describe a person's personality and do not describe a separate "spiritual" part of human beings. Only in later books is a person's spirit or soul thought to be separated from the body. This view is also presented in the Talmud. In order to show that the body and soul are separated, the sages of the Talmud compare the soul's relationship to the body to God's relationship to the world. According to the Talmud, the soul outlives the body just as God outlives the world (Lev. R. 4:8).

In the Second Temple period, the PHARISEES believed in the immortality of the soul, but the SADDUCEES did not. The rabbis' opinion was that the soul is an important part of a human being, given by God; and that throughout life, it is the individual's responsibility to make sure that the soul is not influenced by evil. The medieval Jewish philosophers tried to combine these rabbinic teachings with elements of consciousness such as mind, emotions, memory, will, and reason.

SAADIAH GAON's view is that the soul is created with the body. It is separated from the body at death but they are reunited at the time when final REWARD AND PUNISHMENT are given. MAIMONIDES says that the soul is one, but it expresses itself in different aspects. Unlike most of these aspects that die together with the body, the rational aspect lives on. According to Maimonides, immortality of the soul can be achieved by developing this rational aspect, by learning and gaining knowledge. In contrast, JUDAH HALEVI and Hasdai CRESCAS claim that the development of the soul towards immortality depends on moral actions and the love of God, not on intellectual activity.

A few hints of belief in the AFTERLIFE can be found in the Bible (II Kings 2; Prov. 12:28; Dan 12:2), but there is no concept connecting human destiny and Divine justice to immortality. In the Talmud, different terms refer to the ultimate REDEMPTION. The terms *yemot ha-mashi'ah* (the days of the MESSIAH) and *ketz* (the end) relate to the historic role of the People of Israel in the establishment of the future Kingdom of Heaven. The terms *Olam ha-Ba* (World to Come) and *tehiyyat ha-metim* (RESURRECTION of the dead) refer to Divine justice, individual destiny, and salvation. According to the rabbis, in the World to Come, after physical death, the soul has a completely spiritual existence in a place "where the righteous sit and enjoy the splendor of the Divine Presence" (*Ber.* 17a). This place is also called *Gan Eden* (Garden of Eden), and the place where the wicked are punished is *Gehinnom*. The rabbis of the Talmud considered the physical resurrection of the righteous to be a basic principle of Judaism. Maimonides included this principle in his 13 PRINCIPLES OF FAITH.

Many modern Jewish thinkers stress the idea of immortality of the soul rather than the resurrection of the dead, although both are important for Orthodox Jews. REFORM JUDAISM also believes in the immortality of the soul, but it does not believe in resurrection or in *Gehinnom* and Eden (hell and paradise) as places of punishment and reward.

SPEKTOR, ISAAC ELHANAN (1817–1896). Lithuanian rabbi, halakhic (Jewish legal) scholar and authority, and communal leader. Spektor served as a rabbi in numerous Jewish communities in Lithuania throughout his life. When he was the rabbi of Kovno (1864–1896), he established the "Kovno Kolel," a graduate school for advanced TALMUD studies, and became one of the most important rabbis in Eastern Europe. He also helped change the Russian government's goal of closing down traditional Jewish religious elementary schools (see HEDER).

Spektor supported the Love of Zion (*Hibbat Zion*) movement and joined its spiritual leaders, R. Samuel Mohilewer and R. Naphtali Tsevi Judah BERLIN. He declared that settling in Erets Israel is a religious obligation. During his lifetime, the Jewish pioneers in Erets Israel faced the halakhic-agricultural problem of how to work the land during the SABBATICAL YEAR (*shemittah*). Spektor had a solution for this problem. He told the farmers that if they sold the land to non-Jews for a period of two years, they could then farm it, even during the *shemittah*.

Spector wrote many halakhic works, which include five volumes of RESPONSA, answers to Jewish legal questions. He also published 158 responsa on the issue of the AGUNAH, the deserted wife who cannot be sure of her husband's death and therefore cannot remarry. Spektor developed a series of halakhic principles that allow the *agunah* to remarry. These principles were also put into practice after the HOLOCAUST, in order to enable women whose husbands did not return after the end of the war to remarry.

Two *yeshivot* were founded in 1897 in Spektor's memory. The first, Keneset Beit Yitshak, was originally part of the Slobodka YESHIVAH but later moved to Kovno. The second *yeshivah*, the Rabbi Isaac Elchanan Theological Seminary, was established in New York and later became Yeshiva University, America's largest Jewish institute of higher learning.

SPICEBOX Container for the spices (*besamim*) used in the HAVDALAH ceremony at the end of the SABBATH. During this ceremony, a special blessing is recited before smelling the spices. The use of a special container for the *havdalah* spices is already mentioned in 12th century Jewish literature. During the Middle Ages, myrtle (*hadas*) was the spice used most for *havdalah*; the container itself was also often called *hadas*.

The oldest spicebox existing today is from Germany, dating from the middle of the 16th century. It is made of silver and is shaped like a tower. Since there are no halakhic (Jewish legal) rules that deal with spiceboxes, any container can be used for the spices, and artists are free to use their imagination when creating a spicebox. The shape and size of the spicebox is always changing, but the tower is still the most popular design.

SPINOZA, BARUCH (BENEDICT) (1632–1677). Philosopher. Spinoza was born in Amsterdam to a MARRANO family from

Portugal that fled to Holland to escape persecution and returned to Judaism. As a child, he received a formal Jewish education. When he completed his studies, he started doing research on the works of medieval Jewish philosophers, such as Gersonides (LEVI BEN GERSHOM) and MAIMONIDES. From the age of 22, Spinoza began to draw closer to Christian circles and was interested in general studies. His new interests and the views that he expressed alarmed the Amsterdam Jewish community and led to his EXCOMMUNICATION by the community in 1656. He then left Amsterdam and spent most of the rest of his life in The Hague.

Spinoza's philosophy is very complicated. It offers man an alternative to traditional religions. His first great work was the *Theologico-Political Treatise* (1670), in which he criticized the major principles of religion, supported freedom of spirit and thought, and expressed his opinions about the Bible. The book caused a big uproar, and Spinoza did not dare to publish any more of his ideas. His most important work, the *Ethics*, was published only after he died. Its main idea is that God and nature are one. Spinoza denied the belief that the world is run according to God's will. He claimed that everything that happens in the world happens naturally, as a direct result of God's existence.

Spinoza also discussed the importance of the new political situation in Europe and its effect on the Jewish people. He criticized the Jewish heritage and concluded that HALAKHAH (Jewish law) is not appropriate for the new culture of the modern world. Because of his views both Christians and Jews banned his teachings, even after his death. Philosophers only started studying his ideas at the end of the 18th century. Since then, his writings have become an important part of modern philosophy.

STUDY The study of TORAH, which includes the study of classical Jewish religious texts and commentaries, is a very important part of Jewish life. The Mishnah says that the study of Torah is equivalent to all the other commandments together (*Pe'ah* 1:1; *Shab.* 127a). The Talmud debates which is more important, action or study, and decides on study, "for it leads one to action" (*Kid.* 40a). If possible, one should divide one's free time between study of the Bible, Mishnah, and Talmud (*Kid.* 30a).

When fulfilling a commandment, a blessing is usually recited before the action itself is performed. The blessing for Torah study is recited as part of the MORNING PRAYERS, followed by a small portion of Torah study from the PENTATEUCH (the PRIESTLY BLESSING, Num. 6:24–26), the Mishnah (*Pe'ah* 1:1), and the Talmud (*Shab.* 127a). Ideally, one should study Torah throughout the day.

According to *Sifrei* (*Ekev*), a father must start teaching his son Hebrew as soon as he starts talking, even if Hebrew is not his mother tongue. *Sifrei* (*Ha'azinu*) also advises that rather than learning specific facts, a person should first learn general principles, because they can be put into practice more easily

An engraving of the Dutch-Jewish philosopher Baruch Spinoza (left); Document excommunicating Spinoza from the Amsterdam community (top right); A page from his writings (bottom right).

than facts. The rabbis encouraged setting aside time for Torah study every day and stressed the advantages of studying with another student or students. The BET MIDRASH (study house) was a permanent part of all Jewish communities.

See also EDUCATION; TALMUD TORAH.

SUICIDE   According to Judaism, life is holy because it is given by God. Therefore, man is only the guardian of his life, not its owner. This is why suicide is not allowed and is considered a form of MURDER. Because life is very precious, one is not allowed to sacrifice it, even to avoid breaking the laws of the Torah. The three most serious SINS in Judaism are an exception to this rule: one must rather die than commit IDOLATRY, murder, or INCEST.

Although there have been cases of mass suicide, as during the fall of Masada to the Romans in 73 CE, the HALAKHAH (Jewish law) does not approve of suicide except in very special circumstances.

SUKKAH   The booth (or tabernacle) built for the SUKKOT festival. The laws of the *sukkah* can be found in the tractate called SUKKAH in the Mishnah and both Talmuds.

The *sukkah* is a temporary house, meant to remind the Jews of the booths that the Israelites lived in after they left Egypt, while they wandered in the Wilderness. Its walls can be made of wood, stone, or canvas over a metal frame, as long as they are strong enough to withstand a "normal wind." It must have at least two walls of certain measurements, and part of a third wall in order to be considered a valid *sukkah*. The roof covering (known as *sekhakh*) must be made from plants, such as branches or bamboo shoots, which have been cut and are no longer rooted to the ground. The *sekhakh* must be thick enough to prevent too much sunlight in the *sukkah* during the day, but thin enough to allow one to look up and see the stars at night. Minimally, the *sukkah* must be big enough to hold "the head and most of the body" of one person, and a table at which to eat. The *sukkah*'s exact measurements are given in the *halakhah*. A *sukkah* is not valid if it is built under another roof or ceiling; it must be built outdoors.

All food products made from flour must be eaten in the *sukkah* during the holiday, although some observant Jews do not eat anything outside the booth and also sleep in it. A special BENEDICTION is said when eating in the *sukkah*: "… Who has commanded us to reside in the *sukkah*."

Special prayers are said when first entering the *sukkah* at the beginning of the festival and when leaving it at the end of Sukkot. It is also customary to invite the traditional symbolic guests, the USHPIZIN, every day when sitting in the *sukkah*.

SUKKAH ("Booth"). Sixth tractate (book) of the Order of MO'ED in the Mishnah. Its five chapters discuss the laws of building and living in the SUKKAH during the seven days of the SUKKOT (Tabernacles) festival. It also includes the laws of the FOUR SPECIES that one must wave on the festival (cf. Lev. 23:33–43; Num. 29:12–38; Deut. 16:13–15). The WATER-DRAWING FESTIVAL is also mentioned.

SUKKOT Festival of Tabernacles, one of the three PILGRIM FESTIVALS when, in ancient times, the Jews would to travel to the TEMPLE in JERUSALEM. In Israel (and in Reform communities), Sukkot is celebrated for seven days, 15–21 Tishri, but in the Diaspora it is celebrated for eight days, 15–22 Tishri. Work is not permitted during the first and last days, but is permitted during the middle days of Sukkot, the days of HOL HA-MO'ED.

Sukkot's historical meaning is to remind the Jews of the booths in which the Israelites lived after they left Egypt, during their 40-year journey through the Wilderness, on their way to the Promised Land. Sukkot also has an agricultural meaning. Since the festival takes place in the fall harvest season, it was also observed as a time of thanksgiving for the last year's crops (Ex. 23:16; Deut. 16:13). After the destruction of the Second Temple, Sukkot became a less central festival. Today, the observance of Sukkot involves eating all meals during the festival in the SUKKAH, unless bad weather prevents one from doing so.

In the 16th century, the mystics established the custom of USHPIZIN ("guests"). The word *ushpizin* refers to seven important people in Jewish history (Abraham, Isaac, Jacob, Joseph, Moses, Aaron, and David), who are symbolically welcomed into the *sukkah*, one each day.

The FOUR SPECIES (*arba'ah minim*) are an important part of the festival. These Four Species of plants are the *lulav* or palm branch, the *etrog* or citron, the *hadassim* – three myrtle branches – and the *aravot* – two willow branches. The set of plants are held together and waved in all directions every day of the festival, except the SABBATH, during the full-version HALLEL prayer (Ps. 113–118) that is said on Sukkot.

As on all other holy days, an ADDITIONAL SERVICE follows the MORNING SERVICE and the READING OF THE LAW. Special HOSHANOT prayers are also added to the service throughout the festival, including a procession around the synagogue together with the Four Species (except on the Sabbath). On the seventh day of Sukkot, HOSHANA RABBAH ("the Great *Hoshana*"), the synagogue is circled seven times (see HAKKAFOT) and a bundle of *aravot* is held after the waving of the Four Species. At the end of the *hakkafot*, the *aravot* are struck three times so that some of the leaves fall off. This is a symbol of the rebirth of both nature and humanity.

On the eighth day, the SHEMINI ATSERET festival is celebrated

Celebrating the festival of Tabernacles in a Sukkah.

("Eighth Day of Solemn Assembly"), and the Prayer for RAIN to fall in Erets Israel is recited. In Israel, this day (and in the Diaspora the following day) is also the festival of SIMHAT TORAH ("the Rejoicing of the Law"), during which the annual Torah reading cycle ends and a new one begins.

In ancient days, the joyous WATER-DRAWING FESTIVAL, *Simhat Bet ha-Sho'evah,* took place on Sukkot, when water would be poured on the ALTAR in the Temple. In modern Israel, special *Simhat Bet ha-Sho'evah* celebrations are held in religious circles and kibbutzim. Another ceremony that was reestablished in modern times is the HAKHEL ceremony, which is described in the Bible (Deut. 31:10–13). In Temple times, people would assemble on Sukkot after the SABBATICAL YEAR and portions of the Torah would be read to them by the king or by another religious leader. Today, the President of Israel reads from the Torah to a big assembly gathered at the WESTERN WALL in Jerusalem.

SUPERSTITION The Bible (Deut. 18:9–11) forbade the Israelites to follow certain actions of the non-Jewish nations, whose land they were going to inherit. These include using divination to predict the future and using enchantments, charms, and witchcraft. Some of the prophets also condemned superstition (Jer. 27:9). However, at various times, certain superstitions still existed. The Talmud, for example, discusses ASTROLOGY and the significance of being born on a specific day of the week.

When discussing the biblical prohibition in Deuteronomy 18, the Talmud (*Sanh.* 65a–b) lists some of the superstitions that the non-Jewish nations believed in: they believed in the *me'onen,* "the observer of times," who advised people on when it is a lucky time to go on a journey; and in the *menahesh,* "the enchanter," who saw bad omens. Belief in these superstitions is against Jewish law.

Great attention is given to DREAMS and their interpretations and in Jewish writing, much has been written on how to "cure" bad dreams. The KABBALAH talks about the EVIL EYE superstition and the effects of evil spirits and DEMONS. According to the Talmud, various AMULETS can be used for protection against evil.

Many superstitions existed during the Middle Ages. In his *Sefer Hasidim* (Sect. 59), R. JUDAH HE-HASID mentions some superstitious customs that are against Torah law, but lists other customs which he considers valid and recommended, otherwise "one's life is in danger from the demons."

Some of the customs which are still practiced today have been criticized as being superstitious, but some classic sages and rabbis believed in them. These include the TASHLIKH ceremony on ROSH HA-SHANAH, where all one's sins are symbolically thrown into the water, and KAPPAROT before the DAY OF ATONEMENT, in which sins are symbolically passed on to the hen or rooster used in the ceremony.

SYNAGOGUE (Heb. *bet keneset*). The central religious institution of Judaism, the center for public PRAYER and for other religious and community activities; the model for the parallel institutions in CHRISTIANITY and ISLAM.

Origins Although some historical sources prove that synagogues already existed in the first century BCE, their origin is unclear. Some authorities claim that the synagogue was established during the Babylonian EXILE (after 586 BCE), when the people would meet from time to time to comfort each other after the loss of their land, to study Bible, and maybe to pray. The Talmud (*Meg.* 29a) finds a direct reference to the synagogues of Babylonia in the phrase "small sanctuary" used in Ezekiel 11:16. Over the years, this phrase was often used to describe a synagogue. Other theories date the origin of the synagogue to the First Temple period, to the Hellenistic age, and to the Hasmonean period.

Ancient Period Synagogues in Erets Israel probably developed after the exiles returned from Babylonia and rededicated the TEMPLE. Both the Mishnah (*Sot.* 7:7–8; *Yoma* 7:1) and the Talmud (*Meg.* 3:1) refer to many synagogues that existed in Jerusalem before the destruction of the Second Temple. Synagogues also developed in the Diaspora. An Egyptian synagogue from the third century BCE is the first one in the Diaspora known to us. Different historic sources mention other synagogues in Rome, Damascus, Asia Minor, Cyprus, and Alexandria. By the end of the first century CE, synagogues could be found wherever Jews lived. They were essential for the survival of Jewish life after the destruction of the Second Temple.

In order to prevent Temple rituals from being forgotten after its destruction, some of the Temple rituals continued to be practiced in the synagogues. Other Temple rituals were forbidden, in order to emphasize the difference between the synagogue and the Temple. Prayers in the synagogue were considered a replacement for the Temple sacrifices. In addition, many customs surrounding the synagogue services were established. Most of these customs still exist today. Unlike the Temple ritual's many requirements, the only requirement for a synagogue service was a quorum (MINYAN) of ten worshipers. Because every individual was expected to take part in the synagogue services, the human relationship to God became more personalized. Throughout history, in different ages the synagogue took on additional changing roles.

According to Jewish tradition, the synagogue has a unique importance. All synagogues are thought to have part of the holiness of the Temple, and they are seen as extensions of Erets Israel. It was also believed that at the End of Days, all synagogues would be miraculously moved to the Holy Land (*Meg.* 29a). Jewish law also introduces special rules regarding the synagogue: one must neither gossip or chatter, nor eat or sleep, in the synagogue. Because of its holiness, it has become customary to cover one's head in the synagogue, even in communities where people do not cover their heads at all times (see COVERING THE HEAD). According to Jewish law, a synagogue's holiness stays in effect even when it is not used any more. Selling a synagogue is allowed only under specific circumstances and requires consultation with a halakhic (Jewish legal) authority.

The oldest existing synagogues are located in Israel. They can be found at Masada, in the Judean Desert; at Herodion, south of Jerusalem; and at Gamla, on the Golan Heights. They were in use before the destruction of the Second Temple. These three synagogues, and other ancient synagogues discovered both in Israel and in the Diaspora, were all built to face towards Jerusalem. Many of them were the most impressive buildings in the land at the time and were built, whenever possible, at the town's highest point.

Middle Ages During the Middle Ages, the synagogue was the center of Jewish life, and Jews tried to live as close to one as possible. In many communities, it was built in the heart of the Jewish quarter of the city and was in use at all hours. Most prayers were recited aloud in the synagogue. As a result, the worshipers felt that they were really speaking to the Creator and had a close relationship with Him. The synagogue was a relatively democratic institution. All men could be counted for the prayer quorum, and being called to the READING OF THE LAW or leading the service did not depend on a person's qualifications or social status. Communal offices, the library, the ritual bath (MIKVEH), ovens for baking bread, a social hall, the GENIZAH, and other institutions, were often located in synagogue rooms or in nearby buildings.

During the Middle Ages, special sections for women in the synagogue became standard. The reader's platform (BIMAH) at the center of the synagogue and the ARK, on the wall facing Jerusalem, became the two main points in the synagogue. Ashkenazi communities changed their seating arrangements by placing the Ark at the front, so that their synagogues would become more spacious. Many of the Spanish synagogues, which were very impressive buildings, were confiscated and turned into churches after the expulsion of the Jews from Spain in 1492. In Italy, from the 16th century, the Jews were restricted to ghettos and the building of synagogues was limited. Nevertheless, they were able to build beautiful synagogues. In Rome, the Jews were only allowed one synagogue. They overcame this problem by building five synagogues within one building. The synagogues of Poland built in the Middle Ages were very special. They were made of wood, and their walls and ceilings were completely covered with decorations. Another special type of synagogue was the "fortress" building, which helped the Jews defend themselves during difficult times. In Muslim countries, the law restricted the height of the synagogues. Therefore, the Jews built modest synagogues in the hope that the Muslims would not disturb their services. In some places Jews were influenced by Muslim customs and removed their shoes before entering the prayer hall. A special characteristic of Oriental synagogues is having more than one Ark. The synagogues of the Hasidic movement, from the 18th century, were small and informal (see SHTIBL).

Modern Period   In the 19th century, the REFORM movement introduced major changes into its synagogues. Reform Jews called their synagogues "temples," because they believed that the synagogue fully replaced the ancient Jerusalem Temple in modern times. ORGANS were used during services, and men and women no longer sat separately and did not have to wear head coverings. In addition, the position of the readers' platform was changed, and decorum and esthetics were emphasized. Orthodox congregations in Western countries also started emphasizing decorum and esthetics, but these were emphasized within the limits of *halakhah* (Jewish law). CONSERVATIVE JUDAISM similarly introduced mixed seating, but head coverings were still required for men and customary for women. In Western countries, especially in North America, most synagogues today also fulfill the role of social community centers, as in the Middle Ages. They often have halls for celebrating weddings, bar mitzvahs, etc.; schools and clubs; and also sponsor many social activities. In the Diaspora, synagogue membership is considered a way for people to express their Jewish identity, even if they do not attend the synagogue on a regular basis. In Israel, on the other hand, there are numerous ways of expressing Jewish identity, and Israeli synagogues are therefore largely places of prayer and religious study; their role as a community center is minimal.

SZOLD, HENRIETTA   (1860–1945). U.S. Zionist leader, founder of Hadassah and Youth Aliyah. Szold was born in Baltimore after her family emigrated from Hungary. In her late teen years she taught at a night school and soon became a Zionist (see ZIONISM). Later, she was the first female to study at the Jewish Theological Seminary. In 1909 she visited Erets Israel for the first time. When she returned to America, Szold helped establish the Hadassah Organization. She became its president in 1914. In 1920, she moved to Palestine permanently and assisted in creating a network of medical facilities throughout the country. During World War II, Szold organized Youth Aliyah, rescuing Jewish children from Nazi Germany. She never married and died of pneumonia in the Hadassah hospital that she was very active in founding.

In Israel, Szold's Hebrew birthday, the first day of the Hebrew month of ADAR, was declared to be Mothers' Day. This is because although she never had any children of her own, Szold was a "mother to thousands" in her Youth Aliyah villages.

Henrietta Szold

T

TA'ANIT ("Fast Day"). Ninth tractate (book) of the Order of MO'ED in the Mishnah. Its four chapters discuss the laws of declaring a public fast day and include various laws of the fixed fast days: the 17th of Tammuz, TISHAH BE-AV, and the DAY OF ATONEMENT.

TABERNACLE (MISHKAN)   See SANCTUARY

TABERNACLES FESTIVAL   See SUKKOT

TABLETS OF THE COVENANT   Two stone tablets received by MOSES from God on Mount SINAI; also known as "two tablets of the law" or "two tablets of testimony." God told Moses to climb Mount Sinai in order to receive "the tablets of stone and the Torah and the commandments which I have written" (Ex. 24:12). The TEN COMMANDMENTS were carved into the tablets "by the finger of God" (Ex. 31:18).

When Moses saw the Children of Israel worshiping the GOLDEN CALF, which was the sin of IDOLATRY, he smashed the two tablets (Ex. 32:19). He was told by God to make a second pair, identical to the first, and to climb the mountain top, where He would again carve the words of the first (Ex. 34:1–4). Moses brought the two new tablets down from the mountaintop and put them in the ARK OF THE COVENANT (Deut. 10:2), which Solomon kept in the First TEMPLE until it was destroyed in 586 BCE.

In the times of the Talmud the two tablets of the covenant took on a symbolic meaning. They represented not only the WRITTEN LAW and all 613 commandments, but the ORAL LAW as well (Ex. R. 46:1).

In the late Middle Ages, the two tablets of the covenant became a Jewish religious symbol. They appear as two connected rectangular slabs with rounded tops. They were often displayed on the outside of synagogues in Central and Western Europe. They were also used to decorate ritual objects, jewelry, and art, and were often guarded on either side by the lions of Judah and decorated with a Shield of David.

TAHANUN ("supplication"). Prayer of repentance added after the reader's repetition of the AMIDAH of the weekday MORNING and AFTERNOON SERVICE. It is not recited on days with any degree of festivity. It is also not recited in the Afternoon Service of the day before any festival. *Tahanun* includes *nefilat appayim*, ("falling upon the face"), when the worshiper lays his forehead on his left hand and recites II Samuel 24:14. In the Morning Services on MONDAYS AND THURSDAYS, longer prayers are added to *nefilat appayim*. On fast days (see FASTING AND FAST DAYS) and during the TEN DAYS OF REPENTANCE, both the Morning and Afternoon Services include the AVINU MALKENU ("Our Father, our King") prayer.

The *Tahanun* is not recited on the Sabbath and festivals, the New Moon, throughout the month of Nisan, on 14 Iyyar, on LAG BA-OMER, from the beginning of the month of Sivan until the ninth of the month, from the day before the DAY OF ATONEMENT until the second day after SHEMINI ATSERET, on HANUKKAH, TU BI-SHEVAT, PURIM, and Shushan Purim. Nor is it said on TISHAH BE-AV, the day of mourning for the destruction of both Temples, because the rabbis believe that the day will eventually become a festival. In Israel, it is not recited on INDEPENDENCE DAY and JERUSALEM DAY.

TAKKANAH (pl. *takkanot*). Rules made either by the scholars of the Talmud that obligate all Jews, or by the leaders of the community for the members of their community (*Takkanot ha-Kahal*). *Takkanot* were made by the rabbis to adapt Jewish life to new situations, for example, the *takkanot* of JOHANAN BEN ZAKKAI after the destruction of the Second Temple (*RH* 4:1–3). In ancient times, *takkanot* were made to regulate taxes and the collection and distribution of charity (*BM* 7:1; *BB* 7b–8b). *Takkanot*, such as the 18 measures of BET SHAMMAI, limited contact with the Romans so as to "remove the danger of sin." These *takkanot* were known as *gezerot* ("decrees"). Throughout the Middle Ages, the elders of Jewish communities continued to make *takkanot*, although some were accepted only by their community (such as those of Rabbenu GERSHOM, *Me'or ha-Golah,* in the 11th century for ASHKENAZIM). In modern times, Sephardi and Oriental rabbis continued to exercise this right, while Ashkenazi rabbis prefer not to. For further details, see GEZERAH and HALAKHAH.

EXAMPLES OF TAKKANOT

One who divorces his wife for misconduct is forbidden to remarry her.

Elementary school teachers must be appointed in every community (R. Joshua ben Gamla, 1st cent. CE).

Jews are not to engage in breeding pigs.

One should not give in to extortion when ransoming Jewish captives.

Bigamy is forbidden (Rabbenu Gershom).

A woman may not be divorced except by her own consent (Rabbenu Gershom).

A Jew forced to convert to another faith, but who has returned to Judaism, must not be put to shame (Rabbenu Gershom).

Unauthorized reading of someone else's letters is prohibited (Rabbenu Gershom).

Informers and those requesting Gentile intervention in the community's internal affairs should be excommunicated (Rabbenu TAM).

No conversation is permitted in the synagogue during the *Amidah* and the Reading of the Law (*Takkanot Shum*, 13th cent.).

Lavish celebrations and fancy jewelry or dress are to be avoided.

When money is owed to both a Jew and a non-Jew and the debtor is able to pay only one of them, the non-Jew must be paid first.

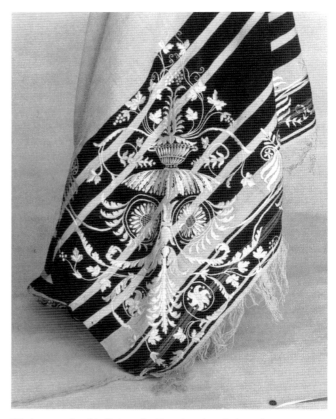

Wool prayer shawl (tallit) *with silk embroidery. Italy, 18th century.*

TALLIT   A four-cornered garment worn as a shawl during certain prayers to fulfill the commandment of fringes (TSITSIT; Num. 15:38). This garment is often called the *tallit gadol* ("large *tallit*"). The *tallit katan* ("small *tallit*") or *tsitsit* is worn under the shirt. When putting on the *tallit*, the BENEDICTION, *le-hi-tattef be-tsitsit* – "Who has commanded us to wrap ourselves is *tsitsit*," – is recited. After the blessing, the wearer wraps oneself entirely in the *tallit*, covering the head, for the amount of time it takes to walk about two yards, and only then arranges the *tallit* around the shoulders.

Traditionally only males wear the four-cornered garment, and the commandment is performed only in the daytime. Women in the REFORM, CONSERVATIVE, and RECONSTRUCTIONIST movements, as well as a number of ORTHODOX women, now also wear a *tallit* during prayers. In most cases, Ashkenazi Jews begin wearing it only after marriage.

The *tallit* is worn for every MORNING SERVICE and ADDITIONAL SERVICE, except on TISHAH BE-AV, when it is worn at the AFTERNOON SERVICE instead. On the DAY OF ATONEMENT, it is worn for all five prayer services. The reader wears a *tallit* at the Afternoon Service and in some commu-

nities, the EVENING SERVICE as well. A person called to the READING OF THE LAW puts on a *tallit* before reciting the Torah blessings.

When the PRIESTS bless the people, they place their *tallit* over their heads and hands, because God's Presence rests on their hands when they recite the PRIESTLY BLESSING.

Ideally, the *tallit* should be made of wool, but other materials may be used. The fringes are made of wool or the material from which the *tallit* is made. Each of the four corners of the garment must have a fringe made of four double threads, giving eight threads. These are then tied with one longer thread that is wound around the other seven and double-knotted.

TALMID HAKHAM   (lit. "student of the wise"; pl. *talmidei hakhamim*). Term from the Mishnah for a learned Jew, especially a rabbinic scholar. A "student of the sages" learned through "attendance on the sages" (*Avot* 6:5): accompanying a scholar in order to watch and learn from all of his ways (*Ber.* 47b). The rabbis of the Mishnah described different levels of achievement, from the student who absorbed everything to the one who retained only essential information (*Avot* 5:5).

A *talmid hakham* had certain privileges, such as not paying taxes, but he had many more responsibilities than the average citizen. All of his ways, including his manners, habits, and clothing, had to be an example to the other members of the community (*Suk.* 21b). He was expected to deal with questions of Jewish law at any time (*Shab.* 114a).

In the Talmud, a scholar had a very high status. A person who was born a *mamzer* (see ILLEGITIMACY) and reached the rank of *talmid hakham* was considered more holy than an ignorant HIGH PRIEST (*Hor.* 3:8, 13a). If necessary, a man should sell off his possessions in order to marry a scholar's daughter (*Pes.* 49a). The punishment for insulting a *talmid hakham* was a heavy fine (TJ, *BK* 8:6) or even EXCOMMUNICATION (*MK* 15a). In modern times, any Jew well versed in Jewish law and literature is described as a *talmid hakham*.

TALMUD

The central body of Jewish law and folklore accumulated over a period of seven centuries (c. 200 BCE–c. 500 CE) in Erets Israel and in Babylonia. The Talmud is made up of the MISHNAH and the discussions of the rabbis on the Mishnah, known as the GEMARA. There are two Talmuds, the Jerusalem (Erets Israel or Palestinian) Talmud (*Talmud Yerushalmi*) and the Babylonian Talmud (*Talmud Bavli*). Another common name for the Talmud is SHAS, the Hebrew acronym for the six Orders (*shishah sedarim*) of the Mishnah.

The ORAL LAW, was given to MOSES on Mount SINAI, passed down through the generations orally, and finally written down in the form of the Mishnah, c. 200 CE. The Gemara presents the discussions that took place in the rabbinic ACADEMIES about the Mishnah during the centuries that followed.

The period of the Talmud is divided into two parts, that of the Mishnah and that of the Gemara. HALAKHAH, Jewish law, is based on a hierarchy of sources. The older a source, the greater its authority. Thus, laws mentioned in the Bible have more authority than those quoted in the Mishnah; laws in the Mishnah have more weight than those found in the Gemara, and so on. The rabbis of the Mishnah are called *tannaim* (pl. of TANNA); those of the Gemara are called *amoraim* (pl. of AMORA).

The Mishnah contains only the end result of rabbinic discussions of *Halakhah*. The original method of studying the Oral Law was preserved in four volumes of MIDRASH HALAKHAH. MIDRASH is the term for any comment or interpretation on the text of the Bible. *Midrash Halakhah* is the collection of interpretations of the legal texts in the Bible.

The many statements that were not included in either the Mishnah or the *Midrash Halakhah* are called *baraitot* (pl. of BARAITA). A collection of these *baraitot*, called TOSEFTA, was edited a number of generations after Rabbi JUDAH HA-NASI edited the Mishnah. Many of the remaining *baraitot* were preserved in the Gemara section of the Talmud. Once the Mishnah was complete, rabbis began to analyze the Mishnah as opposed to writing new *mishnayot*.

By the time Rabbi Judah ha-Nasi published the Mishnah, the Babylonian academies were growing larger and more important. (Jews had lived in Babylonia from the time of the destruction of the First Temple.) As a result, the Gemara developed in two centers: Erets Israel and Babylonia.

Talmudic Methodology   The basic methodology of the Talmud

was the same both in Erets Israel and in Babylonia. The Gemara is the record of the discussion that took place in the academies concerning a particular Mishnah. A typical chapter of Talmud begins with a single Mishnah, usually not longer than a paragraph. This is followed by the Gemara, which usually covers many pages. Then another Mishnah is quoted, followed by the relevant Gemara discussions, and so on.

The Gemara text is broken up into units, each of which is called a *Sugya* (topic). The *Sugya* immediately following the Mishnah begins by analyzing the Mishnah text. The text of the Gemara is usually in the form of questions and answers. The discussion then proceeds to discover the biblical source of the law in the Mishnah. The next step is to compare and contrast it with similar texts from other *mishnayot* or *baraitot*. The Gemara often comes to the conclusion that the author of the Mishnah and the author of the *baraita* or other source agree, by saying that the Mishnah was missing a detail. After inserting the missing detail, the meaning of the Mishnah was changed and the two sources could be in agreement.

Tractate Middot *from the* Talmudis Babylonici Codex Middoth.

The discussions in the Gemara are not limited to the content of the Mishnah. The rabbis sometimes continued on to topics that were associated with the topic of the Mishnah. Sometimes the Gemara discusses at great length opinions that were not accepted as law and other purely theoretical matters. Along with legal debates, the Gemara also includes large sections of MIDRASH (commentaries on the biblical text), AGGADAH (stories about characters and events in the Bible), stories about rabbis, medical advice, science, philosophical debates, and demonology.

While the starting point of the Gemara discussions is the analysis of the Mishnah, the end point is the decision about what is to be accepted as law. Very often a new principle of law is established along with the final legal decision. Some *Sugiot* end with the word "*Teku*," which is an acronym that means that the prophet ELIJAH will solve the legal debate when the MESSIAH comes.

Over the years, the Jewish community in Erets Israel deteriorated. The rabbis saw the need, once again, to write down the Oral Law. By 425 CE, the first edition of the Talmud (Mishnah and Gemara) began to circulate in Erets Israel. It was later called *Talmud Yerushalmi*.

Jerusalem (Palestinian) Talmud (*Talmud Yerushalmi*). Despite its name, the Jerusalem Talmud was not edited in Jerusalem. It was edited in the academies of Caesarea, Sepphoris, and Tiberias.

The Jerusalem Talmud is only about a third of the size of the Babylonian Talmud. There is no Gemara for the last two Orders of the Mishnah (KODASHIM and TOHOROT). On the other hand, it does include Gemara on the entire first division of the Mishnah, ZERA'IM, dealing with agricultural laws. Although the Temple was destroyed, the Jews of Erets Israel still observed the agricultural laws that were not directly connected to the Temple, such as tithes. They studied these laws in their academies because of their daily use.

The political situation in Erets Israel was getting worse and worse, so the rabbis worked quickly to complete the Jerusalem Talmud. The Jerusalem Talmud was completed in c. 400 CE. Much of the credit belongs to the third-century Rabbi JOHANAN BAR NAPPAHA.

The Jerusalem Talmud was basically ignored for many generations because the Babylonian *ge'onim* declared the Babylonian Talmud authoritative. SAADIAH GAON was one of the few rabbis who quoted it in his RESPONSA. It was studied in Erets Israel, North Africa, and southern Italy. Medieval Spanish Talmud scholars studied it more than did Franco-German scholars. In the 18th century, scholars such as Rabbi ELIJAH the Vilna Gaon began to take more interest in the Jerusalem Talmud. In the 20th century, scholars including Saul Lieberman, Louis Ginzberg, and Adin Steinsaltz wrote commentaries on the Jerusalem Talmud.

Babylonian Talmud (*Talmud Bavli*). This second version of the Talmud is quite different from the first. The discussions are longer and more outside material is included.

The Babylonian Talmud contains Gemara on the first book in the Order of ZERA'IM, dealing with the laws of prayer, but since the agricultural laws did not apply outside of Erets Israel, there is no Gemara on the rest of the Order of *Zera'im*. On the other hand, it contains Gemara on each of the books in the Order of *Kodashim* (laws of the sacrifices), despite the fact that these laws were only relevant when the Temple stood. It has Gemara on only one book in the last Order, *Tohorot* (laws of ritual purity), namely, the book of *Niddah* dealing with the laws of menstruating women. Altogether, the Babylonian Talmud contains about two and a half million words and nearly 5,900 folio pages (two sides of a sheet) in 36 separate books.

The two Talmuds differ in language, style, content, and range of subject matter. Over the years and centuries, the Babylonian Talmud has been accepted as the authority in matters of Jewish law. Later halakhic authorities claimed that it includes all of the rulings made in the Erets Israel academies.

According to tradition, the Babylonian Talmud was edited by Rav ASHI and Ravina. Modern scholars believe that the process of editing and arranging the material took place in a number of stages over a period of several generations. The Babylonian academies became the center of world Jewry in the generations after the publication of the Talmud. As a result, less than two centuries later, the *ge'onim* used the Babylonian Talmud as the basis for the law.

Influence of the Talmud on Jewish Life The Talmud is a written edition of the Oral Law as it developed over a 900-year period. That fact alone is enough to guarantee its influence on Jewish religious observance throughout the ages.

The commandment of Torah study (see Deut. 6:7 and 11:19) was interpreted to mean the study of Talmud. To this day, Talmud study is the main aspect of the rabbinic academies throughout the world. Ultimately, the Talmud shaped the very nature of Judaism and Jewishness and its laws made Judaism into a way of life. See also TALMUDIC COMMENTARIES.

TALMUDIC COMMENTARIES

Babylonian Talmud Almost no commentary was written on the Talmud until the 11th century. Until this time, the language and world of the Talmud was familiar to the Jewish communities, making interpretations less necessary. In North Africa and Franco-Germany, by the 11th century, Aramaic was no longer the spoken language and the daily life no longer resembled that of the Talmud period. At this point, rabbis began to write commentaries on the Talmud.

In the early 11th century, Rabbenu GERSHOM BEN JUDAH wrote a commentary on several books of the Talmud. In the same period, Rabbi Hananel ben Hushiel of Kairouan in North Africa wrote a running commentary on a large number of the books. It is possible that his commentary covered the whole Talmud, but that only parts of it still exist.

The most important commentary is that of RASHI on the entire Talmud. It illuminates difficult passages, although it is clearly meant for students who are familiar with the language and content of the Talmud. Without Rashi's commentary, the Talmud would have remained a closed book, even to those who study it regularly.

Rashi's own students were the authors of TOSEFOT, which clarifies points that were still unclear after Rashi's commentary.

Jerusalem Talmud   The first known commentary on the Jerusalem Talmud was written by Rabbi Solomon Sirillo in Erets Israel, c. 1530. At about the same time, another scholar, Rabbi Eleazar Azikri of Safed, wrote *Sefer Haredim* ("Book of Trembling") on a number of books. It is found in the standard version of the Jerusalem Talmud.

The most complete commentary was written by Rabbi Moses Margolies, a Lithuanian Talmud scholar (d. 1780). It covers the entire work and is divided into two sections; *Penei Mosheh* ("The Face of Moses") and *Mareh ha-Penim* ("Showing the Face"). The first is a running commentary and the second is a series of NOVELLAE (original ideas). Other commentaries on the Jerusalem Talmud include that of ELIJAH, the Gaon of Vilna, *Sha'arei Yerushalayim* by Rabbi Dov Berish of Slonin; *No'am Yerushalayim,* by Rabbi Joshua Isaac Schapiro; and *Ha-Yerushalmi ha-Meforash* by Rabbi Shlomo Goren.

TALMUD TORAH   (lit. "study of Torah"). Name given to Jewish community schools, especially in Eastern Europe. The Talmud Torah, unlike the HEDER, had various classes, each taught by its own *rebbe* (master). The Talmud Torah was supported by taxes collected from all members of the community. The Amsterdam Talmud Torah, founded in the 16th century, was attended by all, rich and poor. In Eastern Europe, on the other hand, only children whose parents could not afford a private teacher attended the Talmud Torah. Because the Talmud Torah was sponsored by the COMMUNITY, the community often supervised EDUCATION. Students in the Talmud Torah studied classic Jewish texts, such as the Bible and the Mishnah. Children, especially in the younger grades, were expected to learn passages by heart, including their translation into Yiddish. Older students concentrated on Talmud study. Students who completed their studies at the Talmud Torah could go on to study in a YESHIVAH, but most joined the work force. Today some Jewish afternoon schools are still called Talmud Torah.

TAM, RABBENU   (Jacob ben Meir; 1100–1171). The most important of the French Tosafists (see TOSAFOT). He was almost killed during the Second Crusade, but his life was saved by a passing nobleman who promised the mob that Jacob would convert to Christianity. He was the son of RASHI's daughter and studied under his own father, and brother SAMUEL BEN MEIR (*Rashbam*). Tam was the greatest scholar of his time, and questions of Jewish law were sent him from all over the world. He was the head of the academy in his home town, where more than 80 Tosafists studied at a time.

Rabbenu Tam's explanations appear throughout the *Tosafot* on the Babylonian Talmud. His main work was *Sefer ha-Yashar,* which contains *Tosafot* and decisions as well as RESPONSA. He tried to give lenients decision within the framework of the HALAKHAH.

Rabbenu Tam disagreed with his grandfather Rashi on the proper order of the four sections of the Bible that are placed in the TEFILLIN. As a result, to this day some Jews put on two pairs of *tefillin* – one pair according to the opinion of Rashi and one according to the opinion of Rabbenu Tam.

TAMID   ("Continuous Offering") Ninth tractate (book) of the Order of KODASHIM in the Mishnah. Its seven shapters describe the ritual of the daily burnt-offering in the TEMPLE, brought by the priests every morning and afternoon (cf. Ex. 29:38–42, 30:7, 8; Num. 28:3–8; see SACRIFICES AND OFFERINGS).

TAMMUZ   Fourth month of the Jewish religious CALENDAR; tenth month of the Hebrew civil year, counting from TISHRI. It has 29 days and coincides with June–July. Its zodiac sign is Cancer. In the Bible, it is called "the fourth month." When the Jews returned from the Babylonian EXILE they began to call the month Tammuz, the name of a Mesopotamian god. The fast of 17 Tammuz (SHIVAH ASAR BE-TAMMUZ) is in memory of the breaking of the walls of JERUSALEM by the Babylonian army in 586 BCE and, again, by the Roman army in 70 CE. This fast begins the mournful THREE WEEKS, which end with TISHAH BE-AV.

TAMMUZ, SEVENTEENTH OF   See SHIVAH ASAR BE-TAMMUZ

TANAKH   See BIBLE

TANHUMA   A number of works of MIDRASH (commentary) on the PENTATEUCH written by Tanhuma bar Abba, a rabbi of the Jerusalem Talmud (fourth century CE). The *Tanhuma* is based on the TRIENNIAL CYCLE (three-year cycle) of Torah readings used at that time in Erets Israel. Many manuscripts of *Midrash Tanhuma* exist, none of which are complete.

TANNA   ("teacher," pl. *tannaim*). Scholars of the ORAL LAW who lived from around 20 CE until the days of JUDAH HA-NASI (c. 200 CE). The *tannaim* were the first to put the Oral Law into writing. They produced the MISHNAH (edited by Rabbi Judah ha-Nasi), the TOSEFTA, BARAITA literature, and the MIDRASH HALAKHAH. Over 120 *tannaim* are mentioned by name in the Mishnah; others are referred to in the *baraita* literature. Most were born and educated in Erets Israel.

There are five generations of *tannaim*. Rabban GAMALIEL and Rabbi JOHANAN BEN ZAKKAI were the heads of the first generation. After the Second Temple was destroyed in 70 CE, Johanan ben Zakkai moved the academy of Jewish law to Yavneh to establish a center of learning in Erets Israel (see ACADEMIES).

The leading *tannaim* of the second generation were Gamaliel II, Rabbi ELEAZER BEN AZARIAH, ELIEZER BEN HYRCANUS, and JOSHUA BEN HANANIAH.

They were influenced by the collapse of the BAR KOKHBA revolt in 135 CE. Rabbi Gamaliel II, Rabbi Joshua, and Rabbi Eliezer traveled to Rome to make contact with the Jewish community and to negotiate with the Roman authorities. Rabbi AKIVA, a third generation *tanna,* also traveled around the Diaspora making contact with Jewish communities. He, Rabbi ISHMAEL BEN ELISHA, and Rabbi Hananiah ben Teradyon, were among the TEN MARTYRS to be put to death by the Roman authorities. The halakhic Midrashim (Mekhilta, SIFREI, etc.) were written in the academies of Rabbi Akiva and Rabbi Ishmael, who developed the principles of HERMENEUTICS for interpreting the Bible.

The fourth generation of *tannaim* was made up of Akiva's students SIMEON BAR YOHAI, YOSE BEN HALAFTA, MEIR, Rabbi Simeon ben Gamaliel II, and JUDAH BAR ILAI. Judah ha-Nasi was the outstanding *tanna* of the fifth generation. The period of the *tannaim* ended with his publication of the Mishnah.

TARGUM   The ancient ARAMAIC translations of the Hebrew Bible. They were often an interpretation as well. The earliest manuscripts of Targum were discovered among the DEAD SEA SCROLLS and are dated to the mid-second century BCE. The Targums were probably used in the synagogue to help people understand the READING OF THE LAW and as an aid to private and public study.

Two separate Targums were produced, one in Erets Israel and one in Babylonia. The Erets Israel Targum was written in Galilean Aramaic, while the Babylonian Targum was written in Babylonian Aramaic. The Babylonian Targum was a literal word-for-word translation of the Hebrew original. The Erets Israel version often included interpretations of difficult passages that went beyond the original Hebrew version. The Babylonian Talmud, which is the accepted source of Jewish law, held that the Targum of Onkelos (2nd cent. CE) was written under the guidance of the students of Rabbi AKIVA, which gave it great authority. It refers to Targum Onkelos as "our Targum." As a result, the Erets Israel Targum was displaced by Targum Onkelos.

The Targum often adds missing information, such as names and places, that are not mentioned in the Hebrew Bible. It updates legal passages to match later practice of HALAKHAH. The Erets Israel Targum sometimes adds legends to the stories of the Bible. Targums were written on the entire Bible, except for those books that are originally in Aramaic.

According to the Talmud, the Targum of the PROPHETS was written by the *tanna* Jonathan ben Uzziel. It is therefore called Targum Jonathan. The Targum to the earlier prophets follows Onkelos in both language and content. The Targums to the later prophets and to the Writings (see HAGIOGRAPHA) are closer to the Erets Israel Targums. Some books have more than one Targum.

Nowadays, both Jewish and Chrisitan scholars use the Targum texts as a source for the study of ancient Semitic languages. They also contain information about ancient synagogues and customs.

TASHLIKH   Ceremony performed on the first afternoon of ROSH HA-SHANAH (the New Year). If the first day of the holiday falls on a SABBATH, *tashlikh* is pushed off to the next day. The custom is to go to a body of water and throw in a few crumbs of bread while reciting verses from the prophets Micah and Isaiah. The verse in Micah 7:19 reads, "You will cast all their sins into the depths of the sea."

The custom is first mentioned in the 15th century *Sefer ha-Maharil* by Jacob MÖLLN of Germany. Varied versions of the custom are observed in different communities. Among Kurdish Jews it is customary to jump into the water. Kabbalists shake their clothing to free themselves of the "shells" of the sins of the previous year. The Syrian ceremony includes many quotes from the ZOHAR.

Some rabbis claim that the custom of *tashlikh* is a superstition with non-Jewish origins.

Casting sins into the water (tashlikh).

TEFILLIN   ("phylacteries"). Two small black leather boxes containing four passages of the Bible. Traditionally, Jewish males over the age of 13 wear them on the left arm ("*shel yad*") and head ("*shel rosh*") during the weekday MORNING SERVICE.

Originally, *tefillin* were worn throughout the day. The Bible gives the commandment to wear *tefillin*, but does not specify how they are to be made. These details were added by the rabbis (*Men.* 34a–37b).

The *tefillin* are made up of parchments taken from a KOSHER animal, written upon with permanent black ink, and placed in a square black box upon which is written the Hebrew letter *shin.* The box has a wider base through which the straps are passed.

The commandment to wear *tefillin* is found in four passages in the Bible (Ex. 13:1–10 and 13:11–16; Deut. 6:4–9 and 11:13–21) that are written by a SCRIBE each on a separate piece of parchment and inserted into the the box for the arm. The same passages are written on four separate pieces of parchment for the head box. Other important elements of Judaism that are mentioned in the four biblical passages include: accepting God's rule, that God is One, God's PROVIDENCE, the EXODUS from

---

HOW TO DON TEFILLIN

1. The hand *tefillin* is placed on the bicep of the inner side of the left forearm ("opposite the heart"); the BENEDICTION is recited; the strap is wound seven times around the arm between the elbow and wrist and three times around the middle finger. Lefthanded people place the *tefillin* on the right forearm.

2. The head *tefillin* is placed on the head so that the front edge of the case lies just above the line where the hair begins to grow and directly above the space between the eyes. Its strap circles the head and is fastened in a knot at the nape of the neck, allowing the loose ends to hang down in front. The benediction for the binding of the *tefillin* is said while this is done, followed by the words, "Blessed be the name of His glorious Kingdom forever."

3. The remaining part of the strap of the hand *tefillin* is bound around the palm forming the Hebrew letter *shin* while Hosea 2:21–22 is recited.

4. When the *tefillin* are removed at the end of the service, the order is reversed.

Egypt, and faith in the final REDEMPTION. The act of putting on the *tefillin* reminds a Jew of his service to God.

Father helping his son put on tefillin *(phylacteries).*

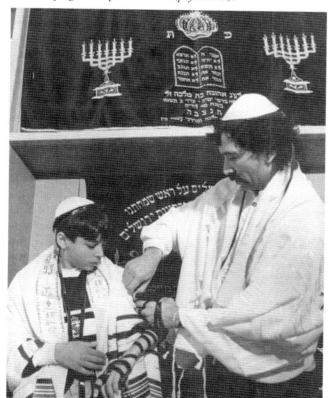

Tefillin are worn daily for the Morning Service. They are not worn on the SABBATH nor on major FESTIVALS because these holidays themselves remind a person of his service to God. They are also not worn in the earliest period of MOURNING, by a groom on his wedding day, by a leper, or by one who has been excommunicated (see EXCOMMUNICATION). On TISHAH BE-AV, they are worn for the AFTERNOON SERVICE instead of the Morning Service.

In the Middle Ages, there was a dispute between RASHI and his grandson Rabbenu TAM about the order of the passages in the *tefillin*. As a result of this dispute, many Hasidic and Oriental Jews put on two sets of *tefillin*, one according to Rashi and the other according to Rabbenu Tam.

Abraham GEIGER, the pioneer of REFORM JUDAISM, claimed that *tefillin* were originally pagan amulets. As a result, they were excluded from Reform prayer until its most recent prayer book. They remain a part of CONSERVATIVE ritual. Today some Jewish women who have made it a practice of taking on commandments originally designated for men also wear *tefillin* to express their closeness to God.

TEHINNAH   (pl. *tehinnot;* "supplication"). Private prayers added by the individual worshiper, usually in addition to the regular prayers. The Mishnah teaches that PRAYER should never become a fixed routine, but rather a plea before God for mercy (*Avot* 2:18). During the times of the Talmud, the individual added improvised *tehinnot* after the AMIDAH. These were later replaced with the fixed TAHANUN prayer. Individuals now have the opportunity of adding *tehinnot* in the framework of the *Amidah*.

Over the years, large numbers of *tehinnot* have been composed in many different languages and styles. Some have been incorporated into the regular prayer book. Mystical *tehinnot* can be identified by the opening phrase "May it be Your will" or "Master of the Universe." There are *tehinnot* for lighting the Sabbath candles, traveling overseas, and many other occasions. Some of these *tehinnot* have been collected in books or pamphlets.

TEMPLE   Main center of Jewish worship in ancient times. It was located on Mount MORIAH (*har ha-bayit*, TEMPLE MOUNT) in JERUSALEM. The First Temple was built by King SOLOMON, c. 960 BCE, and destroyed by the Babylonians under Nebuhadnezzar in 586 BCE. The Second Temple was dedicated c. 520 BCE and destroyed by the Romans under Titus in 70 CE.

First Temple   Originally, King DAVID had wanted to build the Temple, but God rejected this wish, because David had fought so many battles and had too much blood on his hands. David's son, Solomon, built the Temple instead (II Sam. 7:12–13).

When Solomon became king he enlisted the help of Hiram, the king of Tyre, who supplied him with the necessary building materials. The Temple was a magnificent structure, made of the finest materials. It was a stone building standing within a royal compound which also housed the palace, the Hall of Judgment, the Hall of Cedars, and a house for Solomon's wife, Pharaoh's daughter. The main structure of the Temple was surrounded by a three-story building divided into chambers, with the levels connected by trapdoors. These were probably storerooms for the Temple's treasures. The main building was divided into an inner room, the HOLY OF HOLIES, on the west, and an outer room (the *azarah*) on the east. Around the Temple was a walled-in compound. The entrance to the Temple was through the porch, on each side of which stood a massive bronze pillar. The pillars' were called Jachin and Boaz.

The inner walls of the Temple were paneled with cedar wood. The floor of the Holy of Holies was also made of cedar wood, while the floor of the outer room was of a less expensive cypress wood. The walls were decorated with carvings and encrusted in gold. Both the outer room and the Holy of Holies had doors dividing them from the other spaces. The walls of the Holy of Holies were decorated on both sides and its floor was plated with gold (1 Kings 6:29–30). The Holy of Holies was entered only once a year, on the DAY OF ATONEMENT, by the HIGH PRIEST.

The most important object in the Temple was the ARK, which was placed inside the Holy of Holies. Inside the Ark stood the TWO TABLETS OF THE COVENANT with the TEN COMMANDMENTS. Two wooden cherubs with outspread wings surrounded the Ark, as a symbol of the Presence of God.

The outer room of the Temple housed an INCENSE altar, the table for the SHOWBREAD, and ten lampstands (see MENORAH). These were all made of or covered in gold. In front of the Temple stood a huge bronze water basin supported by 12 bronze cattle. Along the east front of the building stood ten smaller water basins. A bronze ALTAR also stood in the courtyard, which was used for various sacrifices.

Within the Temple were three areas meant for specific groups of people: the *ezrat kohanim* ("the priestly enclosure") for the PRIESTS working in the Temple, the *ezrat yisra'el* ("the enclosure for Israelites") for male worshipers, and the *ezrat nashim* ("the women's enclosure") for female worshipers.

During Solomon's reign, the Temple was the main place of Jewish worship and pilgrims came to it from all the tribes of Israel (see PILGRIMAGE, PILGRIM FESTIVALS). However, during the reign of Solomon's son Rehoboam, the kingdom of Israel was divided, and two other temples were built in the Northern Kingdom of ISRAEL.

The Temple was a place to bring SACRIFICES AND OFFERINGS to God. In addition to the daily sacrifices and the additional sacrifices offered on special days, people could bring their own sacrifices, either in thanks or as part of their atonement for sins. The OMER (first barley measure, harvested on the second day of PASSOVER) and the FIRST FRUITS (on SHAVU'OT) were brought to the Temple. On Passover eve, all families had to come to Jerusalem to offer the paschal sacrifice. Many of the PSALMS were originally composed to be sung in the Temple.

Second Temple   The Second Temple was dedicated in Jerusalem some time between 521 and 517 BCE, some 65–70 years after the destruction of the First Temple. It was rebuilt after Cyrus' decree permitting the return of the exiled Jews from Babylonia to Judah. The rebuilt Temple was but a shadow of its former glory. Zadok had been the High Priest under King Solomon, and Zadok's descendants took up this role in the Second Temple.

About 70–80 years after the rededication of the Temple, in the times of EZRA and NEHEMIAH the Second Temple took a central position in the history of the people. Ezra and Nehemiah saw to it that the priestly and Levite lists were reexamined and Temple services renewed accordingly.

When Antiochus IV (Epiphanes) ascended to the Seleucid throne, the Temple's fortunes took a dramatic turn for the worse. The Temple was converted into a place of pagan worship. This and other persecutions of the Jews brought on the revolt of the HASMONEANS, which eventually led JUDAH MACCABEE to restore the Temple's Jewish character. The date of the Temple's rededication, 25 Kislev, is commemorated by the HANUKKAH festival.

Judah's brother Jonathan was the first of the Hasmoneans to put on the High Priestly clothing, ending the eight-century-old Zadokite line. The Hasmoneans were High Priests until HEROD became king, about a century later. At this point, High Priests were installed and removed at the whim of King Herod and those who came after him. When the Revolt against Rome broke out in 66 CE, the sacrifices on behalf of the Roman emperor and his family were stopped.

Structure No real picture is available of the structure other than the knowledge that the Second Temple, up until and including the times of the Hasmoneans, was but a faint shadow of its former glorious self. The little information available is from the Bible, the Talmud, Josephus, and more recent archeological excavations.

The available picture is that of a much enlarged and magnificent building begun by Herod in 20/19 BCE. Although the rebuilt Temple was dedicated a year and a half later, work on the structure continued for decades, with the finishing touches being made only two years before the beginning of the Revolt in 66 CE.

The Temple Mount was now surrounded by massive walls. The outer area of the Temple was huge and contained the inner forecourt. A flight of steps led to the forecourt, which had a railing around it with warning signs in Greek and Latin banning the entrance of non-Jews beyond this area.

According to the Talmud, the seat of the Great SANHEDRIN was within the forecourt of the Temple Mount. Some sort of SYNAGOGUE was also in use there. The rabbis said: "He who has not seen the House of Herod (i.e. the rebuilt Herodian Temple) has never in his life seen a beautiful structure."

Ritual The daily services were performed by the priests. The LEVITES helped the priests with the daily service, while also serving as Temple singers (see MUSIC AND SONG), gatekeepers, and Temple servants. The highest-ranking member of the priestly hierarchy was the High Priest.

The entire priesthood was subdivided into 24 groups (see MISHMAROT AND MA'AMADOT) that took weekly turns. The Levites were divided into corresponding groups. There was also a Temple physician, a choirmaster, and a special person in charge of the priestly clothing.

The services at the Second Temple included prayers, blessings, and readings from the PENTATEUCH. At the end of the incense offering, the priests blessed the congregation. The PRIESTLY BLESSING is still recited in synagogues throughout the world.

After the Destruction   According to the sages, the First Temple was destroyed because of immorality and bloodshed. The Second Temple was destroyed because of hatred among Jews. The destruction of the Second Temple affected nearly every aspect of religious thought and practice. Longings for the destroyed Temple were expressed on the one hand by MOURNING practices and on the other hand by undying hope for its reconstruction. The DIETARY LAWS reflect the laws of animal sacrifices; the schedule of PRAYER services were based on the schedule of sacrifices; a prayer for the restoration of the Temple was added to the AMIDAH. Throughout the centuries, descendants of the priests have studied the laws of the Temple service so they would be prepared to do their jobs when the Temple was rebuilt.

The mourning was expressed in many ways. When a Jew paints his house, he leaves a corner unfinished, in memory of the Temple. The annual fast of TISHAH BE-AV is observed in memory of both Temples. The groom breaks a glass at the end of the MARRIAGE ceremony as an expression of mourning for the destruction of the Temple.

According to the *halakhah* (Jewish law) there are several conditions that must be met before the Temple can be rebuilt: the majority of Jews must be living in Erets Israel; there must be conditions of peace; the desire for a Temple must come from genuine religious feeling among the Jewish people; a sign of God's approval must be given; and a true prophet must order the rebuilding. According to MAIMONIDES, the Temple will not be built by human hands. He holds that it has been constructed in heaven, from where it will miraculously descend at the right time.

TEMPLE MOUNT   (Heb. *Har ha-Bayit*). Elevated area in the southeastern corner of the Old City of JERUSALEM, site of the First and Second TEMPLE. Four large walls built in the days of HEROD the Great (1st cent. BCE) enclose the area of the Temple Mount. Archeologists as well as rabbis disagree about the exact location of the Temple, and because of the holy status of the area, it is impossible to excavate.

According to the Bible, the binding of Isaac (AKEDAH) took place on a mountain in the Land of Moriah. From an early period, Mount MORIAH was identified as being the mountain upon which the Temple was built (II Chr. 3:1). After King SOLOMON built the Temple, the Temple Mount was recognized by Jews as the holiest place on earth. Since the seventh century, it was under Muslim control, and it became a holy site for them as well. More than 100 Muslim buildings now stand on the

Aerial view of the Temple Mount, Jerusalem.

Temple Mount. The most important buildings are the Dome of the Rock and the Mosque of El Aksa.

Because the Temple Mount is holy for Jews, people in certain states of impurity may not enter. Out of respect for the Temple Mount, the Mishnah forbade one to enter "with his staff, or wearing his shoes, or with his feet dust-stained; nor should one make of it a short cut, and spitting is forbidden" (*Ber.* 9:5).

When the Temple was destroyed in 70 CE, the holiness of the Temple Mount became an issue. Most rabbis agreed that the Mount remained holy even after the destruction. Since, in the post-Temple period, it is impossible to become pure without the ashes of the RED HEIFER (see Num. 19), most rabbis agree that since the destruction, no one may enter the Temple Mount (see Maimonides, *Yad, Bet ha-Behirah* 6:14–16). After the Old City of Jerusalem was recaptured by Israel from the Jordanians in 1967, the issue arose again, However, most Jews still do not enter the area of the Temple Mount.

In 1967, the Israeli government decided to ban Jewish worship on the Temple Mount in order to avoid confrontations with the Muslim world. Today the Temple Mount is run by the Muslim Religious Council (*Wakf*).

TEMURAH   ("Exchange"). Sixth tractate (book) of the Order of KODASHIM in the Mishnah. Its seven chapters deal with the laws of exchange of objects dedicated to the TEMPLE (cf. Lev. 27:9, 10. 32. 33). The book also talks about other laws connected with SACRIFICES AND OFFERINGS.

TEN COMMANDMENTS   (or Decalogue; *Aseret ha-Dibrot*). The commandments spoken by God from the top of Mount SINAI to the Children of Israel seven weeks after the EXODUS

THE TEN COMMANDMENTS
(EXODUS 20:2–17)

God spoke all these words, saying:

1. I am the Lord your God who brought you out of the land of Egypt, the house of bondage: You shall have no other gods besides Me.

2. You shall not make for yourselves a sculptured image, or any likeness of what is in the heavens above, or on the earth below, or in the waters under the earth. You shall not bow down to them or serve them. For I the Lord your God am an impassioned God, visiting the guilt of the parents upon the children, upon the third and upon the fourth generations of those who reject Me, but showing kindness to the thousandth generation of those who love Me and keep My commandments.

3. You shall not swear falsely by the name of the Lord your God; for the Lord will not clear one who swears falsely by His name.

4. Remember the Sabbath day and keep it holy. Six days you shall labor and do all your work, but the seventh day is a Sabbath of the Lord your God; you shall not do any work, you, your son or daughter, your male or female slave, or your cattle, or the stranger who is within your settlements. For in six days the Lord made heaven and earth and sea, and all that is within them, and He rested on the seventh day; therefore the Lord blessed the Sabbath day and made it holy.

5. Honor your father and your mother, that you may long endure on the land that the Lord your God is assigning to you.

6. You shall not murder.

7. You shall not commit adultery.

8. You shall not steal.

9. You shall not bear false witness against your neighbor.

10. You shall not covet your neighbor's house; you shall not covet your neighbor's wife, or his male or female slave, or his ox or his ass, or anything that is your neighbor's.

from Egypt. They were later written by God on the two stone TABLETS OF THE COVENANT and given to MOSES to be placed in the ARK OF THE COVENANT in the SANCTUARY and later in the TEMPLE. According to the Bible, the Ten Commandments are the terms of the COVENANT between God and the Israelites at Sinai (Ex. 34:27–28). The Israelites had to prepare themselves to receive the Ten Commandments by washing themselves and their clothing and not having sexual relations. The words were accompanied by thunder and lightning and blasts of the SHOFAR ("ram's horn"; Ex. 20:18–19).

The Ten Commandments are at the core of Judaism. They are the basic moral and ritual code to which more commandments were added. When the Ten Commandments are read in the SYNAGOGUE, the congregation stands and the reader uses a special melody that joins all the commandments into one verse.

Many commentaries were written on the Ten Commandments in the Middle Ages. In the first two commandments God speaks directly to the people in the first person and in the other commandments He speaks in the third person. From this the rabbis learned that the Israelites heard only the first two commandments and that the others were transferred to them through Moses (*Mak.* 24a).

The words of the Ten Commandments are recorded twice in the Pentateuch: in Exodus 20:2–17 and in Deuteronomy 5:6–18. There are many explanations for the differences between the two versions. For example, in the second version, 40 years after the Exodus, it was appropriate to remind the Jews of their slavery in Egypt. This was not necessary in the first version, spoken only seven weeks after the Exodus.

The rabbis taught that the stone tablets on which the Ten Commandments were written were prepared before CREATION and that therefore the Ten Commandments apply to the whole universe, outside of time and place. They also suggested that when God spoke the words, it was simultaneously translated into 70 languages so that all peoples could understand it.

According to the AGGADAH (rabbinic legend), God offered the Torah to the Edomites, Moabites, and Ishmaelites. When they heard that it forbade murder, theft, and adultery, they refused the offer saying that it would interfere with their way of life (*Sif.* to Deut. 33:2). In CHRISTIANITY and ISLAM the Ten Commandments are also central.

TEN DAYS OF REPENTANCE (*aseret yemei teshuvah*). Ten days in September/October, beginning with ROSH HA-SHANAH (1 Tishri) through the DAY OF ATONEMENT (10 Tishri) that are considered the most serious time of the year. Judaism holds that all mankind is judged then and its fate determined for the coming year. The Talmud (*RH* 16b) teaches that on the New Year, those who are completely righteous are written in the BOOK OF LIFE, those who are wholly evil in the Book of Death, and the fate of all the others remains hanging until the Day of Atonement. During this time a person must try to improve and undergo REPENTANCE. Before the MORNING SERVICE, penitential prayers (*selihot*) are said, and various additions are made to the prayers. According to Jewish law, people must beg forgiveness of anyone they have hurt during the past year. The Sabbath between the New Year and the Day of Atonement is called *Shabbat Teshuvah*, the Sabbath of Repentance (see SABBATHS, SPECIAL).

TEN MARTYRS Ten RABBIS of the second century who were tortured and executed on the orders of the Roman emperor Hadrian. The story appears several times in the MIDRASH (rabbinic legend), including the medieval *Eleh Ezkerah*. According to this *midrash*, the Roman ruler asked the rabbis what is the punishment, according to Jewish law, for one who kidnaps and sells a fellow Jew. The rabbis told him that the Bible teaches that the criminal should be put to death. The emperor then brought up the case of JOSEPH, who was kidnapped by his ten brothers and sold as a slave in Egypt. He argued that since the brothers were not killed, ten rabbis of Israel must die instead. The ten included the most important scholars of the time, such as Rabbi AKIVA, Hananiah ben Taradyon, Eleazar ben Shammua, Hananiah ben Hakhinah, the High Priest Ishmael, and the president of the SANHEDRIN, Simeon ben GAMALIEL.

The story is probably not historically correct. The mentioned rabbis did not all live at the same time, and although some were killed by the Romans, various reasons are recorded. Some were not even killed by the Romans. Nevertheless it portrays the tragic story of the Jews of Erets Israel under the rule of the Romans, especially in the times of Hadrian, after the BAR KOKHBA revolt (132–135 CE). It was a time of terrible persecution, when the Romans made laws prohibiting the study of Torah and the practice of Judaism, and many Jewish leaders were killed.

The story of the Ten Martyrs is read during the ADDITIONAL SERVICE of the DAY OF ATONEMENT and as part of the KINOT for TISHAH BE-AV. Some communities have also added sections about the victims of the HOLOCAUST.

TEN PLAGUES   See EXODUS

TEREFAH U-NEVELAH   (lit. "torn and a carcass"). Term used for the meat of an animal or fowl that would have been permitted for food by the DIETARY LAWS but is forbidden to eat because of the way it met its death. According to Jewish law, all KOSHER animals must be slaughtered in a certain way (see SHEHITAH). After it is slaughtered, the animal must be examined to make sure it does not have any defects that would have caused its death within a year. If it is found, for example, that it had a punctured lung, the animal would be considered a *terefah* and its meat could not be eaten. If an animal died by any means other than ritual slaughter, or if the ritual slaughterer did not kill the animal according to all the laws, the carcass is known as a *nevelah*. The word *treif* has been extended to mean any food which may not be eaten according to Jewish law.

TERUMOT   ("Heave Offering"). Sixth tractate (book) of the Order of ZERA'IM in the Mishnah. Its 11 chapters deal with the laws of separating the priests' share of agricultural produce (cf. Lev. 22:12; Num. 18:8, 11, 12, 24–32; Deut. 12:6, 18:4), the mixing of *terumah* ("food set aside for holy purposes") with regular produce, who may and may not eat the *terumah*, and the prohibition against using *terumah* for other purposes (see TITHES).

TETRAGRAMMATON   See GOD, NAMES OF

TEVET   Tenth month of the Jewish religious CALENDAR; fourth month of the Hebrew civil year counting from TISHRI. It has 29 days and coincides with December–January. Its zodiac sign is Capricorn. In the Bible, it is usually called the tenth month and is the beginning of the winter rains in Erets Israel (*Er.* 56a). On 10 Tevet, the Babylonian armies put a siege on JERUSALEM (II Kings 25:1; Ezek. 24:1–2), which eventually led to the destruction of the TEMPLE. This day is commemorated by *Asarah be-Tevet,* "the fast of the tenth month" (see TEVET, TENTH OF).

TEVET, TENTH OF   (Heb. *Asarah be-Tevet*). Minor fast in memory of the beginning of the siege of JERUSALEM by the Babylonian armies (II Kings 25:1). This siege led to the destruction of the First Temple in 586 BCE.

The fast begins at dawn and ends at nightfall (see FASTING AND FAST DAYS). Special prayers of repentance (SELIHOT) are said, and passages from the PENTATEUCH and the PROPHETS are read in the synagogue.

The Israel Chief Rabbinate has declared the Tenth of Tevet as the remembrance day for the victims of the Nazi HOLOCAUST. Some recite KADDISH on this day for the six million victims. Outside Israel, and even within Israel, *Yom ha-Sho'ah*, Holocaust Memorial Day on 27 Nisan, is the more widely observed memorial.

THANKSGIVING OFFERING   See SACRIFICES AND OFFERINGS

THEFT   Theft is forbidden in Judaism, as is written in the Bible: "You shall not steal" (Lev. 19:11). A similar verse in the TEN COMMANDMENTS was interpreted not as theft, but as kidnapping (theft of a person). Theft is carried out in secret, with the thief making every effort not to be seen. By contrast, robbery involves a direct confrontation between the robber and his victim (for example, mugging). A thief who is caught must repay twice the value of what he has stolen as a fine. A thief who voluntarily returns what was stolen does not have to pay the fine. Unlike the thief, a robber who is caught must only return the stolen goods and does not pay a fine. The rabbis explain that the reason for the difference is that the thief is worse than the robber. The robber, by his actions, shows that he fears no one. The thief, on the other hand, shows fear, which is why he avoids confrontation. If he is afraid, he should at least show equal fear of God. According to the Bible, a person who steals and does not have the money to repay his theft may be sold into slavery for up to six years to pay for the theft. The HALAKHAH (Jewish law) teaches that *genevat da'at* – literally "theft of the mind" (deceiving another) – is also considered theft. It is forbidden to buy stolen property because this helps a thief operate.

THEOLOGY   Theology is systematic thought about religious beliefs. Generally, religion is first experienced and only later thought about. The Bible is a record of primary religious experience and contains very little thought about religion. This is true of the first two sections of the Bible, the PENTATEUCH and the PROPHETS. The last section, the HAGIOGRAPHA ("Writings"), contains the beginnings of human response and thought in areas where experience conflicts with religious beliefs. The books of JOB, ECCLESIASTES, and some of PSALMS try to understand the justice of God and deal with questions such as why do the righteous suffer.

While the Bible itself contains very little theology, the fact that Job's questioning of God is not rejected paves the way for theology in Jewish thought. The Talmud contains much theological thought. It is scattered throughout the many volumes and is not developed systematically. The rabbis' thoughts on a certain topic are usually phrased in a general saying. For example, on the subject of FREE WILL versus God the all-powerful the sages said: "Everything is foreseen, yet permission is given; the world is judged with mercy yet the verdict is according to one's deeds" (*Avot* 3:15). The Talmud accepts various opinions on a particular subject.

The RABBIS explored and broadened their understanding of certain basic ideas in the Bible. The Bible calls for both fear and love of God (Deut. 10:12). The rabbis asked: What does that mean? How is this done? Is there not a conflict between love and fear? Sometimes they would discuss an idea that was not related to the text of the Bible. "For two and a half years, the school of HILLEL and the school of SHAMMAI debated whether people would have been better off if they had not been created …" (*Er.* 13b).

The rabbis of the Talmud taught that if one accepts the Bible, one must also believe in a moral God, PROVIDENCE, REWARD AND PUNISHMENT, MIRACLES, REPENTANCE, REVELATION, and REDEMPTION. These were considered norms of faith.

PHILO of Alexandria (20 BCE–50 CE) has been called "the first theologian." During his lifetime, Alexandria was the place where Greek-speaking Jews were exposed to the rich Hellenic culture. Philo believed that both Hellenic wisdom, which was the fruit of human reason, and the Bible, as the word of God, represented the truth. He set out to show both his fellow Jews and the Greeks that the teachings of the holy Jewish tradition conformed to Greek philosophy. In this way, Philo made it clear that Judaism was the universal truth. Philo's ideas were the basis for European philosophy for the next 17 centuries.

Theology became important again in the Middle Ages. The movement lasted from the ninth century until the 15th century and produced religious poetry, Bible commentaries, popular sermons, and special philosophical works.

In the Middle Ages, philosophy became the central Jewish value in many circles. The Jews lived among the Muslims, which stimulated them to develop their own theology. They were also attacked by the KARAITES, who were a Jewish sect that accepted only the authority of the Bible. The Jews had to defend their religion against Karaites, ISLAM, and CHRISTIANITY, all of whom attacked Judaism constantly. The Parsee religion also attacked all monotheistic religions and especially the idea of CREATION.

In the midst of all this, it was difficult to preserve the naive faith in traditional authority. In order to "answer the heretic" both among the Jews themselves and on the outside, Jewish thinkers were forced to look at the theology of Judaism. As in the case of Philo, the sources to be used were not only the Bible and Talmud, but human logic as well. It was an attempt to reconcile religious tradition and the "philosophy" of the time.

The major figures and works of Jewish theology start with SAADIAH GAON of Egypt and Babylonia (882–942) and his *Emunot ve-De'ot* ("Book of Beliefs and Opinions"); Solomon IBN GABIROL (c. 1021–1057) of Spain and his *Mekor Hayyim* ("Source of Life"); and BAHYA IBN PAKUDA (11th cent.) and his *Hovot ha-Levavot* ("Duties of the Heart"). JUDAH HALEVI of Toledo was a famous Jewish poet who wrote the *Kuzari*, a philosophical work in the form of a dialogue between the king of the KHAZARS and a Jewish scholar. Abraham Ibn Daud (c. 1110–1180) of Toledo wrote *Emunah Ramah* ("The Exalted Faith") based on Aristotle. Moses MAIMONIDES (1135–1204) was the leading Jewish philosopher of the time. He wrote the major philosophical work, *Moreh Nevukhim* (*Guide for the Perplexed*), combining Judaism with Aristotle's philosophy. LEVI BEN GERSHOM (1288–1344) of southern France wrote *Milhamot Adonai* ("Wars of the Lord") and Joseph ALBO (c. 1360–1444) discusses the principles of Judaism in his *Ikkarim* ("Basic Principles").

Jewish, Muslim, and Christian philosophers of the Middle Ages agreed that God had provided man with two sources of truth: the Bible, or God's revelation, and human reason. Some men used human reason to discover the same truths found in the Bible and other truths that are not found in the Bible but also do not contradict them. The second kind of truths are called philosophy. Since God is the source of both types, there can be no conflict between them. Misunderstanding the Bible or mistakes made in reasoning can cause a person to think there is conflict. The Bible must be understood in light of what is known to be true from reason, while human reason has to be checked by what is given in the Bible.

In defending Judaism against other religions, Jewish theologians had to answer the questions: Why believe in Judaism rather than some other religion? Why is the revelation at Sinai more meaningful than any other revelation? In order to answer these questions it was necessary to be involved in the field of general philosophy. All of the issues related to the idea of God – His characteristics; the conflict between God's power and man's freedom; and His relationship to time, space, and the world of nature – are discussed by Jewish medieval theologians. Their understanding of these subjects was based on their knowledge of physics, psychology, and other sciences. Some of these Jewish thinkers were able to challenge the assumptions of the times.

Not all Jews were happy with the acheivements of Jewish theology. Maimonides' works caused violent arguments that lasted into the 13th century.

Moses MENDELSSOHN (1729–1786), the first modern Jewish philosopher, was also a major theologian of Judaism. Beginning with the German Enlightenment, when Jews were welcomed into the general society (see EMANCIPATION), philosophers began to justify the idea of a universal religion. Unlike the medieval philosophers, Mendelssohn contributed in the general areas of metaphysics, psychology, and esthetics. He tried to justify belief in the existance of God and the immortal soul.

Mendelssohn belived that the source of all truth could not be a particular revelation to a particular group of people. All human beings need truth, therefore the source of truth could not belong to one nation. Revelation is based on rational truth, which is available to all people including the Jews. Judaism, therefore, is not a revealed religion, but a revealed law that teaches proper behavior for the Jewish people. The Torah is based on worldwide religious truths, so that the Jewish people has the mission "by its very existence to proclaim them continually to the nations, to teach, to preach, and seek to maintain them."

The great changes in the position of the Jewish people brought about by the Enlightenment and Emancipation created social pressures for religious change across Western Europe. More and more Jews found themselves leading a life that was mostly secular, with a small portion of it set aside for "religion." The next generation began to demand that Judaism itself be westernized.

In the early 19th century, mainly in Germany, a group of scholars began to work out a theology of Judaism that could be adapted to the advanced thought of their time, This was the ideology of the REFORM movement. Scholars such as Solomon Ludwig Steinheim (1790–1866), Samuel Holdheim (1806–1860), and Abraham GEIGER (1810–1874) believed that all laws, even those given by revelation, may be given only for certain circumstances. Judaism was moving towards an ideology that would be suitable for the entire world. That is why they thought that ideas like the CHOSEN PEOPLE and ZIONISM must be eliminated.

Not many traditional Jewish scholars were involved in philosophy. As exeption was Samson Raphael HIRSCH (1808–1888), who was the first traditional theologian to engage in modern philosophy. He is considered the founder of Modern or NEO-ORTHODOXY, and believed that a Jew must learn the physical and social sciences, since God reveals Himself in nature and in history. He criticized Maimonides and Mendelssohn for giving too much weight to the philosophy of their times. Judaism must be understood "from within itself" in order to understand what it demands and what it is trying to achieve.

Zacharias FRANKEL (1801–1875) adopted a central position. He was a rabbi and scholar who founded the "positive-historical" school, which in America became the CONSERVATIVE movement. His approach was continued by Solomon SCHECHTER (1847–1915).

The works of German thinkers, Hemann COHEN (1842–1918), Franz ROSENZWEIG (1886–1929), and Martin BUBER (1878–1965), have influenced modern Jewish thought. These scholars did not associate themselves with any particular stream of Judaism. Cohen concentrated on the ethical values of Judaism. Buber examined the relationship between the individual and God and the idea of community.

More recently, Jewish theology has been enriched by theologians who address the issues of today, such as the HOLOCAUST and the State of Israel. These include Abraham Joshua HESCHEL, Joseph Baer SOLOVEICHIK, Eliezer Berkovits, Emil Fackenheim, Louis Jacobs, Andre Neher, Abraham Isaac KOOK, Arthur A. Cohen, and Jakob J. Petuchowski.

THREE WEEKS   The period beginning with the 17th of the Hebrew month of Tammuz (SHIVAH ASAR BE-TAMMUZ, falling in June/July) and ending on the ninth of the Hebrew month of Av (TISHAH BE-AV, falling in July/August). On the 17th of Tammuz, 586 BCE, the Babylonian army of Nebuchadnezzar broke down the walls of Jerusalem, beginning the destruction of Jerusalem. According to tradition, both the First and Second Temples were destroyed on the ninth of Av. This is the saddest time in the Jewish CALENDAR. There are many customs of mourning and sadness observed by different Jewish communities. Throughout the three weeks, one may not have a haircut or get married. It is also forbidden to do anything that would require the SHE-HEHEYANU blessing for special occasions, such as wearing new clothing. Beginning with the first day of Av, Jews do not eat meat or drink wine, except on the SABBATH. On the ninth of Av itself one may not eat or drink at all, wear leather shoes, anoint oneself with oil, wash, or have sexual relations (see FASTING AND FAST DAYS). On each of the three Sabbaths during the three weeks, a special portion of the Prophets (HAFTARAH) is read in the SYNAGOGUE. These three *haftarot* are called *Telata de-Poranuta* – "the three of disaster" (Jer. 1 and 2; Isa. 1).

THRONE OF GOD   The idea of God sitting on a throne, which is a symbol of the power of His rule, appears quite often in the Bible. The Throne of Glory is often mentioned in the Talmud, in prayer poetry (PIYYUT), and in the mystical literature.

The prophets had visions of God sitting on a "lofty and exalted throne" (Isa. 6:1). According to the rabbis, the Throne of God was one of the objects that existed before the creation of the world, with "the souls of the righteous kept underneath the Throne of Glory" (*Shab.* 152b). The rabbis also mention the Throne of MERCY and the Throne of JUSTICE. In the Talmud we read that when God "sees that the world deserves to be destroyed, He gets up from the Throne of Justice and sits on the Throne of Mercy" (*AZ* 3b). The mystical *hekhal* literature contains descriptions of the Throne of God, where it is identified as a *merkavah* (chariot). It sings praises to God, inviting God to sit on it. "And three times a day His Throne of Glory prostrates itself before Him and says, 'O Radiant God, the God of Israel, honor me and sit on me, O Glorious God, because your sitting is precious to me, and is no burden to me'" (see MYSTICISM).

In the Middle Ages, the philosophers and mystics gave the Throne symbolic interpretations. For example, MAIMONIDES thought that the Throne shows the greatness and essence of God. He wrote that *Ma'aseh Merkavah*, the practice of throne mysticism, really meant philosophy. The mystics also saw God's Throne as part of God and understood it as a symbol of one of the SEFIROT ("layers of divine holiness in the universe"; sing. *sefirah*.)

According to the *Sefer* BAHIR, the Throne of Glory symbolizes the *sefirah* of *binah* ("understanding"). According to the ZOHAR, the throne symbolizes the *sefirah* of *malkhut* ("majesty") and God sits upon the *sefirah* of *tiferet* ("glory"). God's sitting on his throne means harmony in the world of God: "When is there perfection above? When God sits on His Throne. And until He sits on His Throne, there is no perfection" (III:48a).

TIKKUN   See LURIA, ISAAC AND LURIANIC KABBALAH; TIKKUN OLAM

TIKKUN HATSOT   (lit. "midnight repairing"). A ceremony, mostly practiced by mystics, at which prayers are recited at midnight to mark the exile (GALUT) of God's Presence (SHEKHINAH) and its REDEMPTION.

The custom of rising at midnight and reciting hymns began at the time of the *ge'onim*. ASHER BEN JEHIEL (13th cent.) said that "it is fitting for every God-fearing person to be grieved and distressed at midnight, and to mourn the destruction of the Temple" (commentary on *Ber.* 3a).

The mystics adopted this custom and saw it as a *tikkun* – an action that restores God's presence to the world. The ZOHAR teaches that midnight is a good time to study the Torah, since it is an ideal time to have a good influence both on the upper worlds and on the person who is studying.

The 16th century mystics of Safed wrote the text for *Tikkun Hatsot*. It is made up of two parts: *Tikkun* RACHEL, which symbolizes the Presence of God in exile, and *Tikkun* LEAH, which stresses redemption. This custom later spread to other Jewish communities.

TIKKUN OLAM   ("repairing/perfecting the world"). Often used to describe the Jewish commitment to social action. The phrase appears in the ALEINU prayer, where it is used in the sense of perfecting the world under the future rule of God. The phrase also appears in a number of RESPONSA. A person's responsibility toward others is discussed in *Pirkei* AVOT (2:4) "Do not separate yourself from the community."

With the Emancipation in the 18th century, the Jews were able to enter general society and contribute to the struggle for social causes. In the United States, Jews were active in the civil rights movement, the American Civil Liberties Union, and the labor movement. All streams of Judaism stress *tikkun olam* as an important aspect of Judaism.

Tikkun Olam is also a basic mystical idea. The KABBALAH sees the world as shattered, to be restored to its earlier perfection only through *tikkun olam*. In the Kabbalah, *tikkun olam* is directed more toward religious self-improvement as a way of perfecting the world rather than reaching out to help others. (See also LURIA, ISAAC AND THE LURIANIC KABBALAH.)

TISHAH BE-AV   ("Ninth of Av"). Fast day in memory of the destruction of the First TEMPLE by the Babylonians under Nebuchadnezzar in 586 BCE and the destruction of the Second Temple by the Roman legions of Titus in 70 CE. The Fast of Av begins at sunset and lasts for over 24 hours. In addition to the fast, there are other restrictions (see FASTING AND FAST DAYS). If the Ninth of Av falls on a Sabbath, the fast is observed from Saturday night to Sunday. Unlike the minor fasts in memory of the destruction of the First Temple, Tishah be-Av was observed throughout the period of the Second Temple.

The Bible mentions both the seventh and the tenth of the Hebrew month of AV (July/August) as the date the First Temple was destroyed (II Kings 25:8–9; Jer 52:12–13), but there is no mention of the ninth. Ancient opinion was that the Second Temple was destroyed on the tenth of the month as well. Why then is the fast on the ninth? The Talmud (*Ta'an.* 29a) suggests that in the last days of the First Temple the enemy entered on the seventh of Av, attacked on the eighth, started the fire on the ninth, and the Temple burned to the ground on the tenth. Because the fire was actually started on the ninth, that day seemed appropriate for fasting and prayer. Later, when the Second Temple was destroyed, the original fast day on the Ninth of Av served to commemorate both disasters.

The Ninth of Av is associated with many dark times in history. BAR KOKHBA's last surviving fortress fell to Hadrian's armies on Tishah be-Av, in 135 CE. On 18 July 1290 (the Fast of Av) Edward I signed the decree banishing all Jews from England. The Nazis deliberately carried out many deportations and murders on this day during the Holocaust. Tishah be-Av became one of the gloomiest days of the Jewish calendar.

There are several degrees of MOURNING that are observed beginning three weeks before with the fast of SHIVAH ASAR BE-TAMMUZ. The following THREE WEEKS have special laws of mourning that become more severe in the NINE DAYS, which begin on the New MOON of Av and reach a climax on the eve of Tishah be-Av. The last meal before the fast includes an egg dipped in ashes, which is a sign of mourning. Eating and drinking are forbidden during the fast day. One may not shave, bathe, wear leather shoes, have marital relations, or even study Torah (except for mournful sections). The curtain is removed from the Holy Ark in the synagogue, and the lights are dimmed. People sit on low stools or on the floor and do not greet one another. The synagogue is transformed from a joyous house of prayer to a house of MOURNING.

On this day, the TALLIT and TEFILLIN are worn during the AFTERNOON SERVICE instead of during the MORNING SERVICE. Regular seats are used during the Afternoon Service. No meat meals are eaten until late in the following day.

The scroll of LAMENTATIONS (*Megillat Ekhah*) is the special reading for Tishah be-Av. Most congregations read it at night, while some also read it in the morning. It describes the horrors of the destruction of Jerusalem and the Temple. KINOT, which are a collection of mournful religious poems, are also read. These poems were written at different dark times in Jewish history (such as the Crusades) and they describe the suffering of the Jews and their hope to return to Erets Israel.

Despite the gloomy atmosphere of Tishah be-Av, the rabbis teach that it will one day become an occasion for celebration. It has also been identified as the birthday of the MESSIAH.

In the State of Israel, thousands attend services at the WESTERN WALL, and Tishah be-Av is a day of public mourning. All restaurants and places of entertainment are closed, and radio and television programs are more solemn.

TISHRI Seventh month of the Jewish religious CALENDAR and the first month of the Jewish civil calendar. Tishri has 30 days and falls in September/October. It zodiac sign is Libra, the Balance, which was associated with the Justice of God and the weighing of man's deeds. The Jewish New Year, ROSH HA-SHANAH, which falls on the first day of Tishri, is traditionally a Day of Judgment for the whole world. In the Bible, Tishri is referred to as the seventh month, and is also called Ethanim (1 Kings 8:2). Tishri is the beginning of the fall season in Erets Israel.

The third day of the month is the fast of GEDALIAH, originally called the "fast of the seventh month" (Zech. 8:19). The TEN DAYS OF REPENTANCE, which begin on Rosh ha-Shanah, reach a solemn climax on the DAY OF ATONEMENT (Yom Kippur) on 10 Tishri. SUKKOT, the Feast of the Tabernacles, is celebrated on 15–22 Tishri in Israel (15–23 Tishri in the Diaspora). It includes HOSHANA RABBAH on the 21st of the month and ends with SHEMINI ATSERET and SIMHAT TORAH (the Rejoicing of the Law).

TITHE (Heb. *ma'aser*). A tenth part of produce or livestock that was set aside for the Lord (Lev. 27:30–32). The Bible teaches that certain percentages of a person's crop must also be set aside for different groups of people. These rules apply only to crops that grow in Erets Israel in the first six years of the seven-year cycle. During the seventh year, the SABBATICAL YEAR (*shemittah*), the farmers did not plant crops and anything that grew naturally was public property.

At first, the farmer had to give *terumah* (a "heave offering") to the PRIEST (Ex. 29:28). The Bible does not specify how much a person must give. The rabbis reasoned that the *terumah* had to be no less than 1/60 of a farmer's crop. According to the Mishnah the average person gave 1/50, while a generous person would give 1/40 (*Ter.* 4:3). See also TERUMOT.

Each year, after separating the *terumah*, a farmer had to set aside one-tenth of his crop for the LEVITES as the regular "first tithe," *ma'aser rishon* (Num. 18:21). Since the Levites lived in cities, unlike the other tribes, and were not given farmland of their own, the tithe allowed them to live comfortably and teach TORAH to all Israel. The book of MA'ASEROT in the Mishnah and Jerusalem TALMUD lists the rules for this tithe.

In the first, second, fourth, and fifth years of the seven-year cycle, the farmer had to set aside one-tenth of his remaining crop as the "second tithe" (*ma'aser sheni*). This had to either be brought to Jerusalem and eaten there or it could be sold and the money used to buy food that was to be eaten in Jerusalem (Deut. 14:22–26). The law of the second tithe made it possible for Israelites who traveled to Jerusalem during the PILGRIM FESTIVALS to maintain themselves during their trip. The laws of this tithe can be found in the book of MA'ASER SHENI in the Mishnah and the Jerusalem Talmud.

In the third and sixth years of the *shemittah* cycle, the "poor man's tithe," *ma'aser ani*, replaced the normal second tithe (Deut. 14:28–29, 26:12). This had to be given to the Levites, the WIDOW AND ORPHAN, and strangers living among the Israelites.

Untithed crops, known as *tevel*, could not be eaten until the tithes had been separated. The rabbis of the Talmud worried that unlearned people might only give the *terumah* and not the other tithes. They therefore ruled that any produce that was suspected of not having been tithed also had to be separated.

While the Jews who were exiled after the destruction of the Second Temple were not expected to observe these laws, the rabbis still required tithing of produce grown in Erets Israel. Today, observant Israelis still uphold this practice in a symbolic way. They separate a small amount from the produce that they grow or buy from another Jew, recite a blessing, and then destroy the *terumah*.

Since tithes are no longer given to priests or Levites, but may be fed to animals, large Israeli companies send their tithes to the various zoos in Israel. Today, the memory of *terumot uma'aserot* can be seen in the practice of donating up to one-tenth of one's income to CHARITY.

TOHORAH See PURITY, RITUAL

TOHOROT (lit. "Cleannesses"). Sixth and last Order of the Mishnah. Its books (KELIM, OHALOT, NEGA'IM, PARAH, TOHOROT, MIKVA'OT, NIDDAH, MAKHSHIRIN, ZAVIM, TEVUL YOM, YADAYIM, and UKTSIN) deal with ritual uncleanness. Four general categories are mentioned: 1) having to do with menstruation and childbirth; 2) passed on by food and drink; 3) having to do with disease (such as leprosy); 4) passed on by a corpse (see PURITY). Since the destruction of the TEMPLE, most of these laws have not been in effect.

The name was also given to the fifth book of the Order. Its ten chapters deal with the rules the lesser degrees of ritual uncleanness (cf. Lev. 11:34).

TOMBSTONE The first tombstone mentioned in the Bible is the one JACOB placed over the grave of his wife RACHEL (Gen. 35:20). During the times of the Talmud, tombstones were put up mainly to prevent priests from coming into contact with graves.

The Mishnah teaches that if money is collected for a person's burial, and there is some left over, it should be used for a tombstone as a memorial (*Shab.* 2:5). The Jerusalem Talmud notes that tombstones should not be placed over the graves of the righteous, because their teachings are their memorial. MAIMONIDES and Rabbi Joseph CARO both ruled that tombstones were not necessary. The kabbalist Rabbi Isaac LURIA, on the other hand, believed that the tombstone was important for the well-being of the deceased. In recent centuries, the accepted Jewish custom has been to place a tombstone to mark the grave of the deceased.

In Israel, the custom is to dedicate the tombstone 30 days after death, but in the rest of the world this is usually done only after the first year. The ceremony usually includes readings from Psalm 119 (which contains several verses beginning with each letter of the alphabet) that can spell out the name of the deceased, followed by verses to spell the Hebrew word for soul (*neshamah*). This is followed by the EL MALEI RAHAMIM prayer and the mourners KADDISH.

Traditionally, epitaphs on Jewish tombstones are engraved in Hebrew. They usually begin with "here lies" and end with sayings such as "May his/her memory be a blessing." Since the 19th century, other languages have been used as well.

In certain communities, when visiting a grave, it is customary to place a stone on the tombstone, as a sign of respect for the deceased and to show that the grave has been visited.

TORAH The word Torah comes from the Hebrew root *yoreh* ("to teach"). It is best translated as "teaching" or "instruction." The Torah is often called "law," although not all of it deals with law The term Torah usually refers to the PENTATEUCH, the Five Books of Moses. These first five books are called "the Torah of the Lord" or the "Torah of Moses" in the later books of the Bible. According to tradition, MOSES wrote the Torah under the influence of God's spirit. It expresses the COVENANT between God and the people of Israel. The Pentateuch ends with the death of Moses and with the people of Israel about to enter the Promised Land, Erets Israel. Because of Moses' special status as prophet and spokesman for God (Deut. 34:10) *Torat Mosheh* alone is considered the basis of Jewish law.

All of the written Bible (the Jewish canon consisting of 24 books) is sometimes called "the Torah" (Dan. 9:10–13). According to Jewish tradition, these books were written with the help of the HOLY SPIRIT (*ru'ah ha-kodesh*); however, they are divided into three categories according to the level of their holiness, the level of prophecy and, therefore, the level of authority (*BB* 14, 15; *Ta'an.* 8; *Shab.* 88a). After the Pentateuch, the remaining 19 books are divided into two parts. The *Nevi'im*, or Prophets was considered the word of God spoken by the prophets and the HAGIOGRAPHA ("Writings") was the personal expression of the individual writer, inspired by God.

Originally, it was forbidden to write down any additional material connected to the Torah, in order to keep the written Torah (see WRITTEN LAW) separate from customs, interpretations, and practices. However, there came to be so much

material, and it was so disorganized, that it would have been forgotten. The rabbis therefore lifted the ban on writing down the ORAL LAW. The Oral Law was organized into the MISHNAH, the TALMUD, and other rabbinic works. The rabbis taught that two Torahs were given at SINAI, a Written Torah and an Oral Torah, and at least some of the teachings in the Oral Torah are as important as the ones in the Written Torah (see HALAKHAH LE-MOSHEH MI-SINAI). In a sense, the Oral Torah became just as important as the Written Torah, because it was needed in order to understand the Written Torah. A third meaning of the word "Torah" therefore includes parts of the Oral Torah that are considered *de-oraitah*", or "from the Torah".

Finally, the word "Torah" is sometimes used to refer to the entire body of HALAKHAH (legal writings) and AGGADAH (commentaries, stories), written and oral, from the Bible up to and including the latest RESPONSA (legal questions and responses) and interpretations of the rabbis.

The recording of the different stages showed that the chain of TRADITION was reliable, and the Written and Oral law that was handed down was authentic: "Moses received the Torah at Sinai and handed it down to JOSHUA; Joshua to the elders; the elders to the prophets; and the prophets to the Men of the Great Assembly" (*Avot* 1:1).

The idea that God revealed the Torah caused people to believe that there is more to be found in the text than the literal meaning of the words and sentences. The rabbis developed the MIDRASH, which was a special method of understanding additional meanings of the text, with the help of God.

According to the teachings of the Historical School of Judaism (19th cent.) and the CONSERVATIVE movement, the Pentateuch contains the revealed message of God, but the words were recorded by different authors at different times. Later, the material was gathered together and edited into one work. The important point is that in his search for God, Moses experienced God's message. The actual text of the Torah did not come from God, but it is the inspired and revealed message, including His laws, and has the stamp of God.

Preexistence Many rabbis believed that the Torah existed in heaven before the creation of the world (*Pes. 54a*; Gen. R. 1:4; Lev. R. 19:1). According to another Midrash, the Torah was the blueprint of the universe, which God used to create the world (Gen. R. 1:1).

PHILO and other Greek philosophers believed that the ultimate reality is a world of ideas of which the world that man experiences is only a poor reflection. The Jewish mystics adopted this idea. They believed that the Torah is one of the early expressions of true reality and of God. Another mystical view claims that the entire Torah is made up of Names of God (*Zohar, Yitro* 87:1), meaning that the letters can be rearranged to form strings of God's names. It also claimed that the same letters of the Torah will be rescrambled in the times of the MESSIAH to spell out a new reality.

The scholars of the Middle Ages interpreted this belief to mean that God created the world very wisely (SAADIAH

GAON) or that the Torah is the very purpose of creation (JUDAH HALEVI).

Eternity of the Torah The idea that the Torah existed before the world proved to Philo and others that the Torah will remain valid and effective forever.

The newer religions, CHRISTIANITY and ISLAM, acknowledged the Torah but argued that Jesus and Muhammad revealed new and improved works of God. In light of this challenge, the question of the eternity of the Torah became crucial. In the Middle Ages, this was one of the main issues that occupied Jewish thinkers. MAIMONIDES included the eternity of the Torah as one of his 13 PRINCIPLES OF FAITH. Joseph ALBO had a more flexible view. He believed that as the covenant between God and Israel, the Torah will always be relevant. However, people and society do change. It is at least possible that as human society gets closer to the times of the Messiah, some changes in the Jewish way of life may be made. According to Albo, it is possible for a Jew to believe that a new Torah can come from God. It will, however, be taken seriously only if it is revealed in the same public manner of the original Torah (*Ikkarim* III, 19), rather than to individual prophets or disciples.

According to REFORM Jewish thinkers, the Oral Torah that developed in the first and second centuries CE changed Judaism and made it relevant to new situations. It began the process of change that can be continued by any generation of learned Jews. Reform Judaism holds that God's will can be known by people in every age and not merely through documents from ages past. Torah can change; and if necessary, radically. The individual Jew makes the final choice of what is living Torah.

TORAH BLESSINGS (Heb. *Birkot ha-Torah*). Special BENEDICTIONS recited daily in the MORNING SERVICE or when one is called to the READING OF THE LAW in the synagogue. Each Morning Service contains three blessings "on studying Torah" (*Ber.* 11b). These blessings praise God for the privilege of "occupying ourselves with the words of Torah" and thank God for having given the Torah to His CHOSEN PEOPLE. The second blessing is the hope that all study of Torah may be performed

li-shemah – "for its own sake" (see ALTRUISM). The third blessing is the same as the first blessing recited by one who has been called to the Torah reading. Sections from the Pentateuch, the Mishnah, and the Talmud are added.

When someone is called to the Reading of the Law, the reader points to the place in the Torah scroll, the person touches that section with the edge of a prayer shawl, kisses it, grasps both wooden rollers, and winds them together. The person then recites *Barekhu* and the first Torah blessing. The reader then unwinds the scroll for the portion to be chanted. When the reading is completed, the person called up again winds the rollers together and holds them while reciting the second blessing.

The first blessing over the Torah emphasizes God's choice of Israel as His holy nation (cf. Ex. 19:5–6) and the receivers of the Torah. The second blessing is about Israel's acceptance of the Torah and Jewish law.

TORAH ORNAMENTS Jewish communities often express their desire to honor the Torah by decorating the SCROLLS OF THE LAW.

The ARK, where the scrolls are kept, was usually decorated to the best of the community's ability. It was placed along

Breastplate over the mantle of the Torah scroll.

BLESSING BEFORE THE READING OF THE TORAH

Praise the Lord who is praised! Praised be the Lord who is to be praised for all eternity.

Blessed are You, the Lord our God, King of the universe, who has chosen us from among all peoples and given us His Torah.

Blessed are You, the Lord, Giver of the Torah.

BLESSING AFTER THE READING OF THE TORAH

Blessed are You, Lord our God, King of the universe, who has given us the Torah of truth and given us eternal life.

Embroidered ribbon for binding Torah scroll.

the wall facing Jerusalem, indicating the direction a person should face when praying. It was decorated with symbols used in Jewish ART.

The scroll has a cloth cover, and a metal breastplate is often hung over the cover. The parchment of the scroll is attached to the rollers (*atsei hayyim;* "trees of life"), which are made of wood and are often topped with decorative silver pomegranates. Torah scrolls can also be topped with a *keter* ("crown"), which fits over the top of the two rollers.

When the Torah is taken out of the Ark and taken to the BIMAH (platform) for the READING OF THE LAW, the decorations are removed and only the YAD (the silver "hand" used as a pointer) is used.

The custom of putting a breastplate on the Torah scrolls began in the 17th century because of the need to identify the Torah scrolls for the different FESTIVALS for which they were used. The breastplates were used mainly in European countries, and many were made of precious metals and decorated with precious and colorful stones. The most common motifs are pillars, a crown, lions, eagles, roses, trees of life, seven-branched candelabra, and the two TABLETS OF THE COVENANT.

The *keter* dates back to the Middle Ages, but the oldest surviving examples are from the 18th and 19th centuries. The *keter* decorates the Torah like royalty. They were often made of a number of layers, one on top of the other, and their designs included eagles, birds, zodiacal signs, and floral designs.

Torah covers are most often made of velvet, and their designs often resemble those on the PAROKHET (Ark cover). The Torah containers used in Islamic lands and in India were fine and complicated works of art. Some were made of silver with precious stones and others were carved of wood.

It is an ancient custom to prepare the inner Torah wrapping from the swaddling clothes used to wrap infant boys on the day of their CIRCUMCISION. Families would decorate the cloth with pictures or embroidery including wishes for the future of the child. When the child grew up, the cloth was donated to the synagogue and used to wrap the Torah on the occasion of his BAR MITZVAH or wedding.

TORAH READING   See READING OF THE LAW

TORAH SHE-BE'AL-PEH   See ORAL LAW

TOSAFOT   ("additions"). Series of commentaries on 30 of the books of the TALMUD. They were written as an addition to RASHI's commentary on the Talmud.

The *Tosafot* were not written by one person, but by an entire school of scholars, known as the Tosafists. They were about 300 people who lived in France and then later in Germany between the 12th and 14th centuries. The school of Tosafists began with Rashi's two sons-in-law, rabbis Meir ben Samuel and Judah ben Nathan, although the leading Tosafist was Rabbi Meir's son, Rabbenu TAM. The *Tosafot* were recorded by a number of people and edited and re-edited over a long period of time.

Unlike Rashi's commentary on the Talmud, which is a running explanation of the text, the *Tosafot* deal with specific topics. They often use Rashi's commentary as a starting point, but arrive at different conclusions. Authors who tried to defend Rashi against the questions posed by the Tosafists wrote many books.

In the traditional editions of the Talmud, the Talmud text is at the center of the page, Rashi's commentary is printed on the inner margin of each page, and the *Tosafot* on the outer margin (see TALMUDIC COMMENTARIES).

The Tosafists also wrote a commentary on the Bible, known as *Da'at Zekenim mi-Ba'alei ha-Tosafot.*

Opposite page: The Judgment of Solomon. Florence, Italy, 15th century.
Overleaf left: The Day of Atonement, Painting by Maurycy Gottlieb, Poland (1856–1879).
Overleaf right: Celebration of Simhat Torah (Rejoicing of the Law) in the Leghorn Synagogue, by Solomon Hart, 19th century.

TOSEFTA ("addition"). Collection of teachings of the *tannaim* (rabbis of the Mishnah period) that supplement those in the Mishnah. It is about four times as long as the Mishnah, is divided into the same six "Orders" and corresponds to the books within each Order. The *Tosefta* is made up of *baraitot* (teachings of the *tannaim* not included in the Mishnah; see BARAITA). They are a major source for talmudic discussion on any topic. Some of them are an alternative version of the text of the Mishnah; others explain the Mishnah; while others add to the Mishnah or deal with fresh material.

It is not clear who wrote the *Tosefta*. The Talmud says that it was written by Rabbi Nehemiah and that the Mishnah was written by Rabbi MEIR (*Sanh.* 61a). Both of these rabbis were students of Rabbi AKIVA, which would explain why the two works are so similar. However, there is no clear evidence that Rabbi Nehemiah is the author of the *Tosefta*. Many scholars believe that the work was written by a collection of scholars, possibly made by putting together a number of oral traditions. Like the Mishnah, the *Tosefta* often presents two sides to a dispute without reaching a final decision.

There are many cases were the *baraitot* in the *Tosefta* contradict the Mishnah. As a rule, the Talmud accepts the opinion in the Mishnah. The official published edition of the *Tosefta* is that of Saul Lieberman, *Tosefta ki-Peshuta* ("Plain Meaning of the Tosefta").

TOWER OF BABEL   See BABEL, TOWER OF

TRADITION   (Heb. *masoret*). The legal norms and folkways handed down orally from one generation to another, from teacher to student, father to son. The rabbis took these traditions very seriously. Although they were not based on the Bible, they were made part of Jewish law (see ORAL LAW). Many of them were recorded in the book of EDUYYOT of the Mishnah. The rabbis said: "Tradition is a fence around the Torah" (*Avot* 3:13), meaning that the oral tradition safeguards the observance of the biblical law. They were sometimes referred to as HALAKHAH LE-MOSHEH MI-SINAI ("the law of Moses from SINAI").

In time, rabbis began to consider customs (see CUSTOM) and traditions that were not necessarily based on a particular law. These traditions were as binding as law, as in the saying: "The custom of the people of Israel is [just like] Torah." Later on, rabbis, especially followers of HASIDISM, considered traditions in dress, customs at religious ceremonies, and special chants at synagogue services to be holy.

TRANSMIGRATION OF SOULS   The idea of the soul's reappearance after death and entry into a new body. This idea is first discussed in a positive sense in the Kabbalah (see also Jewish MYSTICISM), from the late 12th century. It does not appear at all in ancient Judaism, and the early medieval Jewish philosophers condemn it. The earliest work of the Kabbalah, the Book of BAHIR, presents it as God's way of giving human beings another chance to atone for their sins after spending their first life as a wicked person. Rabbi Isaac the Blind (Provence, late 12th–early 13th cent.) was rumored to be able to tell the difference between a "new" soul and an "old" soul. In Jewish mystical literature from the 13th century on, the most common term for this idea was *gilgul-neshamot*.

The idea of *gilgul-neshamot* reached its peak in 16th century Safed, after the expulsion from Spain. The idea was that the being into which a person is transformed is the result of the amount and type of sins in the previous life. It was believed that the human soul could even reappear in animals. For example, Rabbi Isaac LURIA identified a certain deceased person who had engaged in sexual sin during his lifetime in a large black dog in Safed.

Rabbi Hayyim VITAL, a student of Rabbi Luria, wrote a systematic study of *gilgul-neshamot*. In his understanding, the soul is made up of five parts, each of which moves on to a different body. Every soul is a combination of elements that have lived several times in the past in different places and circumstances. Each one of these elements required some form of *tikkun* (repair).

TREE OF LIFE   Tree whose fruit makes the person who eats it immortal. The tree of life is mentioned three times in the story of ADAM AND EVE in the Garden of EDEN. The tree of life is said to be "in the middle of the garden" (Gen. 2:9). After the first humans disobey God, God says "… what if [Adam] should stretch out his hand and take also from the tree of life and eat and live forever!" (Gen. 3:22). Finally, after Adam and Eve were expelled from the Garden of Eden, God put "cherubim and a fiery ever-turning sword, to guard the way to the tree of life" (Gen. 3:24).

The magical quality of the tree of life fascinated the authors of the Pseudepigrapha (See APOCRYPHA AND PSEUDEPIGRAPHA) and the rabbis of the MIDRASH. According to the Midrash, the tree of life gave shade to the entire region and had no fewer than 15,000 tastes. It was so large that it would take a person 500 years to circle it. From beneath its roots, there flowed the waters that watered the earth and then emptied into the four rivers mentioned in the story of the Garden of Eden.

According to the writers of the Pseudepigrapha, the tree was transplanted from the Garden of Eden to paradise in the AFTERLIFE. This idea was later taken up by the scholars of the Midrash. Many of the scholars throughout the ages have tried to interpret the story of the tree of life literally. MAIMONIDES interpreted it symbolically, as does the Kabbalah (see MYSTICISM).

TRIBES, TEN LOST   The ten "lost" tribes were Reuben, Simeon, Dan, Naphtali, Gad, Asher, Issachar, Zebulun, Ephraim, and half the tribe of Manasseh. They lived in the northern kingdom of ISRAEL, which broke away from the kingdom of JUDAH after the death of King SOLOMON. In 772 BCE, the kingdom of Israel fell to the Assyrians under King Shalmaneser, who deported most of the leading and wealthier Israelites to Halah and Habor

Opposite: Chapel of the U.S. Air Force Academy, Colorado Springs.

and to the cities of the Medes (II Kings 17:6; 18:11). Not all Israelites were deported (see Chr. 35:17–19).

Although it was generally believed that the Israelites who were "carried away into Assyria" (II Kings 17:3) assimilated, a passage in I Chronicles 5:26 suggests that the lost tribes survived "until this day." This belief was kept alive by the promises of the PROPHETS that God would gather in the "remnants of Israel" from the four corners of the globe (Isa. 11:12).

Belief in the existence of the "lost" ten tribes continues throughout Mishnah and Talmud times. According to popular legend, they live on the other side of the Sambatyon River, whose waters run fiercely through the week and rest on the SABBATH. The Jerusalem Talmud says that only a third of the exiles live beyond the Sambatyon River, but all will eventually return (*Sanh.* 10:6, 29c). Rabbi AKIVA, however, said that "the ten tribes shall not return again" (*Sanh.* 10:3).

During times of false messiahs, reports have been received of the "discovery" of the lost tribes. The ninth-century traveler Eldad ha-Dani claimed to be from the tribe of Dan. In the second half of the 12th century, the Spanish traveler Benjamin of Tudela claimed that the four tribes of Dan, Asher, Zebulun, and Naphtali were living near the river Gozan. He also mentioned the tribes of Reuben, Gad, and half the tribe of Manasseh as living in Khaibar in Yemen. In the 16th century, David Reuveni, supposedly of the tribe of Reuben, claimed to be a descendant of King Solomon and the brother of Joseph, the king of the descendants of the tribes of Reuben, Gad, and half of Manasseh. He claimed he was sent on a mission to Rome by the king of the "lost" tribes in order to speed up the process of redemption.

In the 19th century, many Jews left Erets Israel in search of the "lost" tribes. Jacob Sapir (1822–1888) visited Yemen and India and reported their existence in those countries.

Today, there are many stories of the "lost" tribes. Jewish communities of Kurdish, Bokharan, and Indian (BENEI ISRAEL) origin claim their forefathers were exiled from the Kingdom of Israel. The Chief Rabbinate of Israel has taken the position that the Jews of Ethiopia come from the tribe of Dan. In addition, a wide range of non-Jewish tribes and groups have claimed to be descendants of the Israelites. A tribe called the Pathans, spread over Afghanistan and Pakistan, are divided into sub-tribal groupings with names like Reubeni, Efridar (Ephraim), and Ashuri. This leads to the suggestion that they come from the lost tribes.

TRIBES, TWELVE   The tribes into which the Israelites were originally divided. Traditionally, the tribes are traced back to JACOB's 12 sons, born to him by his two wives and their two maidservants. They were: LEAH's sons Reuben, Simeon, Levi, Judah, Issachar, and Zebulun; her maidservant Bilhah's sons Dan and Naphtali; RACHEL's sons JOSEPH and Benjamin; and her maidservant Zilpah's sons Gad and Asher.

Sometimes Joseph is counted as two tribes, Manasseh and Ephraim, as Jacob said to Joseph: "Your two sons, Manasseh and

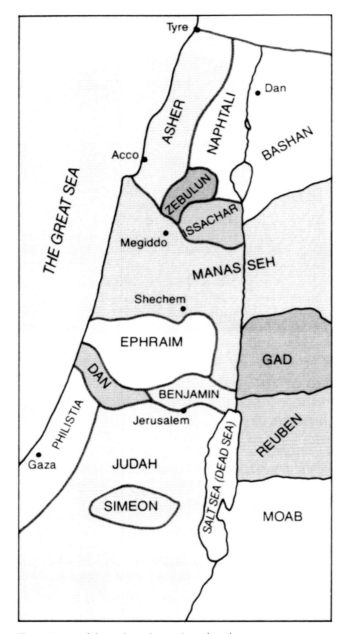

The territories of the twelve tribes in the 12th–11th centuries BCE.

Ephraim … as Reuben and Simeon, they shall be mine" (Gen. 48:5). When Manasseh and Ephraim are counted as two tribes, Levi is left out, because Levi was selected from the other tribes to serve God and teach the people and did not receive its own territory (see LEVITES). In the desert, the tribes were sub-divided into clans and the clans were sub-divided into families. The tribes were headed by *nesi'im* (pl. of NASI), translated as princes. A representative of each tribe helped MOSES in the first census (Num. 1, 2, 4) and one leader from each tribe was sent to spy out the land of Canaan (Num 3:2–15).

Once the tribes conquered Canaan (Erets Israel), they each

received their own territory. As time passed, the Israelites reached the point when they did not have a central leader. They were bound together by their common belief in one God. SAUL was the first Jewish king who attempted to bring the tribes together. This continued under DAVID's reign. SOLOMON divided his kingdom into 12 districts, which often cut across tribal lines.

Later, the tribes split into two kingdoms; the southern kingdom of JUDAH included only Judah and Benjamin and the northern kingdom of ISRAEL included the other ten tribes. The Levites and PRIESTS lived in both kingdoms. At times the two kingdoms were allies, and at other times they went to war against each other. In 722, the Assyrians conquered the northern kingdom and exiled the people living there (see TRIBES, TEN LOST). That was the end of the northern kingdom. The southern tribes of Judah and Benjamin were eventually conquered later as well. However, they never became "lost," since they returned from their exile in Babylonia to Erets Israel.

Twice in the Bible the 12 tribes are blessed. Jacob blesses his sons just before his death (Gen. 49) and MOSES blesses the 12 tribes of Israel, also before his death (Deut. 33).

TRIENNIAL CYCLE The READING OF THE LAW in the synagogue based on completing the PENTATEUCH every three years. This practice of reading developed gradually in Erets Israel.

The Babylonian annual cycle, in which the Pentateuch is finished and begun again every year became the standard practice in the Diaspora. However, the Triennial Cycle remained in certain places. The traveler Benjamin of Tudela reported (c. 1165) that in Cairo, a community of Jews from Erets Israel still followed the Triennial Cycle. MAIMONIDES also mentioned the practice but noted that it was not widespread.

In the 19th century, the German REFORM movement suggested using the Triennial Cycle. The suggestion was not adopted. Instead it became the custom in Reform synagogues to read about a third of the weekly Torah reading (PARASHAH). This practice of reading is also followed in a number of synagogues of the CONSERVATIVE movement and RECONSTRUCTIONISM in the United States.

TRUTH In Judaism, truth is an ultimate ethical value both for the individual and society as a whole. The rabbis teach: "The world stands on three things, on truth, on JUSTICE, and on PEACE" (*Avot.* 1:18), for where there is truth, justice will necessarily follow, and then will come peace – the greatest blessing for society. In Jewish ethical teachings, truth is considered one of the supreme human values.

Jewish ETHICS stresses the value and importance of truth in thought, speech, and behavior. However, recognizing that a person's judgment may not always be reliable, the advice is not to judge things as an individual but to aim for truth through general agreement. Furthermore, since one cannot be sure that one's view represents the truth, people should consider the other view before making a final judgment. This was the approach of the School of Hillel in its arguments with the School of Shammai (see BET SHAMMAI AND BET HILLEL). The Hillelites opinion was chosen in most cases, because they also studied the opinions of their opponents (*Er.* 13b).

While truth is a central value, in certain circumstances an even higher value can be favored. For example, in the case of a conflict between life and truth, life takes precedence.

According to the rabbis, total truth belongs to God and God alone. They declare, "The seal of God is truth" (*Shab.* 55a). Franz ROSENZWEIG said that truth is a value that can only be associated with God. However, it is a good idea for people to try to imitate God and, as far as humanly possible, to live a life of truth.

TSADDIK (pl. *tsaddikim;* "righteous," "just," and "charitable"). A person of outstanding piety and faith; in later usage, a Hasidic rabbi.

The Bible compares the *tsaddik* with the *rasha* (wicked person), as in Genesis 18:25, when ABRAHAM tries to convince God not to destroy the righteous of Sodom and Gomorrah along with the wicked. The prophet Habakkuk says, "The righteous man is rewarded with life for his fidelity" (2:4). ISAIAH believed that the Jewish people would be righteous at the End of Days and thereby fit to reclaim their ancient homeland forever (60:21).

According to the Talmud, the world rests upon the righteousness of 36 *tsaddikim* without whom it would collapse (see LAMED VAV TSADDIKIM). Several figures have been called *tsaddikim* by the rabbis: NOAH, JOSEPH, SAMUEL, Mordecai, and ESTHER (*tsaddikah,* in the feminine).

The mystics believed that the *tsaddik* had supernatural powers and could serve as a go-between between God and the Jewish people. Following this tradition, Hasidim crowned their leaders with the title *tsaddik,* since they saw him as the channel through which God communicated with the common people. They were visited regularly by their followers, who sought advice and *segullot* (formulae for success and recovery from illness). In return, the followers would make donations to CHARITY or contribute to the support of the *tsaddik.* In general, the title was passed on from father to son. In modern Hasidic communities, the Hasidic leader is also called *Rebbe* (Yiddish for Rabbi), or in Israel, *Admor.*

TSEDAKAH See CHARITY

TSIMTSUM See LURIA, ISAAC AND LURIANIC KABBALAH

TSITSIT ("fringes"; also known as *arba kanfot,* "four corners"). Four-cornered fringed undergarment traditionally worn by Jewish males. The source of the commandment is Numbers 15:38: "They shall make for themselves fringes on the corners of their garments for all generations ..." It became customary for Jewish boys to begin wearing *tsitsit* at the age of three. The *tsitsit* is usually made of linen or wool.

Until the 13th century, Jews traditionally wore a four-cornered garment to which the *tsitsit* was attached. From then on, they wore a special garment called the *tallit katan* ("little prayer shawl") under the shirt.

The *tsitsit* is worn only in the daytime and women are traditionally exempt from the commandment. In the reading of SHEMA it is customary to take out the *tsitsit* and to kiss the fringes at every mention of the word *tsitsit* in the prayer.

TU BE-AV   See AV, FIFTEENTH OF

TU BI-SHEVAT   See NEW YEAR FOR TREES

UKTSIN ("Stems of Fruit and Produce"). Twelfth and last tractate (book) of the Order of TOHOROT in the Mishnah. It has three chapters that deal with the laws of food becoming unclean. The Mishnah deals specifically with the parts of a fruit or vegetable (stem, stalk, shell, etc.) that do or do not protect against ritual uncleanness. This is the last book of the Mishnah.

U-NETANNEH TOKEF ("Let us declare [the utter holiness of this day]"). Opening words and name of a key prayer chanted in SYNAGOGUES by ASHKENAZIM during the AMIDAH for the ADDITIONAL SERVICE on ROSH HA-SHANAH (the New Year) and the DAY OF ATONEMENT. It is very dramatic and includes such phrases as "the great *shofar* is sounded; the still small voice is heard; the angels are dismayed." It describes how God's decree about the fate of all humankind is written on the New Year and sealed on Atonement Day. Each and every person symbolically passes under God's watchful eye, as do sheep under the shepherd's staff.

The poem was probably written about 800 CE. According to Jewish tradition, it was first recited by the legendary martyr R. Amnon of Mainz, Germany, who had his hands and feet cut off by a Christian archbishop for refusing to embrace CHRISTIANITY. He was carried into the synagogue on Rosh ha-Shanah and recited it with his dying breath. Since the 11th century it has been a central part of the HIGH HOLIDAY service.

UNIVERSALISM AND PARTICULARISM The religious concern for all of the human race, as opposed to concern for those belonging to one's own faith. Since Bible times, both trends have existed in Judaism. In fact, the opening of the Bible is written from a universal point of view. It focuses on the origin of the human race and on God's concern for humanity. Beginning with the story of the COVENANT of ABRAHAM, the Bible begins to focus on Abraham and his descendants as the CHOSEN PEOPLE of God. Even so, the universal element is not ignored, as God explains: "Through you and your descendants the families of the earth will be blessed" (Gen. 28:14).

The PROPHETS contribute most to the expression of universalism in Judaism. For example, ISAIAH describes the End of Days when all nations shall say, "Let us go up to the mountain of the Lord, to the House of the God of Jacob who will teach us His ways and we will go in His paths … Nation shall not take up sword against nation and they will never again know war" (Isa. 2:3–4). The prophet AMOS directs his prophecies not only to Israel but also to the surrounding nations.

The rabbis also developed a universal message that stresses those teachings of Judaism that apply to all peoples of the world. The NOACHIDE LAWS are a basic code of behavior for non-Jews. According to the Talmud, if non-Jews observe these seven laws, they are guaranteed life in the world to come without having to convert to Judaism. At the same time, the rabbis expressed the particularistic message that God offers special salvation to the Jewish people, delivering it from its enemies.

Throughout history, the type of relationships that existed between Jews and the surrounding population have influenced the degree to which the universalist idea was expressed. Hostile relations led to greater emphasis on particularism. At those times, Jews devoted themselves to their own culture and ceased any attempts to win souls for Judaism. In their anger and frustration, they developed anti-Gentile feelings. In times of relative calm, Jewish thinkers stressed the idea that CHRISTIANITY and ISLAM were extensions of Judaism. MAIMONIDES wrote: "All the matters concerning Jesus and Muhammad were only to lay out the path for the MESSIAH and to repair the whole world in order to serve God together. The whole world is now filled with the idea of the Messiah, of TORAH, and of the COMMANDMENTS."

The era of EMANCIPATION and Enlightenment, when Jews were welcomed into general society, began in the 18th century in Western and Central Europe. It was a time marked by relative calm and freedom for Jews. As might be expected, this era brought with it renewed interest in universalism among Jews. Moses MENDELSSOHN believed that some aspects of Judaism made it a universal "religion of reason." For him, Jews and non-Jews are both entitled to Divine love and salvation, while Judaism remained the private concern of the Jews. REFORM JUDAISM adopted the traditional concept of the Jewish mission to the human race. The Reform movement went so far as to remove all mention of Jews as the "chosen people" from its prayer book.

UNLEAVENED BREAD See MATZAH

URIM AND THUMMIM (meaning of words unclear). A device used for telling the future, worn by the HIGH PRIEST inside his breastplate. The *Urim* and *Thummim* was used to discover God's judgment. The Bible commands (Ex. 28:30), "Inside the breastplate of decision you shall place the *Urim* and *Thummim*," but it does not explain what they are. The breastplate in which they were placed was one of the eight holy garments worn by the High Priest. It had four columns of precious stones, on which the names of the TWELVE TRIBES were engraved (see PRIESTLY GARMENTS). According to tradition, when the High Priest asked it a question, the *Urim* and *Thummim* would light up certain letters on the breastplate. The High Priest could then spell out the answers to his questions.

The Bible mentions many cases of questions asked of the *Urim* and *Thummim*, mostly about whether or not to go to war. Other questions concerned how to divide up the land of Erets Israel among the tribes, the fate of King SAUL, and the identity of the true PRIESTS after the people returned to Israel from EXILE in Babylonia (Ezra 2:63).

USHPIZIN (Aram. "guests"). The seven symbolic guests who, according to Jewish MYSTICISM, visit the SUKKAH in turn during each day of the SUKKOT festival. They are: ABRAHAM, ISAAC, JACOB, JOSEPH, MOSES, AARON, and DAVID. The idea of their visit comes from the ZOHAR, which says: "When one sits in the *sukkah*, Abraham and six righteous men come to share one's company" (5:103b). The mystics used to invite the guests to their *sukkah* each night saying, "May it be Your will, Lord my God, and God of my fathers, that the Divine Presence will dwell in our midst … I hereby invite these exalted guests to dinner: Abraham, etc." This custom spread to HASIDISM and has now been adopted by many Orthodox Jews.

The sages taught that in order to merit the visit of one of these seven distinguished guests, the host must also invite human guests to share the hospitality of the *sukkah*. It became the custom to invite a needy student to sit next to the host during the meal, to "hold the place" for the symbolic guest.

USURY Usually understood to mean unfairly high levels of interest charged on a loan. In Judaism, however, it refer to any interest charged by one Jew to another. The Bible stresses that no interest may be charged on a loan to "the poor among your people" (Ex. 22:24). Interest was also expressly forbidden on loans to resident aliens and on loans of food (Lev. 25:35–37).

The Bible uses two terms for interest, *neshekh* and *tarbit*. According to the Talmud there is no difference between the terms – both are used to teach us that a person who takes interest violates two negative commandments. It assigns guilt not only to the person who charges interest, but also to the scribe who may have written the promissory note and even the witnesses to the document.

Already in Talmud times, the rabbis looked for ways to ease the prohibition against charging interest. If the biblical law is strictly enforced it becomes impossible for people to do business. Those who had money wanted to use their money to make money; those who did not have money needed to be able to borrow some. In one legally acceptable arrangement, worked out by the rabbis, the lender becomes a partner in the borrower's business, shares in the profits, and is guaranteed against loss.

VENGEANCE See RETALIATION

VIDDU'I See CONFESSION OF SINS

VILNA GAON See ELIJAH BEN SOLOMON ZALMAN

VIOLENCE The Bible concerns itself early on with the issue of violence. The first violent crime recorded in the Bible is the killing of Abel by Cain (Gen. 4:8; see CAIN AND ABEL). The fist crime mentioned in the TEN COMMANDMENTS is MURDER. The FLOOD, in the time of Noah, was brought upon the world as punishment for lawlessness and violence (*hamas*, Gen. 6:11–13). JACOB condemns his sons Simeon and Levi for their ruthless violence against the men of Shechem (Gen. 34:30, 49:5–7).

Jewish law places violence in a larger context. Although it does not condone violence, it also does not call for blanket pacifism. It point out the difference between aggressors and victims, with the sages unanimously approving of self-defense: "If one comes to slay you, slay him first!" (*Sanh.* 72a). The aggressor may be killed by the potential victim. We read in the Talmud that someone told RAVA (*Pes.* 25b) that he had been ordered to kill another man or forfeit his own life. Rava replied: "Rather allow yourself to be killed than commit murder. Is your blood redder than that other man's? Perhaps his blood is redder than yours."

The HALAKHAH (Jewish law) describes a range of actions for dealing with violence. These include: self-defense, choosing martyrdom, running away, or seeking an accommodation (the MARRANO solution, i.e. pretending to take on another religion, if that had been the demand of the aggressors). Extreme violence in self-defense is allowed only as a means of preserving life. Limited violence was allowed to defend one's religious convictions or property, but killing a burglar is permitted only when the householder has reason to fear for his own life. In defending oneself or others, where life can be saved through wounding the aggressor it would be considered murder to cause death (*Sanh.* 72b). Violence is not permitted for the sake of revenge, although violent action may be considered lawful by a court when dealing with criminals.

VIRGINITY In Jewish tradition, unmarried women are expected to remain virgins. According to the Bible, the HIGH PRIEST could marry only a virgin (Lev. 21:14); the other priests could also marry widows, but not divorced women.

It is assumed by Jewish law that all women are virgins prior to marriage. Virginity was both the ideal and the norm within the context of the marriage contract. An engaged girl was regarded as a virgin (Heb. *betulah*) between the time of betrothal and MARRIAGE. Therefore, if a man married a woman presumed to be a virgin and proved that she had ceased to be a virgin through intercourse with another man during the betrothal period (*Sanh.* 7:4), the woman could be put to death by stoning (Deut. 22:20–21). If his charge of unchastity against her was proven false, he had to pay a fine to her father, and he could never divorce her (Deut. 22:19). A girl below the age of three who is sexually abused does not lose her status as a virgin (*Nid.* 5:4).

VISITING THE SICK (Heb. *bikkur holim*). It is a major commandment in the Jewish tradition to visit and comfort the sick and attend to their needs. The Talmud says that visiting a sick person takes away 1/60 of the sickness, while failing to do so may lead to the sick person's death (*Ned.* 39b). According to the Midrash, God Himself visited ABRAHAM when the Patriarch was recovering from his CIRCUMCISION.

The HALAKHAH (Jewish law) sets out proper behavior when visiting the sick. One may not sit on a high chair, on the bed, or above the patient's head. One may ask sick people what they require and whether they need financial assistance (*Kol Bo* 112). It is customary to recite a prayer on behalf of the sick person when leaving.

Jewish communities, from early times until today, have organized *bikkur holim* societies, whose members visit the sick and attend to their needs.

VITAL, HAYYIM (1542–1620). Mystic who studied in Safed with Moses Alshekh. When Isaac LURIA came to Safed in 1570. Vital became his most prominent follower. After Luria's death, Vital claimed that he alone possessed accurate notes on his master's teachings and rejected other versions. From 1577 to 1585, he headed a YESHIVAH in Jerusalem.

In his lifetime, Vital refused to publish any of his works. However, when he was ill, others managed to remove his manuscripts and copy them. His account of Luria's teachings were eventually published under the title *Ets ha-Hayyim* ("The Tree of Life") and are regarded as the basic work of Lurianic Kabbalah (see LURIA, ISAAC AND LURIANIC KABBALAH; MYSTICISM, JEWISH).

VOWS AND VOWING   A commitment to God to perform a particular act or to abstain from committing an act otherwise permitted. Vows are discussed in Numbers 30:1–16: "When a man vows a vow to the Lord or takes an oath imposing an obligation upon himself, he shall not break his pledge; he must carry out all that has crossed his lips." The passage also includes a provision that allows a husband to cancel the vows of his wife and a father to cancel the vows of his minor daughter.

The most common vow in ancient times was a pledge to bring a voluntary SACRIFICE (Lev. 7:16–17). Such vows might be made in times of danger or distress (Ps. 66:13–16). They were sometimes conditional upon God's granting a favor. For example, Hannah vowed that if she had a male child, he would be devoted to the service of God (1 Sam. 1:11). A NAZIRITE VOW is essentially a vow that pledges abstinence from eating meat, drinking wine, and other practices. Jewish law uses three terms for the vow: *neder*, the most general term; *nedavah*, the freewill offering, pledging a gift to God; and *shevu'ah*, an oath undertaking to pursue or not pursue certain courses of action.

In all eras, the possibility of failing to fulfill a vow made in haste was recognized. Ecclesiastes (5:3–4) warns: "Better not to vow than to vow and not pay." The sages of the Talmud also dealt with the problem. They both discouraged the taking of vows (*Ned.* 22a) and provided a way for the annulling of a vow after it was taken. The annulment procedure involved searching for factors that the individual had not taken into account when making the vow or facts that were unknown at the time of taking the vow.

For the most part, the practice of taking vows has disappeared. The one widespread exception is the practice of vowing a contribution to the synagogue or to some charity upon being called to the READING OF THE LAW. The KOL NIDREI formula recited on the eve of the Day of Atonement concerns the annulment of rash vows.

WAR Armed conflict between states and peoples. In the ancient world, war also involved their gods. If a nation was defeated, so was its deity. The Bible portrays God as "the Warrior" (Ex. 15:3), "valiant in battle" (Ps. 24:8), who "goes forth like a man of war, a fighter" (Isa. 42:13), and marches at the head of His army (Ps. 68:8). Israel's wars are God's wars. For example, the Amalekites had attacked the weaker stragglers among the Israelites in the Wilderness. They were therefore considered an enemy who had violated God's laws of compassion for the weak, and had dared to attack His people (Deut. 25:17–19). Similarly, the wars against the Canaanite nations were fought in an effort to uproot IDOLATRY from the land. Israel, because of its COVENANT with God, owes Him allegiance. This allegiance means the responsibility to wage war on God's behalf.

Deuteronomy (20:1–20) spells out the laws of warfare, which are further discussed in the Mishnah (*Sot.* 8). Before going into battle, soldiers are warned by the PRIESTS not to panic at the sight of the enemy. Officers then grant exemption to four categories of men: those who had built a new home but had not yet dedicated it; those who had planted a vineyard but had not yet tasted its fruit; those who had betrothed a wife but had still to consummate the marriage; and anyone whose faintheartedness might weaken the army's morale. In addition, both the soldiers and their camp had to be in a state of holiness (Deut. 23:10–15). Before a town is stormed, its inhabitants should be offered terms of surrender; their fruit trees are not to be cut down, even in the event of a long siege. When the Israelites conquered Erets Israel, they were expected to abide by God's battle orders. If any Canaanite town refused to surrender peacefully, all of its inhabitants were to be destroyed. In the case of towns captured far away, where permanent occupation was not possible, only adult males are to be killed; everyone else could be taken as slaves, the spoils of war.

The Mishnah (*Sot.* 8:7) defines three categories of war: *milhemet mitzvah*, "commanded by God"; *milhemet hovah*, "obligatory" because of enemy aggression; and *milhemet reshut*, an "optional" war for political gains only. The first type includes wars of annihilation against AMALEK and the Canaanite nations. Wars of the second type include wars of self-defense and national survival. The third type are wars for the purpose of extending Israel's borders for economic gain, and may be waged

only after the king has obtained the consent of a 71-member Sanhedrin.

During the Middle Ages, Jews experienced horrific suffering at the hands of various conquering armies, particularly the European Crusaders. During this period, there are some examples of Jewish participation in military operations. In Arabia and Maghreb, Jewish tribes fought unsuccessful campaigns against the Muslims. In Ethiopia, the BETA ISRAEL met defeat at the hands of the Christians. In southern Russia and the Caucasus region, the KHAZARS formed a wedge between Christian Byzantium and Muslim Persia. Most uniquely, SAMUEL HA-NAGID (993–1055), Granada's Jewish vizier, led the Spanish army in battle against the rival Muslims. He eventually died during one such campaign.

Beginning in the late 18th century, the freedom that came with the Emancipation, when Jews were welcomed into general society, also brought with it the issue of military service. Halakhic (Jewish legal) authorities such as Moses SOFER were asked to decide whether a Jew should risk his life in non-Jewish wars. While his decision was negative, most believed that Jews should serve the country in which they lived. The HAFETS HAYYIM and others noted that all laws that apply to Jewish kings also apply to non-Jewish rulers who benefit their Jewish subjects by maintaining law and order. This applies to serving in the army of the motherland. However, all opinions condemn a Jew who opts to serve as a mercenary (soldier for hire).

In the modern period, Israel's War of Independence (1948–49) was regarded by most Orthodox religious leaders as a *milhemet hovah*, justified war. The same approval was given to Israel's other wars, since they were fought in self-defense. The one exception is the 1982 Lebanon War, which some rabbis defined as a *milhemet reshut*, an optional war, undertaken for purposes beyond self-defense.

WASHING OF HANDS   See ABLUTIONS

WATER-DRAWING FESTIVAL   Ceremony held in the TEMPLE on the night following the first day of the SUKKOT festival and on each following night of the festival. It celebrated the water libation (pouring) that followed the morning SACRIFICE on each day of the festival. The name "water-drawing ceremony" comes from Isaiah 12:3: "Joyfully shall you draw from the fountains of triumph." The Mishnah states: "He who has not seen the rejoicing of the water-drawing ceremony [in the Temple] has never seen rejoicing in his life" (*Suk.* 45:1). Even the sages joined in the festivities. R. Simeon ben GAMALIEL I was said to have juggled with eight lighted torches at the water-drawing ceremony, without allowing a single torch to touch the ground (*BB* 53). The sages danced with the people to music supplied by the LEVITES and would not sleep the entire night. In JERUSALEM, huge bonfires were lit illuminating the entire city.

WEDDING   See MARRIAGE

WEEKLY PORTION   See PARASHAH

WEEKS, FESTIVAL OF   See SHAVU'OT

WESTERN WALL   (Heb. *Ha-Kotel ha-Ma'aravi*). A portion of the western retaining wall of the TEMPLE MOUNT in JERUSALEM, most important of the Jewish HOLY PLACES. During the reign of HEROD the Great (1st cent. BCE), the Temple Mount was expanded by building great retaining walls around it, filling the gap between the retaining walls and the original slopes with a system of domed vaults, leveling the summit, and covering the vaults with earth. The longest of the retaining walls was the western one. The portion of the wall considered today to be a holy place is a 195 ft. (60-meter) section located near the southern end.

The wall was built from enormous stones, most of which weighed between two and eight tons. Some, however, weighed as much as 40 or 50 tons, with several estimated at more than 100. Today, seven rows of the original stones are visible above ground. The remaining four or five rows were added in the eighth century, at the time of the construction of the El Aksa mosque. There are also several rows of smaller stones whose origin is not known.

According to the MIDRASH (Ex. R. 2:2; Num. R. 11:2; Lam. R. 1:31), the "Western Wall" was never destroyed because the Divine Presence (SHEKHINAH) rests there. It is not likely that the sages were referring to the western wall as we know it today. After all, the retaining walls that supported the Temple walls are not identical with the Temple walls themselves. Nevertheless, the surviving walls of the Temple Mount have taken on greater importance after the destruction of the Temple, if for no other reason than that they survived.

In time, the importance of the present site in comparison to other places of assembly and prayer in Jerusalem has grown. Benjamin of Tudela (12th cent. CE), the well-known medieval traveler, is the only chronicler to mention the western wall. Only after the Ottoman conquest of Palestine (1517) is the western wall mentioned as an important holy place. From then on, the site became increasingly revered by Jews throughout the world. Jewish pilgrims to Jerusalem always visited it, believing the western wall to be the holiest place in Judaism, besides

Praying at The Western ("Wailing") Wall.

the Temple Mount, which it was forbidden to enter. It was at this time also that non-Jews began to call the site the "Wailing Wall," after witnessing Jews there mourning the destruction of the Temple.

Toward the end of the 19th century, the wall began to symbolize the Jewish people's national aspirations. It was at this point that it became a bone of contention between the Muslims and the Jews. The two communities fought over such issues as whether it was permitted to sound the SHOFAR at the wall or to introduce benches or a table from which the SCROLL OF THE LAW could be read.

Prayer offered at the western wall is believed to be particularly powerful. A common custom is to write requests of God on small slips of paper and place them in the wall.

When the Jewish Quarter of the Old City surrendered to the Arab Legion in 1948, the western wall came under Jordanian control. According to the armistice agreement, Jews were to be permitted access to their holy places within Arab-held Jerusalem. The Jordanian government did not honor this agreement. Only on 7 June 1967, when Israeli paratroopers captured the Old City, were Jews again able to worship at their holiest place.

Today, the western wall is the focus of both religious and national sentiment. Many boys celebrate their BAR MITZVAH at the wall. National ceremonies are also held there, with certain units of the Israel Defense Forces being sworn in at the site.

WIDOW AND ORPHAN   Beginning with the Bible, Judaism has always recognized the special needs of the widow and the orphan. Exodus 22:21 states: "You shall not ill-treat any widow or orphan." Elsewhere, we find special laws for their protection (see Deut. 24:7). Protecting the widow and the orphan is taken up by the PROPHETS and later in PSALMS as a matter of ETHICS (see Isa. 1:17; Ps. 94:8). The sages showed the same sensitivities: R. Yose said, "Anyone who robs a widow or an orphan, it is as if he robbed God" (Ex. R., *Mishpatim* 30:8).

The rabbis created a number of laws to benefit the widow and the orphan. For example, since the widow does not inherit her deceased husband's estate (it goes to the children), the rabbis instituted the KETUBBAH. This marriage contract serves as an insurance policy that is paid to the wife after her husband dies (*Ket.* 4:2).

The Talmud also deals with the problems a widow encountered in finding a home. At times, she returned to her father's house. Under other circumstances, she went to live with her in-laws or she became the guardian of her children, which allowed her to remain in her husband's home.

A person who has lost either a father or a mother and is incapable of fending for himself is considered an orphan in Jewish law. There is no age limit to this status. The community is required to assist an orphan in paying for a MARRIAGE celebration.

The widow has a role in two additional COMMANDMENTS. According to Deuteronomy (25:5–6), if a man dies without leaving any children, it is the obligation of a brother-in-law to marry the widow of his deceased brother (LEVIRATE MARRIAGE). The purpose of this commandment is to ensure that the name of the deceased will be carried on, for the firstborn of the levirate marriage is "accounted to the dead brother." The second is the prohibition that states that the HIGH PRIEST may not marry or have relations with a widow. This is because of the special holiness of the High Priest, who may only marry a virgin (see VIRGINITY).

WINE   In the Bible, Noah had the first vineyard, and he made and drank wine from its fruit (Gen. 9:20–21). Wine is one of the products of the Land of Israel, which the Bible cites as a sign of the land's fertility and abundance (Gen. 49:11; Deut. 33:28). Wherever the Bible mentions "cup," it refers to a cup of wine, which is said to "gladden the heart of man" (Ps. 104:15). Wine plays an important role in religious rituals. The Torah mentions the amount of wine to be poured out on the altar as a libation in connection with each type of SACRIFICE.

In the period of the Talmud, both cultivating vineyards and producing wine were prominent features of the economy. A number of the sages were vintners. The Talmud mentions at least ten varieties of wine. Some of these were mixed with

Glass bottle for Kiddush wine inscribed with verses from Genesis.

various spices. It was customary to dilute wine before drinking it by adding one-third water. Wine was usually served with the main meal of the day.

A number of the basic rituals of Jewish life call for drinking wine. At a CIRCUMCISION, one cup of wine is drunk, and a tiny bit of wine is given to the infant to calm it after the ceremony. At a MARRIAGE ceremony, two cups of wine are used, from which both the bride and groom sip. The SABBATH and FESTIVALS are welcomed into the home by the recitation of KIDDUSH over a cup of wine. Similarly, the HAVDALAH ceremony that marks the end of the Sabbath or holiday is made over a cup of wine. During the Passover SEDER, four cups of wine must be drunk. This is also true of the Tu bi-Shevat *seder* developed by Isaac LURIA (see NEW YEAR FOR TREES).

Since wine was widely used by non-Jews in the practice of IDOLATRY, the sages forbade Jews to use wine produced by a non-Jew.

WISDOM   (Heb. *hokhmah*). Wisdom has always been highly regarded in Judaism. The Bible (Deut. 4:6) describes how, when the other nations of the world learn of the Torah's laws, they will say, "Surely that great nation is a wise and discerning people." Throughout the generations, the highest Jewish ideal has been the TALMID HAKHAM, the wise Torah scholar. In contrast, the ignoramus (AM HA-ARETS) is the object of scorn. Respect for the wise is not limited to those wise in Jewish learning. A special

---

ON WISDOM

The beginning of wisdom is: acquire wisdom.

Wisdom cannot reside in the evilhearted.

Never talk to a fool for he despises words of wisdom.

Wisdom increases with years – but so does folly.

Wise men repeat what they have seen:
fools what they have heard.

Make your home a meeting place for the
wise – and drink in their every word.

Who is wise? He who learns from everyone.

Since the destruction of the Temple, the wise
have taken the place of the prophets.

BENEDICTION is called for when a person sees an individual who is exceptionally wise in other fields. This blessing thanks God for "having given of His wisdom to flesh and blood." The comparable blessing upon seeing a TORAH scholar is, "Who has apportioned of His wisdom to those who fear Him."

The Talmud stresses that wisdom must be accompanied by the fear of God, for "the beginning of wisdom is fear of the Lord" (Ps. 111:10). *Avot* (3:9) acknowledges that pure wisdom is worthless if it makes people believe they are above ethical behavior: "A man whose fear of sin is greater than his wisdom – his wisdom will endure; but the man whose wisdom exceeds his fear of sin – his wisdom will not endure."

For the rabbis, wisdom is the product of hard study; natural wisdom is a gift, and therefore not really praiseworthy.

WISDOM LITERATURE Category of ancient literature that praises WISDOM and offers guidance for daily living. In the Bible, this includes the books of JOB, PROVERBS, some of PSALMS, and ECCLESIASTES. In the APOCRYPHA, *Ecclesiasticus* and *Wisdom of Solomon* are examples of wisdom literature.

Wisdom literature, with its proverbs and wise sayings, represents a universal tradition. The truths expressed are universal rather than particular; the concerns are global rather than Jewish (see UNIVERSALISM AND PARTICULARISM). It is often addressed to the young, offering them the benefit of the experience of the elders. The books themselves use a variety of literary devices to make a point. There are similes, metaphors, and allegories. Sometimes, two opposites are contrasted, as the righteous and the wicked in Psalm 1.

WISE, ISAAC MAYER (1819–1900). Pioneer of American REFORM JUDAISM and first president of Hebrew Union College. Wise emigrated to America in 1846, where he was appointed rabbi in Albany. His Reform tendencies and personal conflicts forced him to move on in 1850, when he formed his own con-

gregation. In 1854 he moved to Congregation B'nai Jeshurun, Cincinnati, where he remained for the rest of his life.

Cincinnati proved much more receptive to Wise's brand of Reform. He started an English-language Jewish newspaper and then a German supplement. He also founded a college to train rabbis. In 1855 he took the initiative to summon a rabbinic conference in Cleveland, which established a new American Jewish movement. The movement aimed to publish a uniform prayer book and decide on changes in Jewish practice. Not all these efforts met with success, however, Wise persevered. He published his own prayer book – *Minhag America* (1856) – which was a revision of the traditional prayer book.

In 1875, the Reform rabbinical college, Hebrew Union College, was established. Wise was appointed its first president.

WISSENSCHAFT DES JUDENTUMS (Ger. "Science of Judaism"). Name given to the critical study of Jewish history and culture, which developed among the Jews of the German-speaking world in the 19ᵗʰ century. The EMANCIPATION, when Jews were welcomed into general society, introduced Jews to secular studies. Until then, the Jewish past had been known only through the study of sacred texts using traditional Jewish commentaries. The scientific study of Jewish history, it was felt by supporters of the *Wissenschaft*, would place Jewish culture on a par with that of the German environment. They further felt that intensive scholarship would reveal the richness of the Jewish past and restore the Jews' pride in their heritage. This would also serve to improve Jewish standing in the eyes of the Gentile world. *Wissenschaft* scholars devoted themselves to a pure scholarship, detached from the subjective feelings they might have for the content.

Leopold ZUNZ was the most prominent founding figure in the movement. Zacharias FRANKEL, another key figure, founded the German *Monthly Journal for Jewish History and Science* in 1851. This journal continued to appear until 1939, when the Nazis suppressed it

The *Wissenschaft* had a powerful effect on 20ᵗʰ century scholarship, particularly in America. European-trained scholars made their appearance on American soil and contributed to the *Jewish Encyclopedia*, for example. Likewise in Israel, the first generation of scholars that taught at the Hebrew University (founded in 1925) were European-trained products of the *Wissenschaft*.

WITCHCRAFT Several categories of those who practice witchcraft and sorcery are described in the Bible. These include diviners, soothsayers, those who communicate with ghosts and spirits, sorcerers, etc. Since the Bible calls for the individual's wholehearted allegiance to God, it prohibits all contact with the various forms of witchcraft (see Deut. 18:13). The crime of witchcraft is considered as serious as the crime of human sacrifice (Deut. 18:10) with the same punishment given for both (Lev. 20:27).

The Talmud suggests that witchcraft was mostly found

among women. It reports the story of SIMEON BEN SHETAH, who ordered the execution of 80 witches on the same day (*Sanh.* 6:4). The Talmud lists additional forms of witchcraft, which are all punishable by whipping. These include reading things into certain occurrences, telling fortunes from sand and stones, astrological forecasting, and reciting certain formulas to promote healing (*Sanh.* 65b).

WOMEN   The Bible provides two accounts of the creation of woman. In the first (Gen. 1:27), woman is placed on a par with man, both being created in the image of God. In the second, (Gen. 2:21–25), woman is created from man's rib to be his helper; man is told to leave his parents and cling to his wife. Later, in the Garden of EDEN (Gen. 3:16), woman is told that for her disobedience, she would suffer pain in childbirth and be subservient to man.

In ancient times, Judaism was clearly a patriarchal religion. It was located within the context of the general patriarchal society of the Near East. Social roles were usually based on gender. A woman's primary roles were childbearing and homemaking. Even so, Israelite women fared better under biblical law than women in surrounding cultures. Many of their rights were safeguarded, and their freedom was guaranteed. For example, a husband had to properly provide for his wife.

Rabbinic Attitudes   The Talmud is both positive and critical concerning women. It acknowledges that man is incomplete without woman, and that a man without a wife lives without joy and blessing. It teaches that a man should love his wife as himself and respect her more than himself. The rabbis further contend that each generation is redeemed only because of the righteous women of that generation. At the same time, it criticizes women as being frivolous, greedy, gossipers, and a source of temptation.

As in Bible times, Jewish women fared better under the rule of HALAKHAH (Jewish law) than their non-Jewish counterparts did in surrounding societies. The Jewish woman could not be married against her will. The KETUBBAH (Jewish marriage contract) was a legally binding document that provided for her and guaranteed her a monetary settlement in the event of divorce or the death of her husband.

In terms of religious status, women were exempt from positive time-bound commandments (with some exceptions). They were also disqualified as witnesses in most cases in court. On the other hand, within the family and home, they enjoyed respect and considerable authority. Three positive commandments are specifically assigned to women. They must separate

a piece of dough from the kneading bowl to give to the priests as CHALLAH. They must light the Sabbath CANDLES. And they must uphold the laws of FAMILY PURITY.

The Modern Period   The exemption of women from time-related commandments has presented a problem in the modern period, as women have sought equal status in the observance of Jewish law. Because the law is that women are exempt – for example, from public prayer at specific times – her commitment to performing such a commandment comes from voluntary choice. In the eyes of traditional Jewish law, this does not equal real obligation. For this reason, according to the traditional understanding of the *halakhah*, she cannot lead prayer and exempt a man, who has a real obligation.

Orthodoxy has remained true to this halakhic framework. In certain circles, it has changed the positioning of partitions separating men and women in the SYNAGOGUE (see MEHITSAH) to make women feel more comfortable. In some cases it has even welcomed women's prayer groups, in which women lead prayers and read and are called to the READING OF THE LAW. However, such changes remain within the definitions of traditional male-female roles, without altering the *halakhah* or ritual.

Non-Orthodox movements have been more responsive to the influence and demands of FEMINISM. Within the REFORM and CONSERVATIVE movements and RECONSTRUCTIONISM, women have gained increasing status in Jewish ritual and, in many cases, complete equality. Furthermore, in these movements, women have been ordained as rabbis.

WORLD TO COME   See AFTERLIFE

WRITTEN LAW   (Heb. *Torah she-bi-khetav*). The TORAH, traditionally dictated by God to MOSES; by extension, the entire Bible. Rabbis made a distinction between the Written Law and the ORAL LAW. However the two, taken together, are the source of all basic Jewish law. We read in Leviticus 26:46, "These are the statutes and ordinances and *torahs*, which the Lord made between Him and the children of Israel on Mount Sinai by the hand of Moses." The *Sifra* (54:11) comments: "The use of *torah* in the plural shows that two Torahs were given [by God to Moses], one written and one oral."

In rabbinic tradition, the Written Law was never meant to stand alone and could be understood only through the traditional interpretation of the Oral Law (*Shab.* 31a). According to MAIMONIDES (*Introduction to the Mishnah* 1): "Every commandment was given with its explanation."

Υ

YA'ALEH VE-YAVO ("May [our remembrance] arise and come … [before You]"). Key words and title of a special paragraph added to the AMIDAH prayer and GRACE AFTER MEALS on New MOONS and PILGRIM FESTIVALS. It is also added during HOL HA-MO'ED, the middle days of Sukkot and Passover. The main idea of the *Ya'aleh ve-Yavo* prayer is that God should remember the PATRIARCHS, the entire House of Israel, and JERUSALEM and that he should send his MESSIAH and bring "deliverance, mercy, life, peace" and other blessings to the Jewish people on the holiday.

YAD (lit. "hand"). Pointer used to keep the place when reading aloud from the SCROLL OF THE LAW. The reader is forbidden to touch the scroll directly with the finger, since the hands could be unclean (*Yad.* 3:2).

We first hear of the use of the *yad* as a special ritual object in 1570. It is generally made of silver and shaped like a rod with a tiny hand with pointed finger at its end. In some cases it is carved and beautifully decorated. Sephardi Jews also have the custom of using the fringes of the prayer shawl (TALLIT) to point as they read from the TORAH.

YADAYIM ("Hands"). Eleventh tractate (book) of the Order of TOHOROT in the Mishnah. Its four chapters deal with how hands can become unclean and how to purify them. The last chapter discusses some laws of SACRIFICES AND OFFERINGS, TITHES given by Jews outside of Israel, and disagreements between the PHARISEES and the SADDUCEES.

YAHRZEIT ("anniversary"). Yiddish term for the death anniversary of a parent or other close relative, according to the Hebrew date. Customs associated with the *yahrzeit* observance sprang up in 15th century Germany and spread throughout the Jewish world. These include reciting the KADDISH prayer and kindling a MEMORIAL LIGHT, since these practices are believed to elevate the dead person's soul. A person observing a *yahrzeit* is often the leader of the prayers on weekdays and is called to the READING OF THE LAW on the SABBATH closest to the *yahrzeit*. Already in the Talmud we read that people did not eat meat or drink wine on the anniversary of their parents' death (*Ned.* 12a; *Shev.* 20a). This led to the custom of some Orthodox Jews to fast on the *yahrzeit*, unless it is a joyous day in the Jewish CALENDAR.

Engraved and pierced Torah pointer (yad) *from Poland, 1855.*

Oriental Sephardim call the day *nahalah* ("inheritance"). Spanish and Portuguese Jews often call it *meldado*, a "study session" in memory of the departed in which friends and relatives participate.

YAMIM NORA'IM   See HIGH HOLIDAYS

YEDID NEFESH   ("Beloved of [My] Soul"). A religious poem (PIYYUT) written by Eleazar ben Moses Azikri of Safed in the 16th century. The poem is sung in many congregations just before the service that welcomes the SABBATH on Friday nights and in others later in the service. Its beautiful words begin with: "Beloved of [my] soul, merciful Father, draw your servant to your will…"

YESHIVAH   (pl. *yeshivot*). A school of advanced rabbinic study. It students study almost entirely traditional Jewish texts, especially the TALMUD. Most RABBIS have studied in a *yeshivah*; however, graduating professional rabbis is not the main purpose of the *yeshivah*.

Yeshivot follow the tradition of the ACADEMIES of 3rd–11th century Erets Israel and Babylonia. In the tenth century, there was a *yeshivah* in Jerusalem, which was probably at one time the last remaining academy in Erets Israel. It was moved to Damascus after 1071, since Damascus and Aleppo, Syria, were important centers of learning until the end of the 12th century.

A legend from *Sefer ha-Kabbalah* (mid-12th cent.), by Abraham Ibn Daud, tells of four scholars on their way to study in Babylonia in the year 990. Their ship was seized by pirates. One of the scholars was never heard from again, but the other three were sold as slaves, each in a different port: one in North Africa, one in Egypt, and one in Spain. Each one built a *yeshivah* and created a center of Jewish learning in that area.

Yeshivot existed in North Africa from the eighth to the 11th centuries. Many yeshivot could be found in Spain from the tenth century until the time when the Jews were expelled from that country in 1492. Spanish Jewish scholars such as Moses ben Hanokh, NAHMANIDES, and Solomon ben Abraham ADRET headed these *yeshivot*.

A great contribution to Jewish scholarship was made by the Ashkenazi *yeshivot* of northern Europe. They produced such major authorities as GERSHOM BEN JUDAH and RASHI (11th cent.), as well as the Tosafists (see TOSAFOT). The Ashkenazi *yeshivah* was smaller than the great academies of old. Most had only about 100 students, many of whom lived with the head of the *yeshivah*. The leader of the *yeshivah* raised money to help support those students who did not come from wealthy families. Those who attended the *yeshivah* were already successful scholars. Moses ben Jacob of Coucy noted that French *yeshivah* students were often so dedicated that most slept in their clothes. The golden age of French *yeshivot* ended with the EXPULSION of the Jews from France in 1306.

From the middle of the 16th century, communities in Western

Ner Israel Rabbinical College in Baltimore, Maryland.

Europe began to maintain regional *yeshivot*. Students had their meals at private homes on a rotating basis. Studies centered around discussion and disputation, and many written commentaries came out of these *yeshivot*. The main center of *yeshivot* moved to Eastern Europe, especially Poland, in the 16th century. Their best-known method of study was called PILPUL and involved extremely complicated intellectual discussions of the texts. Ashkenazi *yeshivot* declined during the 17th and 18th centuries, due to terrible persecutions against the Jews (see ANTI-SEMITISM).

The modern era of *yeshivot* began in 1802, with the opening of the Volozhin *yeshivah* in White Russia. It built its own building, and within 50 years had attracted 400 students. Other great *yeshivot* flourished in White Russia, including Kovno, which became the center of the MUSAR MOVEMENT. In *yeshivot* connected with the Musar Movement, Jewish ETHICS was studied along with Talmud. Thousands of students were drawn to these institutions, many of whom became rabbis and teachers. In the world of HASIDISM, most *yeshivot* belonged to particular branches of the Hasidic movement, and only its members studied there.

The great European *yeshivot* were suddenly and brutally destroyed by the Nazi HOLOCAUST. Survivors rebuilt some of the famous *yeshivot* in other places in the world, particularly Israel and the United States.

Before World War II, there were not many *yeshivot* in the United States. The few that developed were Yeshiva University in New York; the Rabbi Aaron Kotler Institute for Advanced Studies in Lakewood, New Jersey; Torah Vo-Da'as in New York; and Ner Israel in Baltimore. In most of these, students were involved in university studies along with their *yeshivah* learning.

By far, the leading center of *yeshivot* today is the State of Israel. It has been estimated that there are more full-time *yeshivah* students in Israel today than there were in pre-war Europe.

The willingness of the Israeli government to defer the army service of full-time *yeshivah* students has enabled *yeshivot* to develop rapidly. In some cases, young men study for a year or two after high school to bolster and prepare themselves for their army service. In the case of HAREDIM, many make a career of full-time *yeshivah* learning. A unique form is the *yeshivat hesder* ("arrangement"), where students combine *yeshivah* learning with their army service. A relatively new development in modern ORTHODOXY is the growth of dozens of women's *yeshivot* in Israel where thousands of women engage in high-level Torah learning, including Talmud study, for the first time in Jewish history.

YEVAMOT ("Levirate Marriages"). First tractate (book) of the Order of NASHIM in the Mishnah. Its 16 chapters deal mainly with LEVIRATE MARRIAGE (*yibbum*). This is the obligation of a man to marry the wife of his dead brother if he dies before she has had any children by him. The purpose is so that the living brother can carry on the dead brother's name to the next generation. The book covers laws about the levirate marriage, who must undertake it, and who is exempt. It also describes a ceremony called *halitsah,* which enables the surviving brother to free himself from the obligation to marry his brother's widow.

YHWH   See GOD, NAMES OF

YIBBUM   See LEVIRITE MARRIAGE

YIDDISH ("Judeo-German"). The everyday spoken language of most ASHKENAZIM from the early Middle Ages until recent times. Beginning in the early 11th century, Jews living in

what is now Germany and France gradually began speaking the Old High German and Middle High German of their Christian neighbors. Hebrew terms and expressions were mixed in, and Hebrew letters were used to write the language. As Jews moved eastward through Europe, due to persecutions (see ANTI-SEMITISM), the Yiddish language spread. Around 1500, Yiddish split into the Western form, spoken in Germany, Alsace, Holland, and Switzerland, and Eastern Yiddish, spoken east of Prussia. This form was often called *mamma-loshen* ("mother tongue"). Both forms included words for ideas and objects related to the SYNAGOGUE and PRAYER, the DIETARY LAWS, and other traditional Jewish practices.

From its earliest beginnings, Yiddish literature was dedicated to sending strong, simple religious messages to the less educated Jew. Dozens of Bible translations and books of stories and teachings from the Talmud were published. Most outstanding were *Taytsh-Hummash* ("Bible Translation"; 1590); *Tse'enah u-Re'enah* ("Go Out and See"; late 16th cent.), an enormously popular commentary on the Bible for women; and *Ma'aseh Bukh* (1602), a collection of instructive and entertaining stories from the Talmud that greatly influenced the development of Yiddish literature. Many historical works, biblical plays, satires, and comedies appeared and greatly influenced Jewish daily life in Europe until World War II. Religious works also continued to be written in Yiddish throughout this period. These include: *Gott fun Avrohom* ("God of Abraham"), a prayer for the family recited by women as they light the Sabbath candles, and *Tales of Rabbi* NAHMAN OF BRATSLAV, which conveyed the teachings of this Hasidic leader. Modern Yiddish literature, such as that of Y.L. Peretz and Chaim Grade, include religious themes as well.

Of the nearly 11 million Jews who spoke Yiddish in 1939, about half were killed in the HOLOCAUST. Today Yiddish is

Passover Seder *plate inscribed with good wishes for the holiday, in Yiddish, in Hebrew letters. Delft, Holland, 18th century.*

spoken mainly among ultra-Orthodox Ashkenazim and in the YESHIVAH world.

YIGDAL ("May He be magnified"). Opening words and title of a popular hymn. It is believed that it was written by Daniel ben Judah of Rome (c. 1300). The hymn is a version of MAIMONIDES' 13 PRINCIPLES OF FAITH that has been set to verse. It is sung in the synagogue at the beginning of the MORNING SERVICE and also at the end of the EVENING SERVICE for the SABBATH and FESTIVALS.

YISHTABBAKH ("Praised [Your Name] shall be"). Opening word of a prayer that ends the PESUKEI DE-ZIMRA ("Passages of Song") section of the MORNING SERVICE. It is also said in the SEDER for PASSOVER. The paragraph contains 15 different words that praise God and is traditionally linked to the 15 Psalms of Ascent (Ps. 120–134) that the LEVITES said when they climbed the 15 steps leading to the TEMPLE. *Yishtabbakh* is meant to put worshipers in the proper frame of mind for worship (see KAVVANAH).

YIZKOR   See MEMORIAL SERVICES

YOMA ("The Day," i.e., Day of Atonement). Fifth tractate (book) of the Order of MO'ED in the Mishnah. Its eight chapters deal with the HIGH PRIEST's preparations and special service in the HOLY OF HOLIES on the DAY OF ATONEMENT (Yom Kippur) in the TEMPLE (Lev. 16:1–34, 23:26–32). The last chapter gives the laws of Yom Kippur itself.

YOM HA-ATSMA'UT   See INDEPENDENCE DAY OF ISRAEL

YOM KIPPUR   See DAY OF ATONEMENT

YOM KIPPUR KATAN ("minor DAY OF ATONEMENT"). The day before each New MOON. According to Jewish mystics, the New Moon is a time of forgiveness for sins. R. Moses Cordovero of Sefad therefore began the custom of full REPENTANCE the day before it so that a person could enter each month free of SIN. The CUSTOMS of the day include FASTING for some or all of the day, special prayers asking for God's forgiveness, and a Torah reading if there is a MINYAN present of people who are fasting. The reading is the one usually read on the afternoon of fast days. Yom Kippur Katan is hardly observed today.

YOM TOV   See FESTIVALS

YOSE BEN HALAFTA (c. 100–c. 160 CE). One of the last students of Rabbi AKIVA in Erets Israel. He is called simply "Rabbi Yose" in the Mishnah, where he is quoted over 300 times. He played a leading role in reestablishing the SANHEDRIN after the TEMPLE was destroyed and was a teacher of Rabbi JUDAH HA-NASI. His opinions in settling legal disputes were greatly respected. He earned his living as a tanner of hides in Sepphoris, where he established a law court (BET DIN) and a rabbinical ACADEMY. His five sons were all noted scholars.

R. Yose took part in religious debates with Christians and pagans who challenged the basics of Judaism. He is famous for saying, "The Holy One is the Place [*ha-Makom*] of the world, but the world is not his place" (*Midr. Ps.* 90:1). By this he meant that God was otherworldly. He first made the rule that a person may not be condemned to death in a capital crime unless two witnesses warned him against committing the crime (*Mak.* 1:9; *Sanh.* 56b).

YOTSEROT (sing. *yotser*) A series of ancient poems used in prayer (*piyyutim*) that add poetic beauty to the two blessings before and the blessing after the recital of the SHEMA of the MORNING SERVICE. The word comes from the opening words of the first blessing before the *Shema, yotser or* ("Creator of light"). These *piyyutim* are recited on the FESTIVALS and on special SABBATHS (see SABBATHS, SPECIAL).

The basic series of *yotserot* was composed of seven *piyyutim*, which were inserted throughout the section of the morning service containing the *Shema* and its blessings. In modern times, the *yotserot* are not usually recited.

ZAKEN MAMREH A "rebellious elder" who, in biblical law, is sentenced to death (Deut. 17:12). In order to be judged a *zaken mamreh*, one must meet a number of conditions: the person must be an ordained TORAH scholar; he must deliberately refuse to accept the decision of the SANHEDRIN; he must have ruled that others must act in accordance with his views; he must be aware that other sages have ruled differently, yet stubbornly hold to his ruling. Also, the ruling in question must involve the punishment of a sin-offering and KARET, "being cut off" from the Jewish people. The purpose of this law was to preserve the unity of the Jewish people.

ZAVIM ("Discharges"). Ninth tractate (book) of the Order of TOHOROT in the Mishnah. It consists of five chapters that deal with the cleanness or uncleanness of a man (*zav*) or a woman (*zavah*) suffering from certain types of bodily discharges (Lev. 15:1–15, 25–30). The book deals with purification rituals, the SACRIFICES that are to be brought, and the transmission of uncleanness through physical contact with a *zav(ah)*.

ZEALOTS Jewish movement active in the war against Rome (66–73 CE). According to Josephus, there were a number of groups that participated in the Jewish Revolt, but the term Zealots is used in a general way to include them all.

The movement developed in the first century, after the fall of the HASMONEANS, a time when there was a great deal of expectation among the people that the MESSIAH was about to come. The national depression that accompanied the fall of the Hasmoneans took several forms. The ESSENES, for example, withdrew from society. The SADUCEES called for compromise with the Hellenists. The Pharisees focused on the people, but stayed away from politics. The Zealots called for action.

Following HEROD's death, the Romans tried to conduct a census in Judea in 6 CE. This enraged the local population and was the spark that ignited the Zealots. Judah the Galilean, the leader of the *Sicarii* ("knife wielders"), rebelled and then his followers retreated to the desert and probably operated a guerilla campaign. The Roman emperor, Caligula, further enraged the population when he tried to install his image in the TEMPLE. Finally, in 66 CE, a full revolt broke out. The following year, the Roman general, Vespasian, was sent to the region along with

---

JOSEPHUS ON THE LAST HOURS OF THE DEFENDERS OF MASADA

… for the husbands tenderly embraced their wives and took their children into their arms, and gave the longest parting kisses to them, with tears in their eyes. Yet at the same time did they complete what they had resolved on, as if they had been executed by the hands of strangers…. Miserable men indeed were they whose distress forced them to slay their own wives and children with their own hands, as the lightest of those evils that were before them…. They then chose ten men by lot out of them, to slay all the rest; every one of whom laid himself down by his wife and children on the ground and threw his arms about them, and they offered their necks to the strokes of those who by lot executed that melancholy office; and when these ten had, without fear, slain them all, they made the same rule for casting lots for themselves, that he whose lot it was should first kill the other nine, and after all, should kill himself;… so, for a conclusion, the nine offered their necks to the executioner, and he who was the last of all, took a view of all the other bodies, lest perchance some or other among so many that were slain should want his assistance to be quite dispatched; and when he perceived that they were all slain, he set fire to the palace, and with a great force of his hand ran his sword entirely through himself, and fell down dead near to his own relations.

60,000 men. He took control of Galilee, the Jordan Valley, and the Coastal Plain. He then attacked Judea. Titus continued the campaign and eventually reached JERUSALEM with four legions in 70 CE. He breached the walls of Jerusalem and then destroyed the Temple. The Zealots at Masada, under the leadership of Eleazar ben Jair, held out until the year 73. The defenders of Masada took their own lives rather than fall into Roman hands. This ended the Jewish Revolt.

The suppression that produced the Zealot movement continued, as did the Zealot spirit in response. In 132 CE, BAR KOKHBA led another revolt against the Romans.

ZEBULUN See TRIBES, TWELVE

ZECHARIAH   Eleventh of the minor prophets. Next to last in the PROPHETS section of the Bible. His first prophecy was made in the second year of the reign of Darius I (520 BCE). He was a contemporary of Zerubbabel the governor, Joshua the High Priest, and HAGGAI the prophet. He prophesied for about two years. Along with Haggai, he pushed the people of Jerusalem to resume work on the rebuilding of the TEMPLE.

The Book of Zechariah, along with those of Haggai and MALACHI, dates after the Babylonian EXILE. The book has two different styles. The first eight chapters are direct in style and relate clearly to the events of the time. The remaining six chapters are written in a mysterious mystical fashion. The different styles of the two parts have led some modern scholars to conclude that there are two authors.

Zechariah places before the people the idea that rebuilding the Temple is necessary in order to bring the messianic kingdom (see MESSIAH). As a result of the combined efforts Zechariah, Haggai, and Malachi, the Temple was completed in 516 BCE.

BOOK OE ZECHARIAH	
1:1–1:7	Call to repentance
1:8–1:17	Vision of the horses
2:1–2:4	The four horns and the four smiths
2:5–2:16	The man with the measuring line; promise of restoration
3:1–3:10	The cleansing of the priesthood
4:1–4:14	The lamp and the olive tree; promises of deliverance
5:1–5:11	The flying scroll and the woman inside the bushel
6:1–6:8	The four chariots
6:9–8:23	The messianic age
9:1–9:8	Punishment of neighboring nations
9:9–9:17	Redemption of Israel
10:1–10:12	Ingathering of Israel's exiles
11:1–11:17	The punishment of the evil shepherds
12:1–14:21	Apocalyptic oracles; end of days

ZEKHUT AVOT   See MERIT

ZEMIROT   (from the Hebrew root *z-m-r*, "to sing"). Table hymns sung during and after the SABBATH meals. The texts are religious poems written through the ages by various Hebrew poets. Most are in Hebrew, though a few are in Aramaic. The subject matter includes Sabbath laws, observances, and customs, the rewards due the Sabbath observer, references to the prophet ELIJAH, and praise of God. Other popular *zemirot* were composed by the kabbalists of the 16th and 17th centuries. There are about 25 *zemirot* that form the core of the table hymns sung among ASHKENAZIM. They are divided into songs associated with Friday evening, Saturday morning, and the end of the Sabbath, particularly at MELAVVEH MALKAH. SEPHARDIM sing some *zemirot* that are unique to their heritage.

What is the origin of the custom of singing at the table? In *Sefer Hasidim* (ed. Wistinetzki, 722) we read that it is praiseworthy to sit and sing praises on the Sabbath, citing Psalm 92:12. *Siddur Rashi* (534) states that the recital of *zemirot* at the conclusion of the Sabbath is a proper CUSTOM; in the same manner that citizens of a country accompany the excursions of the king with voices and lutes and harps, so Jews accompany the exit of the Sabbath Queen in joy and song.

There is no rigid rule about how many songs are to be sung at any of the Sabbath meals. A wide variety of tunes developed, some identified with particular Jewish communities. Others are more generally identified as Ashkenazi or Sephardi. New tunes still continue to be composed.

ZEPHANIAH   Ninth of the minor prophets. Fourth from last in the PROPHETS section of the Bible. Zephaniah was a descendant of King Hezekiah of Judah. This would mean, according to traditional genealogy, that he was a distant relative of King Josiah, during whose reign he prophesied. Therefore, when he criticizes the king's family in his prophecies, we can assume that he was personally familiar with their lifestyle. He lived at the same time as JEREMIAH and the prophetess Huldah. According to tradition, Jeremiah preached in the markets, Zephaniah in the synagogues, and Huldah before the women.

The Book of Zephaniah contains three prophecies delivered during the early years of the reign of King Josiah (639–609 BCE). He rebukes the people for IDOLATRY, calls for REPENTANCE, and denounces Judah's political and religious leaders. He predicts that the surviving remnant of Judah will include ingathered exiles and will practice justice and humility.

BOOK OF ZEPHANIAH	
1:1–1:18	Denunciation of idolatry in Judah and pronunciation of judgment
2:1–3:7	Nations called to repentance
3:8–3:13	After judgment of the wicked, the remnant will be delivered
3:14–3:20	Deliverance of Israel

ZERA'IM   ("Seeds"). First Order of the Mishnah. *Zera'im* opens with the tractate BERAKHOT, which deals with the laws of prayer and the BENEDICTIONS said over food and drink. The remaining ten books (PE'AH, DEMAI, KELA'IM, SHEVI'IT, TERUMOT, MA'ASEROT, MA'ASER SHENI, HALLAH, ORLAH, and BIKKURIM) deal with agricultural laws, such as separating TITHES, sowing mixed seeds, letting the land lie fallow, and bringing the FIRST

FRUITS to the TEMPLE. Most of these laws apply only in Erets Israel.

Why does the Mishnah begin with *Zera'im*? MAIMONIDES explains that the Order is concerned with food, and a man cannot live and serve God without eating. The book about blessings begins the Order because before eating the produce of the land, one must first bless the Creator, whose existence makes all plant and animal life possible.

ZEVAHIM   ("Sacrifices"). First tractate (book) of the Order of KODASHIM in the Mishnah. It consists of 14 chapters that deal with the laws of slaughtering and sprinklinwg the blood of animal and bird sacrifices in the TEMPLE (cf. Lev. 1:1–17, 2:1–4, 4:27–31).

ZIKHRONOT   (lit. "remembrances"). Name given to the second of the three middle blessings of the AMIDAH prayer in the ADDITIONAL SERVICE of ROSH HA-SHANAH (the New Year). This section lists "remembrances," where God is asked to remember His COVENANT with the Jewish people. The actual *zikhronot* are ten verses of the Bible that show God as remembering. Ten blasts on the SHOFAR mark the completion of the section.

ZION   One of the names for the city of JERUSALEM, or a part of it. The original references in the Bible are quite specific: "David took the stronghold of Zion, that is, the city of David" (II Sam. 5:7). This refers to the small hill now southeast of the present city walls. In time, the name "Zion" was extended to cover the original biblical city enlarged by DAVID and later kings of JUDAH. Later, the term was applied to the whole land of Judah (see Isa. 10:24), and even more generally, to the land and even the people of ISRAEL: "And saying to Zion, 'You are my people'" (Isa. 51:16).

In later usage we see both the specific and the general meaning. In the late biblical and early post-biblical period, the name Zion came to refer to the TEMPLE MOUNT (e.g., Joel 3:17). It is also identified with David's tomb, on the western hill just south of the present walls of the Old City.

ZION, RETURN TO   (Heb. *shivat tsiyyon*). The desire of Jews living in the Diaspora to return to the Land of Israel. ZION, originally a synonym for JERUSALEM, came to apply to the whole Land of ISRAEL. The term "Return to Zion" was first applied to a historic event some 50 years after the destruction of the First Temple. Cyrus, the Persian conqueror of Babylonia, proclaimed to the Jews in the Babylonian captivity: "Whosoever there is among you of all His people, his God be with him, let him go up to Jerusalem, which is in Judah …" (Ezra 1:3; II Chr. 36:23).

The Bible mentions small waves of immigration under Zerubbabel, EZRA, and NEHEMIAH that "went up" (the term used for a Jew going to Israel) and reestablished Jewish life in Judah. Most of the exiles, however, chose not to return. The rabbis later said that the destruction of the Second Temple

The word "Zion" inside a Magen David *on the finials of a Torah scroll from Persia.*

was already foreshadowed in the refusal of the exiled Jews of Babylon to return (*Yoma* 9b). It was after the destruction of the Second Temple, in 70 CE, with the loss of Jewish rule in Erets Israel, that the yearning for the Return to Zion became a major factor in Judaism.

There are three factors that contributed to the Jewish people's longing for a Return to Zion. First, there was a natural desire to be in the physical land. A nostalgic memory for the homeland, the birthplace of the people, was embodied in the Bible and other Jewish literature. This nostalgia was strengthened by the many references to Zion in the prayers and rituals of Judaism. Secondly, at the center of the Jewish belief system is a faith in the final REDEMPTION of humanity. The age of the MESSIAH will include the restoration of the full national and religious life of the Jewish people in its land, including a mass return to the location of Zion. Finally, the Return to Zion has become part of HALAKHAH (Jewish law) as a religious obligation of every Jew. The importance of this obligation is considerable. For example, it is a cause for divorce if a spouse refuses to accompany husband or wife in a move to the Land of Israel (*Yad,*

Hilkhot Ishut 13). The sense of religious obligation became part of the national Jewish consciousness.

Historically, the constant trickle of Jews who returned to Zion over the centuries was motivated by religious feelings. It included a number of distinguished rabbis. Groups of refugees arrived from Spain and Portugal after the EXPULSIONS of the late 15th century. Some of them established the great center of Jewish MYSTICISM in Safed. From the end of the 18th century followers of HASIDISM and disciples of ELIJAH BEN SOLOMON, the Gaon of Vilna, settled in the Holy Land, especially in the "Holy Cities" of Jerusalem, Hebron, Tiberias, and Safed. Most of them spent their time in religious study, and many came to the country in order to be buried in holy soil. In the 19th century, the concept of Return to Zion took on new meaning as it was adopted by the political Zionists (see ZIONISM).

ZIONISM   Modern movement for the national independence of the Jewish people in Erets Israel. The ideas of the modern Zionist movement had their origins in the idea of a Return to Zion (see ZION, RETURN TO). However, the early leaders of the modern movement worked to transform the utopian religious goal into a practical set of programs. Judah Alkalai and Tsevi Hirsch Kalischer, both rabbis, took the radical position that REDEMPTION must be brought about through human efforts rather than Divine intervention. Both worked until their deaths in the 1870s to establish Jewish colonies in Erets Israel. Moses Hess, another important figure, published *Rome and Jerusalem* in 1862. He called for the creation of a Jewish homeland in Erets Israel, founded on socialist principles, in a network of agricultural settlements and cooperative communities.

The real practical work of the modern Zionist movement began with the founding of the Hibbat Zion movement in Eastern Europe in 1881. Spurred by the terrible attacks against Jews (pogroms) in Russia, Leo Pinsker effectively led Hibbat Zion in the effort to establish agricultural settlements in Erets Israel all through the 1880s. These settlements included Rishon le-Zion, Rosh Pinnah, Zikhron Yaakov, and Gederah. At the same time, Ahad Ha-am, opposed this brand of practical Zionism as unrealistic. He called for a cultural renaissance through Hebrew language and literature. He saw the Land of Israel as a spiritual center that could strengthen Jewish life in the Diaspora.

Theodor HERZL is responsible for transforming the Zionist idea into a political movement. He convened the First Zionist Congress in Basel in 1897 and founded the World Zionist Organization. The Congress adopted the Basel Program. It established the aim of Zionism as creating a home for the Jewish people in Erets Israel under public law and with the consent of governments. Chaim Weizmann assumed leadership of the World Zionist Organization and was instrumental in bringing about the publication of the Balfour Declaration in 1917. This British document recognized the right of the Jewish people to establish a national home in Erets Israel (called "Palestine" at the time). Jews continued to arrive in Erets Israel, where

the socialist camp dominated under the leadership of David BEN-GURION.

Zionism, in time, became a mass movement. In Europe, numerous Zionist youth groups were actively promoting immigration (*aliyah*) to Erets Israel. American supporters, including such leading figures as Louis Brandeis, Stephen S. Wise, and Abba Hillel Silver, provided money and political support. In Palestine itself, under the British Mandate, Zionist leaders encouraged immigration, land purchases, settlement, and economic development. They established the national institutions that were in fact the governing bodies of the State-in-the-Making. At the same time, the *yishuv* (Jewish community in pre-State Israel) was forced to deal with Arab and British hostility. After World War II, the Zionist leadership directed its efforts to creating "a Jewish commonwealth" based on the partition of the Land of Israel in keeping with the original proposal made by the British in the Peel Commission Report of 1937.

In the final analysis, the Zionist idea achieved the Jewish state. It became the great national force in the Jewish world. Through the efforts of Jews the world over, it set the stage for the establishment of the State of Israel.

ZOHAR   ("Book of Splendor"). The major work of Jewish MYSTICISM; the most influential work of the Kabbalah. The *Zohar* was written in Castile in the last third of the 13th century. The main author of the work was R. MOSES DE LEON. Two sections of the *Zohar*, *Ra'aya Mehemna* and *Tikkunei ha-Zohar*, were probably written later.

The *Zohar* is written in the ARAMAIC language and is essentially a commentary on the TORAH. The commentary is made up of a fabric of MIDRASH and story-like elements. R. SIMEON BAR YOHAI and his son R. Eleazar are featured as the head of a group of *tannaim* (rabbis of Mishnah times) that has supernatural knowledge and powers. They receive spiritual messages from several fictional figures, like the mysterious Sava ("Old Man") and Yenuka ("Child").

The *Zohar* has had lasting impact on Jewish culture. The author of the *Zohar* took many of his symbols from the works of the earlier kabbalists (mystics), especially the *Sefer ha-*BAHIR, the kabbalists of Provence and Gerona, and others. But all of these sources were used creatively, and Moses de Leon added to them his own mystical visions and speculations.

The *Zohar* includes five central myths: (1) the evolving of the ten Divine powers (the SEFIROT), from the eternal Godhead; (2) the dynamic interrelationship within the realm of the *Sefirot*; (3) the symbolic sexual myth of the relationship between masculine and feminine (see SHEKHINAH) elements in the Divine world; (4) the struggle between the holy Divine realm on the right and the evil system – the *Sitra Ahra*, the realm of the satanic powers – on the left; (5) the description of the REDEMPTION, the role of the MESSIAH, and the role of R. Simeon and his group in this process.

The *Zohar* was printed in the 16th century. One of the main motives for its publication was the belief that having knowledge of the *Zohar* is part of bringing the Messiah. The *Zohar* joins the Bible and the Talmud in the trio of the most sacred books of Judaism.

ZUGOT   ("Pairs"). Hebrew term for the five pairs of teachers and transmitters of the ORAL LAW listed in the opening chapter of AVOT in the Mishnah (1:4–15). In each pair, the first member is the president (NASI) and the second is the vice president (AV BET DIN) of the great SANHEDRIN that met in the TEMPLE'S Chamber of Hewn Stone. Their period of activity was from just before the Maccabean Revolt to the era of the *tannaim* (rabbis of the Mishnah). The five pairs were:

1. Yose ben Yoezer and Yose ben Johanan (before 160 BCE)
2. Joshua ben Perahyah and Nittai (or Mattai) of Arbel (about 130 BCE)
3. Judah ben Tabbai and SIMEON BEN SHETAH (about 100–75 BCE)
4. SHEMAYAH and AVTALYON (late 1st cent. BCE)
5. HILLEL and SHAMMAI (end of 1st cent. BCE–before 30 CE)

ZUNZ, LEOPOLD   (Yom Tov Lippman; 1794–1886). One of the founders of the "Science of Judaism" (WISSENSCHAFT DES JUDENTUMS) and pioneer of the scientific study of Jewish literature, prayer writings, and religious poetry. He attended the University of Berlin and in 1821 received his doctorate from the University of Halle. He was ordained as a rabbi by Aaron CHORIN.

In 1818 Zunz published his first major work on Jewish literature. He argues that Jewish literature should occupy a dignified place in all universities. He and others founded a journal the following year. Zunz became the editor of the *Zeitschrift für die Wissenschaft des Judentums* in 1823. Of the articles he personally published in that journal was a biography of RASHI. This was

Leopold Zunz

the first time that the biography of a Jewish scholar had been scientifically presented.

Throughout his career, he continued to publish works on the language of prayer, according to the CUSTOMS of different communities. In order to research these works, he visited the libraries of London, Oxford, Paris, and Parma. However, he was denied access to the Vatican Library because he was a Jew.

FOR FURTHER READING

Artson, Bradley Shavit and Gevritz, Gila. *Making a Difference: Putting Jewish Spirituality into Action, One Mitzvah at a Time.* Springfield, NJ, Behrman House, 2001. 143 p. ISBN: 0874417120.

Bauer, Yehuda, with the assistance of Nili Keren. *A History of the Holocaust.* Revised edition. New York, Franklin Watts, 2001. 432 p. ISBN 0531118843.

Ben-Asher, Naomi. *The Junior Jewish Encyclopedia.* 12th revised edition. New York, Shengold Publishers, 1993. 350 p. ISBN 0884001628.

Cardin, Nina Beth with Blumenthal, Scott. *The Time of Our Lives: A Teen Guide to the Jewish Life Cycle.* Springfield, NJ: Behrman House, 2003. 95 p. ISBN 087441718x.

Cardin, Nina Beth and Gevirtz, Gila. *Rediscovering the Jewish Holidays: Tradition in a Modern Voice.* Springfield, NJ: Behrman House, 2002. 196 p. ISBN 0874416639.

Chaiken, Miriam. *Menorahs, Mezuzas, and Other Jewish Symbols.* New York: Clarion Books, 1990. 102 p. ISBN 0899198562.

Feinstein, Edward. *Tough Questions Jews Ask: A Young Adult's Guide to Building a Jewish Life.* Woodstock, VT: Jewish Lights Publishers, 2003. 136 p. ISBN 158023139.

Fields, Harvey J. *A Torah Commentary for Our Times.* New York, UAHC Press, 3 vols. 1990–1993. (Vol. 1: Genesis, ISBN 087403083; Vol. 2: Exodus and Leviticus, ISBN 0807403342; Vol. 3: Numbers and Deuteronomy, 0807405126.)

Goldin, Barbara Diamond. *A Child's Book of Midrash: 52 Jewish Stories from the Sages.* Northvale, NJ: Aronson, 1990. 110 p. ISBN 876688377.

Greenwald, Zev. *Stories My Grandfather Told Me: Memorable Tales Arranged to the Weekly Sidrah.* 1st edition. New York, Mesorah Publications. 2000–2001. 5 vols. ISBN: 157819525x (vol. 1); ISBN 1578195276 (vol. 2); ISBN 1578195292 (vol. 3); ISBN 1578195314 (vol. 6); 1578195349 (vol. 5).

Grishaver, Joel Lurie. *Learning Torah: A Self-Guided Journey Through the Layers of Jewish Learning.* New York: UAHC Press, 1990. 243 p. ISBN 0807403229.

Grishaver, Joel Lurie. *You Be the Judge: A Collection of Ethical Cases and Jewish Answers.* Los Angeles: Torah Aura Productions, 2000. 128 p. ISBN: 1891662007.

Isaacs, Ronald. *Exploring Jewish Ethics and Values.* Hoboken, NJ: Ktav, 1999. 125 p. ISBN 0881256528.

Issacs, Ronald H. and Olitzky, Kerry, M. *Doing Mitzvot: Mitzvot Projects for Bar/Bat Mitzvah.* Hoboken, NJ: Ktav, 1994. 150 p. ISBN 0881252441.

Kushner, Lawrence. *The Book of Miracles: A Young Person's Guide to Jewish Spiritual Awareness.* 10th anniversary edition. Woodstock, VT: Jewish Lights Publishers, 1997. 92 p. ISBN 1879045788.

Lamm, Maurice. *Living Torah in America: Derekh Hatov.* West Orange, NJ: Behrman House, 1993. 182 p. ISBN 0874415136.

Passachoff, Naomi. *Links in the Chain: Shapers of the Jewish Tradition.* New York, Oxford University Press, 1997. 238 p. ISBN 0195099397.

Posner, Raphael (ed.). *Junior Judaica: Encyclopedia Judaica for Youth*. 3rd edition. Jerusalem: Keter, 1994. 1200 p. ISBN 0895638169.

Salkin, Jeffrey K. *For Kids—Putting God on Your Guest List: How to Claim the Spiritual Meaning of Your Bar or Bat Mitzvah*. 1st edition. Woodstock, VT: Jewish Lights Publishers, 1998. 144 p. ISBN 01580230156.

Samuels, Ruth. *Pathways through Jewish History*. Revised edition. New York: Ktav, 1997. 410 p. ISBN 0879685291.

Schafstein, Sol. *Praying with Spirituality*. Hoboken, NJ: Ktav, 1995. 128 p. ISBN 0881255173.

Schafstein, Sol. *Chronicle of Jewish History: From the Patriarchs to the 21st Century*. Hoboken, NJ: Ktav, 1997. 349 p. ISBN 0881256064.

Schafstein, Sol. *Understanding Jewish Holidays and Customs: Historical and Contemporary*. Hoboken, NJ: Ktav, 1999. 186 p. ISBN 0881256269.

Shamir, Ilana (general editor). *The Young Reader's Encyclopedia of Jewish History*. (Shlomo Shavit, editor). New York, Viking Kestrel, 1987. 125 p. ISBN 0670817384.

Shekel, Michal. *The Jewish Lifecycle Book*. Hoboken, NJ: Ktav, 1989. 137 p. ISBN 0870682603.

Sofer, G. *A Story a Day: Stories from Our History and Heritage, from Ancient Times to Modern Times, Arranged to the Jewish Calendar*. 1st edition. New York, Messorah Publications, 6 vols., 1988–1989.

Syme, David and Daniel B. *The Book of the Jewish Life*. New York: UAHC Press, 1997. 115 p.

Van Dusen, Susan and Berkson, Marc. *The Synagouge: House of the Jewish People*. West Orange, NJ: Behrman House, 1999. 96 p. ISBN 0874416647.

INDEX

The entries preceded by an asterisk indicate articles in the body of the Encyclopedia.

ARTICLES OF FAITH → Principles of Faith.

*ARTIFICIAL INSEMINATION 26 → Feinstein, Moses; Medical Ethics, Jewish.

ARVIT → Evening Service.

ASARAH BE-TEVET → Tevet, Tenth of.

*ASCETICISM 27 → Dov Baer of Mezhirech; Fasting and Fast Days; Holiness; Judaism; Social Ethics.

*ASHAMNU 27 → Confession.

ASHER → Tribes, Twelve.

*ASHER BEN JEHIEL 27 → Codification of Jewish Law; Halakhah; Jacob ben Asher.

*ASHI 27 → Academies; Talmud.

*ASHKENAZI, TSEVI HIRSCH BEN JACOB 28

*ASHKENAZIM 28 → Bar Mitzvah; Bible; Bimah; Bittul ha-Tamid; Book of Life; Burial; Cantillation; Children's Prayers and Services; Consecration; Custom; Day of Atonement; Education; Evening Service; Evil Eye; Ezrat Nashim; Food, Sabbath and Festival; Funeral Service; Hakkafot; Hanukkah Lamp; Hasidei Ashkenaz; Havdalah; Hebrew; Hol ha-Mo'ed; Isserles, Moses; Jewish Languages; Kitel; Liturgy; Marriage; Marriages, Prohibited; Meir ben Baruch of Rothenburg; Melavveh Malkah; Memorial Prayers and Services; Messianic Movements; Minhagim, Book of; Mitnaggedim; Monogamy and Polygamy; Prayer Book; Responses, Liturgical; Sephardim; Three Weeks; Tombstone; Torah Ornaments; Yahrzeit; Yiddish; Zemirot.

*ASHREI 28 → Afternoon Service; Morning Service.

ASSEMBLY GREAT → Great Assembly.

ASSEMBLY OF NOTABLES → Consistory.

*ASSIMILATION 29 → Emancipation; Galut; Gentile; Haskalah.

*ASTROLOGY 29 → Bible; Hukkat ha-Goy; Magic; Posekim; Predestination; Superstition.

*ASYLUM 30 → Altar.

ATHEISM → Agnosticism and Atheism; Humanistic Judaism.

*ATONEMENT 31 → Akedah; Community, Jewish; Day of Atonement; Death; Red Heifer; Sin.

ATSERET → Shavu'ot, Shemini Atseret.

*ATTAH EHAD 31

ATTAH HORETA LA-DA'AT 31

ATTRIBUTES, DIVINE → God; Maimonides, Moses.

AUFRUFEN → Reading of the Law.

*AUTHORITY, RABBINIC 31 → Halakhah; Ordination.

AUTOPSIES AND DISSECTIONS → Medical Ethics, Jewish.

*AV 32 → Three Weeks; Tishah be-Av.

*AV, FIFTEENTH OF 33 → Dance; Festivals.

AV NINTH OF → Tishah be-Av.

*AVELEI ZION 33

*AV HA-RAHAMIM 33 → Memorial Prayers and Services.

*AVINU MALKENU 33 → Day of Atonement; Fatherhood of God; Rosh ha-Shanah; Tahanun; Ten Days of Repentance.

*AVINU SHE-BA-SHAMAYIM 33 → Fatherhood of God.

*AVODAH 34 → Additional Service; Confession; Day of Atonement.

*AVODAH ZARAH 34 → Censorship; Idolatry.

*AVOT 34 → Age and the Aged; Aggadah; Avot de-Rabbi Natan; Baraita; Ethical Literature; Ethics; Study.

*AVOT DE-RABBI NATAN 34 → Schechter, Solomon; Tosefta.

AVTAYLON → Shemayah.

AYIN HA-RA → Evil Eye.

*AZAZEL 34 → Atonement; Avodah; Demons and Demonology.

B

*BAAL 35 → Elijah; Elisha; Idolatry.

*BA'AL KERI'AH 35 → Cantillation; Reading of the Law.

*BA'AL SHEM 35

*BA'AL SHEM TOV 35 → Ba'al Shem; Devekut; Dov Baer of Mezhirech; Hasidism; Levi Isaac of Berdichev; Love of Israel.

*BA'AL TEFILLAH 36 → Prayer.

*BA'AL TEKI'AH 36 → Rosh ha-Shanah.

*BA'AL TESHUVAH 37

*BABEL TOWER OF 37

BABYLONIAN EXILE → Ashi; Exile, Babylonian.

BABYLONIAN TALMUD → Talmud.

*BAECK, LEO 37

*BAHIR, SEFER 37 → Evil.

*BAHUR 37

*BAHYA BEN ASHER IBN HALAWA 37 → Bible Commentary, Jewish.

*BAHYA BEN JOSEPH IBN PAKUDA 38 → Afterlife; Bahir, Sefer; Commandments.

*BAL TASHHIT 38

*BA-MEH MADLIKIN 38

BAN → Excommunication.

*BARAITA 38 → Eliezer ben Hyrcanus; Judah ha-Nasi; Mishnah; Pittum ha-Ketoret; Talmud; Tanna; Tosefta; Yose ben Halafta.

*BAREKHI NAFSHI 38

*BAREKHU 38 → Benedictions; Evening Service; Minyan; Morning Service; Responses, Liturgical; Torah Blessings; Yishtabbah.

*BAR KOKHBA, SIMON 39 → Academies; Akiva ben Joseph; Circumcision; Eschatology; Jerusalem; Merit; Omer; Simeon bar Yohai; Ten Martyrs; Tishah be-Av.

*BAR MITZVAH 39 → Adar; Adult; Ba'al Keri'ah; Barukh she-Petarani; Bat Mitzvah; Children; Confirmation; Father; Haftarah; Home, Jewish; Maftir; Mitzvah; Reading of the Law; Se'udah; Simhat Torah; Western Wall.

*BARRENNESS 40 → Amulet; Birth; Children.

*BARUKH DAYYAN HA-EMET 40 → Benedictions; Death; Funeral Service.

*BARUKH HA-SHEM 40

*BARUKH SHE-AMAR 40 → Morning Service.

*BARUKH SHEM KEVOD MALKHUTO 40

*BARUKH SHE-PETARANI 41 → Adult; Bar Mitzvah; Bat Mitzvah; Benedictions; Father.

*BAT KOL 41 → Authority, Rabbinic; Bet Shammai and Bet Hillel; Eliezer ben Hyrcanus.

*BATLANIM 41

*BAT MITZVAH 41 → Ba'al Keri'ah; Barukh she-Petarani; Haftarah; Home, Jewish; Mitzvah; Reading of the Law; Women.

*BAVA BATRA 41 → Samuel ben Meir.

*BAVA KAMMA 42

*BAVA METSI'AH 42

BEDIKAT HAMETS → Leaven, Search for; Passover.

*BE-EZRAT HA-SHEM 42

BEHEMOTH → Leviathan.

*BEKHOROT 42 → Firstborn, Redemption of.

*BELZ 42

*BENEDICTIONS 42 → Ablutions; Ahavah Rabbah; Ahavat Olam; Akiva ben Joseph; Amen; Amidah; Barukh Dayyan ha-Emet; Blessing and Cursing; Gomel Blessing; Government, Prayer for; Grace Before Meals; Halakhah; Judaism; Life; Liturgy; Mitzvah; Modeh Ani; Priestly Blessing; Torah Blessing; She-Heheyanu.

*BENE ISRAEL 43

*BEN-GURION, DAVID 43 → Jew, Who is a; Zionism.

BENJAMIN → Jacob; Rachel; Tribes, Twelve.

*BENTSHEN 44 → Benedictions; Grace After Meals.

*BERAH DODI 44 → Ge'ulah.

BERAKHOT → Benedictions.

*BERAKHOT (BOOK) 44 → Baraita; Benedictions; Zera'im.

*BERIKH SHEMEH 44

*BERIT MILAH 44 → Circumcision.

*BERLIN, NAPHTALI TSEVI JUDAH 44 → Kook, Abraham Isaac; Yeshivah.

*BERNAYS, ISAAC 45 → Neo-Orthodoxy.

*BERTINORO, OBADIAH BEN ABRAHAM YAREI DI 45

*BERURYAH 45 → Meir.

BESAMIM → Spices.

*BET DIN 45 → Academies; Academy on High; Authority, Rabbinic; Cherub; Conversion to Judaism; Dayyan; Din Torah; Divorce; Hakham; Kol Nidrei; Prosbul; Rebellious Son; Sanhedrin; Slavery.

BET HA-MIKDASH → Temple.

BETH JACOB → Education.

*BET MIDRASH 46 → Academies; Community, Jewish; Midrash; Study; Synagogue.

BETROTHAL → Custom; Family; Kiddushin; Marriage; Nashim; Shadkhan; Virginity.

*BETSAH 46

*BET SHAMMAI AND BET HILLEL 46 → Custom; Divorce; Eduyyot; Hillel; Pharisees; Shammai; Takkanah.

*BIBLE 47 → Acrostics; Age and the Aged; Agricultural Laws; Allegory; Altar; Am ha-Arets; Angels; Anointing; Apocalypse; Apostasy; Aramaic; Ark of the Covenant; Asceticism; Ashkenazim; Ashrei; Asylum; Atonement; Avinu she-ba-Shamayim; Ba'al Keri'ah; Bible; Birth; Blood; Blood Avenger; Bribery; Buber, Martin; Burial; Business Ethics; Cain and Abel; Canaan, Land of; Cantillation; Charity; Chastity; Cherub; Children; Chosen People; Circumcision; Consecration; Conversion to Judaism; Covenant; Covetousness; Creation; Daf Yomi; Dance; David; Day of Atonement; Dead Sea Scrolls; Death; Derash; Divorce; Dowry; Eden, Garden of; Education; Elders; Elijah ben Solomon Zalman; Elisha; Enoch; Ethics; Ethiopian Jews; Eulogy; Evar min ha-Hai; Evil; Exile, Babylonian; Exodus; Ezekiel; Ezra; Faith; Family; Family Purity; Father; First Fruits; Firstborn, Redemption of; Five Scrolls; Flood; Forgiveness; Four Species; Free Will; Galut; God; God, Names of; Golden Calf; Hagiographa; Hakhel; Hallelujah; Hebrew; Holiness; Homiletics; Homosexuality; Humility; Illegitimacy; Imitation of God; Incense; Incest; Ingathering of the Exiles; Inheritance; Intermarriage; Isaac; Isaiah; Islam; Israel; Israelite; Jacob; Jeremiah; Jerusalem; Jewish Languages; Joseph; Jubilee; Judaism; Karet; Keter; King, Kingship; Labor and Labor Laws; Leaven, Search for; Lekah Tov; Lel Shimmurim; Leshon ha-Ra; Levirate Marriage; Life; Liturgy; Love of God; Love of Neighbor; Magic; Mah Tovu; Malachi; Man; Manna; Marriage; Matriarchs; Matzah; Menorah; Mercy; Merit; Messianic Movements; Meturgeman; Midrash; Midrash Aggadah; Midrash va-Yissa'u; Minyan; Monogamy and Polygamy; Moriah; Moses; Mourning; Murder; Music and Song; Nasi; Nazirite; Niddah; Noachide Laws; Parashah; Parent and Child; Passover, Second; Philo; Pilgrimage; Poverty and the Poor; Prayer; Predestination; Prophets and Prophecy; Punishment; Rebellious Son; Red Heifer; Redemption; Remnant of Israel; Rending of Garments; Repentance; Retaliation; Reward and Punishment; Rosenzweig, Franz; Rosh ha-Shanah; Saadiah Gaon; Sabbath; Sabbatical Year; Sacrifices and Offerings; Samuel; Sanctuary; Sarah; Satan; Science; Septuagint; Servant of the Lord; Seven Species; Sex; Shaving; Shavu'ot; Shemini Atseret; Shofar; Showbread; Simhah; Sin; Sinai, Mount; Slavery; Social Ethics; Solomon; Soul, Immortality of; Sukkot; Superstition; Tablets of the Covenant; Targum; Tefillin; Temple Mount; Theft; Theology; Throne of God; Tishah be-Av; Tithe; Tokhahah; Tombstone; Torah; Tree of Life; Tribes, Twelve; Tsaddik; Universalism and Particularism; Urim and Thummim; Usury; Violence; Vows and Vowing; War; Widow and Orphan;